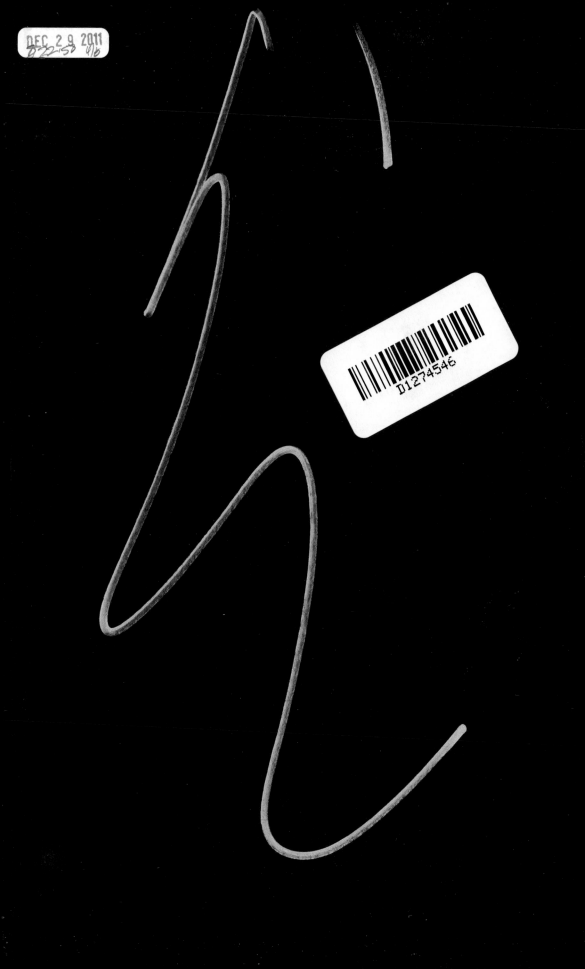

JUSTICE LEAGUE

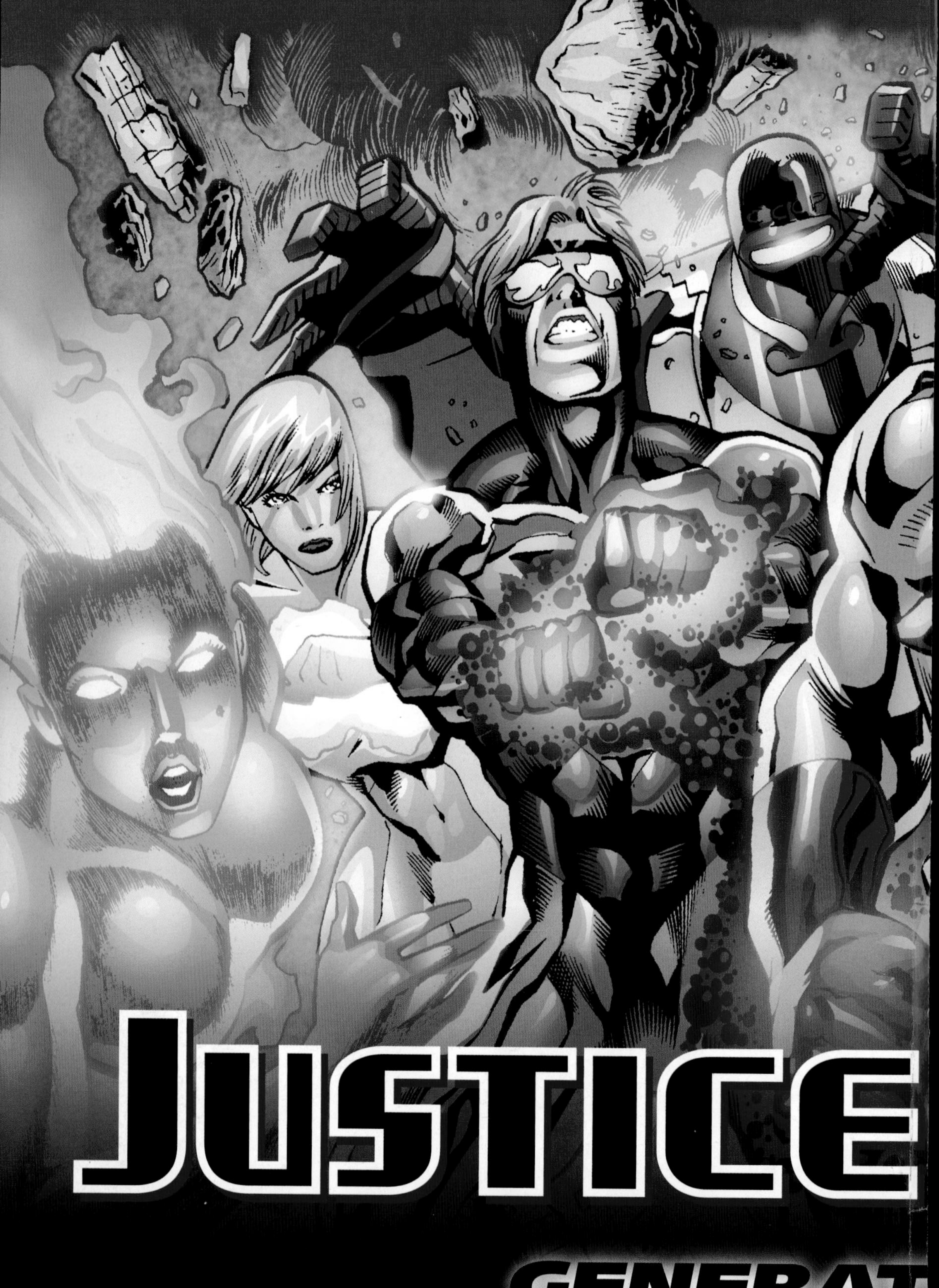
JUSTICE

Cover by Cliff Chiang

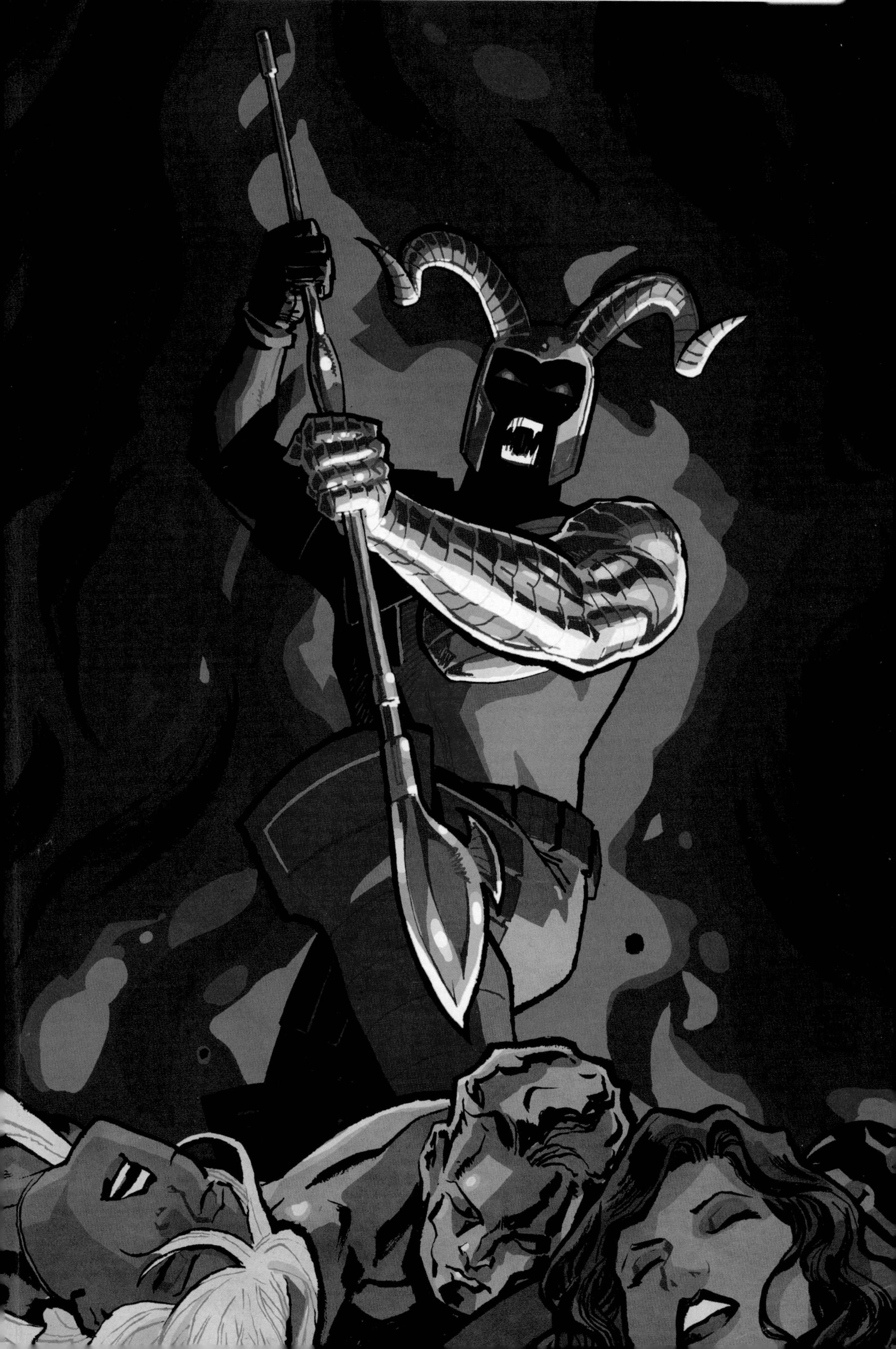

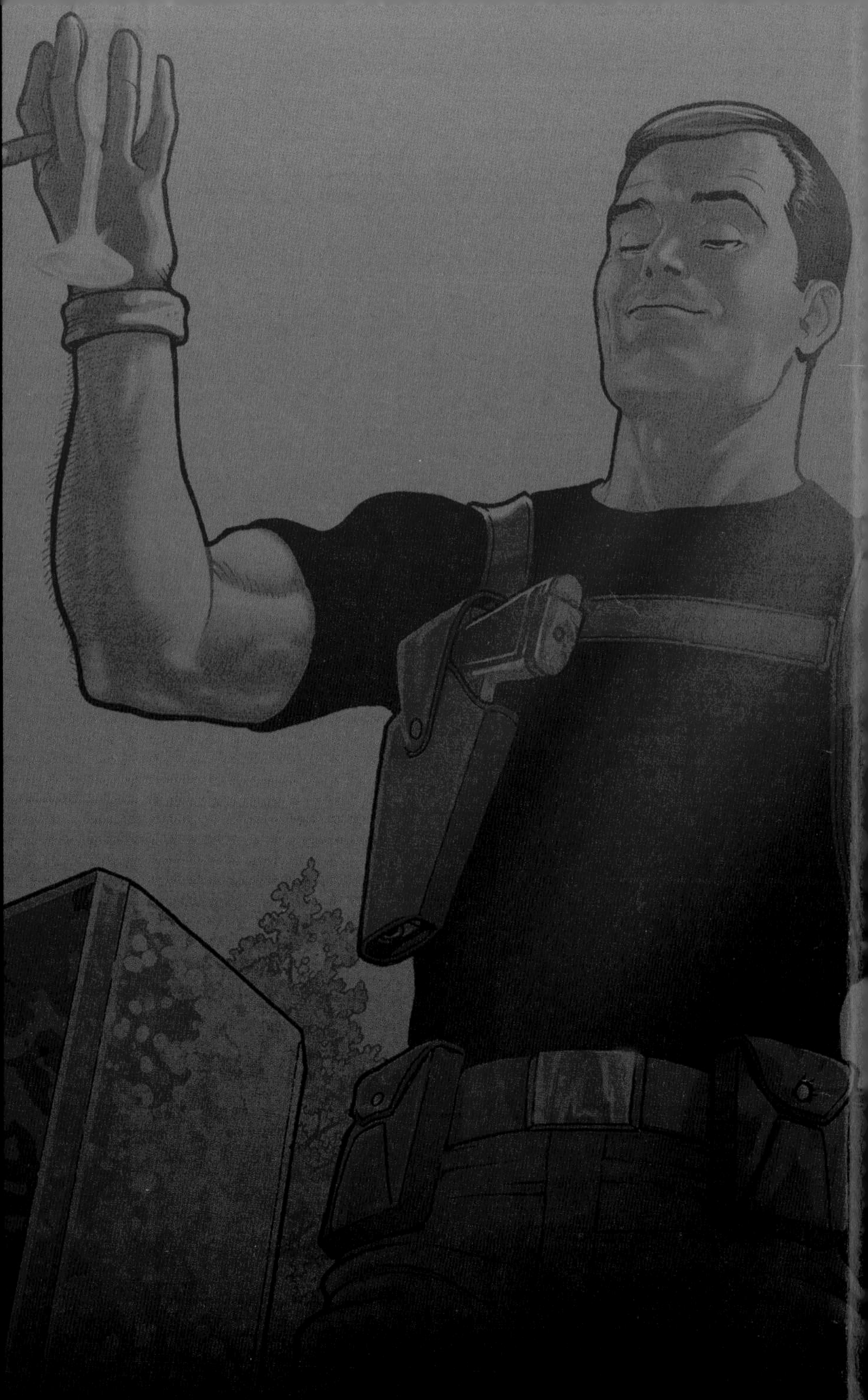

PART THIRTEEN:
OLD SOLDIERS

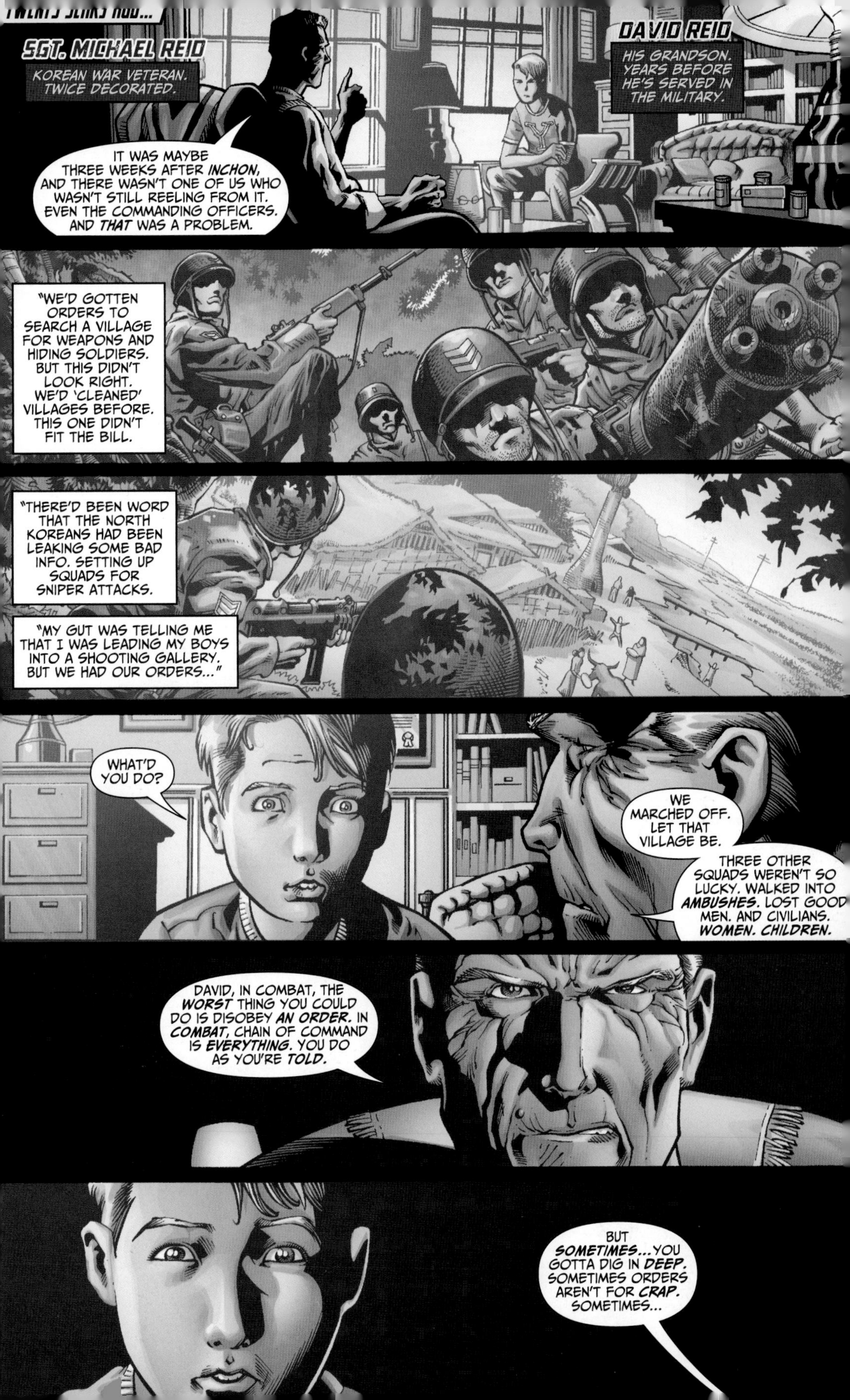
SGT. MICHAEL REID
KOREAN WAR VETERAN. TWICE DECORATED.
DAVID REID
HIS GRANDSON. YEARS BEFORE HE'S SERVED IN THE MILITARY.
IT WAS MAYBE THREE WEEKS AFTER INCHON, AND THERE WASN'T ONE OF US WHO WASN'T STILL REELING FROM IT. EVEN THE COMMANDING OFFICERS. AND THAT WAS A PROBLEM.
"WE'D GOTTEN ORDERS TO SEARCH A VILLAGE FOR WEAPONS AND HIDING SOLDIERS. BUT THIS DIDN'T LOOK RIGHT. WE'D 'CLEANED' VILLAGES BEFORE. THIS ONE DIDN'T FIT THE BILL.
"THERE'D BEEN WORD THAT THE NORTH KOREANS HAD BEEN LEAKING SOME BAD INFO. SETTING UP SQUADS FOR SNIPER ATTACKS.
"MY GUT WAS TELLING ME THAT I WAS LEADING MY BOYS INTO A SHOOTING GALLERY. BUT WE HAD OUR ORDERS..."
WHAT'D YOU DO?
WE MARCHED OFF. LET THAT VILLAGE BE.
THREE OTHER SQUADS WEREN'T SO LUCKY. WALKED INTO AMBUSHES. LOST GOOD MEN. AND CIVILIANS. WOMEN. CHILDREN.
DAVID, IN COMBAT, THE WORST THING YOU COULD DO IS DISOBEY AN ORDER. IN COMBAT, CHAIN OF COMMAND IS EVERYTHING. YOU DO AS YOU'RE TOLD.
BUT SOMETIMES... YOU GOTTA DIG IN DEEP. SOMETIMES ORDERS AREN'T FOR CRAP. SOMETIMES...

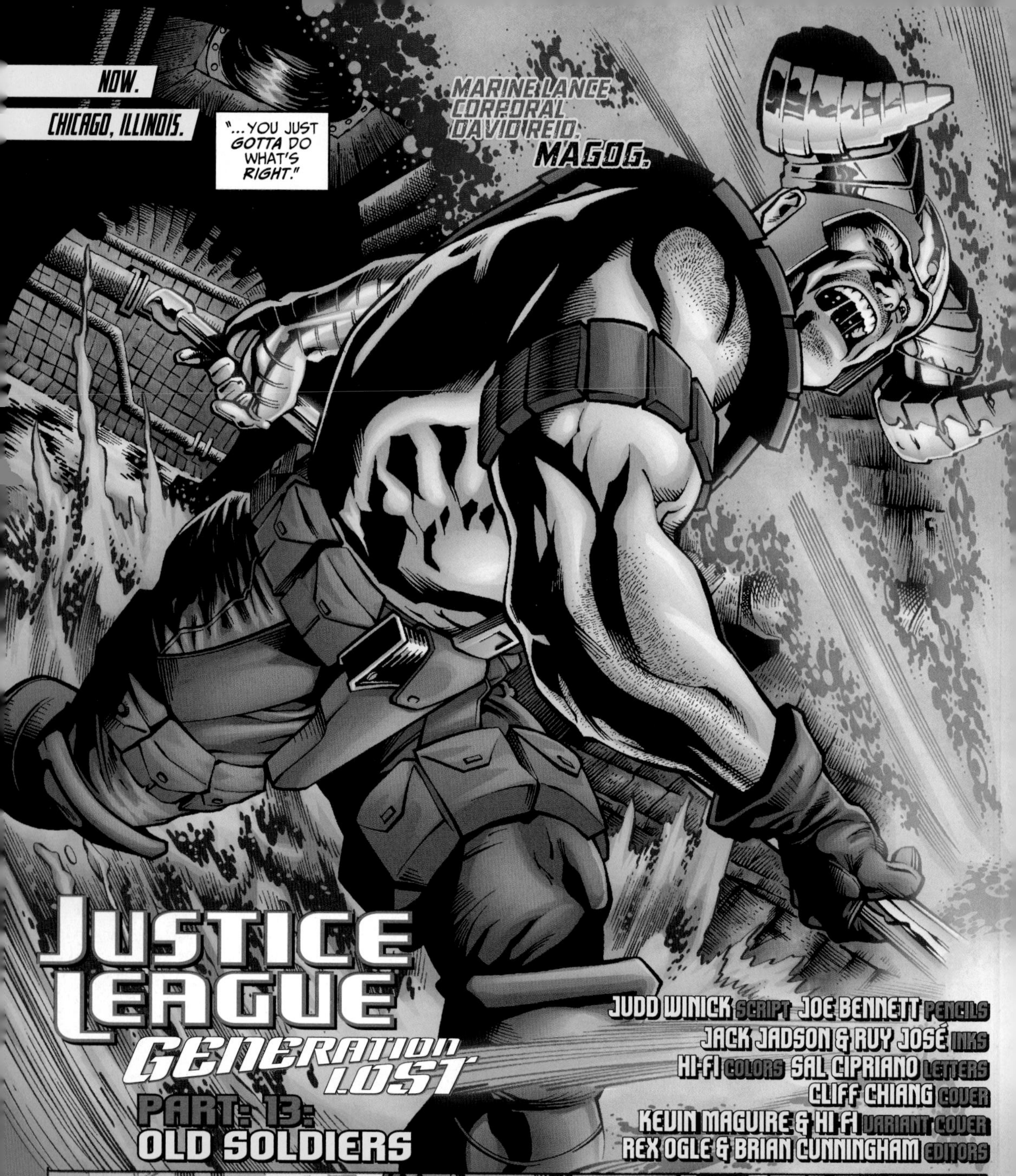
NOW.
CHICAGO, ILLINOIS.
"...YOU JUST GOTTA DO WHAT'S RIGHT."
MARINE LANCE CORPORAL DAVID REID.
MAGOG.
JUSTICE LEAGUE
GENERATION LOST
PART 13:
OLD SOLDIERS
JUDD WINICK SCRIPT JOE BENNETT PENCILS
JACK JADSON & RUY JOSÉ INKS
HI-FI COLORS SAL CIPRIANO LETTERS
CLIFF CHIANG COVER
KEVIN MAGUIRE & HI FI VARIANT COVER
REX OGLE & BRIAN CUNNINGHAM EDITORS
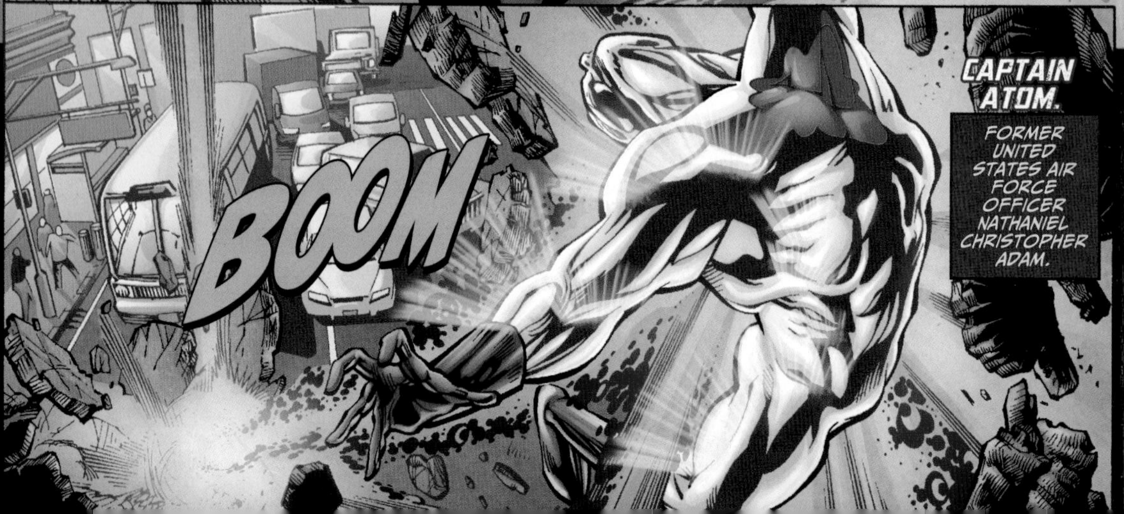
BOOM
CAPTAIN ATOM.
FORMER UNITED STATES AIR FORCE OFFICER NATHANIEL CHRISTOPHER ADAM.

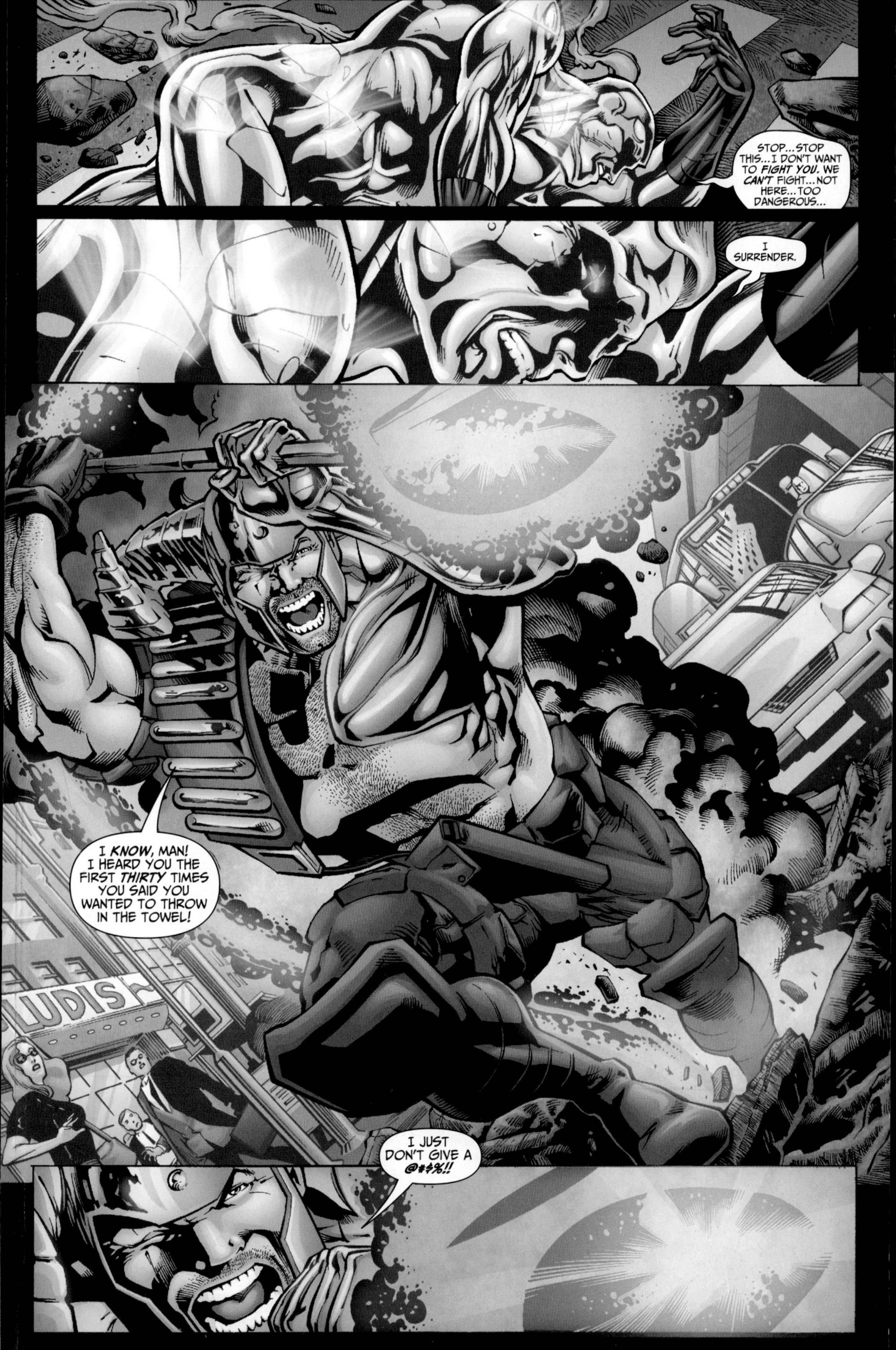
STOP...STOP THIS...I DON'T WANT TO FIGHT YOU. WE CAN'T FIGHT...NOT HERE...TOO DANGEROUS...
I SURRENDER.
I KNOW, MAN! I HEARD YOU THE FIRST THIRTY TIMES YOU SAID YOU WANTED TO THROW IN THE TOWEL!
LUDIS
I JUST DON'T GIVE A @#$%!!

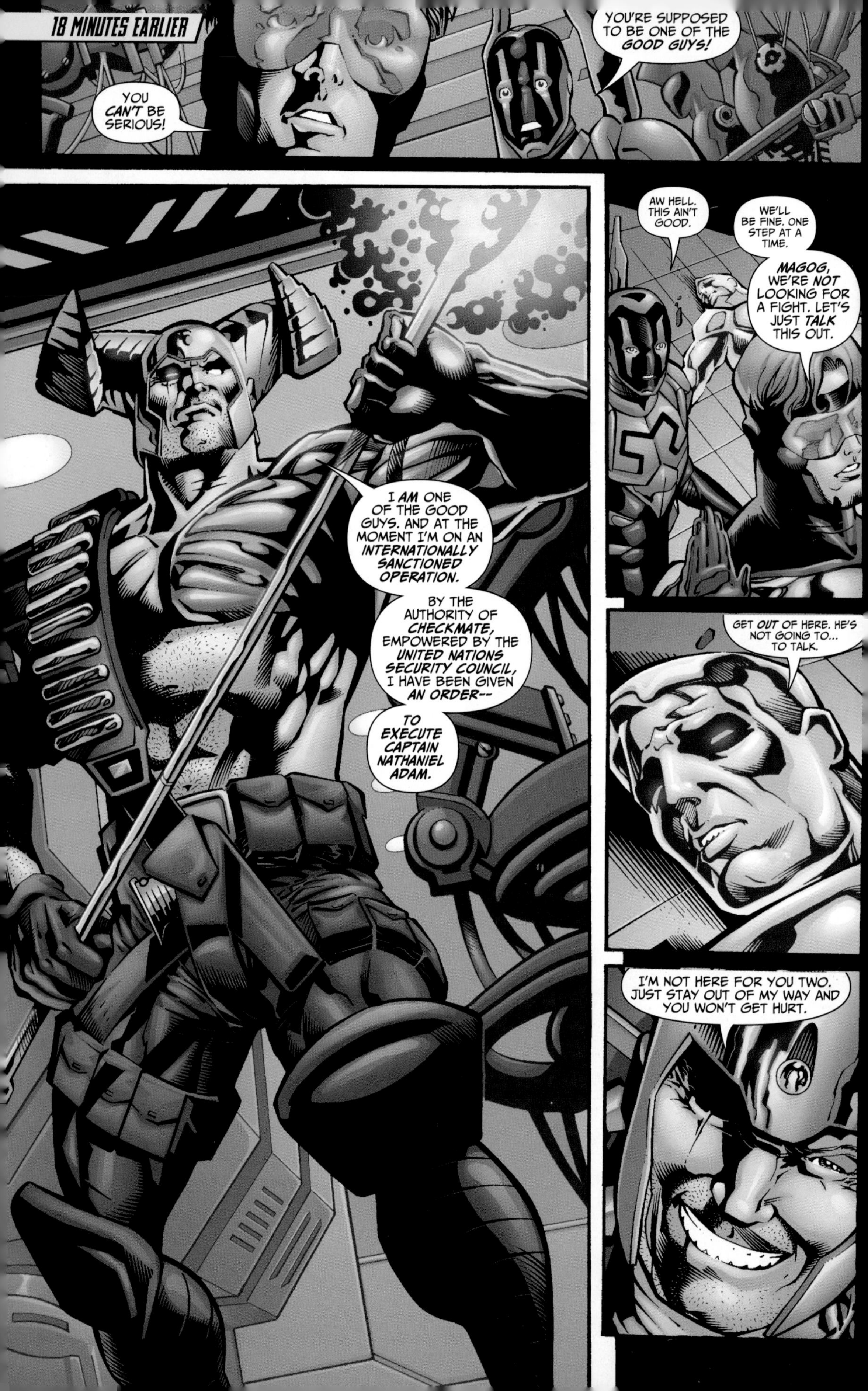
18 MINUTES EARLIER
YOU CAN'T BE SERIOUS!
YOU'RE SUPPOSED TO BE ONE OF THE GOOD GUYS!
I AM ONE OF THE GOOD GUYS. AND AT THE MOMENT I'M ON AN INTERNATIONALLY SANCTIONED OPERATION.
BY THE AUTHORITY OF CHECKMATE, EMPOWERED BY THE UNITED NATIONS SECURITY COUNCIL, I HAVE BEEN GIVEN AN ORDER--
TO EXECUTE CAPTAIN NATHANIEL ADAM.
AW HELL. THIS AIN'T GOOD.
WE'LL BE FINE. ONE STEP AT A TIME.
MAGOG, WE'RE NOT LOOKING FOR A FIGHT. LET'S JUST TALK THIS OUT.
GET OUT OF HERE. HE'S NOT GOING TO... TO TALK.
I'M NOT HERE FOR YOU TWO. JUST STAY OUT OF MY WAY AND YOU WON'T GET HURT.

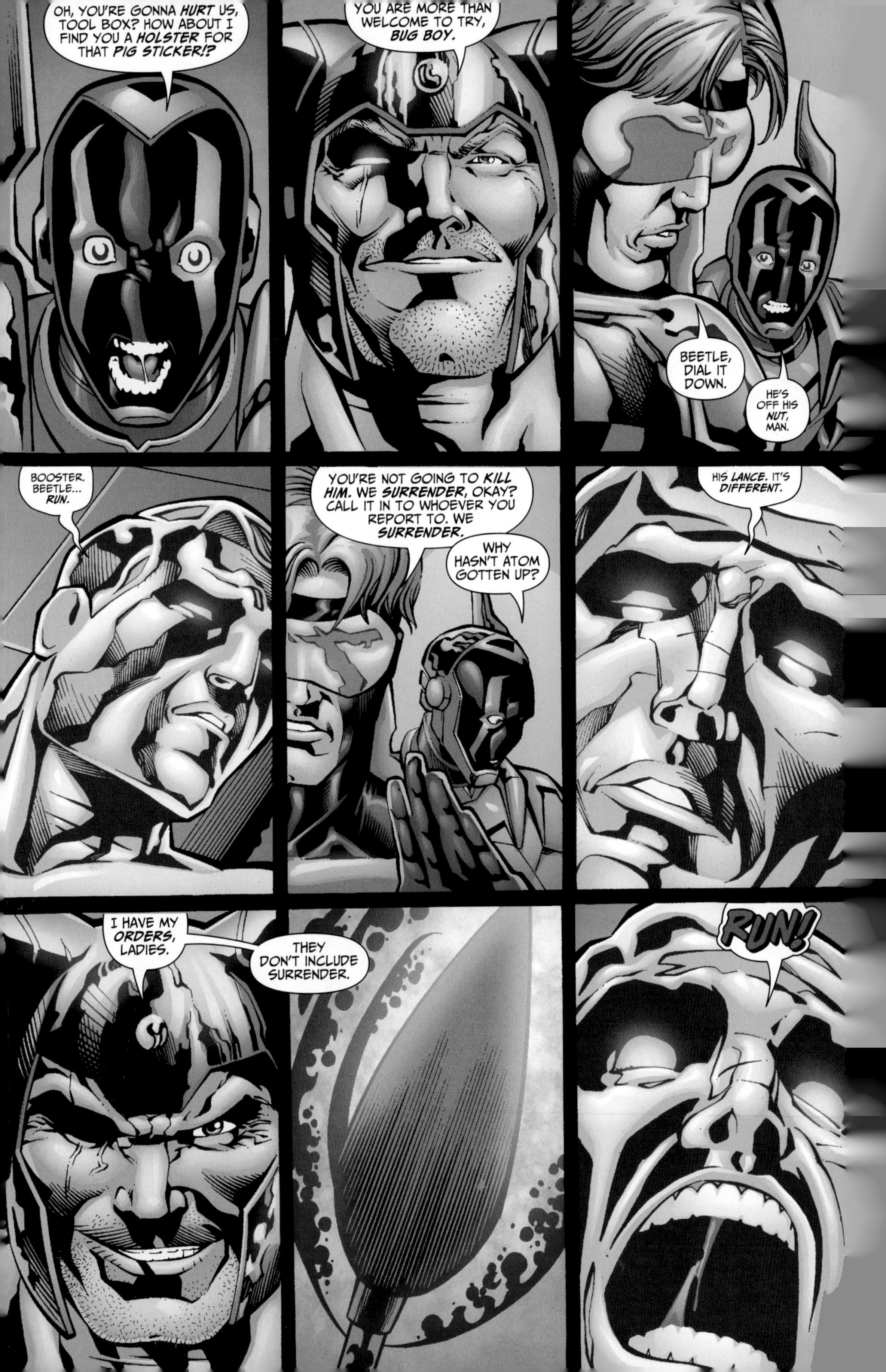

OH, YOU'RE GONNA HURT US, TOOL BOX? HOW ABOUT I FIND YOU A HOLSTER FOR THAT PIG STICKER!?
YOU ARE MORE THAN WELCOME TO TRY, BUG BOY.
BEETLE, DIAL IT DOWN.
HE'S OFF HIS NUT, MAN.
BOOSTER. BEETLE... RUN.
YOU'RE NOT GOING TO KILL HIM. WE SURRENDER, OKAY? CALL IT IN TO WHOEVER YOU REPORT TO. WE SURRENDER.
WHY HASN'T ATOM GOTTEN UP?
HIS LANCE. IT'S DIFFERENT.
I HAVE MY ORDERS, LADIES.
THEY DON'T INCLUDE SURRENDER.
RUN!

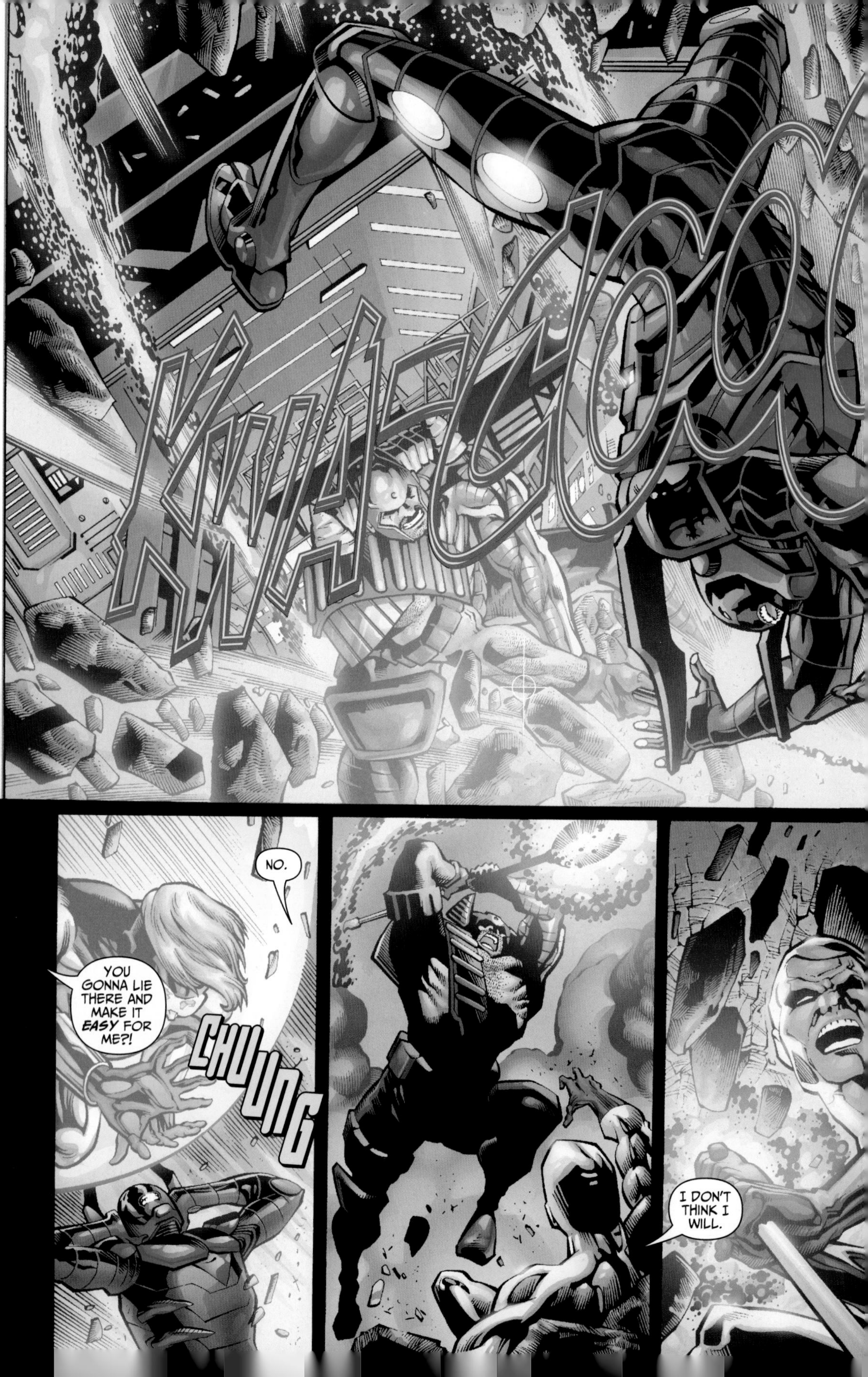
KWHAOOOOM
NO.
YOU GONNA LIE THERE AND MAKE IT EASY FOR ME?!
CHUUNG
I DON'T THINK I WILL.

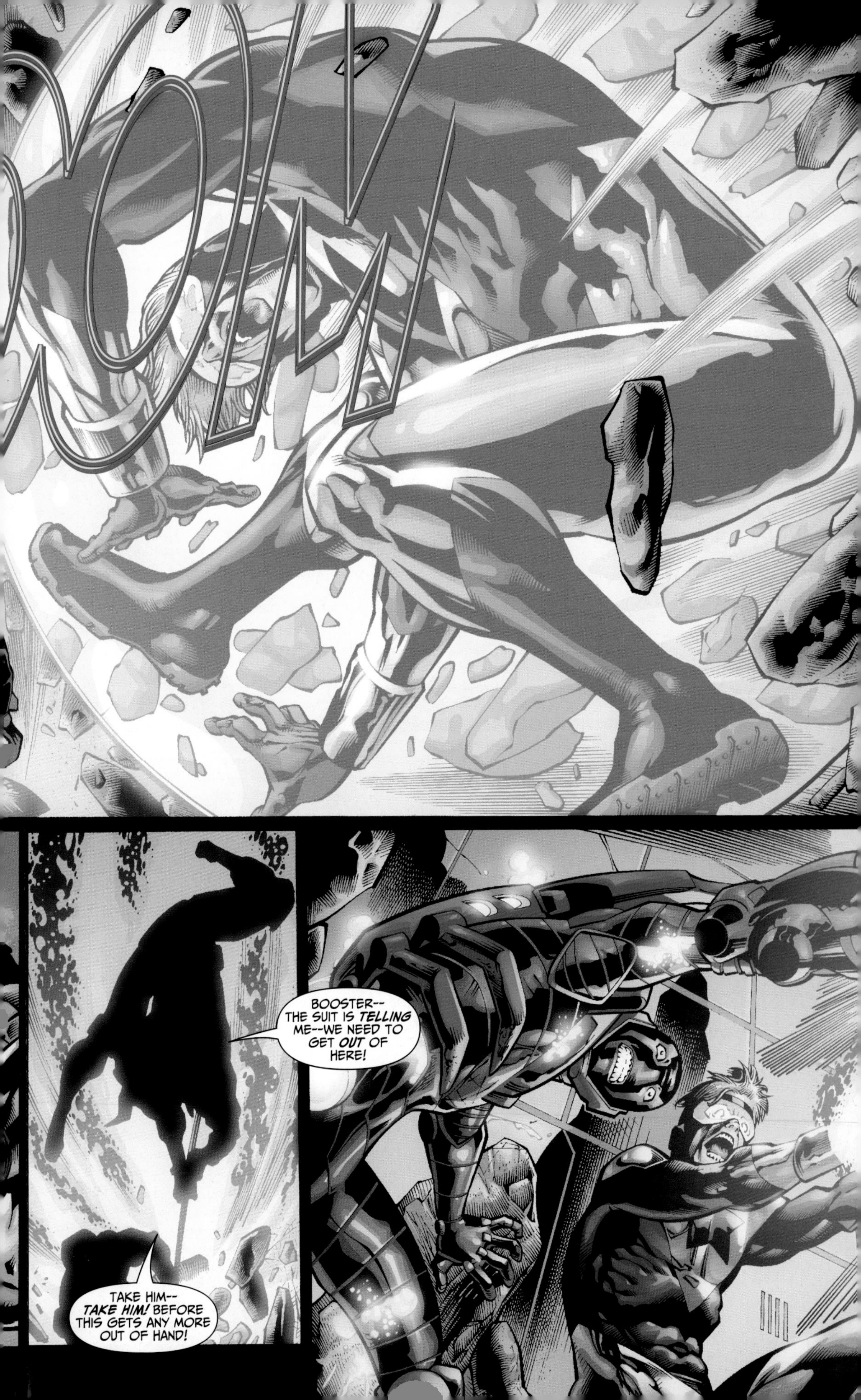
TAKE HIM-- TAKE HIM! BEFORE THIS GETS ANY MORE OUT OF HAND!
BOOSTER-- THE SUIT IS TELLING ME--WE NEED TO GET OUT OF HERE!

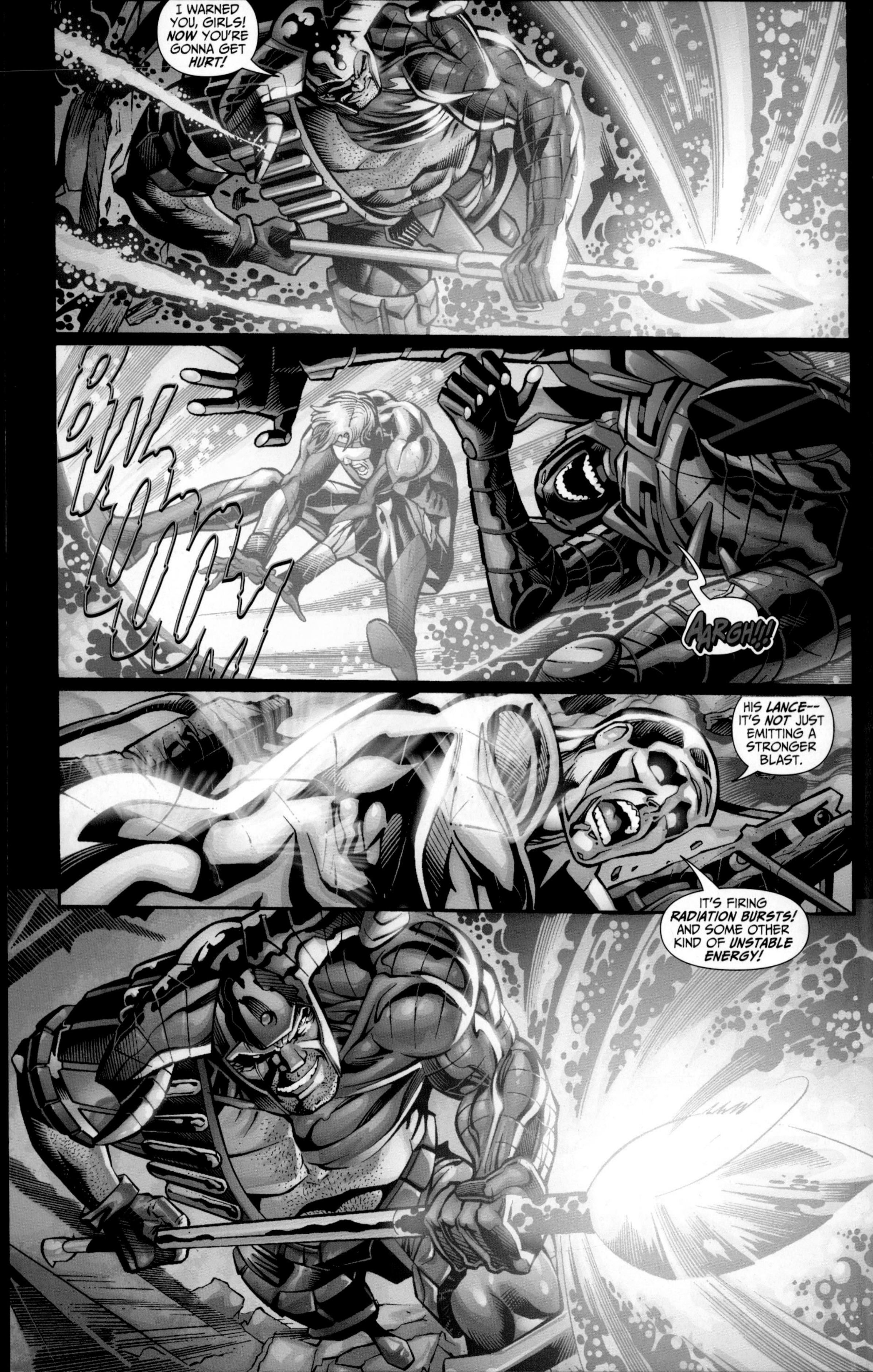
I WARNED YOU, GIRLS! NOW YOU'RE GONNA GET HURT!
AARGH!!!
HIS LANCE-- IT'S NOT JUST EMITTING A STRONGER BLAST.
IT'S FIRING RADIATION BURSTS! AND SOME OTHER KIND OF UNSTABLE ENERGY!

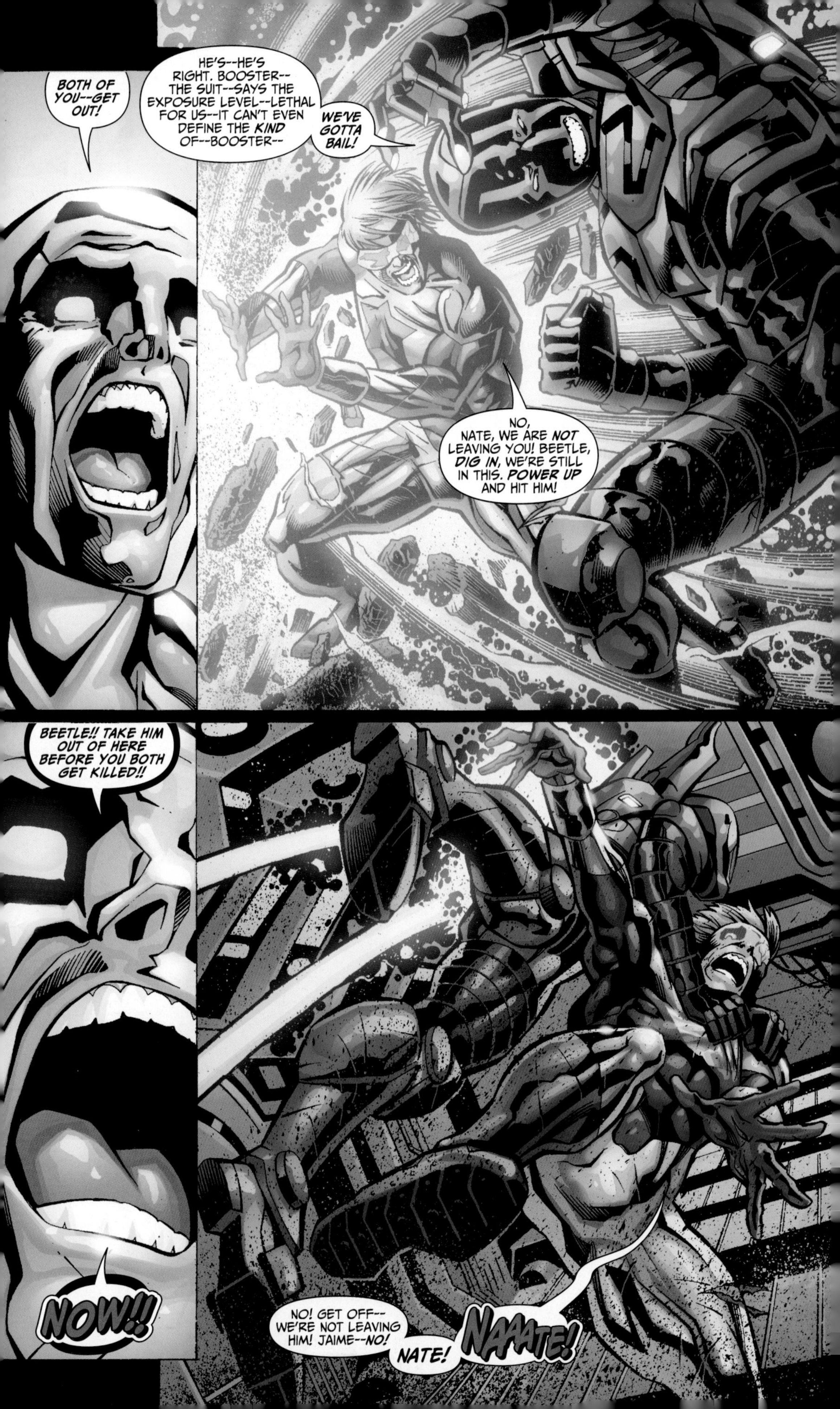

BOTH OF YOU--GET OUT!
HE'S--HE'S RIGHT. BOOSTER--THE SUIT--SAYS THE EXPOSURE LEVEL--LETHAL FOR US--IT CAN'T EVEN DEFINE THE KIND OF--BOOSTER--
WE'VE GOTTA BAIL!
NO, NATE, WE ARE NOT LEAVING YOU! BEETLE, DIG IN, WE'RE STILL IN THIS. POWER UP AND HIT HIM!
BEETLE!! TAKE HIM OUT OF HERE BEFORE YOU BOTH GET KILLED!!
NOW!!
NO! GET OFF--WE'RE NOT LEAVING HIM! JAIME--NO!
NATE!
NAAAATE!

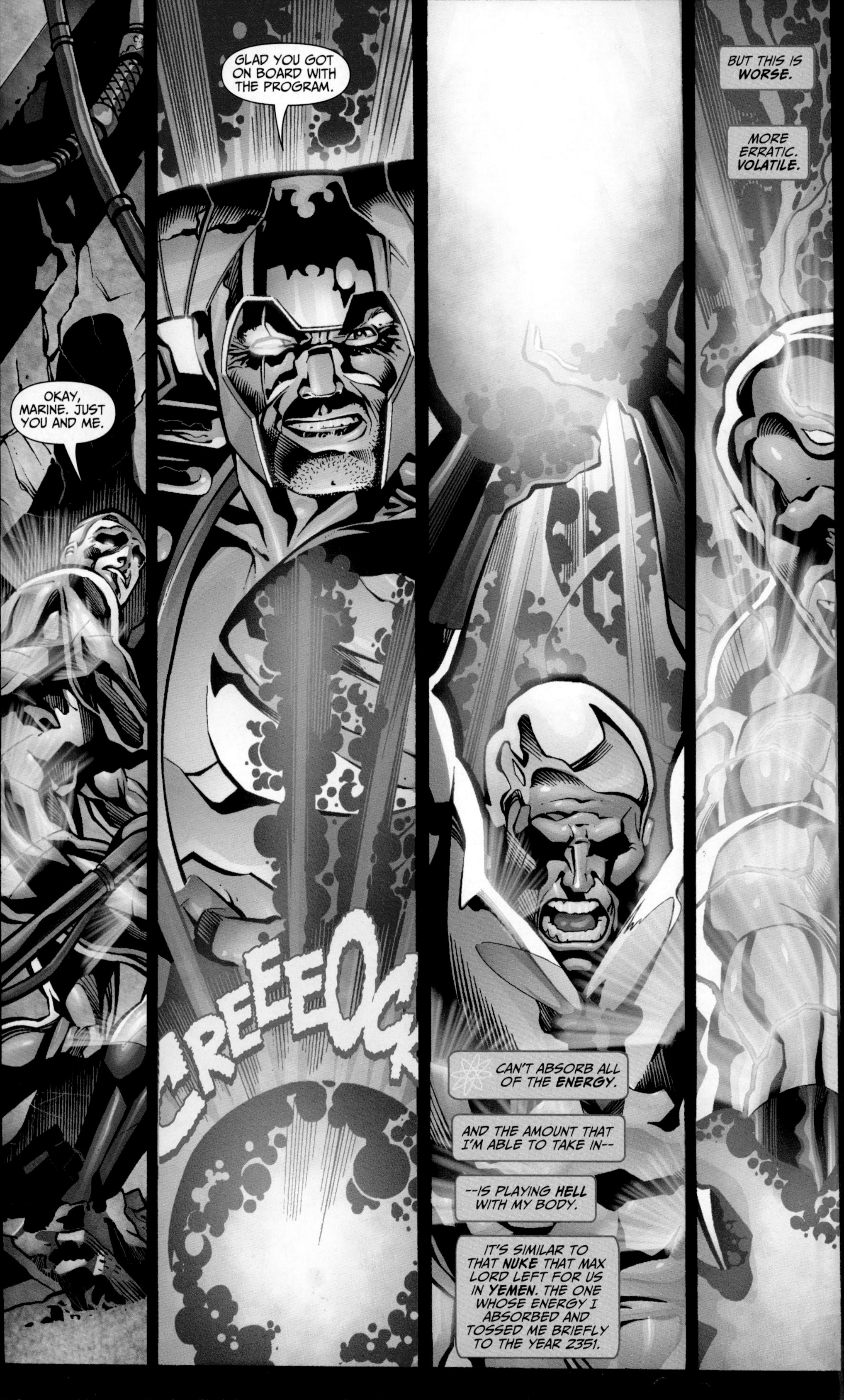
OKAY, MARINE. JUST YOU AND ME.
GLAD YOU GOT ON BOARD WITH THE PROGRAM.
CREEEOCK
CAN'T ABSORB ALL OF THE ENERGY.
AND THE AMOUNT THAT I'M ABLE TO TAKE IN--
--IS PLAYING HELL WITH MY BODY.
IT'S SIMILAR TO THAT NUKE THAT MAX LORD LEFT FOR US IN YEMEN. THE ONE WHOSE ENERGY I ABSORBED AND TOSSED ME BRIEFLY TO THE YEAR 2351.
BUT THIS IS WORSE.
MORE ERRATIC. VOLATILE.

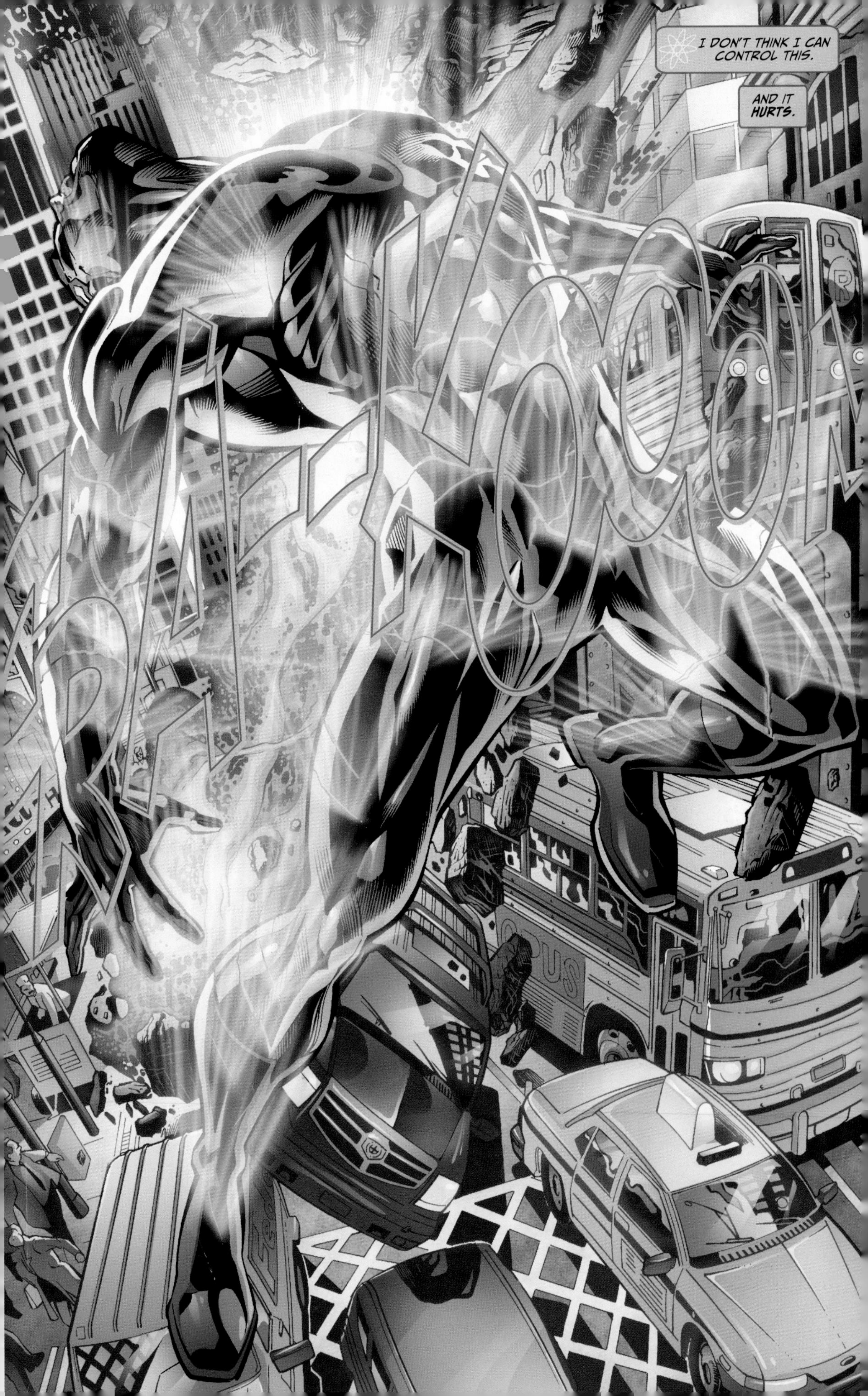
I DON'T THINK I CAN CONTROL THIS.
AND IT HURTS.
OPUS

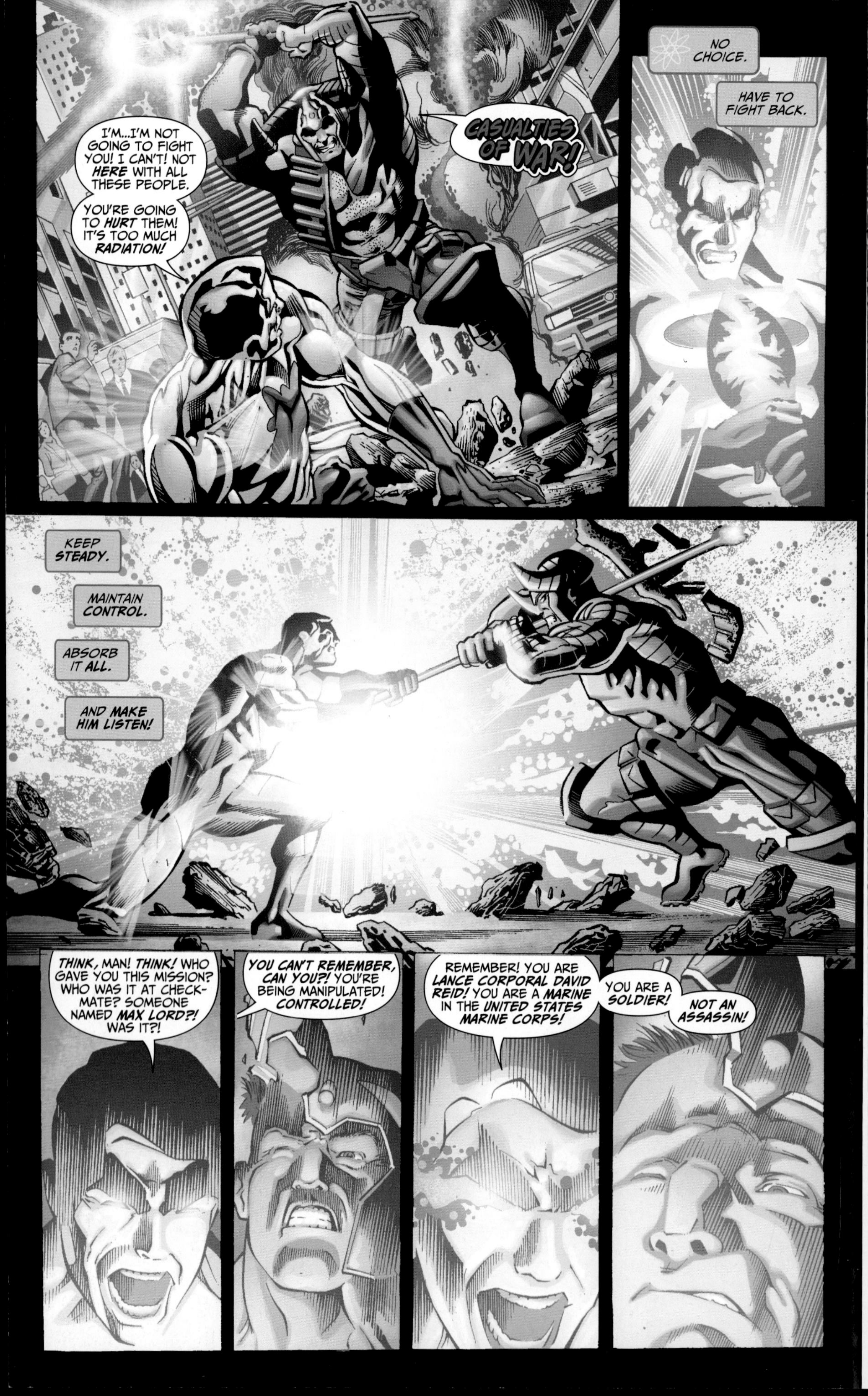
I'M...I'M NOT GOING TO FIGHT YOU! I CAN'T! NOT HERE WITH ALL THESE PEOPLE.
YOU'RE GOING TO HURT THEM! IT'S TOO MUCH RADIATION!
CASUALTIES OF WAR!
NO CHOICE.
HAVE TO FIGHT BACK.
KEEP STEADY.
MAINTAIN CONTROL.
ABSORB IT ALL.
AND MAKE HIM LISTEN!
THINK, MAN! THINK! WHO GAVE YOU THIS MISSION? WHO WAS IT AT CHECK-MATE? SOMEONE NAMED MAX LORD?! WAS IT?!
YOU CAN'T REMEMBER, CAN YOU?! YOU'RE BEING MANIPULATED! CONTROLLED!
REMEMBER! YOU ARE LANCE CORPORAL DAVID REID! YOU ARE A MARINE IN THE UNITED STATES MARINE CORPS!
YOU ARE A SOLDIER!
NOT AN ASSASSIN!

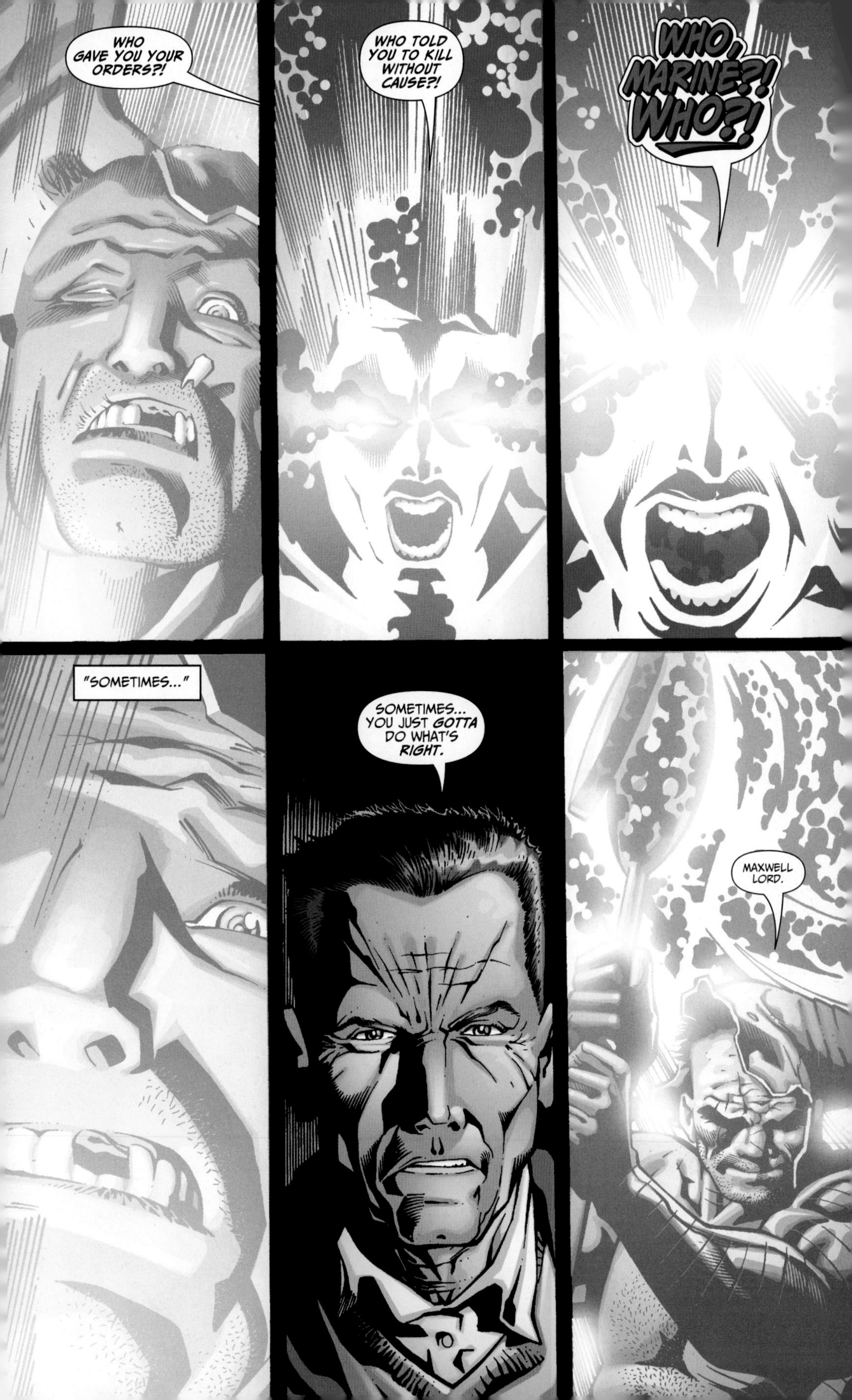
WHO GAVE YOU YOUR ORDERS?!
WHO TOLD YOU TO KILL WITHOUT CAUSE?!
WHO, MARINE?! WHO?!
"SOMETIMES..."
SOMETIMES... YOU JUST GOTTA DO WHAT'S RIGHT.
MAXWELL LORD.

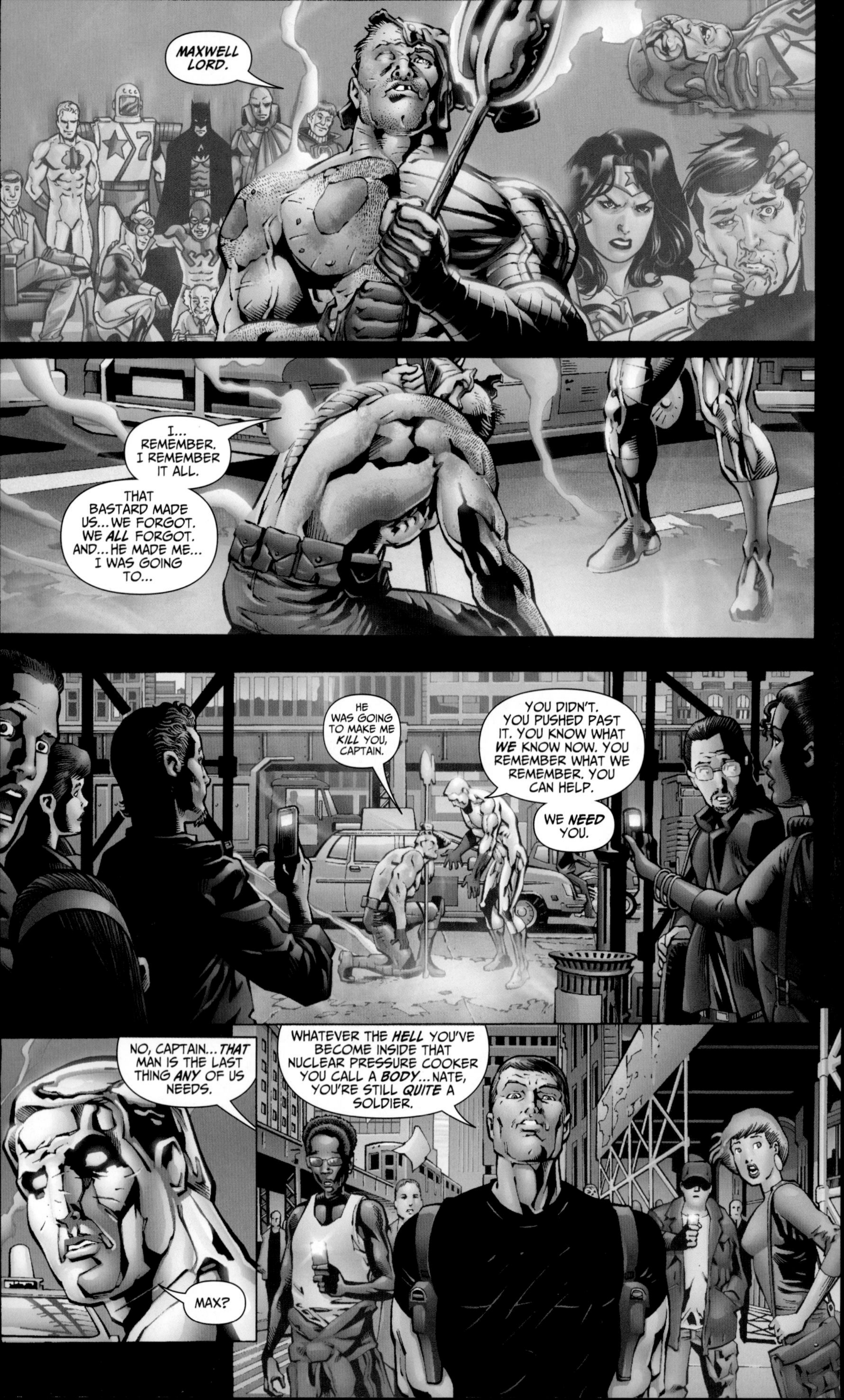
MAXWELL LORD.
I... REMEMBER. I REMEMBER IT ALL.
THAT BASTARD MADE US... WE FORGOT. WE ALL FORGOT. AND... HE MADE ME... I WAS GOING TO...
HE WAS GOING TO MAKE ME KILL YOU, CAPTAIN.
YOU DIDN'T. YOU PUSHED PAST IT. YOU KNOW WHAT WE KNOW NOW. YOU REMEMBER WHAT WE REMEMBER. YOU CAN HELP.
WE NEED YOU.
NO, CAPTAIN... THAT MAN IS THE LAST THING ANY OF US NEEDS.
WHATEVER THE HELL YOU'VE BECOME INSIDE THAT NUCLEAR PRESSURE COOKER YOU CALL A BODY... NATE, YOU'RE STILL QUITE A SOLDIER.
MAX?

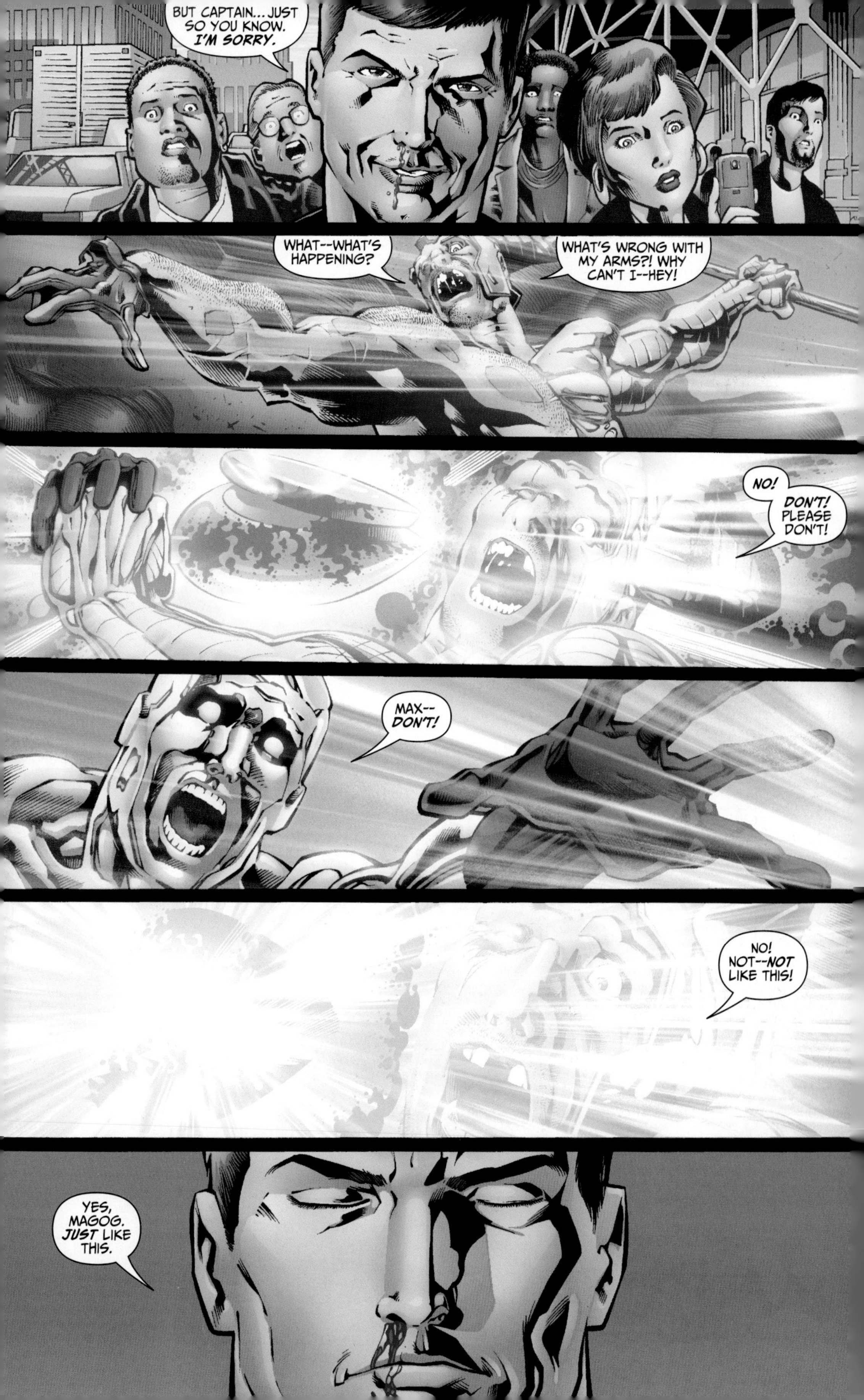
BUT CAPTAIN... JUST SO YOU KNOW. I'M SORRY.
WHAT--WHAT'S HAPPENING?
WHAT'S WRONG WITH MY ARMS?! WHY CAN'T I--HEY!
NO! DON'T! PLEASE DON'T!
MAX-- DON'T!
NO! NOT--NOT LIKE THIS!
YES, MAGOG. JUST LIKE THIS.

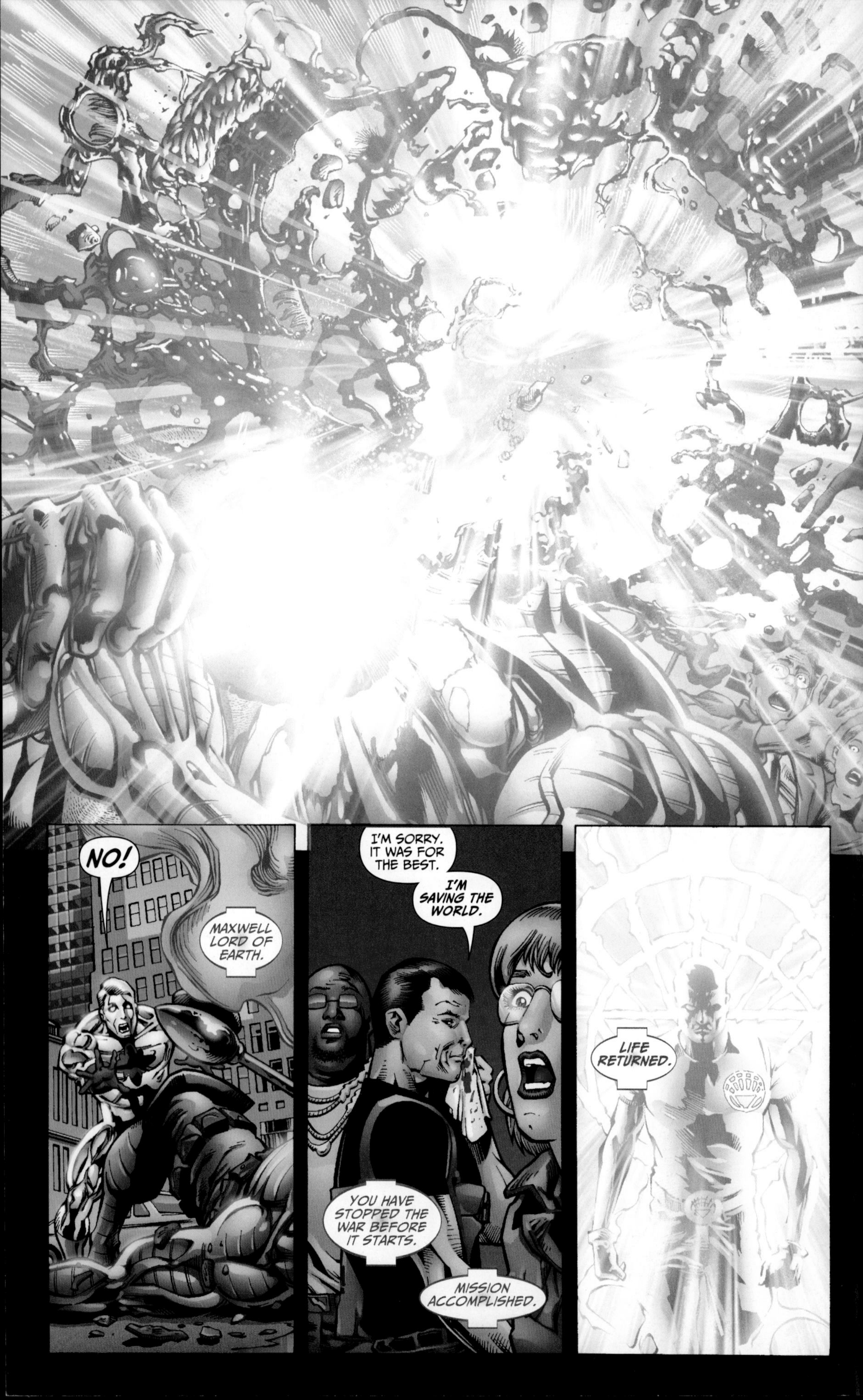
NO!
MAXWELL LORD OF EARTH.
I'M SORRY. IT WAS FOR THE BEST.
I'M SAVING THE WORLD.
YOU HAVE STOPPED THE WAR BEFORE IT STARTS.
MISSION ACCOMPLISHED.
LIFE RETURNED.

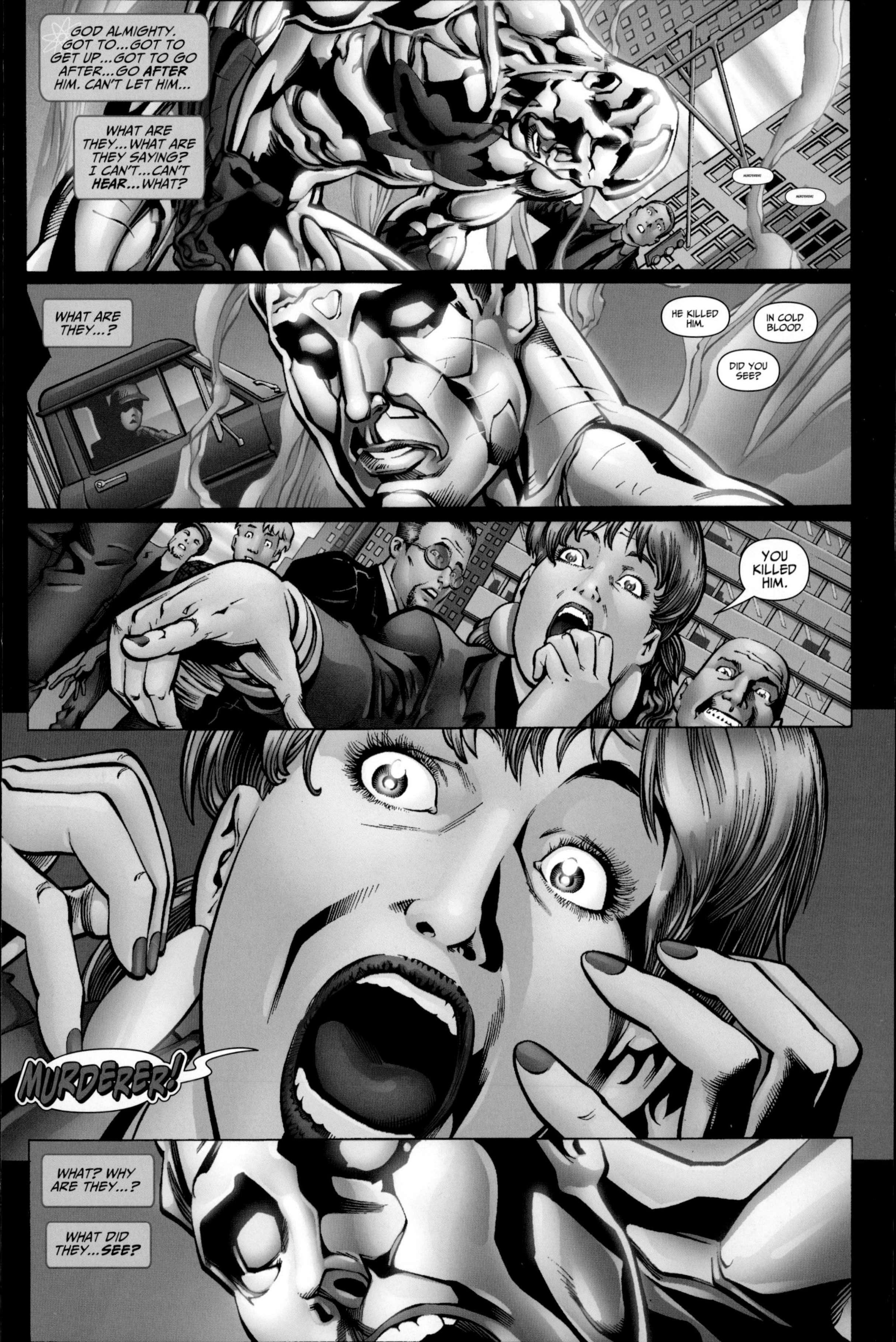
GOD ALMIGHTY. GOT TO...GOT TO GET UP...GOT TO GO AFTER...GO AFTER HIM. CAN'T LET HIM...
WHAT ARE THEY...WHAT ARE THEY SAYING? I CAN'T...CAN'T HEAR...WHAT?
WHAT ARE THEY...?
HE KILLED HIM.
IN COLD BLOOD.
DID YOU SEE?
YOU KILLED HIM.
MURDERER!
WHAT? WHY ARE THEY...?
WHAT DID THEY...SEE?

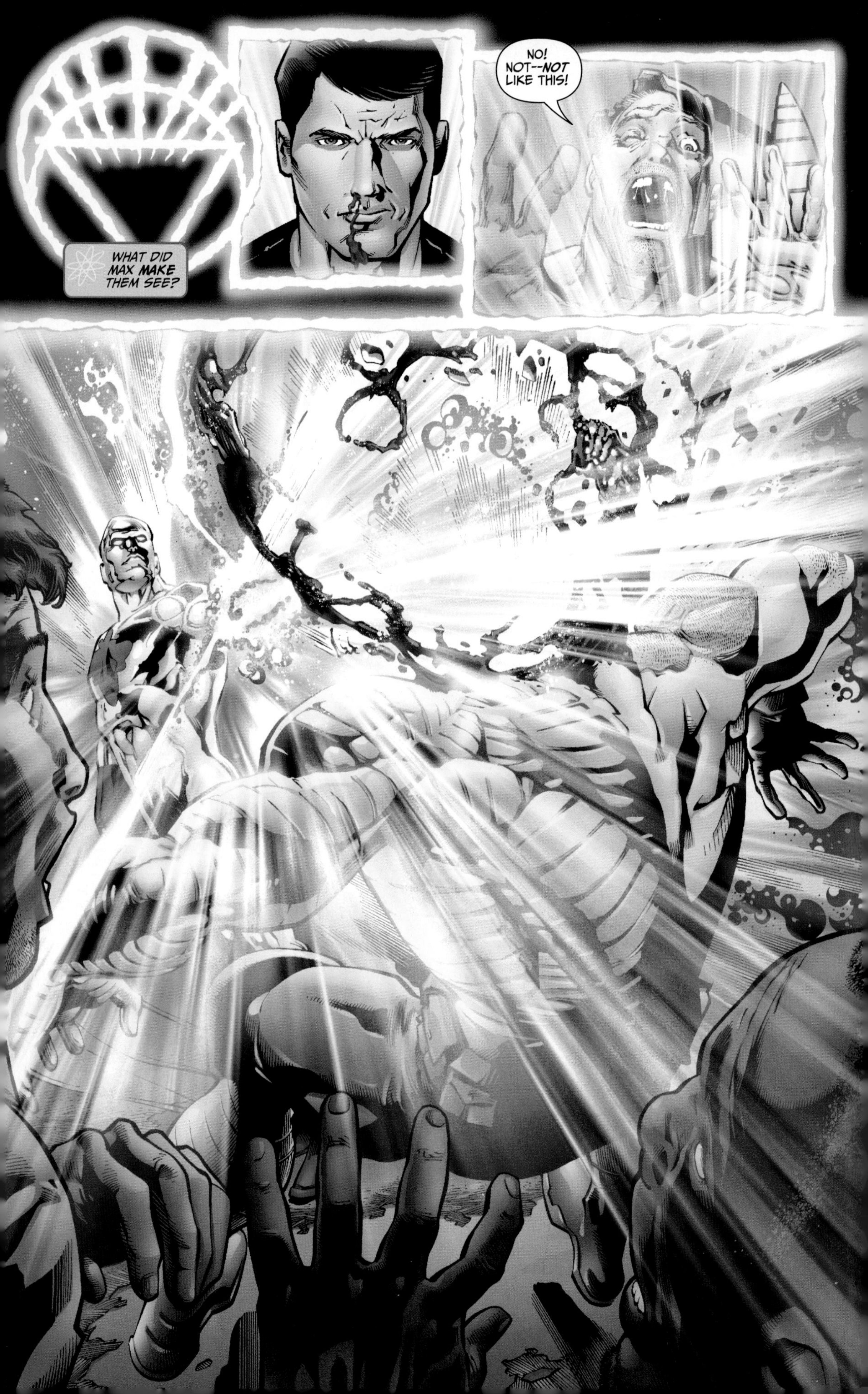
WHAT DID MAX MAKE THEM SEE?
NO! NOT--NOT LIKE THIS!

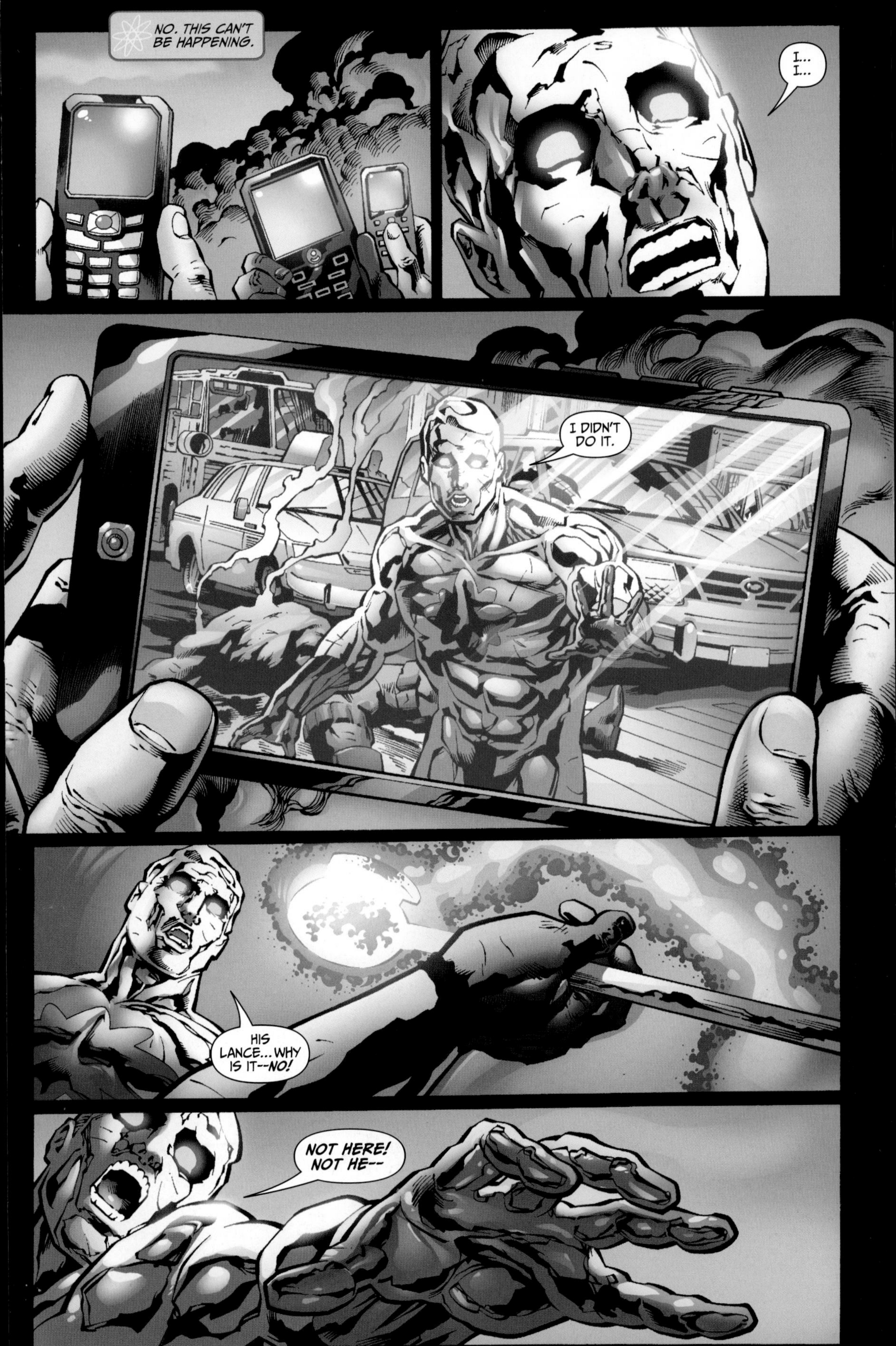
NO. THIS CAN'T BE HAPPENING.
I... I...
I DIDN'T DO IT.
HIS LANCE...WHY IS IT--NO!
NOT HERE! NOT HE--

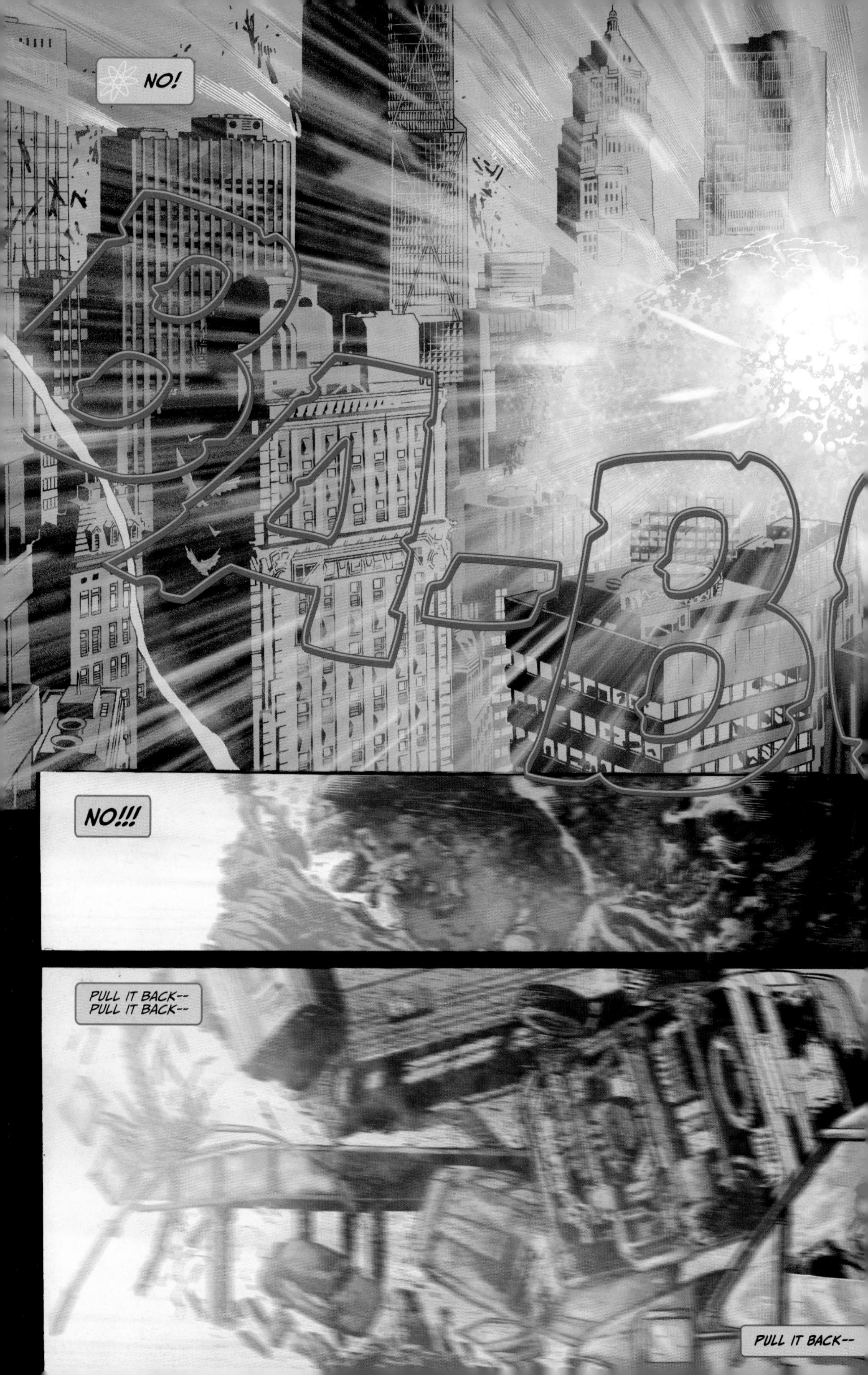
NO!
NO!!!
PULL IT BACK--
PULL IT BACK--
PULL IT BACK--

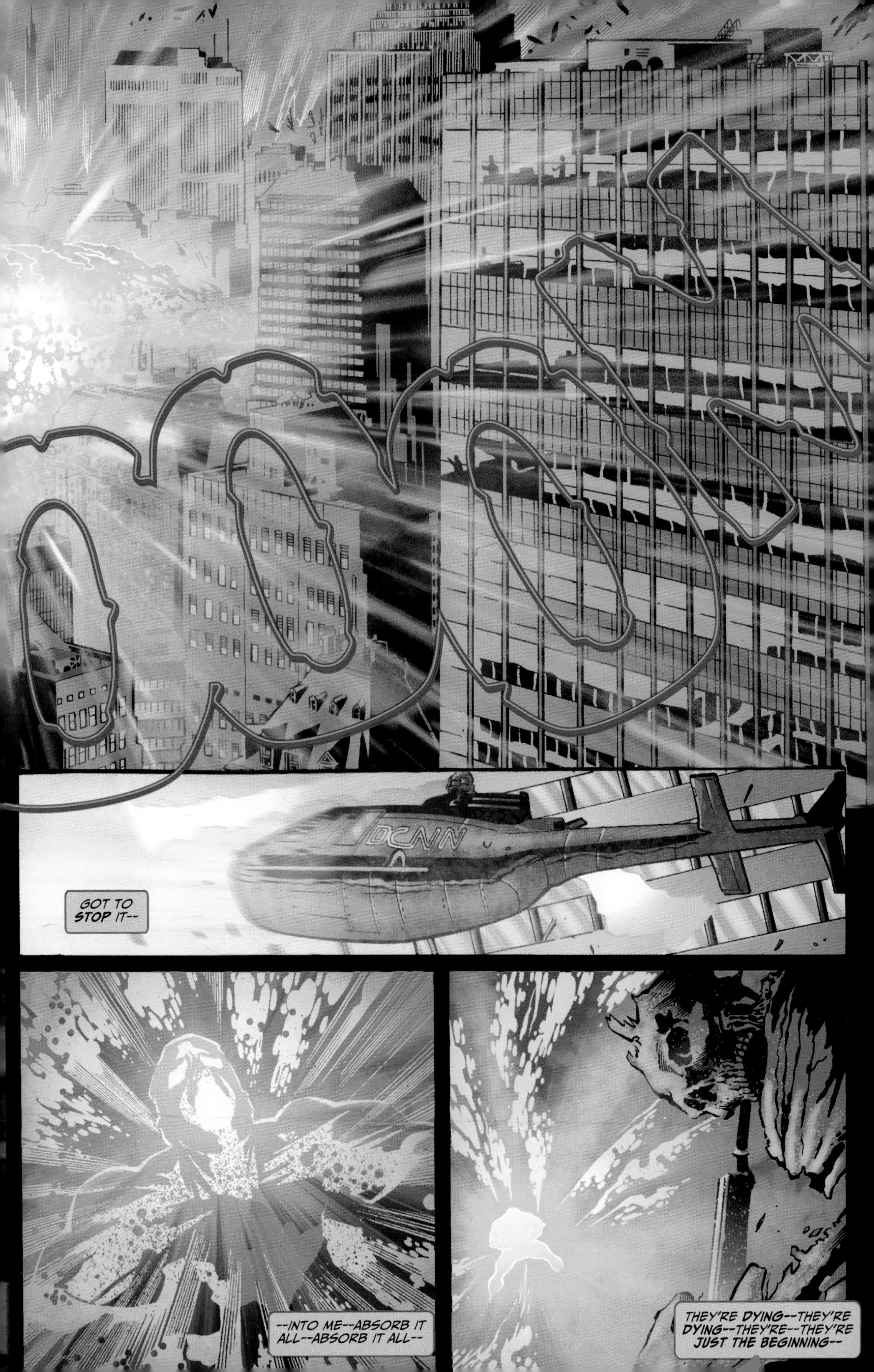
GOT TO STOP IT--
--INTO ME--ABSORB IT ALL--ABSORB IT ALL--
THEY'RE DYING--THEY'RE DYING--THEY'RE--THEY'RE JUST THE BEGINNING--

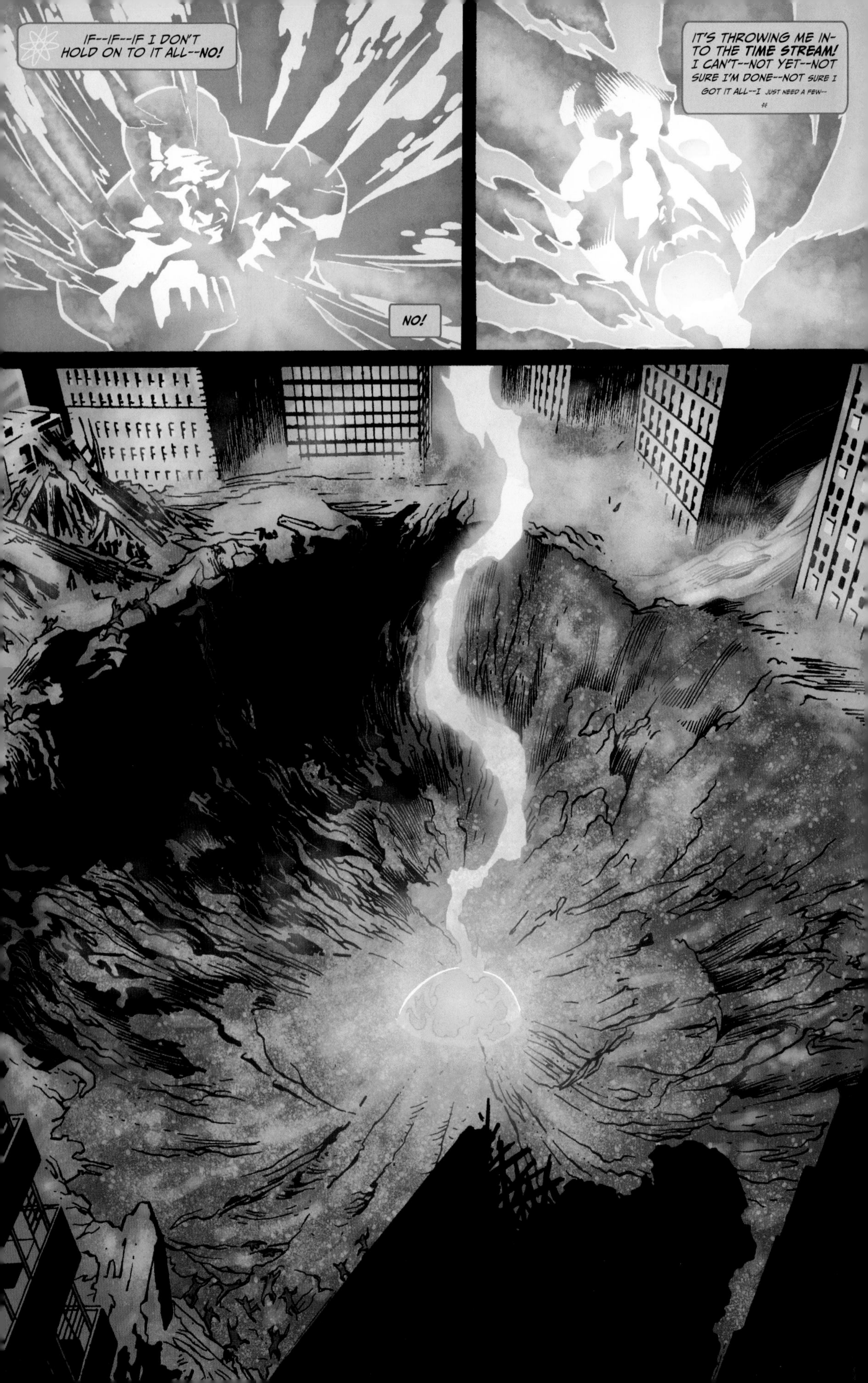
IF--IF--IF I DON'T HOLD ON TO IT ALL--NO!
NO!
IT'S THROWING ME INTO THE TIME STREAM! I CAN'T--NOT YET--NOT SURE I'M DONE--NOT SURE I GOT IT ALL--I JUST NEED A FEW--

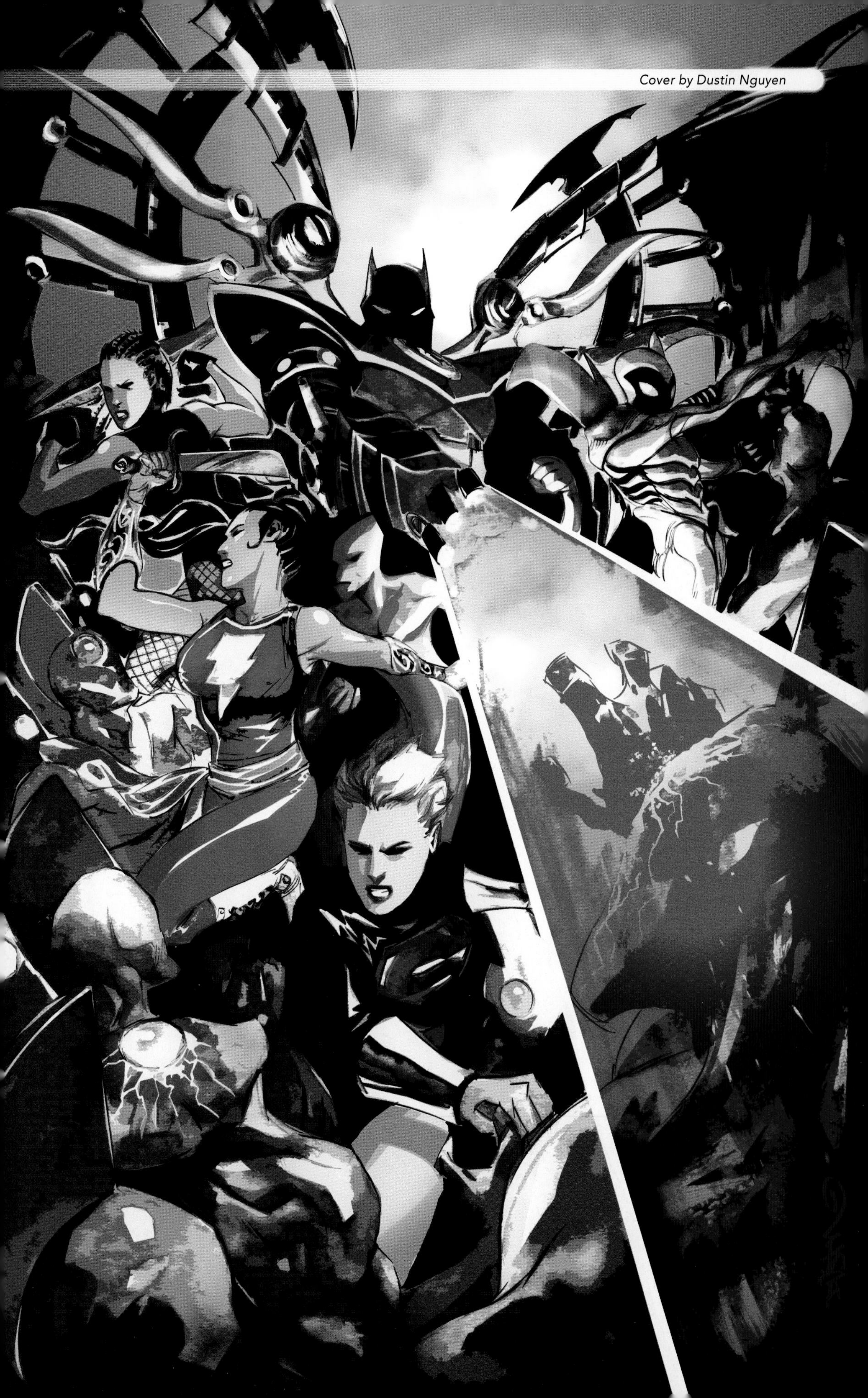

Cover by Dustin Nguyen

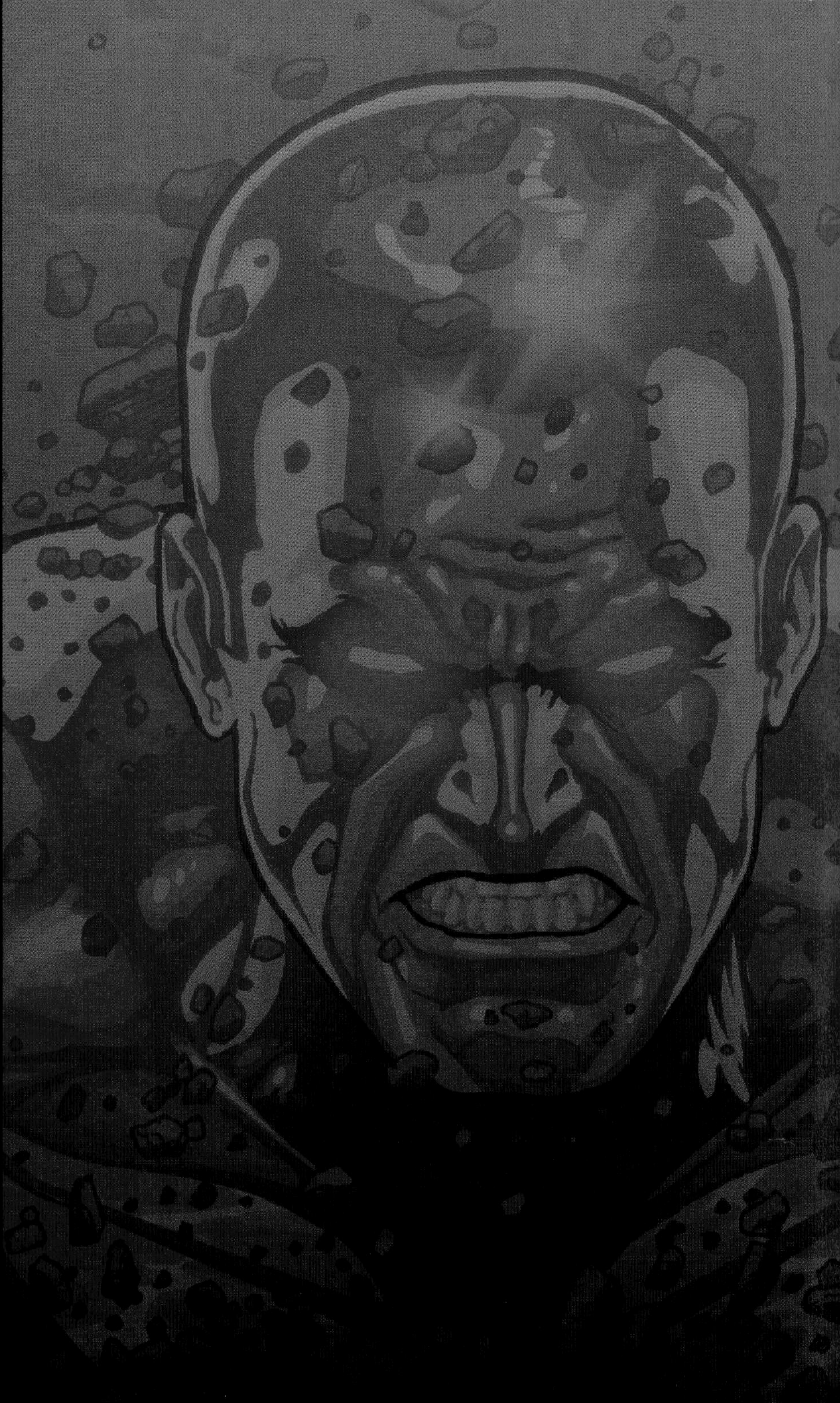

PART FOURTEEN:
TOMORROW IS TODAY

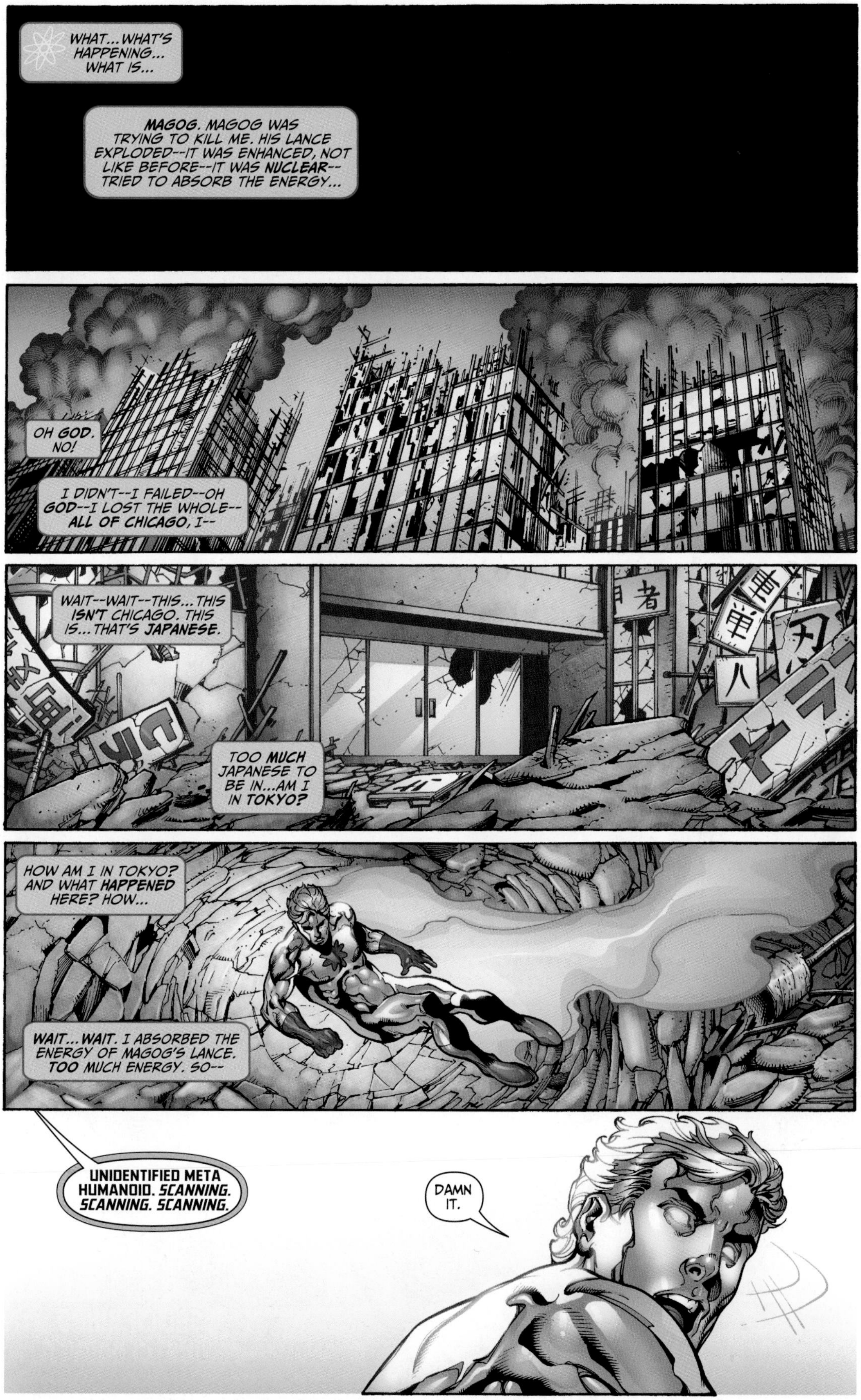
WHAT...WHAT'S HAPPENING... WHAT IS...
MAGOG. MAGOG WAS TRYING TO KILL ME. HIS LANCE EXPLODED--IT WAS ENHANCED, NOT LIKE BEFORE--IT WAS NUCLEAR--TRIED TO ABSORB THE ENERGY...
OH GOD. NO!
I DIDN'T--I FAILED--OH GOD--I LOST THE WHOLE--ALL OF CHICAGO, I--
WAIT--WAIT--THIS...THIS ISN'T CHICAGO. THIS IS...THAT'S JAPANESE.
TOO MUCH JAPANESE TO BE IN...AM I IN TOKYO?
HOW AM I IN TOKYO? AND WHAT HAPPENED HERE? HOW...
WAIT...WAIT. I ABSORBED THE ENERGY OF MAGOG'S LANCE. TOO MUCH ENERGY. SO--
UNIDENTIFIED META HUMANOID. SCANNING. SCANNING. SCANNING.
DAMN IT.

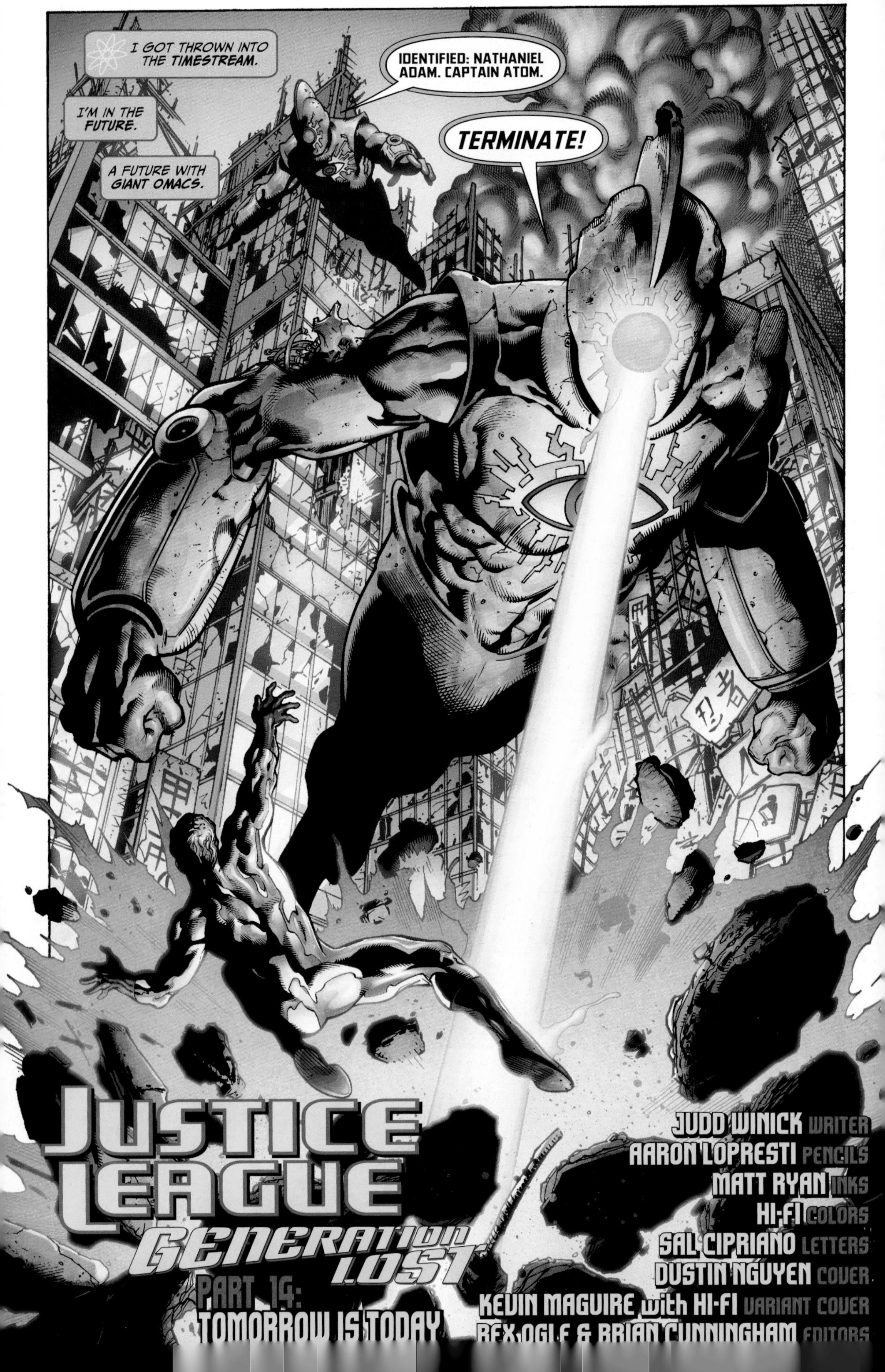

I GOT THROWN INTO THE TIMESTREAM.
IDENTIFIED: NATHANIEL ADAM. CAPTAIN ATOM.
I'M IN THE FUTURE.
TERMINATE!
A FUTURE WITH GIANT OMACS.
JUSTICE LEAGUE
GENERATION LOST
PART 14:
TOMORROW IS TODAY
JUDD WINICK WRITER
AARON LOPRESTI PENCILS
MATT RYAN INKS
HI-FI COLORS
SAL CIPRIANO LETTERS
DUSTIN NGUYEN COVER
KEVIN MAGUIRE with HI-FI VARIANT COVER
REX OGLE & BRIAN CUNNINGHAM EDITORS

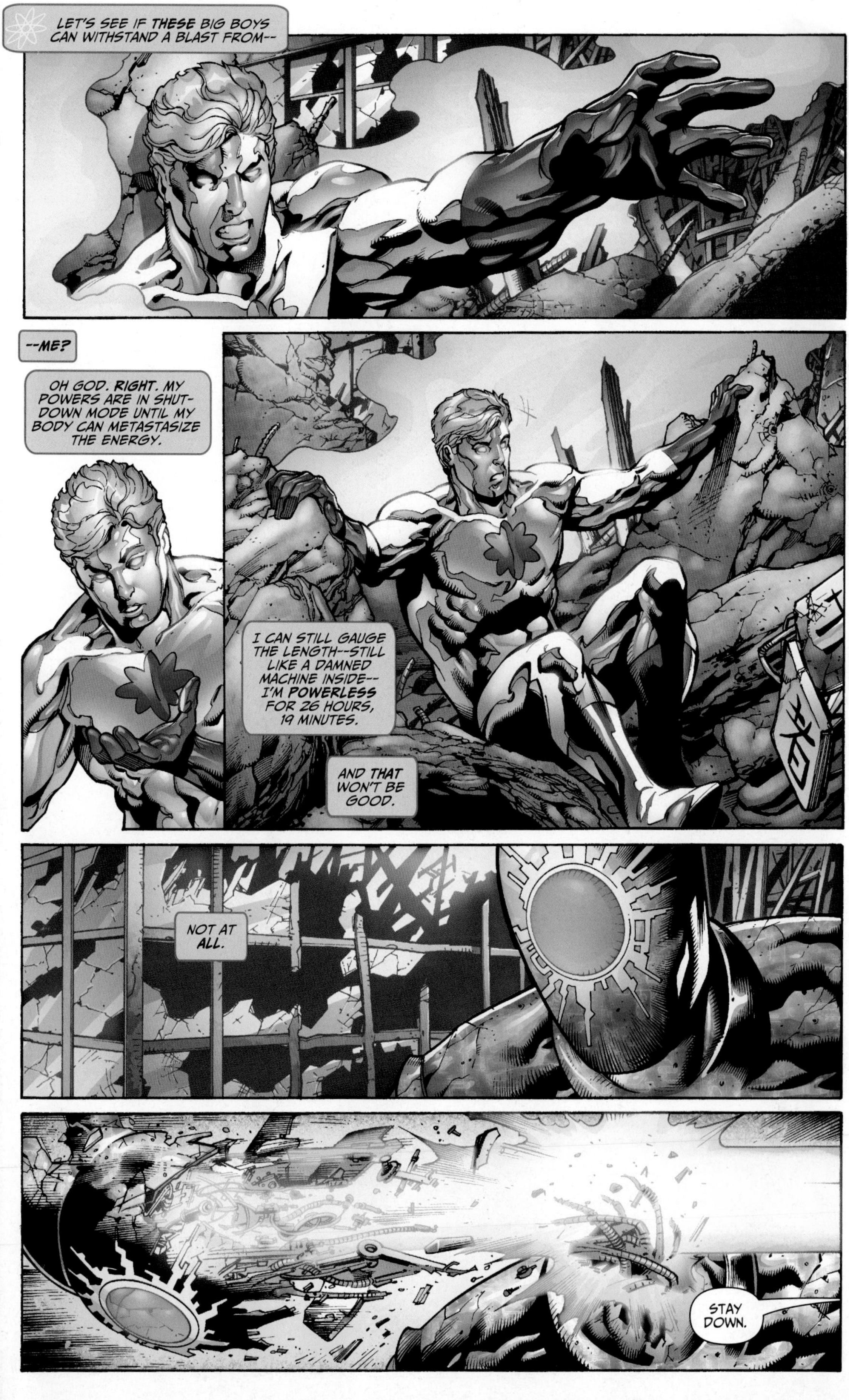
LET'S SEE IF THESE BIG BOYS CAN WITHSTAND A BLAST FROM--
--ME?
OH GOD. RIGHT. MY POWERS ARE IN SHUT-DOWN MODE UNTIL MY BODY CAN METASTASIZE THE ENERGY.
I CAN STILL GAUGE THE LENGTH--STILL LIKE A DAMNED MACHINE INSIDE--I'M POWERLESS FOR 26 HOURS, 19 MINUTES.
AND THAT WON'T BE GOOD.
NOT AT ALL.
STAY DOWN.

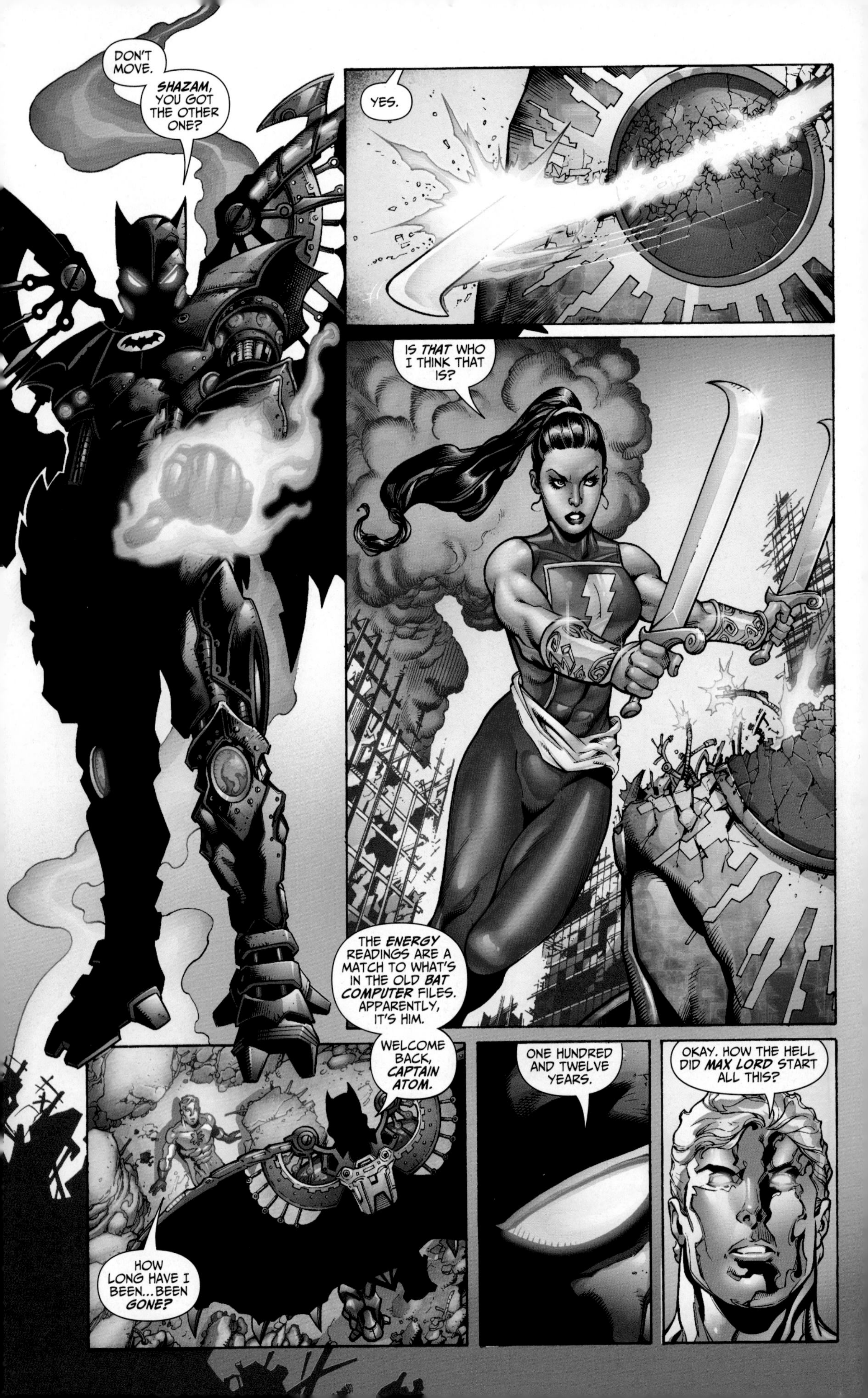
DON'T MOVE.
SHAZAM, YOU GOT THE OTHER ONE?
YES.
IS THAT WHO I THINK THAT IS?
THE ENERGY READINGS ARE A MATCH TO WHAT'S IN THE OLD BAT COMPUTER FILES. APPARENTLY, IT'S HIM.
WELCOME BACK, CAPTAIN ATOM.
HOW LONG HAVE I BEEN...BEEN GONE?
ONE HUNDRED AND TWELVE YEARS.
OKAY. HOW THE HELL DID MAX LORD START ALL THIS?

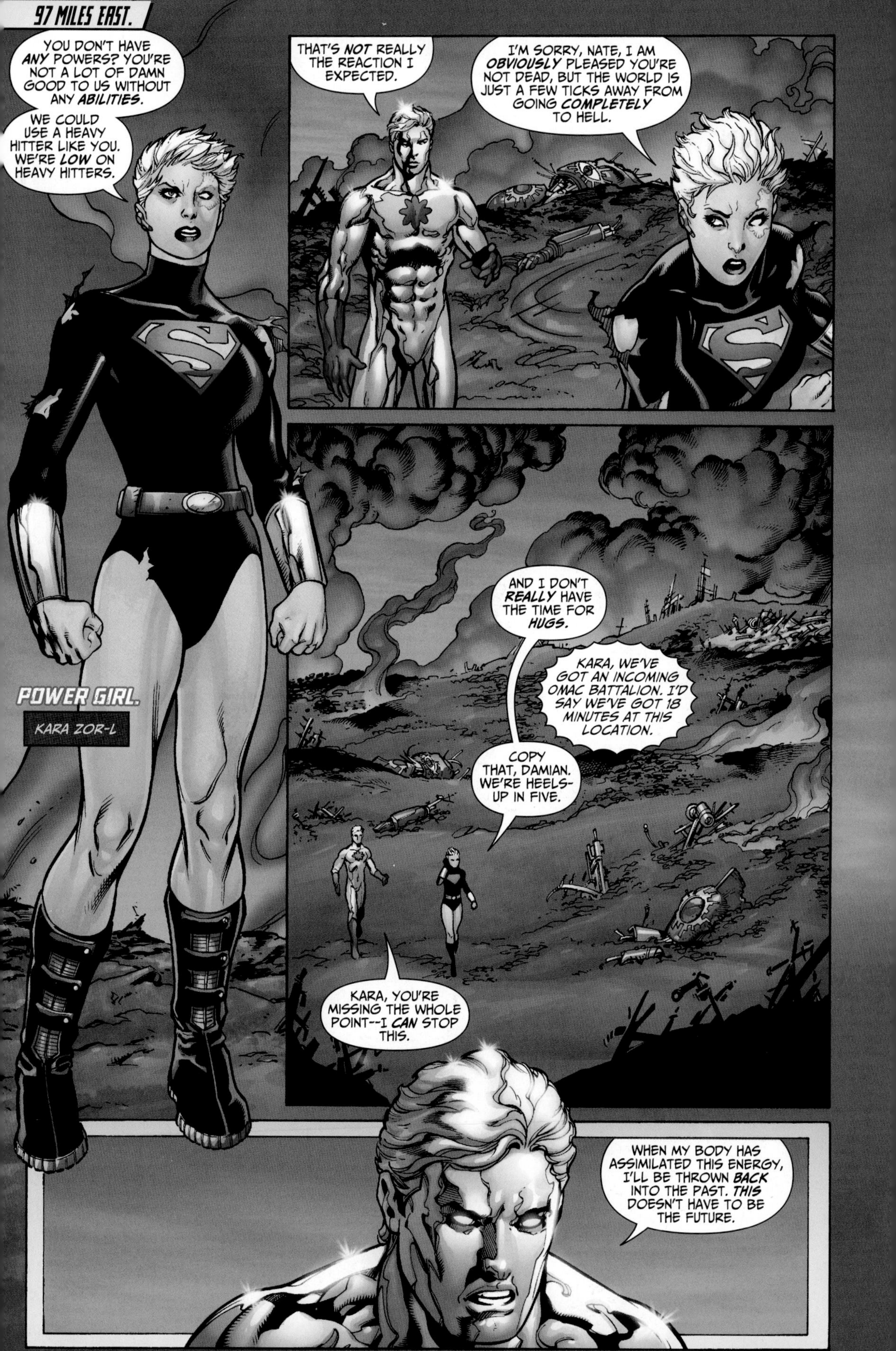
97 MILES EAST.
YOU DON'T HAVE ANY POWERS? YOU'RE NOT A LOT OF DAMN GOOD TO US WITHOUT ANY ABILITIES.
WE COULD USE A HEAVY HITTER LIKE YOU. WE'RE LOW ON HEAVY HITTERS.
THAT'S NOT REALLY THE REACTION I EXPECTED.
I'M SORRY, NATE, I AM OBVIOUSLY PLEASED YOU'RE NOT DEAD, BUT THE WORLD IS JUST A FEW TICKS AWAY FROM GOING COMPLETELY TO HELL.
POWER GIRL.
KARA ZOR-L
AND I DON'T REALLY HAVE THE TIME FOR HUGS.
KARA, WE'VE GOT AN INCOMING OMAC BATTALION. I'D SAY WE'VE GOT 18 MINUTES AT THIS LOCATION.
COPY THAT, DAMIAN. WE'RE HEELS-UP IN FIVE.
KARA, YOU'RE MISSING THE WHOLE POINT--I CAN STOP THIS.
WHEN MY BODY HAS ASSIMILATED THIS ENERGY, I'LL BE THROWN BACK INTO THE PAST. THIS DOESN'T HAVE TO BE THE FUTURE.

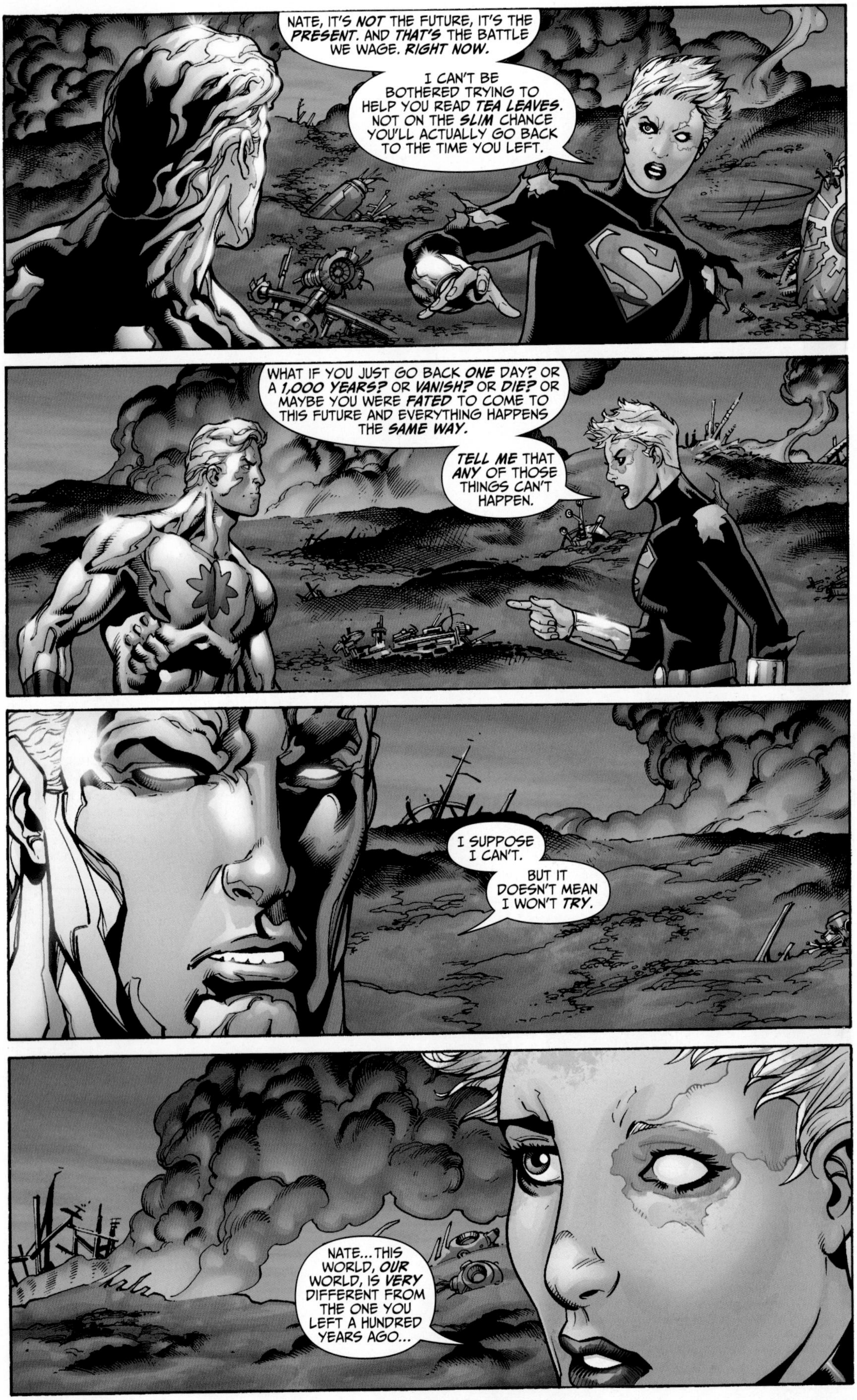
NATE, IT'S NOT THE FUTURE, IT'S THE PRESENT. AND THAT'S THE BATTLE WE WAGE. RIGHT NOW.
I CAN'T BE BOTHERED TRYING TO HELP YOU READ TEA LEAVES. NOT ON THE SLIM CHANCE YOU'LL ACTUALLY GO BACK TO THE TIME YOU LEFT.
WHAT IF YOU JUST GO BACK ONE DAY? OR A 1,000 YEARS? OR VANISH? OR DIE? OR MAYBE YOU WERE FATED TO COME TO THIS FUTURE AND EVERYTHING HAPPENS THE SAME WAY.
TELL ME THAT ANY OF THOSE THINGS CAN'T HAPPEN.
I SUPPOSE I CAN'T.
BUT IT DOESN'T MEAN I WON'T TRY.
NATE...THIS WORLD, OUR WORLD, IS VERY DIFFERENT FROM THE ONE YOU LEFT A HUNDRED YEARS AGO...

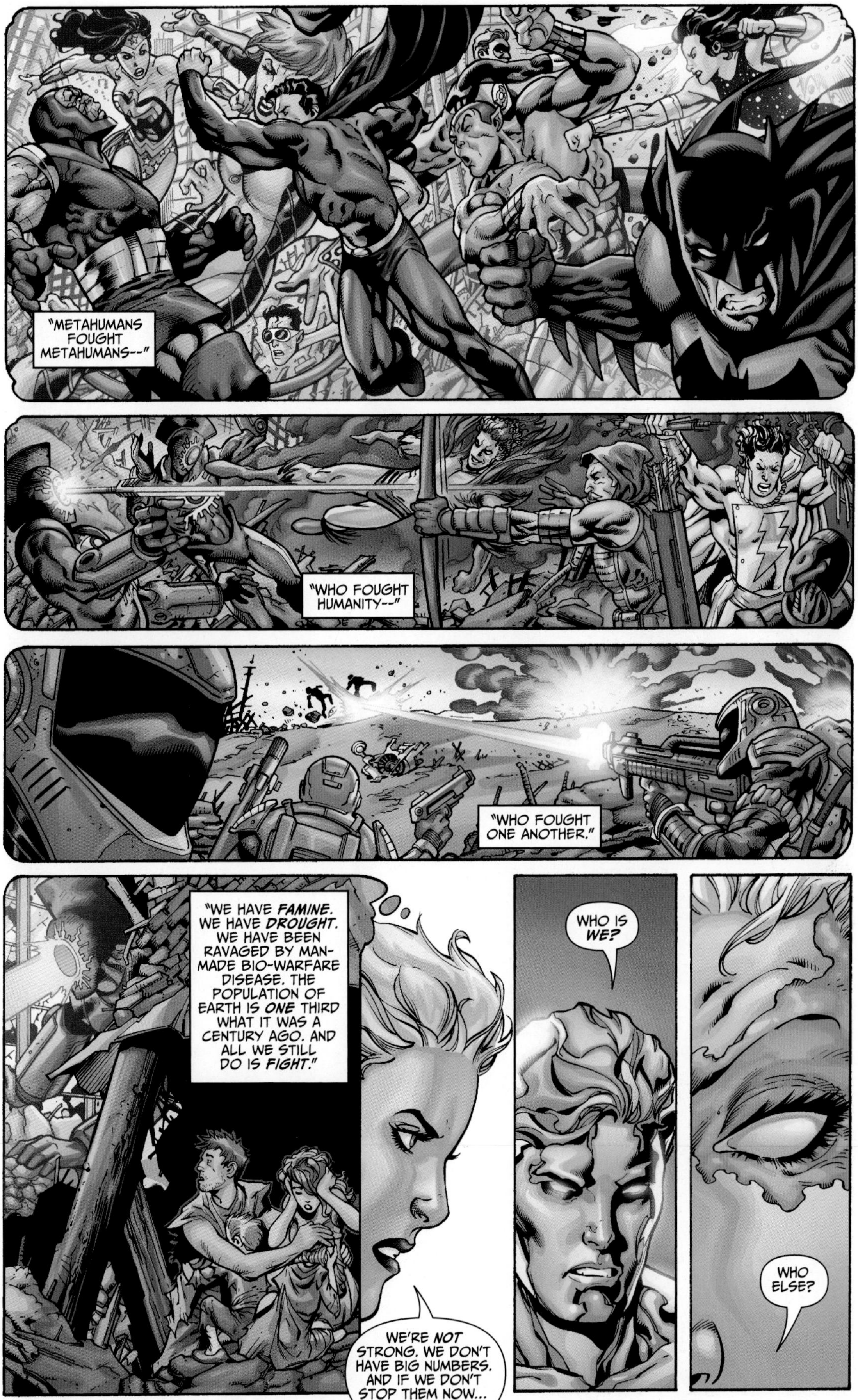
"METAHUMANS FOUGHT METAHUMANS--"
"WHO FOUGHT HUMANITY--"
"WHO FOUGHT ONE ANOTHER."
"WE HAVE FAMINE. WE HAVE DROUGHT. WE HAVE BEEN RAVAGED BY MAN-MADE BIO-WARFARE DISEASE. THE POPULATION OF EARTH IS ONE THIRD WHAT IT WAS A CENTURY AGO. AND ALL WE STILL DO IS FIGHT."
WE'RE NOT STRONG. WE DON'T HAVE BIG NUMBERS. AND IF WE DON'T STOP THEM NOW... IT'S OVER.
WHO IS WE?
WHO ELSE?

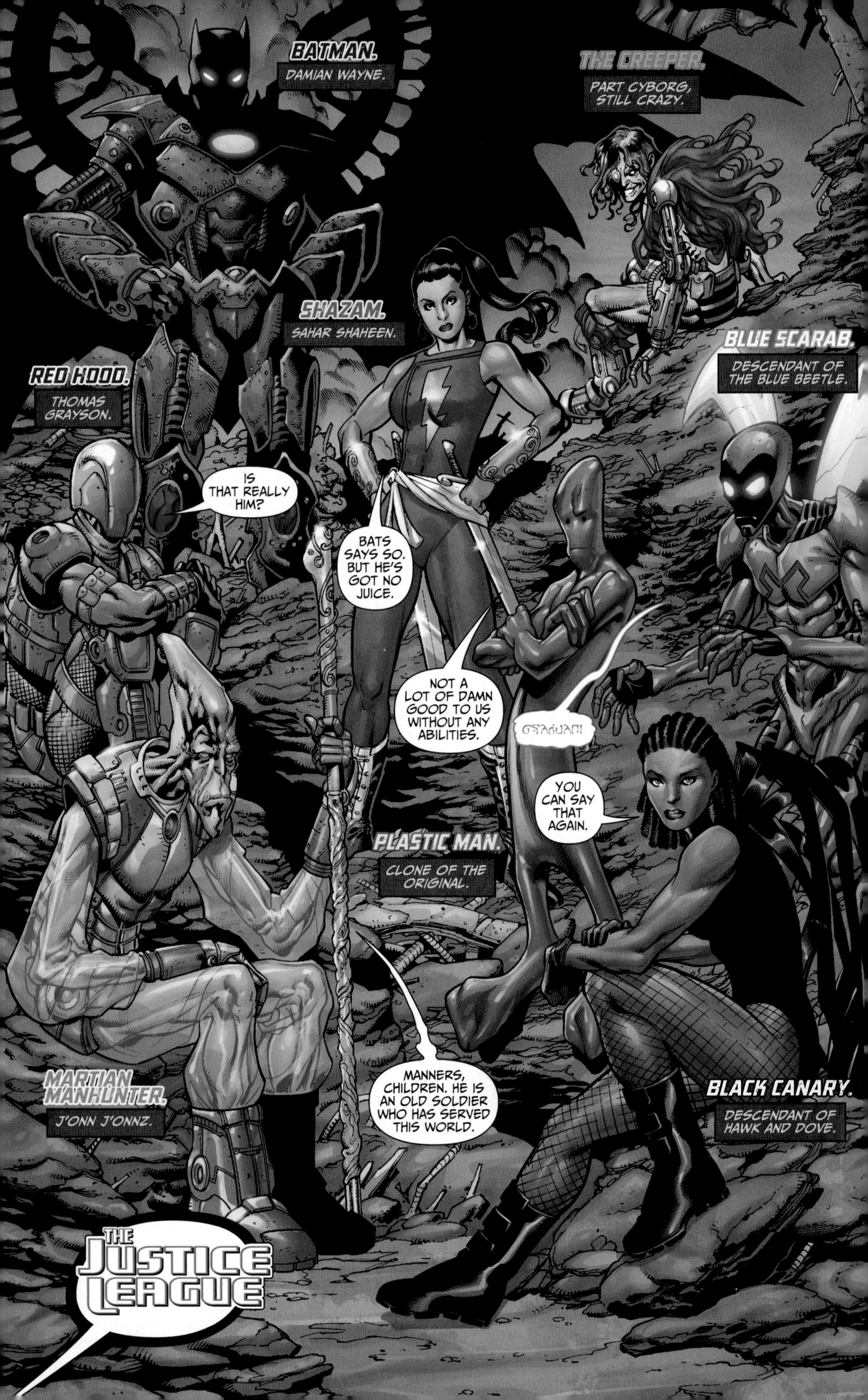
BATMAN.
DAMIAN WAYNE.
THE CREEPER.
PART CYBORG, STILL CRAZY.
SHAZAM.
SAHAR SHAHEEN.
RED HOOD.
THOMAS GRAYSON.
BLUE SCARAB.
DESCENDANT OF THE BLUE BEETLE.
IS THAT REALLY HIM?
BATS SAYS SO. BUT HE'S GOT NO JUICE.
NOT A LOT OF DAMN GOOD TO US WITHOUT ANY ABILITIES.
YOU CAN SAY THAT AGAIN.
PLASTIC MAN.
CLONE OF THE ORIGINAL.
MARTIAN MANHUNTER.
J'ONN J'ONNZ.
MANNERS, CHILDREN. HE IS AN OLD SOLDIER WHO HAS SERVED THIS WORLD.
BLACK CANARY.
DESCENDANT OF HAWK AND DOVE.
THE JUSTICE LEAGUE

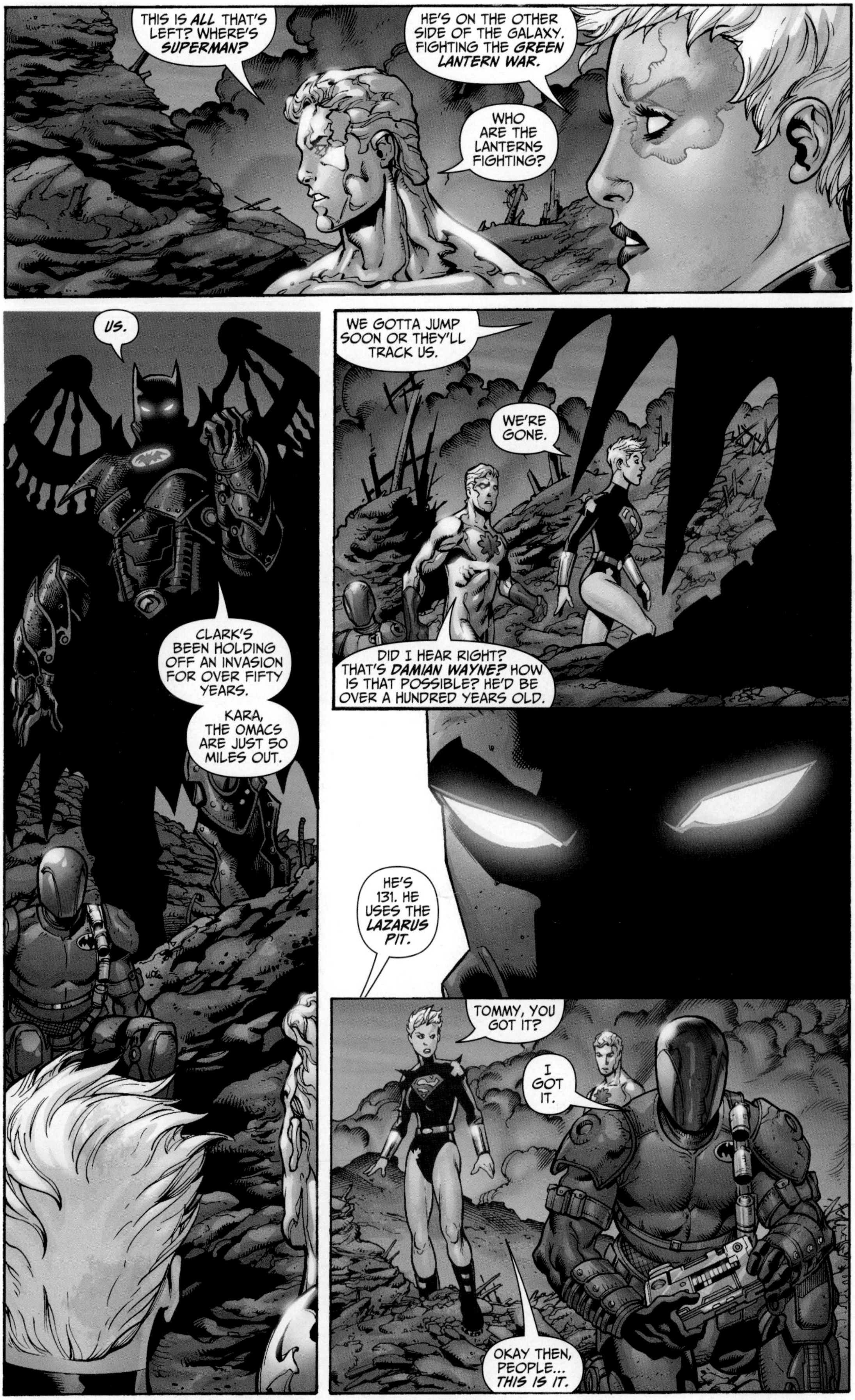
THIS IS *ALL* THAT'S LEFT? WHERE'S *SUPERMAN?*
HE'S ON THE OTHER SIDE OF THE GALAXY. FIGHTING THE *GREEN LANTERN WAR.*
WHO ARE THE LANTERNS FIGHTING?
US.
CLARK'S BEEN HOLDING OFF AN INVASION FOR OVER FIFTY YEARS.
KARA, THE OMACS ARE JUST 50 MILES OUT.
WE GOTTA JUMP SOON OR THEY'LL TRACK US.
WE'RE GONE.
DID I HEAR RIGHT? THAT'S *DAMIAN WAYNE?* HOW IS THAT POSSIBLE? HE'D BE OVER A HUNDRED YEARS OLD.
HE'S 131. HE USES THE *LAZARUS PIT.*
TOMMY, YOU GOT IT?
I GOT IT.
OKAY THEN, PEOPLE... *THIS IS IT.*

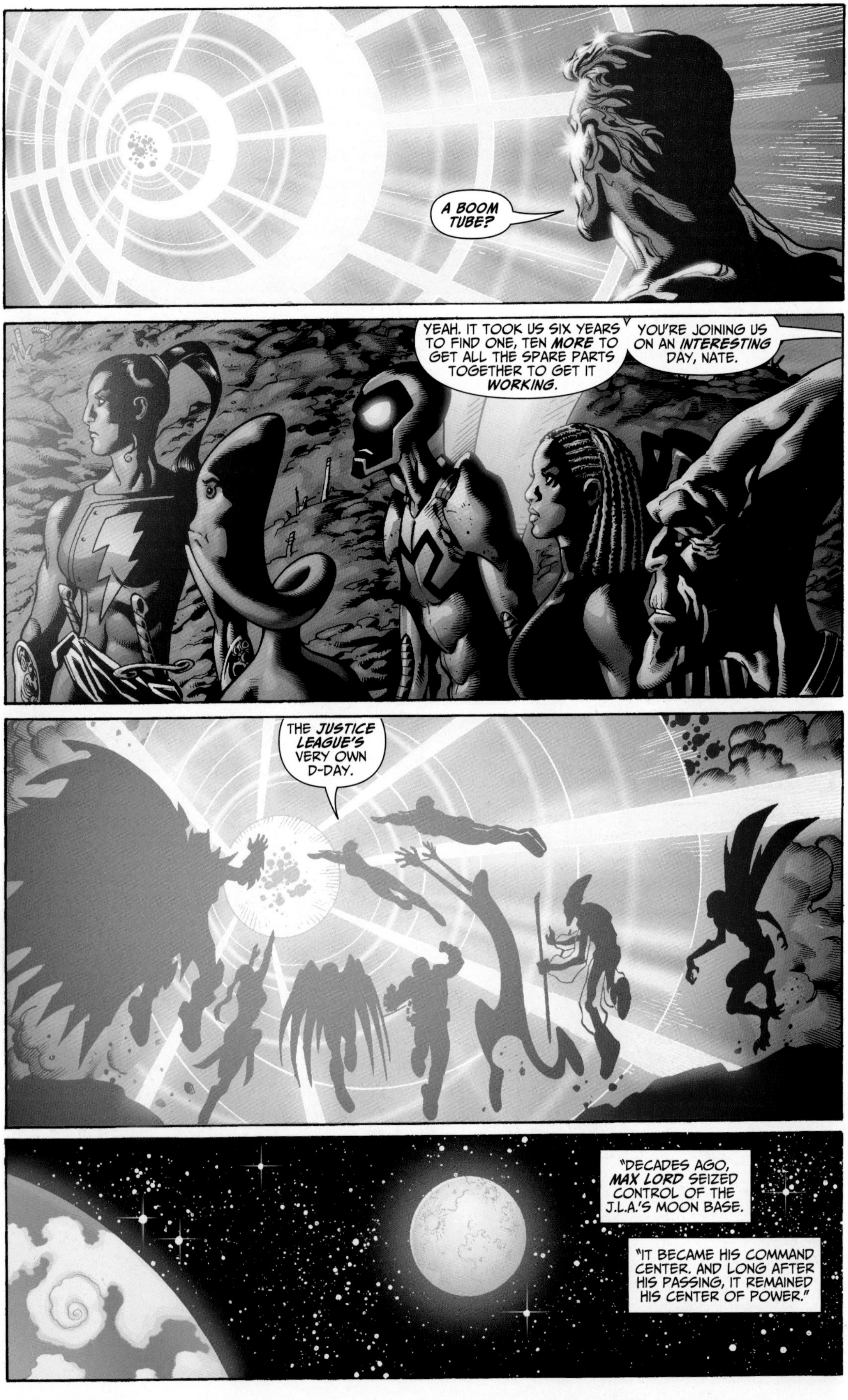
A BOOM TUBE?
YEAH. IT TOOK US SIX YEARS TO FIND ONE, TEN MORE TO GET ALL THE SPARE PARTS TOGETHER TO GET IT WORKING.
YOU'RE JOINING US ON AN INTERESTING DAY, NATE.
THE JUSTICE LEAGUE'S VERY OWN D-DAY.
"DECADES AGO, MAX LORD SEIZED CONTROL OF THE J.L.A.'S MOON BASE.
"IT BECAME HIS COMMAND CENTER. AND LONG AFTER HIS PASSING, IT REMAINED HIS CENTER OF POWER."

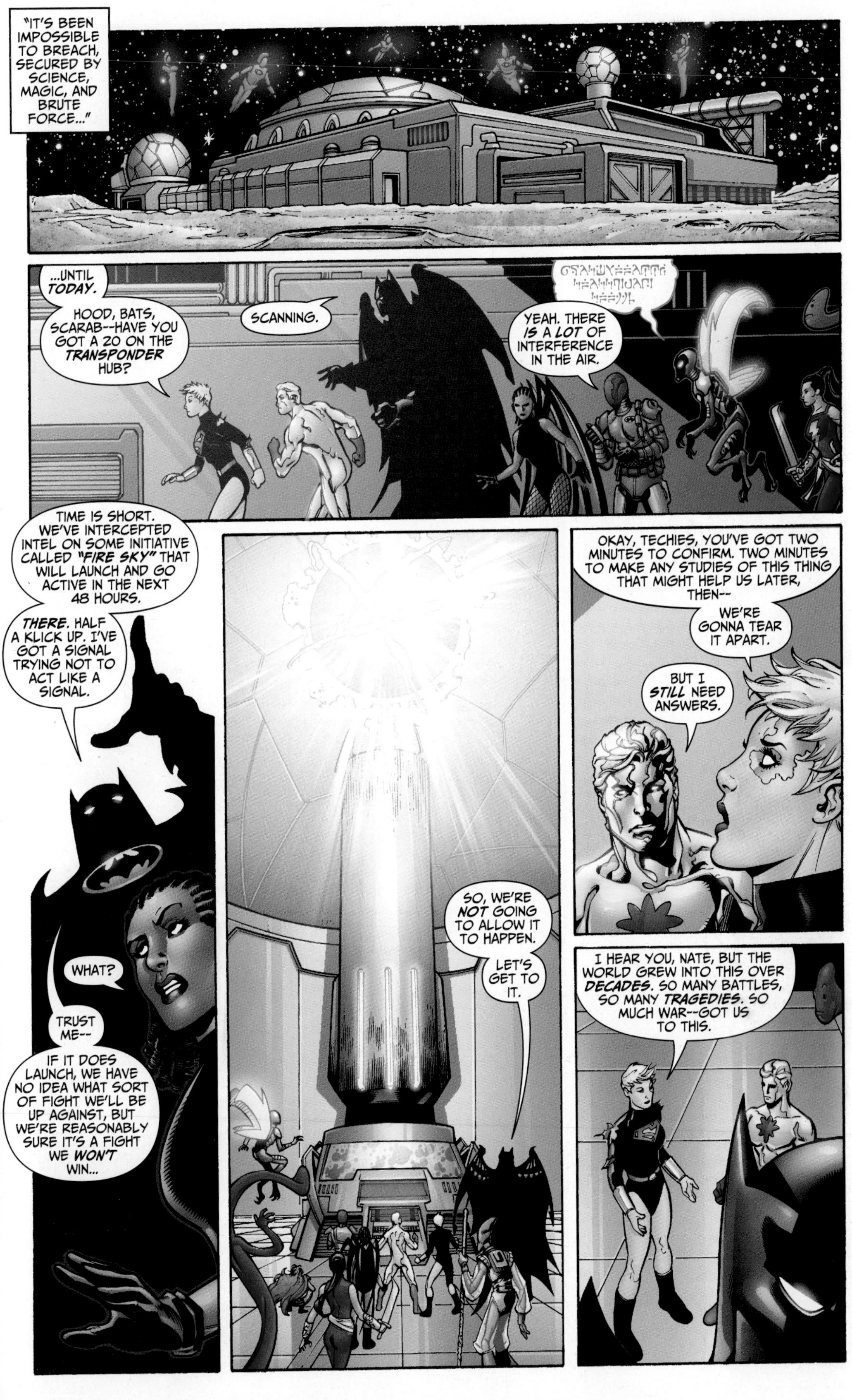
"IT'S BEEN IMPOSSIBLE TO BREACH, SECURED BY SCIENCE, MAGIC, AND BRUTE FORCE..."
...UNTIL TODAY.
HOOD, BATS, SCARAB--HAVE YOU GOT A 20 ON THE TRANSPONDER HUB?
SCANNING.
YEAH. THERE IS A LOT OF INTERFERENCE IN THE AIR.
TIME IS SHORT. WE'VE INTERCEPTED INTEL ON SOME INITIATIVE CALLED "FIRE SKY" THAT WILL LAUNCH AND GO ACTIVE IN THE NEXT 48 HOURS.
THERE. HALF A KLICK UP. I'VE GOT A SIGNAL TRYING NOT TO ACT LIKE A SIGNAL.
WHAT?
TRUST ME--
IF IT DOES LAUNCH, WE HAVE NO IDEA WHAT SORT OF FIGHT WE'LL BE UP AGAINST, BUT WE'RE REASONABLY SURE IT'S A FIGHT WE WON'T WIN...
SO, WE'RE NOT GOING TO ALLOW IT TO HAPPEN.
LET'S GET TO IT.
OKAY, TECHIES, YOU'VE GOT TWO MINUTES TO CONFIRM. TWO MINUTES TO MAKE ANY STUDIES OF THIS THING THAT MIGHT HELP US LATER, THEN--
WE'RE GONNA TEAR IT APART.
BUT I STILL NEED ANSWERS.
I HEAR YOU, NATE, BUT THE WORLD GREW INTO THIS OVER DECADES. SO MANY BATTLES, SO MANY TRAGEDIES. SO MUCH WAR--GOT US TO THIS.

I KNOW THAT, BUT THERE'S ALWAYS A CATALYST. HISTORY HAS ALWAYS SHOWN, *ESPECIALLY* IN *HINDSIGHT*, THAT WE *CAN* FIND THOSE MOMENTS.

FRANZ FERDINAND'S ASSASSINATION LED TO *WORLD WAR I*. THE TREATY OF VERSAILLES LAID THE GROUNDWORK OF THE *WORLD WAR II.*

THE RISE OF THE *ANTI-MONITOR.* THE *MURDER* OF *DARKSEID'S* SON.

MOMENTS--THESE *ACTS*--WERE THE DOMINOES THAT LED TO SO MUCH DEVASTATION.

WAS IT *ALL* MAX LORD? IF I GO BACK AND *KILL* HIM...WILL IT STOP?

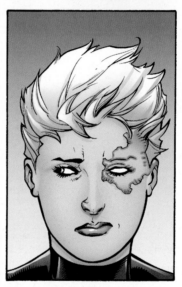

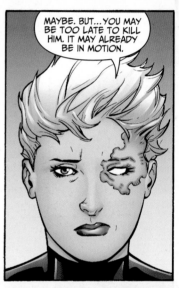

MAYBE. BUT...YOU MAY BE TOO LATE TO KILL HIM. IT MAY ALREADY BE IN MOTION.

WHAT DO YOU MEAN?

IF I HAD TO POINT TO JUST *ONE* THING, ONE MOMENT THAT SEEMED...

THERE *WAS* SOMETHING THAT HAPPENED JUST AFTER YOU DISAPPEARED.

WHAT? WHAT HAPP--

SOMETHING'S WRONG... VERY WRONG.

PLEASE DON'T TELL ME THAT THIS OVERBRED WASHING MACHINE AIN'T THE REAL TRANSPONDER.

NO. THIS IS IT. THIS IS THE MAIN DISPATCH. THIS WILL LAUNCH THE NEW OMAC PROJECT AND ADMINISTER ALL ITS DIRECTIVES. THIS IS THE COMMAND CENTER. IT'S JUST...

WHAT?!

I THINK IT'S ALREADY LAUNCHED.

HOW CAN THAT BE? THERE ARE NO OMACS FLYING TOWARDS EARTH, I'M NOT GETTING ANY MEDIA ON TERRA FIRMA THAT ANY ATTACKS HAVE BEEN...

...BEEN...

ᏩᎦᎮᎢᎭᎴᏔᎢᏋ ᏨᎳᏎᏞᎠᏣᎾᏂᏌᎠᏣᎩ

WHAT THE HELL DO YOU MEAN, "AIRBORNE NANOS ARE FLOODING THE CHAMBER"?

YEAAARGH!

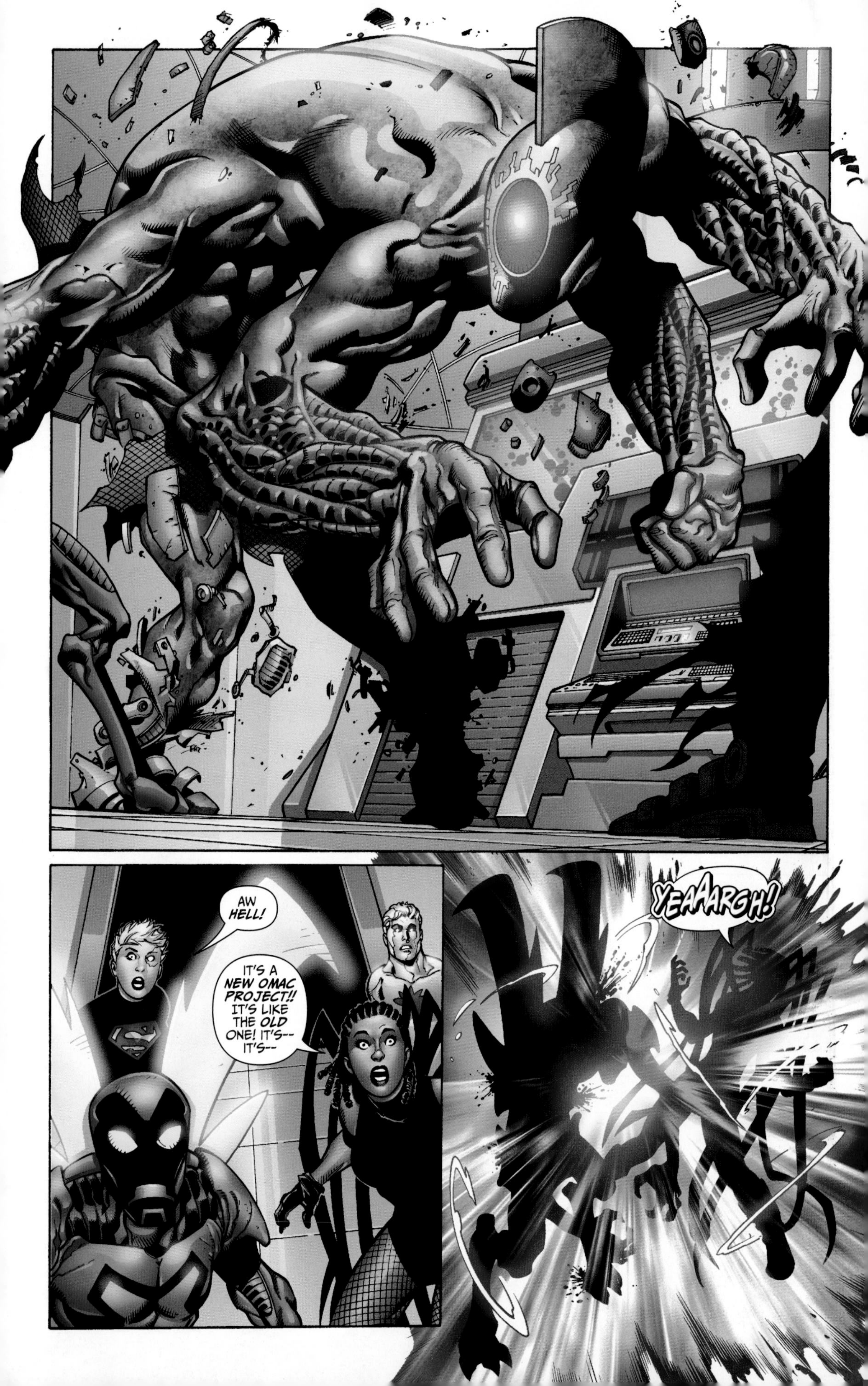
AW HELL!
IT'S A NEW OMAC PROJECT!! IT'S LIKE THE OLD ONE! IT'S-- IT'S--
YEAAARGH!

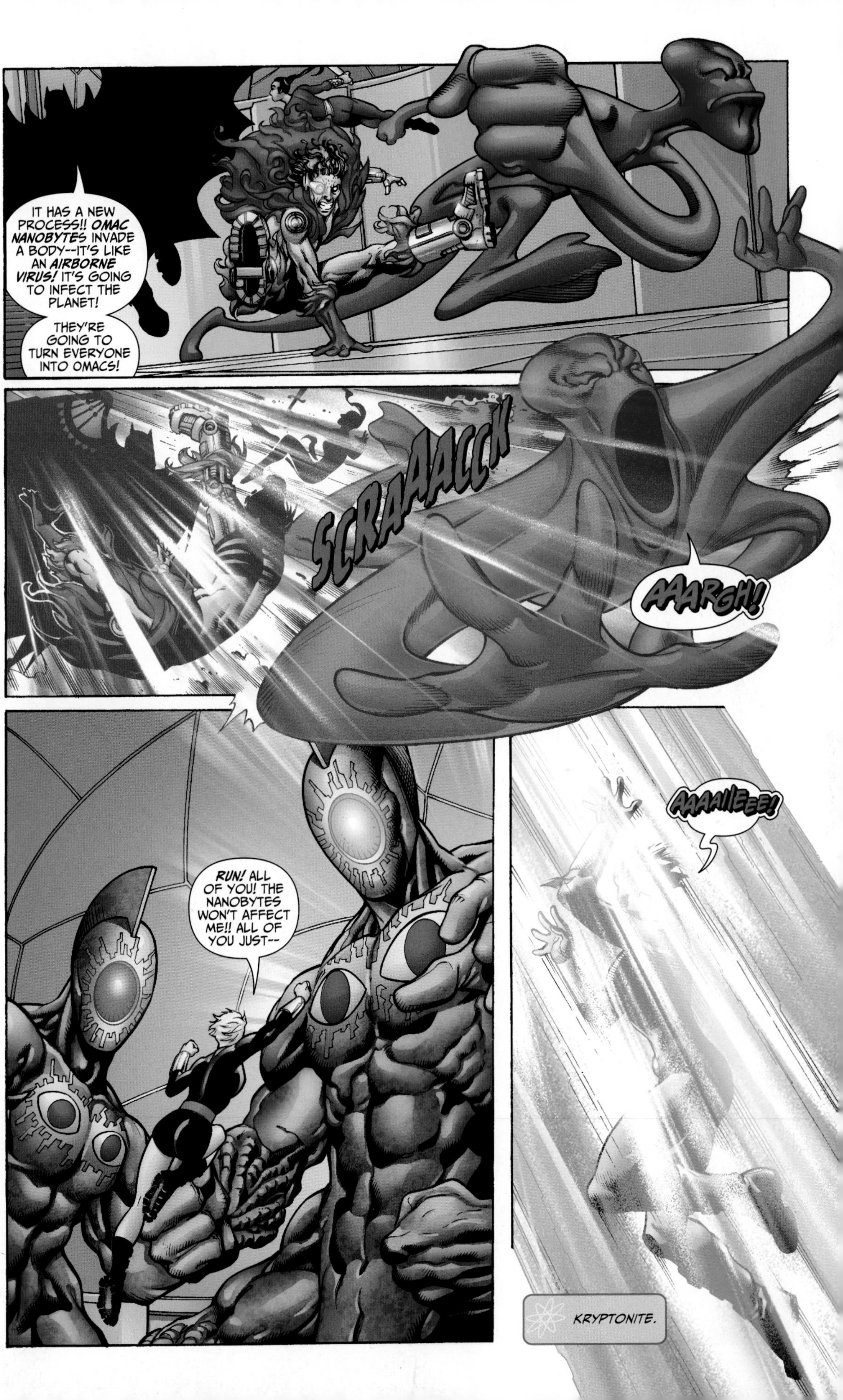
IT HAS A NEW PROCESS!! OMAC NANOBYTES INVADE A BODY--IT'S LIKE AN AIRBORNE VIRUS! IT'S GOING TO INFECT THE PLANET!
THEY'RE GOING TO TURN EVERYONE INTO OMACS!
SCRAAACCK
AAARGH!
RUN! ALL OF YOU! THE NANOBYTES WON'T AFFECT ME!! ALL OF YOU JUST--
AAAAIIEEE!
KRYPTONITE.

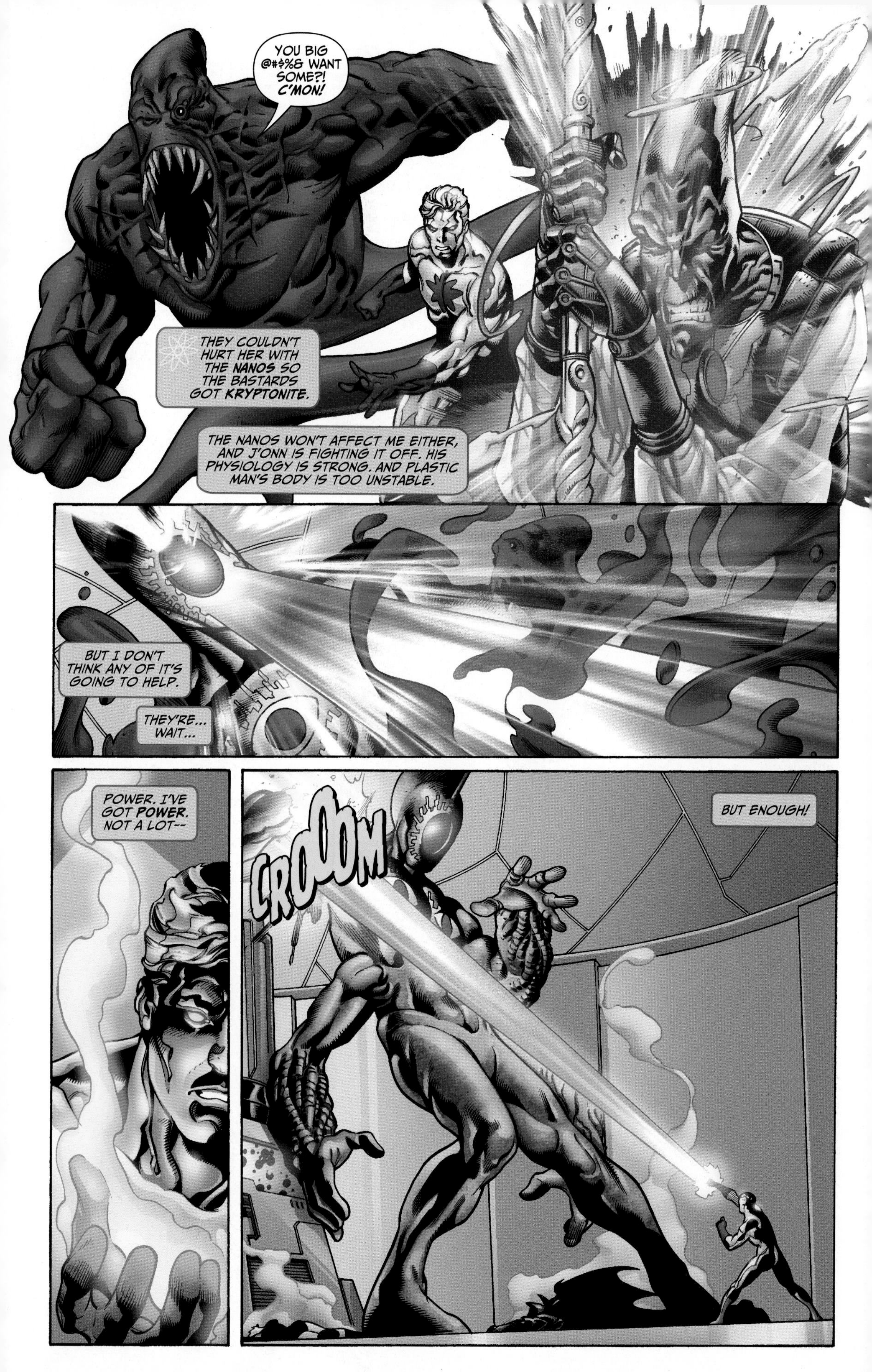
YOU BIG @#$%& WANT SOME?! C'MON!
THEY COULDN'T HURT HER WITH THE NANOS SO THE BASTARDS GOT KRYPTONITE.
THE NANOS WON'T AFFECT ME EITHER, AND J'ONN IS FIGHTING IT OFF. HIS PHYSIOLOGY IS STRONG. AND PLASTIC MAN'S BODY IS TOO UNSTABLE.
BUT I DON'T THINK ANY OF IT'S GOING TO HELP.
THEY'RE... WAIT...
POWER. I'VE GOT POWER. NOT A LOT--
CROOOM
BUT ENOUGH!

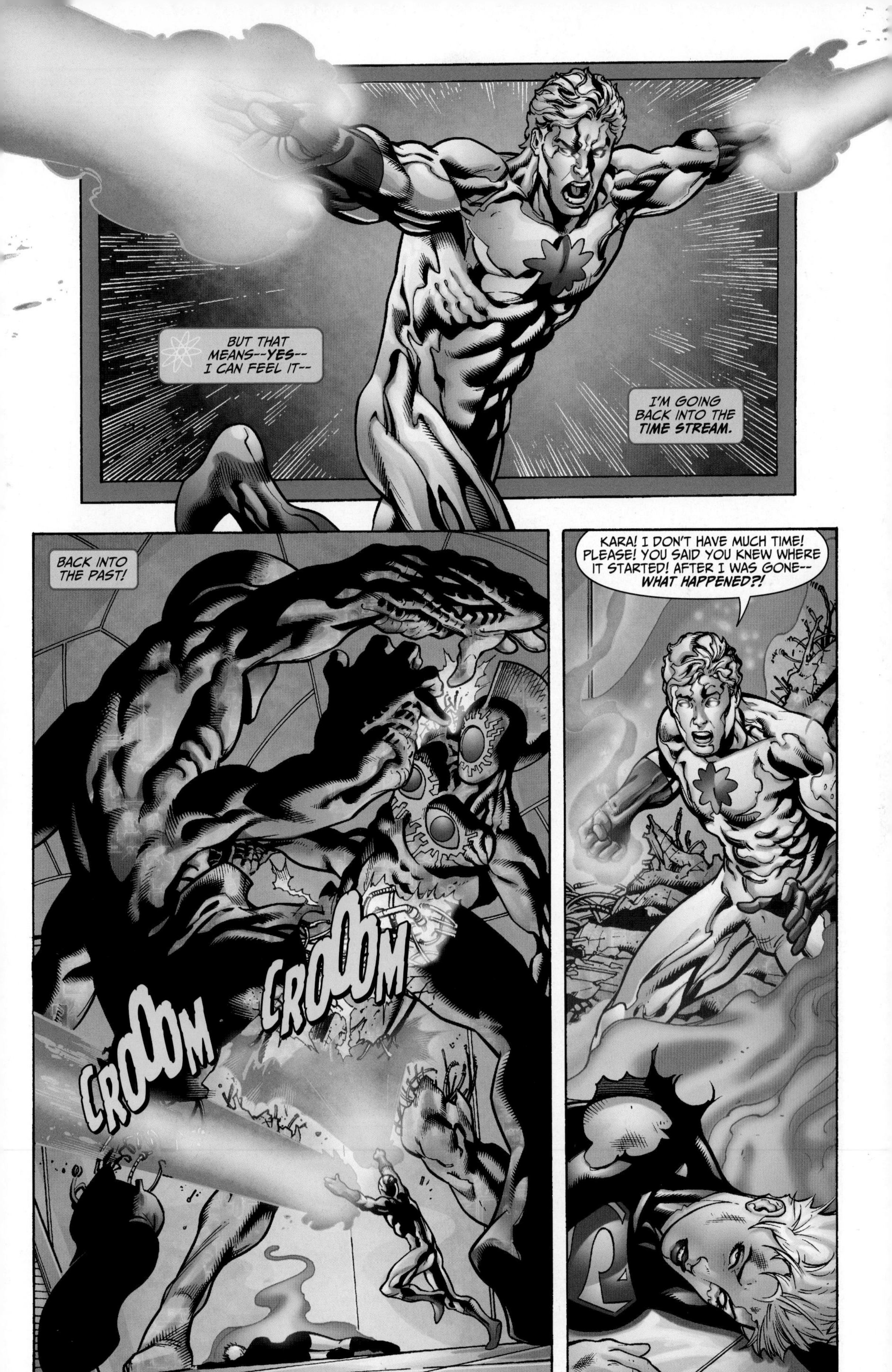
BUT THAT MEANS--YES--I CAN FEEL IT--
I'M GOING BACK INTO THE TIME STREAM.
BACK INTO THE PAST!
CROOOM
CROOOM
KARA! I DON'T HAVE MUCH TIME! PLEASE! YOU SAID YOU KNEW WHERE IT STARTED! AFTER I WAS GONE--WHAT HAPPENED?!

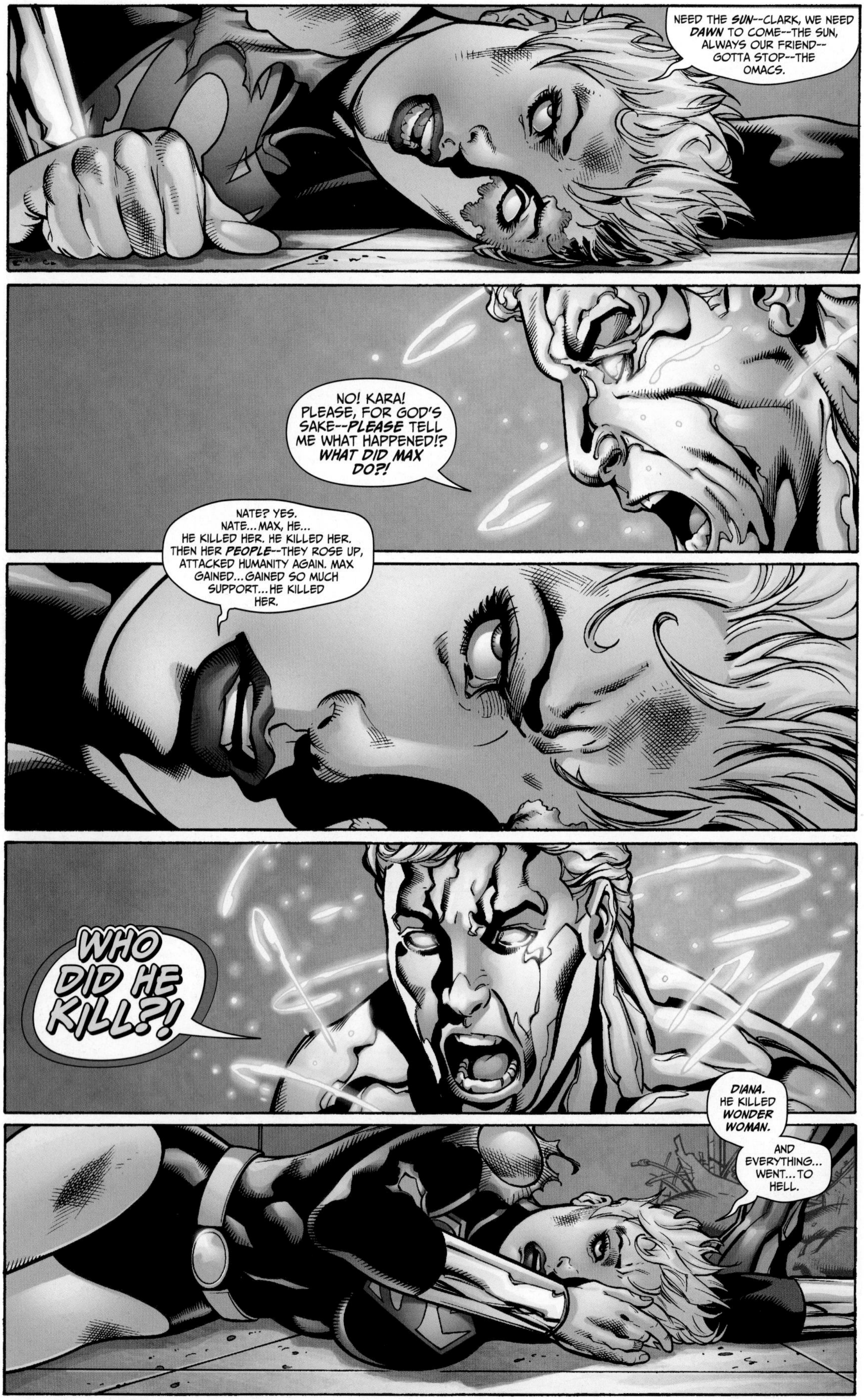
NEED THE SUN--CLARK, WE NEED DAWN TO COME--THE SUN, ALWAYS OUR FRIEND-- GOTTA STOP--THE OMACS.
NO! KARA! PLEASE, FOR GOD'S SAKE--PLEASE TELL ME WHAT HAPPENED!? WHAT DID MAX DO?!
NATE? YES. NATE...MAX, HE... HE KILLED HER. HE KILLED HER. THEN HER PEOPLE--THEY ROSE UP, ATTACKED HUMANITY AGAIN. MAX GAINED...GAINED SO MUCH SUPPORT...HE KILLED HER.
WHO DID HE KILL?!
DIANA. HE KILLED WONDER WOMAN.
AND EVERYTHING... WENT...TO HELL.

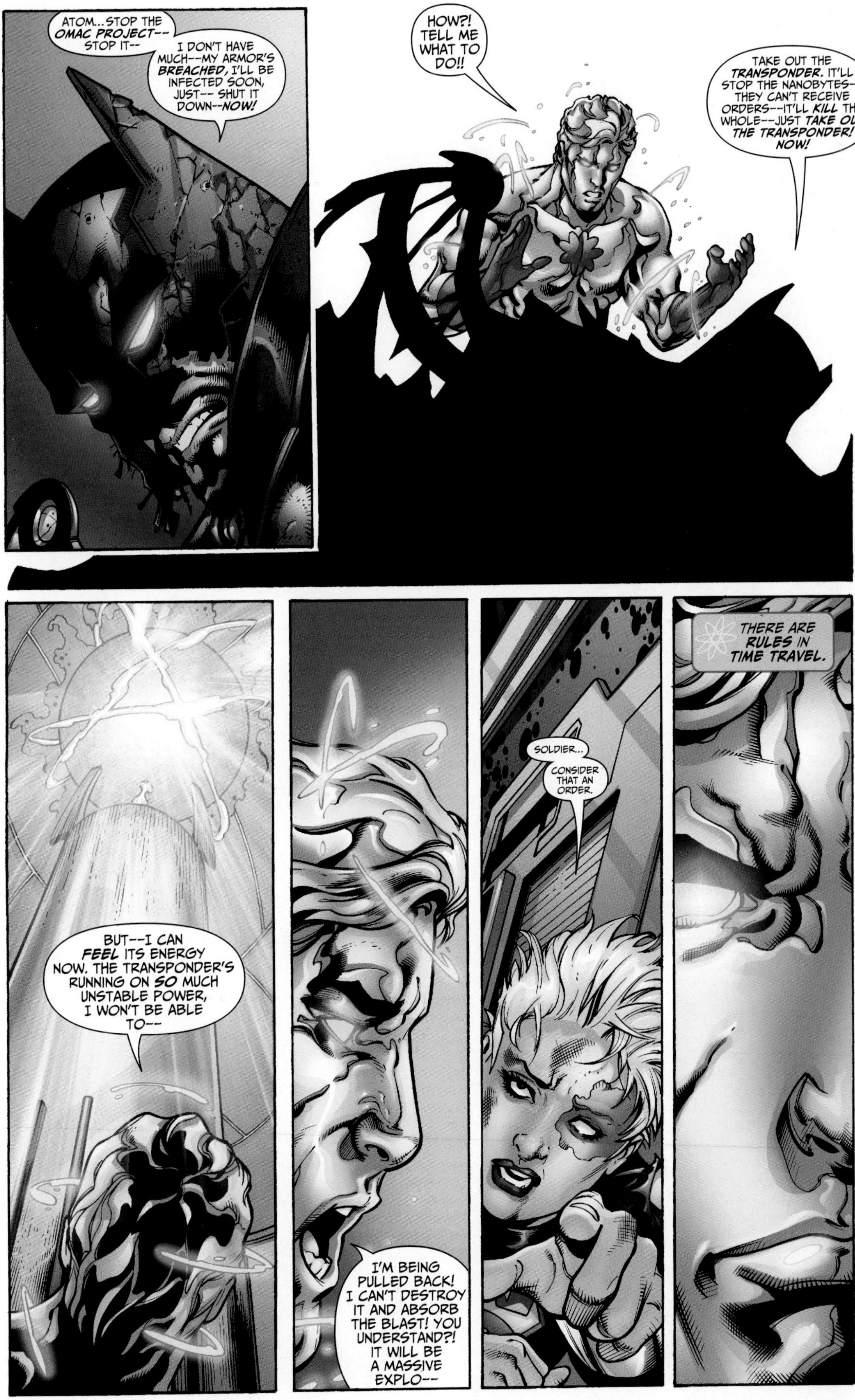
ATOM...STOP THE OMAC PROJECT-- STOP IT--
I DON'T HAVE MUCH--MY ARMOR'S BREACHED, I'LL BE INFECTED SOON, JUST-- SHUT IT DOWN--NOW!
HOW?! TELL ME WHAT TO DO!!
TAKE OUT THE TRANSPONDER. IT'LL STOP THE NANOBYTES-- THEY CAN'T RECEIVE ORDERS--IT'LL KILL THE WHOLE--JUST TAKE OUT THE TRANSPONDER! NOW!
BUT--I CAN FEEL ITS ENERGY NOW. THE TRANSPONDER'S RUNNING ON SO MUCH UNSTABLE POWER, I WON'T BE ABLE TO--
I'M BEING PULLED BACK! I CAN'T DESTROY IT AND ABSORB THE BLAST! YOU UNDERSTAND?! IT WILL BE A MASSIVE EXPLO--
SOLDIER...
CONSIDER THAT AN ORDER.
THERE ARE RULES IN TIME TRAVEL.

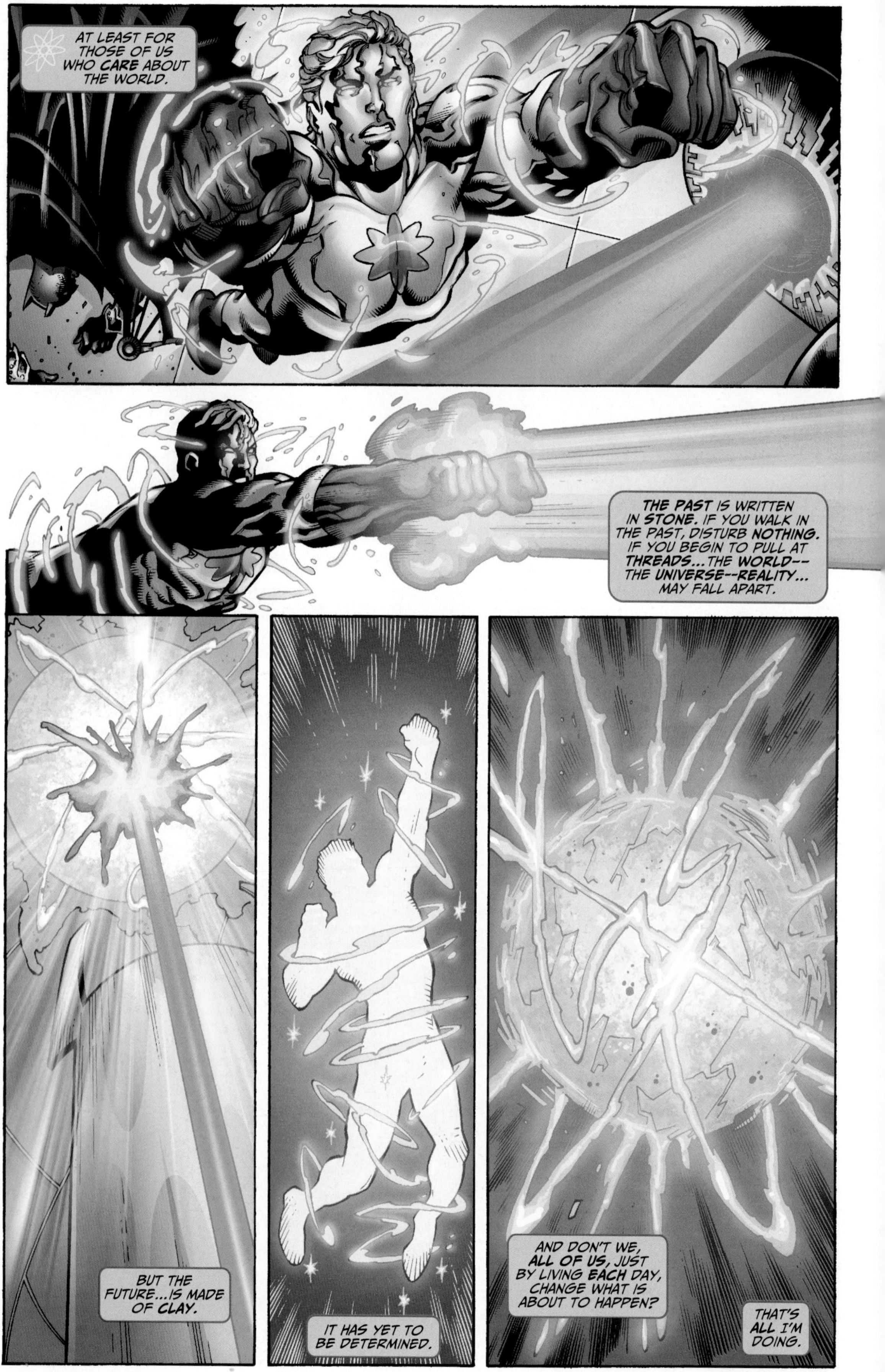
AT LEAST FOR THOSE OF US WHO CARE ABOUT THE WORLD.
THE PAST IS WRITTEN IN STONE. IF YOU WALK IN THE PAST, DISTURB NOTHING. IF YOU BEGIN TO PULL AT THREADS...THE WORLD-- THE UNIVERSE--REALITY... MAY FALL APART.
BUT THE FUTURE...IS MADE OF CLAY.
IT HAS YET TO BE DETERMINED.
AND DON'T WE, ALL OF US, JUST BY LIVING EACH DAY, CHANGE WHAT IS ABOUT TO HAPPEN?
THAT'S ALL I'M DOING.

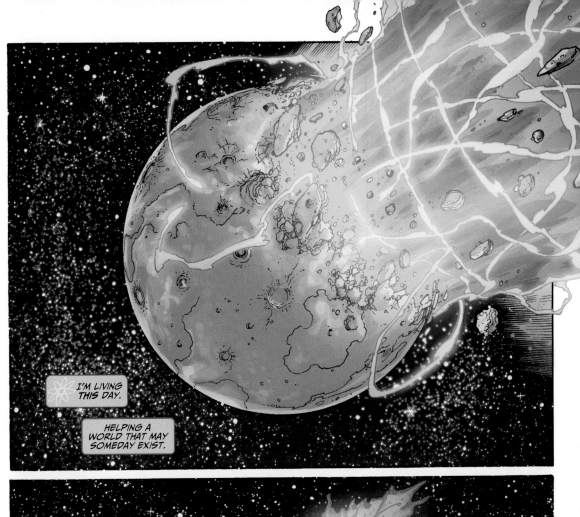

I'M LIVING THIS DAY.

HELPING A WORLD THAT MAY SOMEDAY EXIST.

HELPING MY FRIENDS FIGHT THEIR WAR.

IT'S THE LEAST I CAN DO...

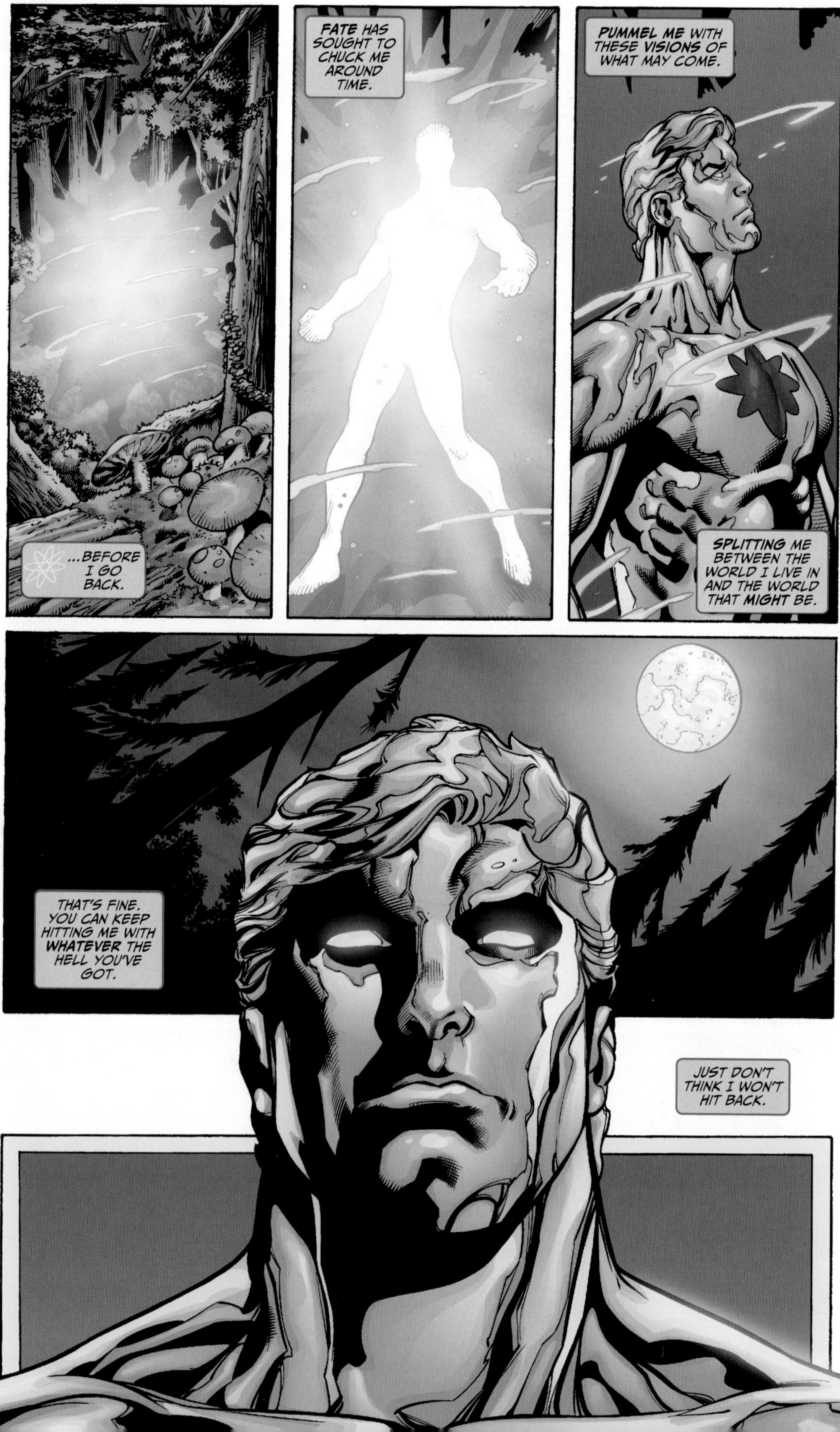
...BEFORE I GO BACK.
FATE HAS SOUGHT TO CHUCK ME AROUND TIME.
PUMMEL ME WITH THESE VISIONS OF WHAT MAY COME.
SPLITTING ME BETWEEN THE WORLD I LIVE IN AND THE WORLD THAT MIGHT BE.
THAT'S FINE. YOU CAN KEEP HITTING ME WITH WHATEVER THE HELL YOU'VE GOT.
JUST DON'T THINK I WON'T HIT BACK.

Cover by Dustin Nguyen

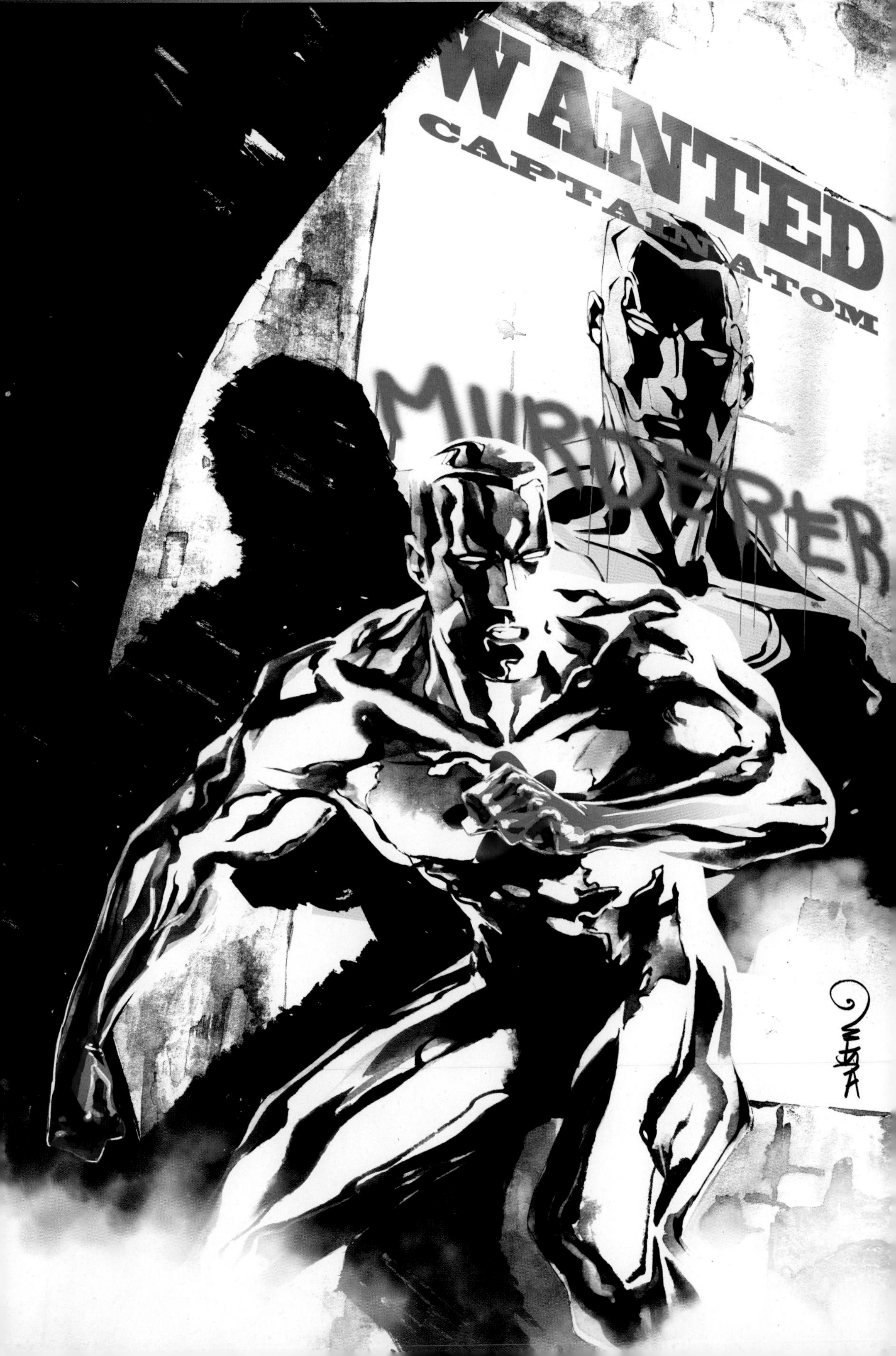
WANTED
CAPTAIN ATOM
MURDERER

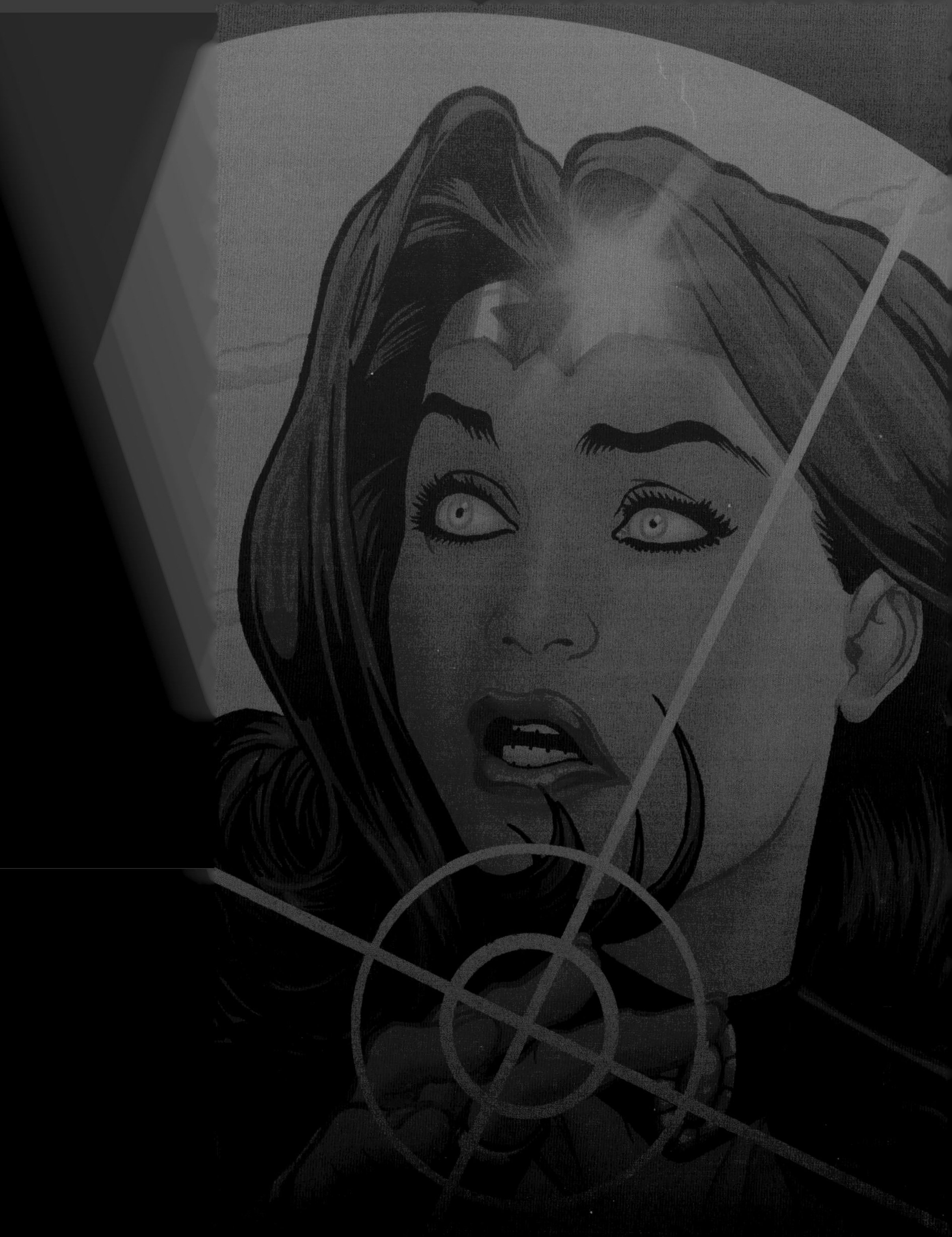

TEEN:
TOMORROW IS TODAY

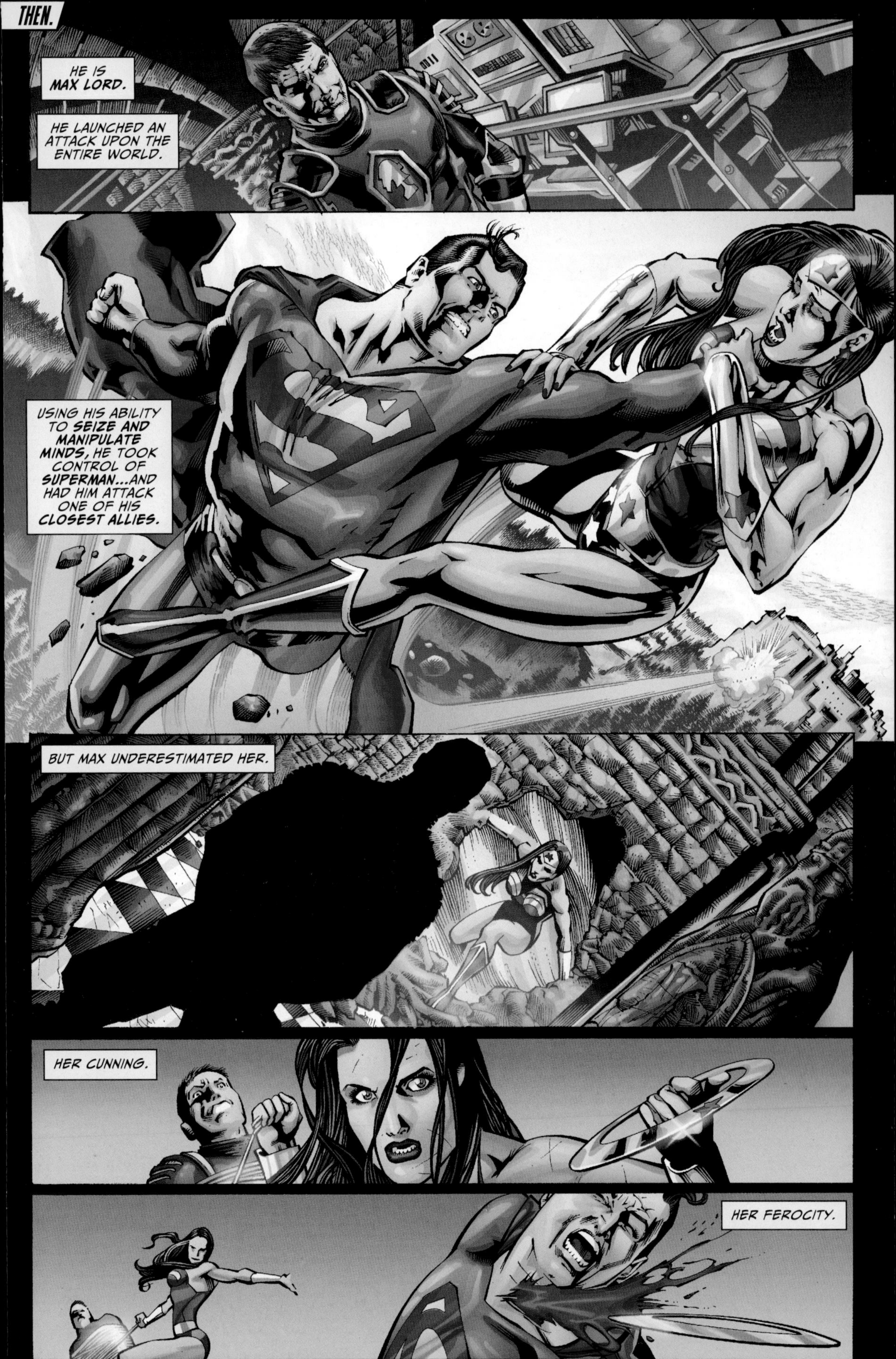
THEN.
HE IS MAX LORD.
HE LAUNCHED AN ATTACK UPON THE ENTIRE WORLD.
USING HIS ABILITY TO SEIZE AND MANIPULATE MINDS, HE TOOK CONTROL OF SUPERMAN...AND HAD HIM ATTACK ONE OF HIS CLOSEST ALLIES.
BUT MAX UNDERESTIMATED HER.
HER CUNNING.
HER FEROCITY.

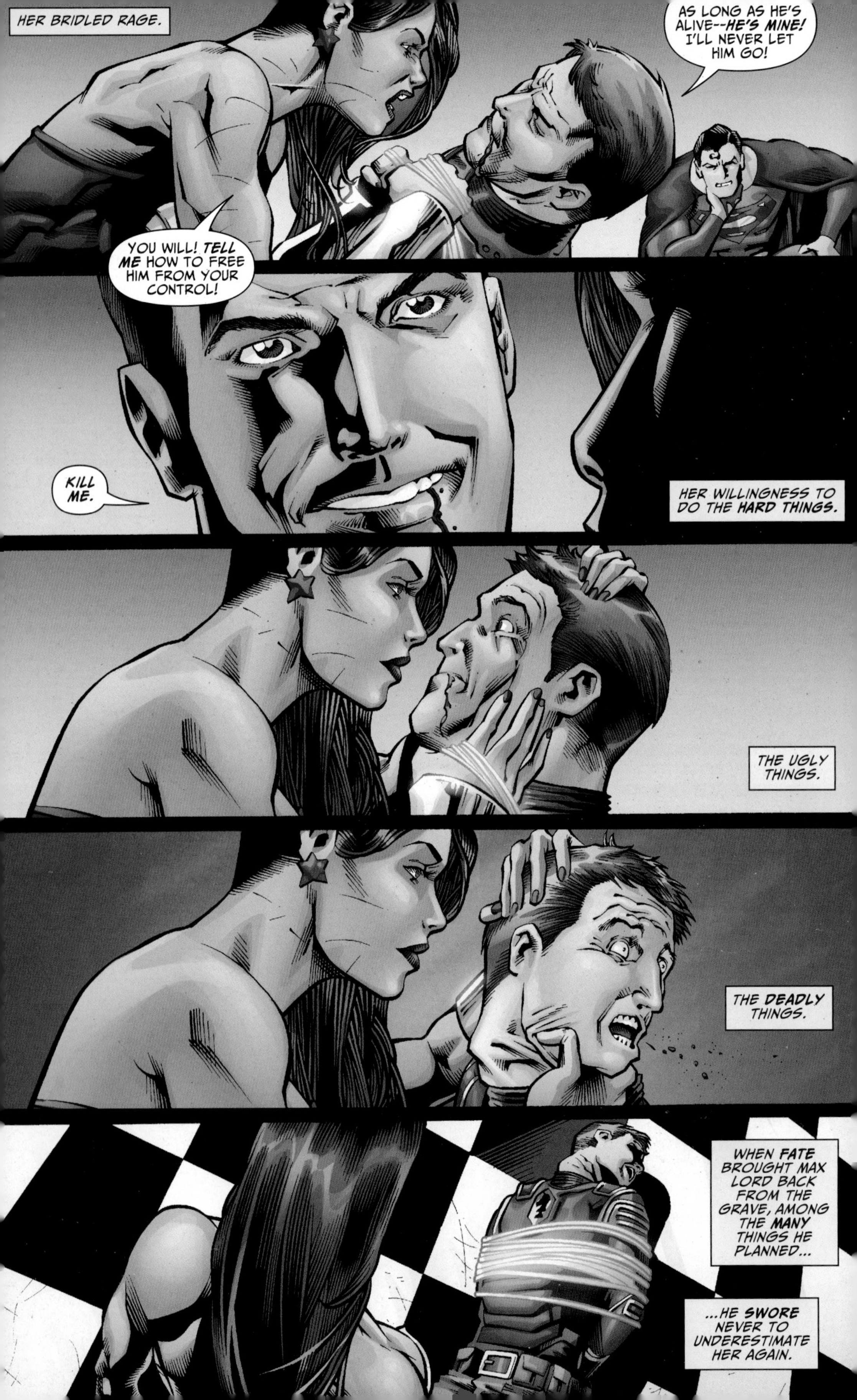

HER BRIDLED RAGE.
AS LONG AS HE'S ALIVE--**HE'S MINE!** I'LL NEVER LET HIM GO!
YOU WILL! **TELL ME** HOW TO FREE HIM FROM YOUR CONTROL!
KILL ME.
HER WILLINGNESS TO DO THE **HARD THINGS.**
THE UGLY THINGS.
THE **DEADLY** THINGS.
WHEN **FATE** BROUGHT MAX LORD BACK FROM THE GRAVE, AMONG THE **MANY** THINGS HE PLANNED...
...HE **SWORE** NEVER TO UNDERESTIMATE HER AGAIN.

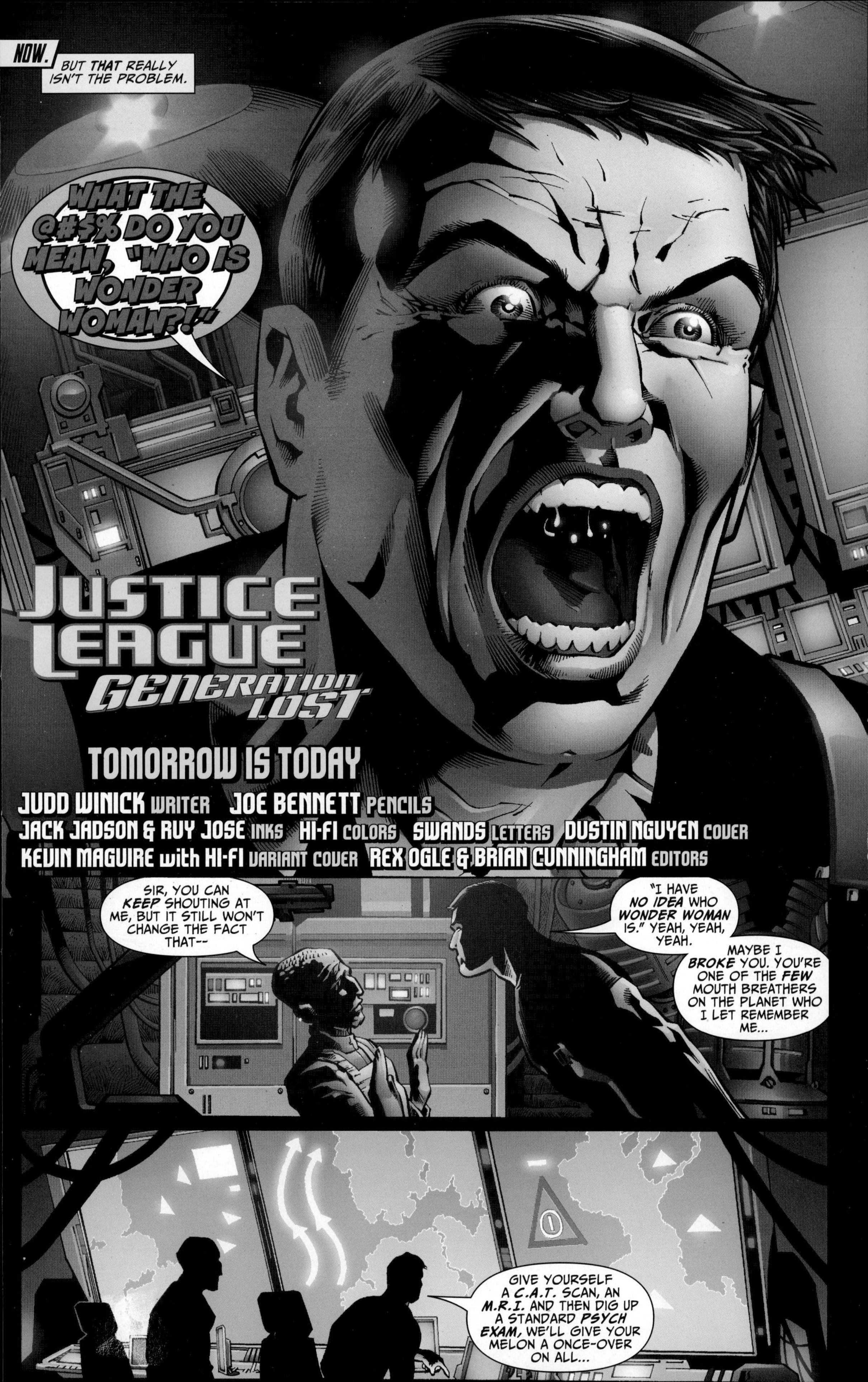
NOW.
BUT THAT REALLY ISN'T THE PROBLEM.
WHAT THE @#$% DO YOU MEAN, "WHO IS WONDER WOMAN?!"
JUSTICE LEAGUE GENERATION LOST
TOMORROW IS TODAY
JUDD WINICK WRITER JOE BENNETT PENCILS
JACK JADSON & RUY JOSE INKS HI-FI COLORS SWANDS LETTERS DUSTIN NGUYEN COVER
KEVIN MAGUIRE with HI-FI VARIANT COVER REX OGLE & BRIAN CUNNINGHAM EDITORS
SIR, YOU CAN KEEP SHOUTING AT ME, BUT IT STILL WON'T CHANGE THE FACT THAT--
"I HAVE NO IDEA WHO WONDER WOMAN IS." YEAH, YEAH, YEAH.
MAYBE I BROKE YOU. YOU'RE ONE OF THE FEW MOUTH BREATHERS ON THE PLANET WHO I LET REMEMBER ME...
GIVE YOURSELF A C.A.T. SCAN, AN M.R.I. AND THEN DIG UP A STANDARD PSYCH EXAM, WE'LL GIVE YOUR MELON A ONCE-OVER ON ALL...

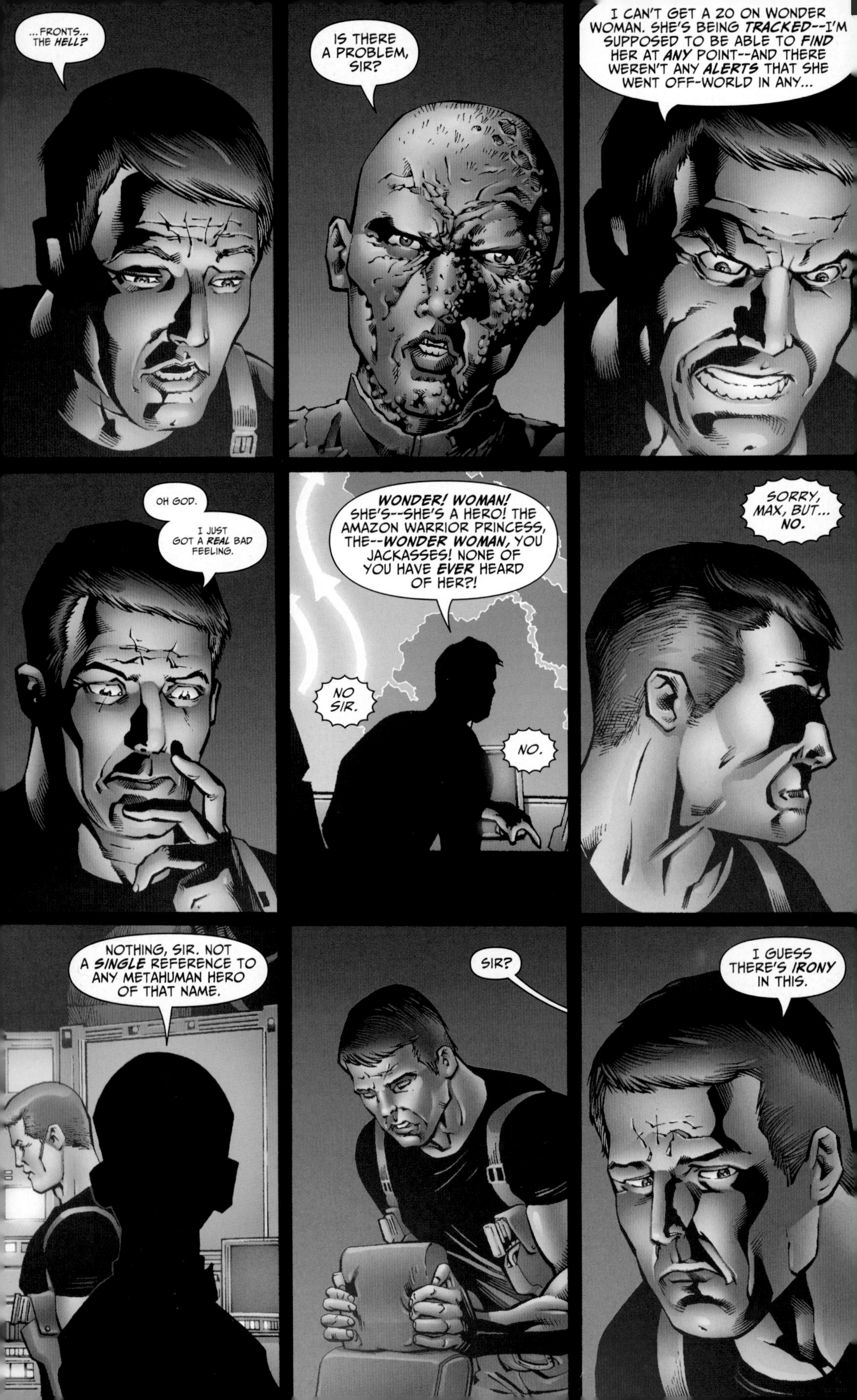

...FRONTS... THE HELL?
IS THERE A PROBLEM, SIR?
I CAN'T GET A 20 ON WONDER WOMAN. SHE'S BEING TRACKED--I'M SUPPOSED TO BE ABLE TO FIND HER AT ANY POINT--AND THERE WEREN'T ANY ALERTS THAT SHE WENT OFF-WORLD IN ANY...
OH GOD.
I JUST GOT A REAL BAD FEELING.
WONDER! WOMAN! SHE'S--SHE'S A HERO! THE AMAZON WARRIOR PRINCESS, THE--WONDER WOMAN, YOU JACKASSES! NONE OF YOU HAVE EVER HEARD OF HER?!
NO SIR.
NO.
SORRY, MAX, BUT... NO.
NOTHING, SIR. NOT A SINGLE REFERENCE TO ANY METAHUMAN HERO OF THAT NAME.
SIR?
I GUESS THERE'S IRONY IN THIS.

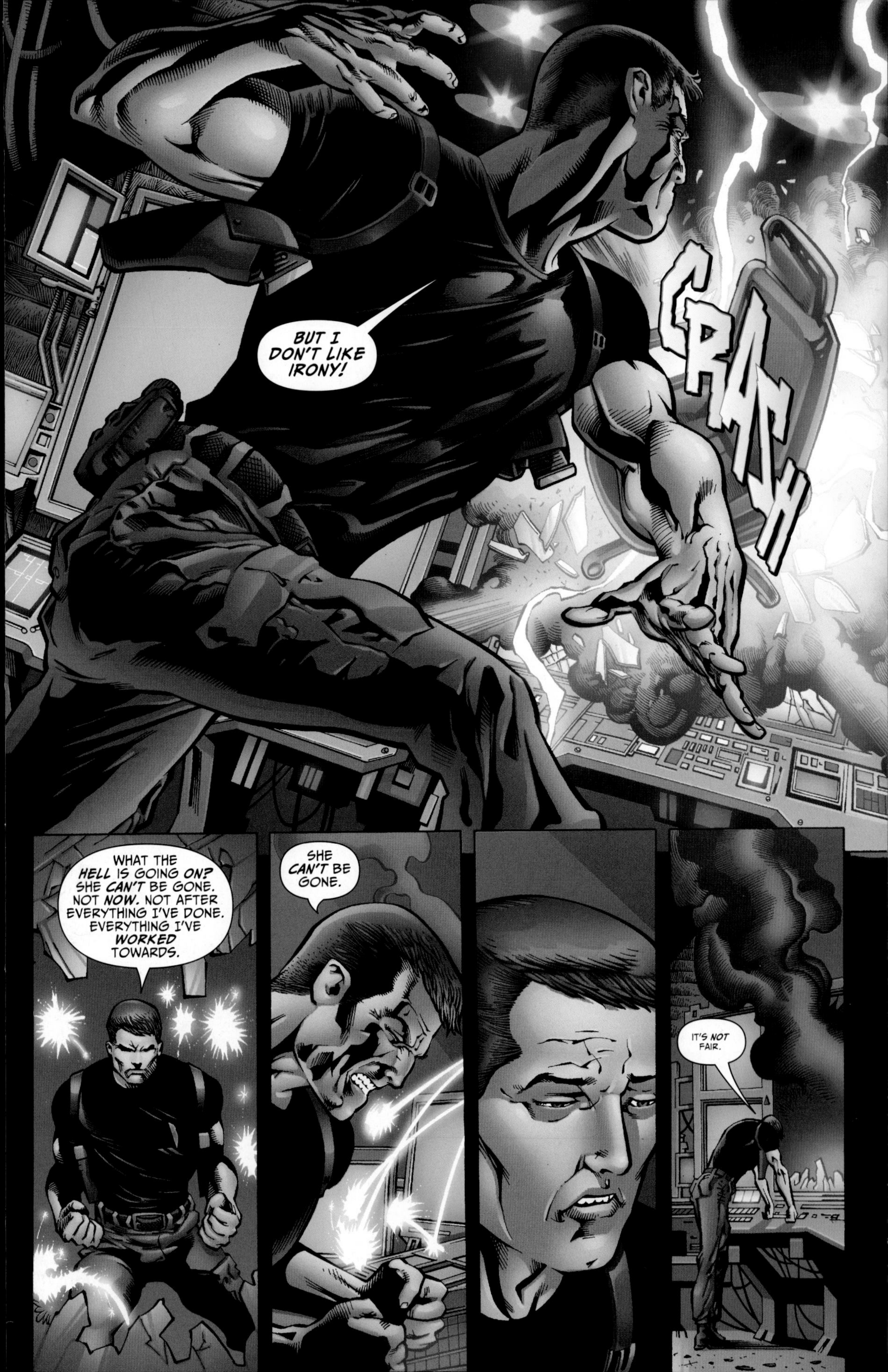
BUT I DON'T LIKE IRONY!
CRASH
WHAT THE HELL IS GOING ON? SHE CAN'T BE GONE. NOT NOW. NOT AFTER EVERYTHING I'VE DONE. EVERYTHING I'VE WORKED TOWARDS.
SHE CAN'T BE GONE.
IT'S NOT FAIR.

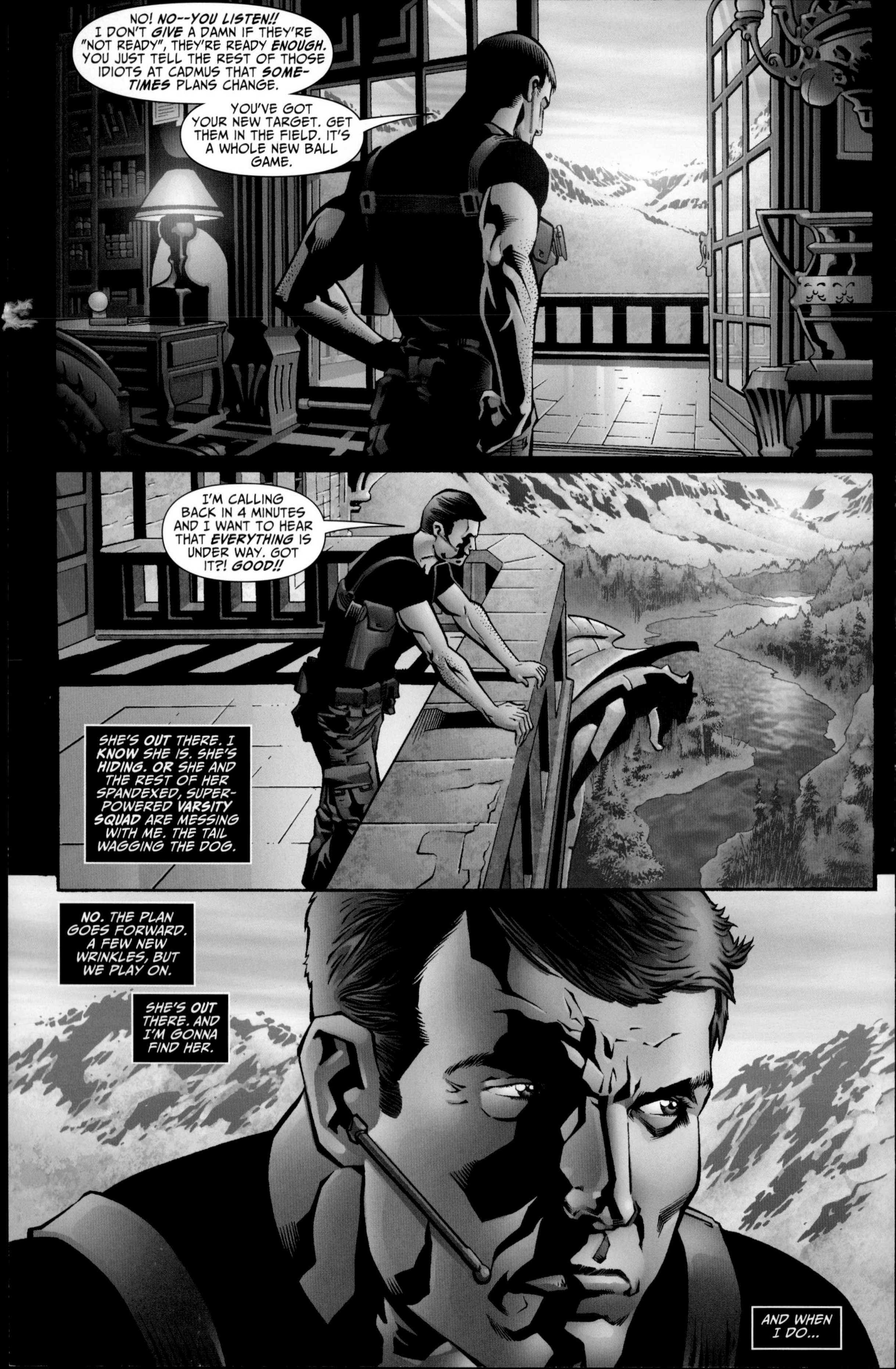
NO! NO--YOU LISTEN!! I DON'T GIVE A DAMN IF THEY'RE "NOT READY", THEY'RE READY ENOUGH. YOU JUST TELL THE REST OF THOSE IDIOTS AT CADMUS THAT SOME-TIMES PLANS CHANGE.
YOU'VE GOT YOUR NEW TARGET. GET THEM IN THE FIELD. IT'S A WHOLE NEW BALL GAME.
I'M CALLING BACK IN 4 MINUTES AND I WANT TO HEAR THAT EVERYTHING IS UNDER WAY. GOT IT?! GOOD!!
SHE'S OUT THERE. I KNOW SHE IS. SHE'S HIDING. OR SHE AND THE REST OF HER SPANDEXED, SUPER-POWERED VARSITY SQUAD ARE MESSING WITH ME. THE TAIL WAGGING THE DOG.
NO. THE PLAN GOES FORWARD. A FEW NEW WRINKLES, BUT WE PLAY ON.
SHE'S OUT THERE. AND I'M GONNA FIND HER.
AND WHEN I DO...

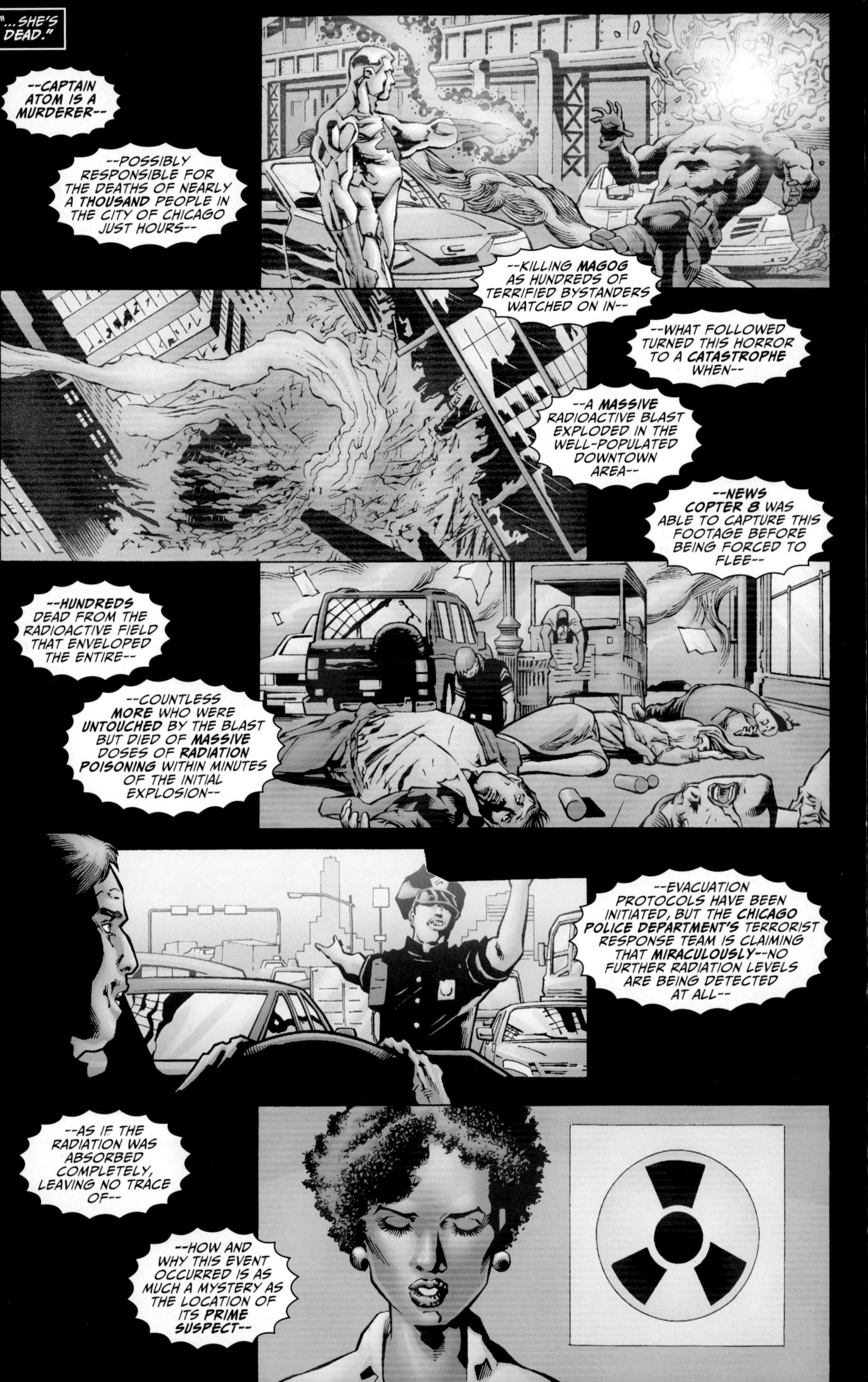
"...SHE'S DEAD."
--CAPTAIN ATOM IS A MURDERER--
--POSSIBLY RESPONSIBLE FOR THE DEATHS OF NEARLY A THOUSAND PEOPLE IN THE CITY OF CHICAGO JUST HOURS--
--KILLING MAGOG AS HUNDREDS OF TERRIFIED BYSTANDERS WATCHED ON IN--
--WHAT FOLLOWED TURNED THIS HORROR TO A CATASTROPHE WHEN--
--A MASSIVE RADIOACTIVE BLAST EXPLODED IN THE WELL-POPULATED DOWNTOWN AREA--
--NEWS COPTER 8 WAS ABLE TO CAPTURE THIS FOOTAGE BEFORE BEING FORCED TO FLEE--
--HUNDREDS DEAD FROM THE RADIOACTIVE FIELD THAT ENVELOPED THE ENTIRE--
--COUNTLESS MORE WHO WERE UNTOUCHED BY THE BLAST BUT DIED OF MASSIVE DOSES OF RADIATION POISONING WITHIN MINUTES OF THE INITIAL EXPLOSION--
--EVACUATION PROTOCOLS HAVE BEEN INITIATED, BUT THE CHICAGO POLICE DEPARTMENT'S TERRORIST RESPONSE TEAM IS CLAIMING THAT MIRACULOUSLY--NO FURTHER RADIATION LEVELS ARE BEING DETECTED AT ALL--
--AS IF THE RADIATION WAS ABSORBED COMPLETELY, LEAVING NO TRACE OF--
--HOW AND WHY THIS EVENT OCCURRED IS AS MUCH A MYSTERY AS THE LOCATION OF ITS PRIME SUSPECT--

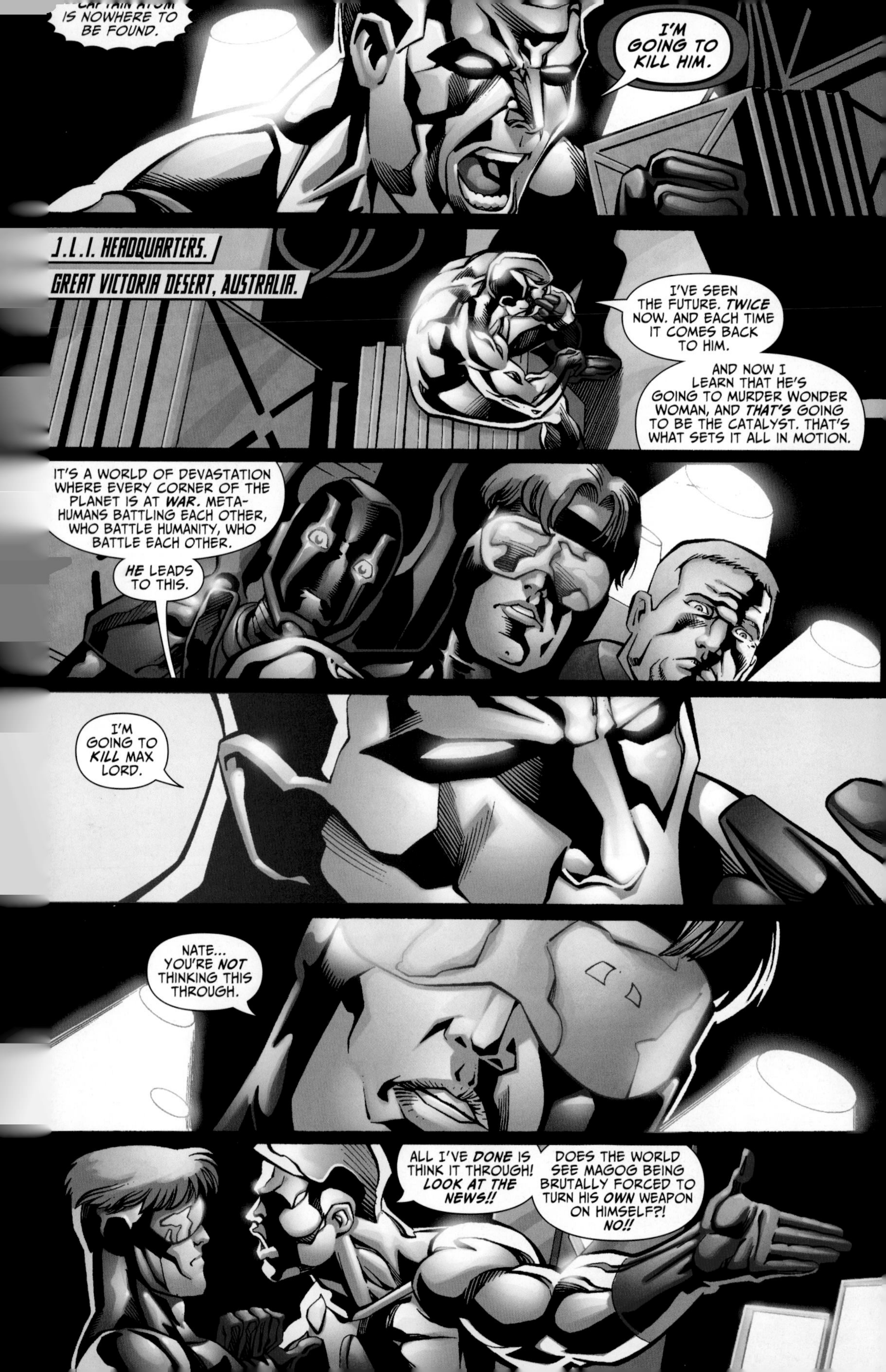
CAPTAIN ATOM IS NOWHERE TO BE FOUND.
I'M GOING TO KILL HIM.
J.L.I. HEADQUARTERS. / GREAT VICTORIA DESERT, AUSTRALIA.
I'VE SEEN THE FUTURE. TWICE NOW. AND EACH TIME IT COMES BACK TO HIM.
AND NOW I LEARN THAT HE'S GOING TO MURDER WONDER WOMAN, AND THAT'S GOING TO BE THE CATALYST. THAT'S WHAT SETS IT ALL IN MOTION.
IT'S A WORLD OF DEVASTATION WHERE EVERY CORNER OF THE PLANET IS AT WAR. META-HUMANS BATTLING EACH OTHER, WHO BATTLE HUMANITY, WHO BATTLE EACH OTHER.
HE LEADS TO THIS.
I'M GOING TO KILL MAX LORD.
NATE... YOU'RE NOT THINKING THIS THROUGH.
ALL I'VE DONE IS THINK IT THROUGH! LOOK AT THE NEWS!!
DOES THE WORLD SEE MAGOG BEING BRUTALLY FORCED TO TURN HIS OWN WEAPON ON HIMSELF?! NO!!

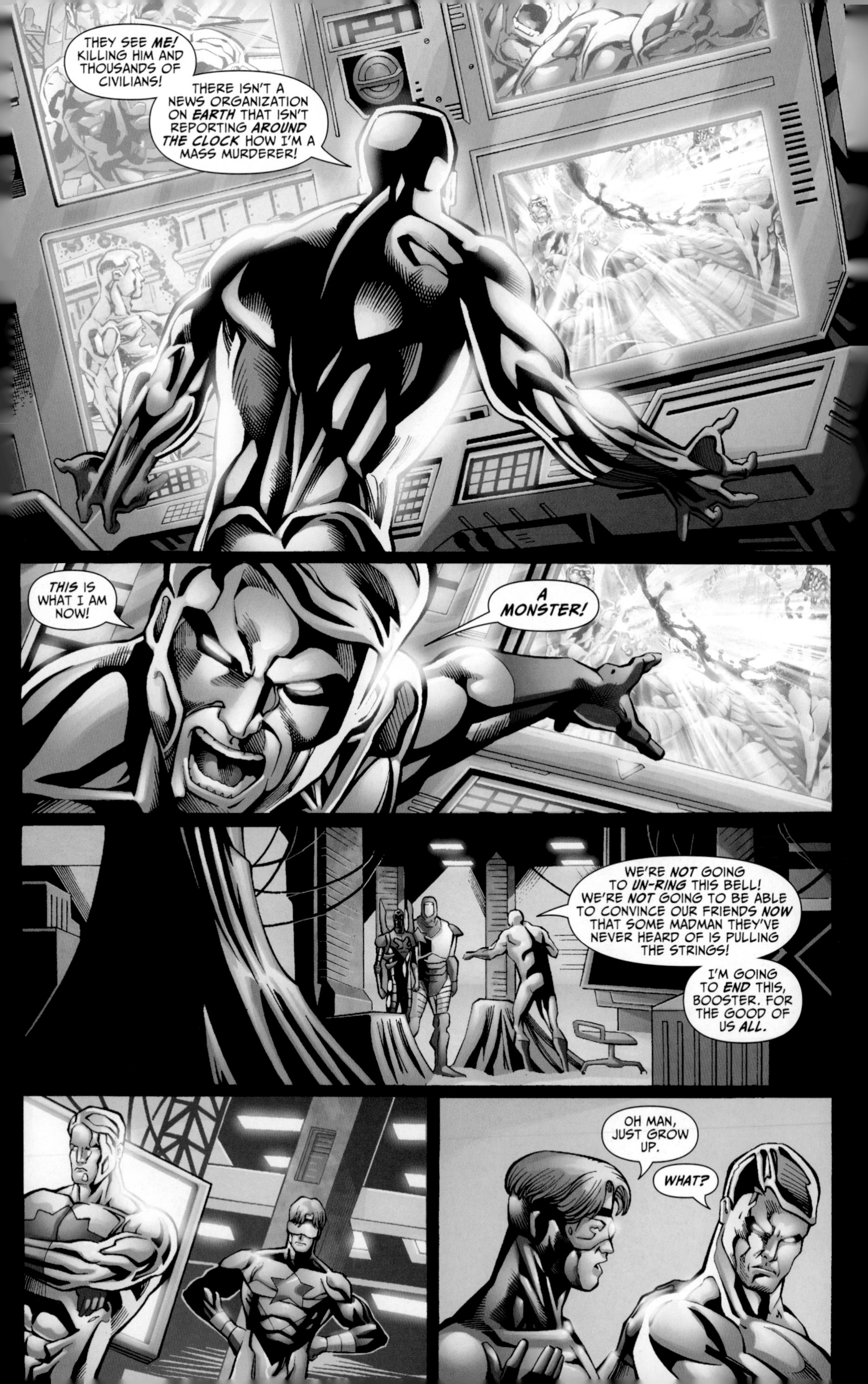
THEY SEE ME! KILLING HIM AND THOUSANDS OF CIVILIANS!
THERE ISN'T A NEWS ORGANIZATION ON EARTH THAT ISN'T REPORTING AROUND THE CLOCK HOW I'M A MASS MURDERER!
THIS IS WHAT I AM NOW!
A MONSTER!
WE'RE NOT GOING TO UN-RING THIS BELL! WE'RE NOT GOING TO BE ABLE TO CONVINCE OUR FRIENDS NOW THAT SOME MADMAN THEY'VE NEVER HEARD OF IS PULLING THE STRINGS!
I'M GOING TO END THIS, BOOSTER. FOR THE GOOD OF US ALL.
OH MAN, JUST GROW UP.
WHAT?

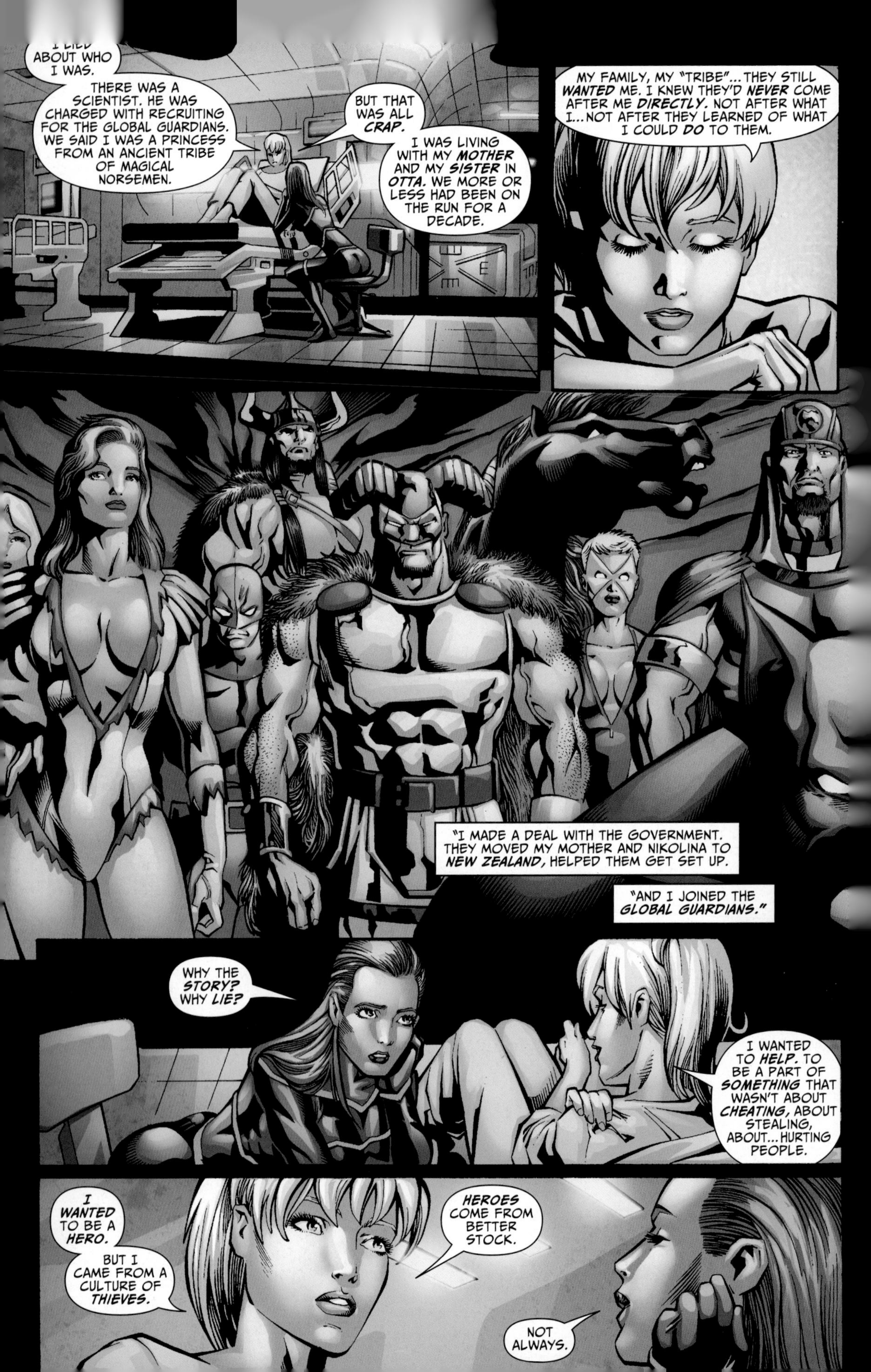
I LIED ABOUT WHO I WAS.
THERE WAS A SCIENTIST. HE WAS CHARGED WITH RECRUITING FOR THE GLOBAL GUARDIANS. WE SAID I WAS A PRINCESS FROM AN ANCIENT TRIBE OF MAGICAL NORSEMEN.
BUT THAT WAS ALL CRAP.
I WAS LIVING WITH MY MOTHER AND MY SISTER IN OTTA. WE MORE OR LESS HAD BEEN ON THE RUN FOR A DECADE.
MY FAMILY, MY "TRIBE"... THEY STILL WANTED ME. I KNEW THEY'D NEVER COME AFTER ME DIRECTLY. NOT AFTER WHAT I... NOT AFTER THEY LEARNED OF WHAT I COULD DO TO THEM.
"I MADE A DEAL WITH THE GOVERNMENT. THEY MOVED MY MOTHER AND NIKOLINA TO NEW ZEALAND, HELPED THEM GET SET UP.
"AND I JOINED THE GLOBAL GUARDIANS."
WHY THE STORY? WHY LIE?
I WANTED TO HELP. TO BE A PART OF SOMETHING THAT WASN'T ABOUT CHEATING, ABOUT STEALING, ABOUT... HURTING PEOPLE.
I WANTED TO BE A HERO.
BUT I CAME FROM A CULTURE OF THIEVES.
HEROES COME FROM BETTER STOCK.
NOT ALWAYS.

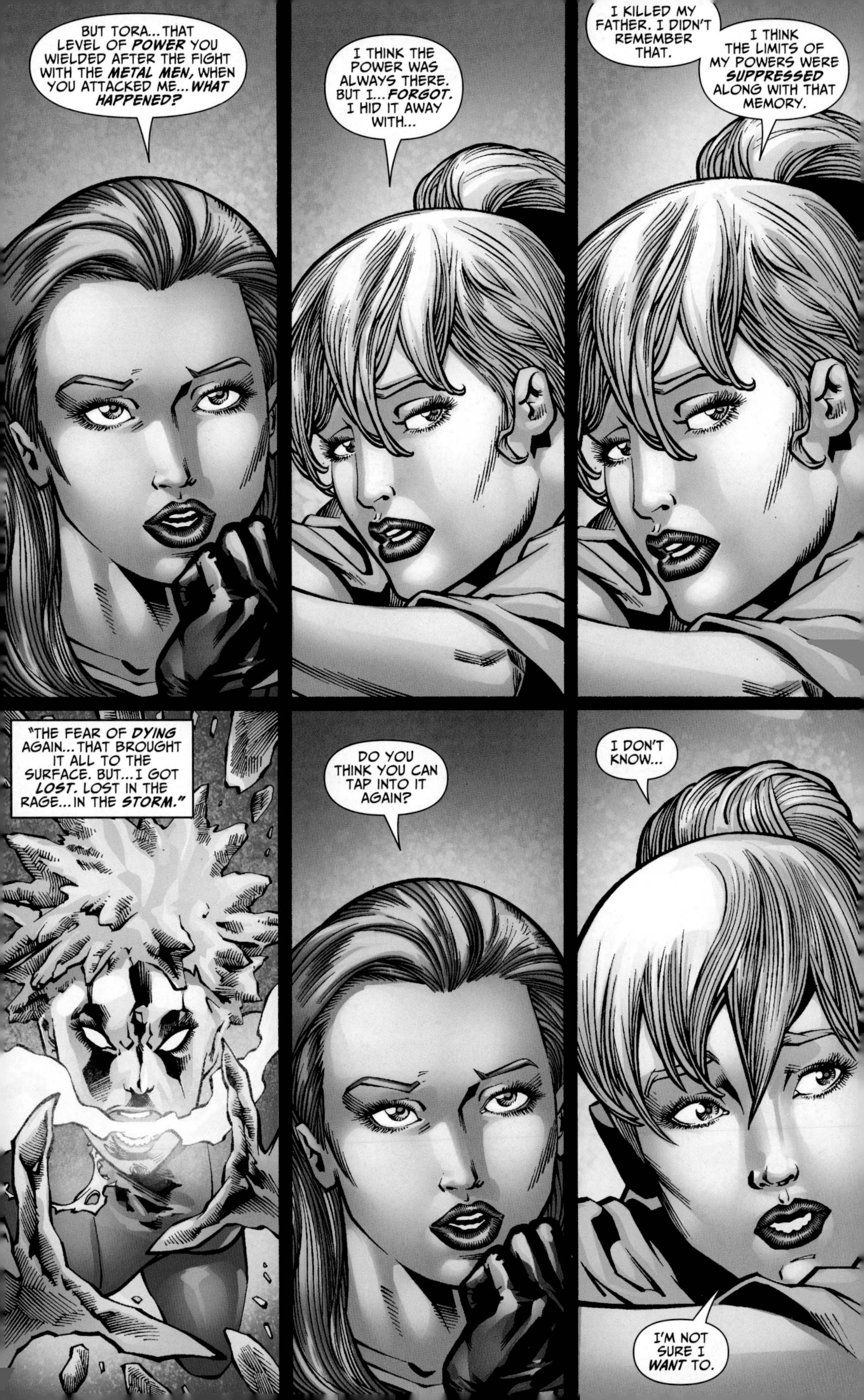
BUT TORA...THAT LEVEL OF POWER YOU WIELDED AFTER THE FIGHT WITH THE METAL MEN, WHEN YOU ATTACKED ME...WHAT HAPPENED?
I THINK THE POWER WAS ALWAYS THERE. BUT I...FORGOT. I HID IT AWAY WITH...
I KILLED MY FATHER. I DIDN'T REMEMBER THAT.
I THINK THE LIMITS OF MY POWERS WERE SUPPRESSED ALONG WITH THAT MEMORY.
"THE FEAR OF DYING AGAIN...THAT BROUGHT IT ALL TO THE SURFACE. BUT...I GOT LOST. LOST IN THE RAGE...IN THE STORM."
DO YOU THINK YOU CAN TAP INTO IT AGAIN?
I DON'T KNOW...
I'M NOT SURE I WANT TO.

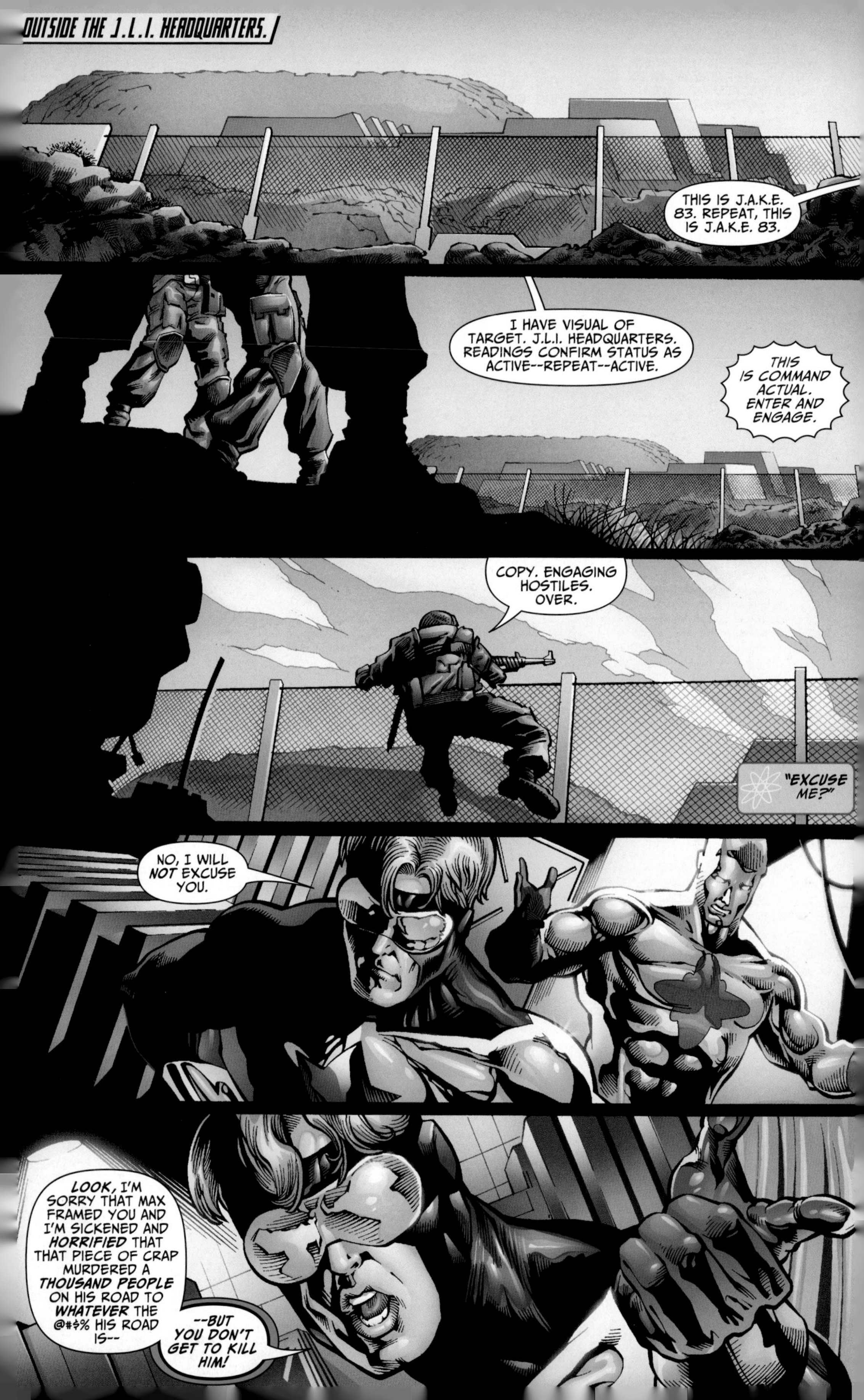
OUTSIDE THE J.L.I. HEADQUARTERS.
THIS IS J.A.K.E. 83. REPEAT, THIS IS J.A.K.E. 83.
I HAVE VISUAL OF TARGET. J.L.I. HEADQUARTERS. READINGS CONFIRM STATUS AS ACTIVE--REPEAT--ACTIVE.
THIS IS COMMAND ACTUAL. ENTER AND ENGAGE.
COPY. ENGAGING HOSTILES. OVER.
"EXCUSE ME?"
NO, I WILL NOT EXCUSE YOU.
LOOK, I'M SORRY THAT MAX FRAMED YOU AND I'M SICKENED AND HORRIFIED THAT THAT PIECE OF CRAP MURDERED A THOUSAND PEOPLE ON HIS ROAD TO WHATEVER THE @#$% HIS ROAD IS--
--BUT YOU DON'T GET TO KILL HIM!

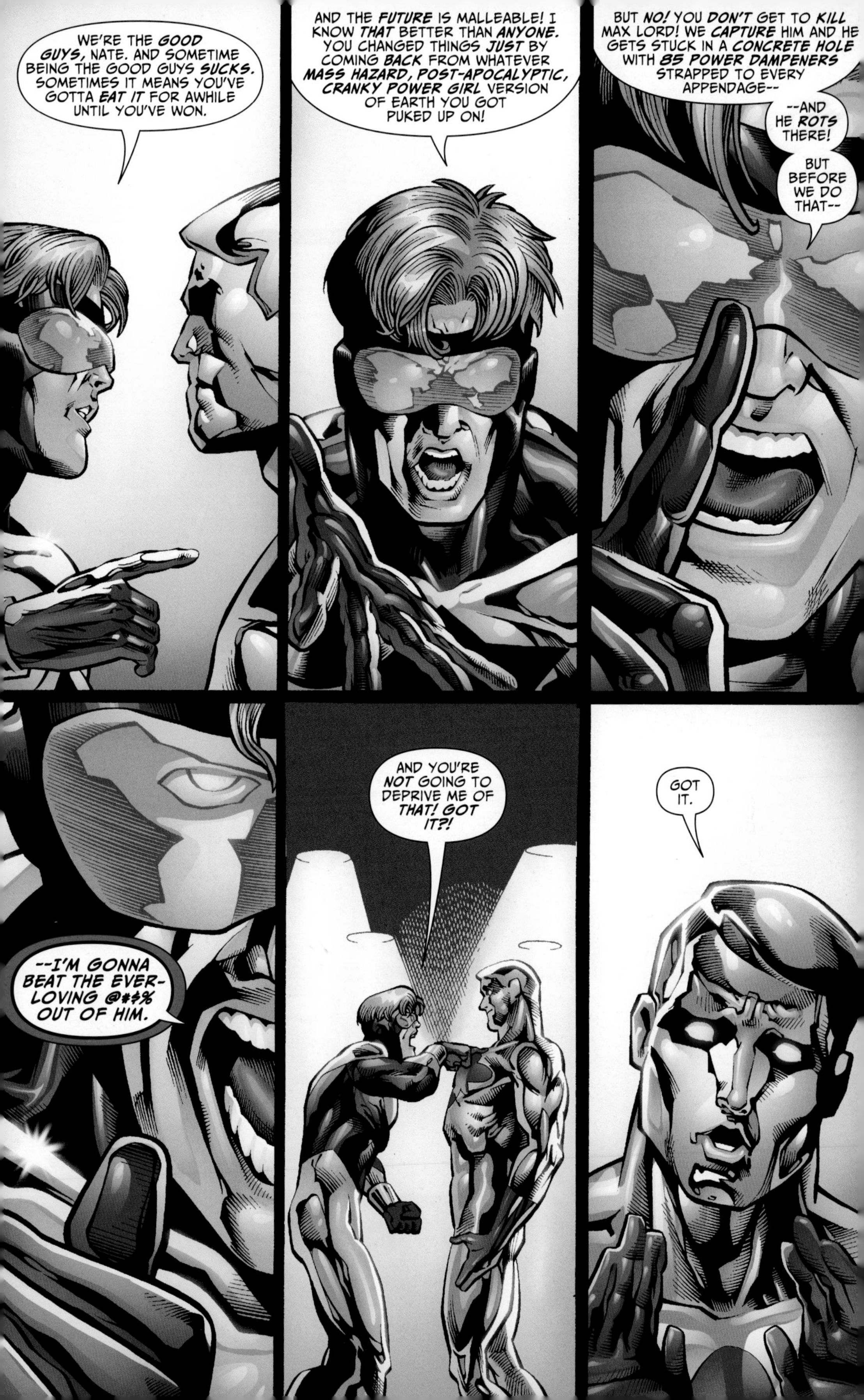
WE'RE THE GOOD GUYS, NATE. AND SOMETIME BEING THE GOOD GUYS SUCKS. SOMETIMES IT MEANS YOU'VE GOTTA EAT IT FOR AWHILE UNTIL YOU'VE WON.
AND THE FUTURE IS MALLEABLE! I KNOW THAT BETTER THAN ANYONE. YOU CHANGED THINGS JUST BY COMING BACK FROM WHATEVER MASS HAZARD, POST-APOCALYPTIC, CRANKY POWER GIRL VERSION OF EARTH YOU GOT PUKED UP ON!
BUT NO! YOU DON'T GET TO KILL MAX LORD! WE CAPTURE HIM AND HE GETS STUCK IN A CONCRETE HOLE WITH 85 POWER DAMPENERS STRAPPED TO EVERY APPENDAGE--
--AND HE ROTS THERE!
BUT BEFORE WE DO THAT--
--I'M GONNA BEAT THE EVER-LOVING @#$% OUT OF HIM.
AND YOU'RE NOT GOING TO DEPRIVE ME OF THAT! GOT IT?!
GOT IT.

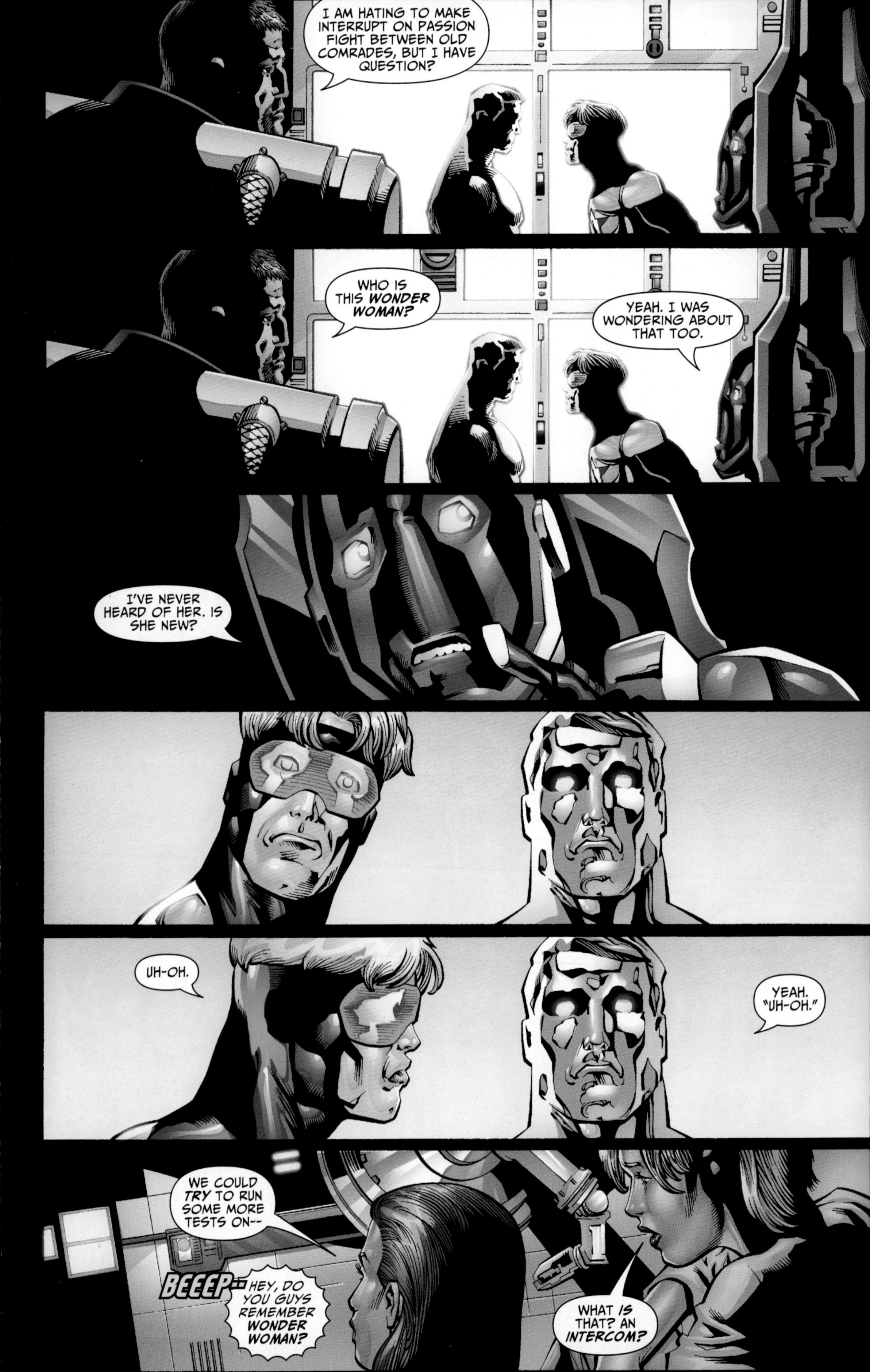
I AM HATING TO MAKE INTERRUPT ON PASSION FIGHT BETWEEN OLD COMRADES, BUT I HAVE QUESTION?
WHO IS THIS WONDER WOMAN?
YEAH. I WAS WONDERING ABOUT THAT TOO.
I'VE NEVER HEARD OF HER. IS SHE NEW?
UH-OH.
YEAH. "UH-OH."
WE COULD TRY TO RUN SOME MORE TESTS ON--
BEEEP
HEY, DO YOU GUYS REMEMBER WONDER WOMAN?
WHAT IS THAT? AN INTERCOM?

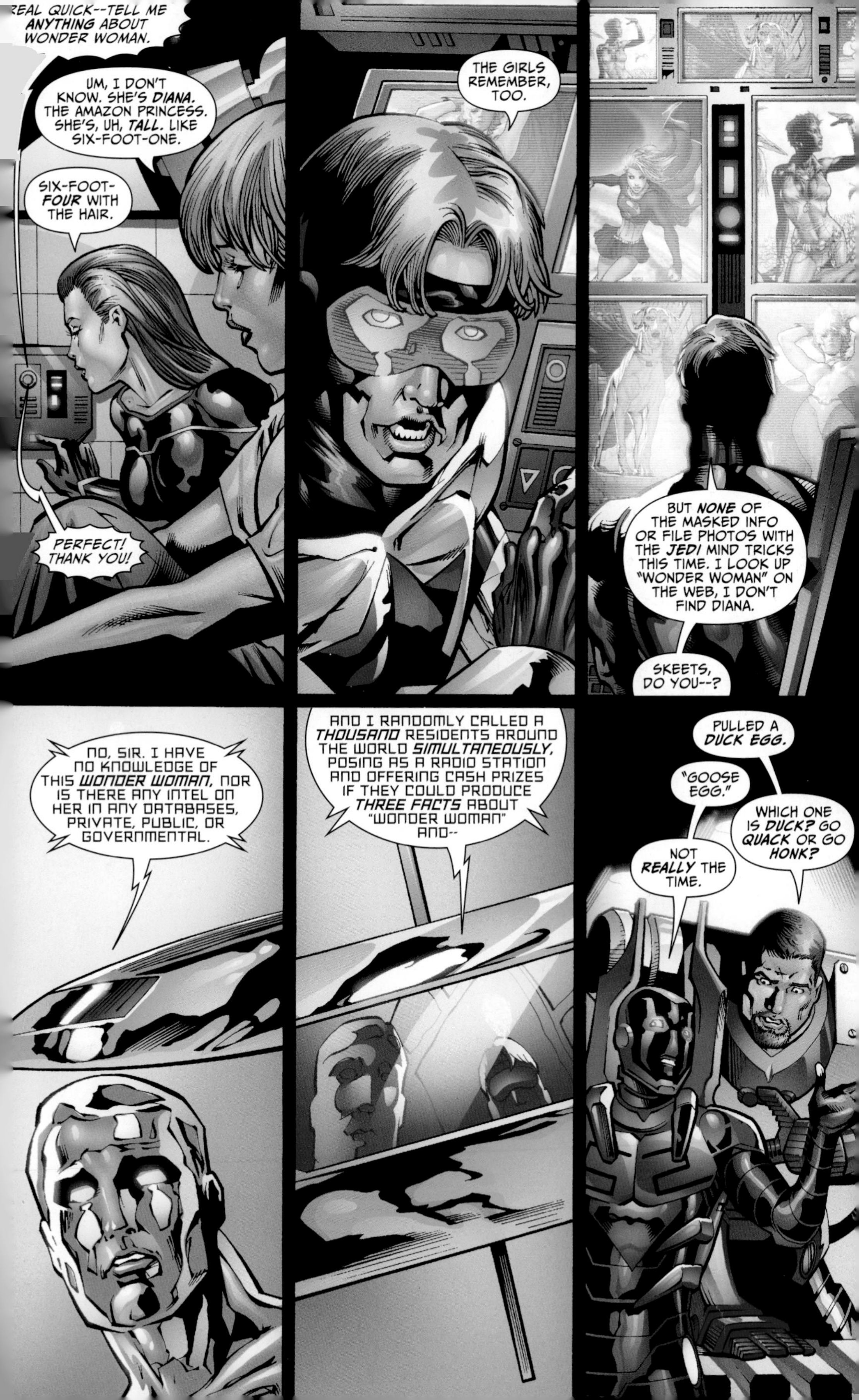
REAL QUICK--TELL ME ANYTHING ABOUT WONDER WOMAN.
UM, I DON'T KNOW. SHE'S DIANA. THE AMAZON PRINCESS. SHE'S, UH, TALL. LIKE SIX-FOOT-ONE.
SIX-FOOT-FOUR WITH THE HAIR.
PERFECT! THANK YOU!
THE GIRLS REMEMBER, TOO.
BUT NONE OF THE MASKED INFO OR FILE PHOTOS WITH THE JEDI MIND TRICKS THIS TIME. I LOOK UP "WONDER WOMAN" ON THE WEB, I DON'T FIND DIANA.
SKEETS, DO YOU--?
NO, SIR. I HAVE NO KNOWLEDGE OF THIS WONDER WOMAN, NOR IS THERE ANY INTEL ON HER IN ANY DATABASES, PRIVATE, PUBLIC, OR GOVERNMENTAL.
AND I RANDOMLY CALLED A THOUSAND RESIDENTS AROUND THE WORLD SIMULTANEOUSLY, POSING AS A RADIO STATION AND OFFERING CASH PRIZES IF THEY COULD PRODUCE THREE FACTS ABOUT "WONDER WOMAN" AND--
PULLED A DUCK EGG.
"GOOSE EGG."
WHICH ONE IS DUCK? GO QUACK OR GO HONK?
NOT REALLY THE TIME.

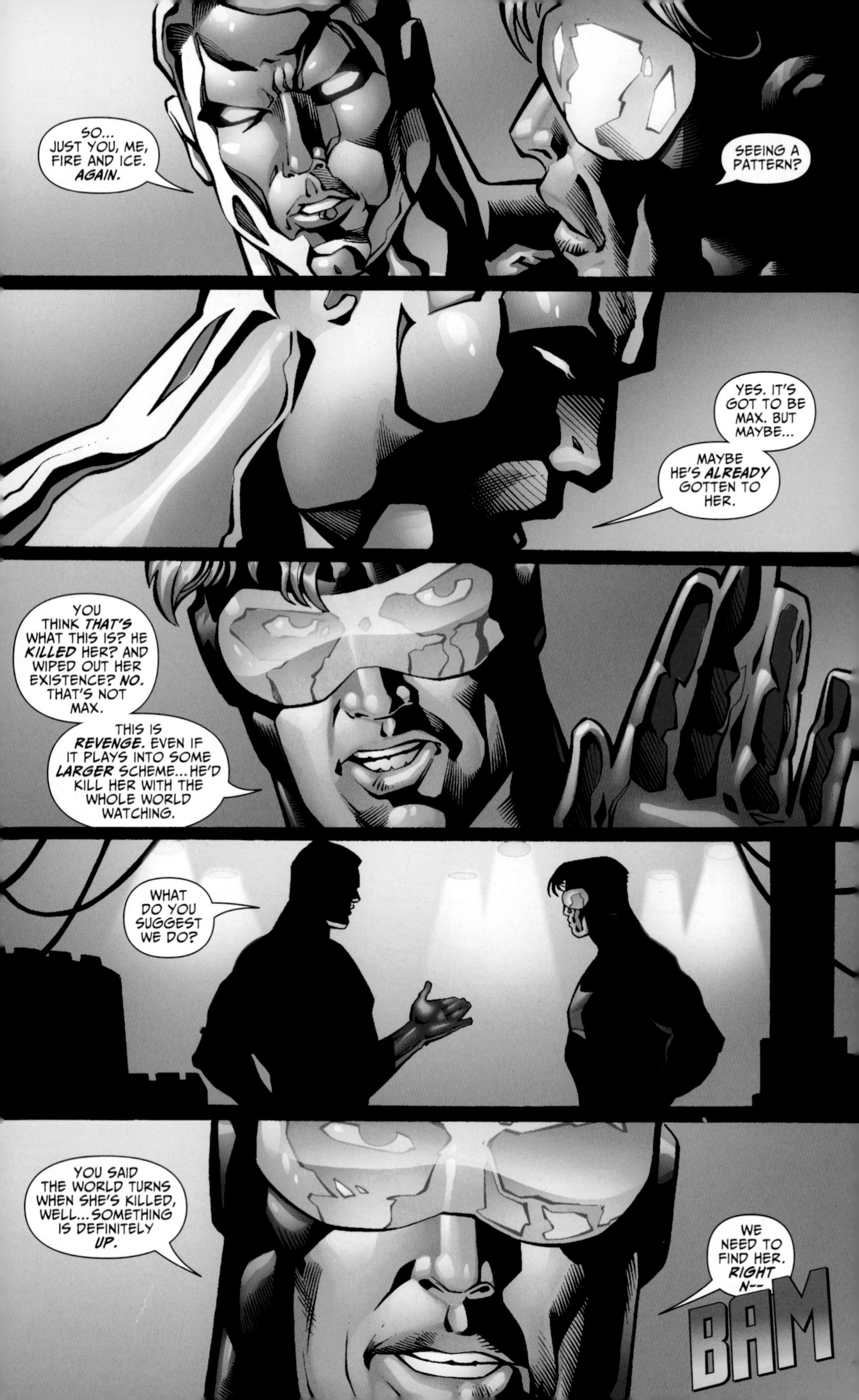
SO... JUST YOU, ME, FIRE AND ICE. AGAIN.
SEEING A PATTERN?
YES. IT'S GOT TO BE MAX. BUT MAYBE...
MAYBE HE'S ALREADY GOTTEN TO HER.
YOU THINK THAT'S WHAT THIS IS? HE KILLED HER? AND WIPED OUT HER EXISTENCE? NO. THAT'S NOT MAX.
THIS IS REVENGE. EVEN IF IT PLAYS INTO SOME LARGER SCHEME...HE'D KILL HER WITH THE WHOLE WORLD WATCHING.
WHAT DO YOU SUGGEST WE DO?
YOU SAID THE WORLD TURNS WHEN SHE'S KILLED, WELL...SOMETHING IS DEFINITELY UP.
WE NEED TO FIND HER. RIGHT N--
BAM

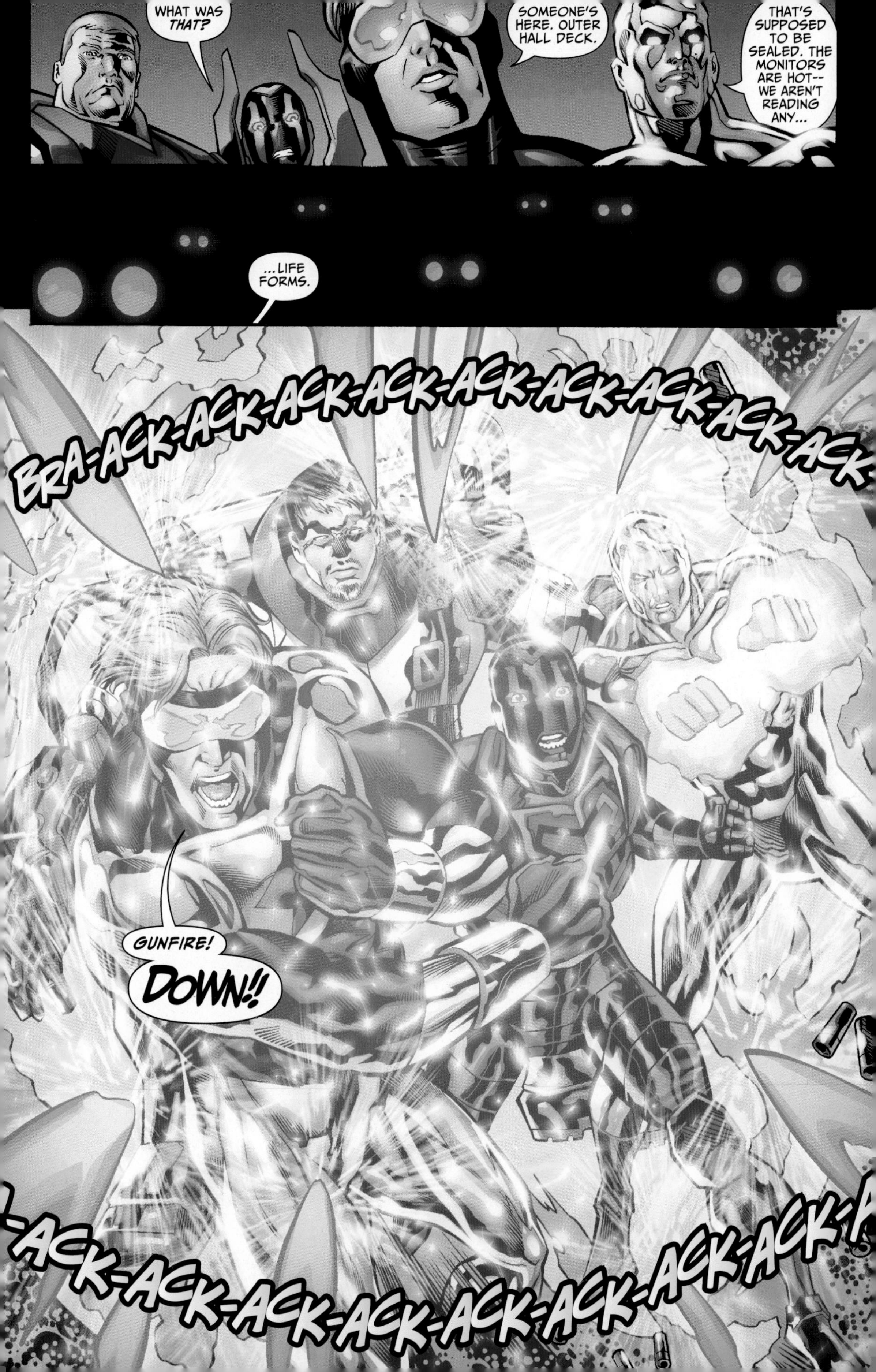
WHAT WAS THAT?
SOMEONE'S HERE. OUTER HALL DECK.
THAT'S SUPPOSED TO BE SEALED. THE MONITORS ARE HOT-- WE AREN'T READING ANY...
...LIFE FORMS.
BRA-ACK-ACK-ACK-ACK-ACK-ACK-ACK-ACK-ACK-ACK-ACK
GUNFIRE!
DOWN!!
-ACK-ACK-ACK-ACK-ACK-ACK-ACK-ACK-ACK-

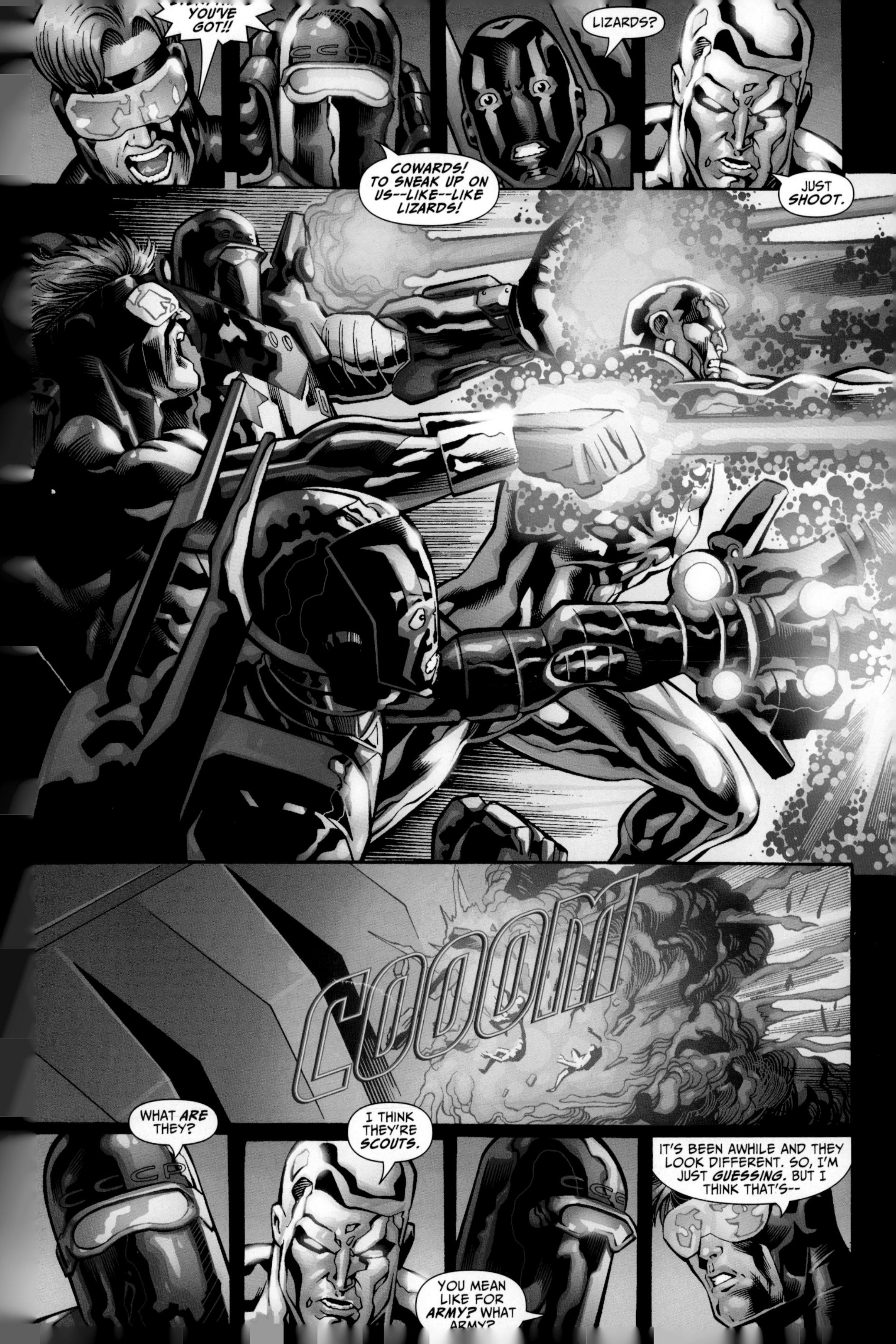
YOU'VE GOT!!
LIZARDS?
COWARDS! TO SNEAK UP ON US--LIKE--LIKE LIZARDS!
JUST SHOOT.
COOOM
WHAT ARE THEY?
I THINK THEY'RE SCOUTS.
YOU MEAN LIKE FOR ARMY? WHAT ARMY?
IT'S BEEN AWHILE AND THEY LOOK DIFFERENT. SO, I'M JUST GUESSING. BUT I THINK THAT'S--

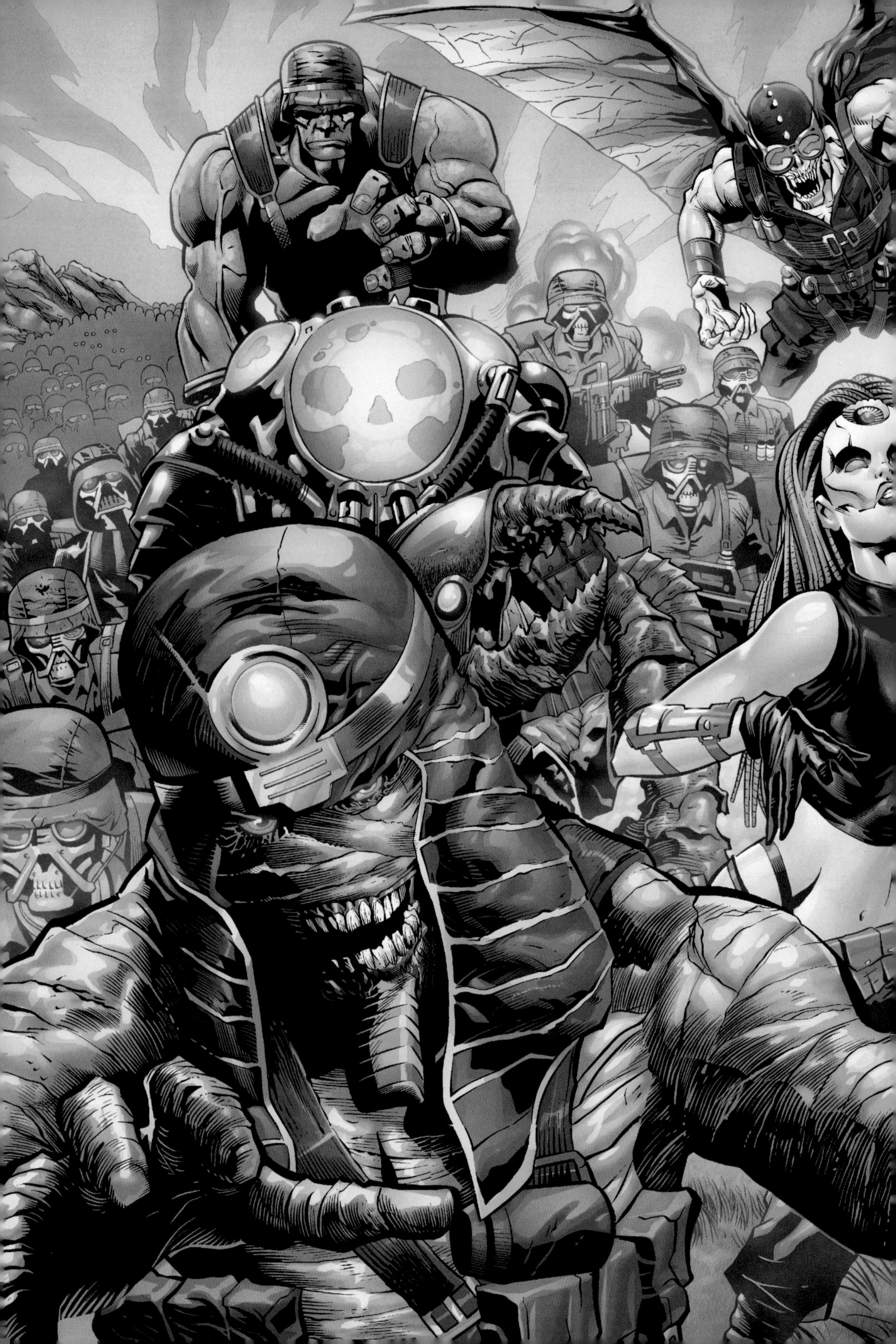

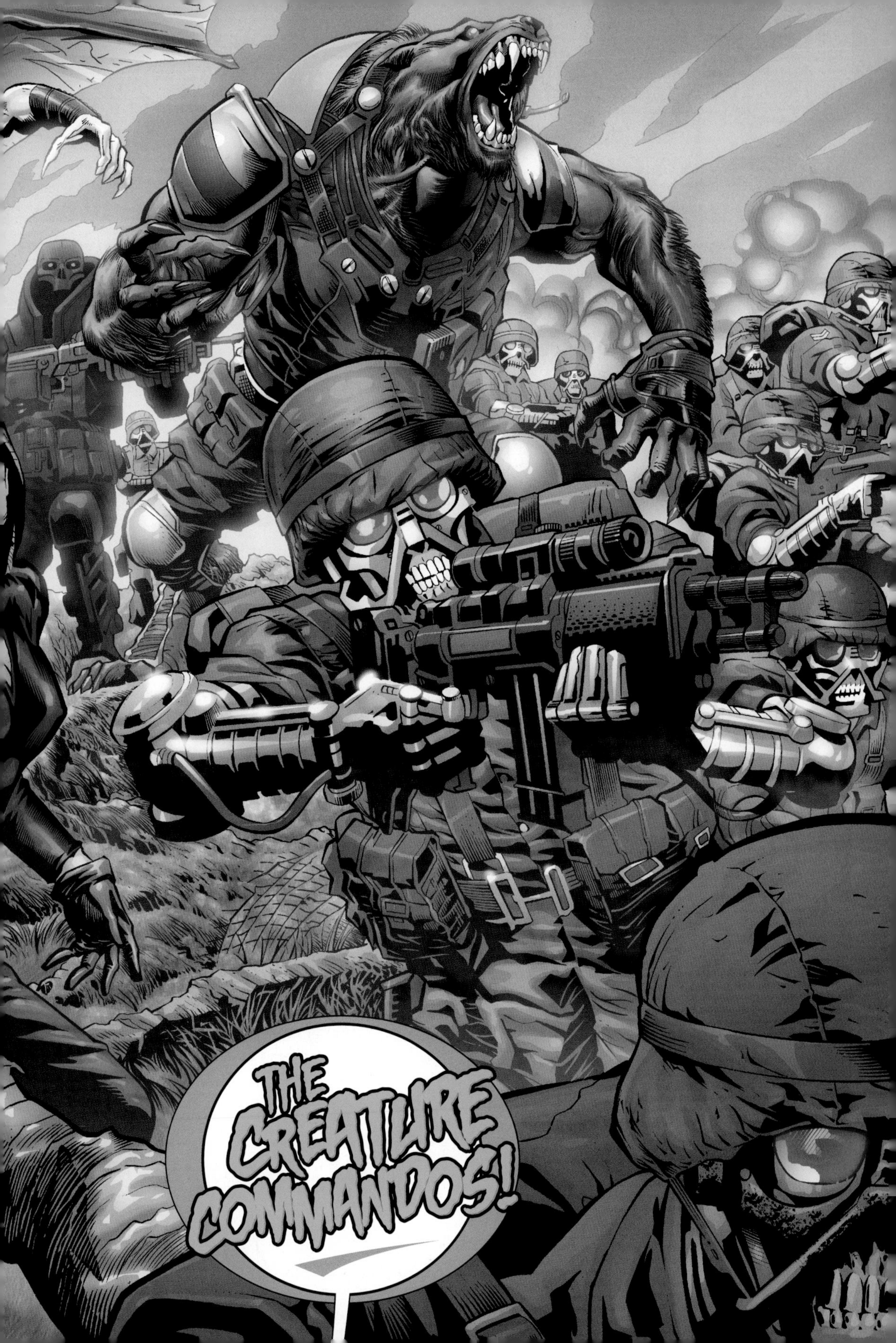
THE CREATURE COMMANDOS!

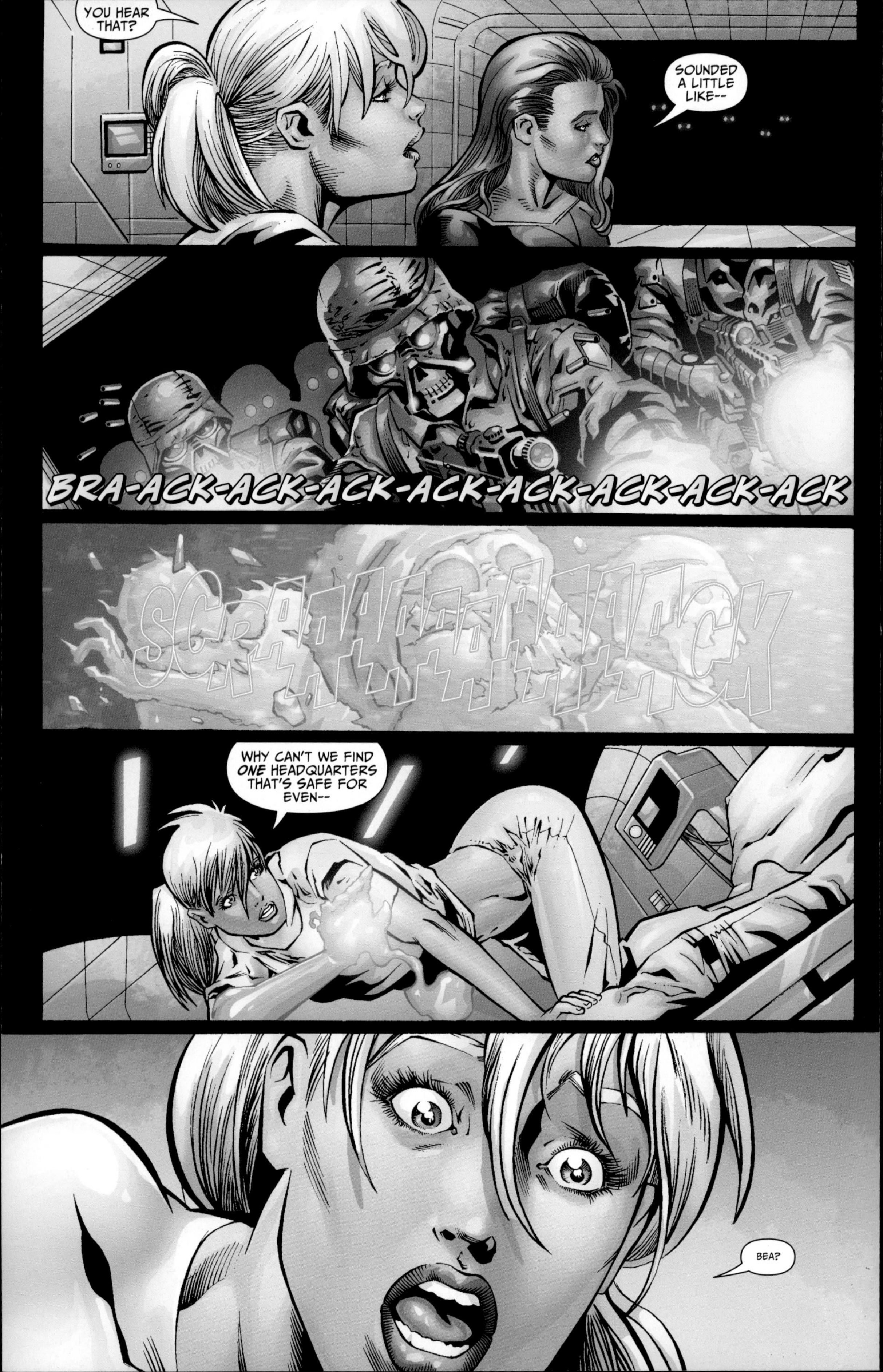
YOU HEAR THAT?
SOUNDED A LITTLE LIKE--
BRA-ACK-ACK-ACK-ACK-ACK-ACK-ACK-ACK
SCRAAAAAAAACK
WHY CAN'T WE FIND ONE HEADQUARTERS THAT'S SAFE FOR EVEN--
BEA?

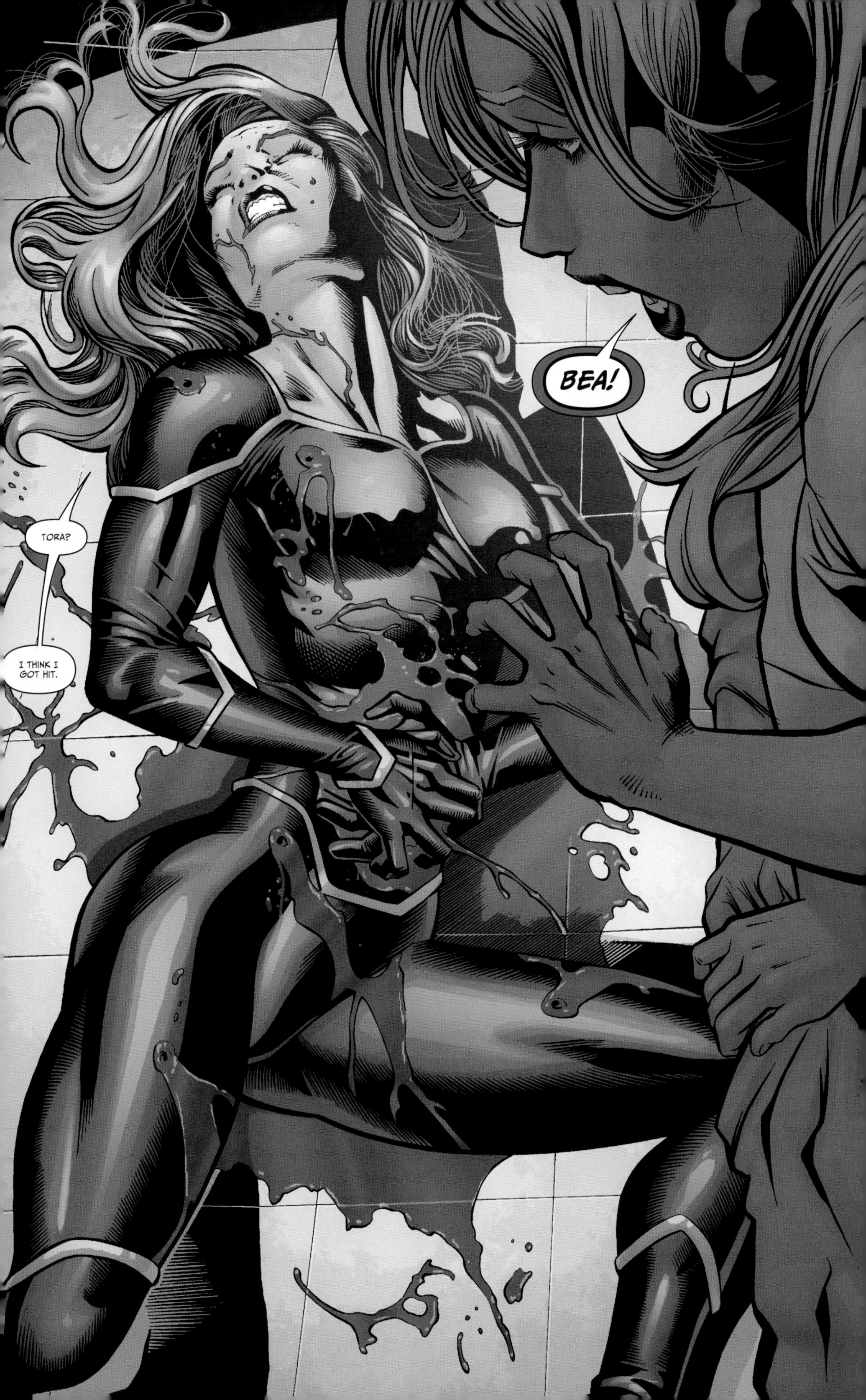
BEA!
TORA?
I THINK I GOT HIT.

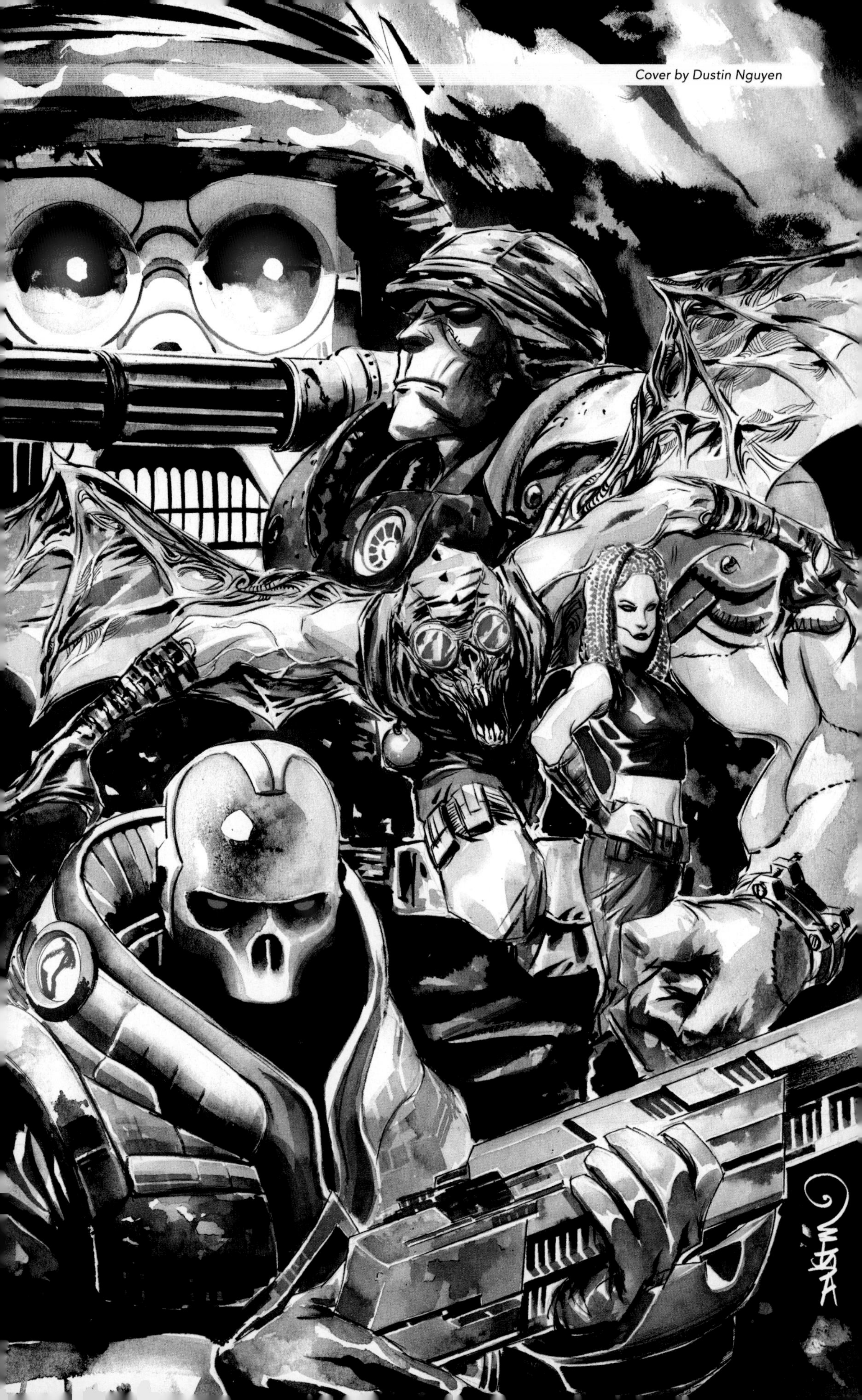

Cover by Dustin Nguyen

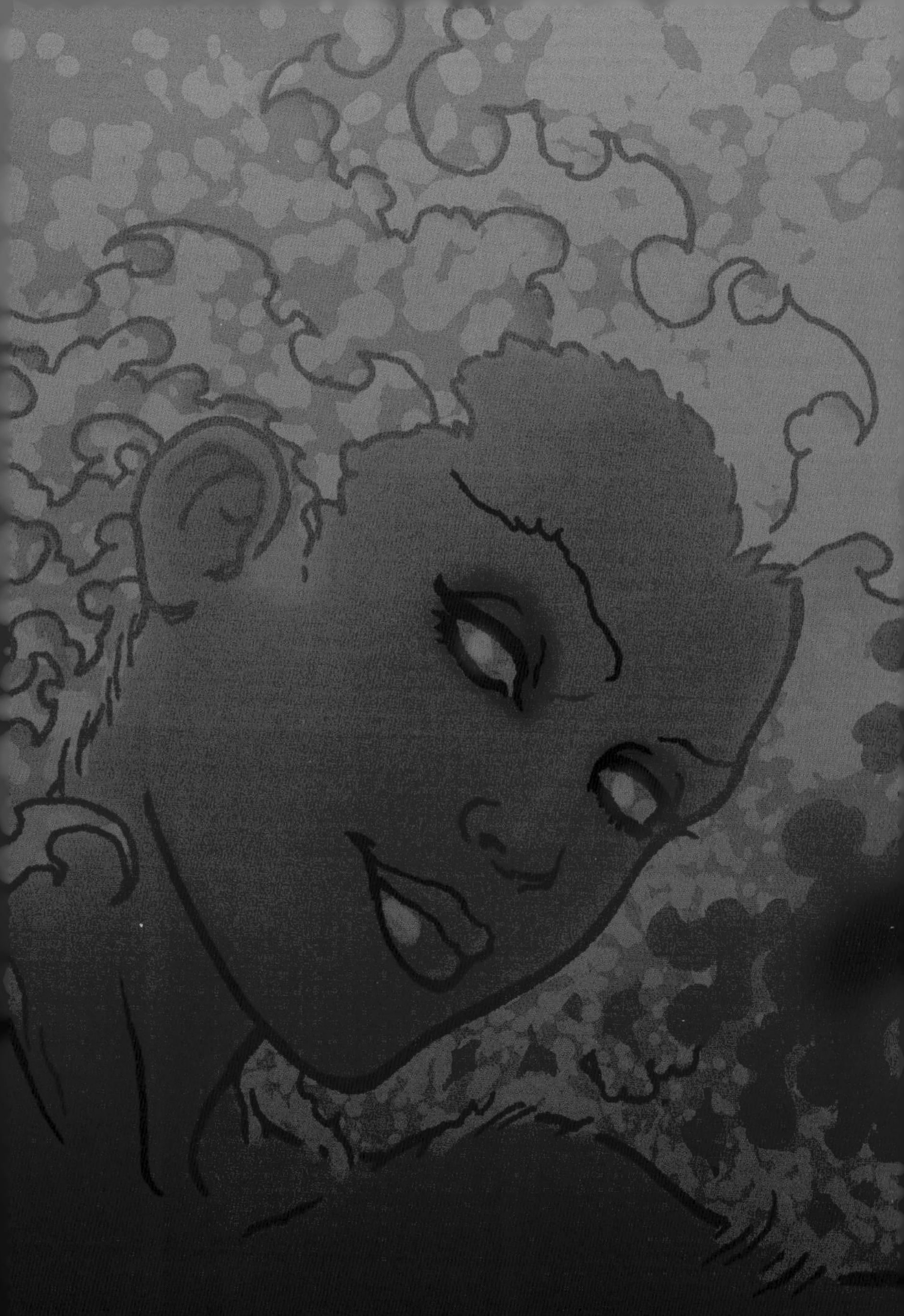

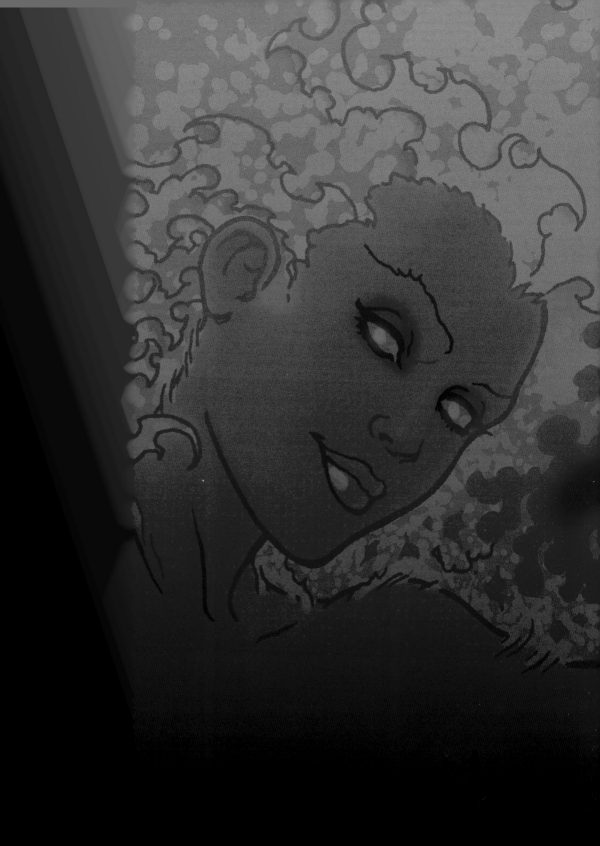

TEEN:
SCARY MONSTERS

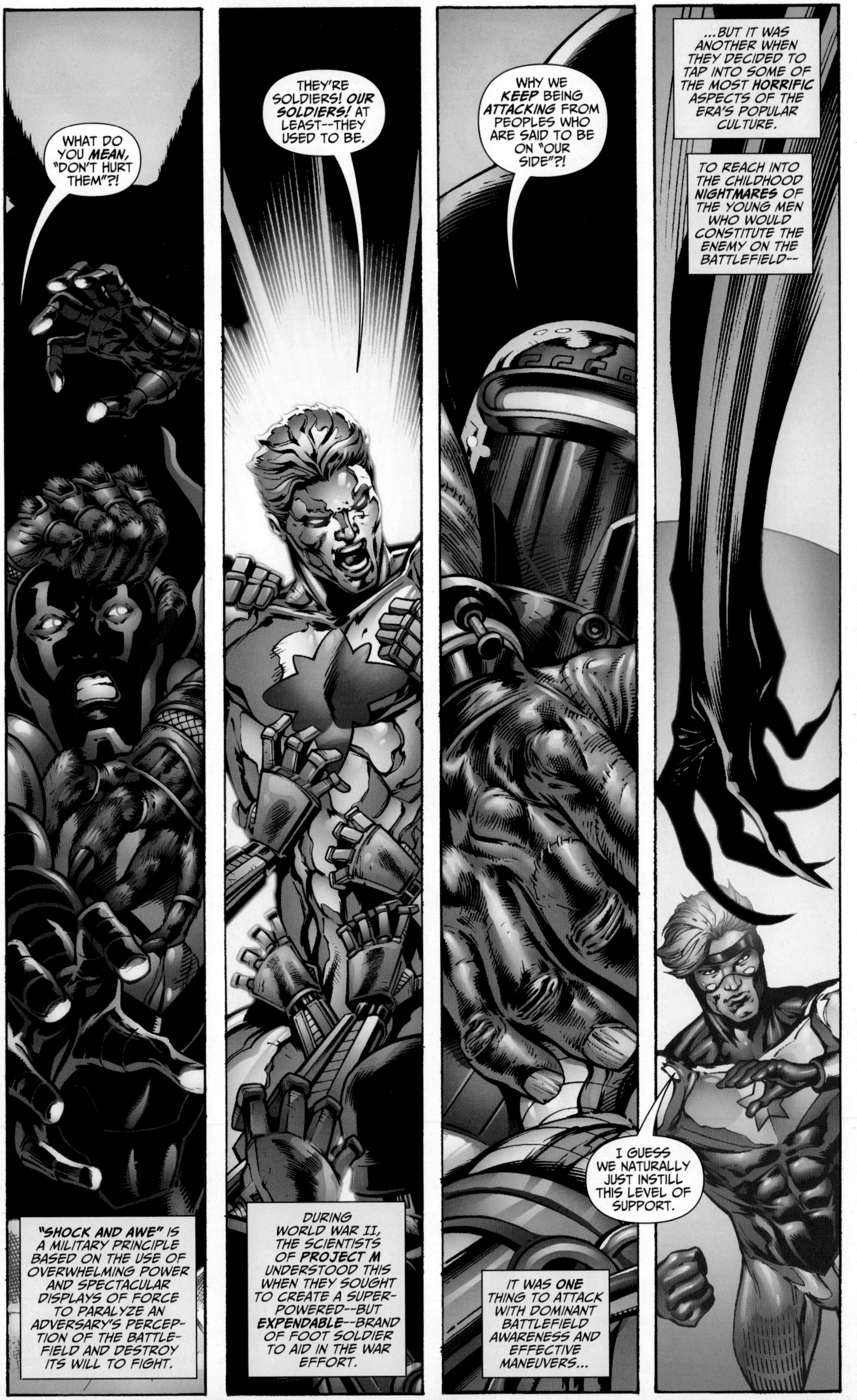

WHAT DO YOU MEAN, "DON'T HURT THEM"?!
"SHOCK AND AWE" IS A MILITARY PRINCIPLE BASED ON THE USE OF OVERWHELMING POWER AND SPECTACULAR DISPLAYS OF FORCE TO PARALYZE AN ADVERSARY'S PERCEPTION OF THE BATTLEFIELD AND DESTROY ITS WILL TO FIGHT.
THEY'RE SOLDIERS! OUR SOLDIERS! AT LEAST--THEY USED TO BE.
DURING WORLD WAR II, THE SCIENTISTS OF PROJECT M UNDERSTOOD THIS WHEN THEY SOUGHT TO CREATE A SUPER-POWERED--BUT EXPENDABLE--BRAND OF FOOT SOLDIER TO AID IN THE WAR EFFORT.
WHY WE KEEP BEING ATTACKING FROM PEOPLES WHO ARE SAID TO BE ON "OUR SIDE"?!
IT WAS ONE THING TO ATTACK WITH DOMINANT BATTLEFIELD AWARENESS AND EFFECTIVE MANEUVERS...
...BUT IT WAS ANOTHER WHEN THEY DECIDED TO TAP INTO SOME OF THE MOST HORRIFIC ASPECTS OF THE ERA'S POPULAR CULTURE.
TO REACH INTO THE CHILDHOOD NIGHTMARES OF THE YOUNG MEN WHO WOULD CONSTITUTE THE ENEMY ON THE BATTLEFIELD--
I GUESS WE NATURALLY JUST INSTILL THIS LEVEL OF SUPPORT.

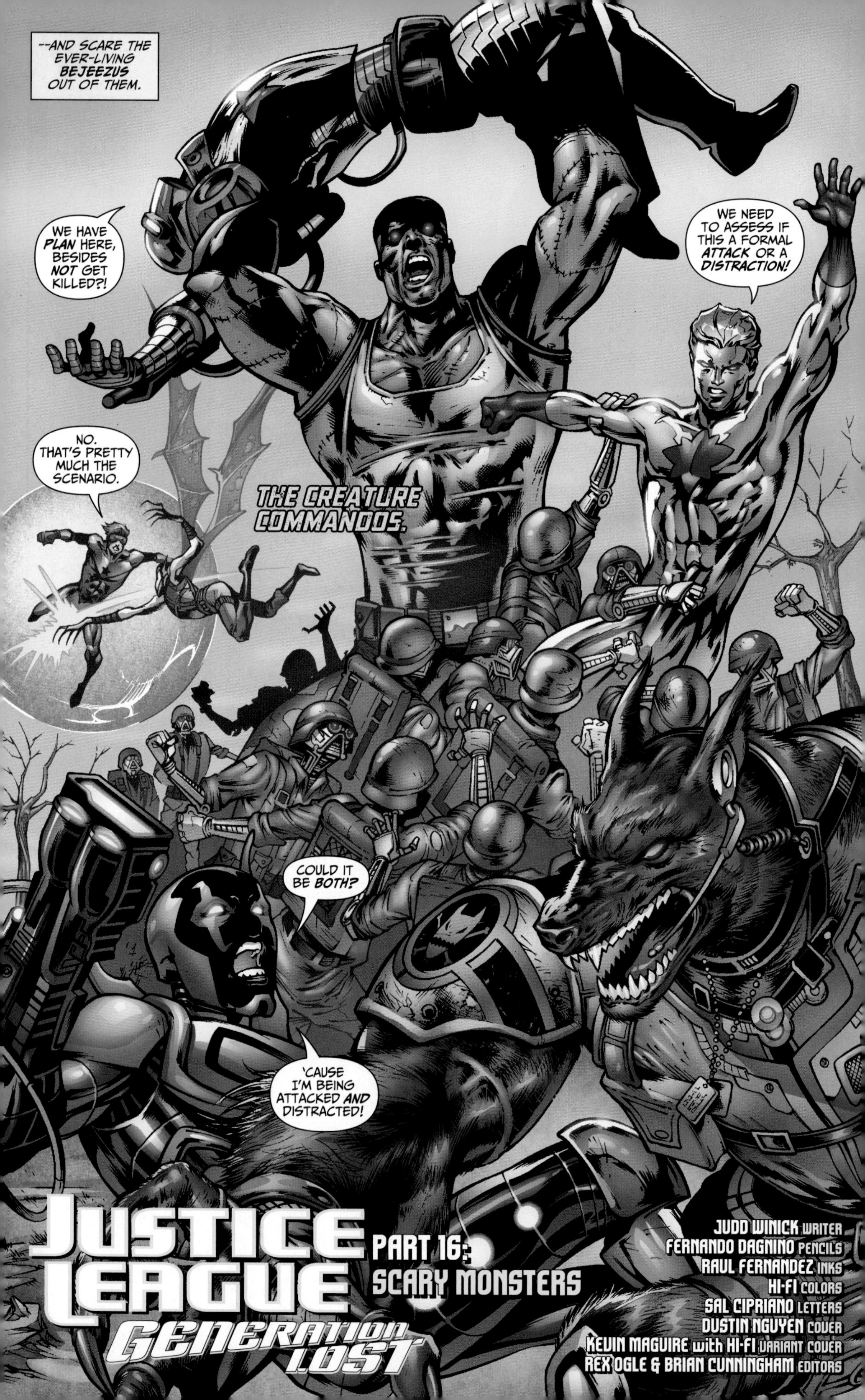

--AND SCARE THE EVER-LIVING BEJEEZUS OUT OF THEM.
WE HAVE PLAN HERE, BESIDES NOT GET KILLED?!
WE NEED TO ASSESS IF THIS A FORMAL ATTACK OR A DISTRACTION!
NO. THAT'S PRETTY MUCH THE SCENARIO.
THE CREATURE COMMANDOS.
COULD IT BE BOTH?
'CAUSE I'M BEING ATTACKED AND DISTRACTED!
JUSTICE LEAGUE GENERATION LOST
PART 16: SCARY MONSTERS
JUDD WINICK WRITER
FERNANDO DAGNINO PENCILS
RAUL FERNANDEZ INKS
HI-FI COLORS
SAL CIPRIANO LETTERS
DUSTIN NGUYEN COVER
KEVIN MAGUIRE with HI-FI VARIANT COVER
REX OGLE & BRIAN CUNNINGHAM EDITORS

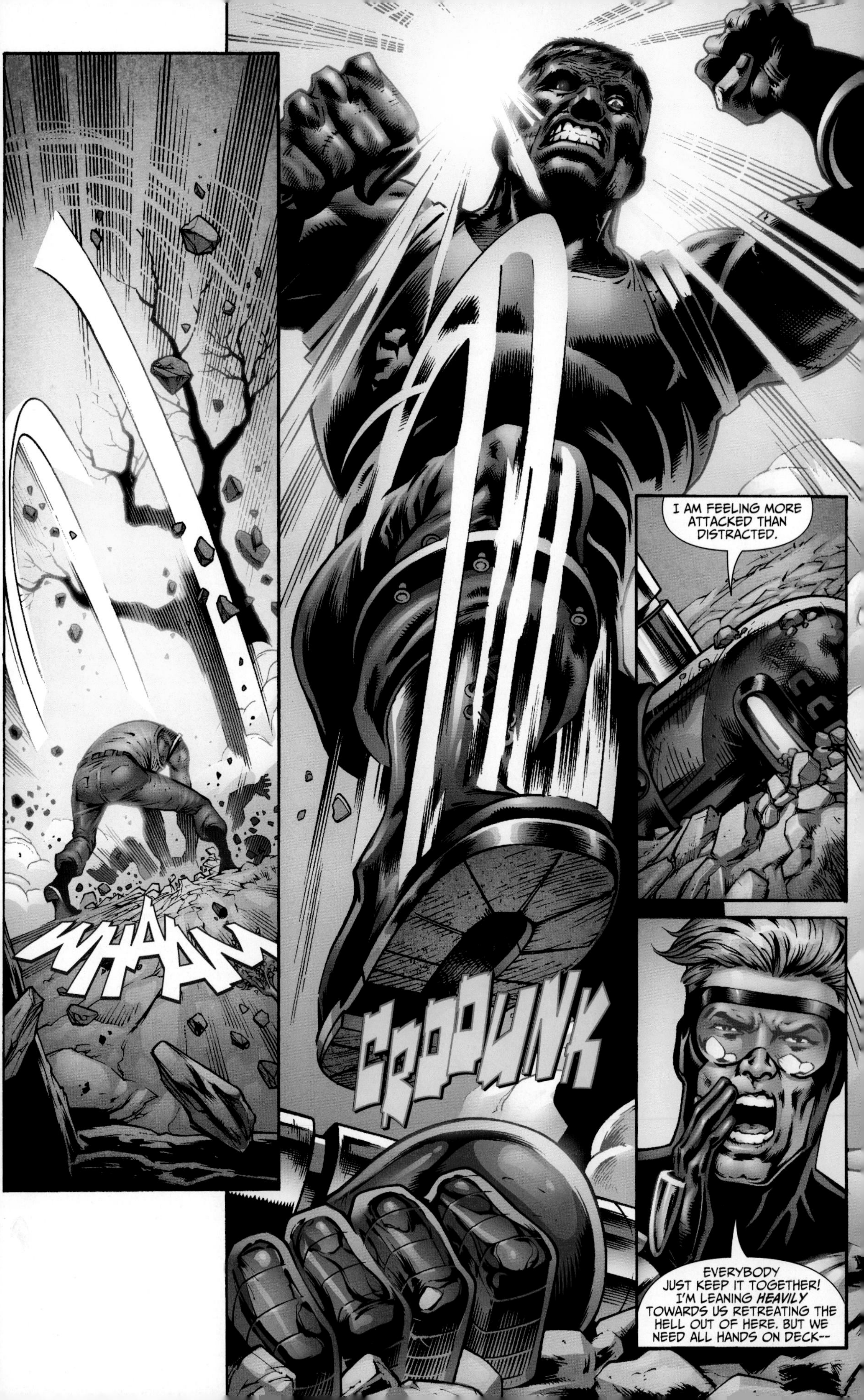
WHAM
CRROUNK
I AM FEELING MORE ATTACKED THAN DISTRACTED.
EVERYBODY JUST KEEP IT TOGETHER! I'M LEANING *HEAVILY* TOWARDS US RETREATING THE HELL OUT OF HERE. BUT WE NEED ALL HANDS ON DECK--

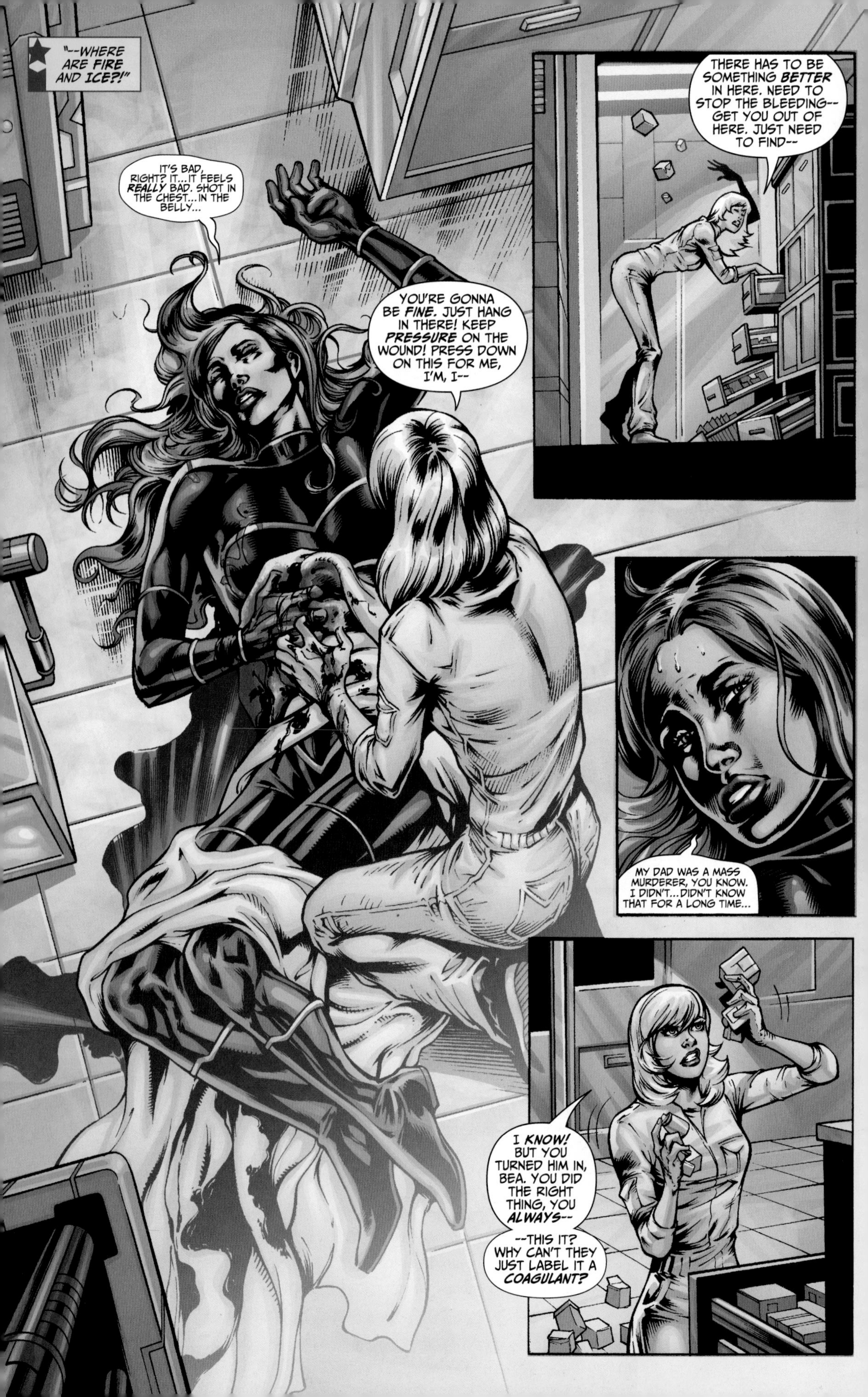
"--WHERE ARE FIRE AND ICE?!"
IT'S BAD, RIGHT? IT...IT FEELS REALLY BAD. SHOT IN THE CHEST...IN THE BELLY...
YOU'RE GONNA BE FINE. JUST HANG IN THERE! KEEP PRESSURE ON THE WOUND! PRESS DOWN ON THIS FOR ME, I'M, I--
THERE HAS TO BE SOMETHING BETTER IN HERE. NEED TO STOP THE BLEEDING--GET YOU OUT OF HERE. JUST NEED TO FIND--
MY DAD WAS A MASS MURDERER, YOU KNOW. I DIDN'T...DIDN'T KNOW THAT FOR A LONG TIME...
I KNOW! BUT YOU TURNED HIM IN, BEA. YOU DID THE RIGHT THING, YOU ALWAYS--
--THIS IT? WHY CAN'T THEY JUST LABEL IT A COAGULANT?

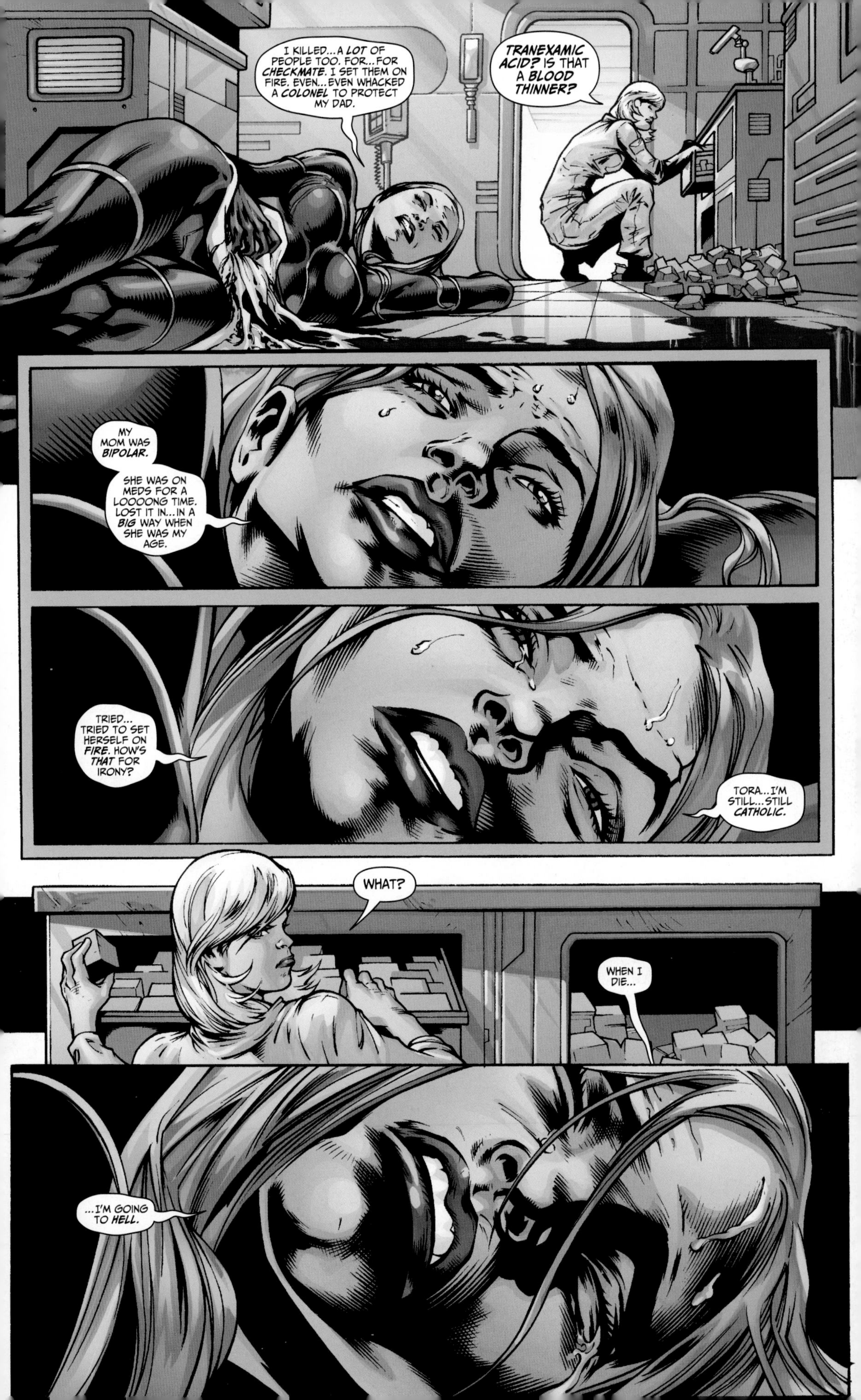
I KILLED...A LOT OF PEOPLE TOO. FOR...FOR CHECKMATE. I SET THEM ON FIRE. EVEN...EVEN WHACKED A COLONEL TO PROTECT MY DAD.
TRANEXAMIC ACID? IS THAT A BLOOD THINNER?
MY MOM WAS BIPOLAR.
SHE WAS ON MEDS FOR A LOOOONG TIME. LOST IT IN...IN A BIG WAY WHEN SHE WAS MY AGE.
TRIED... TRIED TO SET HERSELF ON FIRE. HOW'S THAT FOR IRONY?
TORA...I'M STILL...STILL CATHOLIC.
WHAT?
WHEN I DIE...
...I'M GOING TO HELL.

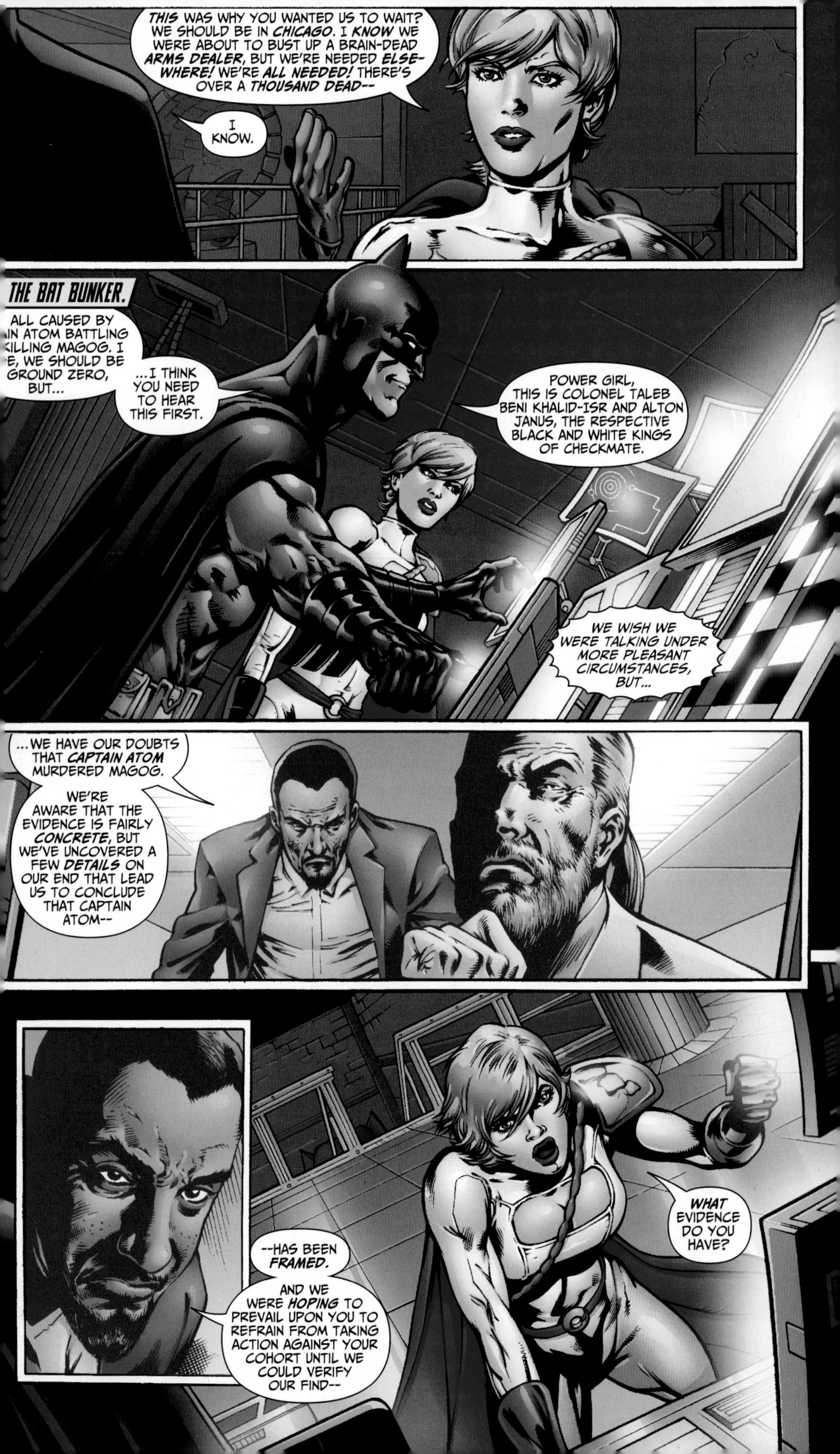
THIS WAS WHY YOU WANTED US TO WAIT? WE SHOULD BE IN CHICAGO. I KNOW WE WERE ABOUT TO BUST UP A BRAIN-DEAD ARMS DEALER, BUT WE'RE NEEDED ELSE-WHERE! WE'RE ALL NEEDED! THERE'S OVER A THOUSAND DEAD--
I KNOW.
THE BAT BUNKER.
ALL CAUSED BY
AIN ATOM BATTLING
KILLING MAGOG. I
E, WE SHOULD BE
GROUND ZERO,
BUT...
...I THINK YOU NEED TO HEAR THIS FIRST.
POWER GIRL, THIS IS COLONEL TALEB BENI KHALID-ISR AND ALTON JANUS, THE RESPECTIVE BLACK AND WHITE KINGS OF CHECKMATE.
WE WISH WE WERE TALKING UNDER MORE PLEASANT CIRCUMSTANCES, BUT...
...WE HAVE OUR DOUBTS THAT CAPTAIN ATOM MURDERED MAGOG.
WE'RE AWARE THAT THE EVIDENCE IS FAIRLY CONCRETE, BUT WE'VE UNCOVERED A FEW DETAILS ON OUR END THAT LEAD US TO CONCLUDE THAT CAPTAIN ATOM--
--HAS BEEN FRAMED.
AND WE WERE HOPING TO PREVAIL UPON YOU TO REFRAIN FROM TAKING ACTION AGAINST YOUR COHORT UNTIL WE COULD VERIFY OUR FIND--
WHAT EVIDENCE DO YOU HAVE?

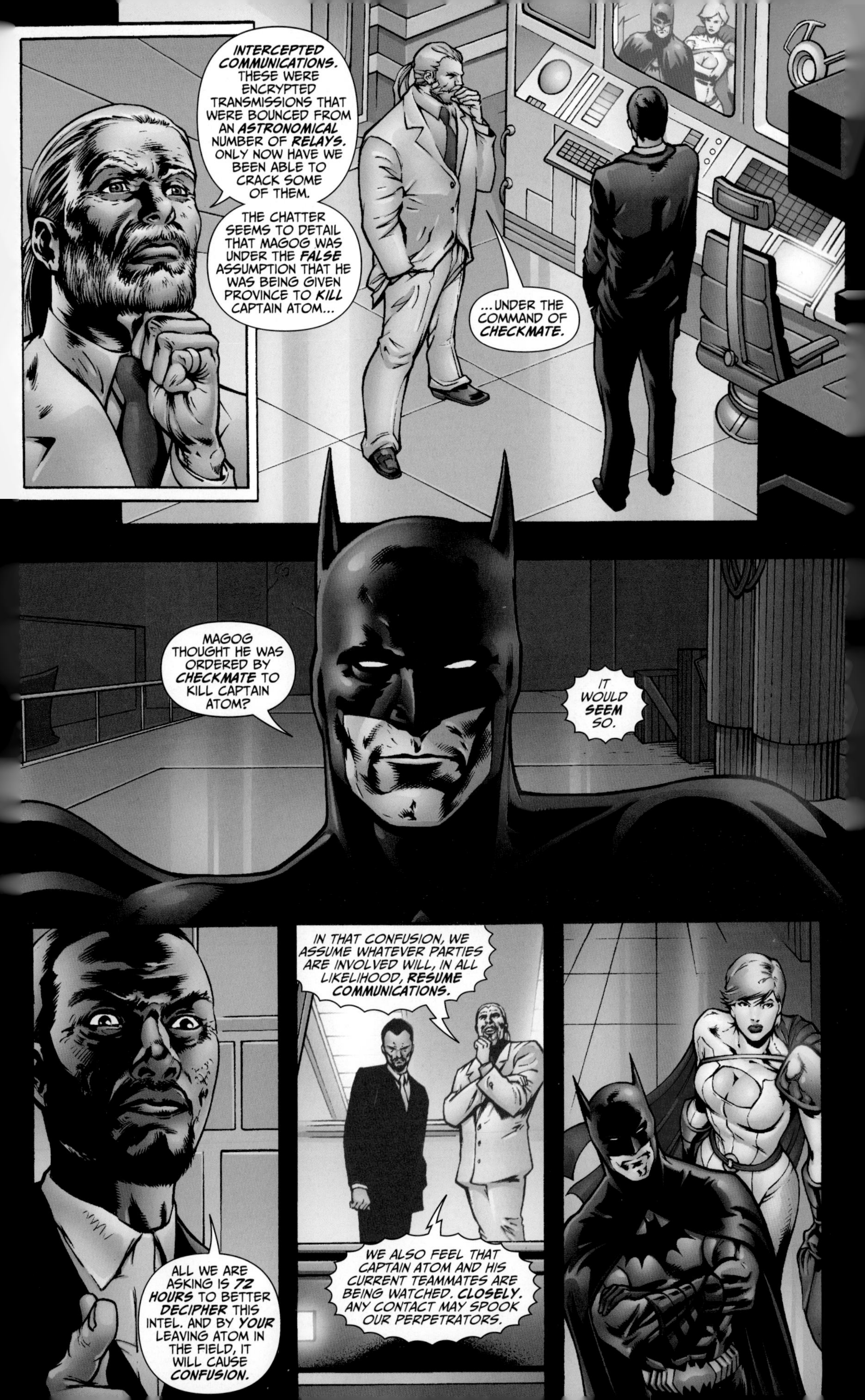
INTERCEPTED COMMUNICATIONS. THESE WERE ENCRYPTED TRANSMISSIONS THAT WERE BOUNCED FROM AN ASTRONOMICAL NUMBER OF RELAYS. ONLY NOW HAVE WE BEEN ABLE TO CRACK SOME OF THEM.
THE CHATTER SEEMS TO DETAIL THAT MAGOG WAS UNDER THE FALSE ASSUMPTION THAT HE WAS BEING GIVEN PROVINCE TO KILL CAPTAIN ATOM...
...UNDER THE COMMAND OF CHECKMATE.
MAGOG THOUGHT HE WAS ORDERED BY CHECKMATE TO KILL CAPTAIN ATOM?
IT WOULD SEEM SO.
ALL WE ARE ASKING IS 72 HOURS TO BETTER DECIPHER THIS INTEL. AND BY YOUR LEAVING ATOM IN THE FIELD, IT WILL CAUSE CONFUSION.
IN THAT CONFUSION, WE ASSUME WHATEVER PARTIES ARE INVOLVED WILL, IN ALL LIKELIHOOD, RESUME COMMUNICATIONS.
WE ALSO FEEL THAT CAPTAIN ATOM AND HIS CURRENT TEAMMATES ARE BEING WATCHED. CLOSELY. ANY CONTACT MAY SPOOK OUR PERPETRATORS.

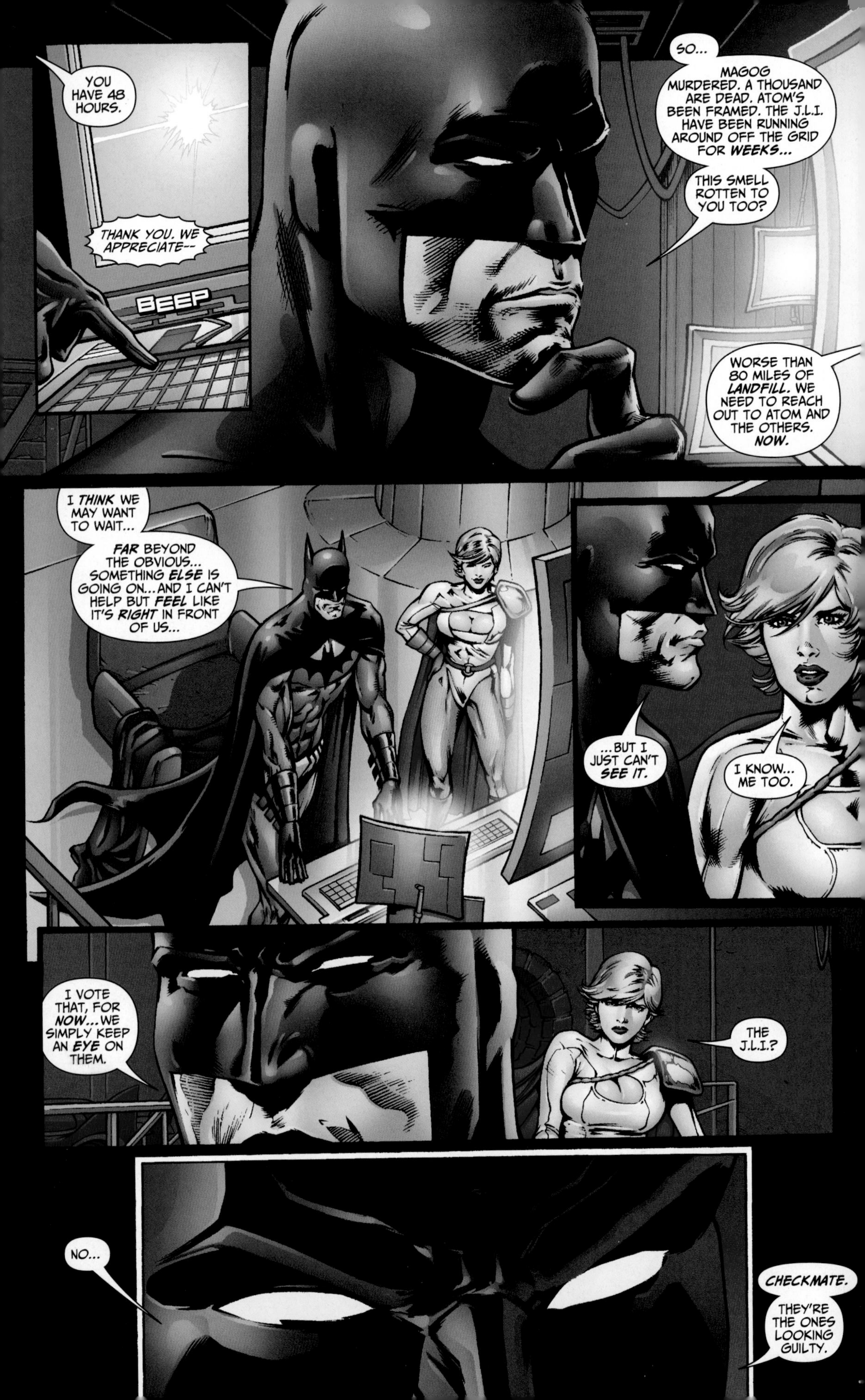
YOU HAVE 48 HOURS.
THANK YOU. WE APPRECIATE--
BEEP
SO...
MAGOG MURDERED. A THOUSAND ARE DEAD. ATOM'S BEEN FRAMED. THE J.L.I. HAVE BEEN RUNNING AROUND OFF THE GRID FOR WEEKS...
THIS SMELL ROTTEN TO YOU TOO?
WORSE THAN 80 MILES OF LANDFILL. WE NEED TO REACH OUT TO ATOM AND THE OTHERS. NOW.
I THINK WE MAY WANT TO WAIT...
FAR BEYOND THE OBVIOUS... SOMETHING ELSE IS GOING ON... AND I CAN'T HELP BUT FEEL LIKE IT'S RIGHT IN FRONT OF US...
...BUT I JUST CAN'T SEE IT.
I KNOW... ME TOO.
I VOTE THAT, FOR NOW... WE SIMPLY KEEP AN EYE ON THEM.
THE J.L.I.?
NO...
CHECKMATE.
THEY'RE THE ONES LOOKING GUILTY.

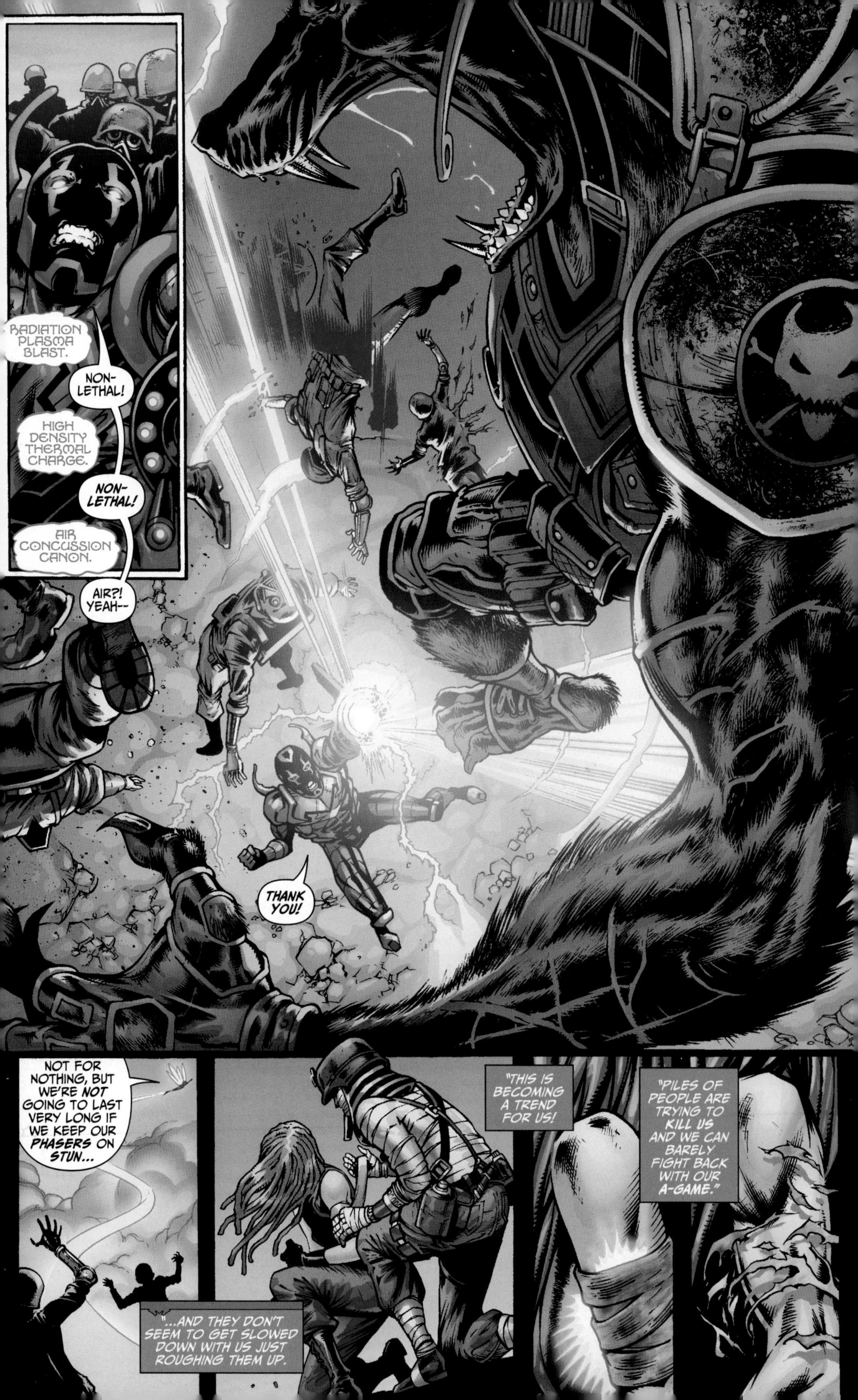
RADIATION PLASMA BLAST.
NON-LETHAL!
HIGH DENSITY THERMAL CHARGE.
NON-LETHAL!
AIR CONCUSSION CANON.
AIR?! YEAH--
THANK YOU!
NOT FOR NOTHING, BUT WE'RE NOT GOING TO LAST VERY LONG IF WE KEEP OUR PHASERS ON STUN...
"...AND THEY DON'T SEEM TO GET SLOWED DOWN WITH US JUST ROUGHING THEM UP.
"THIS IS BECOMING A TREND FOR US!
"PILES OF PEOPLE ARE TRYING TO KILL US AND WE CAN BARELY FIGHT BACK WITH OUR A-GAME."

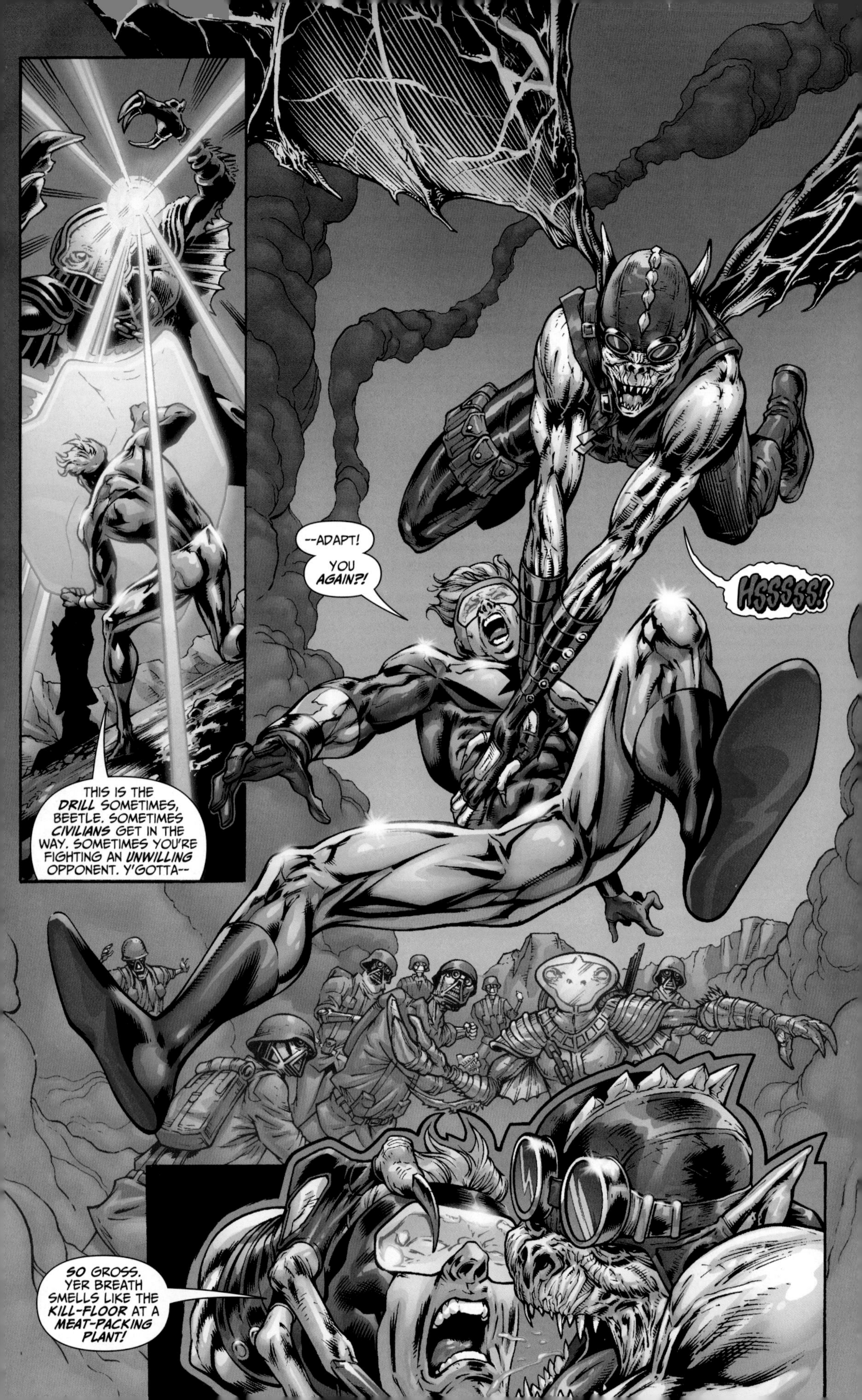
THIS IS THE DRILL SOMETIMES, BEETLE. SOMETIMES CIVILIANS GET IN THE WAY. SOMETIMES YOU'RE FIGHTING AN UNWILLING OPPONENT. Y'GOTTA--
--ADAPT! YOU AGAIN?!
HSSSSS!
SO GROSS. YER BREATH SMELLS LIKE THE KILL-FLOOR AT A MEAT-PACKING PLANT!

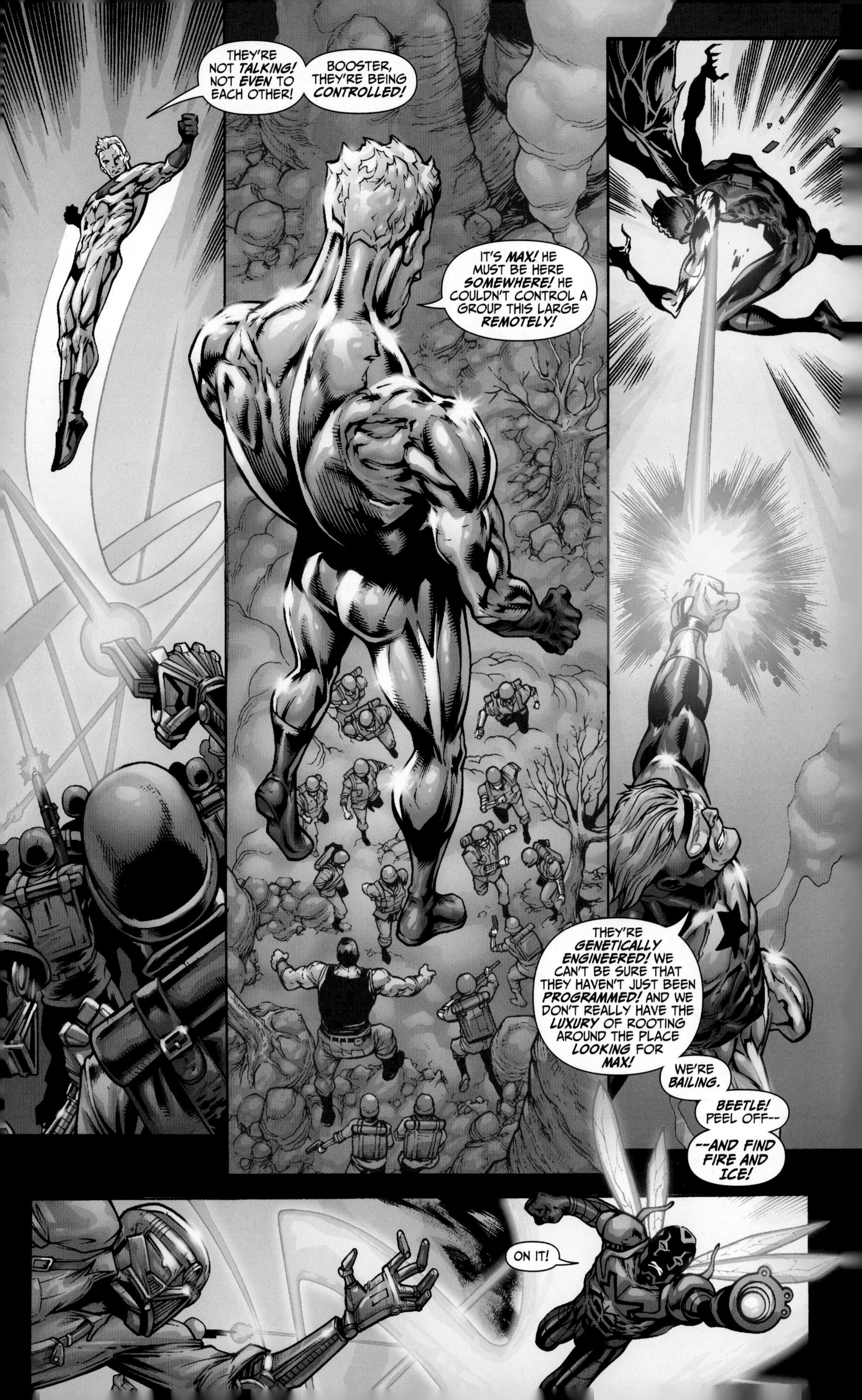

THEY'RE NOT TALKING! NOT EVEN TO EACH OTHER!
BOOSTER, THEY'RE BEING CONTROLLED!
IT'S MAX! HE MUST BE HERE SOMEWHERE! HE COULDN'T CONTROL A GROUP THIS LARGE REMOTELY!
THEY'RE GENETICALLY ENGINEERED! WE CAN'T BE SURE THAT THEY HAVEN'T JUST BEEN PROGRAMMED! AND WE DON'T REALLY HAVE THE LUXURY OF ROOTING AROUND THE PLACE LOOKING FOR MAX!
WE'RE BAILING.
BEETLE! PEEL OFF--
--AND FIND FIRE AND ICE!
ON IT!

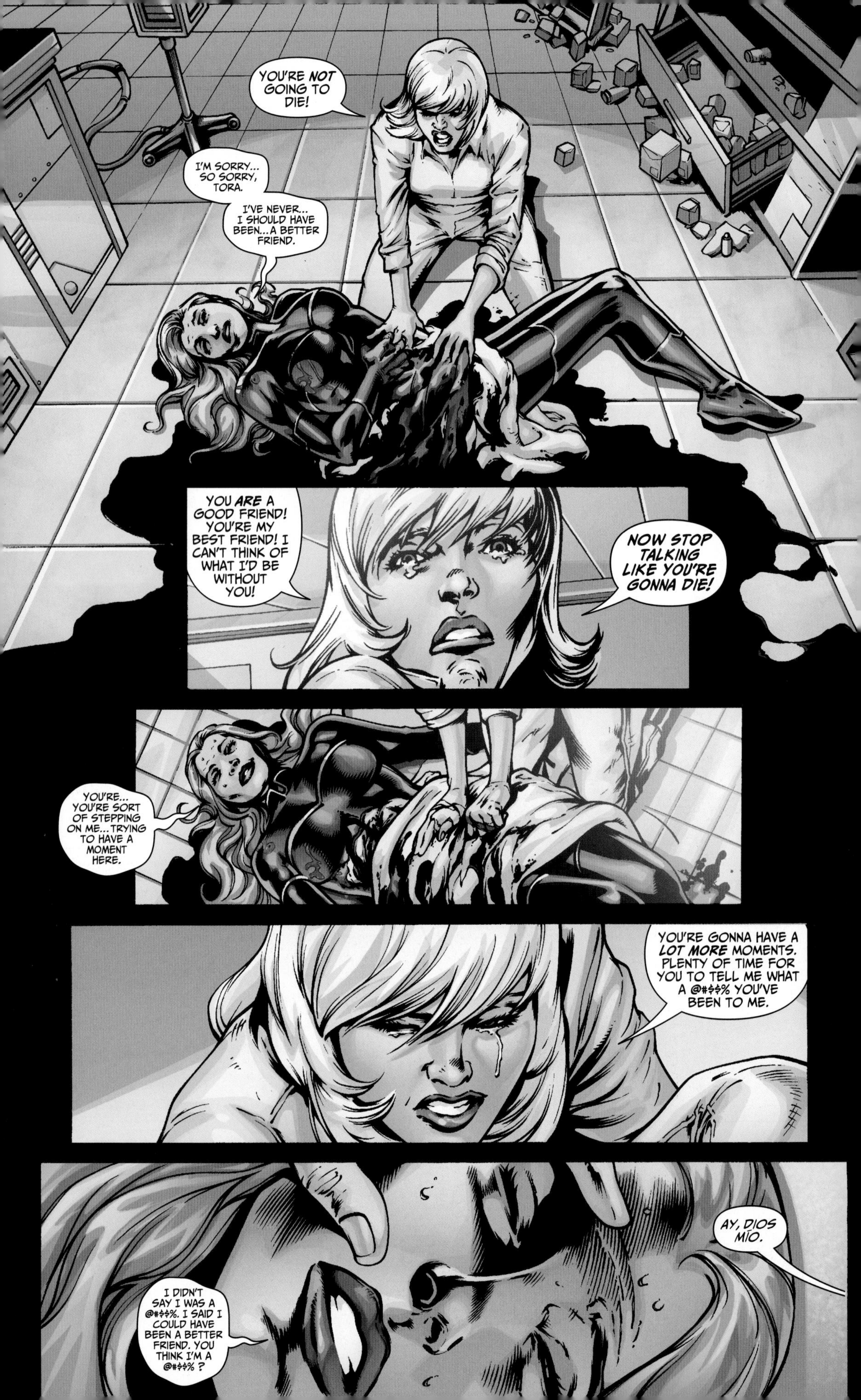
YOU'RE NOT GOING TO DIE!
I'M SORRY... SO SORRY, TORA.
I'VE NEVER... I SHOULD HAVE BEEN... A BETTER FRIEND.
YOU ARE A GOOD FRIEND! YOU'RE MY BEST FRIEND! I CAN'T THINK OF WHAT I'D BE WITHOUT YOU!
NOW STOP TALKING LIKE YOU'RE GONNA DIE!
YOU'RE... YOU'RE SORT OF STEPPING ON ME... TRYING TO HAVE A MOMENT HERE.
YOU'RE GONNA HAVE A LOT MORE MOMENTS. PLENTY OF TIME FOR YOU TO TELL ME WHAT A @#$$% YOU'VE BEEN TO ME.
AY, DIOS MÍO.
I DIDN'T SAY I WAS A @#$$%. I SAID I COULD HAVE BEEN A BETTER FRIEND. YOU THINK I'M A @#$$% ?

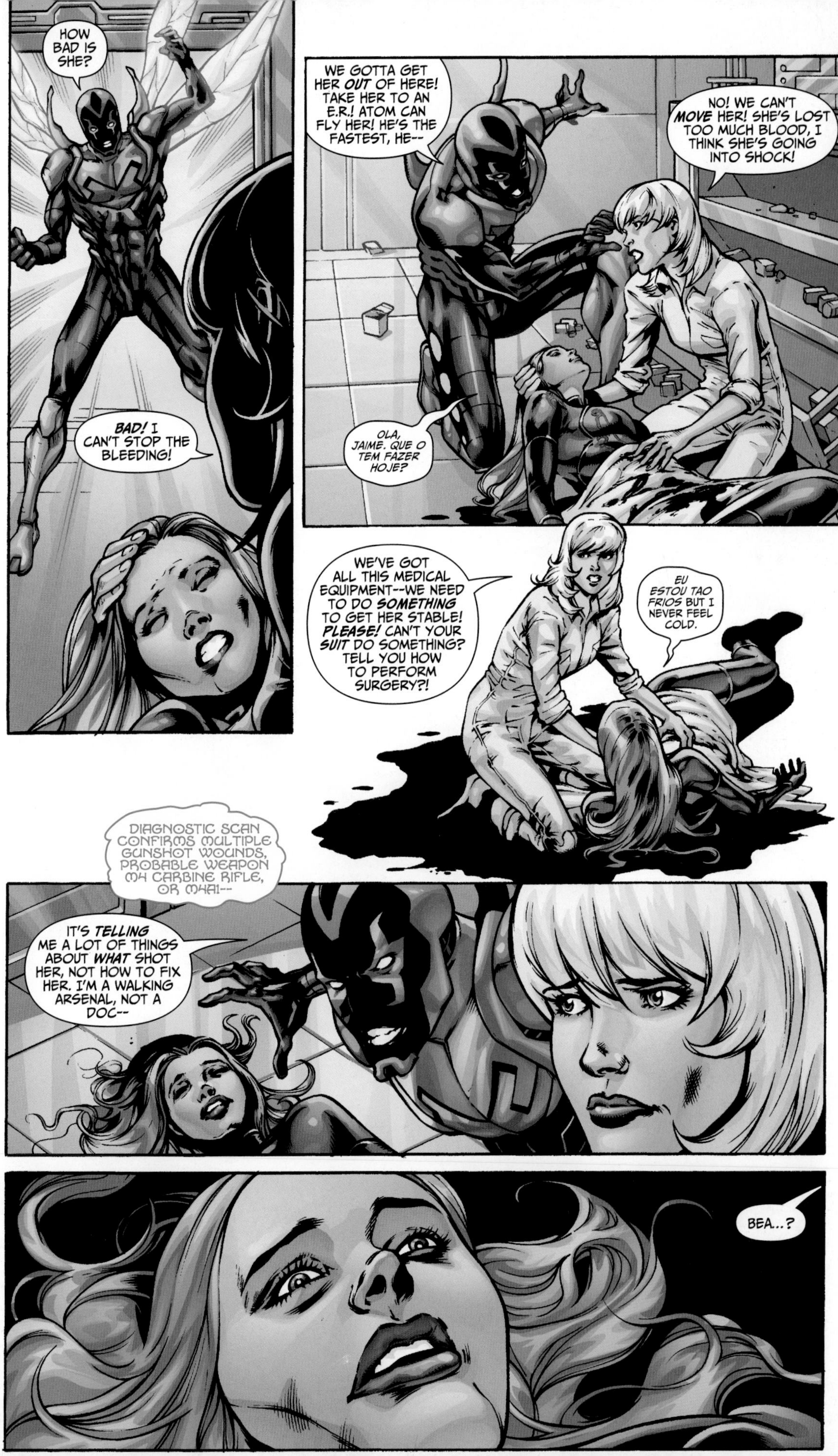
HOW BAD IS SHE?
BAD! I CAN'T STOP THE BLEEDING!
WE GOTTA GET HER OUT OF HERE! TAKE HER TO AN E.R.! ATOM CAN FLY HER! HE'S THE FASTEST, HE--
NO! WE CAN'T MOVE HER! SHE'S LOST TOO MUCH BLOOD, I THINK SHE'S GOING INTO SHOCK!
OLA, JAIME. QUE O TEM FAZER HOJE?
WE'VE GOT ALL THIS MEDICAL EQUIPMENT--WE NEED TO DO SOMETHING TO GET HER STABLE! PLEASE! CAN'T YOUR SUIT DO SOMETHING? TELL YOU HOW TO PERFORM SURGERY?!
EU ESTOU TAO FRIOS BUT I NEVER FEEL COLD.
DIAGNOSTIC SCAN CONFIRMS MULTIPLE GUNSHOT WOUNDS, PROBABLE WEAPON M4 CARBINE RIFLE, OR M4A1--
IT'S TELLING ME A LOT OF THINGS ABOUT WHAT SHOT HER, NOT HOW TO FIX HER. I'M A WALKING ARSENAL, NOT A DOC--
BEA..?

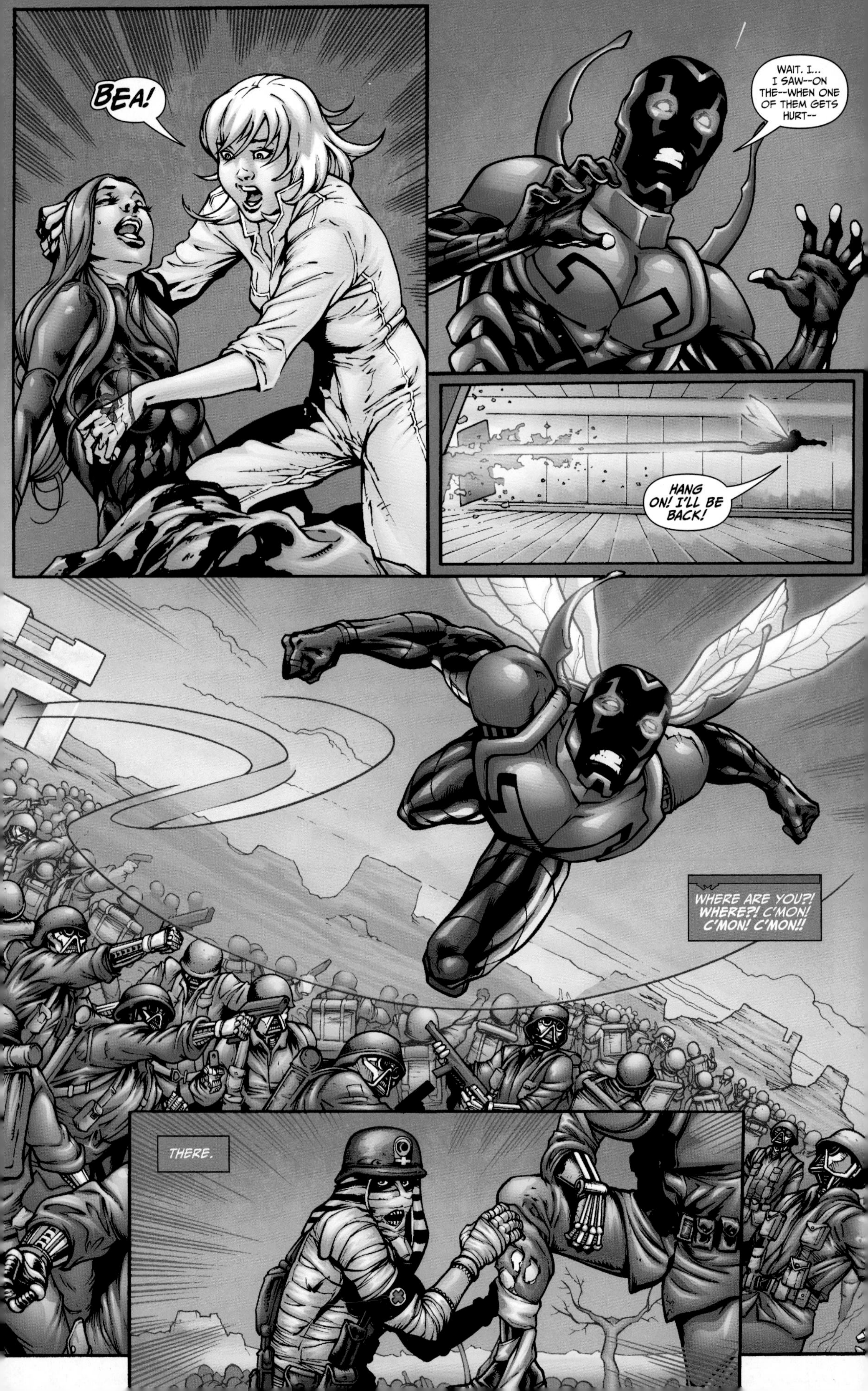
BEA!
WAIT. I... I SAW--ON THE--WHEN ONE OF THEM GETS HURT--
HANG ON! I'LL BE BACK!
WHERE ARE YOU?! WHERE?! C'MON! C'MON! C'MON!!
THERE.

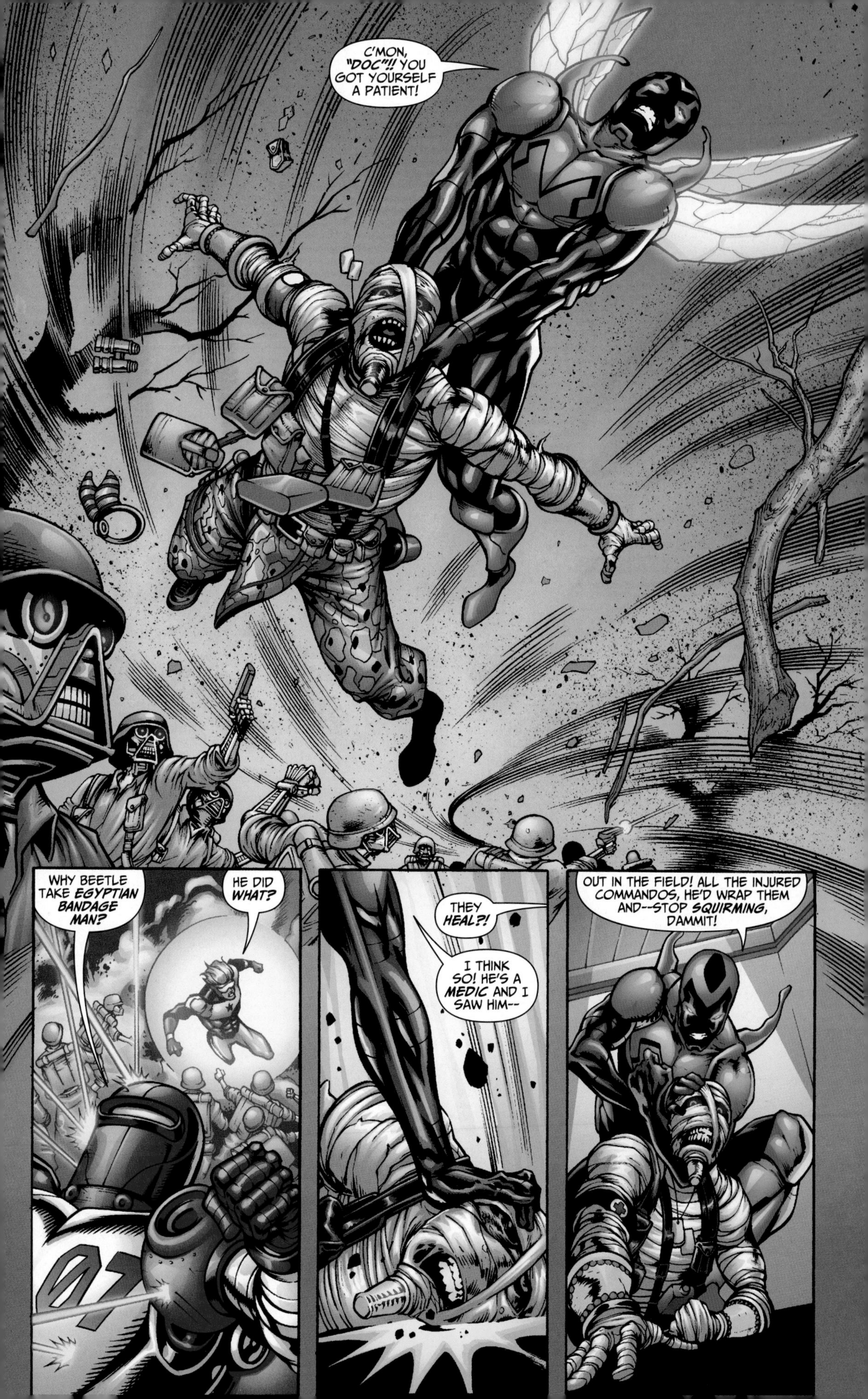
C'MON, "DOC"!! YOU GOT YOURSELF A PATIENT!
WHY BEETLE TAKE EGYPTIAN BANDAGE MAN?
HE DID WHAT?
THEY HEAL?!
I THINK SO! HE'S A MEDIC AND I SAW HIM--
OUT IN THE FIELD! ALL THE INJURED COMMANDOS, HE'D WRAP THEM AND--STOP SQUIRMING, DAMMIT!

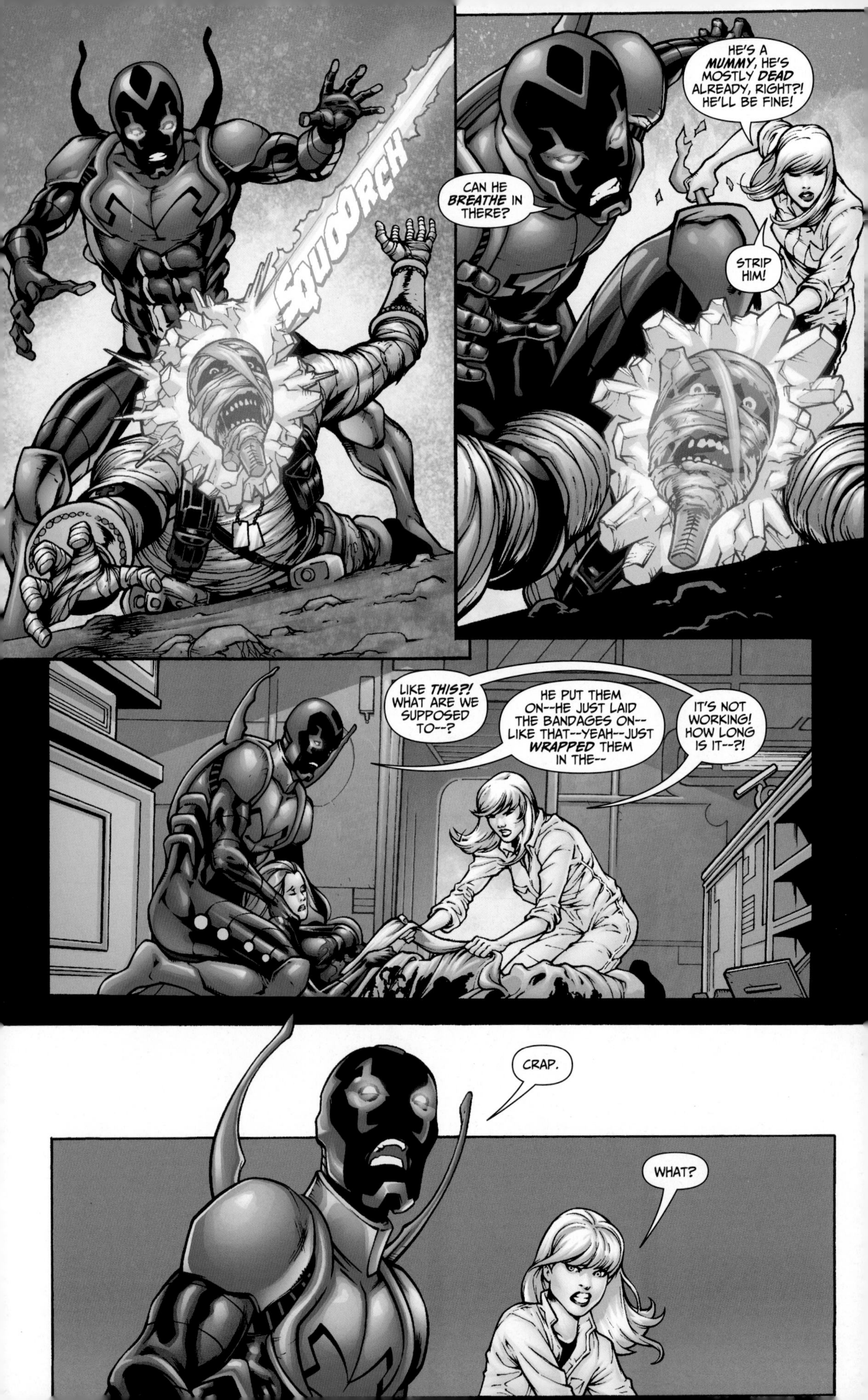
SQUOORCH
HE'S A MUMMY, HE'S MOSTLY DEAD ALREADY, RIGHT?! HE'LL BE FINE!
CAN HE BREATHE IN THERE?
STRIP HIM!
LIKE THIS?! WHAT ARE WE SUPPOSED TO--?
HE PUT THEM ON--HE JUST LAID THE BANDAGES ON--LIKE THAT--YEAH--JUST WRAPPED THEM IN THE--
IT'S NOT WORKING! HOW LONG IS IT--?!
CRAP.
WHAT?

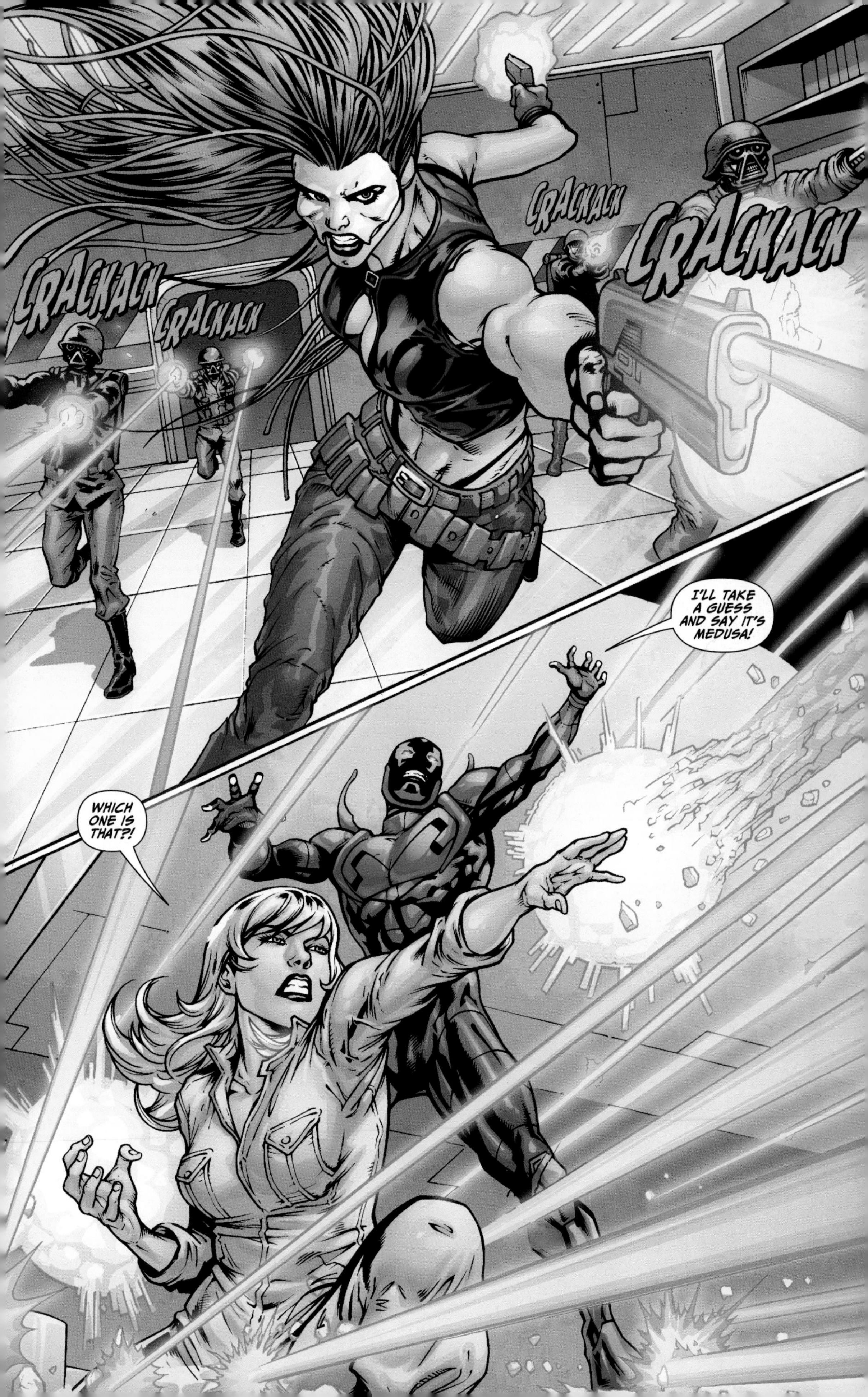
CRACKACK
CRACKACK
CRACKACK
CRACKACK
I'LL TAKE A GUESS AND SAY IT'S MEDUSA!
WHICH ONE IS THAT?!

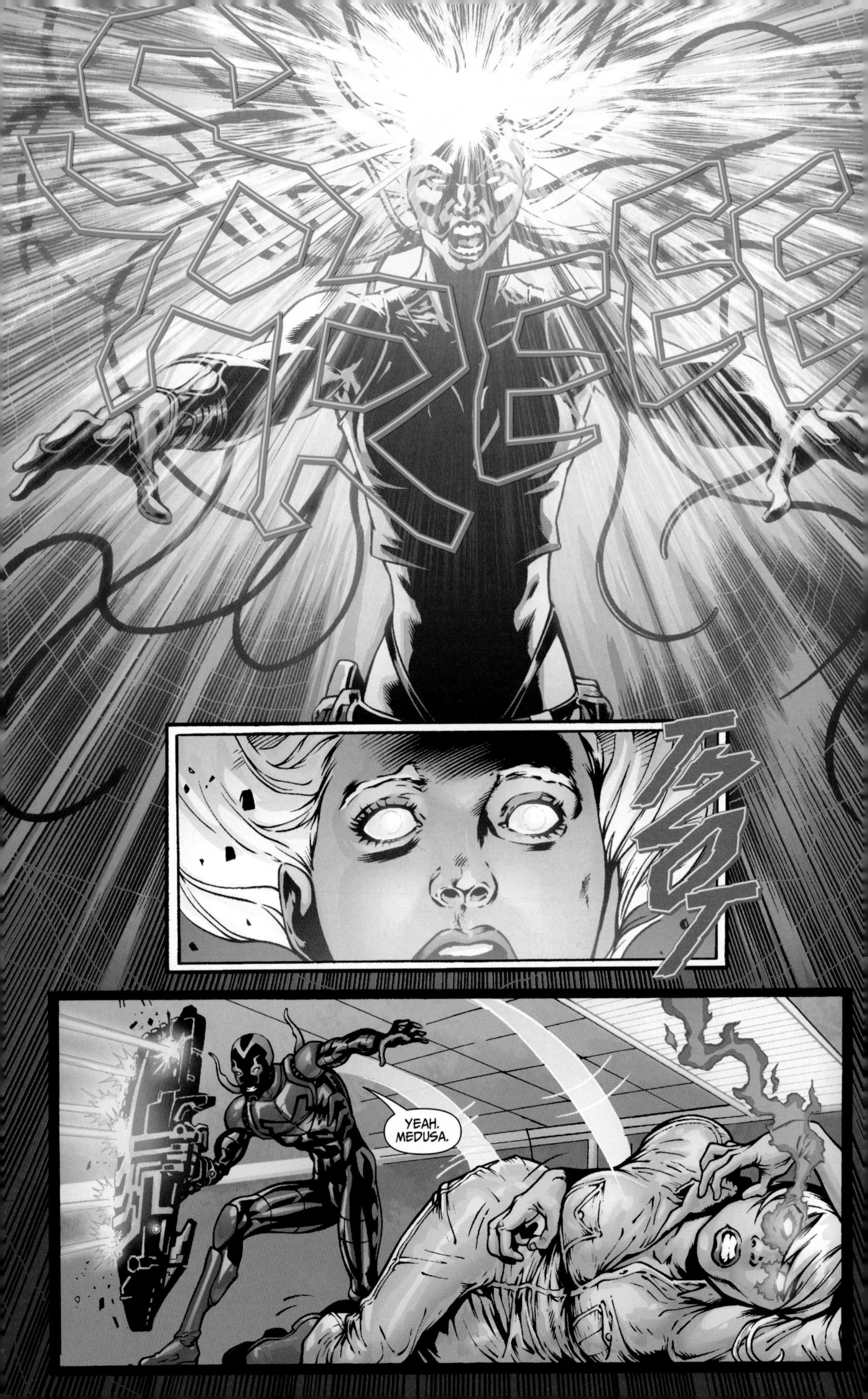
TZOT
YEAH. MEDUSA.

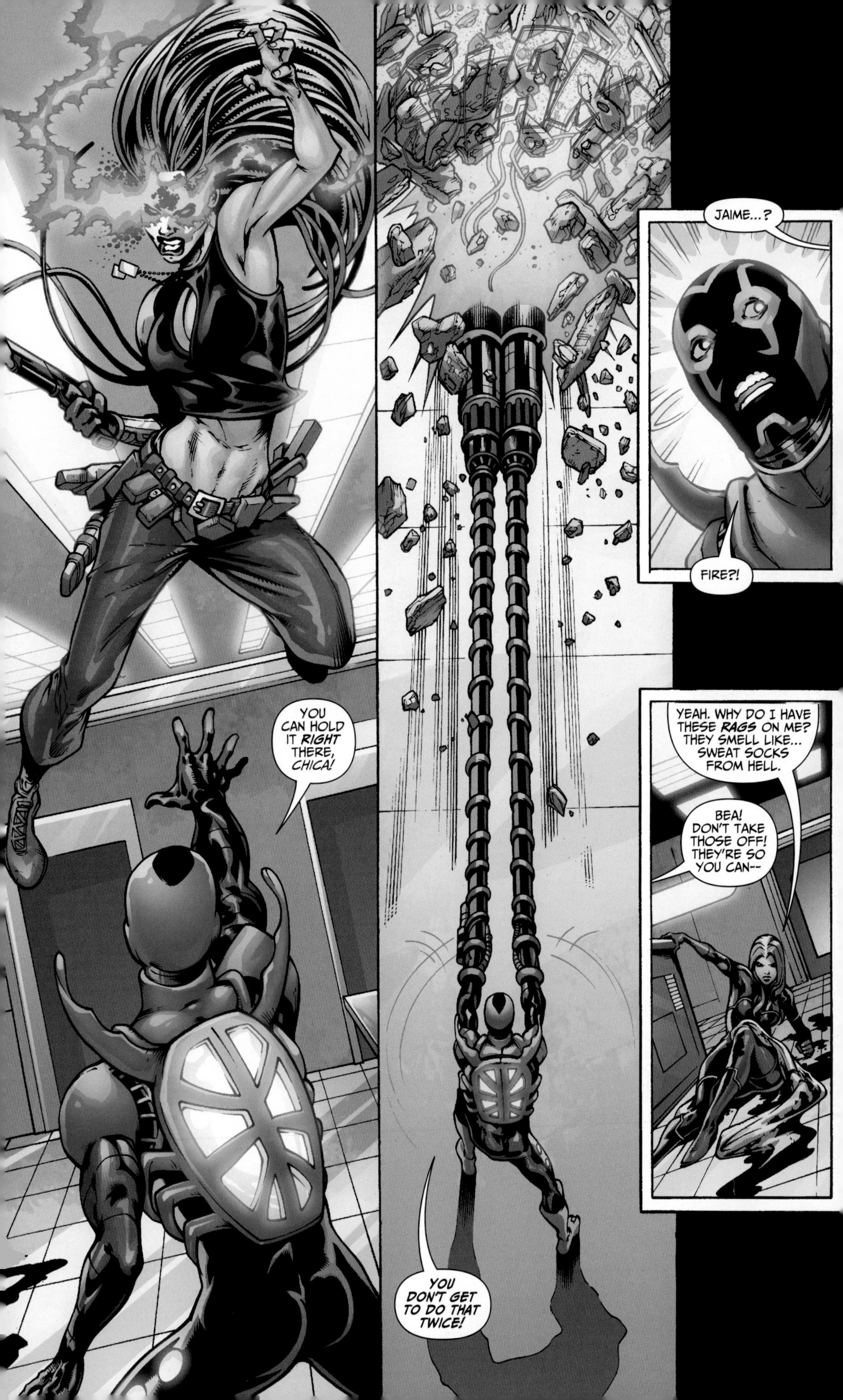
YOU CAN HOLD IT RIGHT THERE, CHICA!
YOU DON'T GET TO DO THAT TWICE!
JAIME...?
FIRE?!
YEAH. WHY DO I HAVE THESE RAGS ON ME? THEY SMELL LIKE... SWEAT SOCKS FROM HELL.
BEA! DON'T TAKE THOSE OFF! THEY'RE SO YOU CAN--

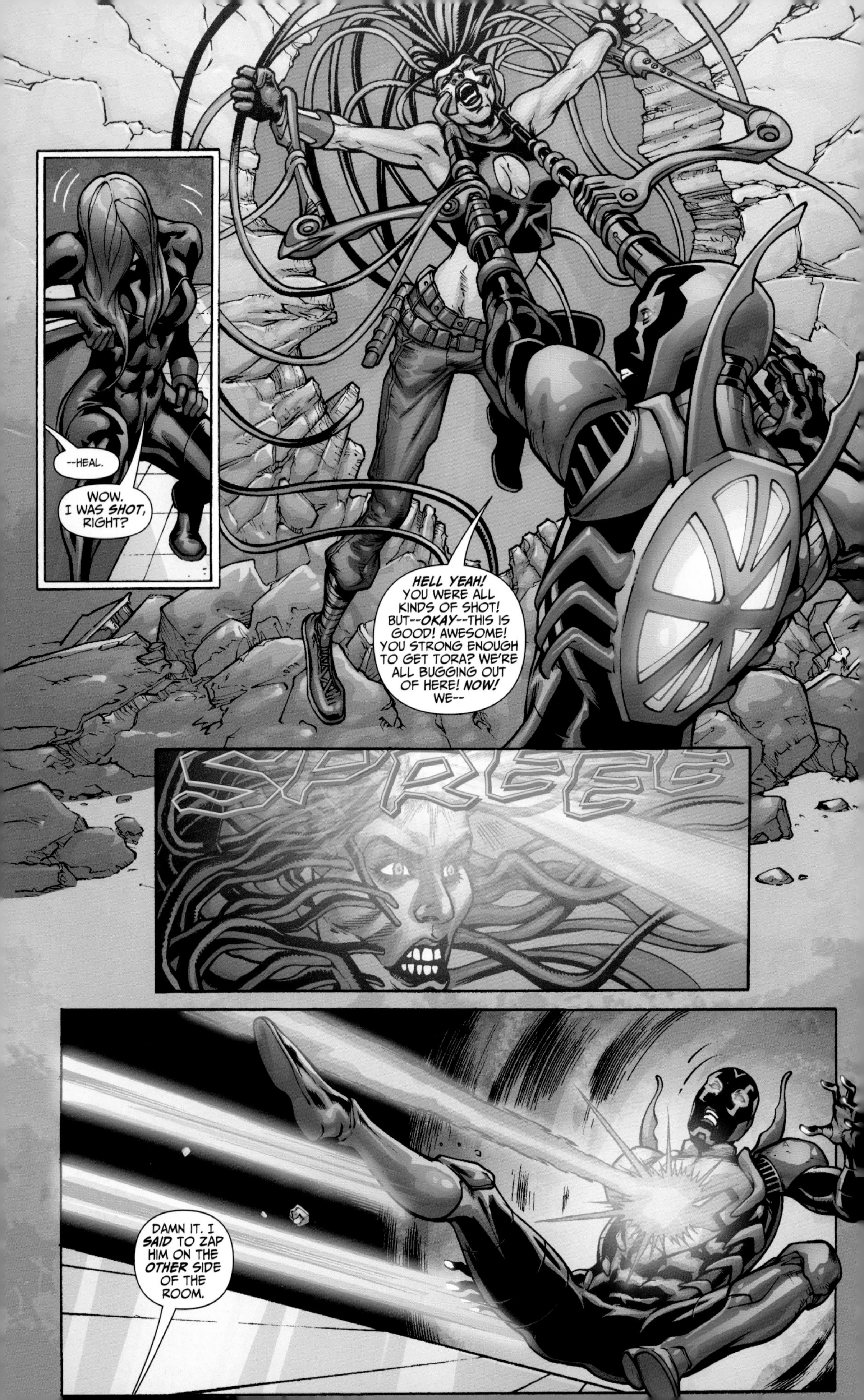
--HEAL.
WOW. I WAS SHOT, RIGHT?
HELL YEAH! YOU WERE ALL KINDS OF SHOT! BUT--OKAY--THIS IS GOOD! AWESOME! YOU STRONG ENOUGH TO GET TORA? WE'RE ALL BUGGING OUT OF HERE! NOW! WE--
SPREEE
DAMN IT. I SAID TO ZAP HIM ON THE OTHER SIDE OF THE ROOM.

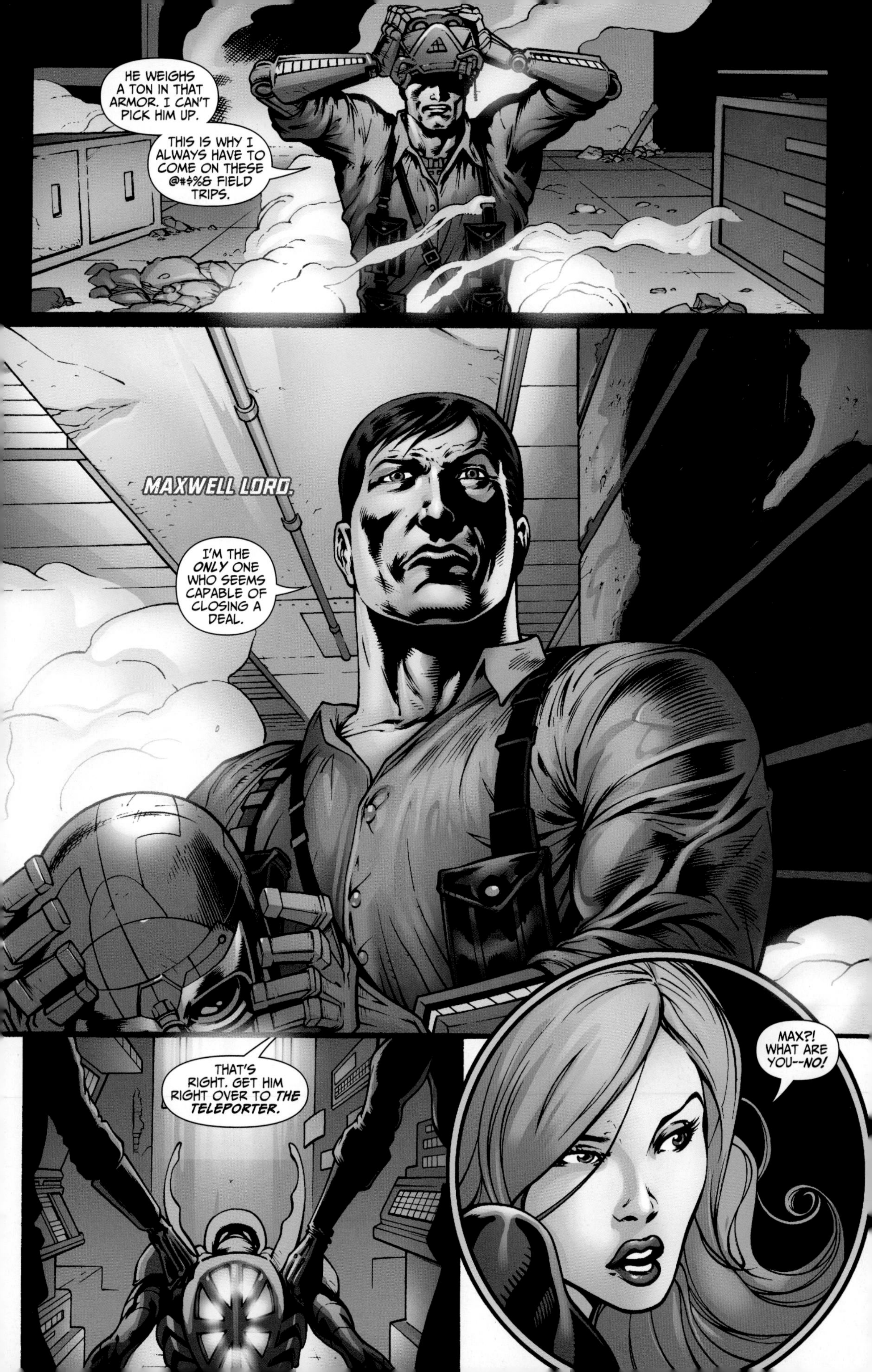
HE WEIGHS A TON IN THAT ARMOR. I CAN'T PICK HIM UP.
THIS IS WHY I ALWAYS HAVE TO COME ON THESE @#$%& FIELD TRIPS.
MAXWELL LORD.
I'M THE ONLY ONE WHO SEEMS CAPABLE OF CLOSING A DEAL.
THAT'S RIGHT. GET HIM RIGHT OVER TO THE TELEPORTER.
MAX?! WHAT ARE YOU--NO!

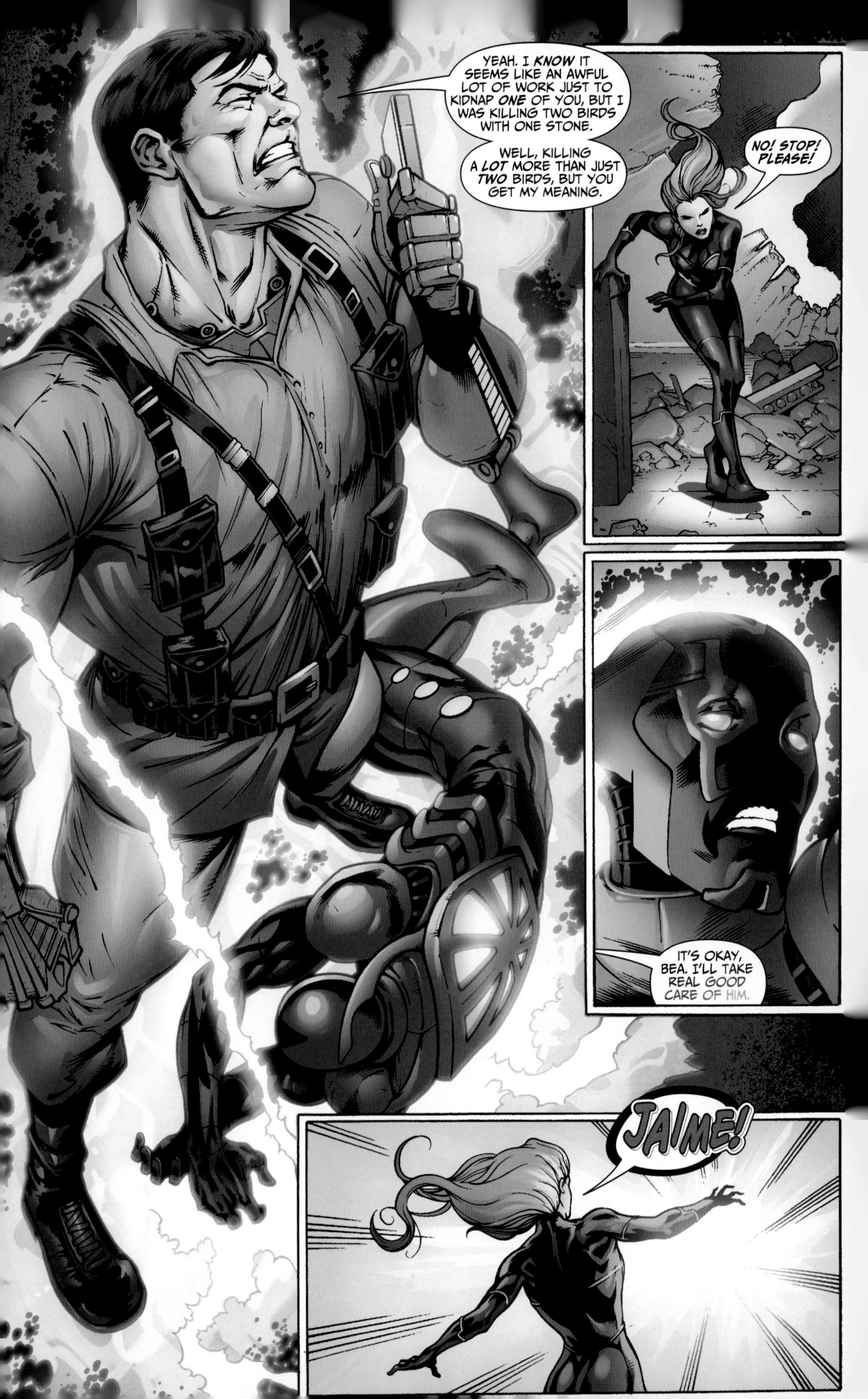
YEAH. I *KNOW* IT SEEMS LIKE AN AWFUL LOT OF WORK JUST TO KIDNAP *ONE* OF YOU, BUT I WAS KILLING TWO BIRDS WITH ONE STONE.
WELL, KILLING A *LOT* MORE THAN JUST *TWO* BIRDS, BUT YOU GET MY MEANING.
NO! STOP! PLEASE!
IT'S OKAY, BEA. I'LL TAKE REAL GOOD CARE OF HIM.
JAIME!

Cover by Aaron Lopresti with Hi-Fi

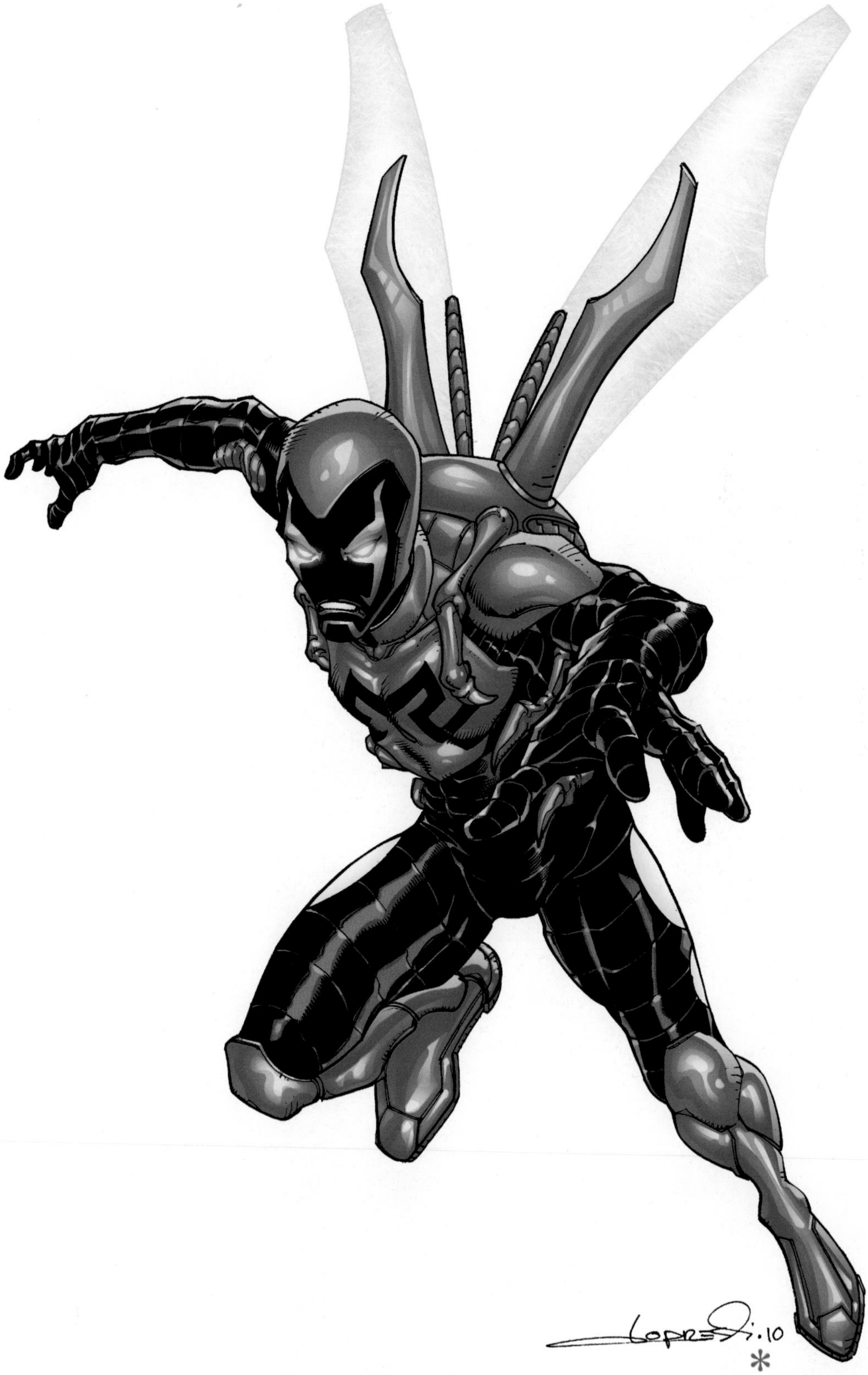

PART SEVENTEEN:
CODE BLUE

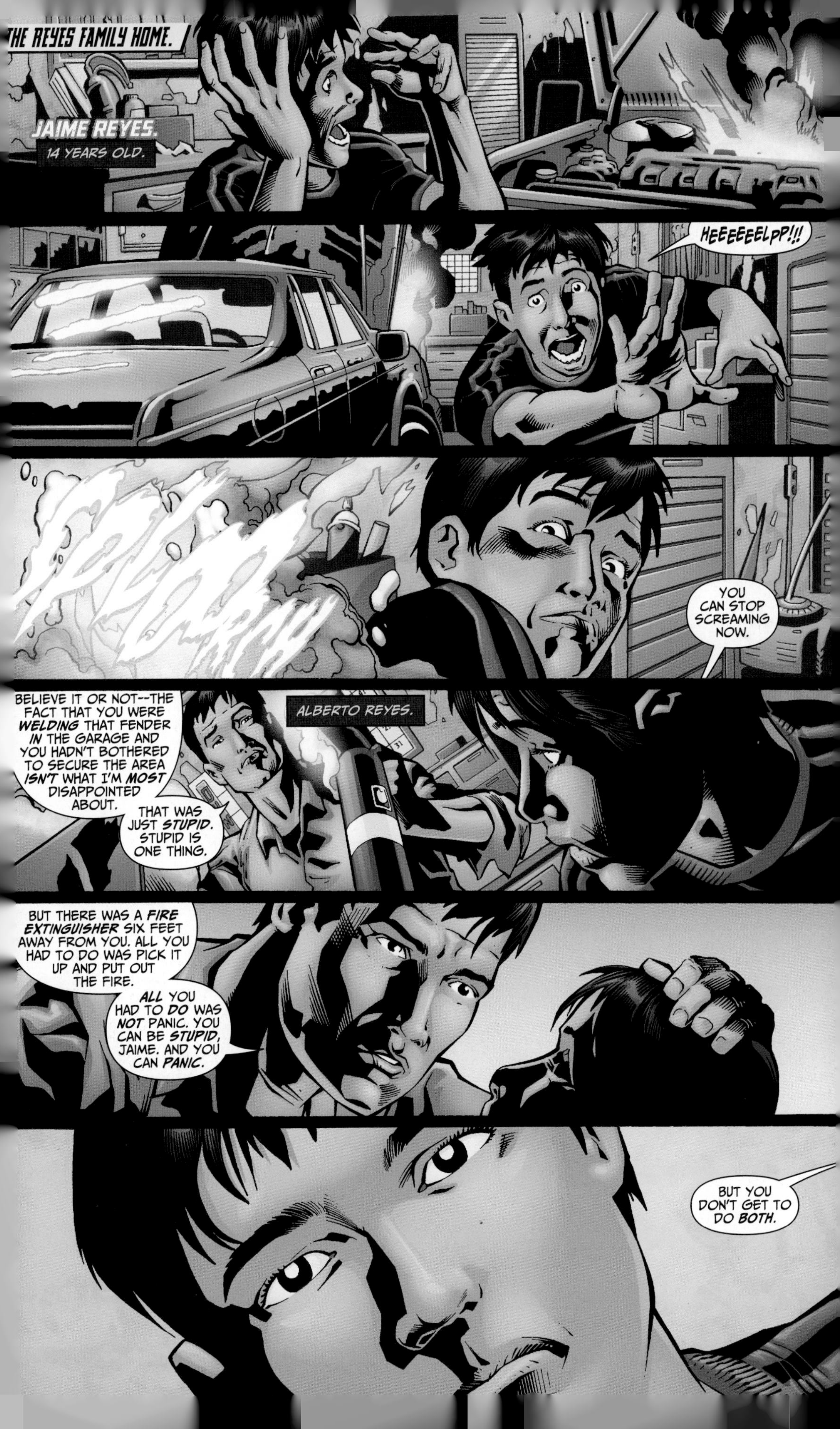

THE REYES FAMILY HOME.
JAIME REYES.
14 YEARS OLD.
HEEEEEELPP!!!
YOU CAN STOP SCREAMING NOW.
ALBERTO REYES.
BELIEVE IT OR NOT--THE FACT THAT YOU WERE WELDING THAT FENDER IN THE GARAGE AND YOU HADN'T BOTHERED TO SECURE THE AREA ISN'T WHAT I'M MOST DISAPPOINTED ABOUT.
THAT WAS JUST STUPID. STUPID IS ONE THING.
BUT THERE WAS A FIRE EXTINGUISHER SIX FEET AWAY FROM YOU. ALL YOU HAD TO DO WAS PICK IT UP AND PUT OUT THE FIRE.
ALL YOU HAD TO DO WAS NOT PANIC. YOU CAN BE STUPID, JAIME. AND YOU CAN PANIC.
BUT YOU DON'T GET TO DO BOTH.

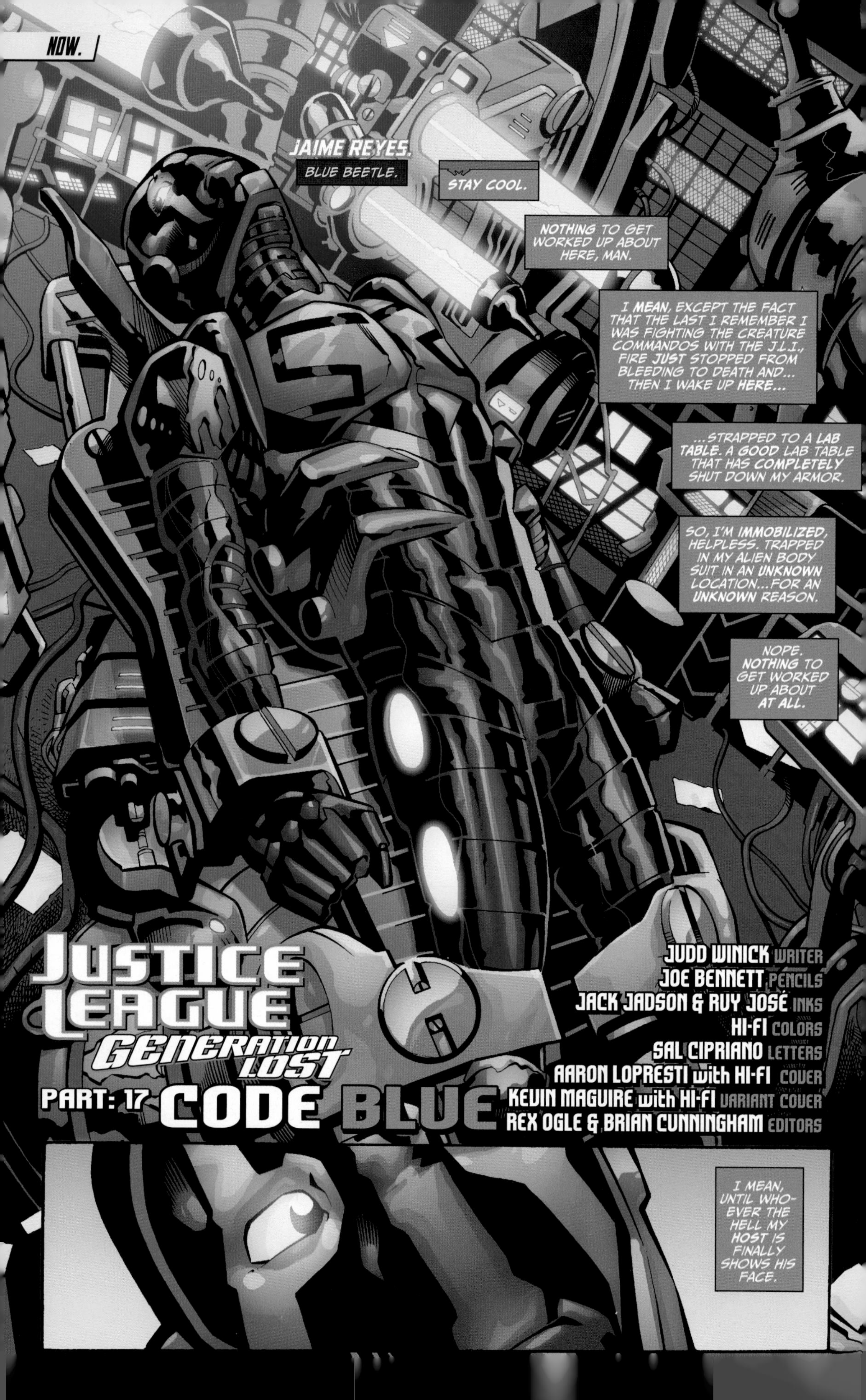

NOW.
JAIME REYES.
BLUE BEETLE.
STAY COOL.
NOTHING TO GET WORKED UP ABOUT HERE, MAN.
I MEAN, EXCEPT THE FACT THAT THE LAST I REMEMBER I WAS FIGHTING THE CREATURE COMMANDOS WITH THE J.L.I., FIRE JUST STOPPED FROM BLEEDING TO DEATH AND... THEN I WAKE UP HERE...
...STRAPPED TO A LAB TABLE. A GOOD LAB TABLE THAT HAS COMPLETELY SHUT DOWN MY ARMOR.
SO, I'M IMMOBILIZED, HELPLESS. TRAPPED IN MY ALIEN BODY SUIT IN AN UNKNOWN LOCATION...FOR AN UNKNOWN REASON.
NOPE. NOTHING TO GET WORKED UP ABOUT AT ALL.
JUSTICE LEAGUE GENERATION LOST
PART: 17 CODE BLUE
JUDD WINICK WRITER
JOE BENNETT PENCILS
JACK JADSON & RUY JOSÉ INKS
HI-FI COLORS
SAL CIPRIANO LETTERS
AARON LOPRESTI with HI-FI COVER
KEVIN MAGUIRE with HI-FI VARIANT COVER
REX OGLE & BRIAN CUNNINGHAM EDITORS
I MEAN, UNTIL WHO-EVER THE HELL MY HOST IS FINALLY SHOWS HIS FACE.

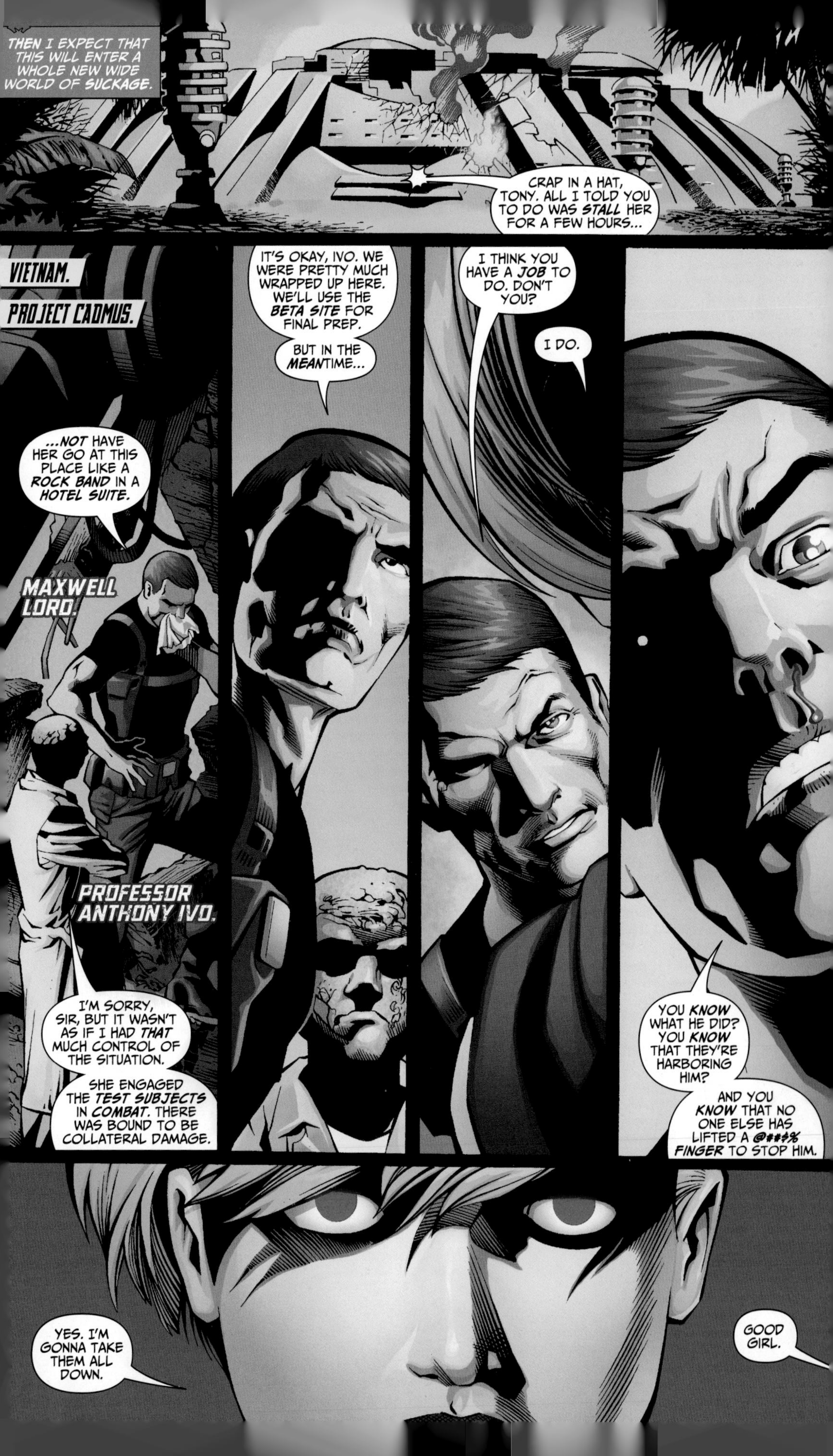
THEN I EXPECT THAT THIS WILL ENTER A WHOLE NEW WIDE WORLD OF SUCKAGE.
CRAP IN A HAT, TONY. ALL I TOLD YOU TO DO WAS STALL HER FOR A FEW HOURS...
VIETNAM.
PROJECT CADMUS.
...NOT HAVE HER GO AT THIS PLACE LIKE A ROCK BAND IN A HOTEL SUITE.
MAXWELL LORD.
PROFESSOR ANTHONY IVO.
I'M SORRY, SIR, BUT IT WASN'T AS IF I HAD THAT MUCH CONTROL OF THE SITUATION.
SHE ENGAGED THE TEST SUBJECTS IN COMBAT. THERE WAS BOUND TO BE COLLATERAL DAMAGE.
IT'S OKAY, IVO. WE WERE PRETTY MUCH WRAPPED UP HERE. WE'LL USE THE BETA SITE FOR FINAL PREP.
BUT IN THE MEANTIME...
I THINK YOU HAVE A JOB TO DO. DON'T YOU?
I DO.
YOU KNOW WHAT HE DID? YOU KNOW THAT THEY'RE HARBORING HIM?
AND YOU KNOW THAT NO ONE ELSE HAS LIFTED A @#*#% FINGER TO STOP HIM.
YES. I'M GONNA TAKE THEM ALL DOWN.
GOOD GIRL.

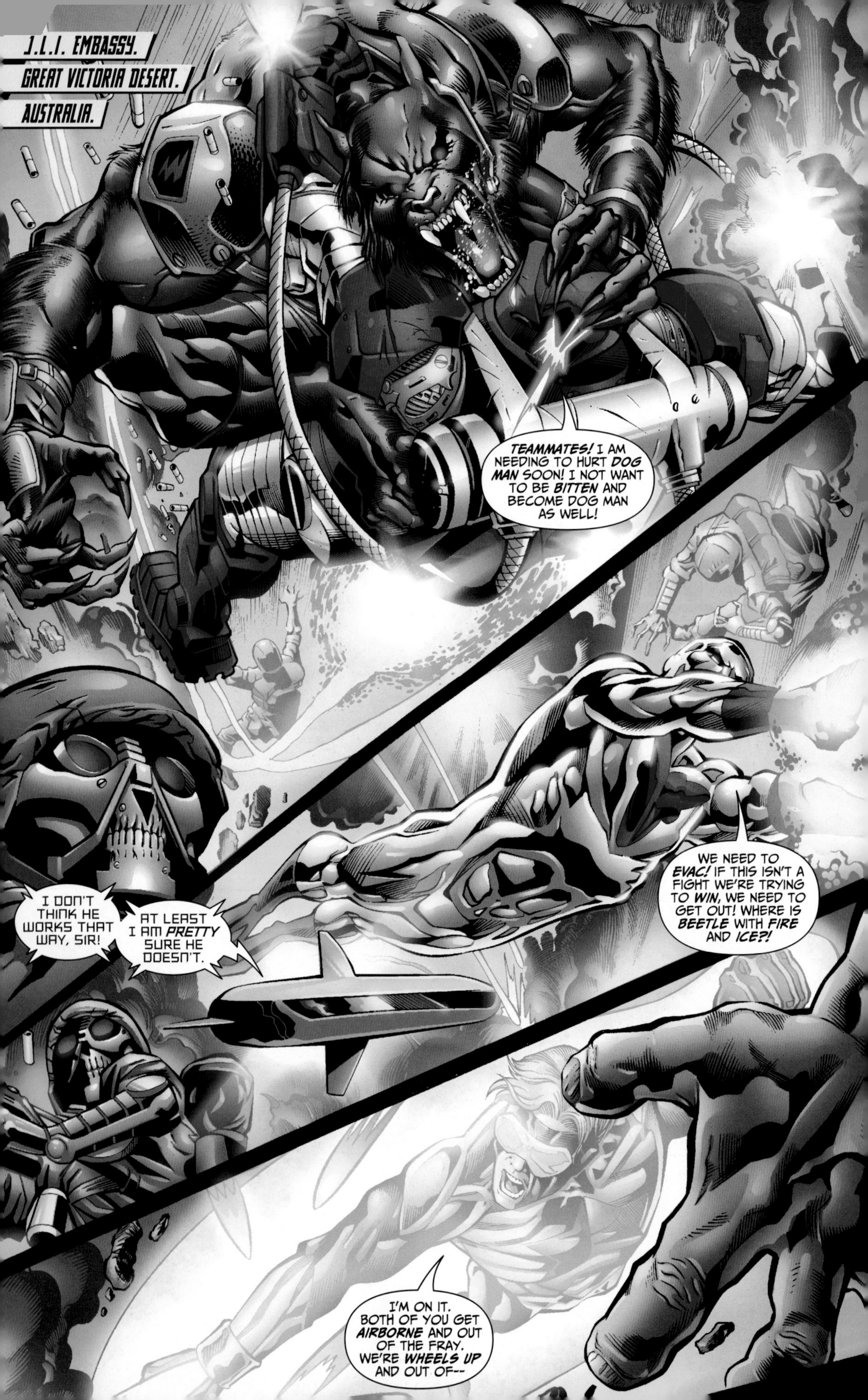
J.L.I. EMBASSY.
GREAT VICTORIA DESERT.
AUSTRALIA.
TEAMMATES! I AM NEEDING TO HURT DOG MAN SOON! I NOT WANT TO BE BITTEN AND BECOME DOG MAN AS WELL!
I DON'T THINK HE WORKS THAT WAY, SIR!
AT LEAST I AM PRETTY SURE HE DOESN'T.
WE NEED TO EVAC! IF THIS ISN'T A FIGHT WE'RE TRYING TO WIN, WE NEED TO GET OUT! WHERE IS BEETLE WITH FIRE AND ICE?!
I'M ON IT. BOTH OF YOU GET AIRBORNE AND OUT OF THE FRAY. WE'RE WHEELS UP AND OUT OF--

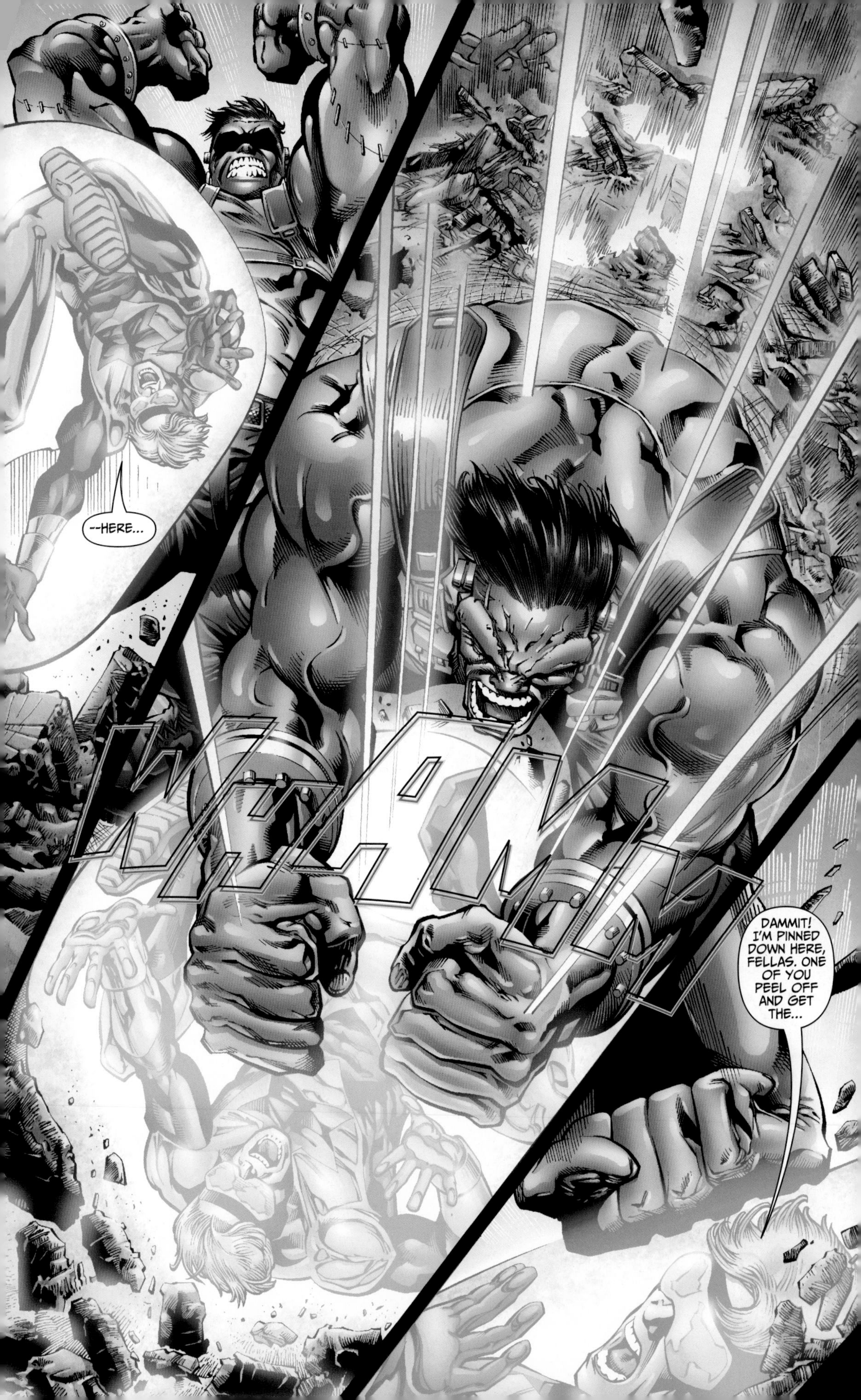
--HERE...
WHAM
DAMMIT! I'M PINNED DOWN HERE, FELLAS. ONE OF YOU PEEL OFF AND GET THE...

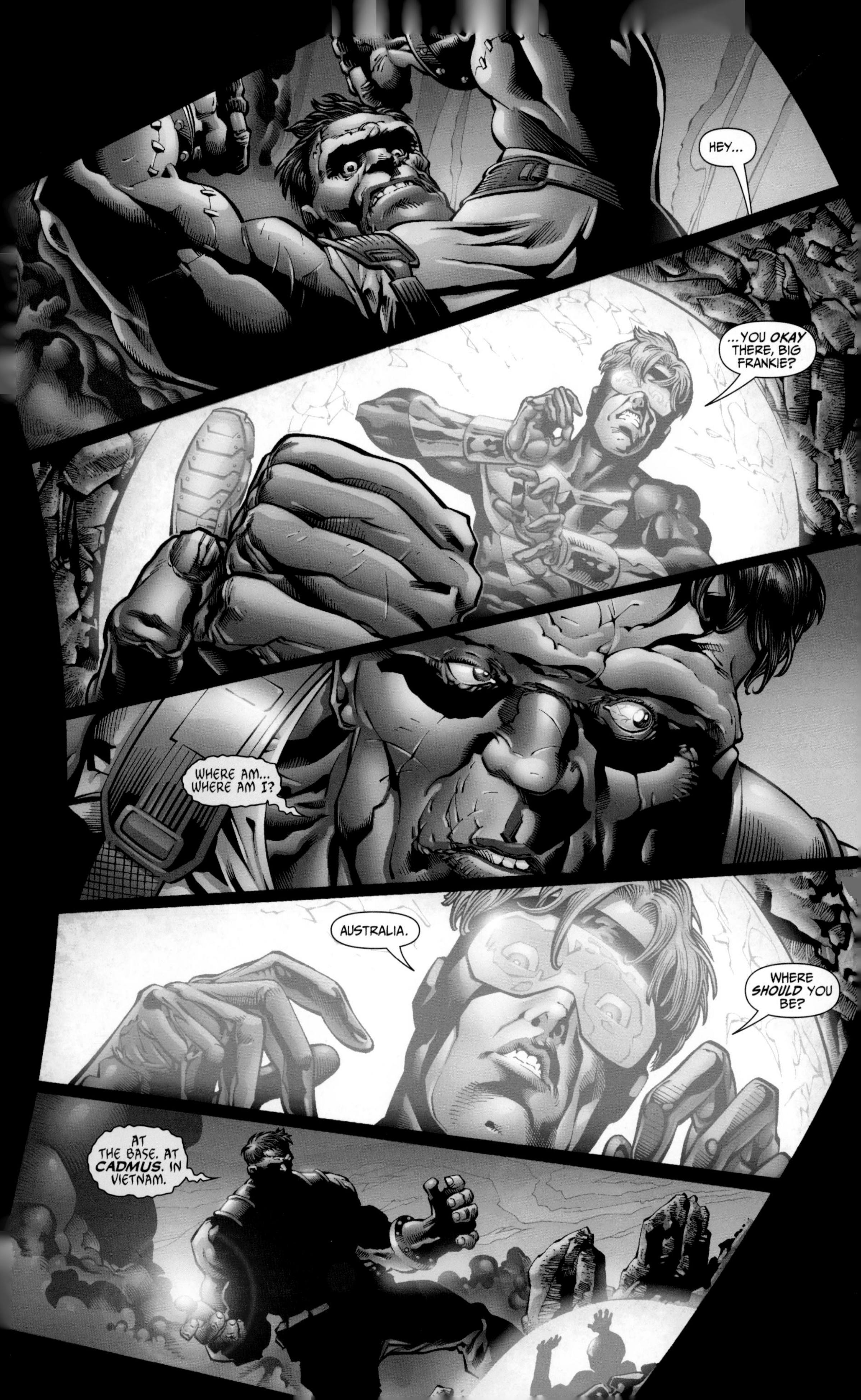
HEY...
...YOU OKAY THERE, BIG FRANKIE?
WHERE AM... WHERE AM I?
AUSTRALIA.
WHERE SHOULD YOU BE?
AT THE BASE. AT CADMUS. IN VIETNAM.

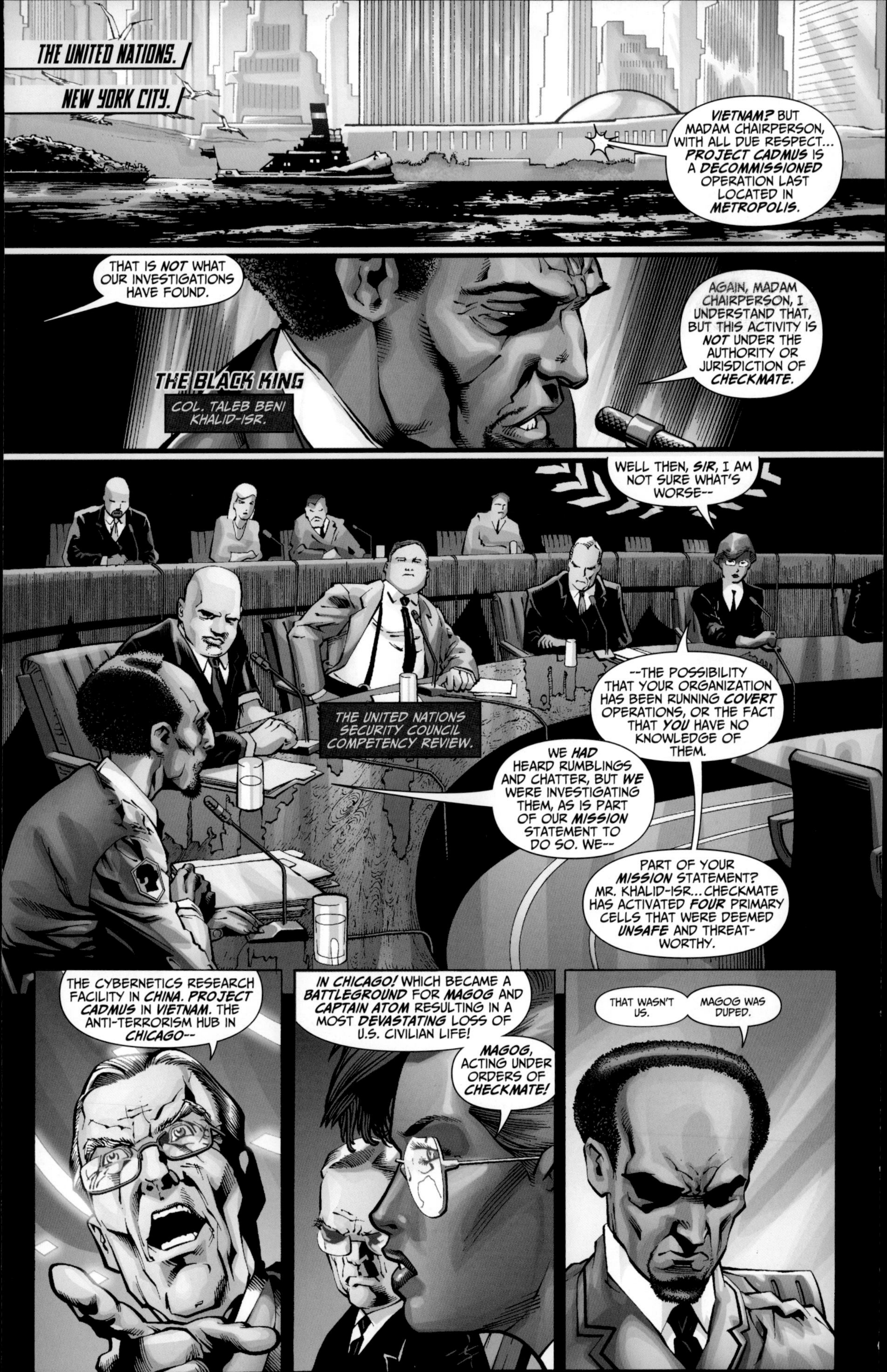
THE UNITED NATIONS.
NEW YORK CITY.
VIETNAM? BUT MADAM CHAIRPERSON, WITH ALL DUE RESPECT... PROJECT CADMUS IS A DECOMMISSIONED OPERATION LAST LOCATED IN METROPOLIS.
THAT IS NOT WHAT OUR INVESTIGATIONS HAVE FOUND.
AGAIN, MADAM CHAIRPERSON, I UNDERSTAND THAT, BUT THIS ACTIVITY IS NOT UNDER THE AUTHORITY OR JURISDICTION OF CHECKMATE.
THE BLACK KING
COL. TALEB BENI KHALID-ISR.
WELL THEN, SIR, I AM NOT SURE WHAT'S WORSE--
THE UNITED NATIONS SECURITY COUNCIL COMPETENCY REVIEW.
--THE POSSIBILITY THAT YOUR ORGANIZATION HAS BEEN RUNNING COVERT OPERATIONS, OR THE FACT THAT YOU HAVE NO KNOWLEDGE OF THEM.
WE HAD HEARD RUMBLINGS AND CHATTER, BUT WE WERE INVESTIGATING THEM, AS IS PART OF OUR MISSION STATEMENT TO DO SO. WE--
PART OF YOUR MISSION STATEMENT? MR. KHALID-ISR...CHECKMATE HAS ACTIVATED FOUR PRIMARY CELLS THAT WERE DEEMED UNSAFE AND THREAT-WORTHY.
THE CYBERNETICS RESEARCH FACILITY IN CHINA. PROJECT CADMUS IN VIETNAM. THE ANTI-TERRORISM HUB IN CHICAGO--
IN CHICAGO! WHICH BECAME A BATTLEGROUND FOR MAGOG AND CAPTAIN ATOM RESULTING IN A MOST DEVASTATING LOSS OF U.S. CIVILIAN LIFE!
MAGOG, ACTING UNDER ORDERS OF CHECKMATE!
THAT WASN'T US.
MAGOG WAS DUPED.

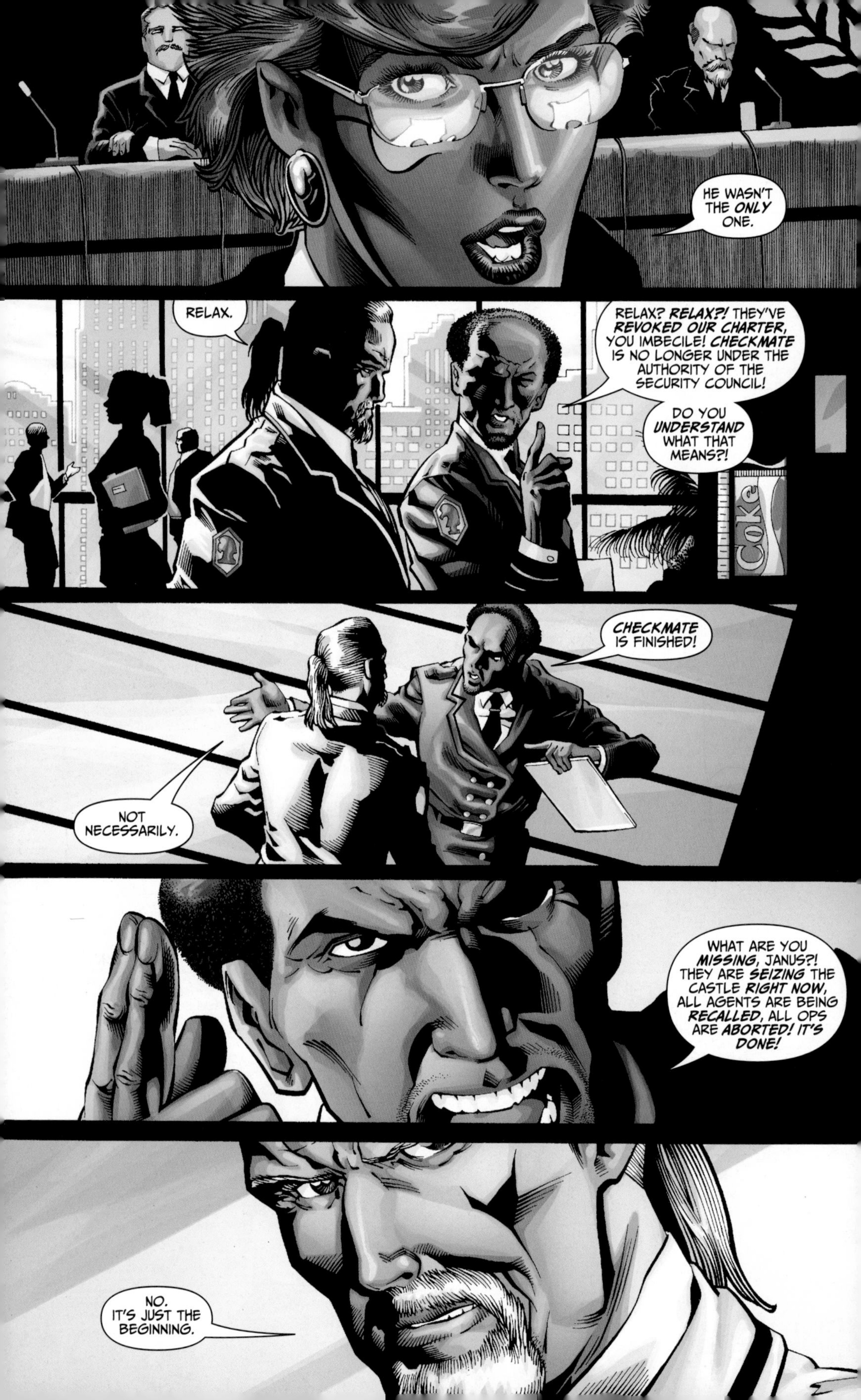
HE WASN'T THE *ONLY* ONE.
RELAX.
RELAX? *RELAX?!* THEY'VE *REVOKED OUR CHARTER*, YOU IMBECILE! *CHECKMATE* IS NO LONGER UNDER THE AUTHORITY OF THE SECURITY COUNCIL!
DO YOU *UNDERSTAND* WHAT THAT MEANS?!
Coke
CHECKMATE IS FINISHED!
NOT NECESSARILY.
WHAT ARE YOU *MISSING*, JANUS?! THEY ARE *SEIZING* THE CASTLE *RIGHT NOW*, ALL AGENTS ARE BEING *RECALLED*, ALL OPS ARE *ABORTED! IT'S DONE!*
NO. IT'S JUST THE BEGINNING.

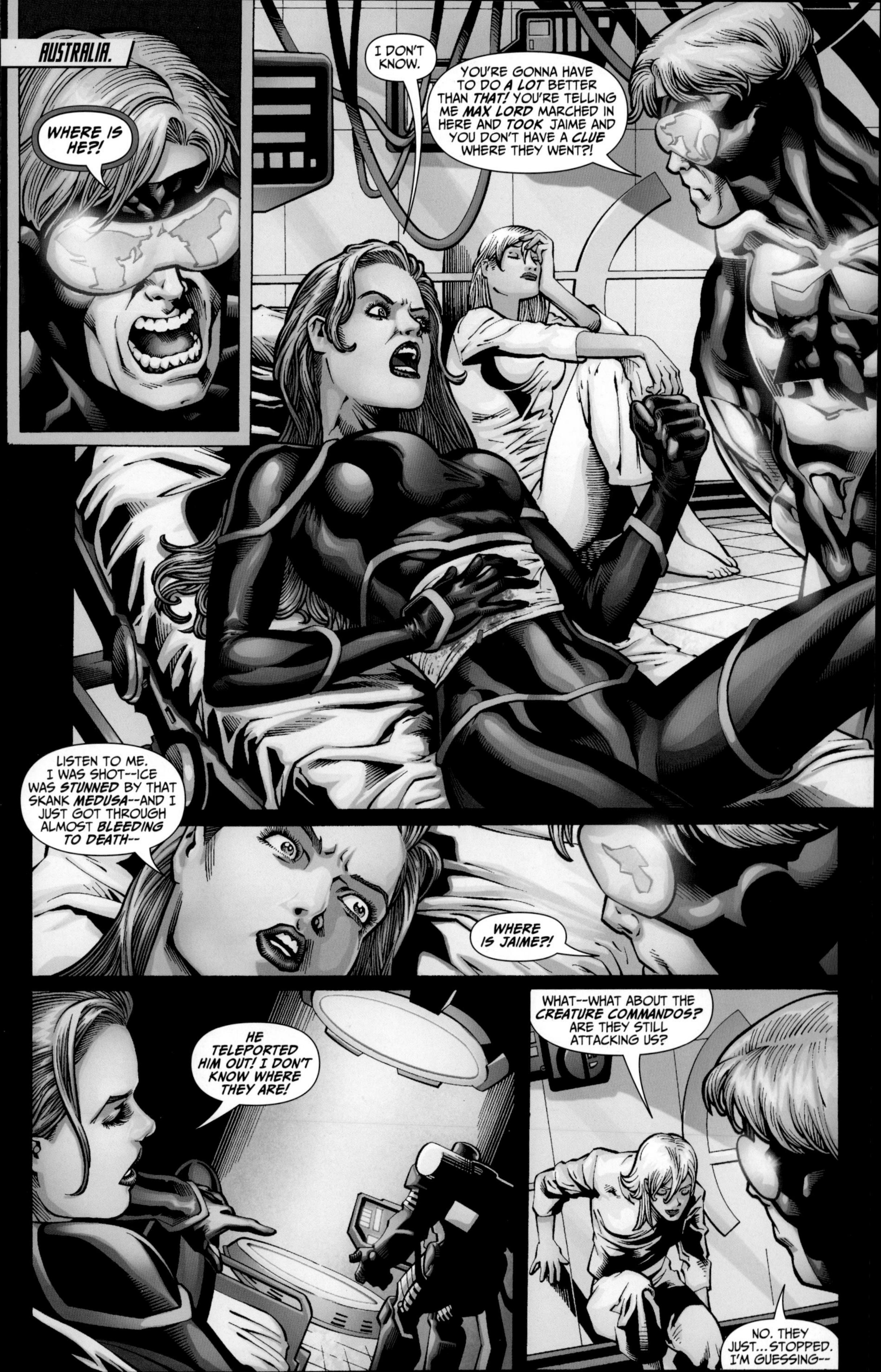
AUSTRALIA.
WHERE IS HE?!
I DON'T KNOW.
YOU'RE GONNA HAVE TO DO A LOT BETTER THAN THAT! YOU'RE TELLING ME MAX LORD MARCHED IN HERE AND TOOK JAIME AND YOU DON'T HAVE A CLUE WHERE THEY WENT?!
LISTEN TO ME. I WAS SHOT--ICE WAS STUNNED BY THAT SKANK MEDUSA--AND I JUST GOT THROUGH ALMOST BLEEDING TO DEATH--
WHERE IS JAIME?!
HE TELEPORTED HIM OUT! I DON'T KNOW WHERE THEY ARE!
WHAT--WHAT ABOUT THE CREATURE COMMANDOS? ARE THEY STILL ATTACKING US?
NO. THEY JUST...STOPPED. I'M GUESSING--

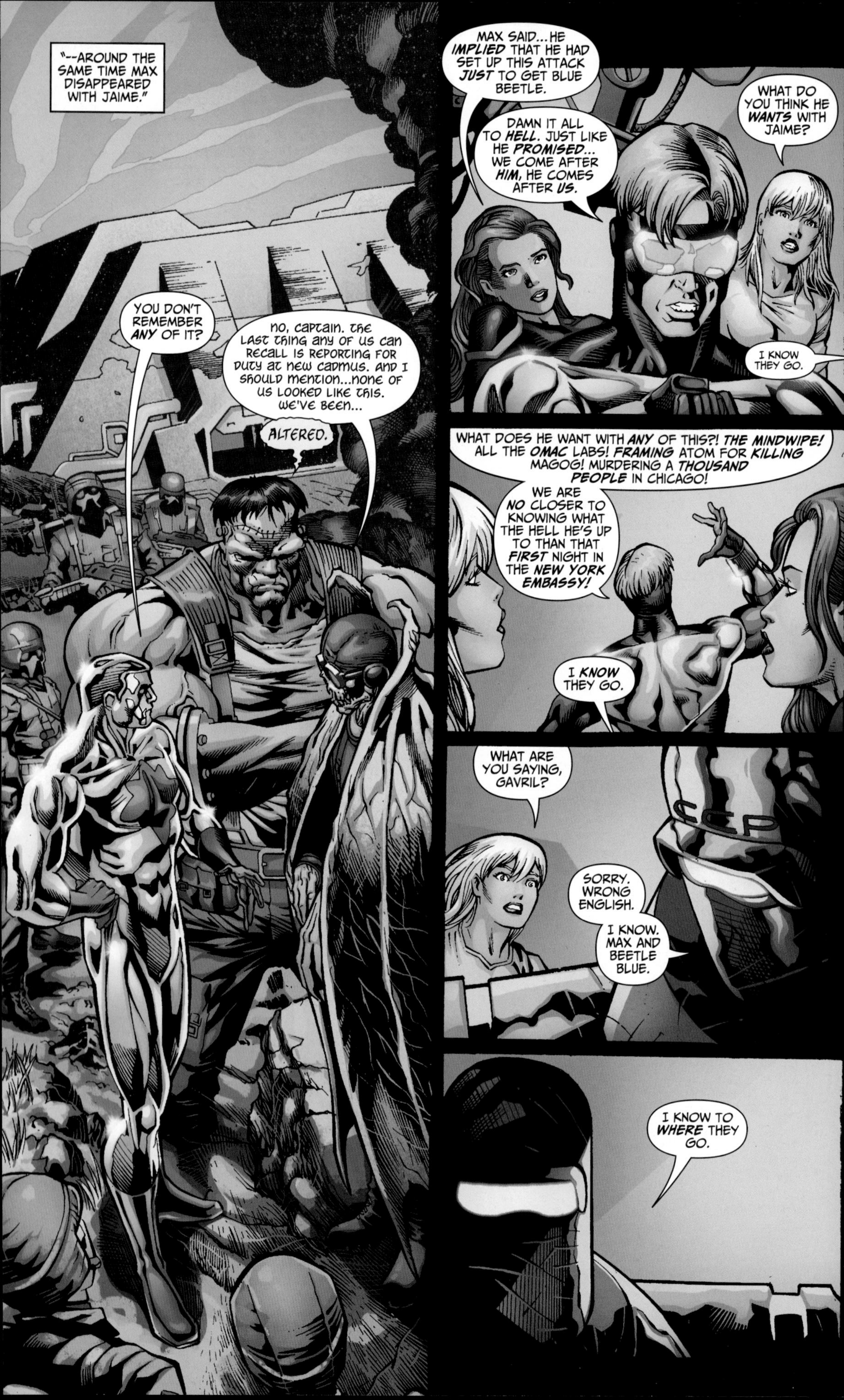
"--AROUND THE SAME TIME MAX DISAPPEARED WITH JAIME."
YOU DON'T REMEMBER ANY OF IT?
NO, CAPTAIN. THE LAST THING ANY OF US CAN RECALL IS REPORTING FOR DUTY AT NEW CADMUS. AND I SHOULD MENTION...NONE OF US LOOKED LIKE THIS. WE'VE BEEN...
ALTERED.
MAX SAID...HE IMPLIED THAT HE HAD SET UP THIS ATTACK JUST TO GET BLUE BEETLE.
DAMN IT ALL TO HELL. JUST LIKE HE PROMISED... WE COME AFTER HIM, HE COMES AFTER US.
WHAT DO YOU THINK HE WANTS WITH JAIME?
I KNOW THEY GO.
WHAT DOES HE WANT WITH ANY OF THIS?! THE MINDWIPE! ALL THE OMAC LABS! FRAMING ATOM FOR KILLING MAGOG! MURDERING A THOUSAND PEOPLE IN CHICAGO!
WE ARE NO CLOSER TO KNOWING WHAT THE HELL HE'S UP TO THAN THAT FIRST NIGHT IN THE NEW YORK EMBASSY!
I KNOW THEY GO.
WHAT ARE YOU SAYING, GAVRIL?
SORRY. WRONG ENGLISH.
I KNOW. MAX AND BEETLE BLUE.
I KNOW TO WHERE THEY GO.

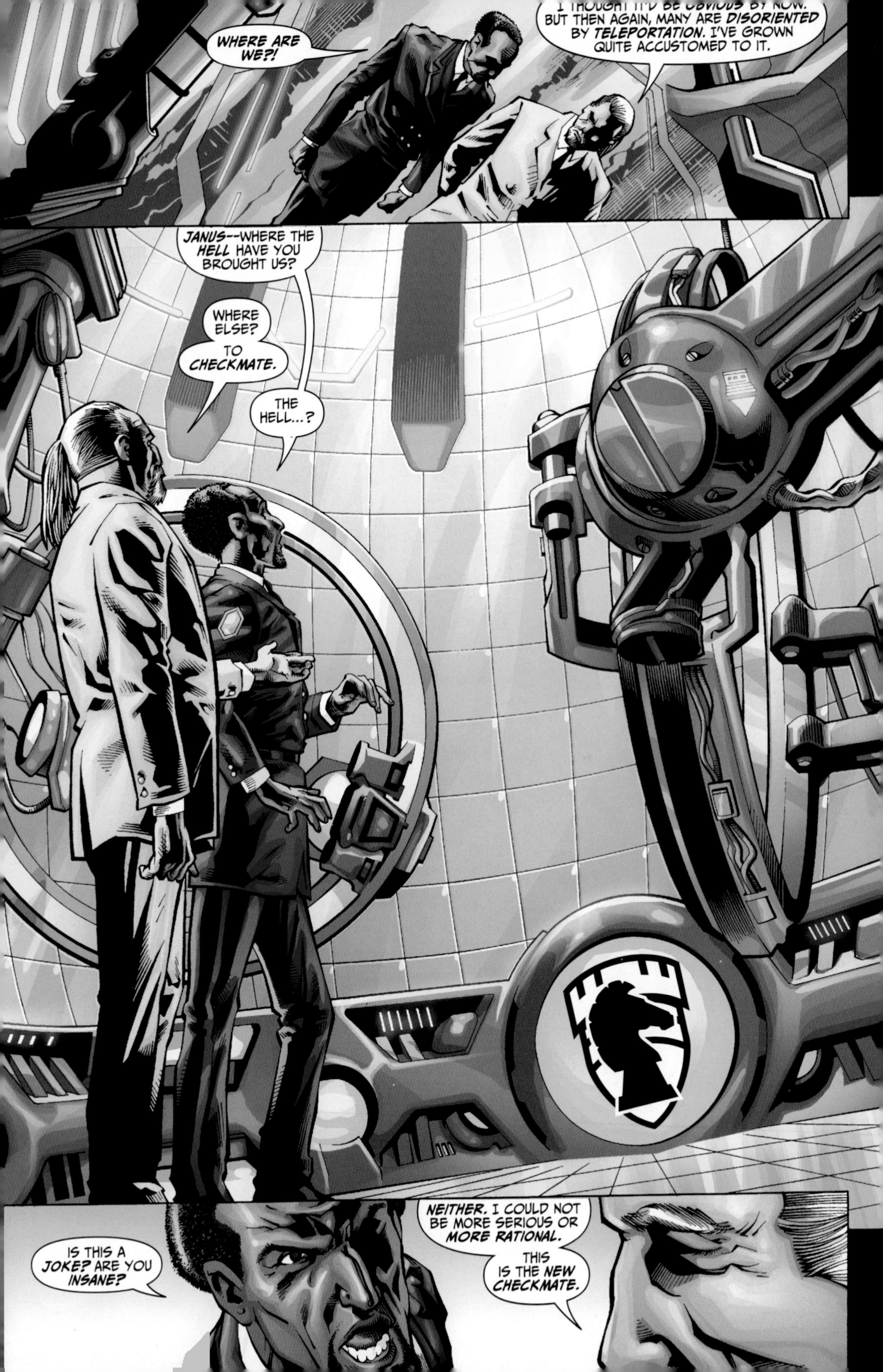

WHERE ARE WE?!
I THOUGHT IT'D BE OBVIOUS BY NOW. BUT THEN AGAIN, MANY ARE DISORIENTED BY TELEPORTATION. I'VE GROWN QUITE ACCUSTOMED TO IT.
JANUS--WHERE THE HELL HAVE YOU BROUGHT US?
WHERE ELSE?
TO CHECKMATE.
THE HELL...?
IS THIS A JOKE? ARE YOU INSANE?
NEITHER. I COULD NOT BE MORE SERIOUS OR MORE RATIONAL.
THIS IS THE NEW CHECKMATE.

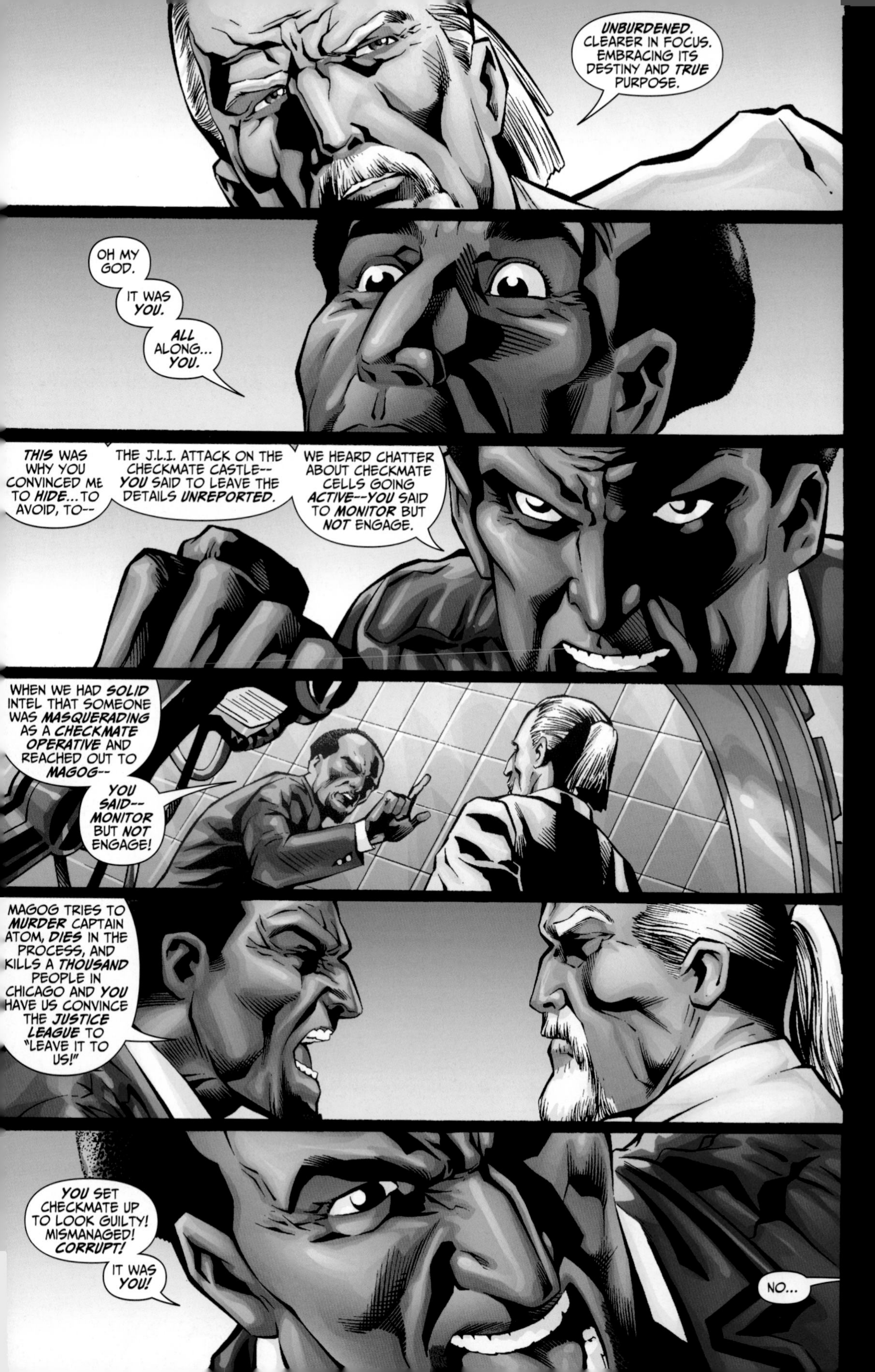
UNBURDENED. CLEARER IN FOCUS. EMBRACING ITS DESTINY AND TRUE PURPOSE.
OH MY GOD.
IT WAS YOU.
ALL ALONG... YOU.
THIS WAS WHY YOU CONVINCED ME TO HIDE...TO AVOID, TO--
THE J.L.I. ATTACK ON THE CHECKMATE CASTLE-- YOU SAID TO LEAVE THE DETAILS UNREPORTED.
WE HEARD CHATTER ABOUT CHECKMATE CELLS GOING ACTIVE--YOU SAID TO MONITOR BUT NOT ENGAGE.
WHEN WE HAD SOLID INTEL THAT SOMEONE WAS MASQUERADING AS A CHECKMATE OPERATIVE AND REACHED OUT TO MAGOG--
YOU SAID-- MONITOR BUT NOT ENGAGE!
MAGOG TRIES TO MURDER CAPTAIN ATOM, DIES IN THE PROCESS, AND KILLS A THOUSAND PEOPLE IN CHICAGO AND YOU HAVE US CONVINCE THE JUSTICE LEAGUE TO "LEAVE IT TO US!"
YOU SET CHECKMATE UP TO LOOK GUILTY! MISMANAGED! CORRUPT!
IT WAS YOU!
NO...

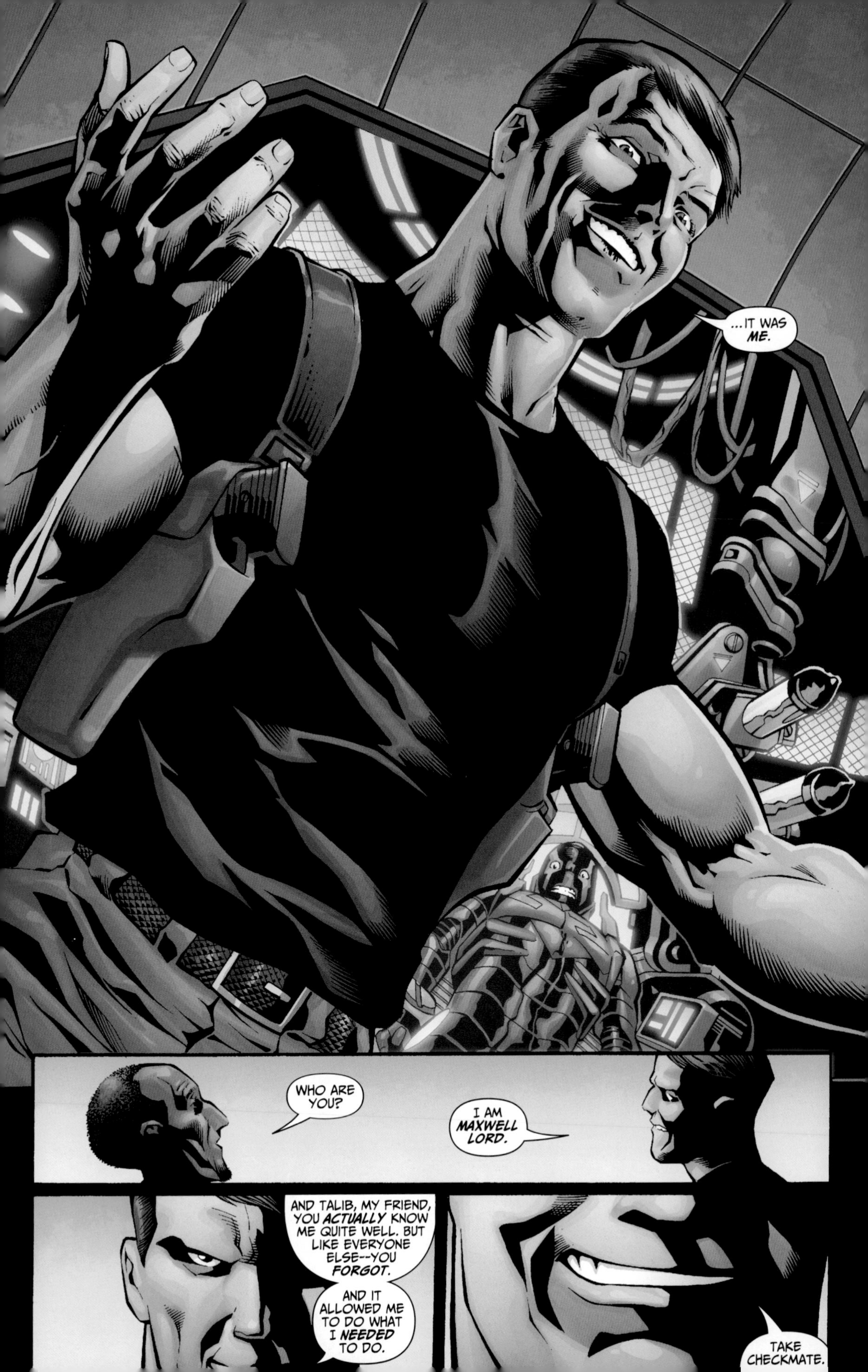
...IT WAS ME.
WHO ARE YOU?
I AM MAXWELL LORD.
AND TALIB, MY FRIEND, YOU ACTUALLY KNOW ME QUITE WELL. BUT LIKE EVERYONE ELSE--YOU FORGOT.
AND IT ALLOWED ME TO DO WHAT I NEEDED TO DO.
TAKE CHECKMATE.

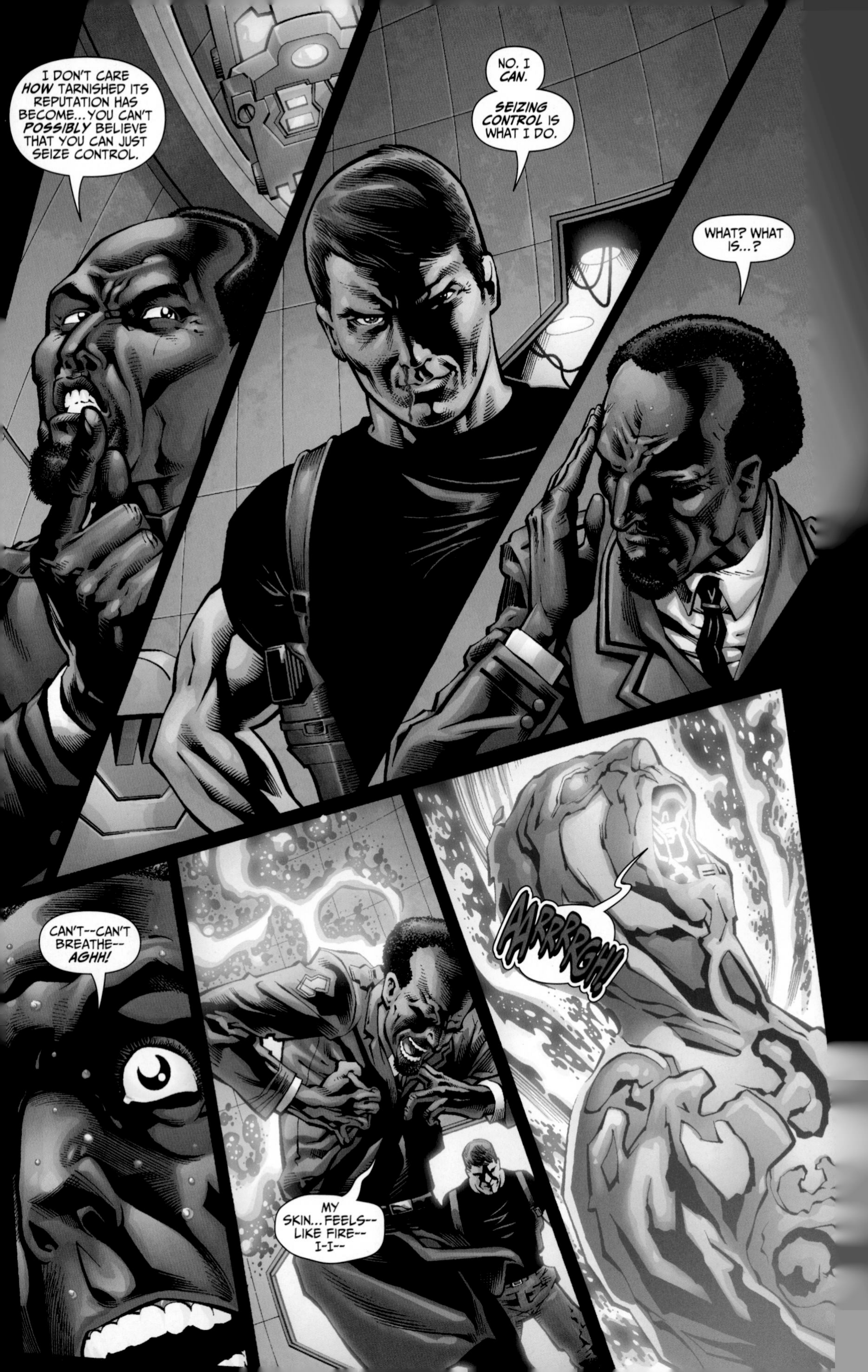
I DON'T CARE HOW TARNISHED ITS REPUTATION HAS BECOME...YOU CAN'T POSSIBLY BELIEVE THAT YOU CAN JUST SEIZE CONTROL.
NO. I CAN.
SEIZING CONTROL IS WHAT I DO.
WHAT? WHAT IS...?
CAN'T--CAN'T BREATHE--AGHH!
MY SKIN...FEELS--LIKE FIRE--I-I--
AARRRRGH!

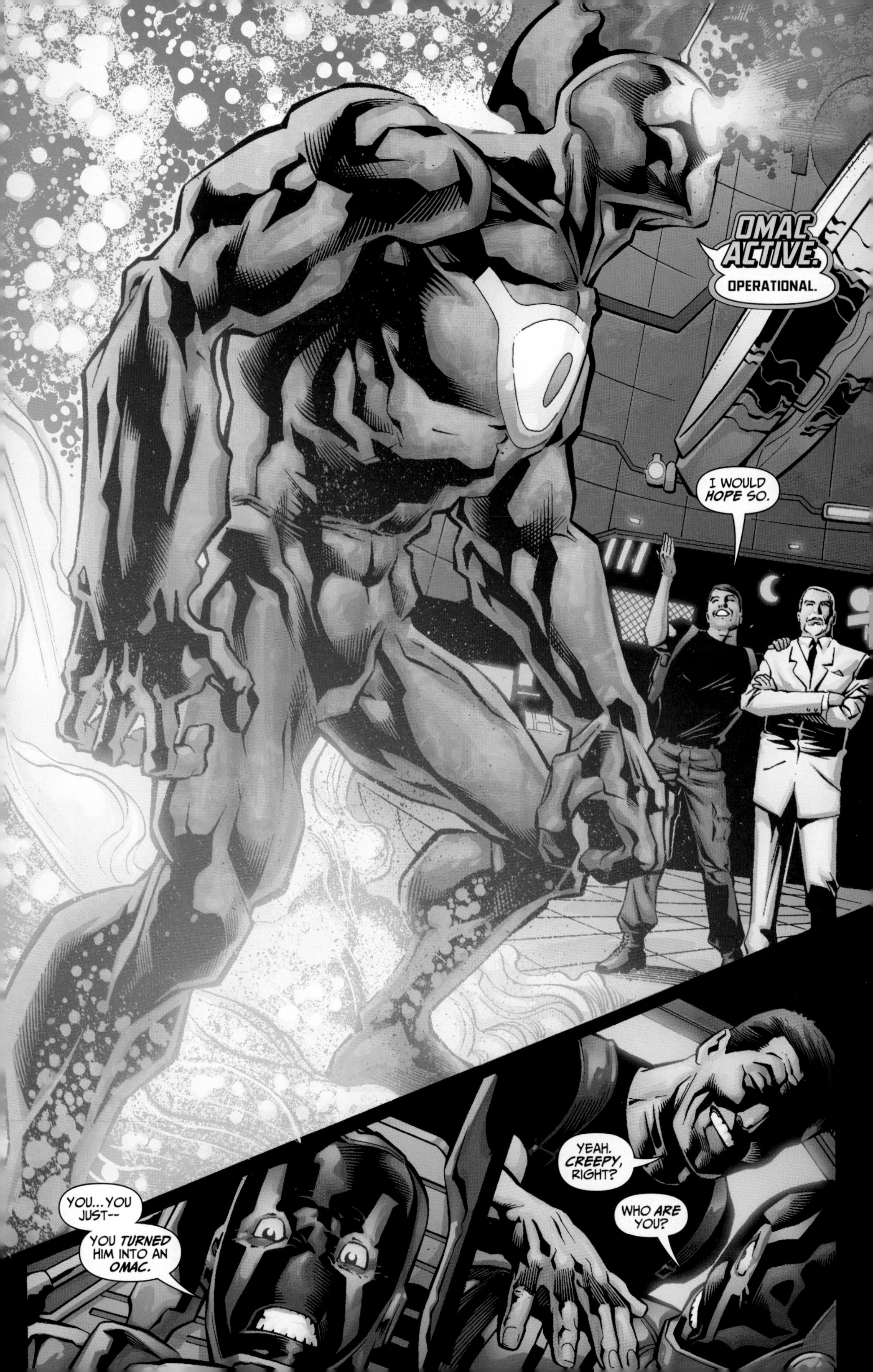
OMAC ACTIVE.
OPERATIONAL.
I WOULD HOPE SO.
YOU...YOU JUST--
YOU TURNED HIM INTO AN OMAC.
YEAH. CREEPY, RIGHT?
WHO ARE YOU?

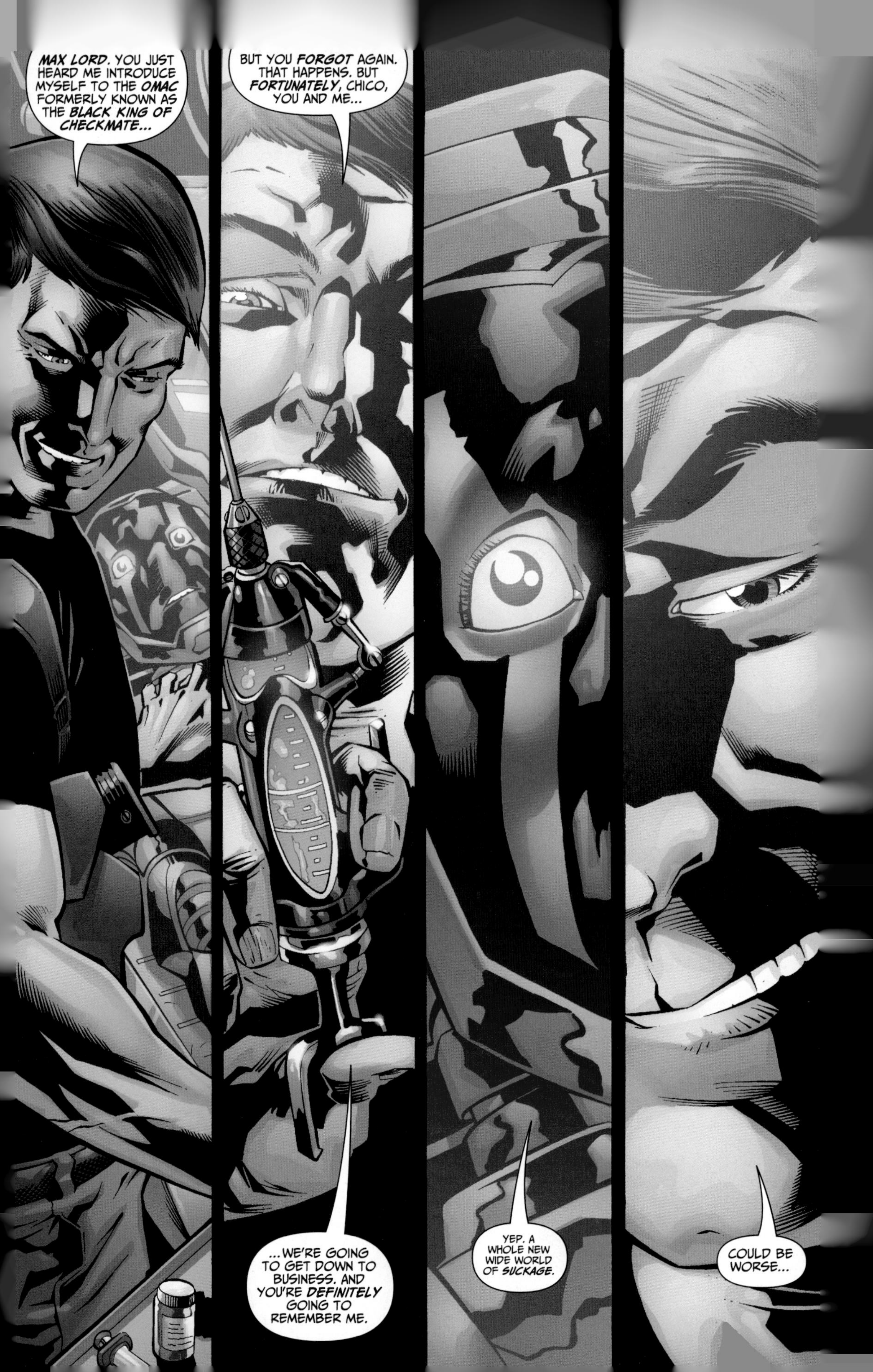
MAX LORD. YOU JUST HEARD ME INTRODUCE MYSELF TO THE OMAC FORMERLY KNOWN AS THE BLACK KING OF CHECKMATE...
BUT YOU FORGOT AGAIN. THAT HAPPENS. BUT FORTUNATELY, CHICO, YOU AND ME...
...WE'RE GOING TO GET DOWN TO BUSINESS. AND YOU'RE DEFINITELY GOING TO REMEMBER ME.
YEP. A WHOLE NEW WIDE WORLD OF SUCKAGE.
COULD BE WORSE...

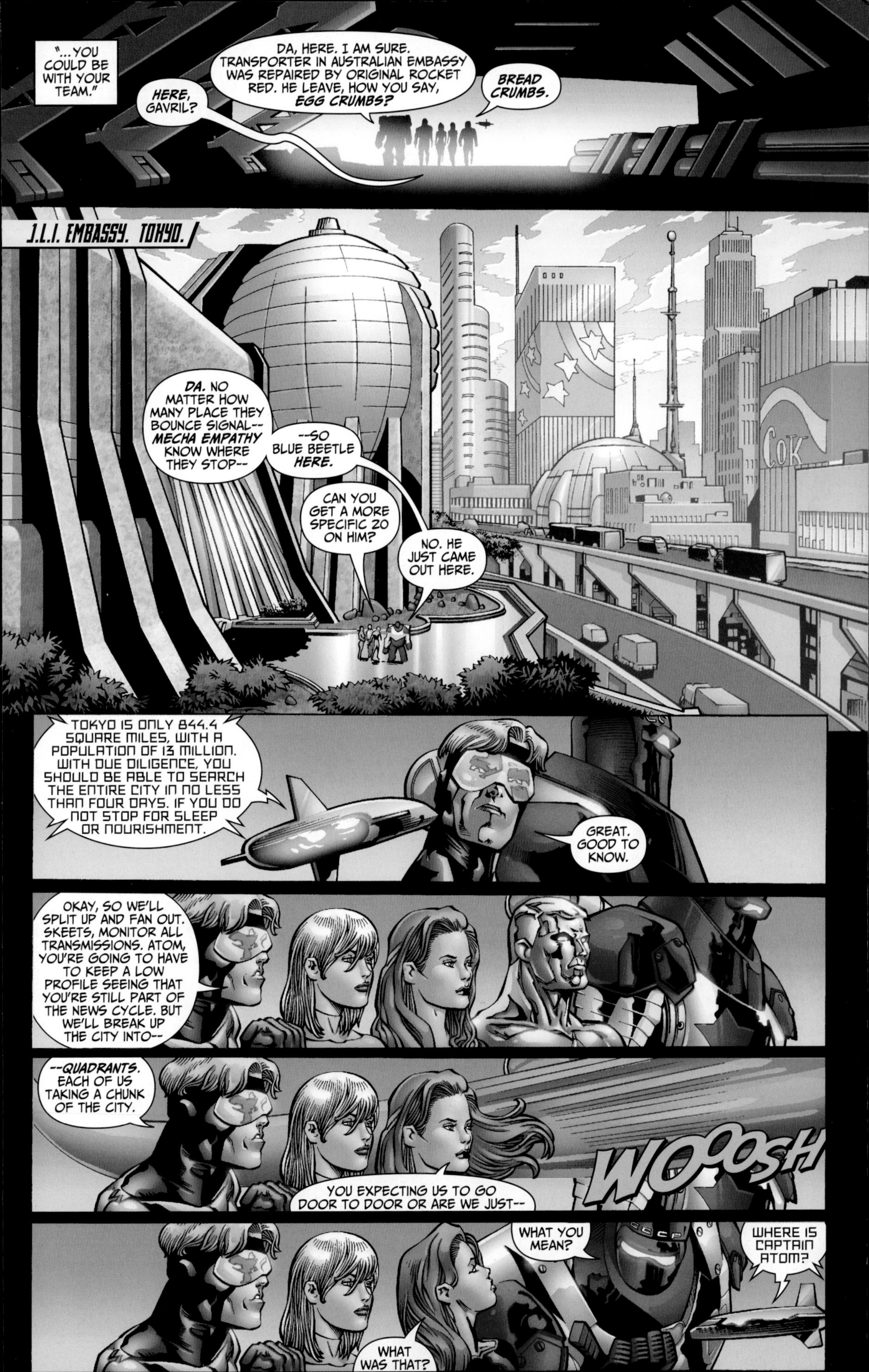
"...YOU COULD BE WITH YOUR TEAM."
HERE, GAVRIL?
DA, HERE. I AM SURE. TRANSPORTER IN AUSTRALIAN EMBASSY WAS REPAIRED BY ORIGINAL ROCKET RED. HE LEAVE, HOW YOU SAY, EGG CRUMBS?
BREAD CRUMBS.
J.L.I. EMBASSY. TOKYO.
DA. NO MATTER HOW MANY PLACE THEY BOUNCE SIGNAL-- MECHA EMPATHY KNOW WHERE THEY STOP--
--SO BLUE BEETLE HERE.
CAN YOU GET A MORE SPECIFIC 20 ON HIM?
NO. HE JUST CAME OUT HERE.
TOKYO IS ONLY 844.4 SQUARE MILES, WITH A POPULATION OF 13 MILLION. WITH DUE DILIGENCE, YOU SHOULD BE ABLE TO SEARCH THE ENTIRE CITY IN NO LESS THAN FOUR DAYS. IF YOU DO NOT STOP FOR SLEEP OR NOURISHMENT.
GREAT. GOOD TO KNOW.
OKAY, SO WE'LL SPLIT UP AND FAN OUT. SKEETS, MONITOR ALL TRANSMISSIONS. ATOM, YOU'RE GOING TO HAVE TO KEEP A LOW PROFILE SEEING THAT YOU'RE STILL PART OF THE NEWS CYCLE. BUT WE'LL BREAK UP THE CITY INTO--
--QUADRANTS. EACH OF US TAKING A CHUNK OF THE CITY.
WOOOSH
YOU EXPECTING US TO GO DOOR TO DOOR OR ARE WE JUST--
WHAT YOU MEAN?
WHERE IS CAPTAIN ATOM?
WHAT WAS THAT?

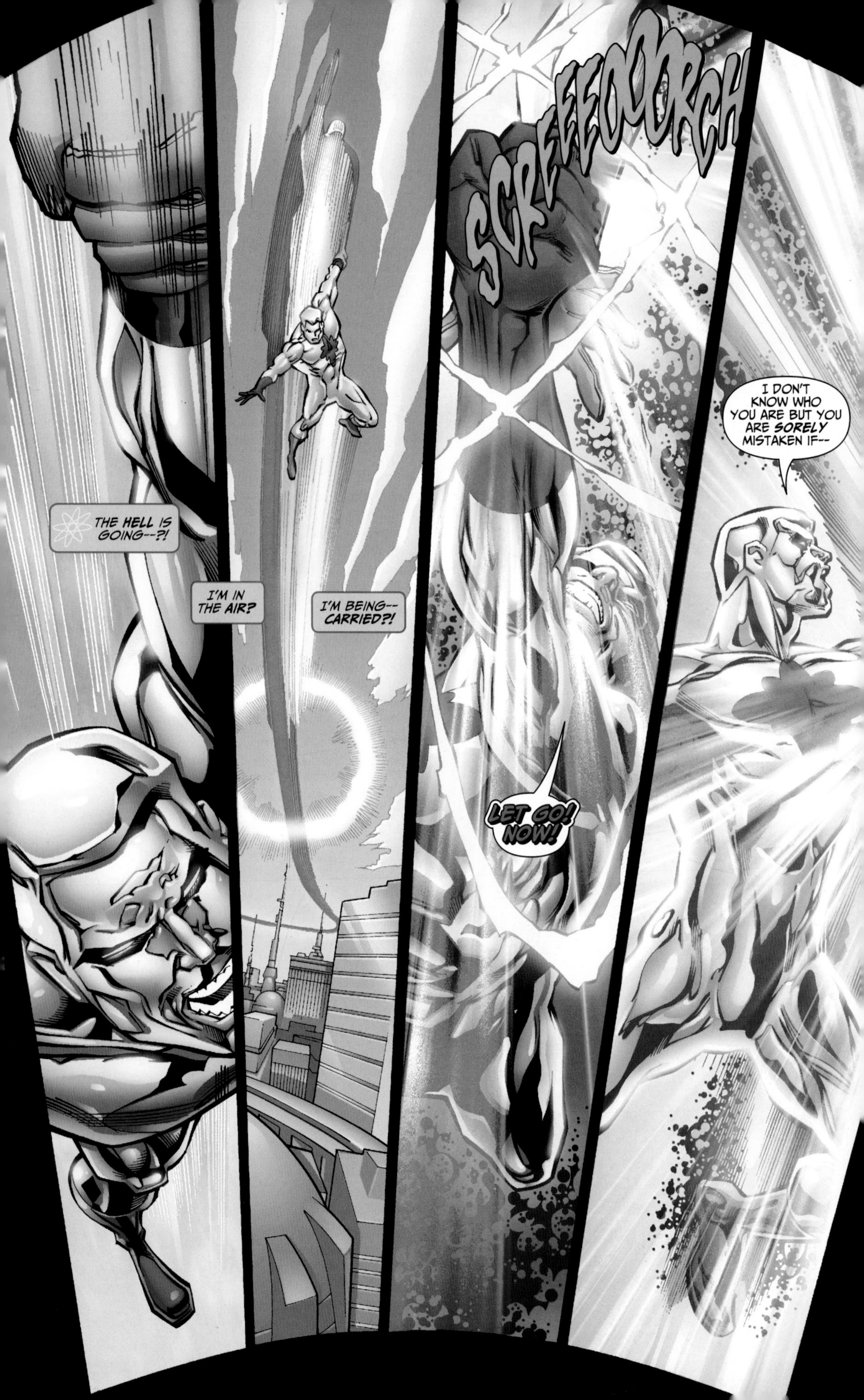
THE HELL IS GOING--?!
I'M IN THE AIR?
I'M BEING-- CARRIED?!
SCREEEOOORCH
LET GO! NOW!
I DON'T KNOW WHO YOU ARE BUT YOU ARE SORELY MISTAKEN IF--

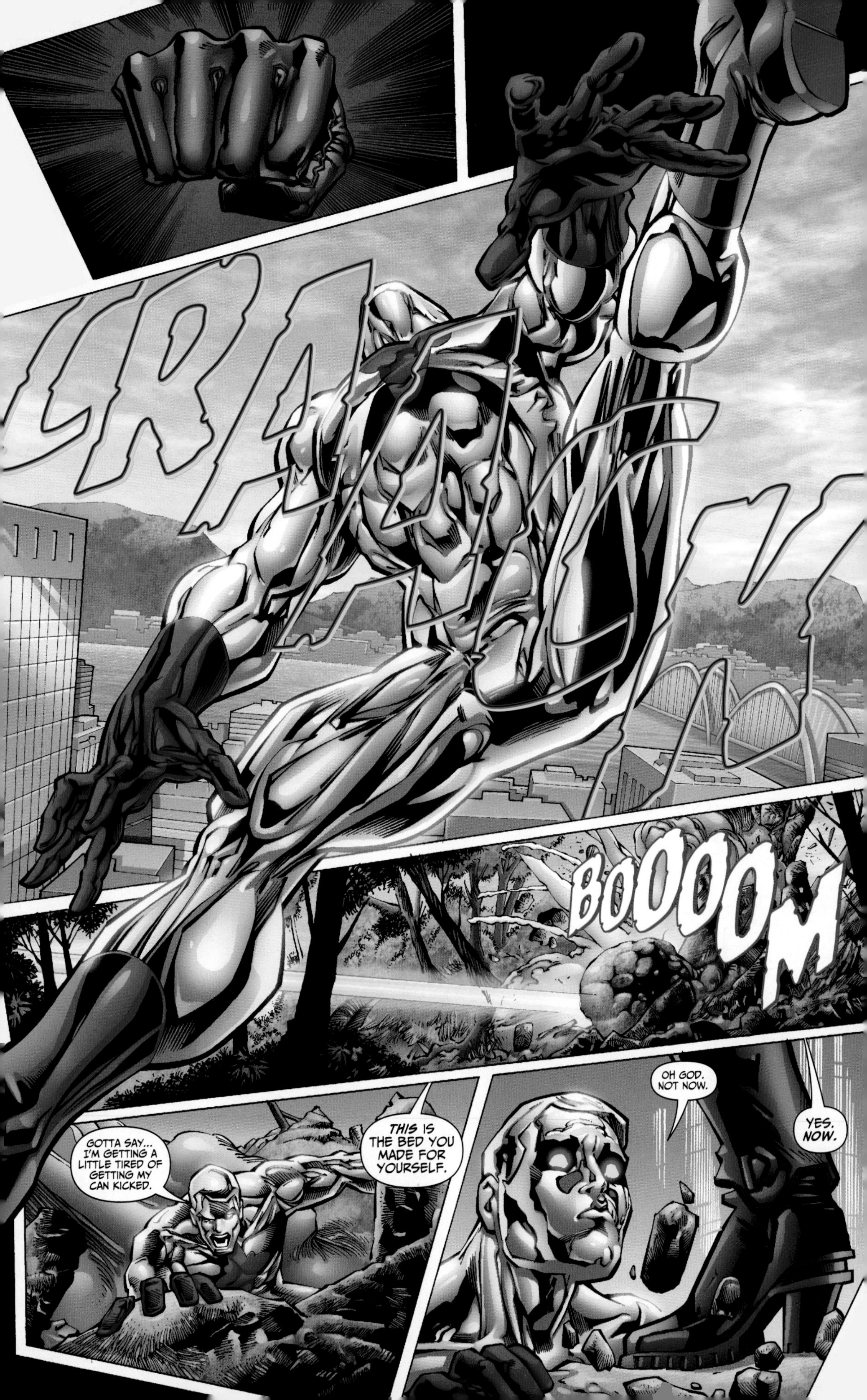
BOOOOOM
GOTTA SAY... I'M GETTING A LITTLE TIRED OF GETTING MY CAN KICKED.
THIS IS THE BED YOU MADE FOR YOURSELF.
OH GOD. NOT NOW.
YES. NOW.

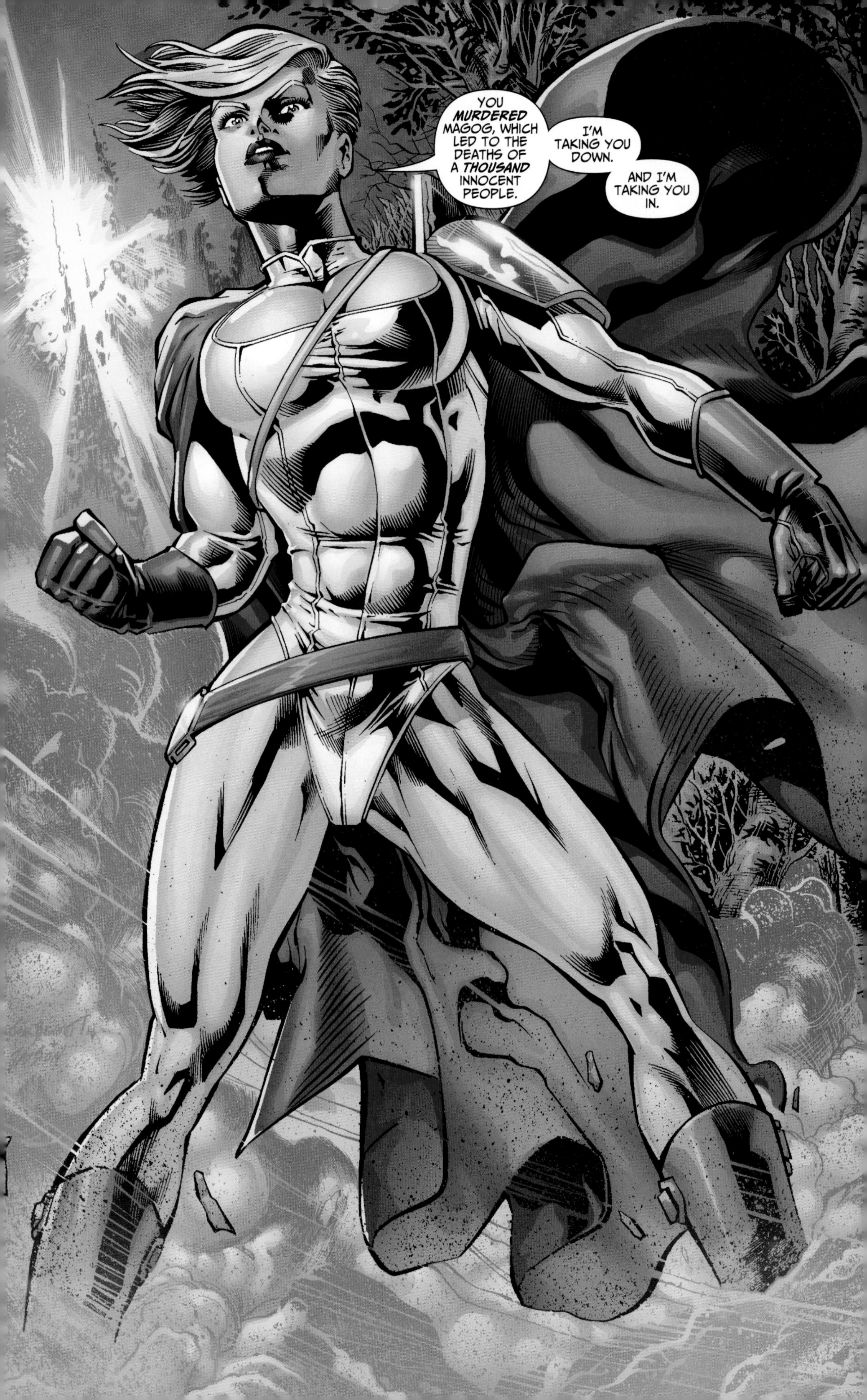
YOU **MURDERED** MAGOG, WHICH LED TO THE DEATHS OF A **THOUSAND** INNOCENT PEOPLE.
I'M TAKING YOU DOWN.
AND I'M TAKING YOU IN.

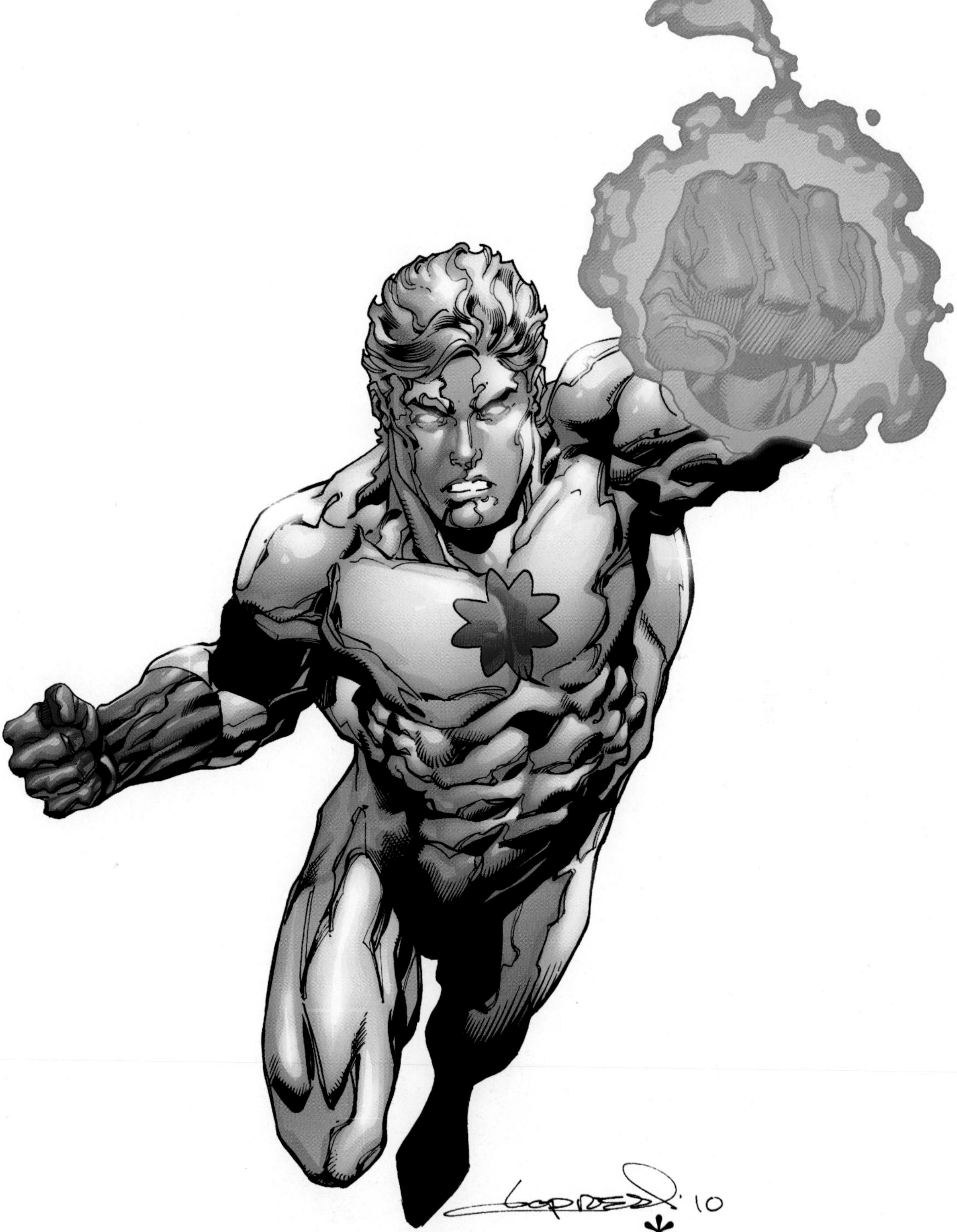

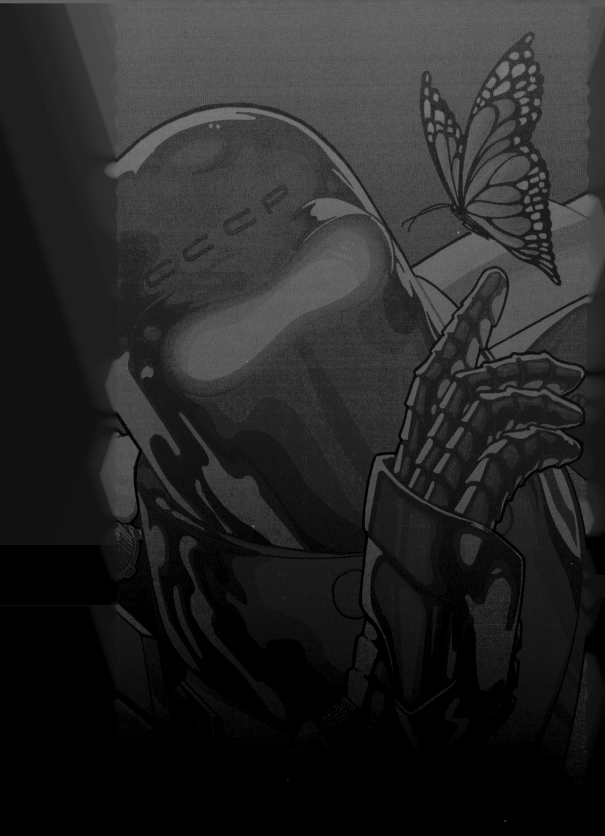

iHTEEN:
OLD FRIENDS

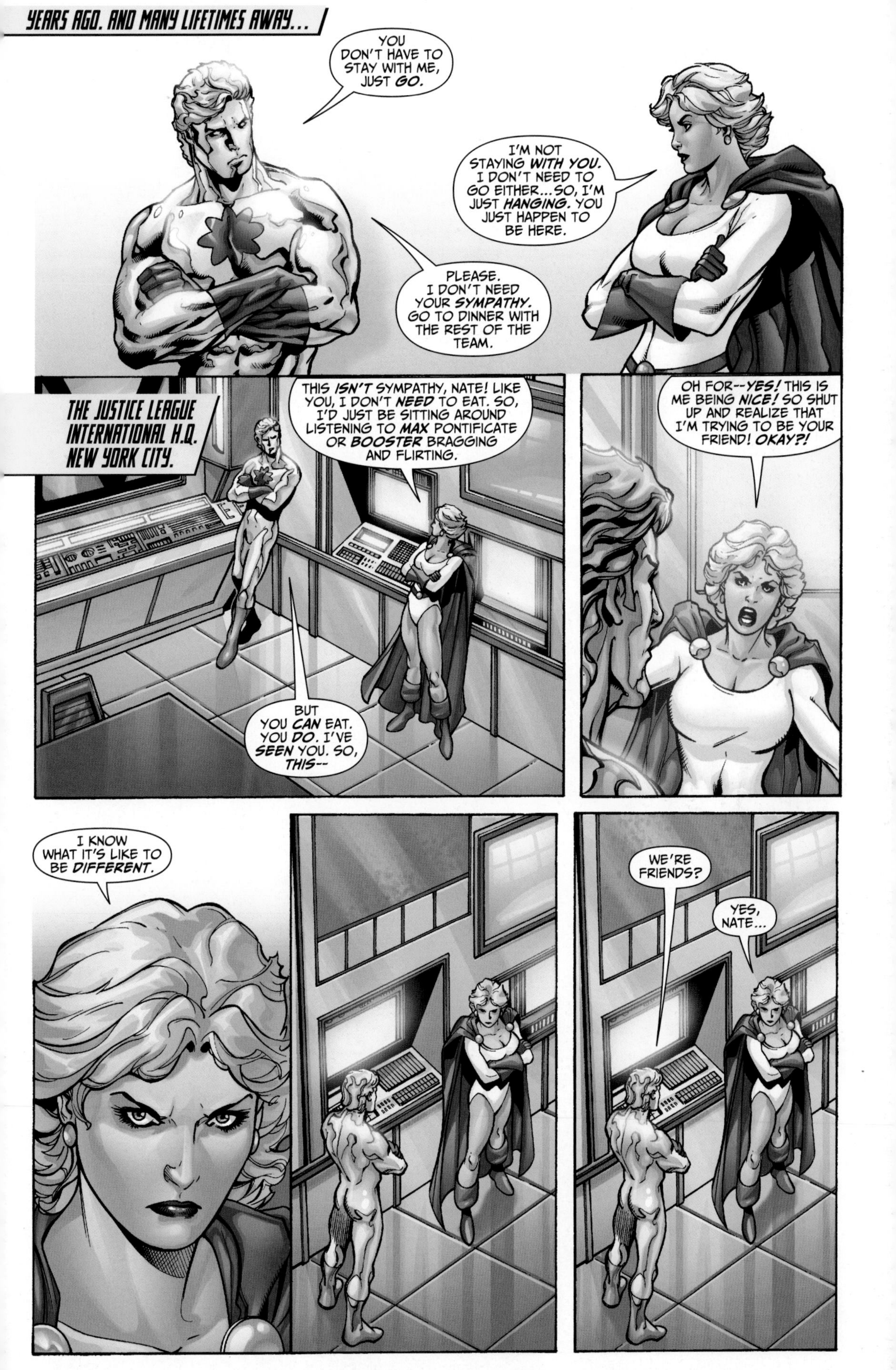
YEARS AGO. AND MANY LIFETIMES AWAY...
YOU DON'T HAVE TO STAY WITH ME, JUST GO.
I'M NOT STAYING WITH YOU. I DON'T NEED TO GO EITHER...SO, I'M JUST HANGING. YOU JUST HAPPEN TO BE HERE.
PLEASE. I DON'T NEED YOUR SYMPATHY. GO TO DINNER WITH THE REST OF THE TEAM.
THE JUSTICE LEAGUE INTERNATIONAL H.Q. NEW YORK CITY.
THIS ISN'T SYMPATHY, NATE! LIKE YOU, I DON'T NEED TO EAT. SO, I'D JUST BE SITTING AROUND LISTENING TO MAX PONTIFICATE OR BOOSTER BRAGGING AND FLIRTING.
BUT YOU CAN EAT. YOU DO. I'VE SEEN YOU. SO, THIS--
OH FOR--YES! THIS IS ME BEING NICE! SO SHUT UP AND REALIZE THAT I'M TRYING TO BE YOUR FRIEND! OKAY?!
I KNOW WHAT IT'S LIKE TO BE DIFFERENT.
WE'RE FRIENDS?
YES, NATE...

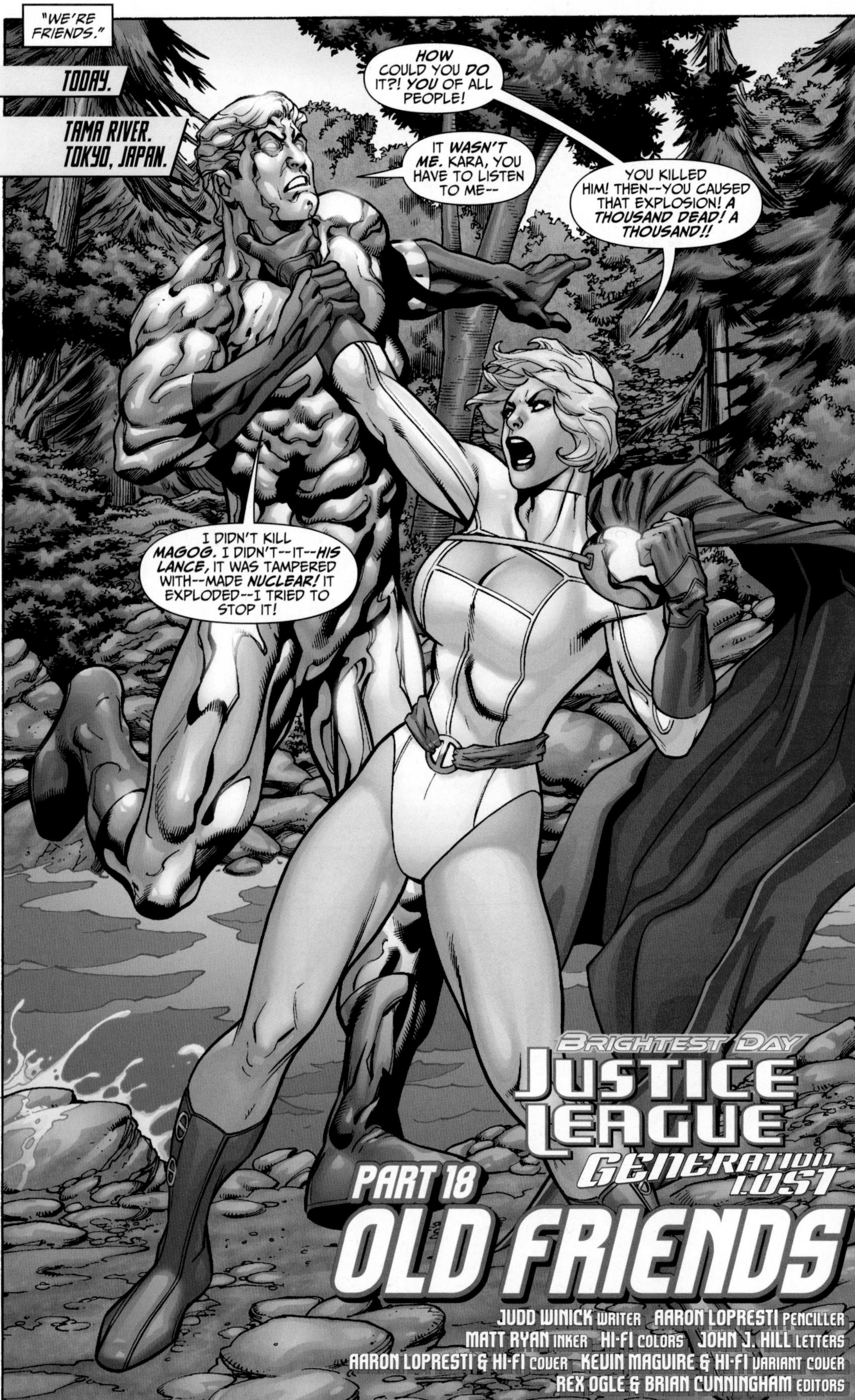

"WE'RE FRIENDS."
TODAY.
TAMA RIVER. TOKYO, JAPAN.
HOW COULD YOU DO IT?! YOU OF ALL PEOPLE!
IT WASN'T ME. KARA, YOU HAVE TO LISTEN TO ME--
YOU KILLED HIM! THEN--YOU CAUSED THAT EXPLOSION! A THOUSAND DEAD! A THOUSAND!!
I DIDN'T KILL MAGOG. I DIDN'T--IT--HIS LANCE, IT WAS TAMPERED WITH--MADE NUCLEAR! IT EXPLODED--I TRIED TO STOP IT!
BRIGHTEST DAY
JUSTICE LEAGUE
GENERATION LOST
PART 18
OLD FRIENDS
JUDD WINICK WRITER AARON LOPRESTI PENCILLER
MATT RYAN INKER HI-FI COLORS JOHN J. HILL LETTERS
AARON LOPRESTI & HI-FI COVER KEVIN MAGUIRE & HI-FI VARIANT COVER
REX OGLE & BRIAN CUNNINGHAM EDITORS

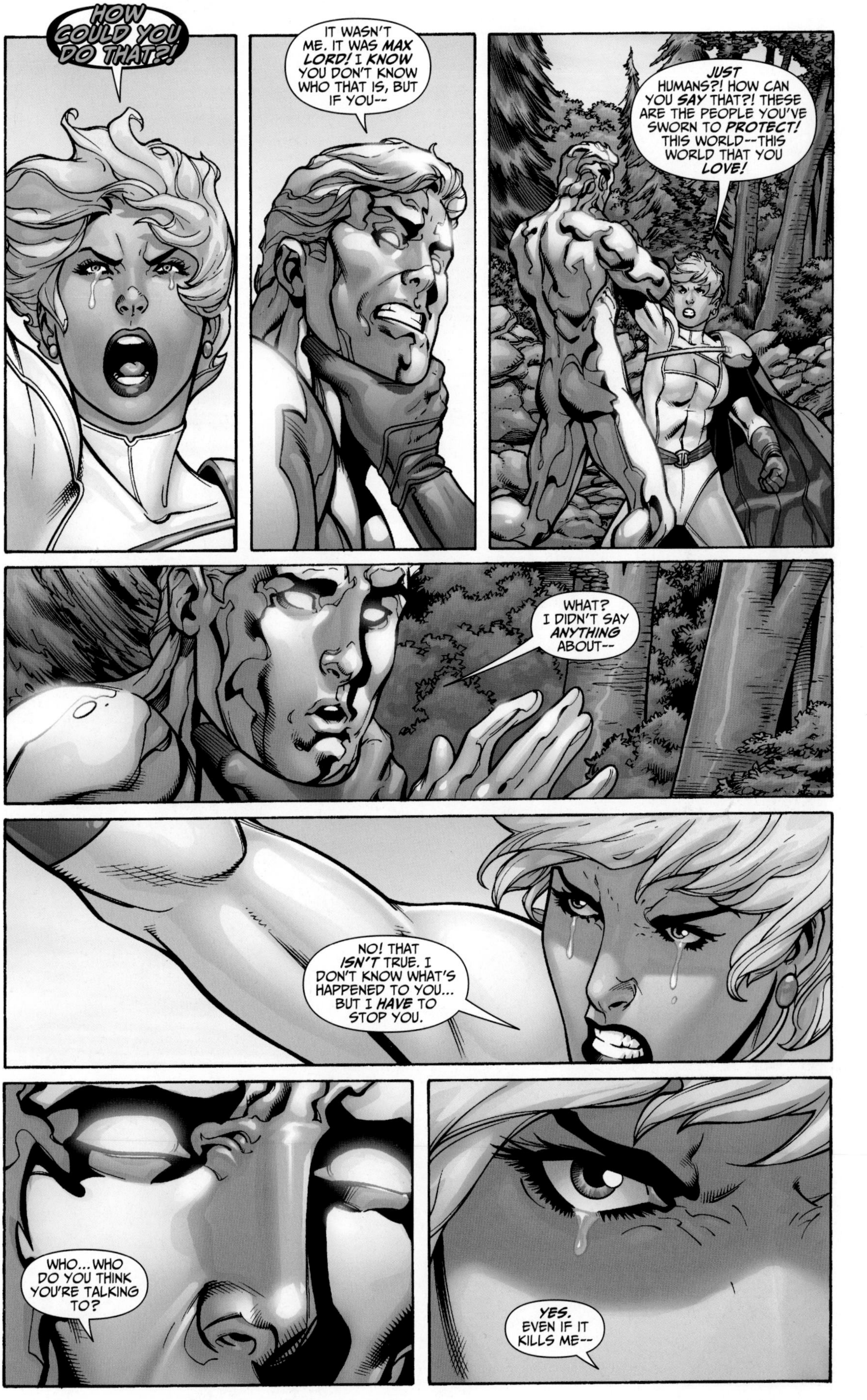
HOW COULD YOU DO THAT?!
IT WASN'T ME. IT WAS MAX LORD! I KNOW YOU DON'T KNOW WHO THAT IS, BUT IF YOU--
JUST HUMANS?! HOW CAN YOU SAY THAT?! THESE ARE THE PEOPLE YOU'VE SWORN TO PROTECT! THIS WORLD--THIS WORLD THAT YOU LOVE!
WHAT? I DIDN'T SAY ANYTHING ABOUT--
NO! THAT ISN'T TRUE. I DON'T KNOW WHAT'S HAPPENED TO YOU... BUT I HAVE TO STOP YOU.
WHO...WHO DO YOU THINK YOU'RE TALKING TO?
YES. EVEN IF IT KILLS ME--

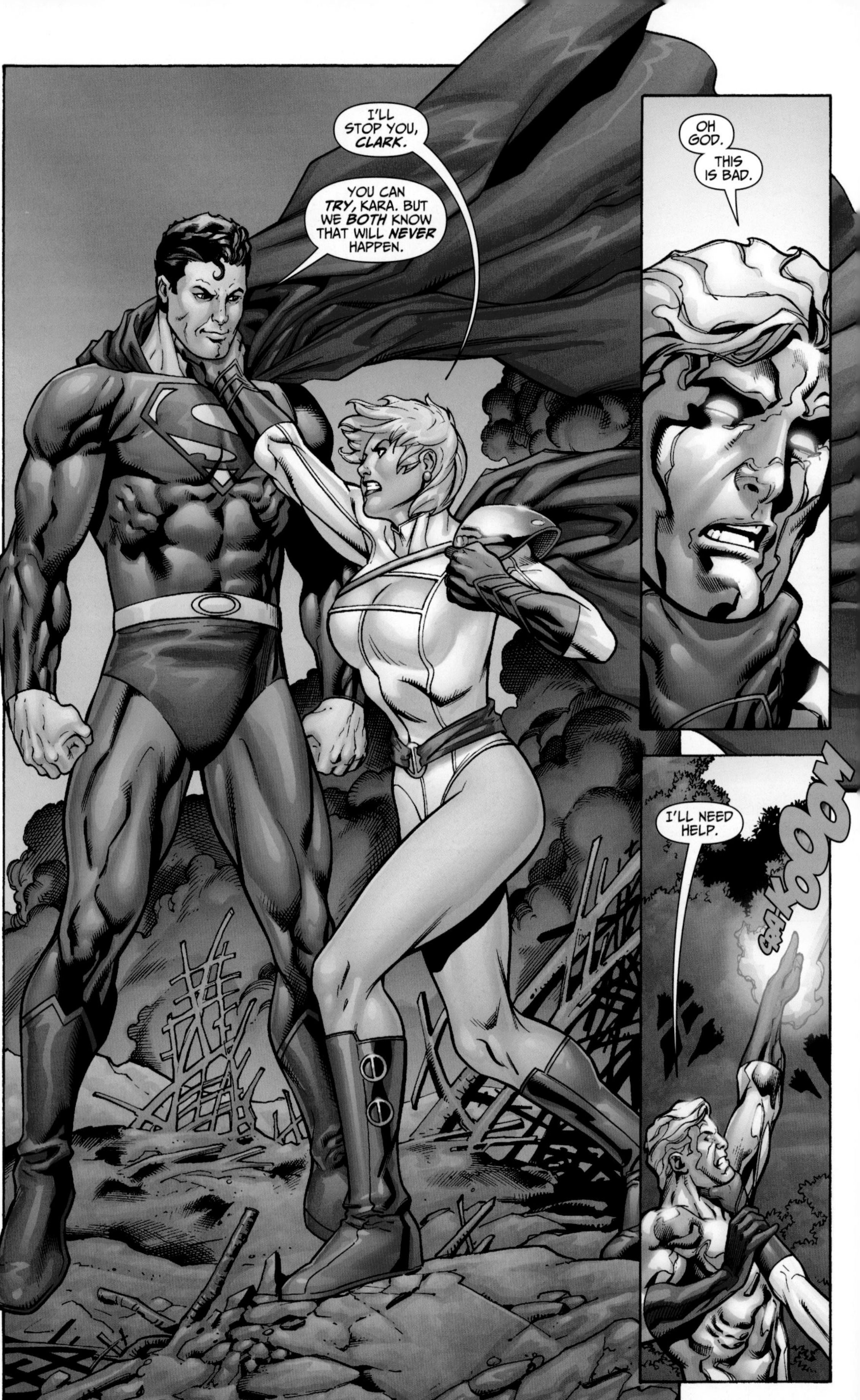
I'LL STOP YOU, CLARK.
YOU CAN TRY, KARA. BUT WE BOTH KNOW THAT WILL NEVER HAPPEN.
OH GOD.
THIS IS BAD.
I'LL NEED HELP.
GRAKOOOOM

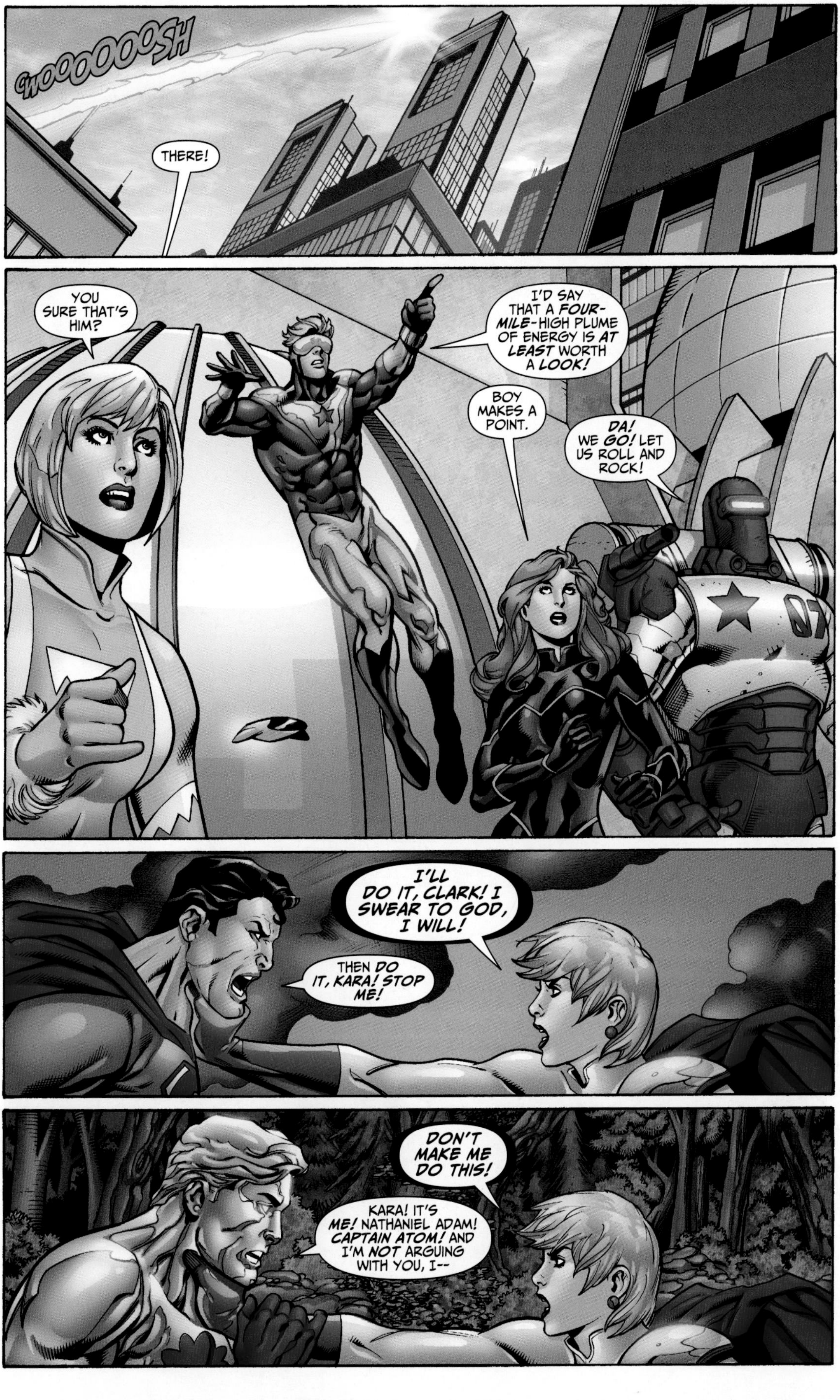
SWOOOOOOSH
THERE!
YOU SURE THAT'S HIM?
I'D SAY THAT A FOUR-MILE-HIGH PLUME OF ENERGY IS AT LEAST WORTH A LOOK!
BOY MAKES A POINT.
DA! WE GO! LET US ROLL AND ROCK!
I'LL DO IT, CLARK! I SWEAR TO GOD, I WILL!
THEN DO IT, KARA! STOP ME!
DON'T MAKE ME DO THIS!
KARA! IT'S ME! NATHANIEL ADAM! CAPTAIN ATOM! AND I'M NOT ARGUING WITH YOU, I--

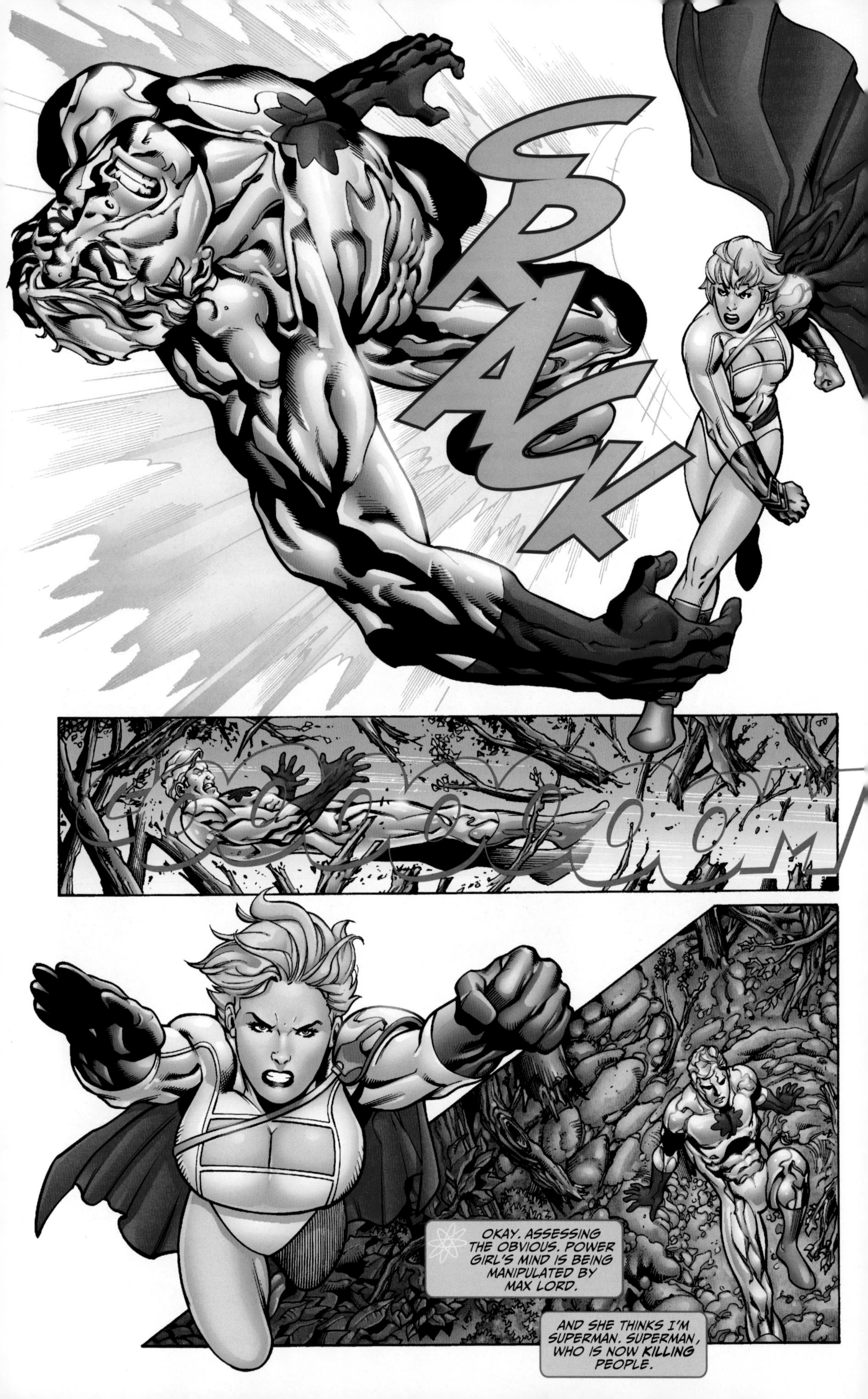
CRACK
BOOOOOOOOOM
OKAY. ASSESSING THE OBVIOUS. POWER GIRL'S MIND IS BEING MANIPULATED BY MAX LORD.
AND SHE THINKS I'M SUPERMAN. SUPERMAN, WHO IS NOW KILLING PEOPLE.

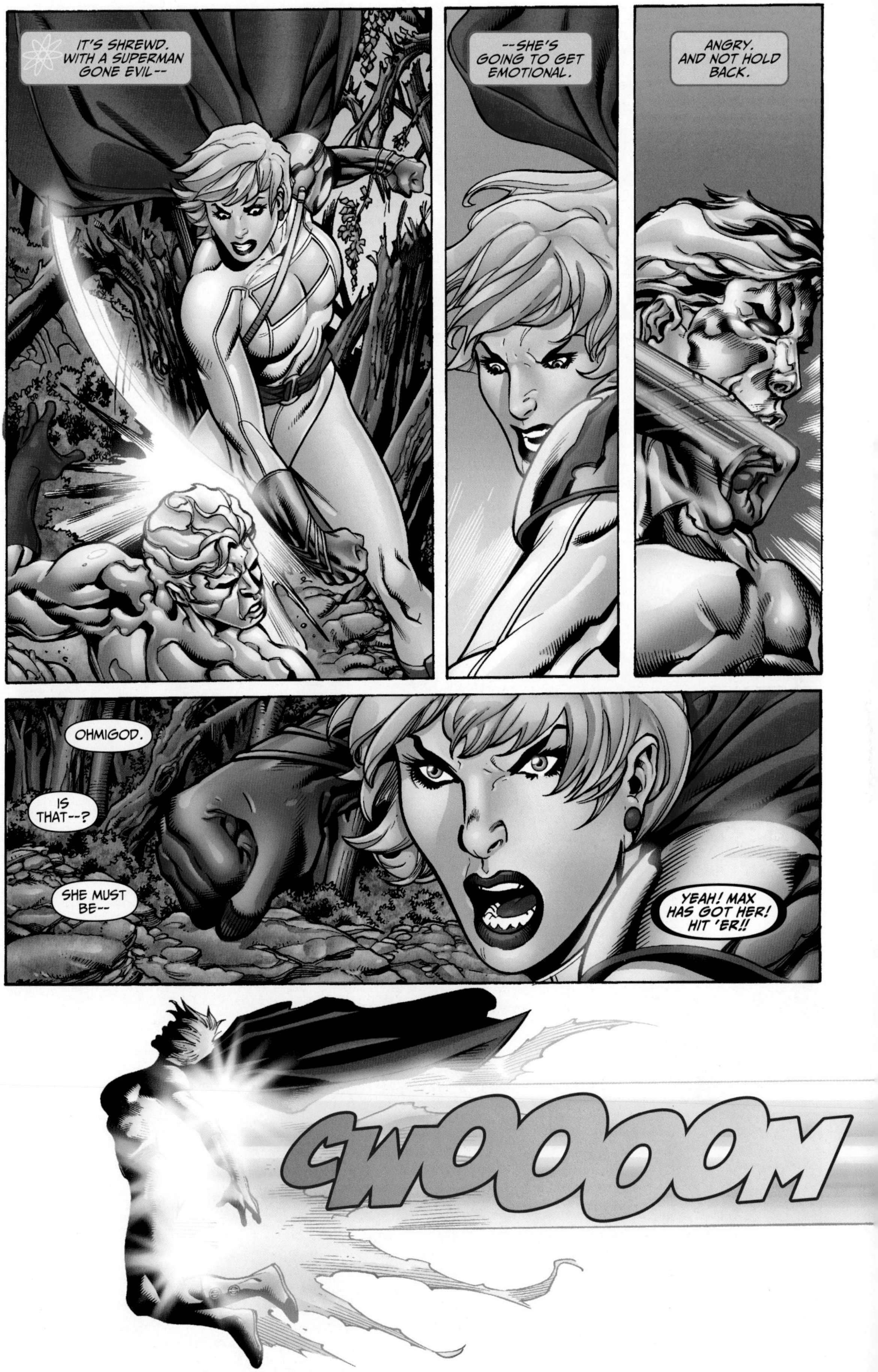
IT'S SHREWD. WITH A SUPERMAN GONE EVIL--
--SHE'S GOING TO GET EMOTIONAL.
ANGRY. AND NOT HOLD BACK.
OHMIGOD.
IS THAT--?
SHE MUST BE--
YEAH! MAX HAS GOT HER! HIT 'ER!!
CWOOOOM

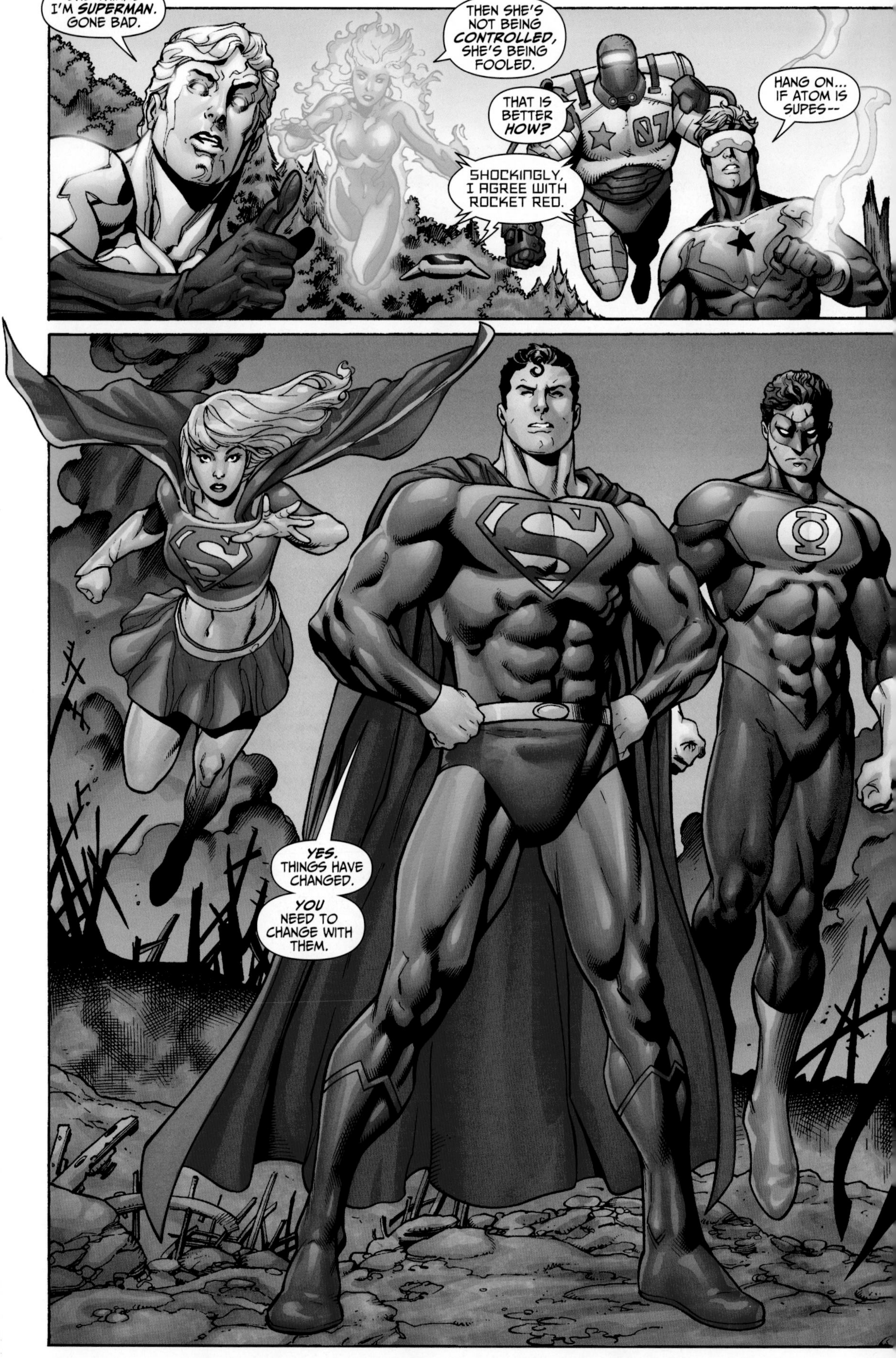
SHE THINKS I'M *SUPERMAN*. GONE BAD.
THEN SHE'S NOT BEING *CONTROLLED*, SHE'S BEING FOOLED.
THAT IS BETTER *HOW?*
SHOCKINGLY, I AGREE WITH ROCKET RED.
HANG ON... IF ATOM IS SUPES--
YES. THINGS HAVE CHANGED.
YOU NEED TO CHANGE WITH THEM.

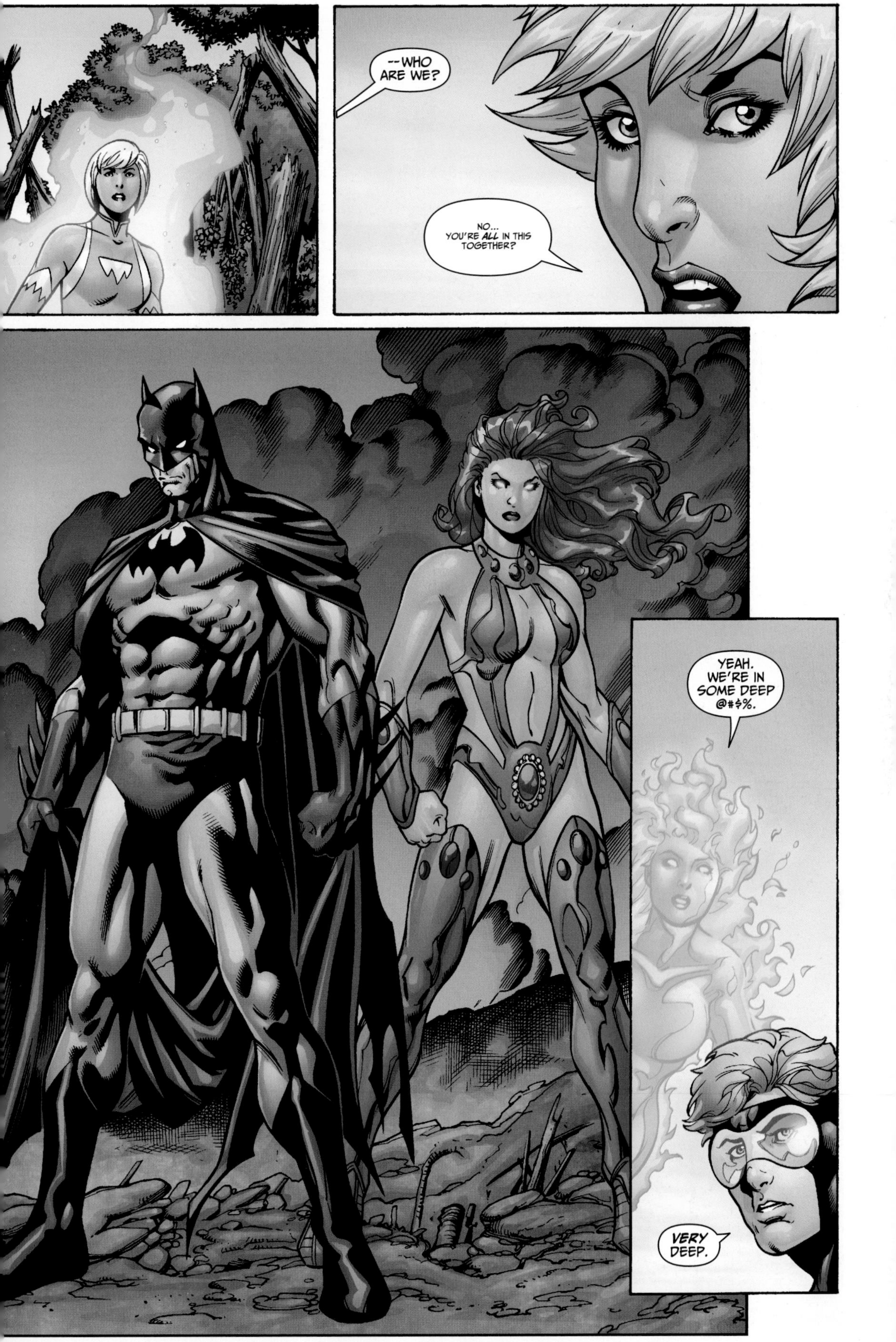
--WHO ARE WE?
NO... YOU'RE ALL IN THIS TOGETHER?
YEAH. WE'RE IN SOME DEEP @#$%.
VERY DEEP.

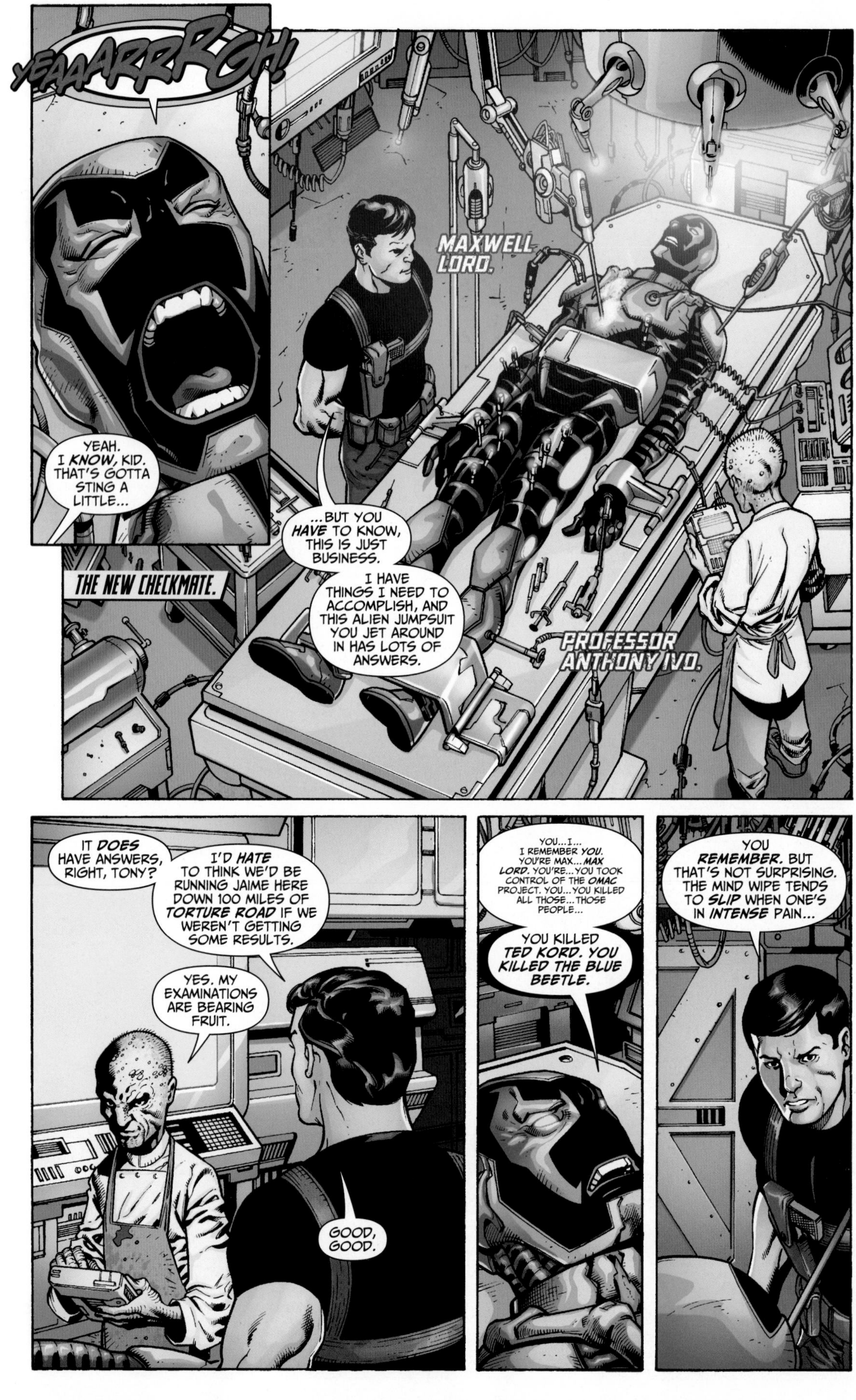
YEAAARRRGH!
YEAH. I KNOW, KID. THAT'S GOTTA STING A LITTLE...
MAXWELL LORD.
...BUT YOU HAVE TO KNOW, THIS IS JUST BUSINESS.
I HAVE THINGS I NEED TO ACCOMPLISH, AND THIS ALIEN JUMPSUIT YOU JET AROUND IN HAS LOTS OF ANSWERS.
THE NEW CHECKMATE.
PROFESSOR ANTHONY IVO.
IT DOES HAVE ANSWERS, RIGHT, TONY?
I'D HATE TO THINK WE'D BE RUNNING JAIME HERE DOWN 100 MILES OF TORTURE ROAD IF WE WEREN'T GETTING SOME RESULTS.
YES. MY EXAMINATIONS ARE BEARING FRUIT.
GOOD, GOOD.
YOU...I... I REMEMBER YOU. YOU'RE MAX... MAX LORD. YOU'RE...YOU TOOK CONTROL OF THE OMAC PROJECT. YOU...YOU KILLED ALL THOSE...THOSE PEOPLE...
YOU KILLED TED KORD. YOU KILLED THE BLUE BEETLE.
YOU REMEMBER. BUT THAT'S NOT SURPRISING. THE MIND WIPE TENDS TO SLIP WHEN ONE'S IN INTENSE PAIN...

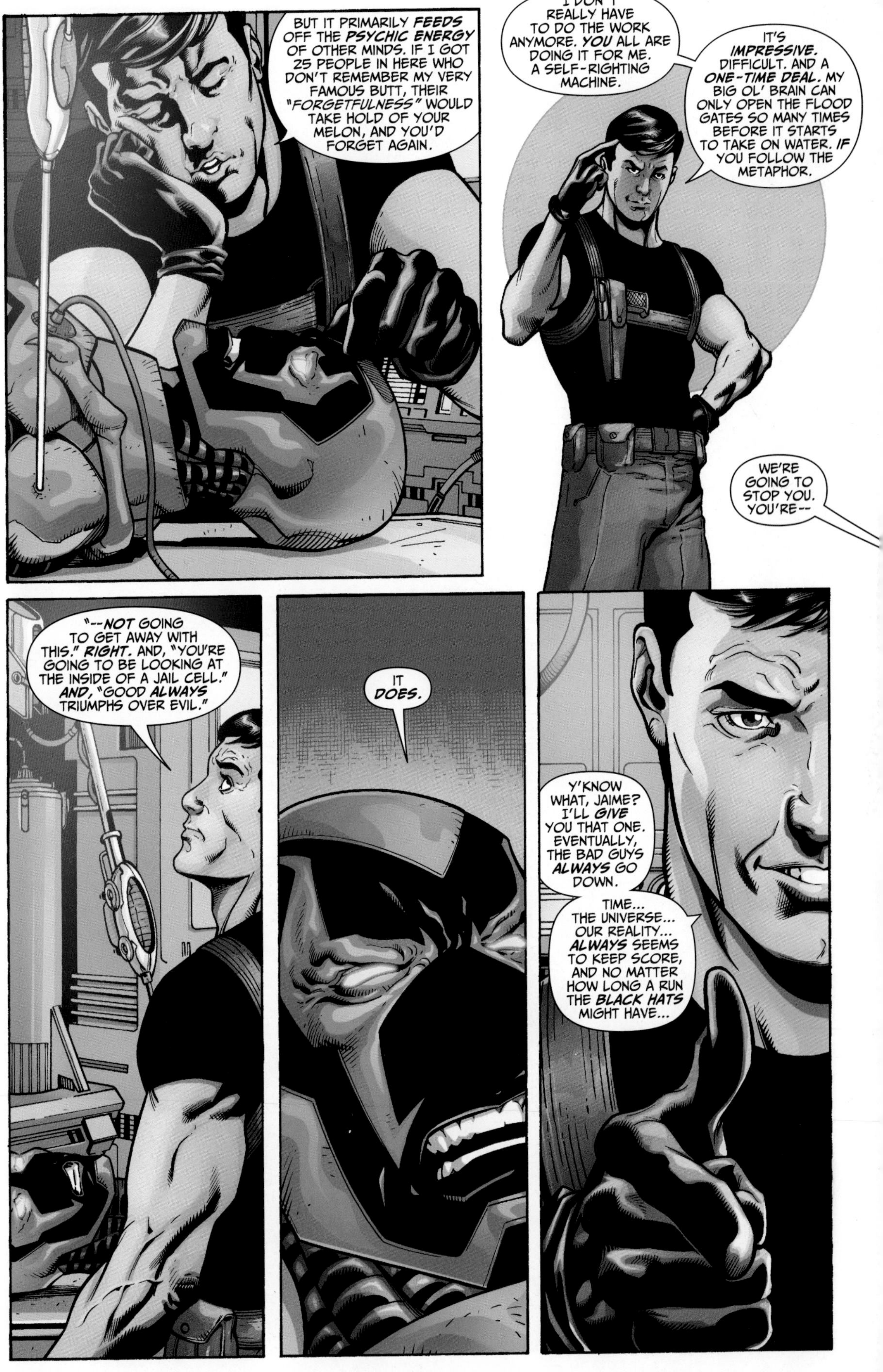
BUT IT PRIMARILY FEEDS OFF THE PSYCHIC ENERGY OF OTHER MINDS. IF I GOT 25 PEOPLE IN HERE WHO DON'T REMEMBER MY VERY FAMOUS BUTT, THEIR "FORGETFULNESS" WOULD TAKE HOLD OF YOUR MELON, AND YOU'D FORGET AGAIN.
I DON'T REALLY HAVE TO DO THE WORK ANYMORE. YOU ALL ARE DOING IT FOR ME. A SELF-RIGHTING MACHINE.
IT'S IMPRESSIVE. DIFFICULT. AND A ONE-TIME DEAL. MY BIG OL' BRAIN CAN ONLY OPEN THE FLOOD GATES SO MANY TIMES BEFORE IT STARTS TO TAKE ON WATER. IF YOU FOLLOW THE METAPHOR.
WE'RE GOING TO STOP YOU. YOU'RE--
"--NOT GOING TO GET AWAY WITH THIS." RIGHT. AND, "YOU'RE GOING TO BE LOOKING AT THE INSIDE OF A JAIL CELL." AND, "GOOD ALWAYS TRIUMPHS OVER EVIL."
IT DOES.
Y'KNOW WHAT, JAIME? I'LL GIVE YOU THAT ONE. EVENTUALLY, THE BAD GUYS ALWAYS GO DOWN.
TIME... THE UNIVERSE... OUR REALITY... ALWAYS SEEMS TO KEEP SCORE, AND NO MATTER HOW LONG A RUN THE BLACK HATS MIGHT HAVE...

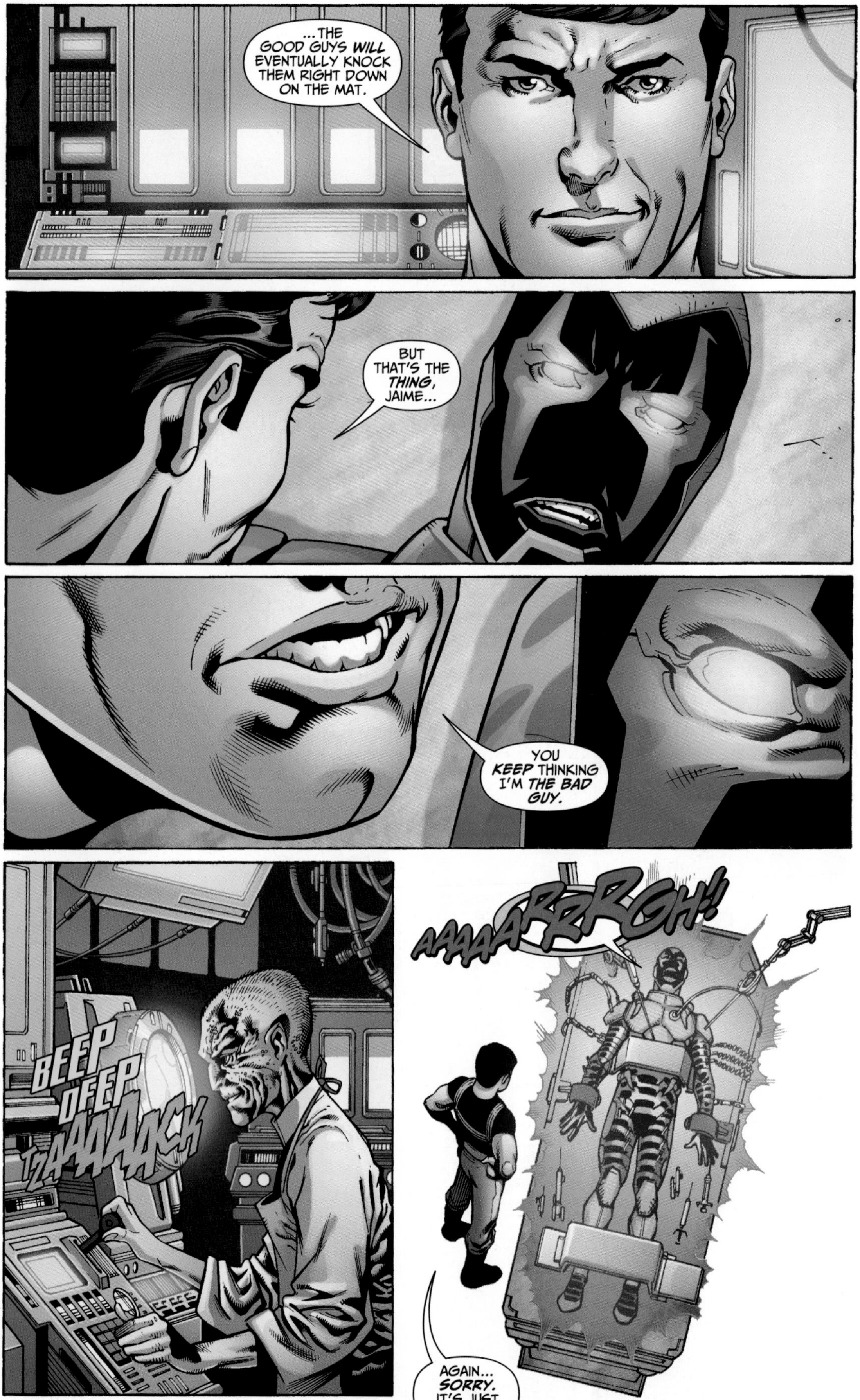
...THE GOOD GUYS WILL EVENTUALLY KNOCK THEM RIGHT DOWN ON THE MAT.
BUT THAT'S THE THING, JAIME...
YOU KEEP THINKING I'M THE BAD GUY.
BEEP DEEP TZAAAAACK
AAAAARRRGH!!
AGAIN... SORRY. IT'S JUST BUSINESS.

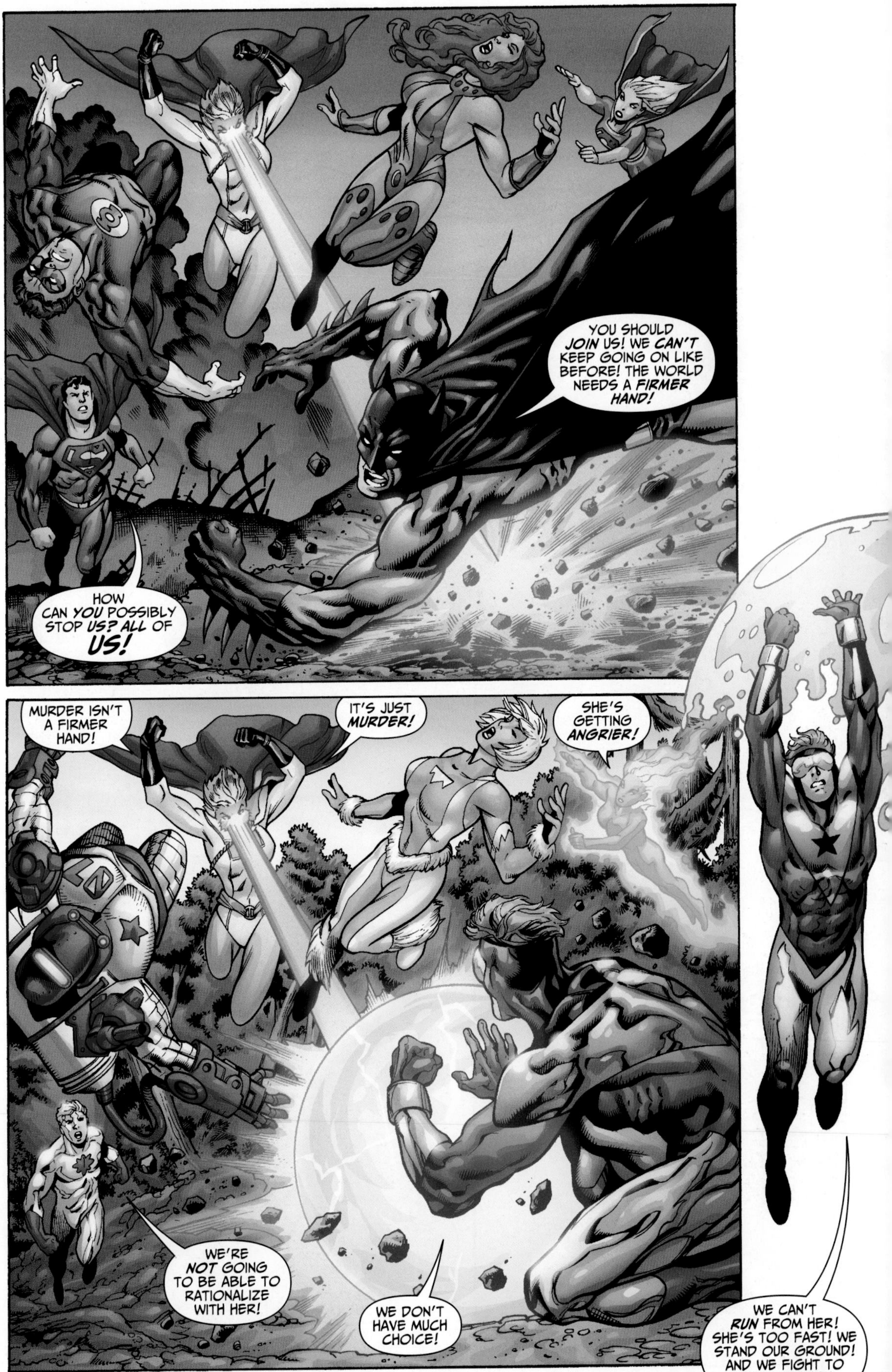
YOU SHOULD JOIN US! WE CAN'T KEEP GOING ON LIKE BEFORE! THE WORLD NEEDS A FIRMER HAND!
HOW CAN YOU POSSIBLY STOP US? ALL OF US!
MURDER ISN'T A FIRMER HAND!
IT'S JUST MURDER!
SHE'S GETTING ANGRIER!
WE'RE NOT GOING TO BE ABLE TO RATIONALIZE WITH HER!
WE DON'T HAVE MUCH CHOICE!
WE CAN'T RUN FROM HER! SHE'S TOO FAST! WE STAND OUR GROUND! AND WE FIGHT TO GET THROUGH TO H--

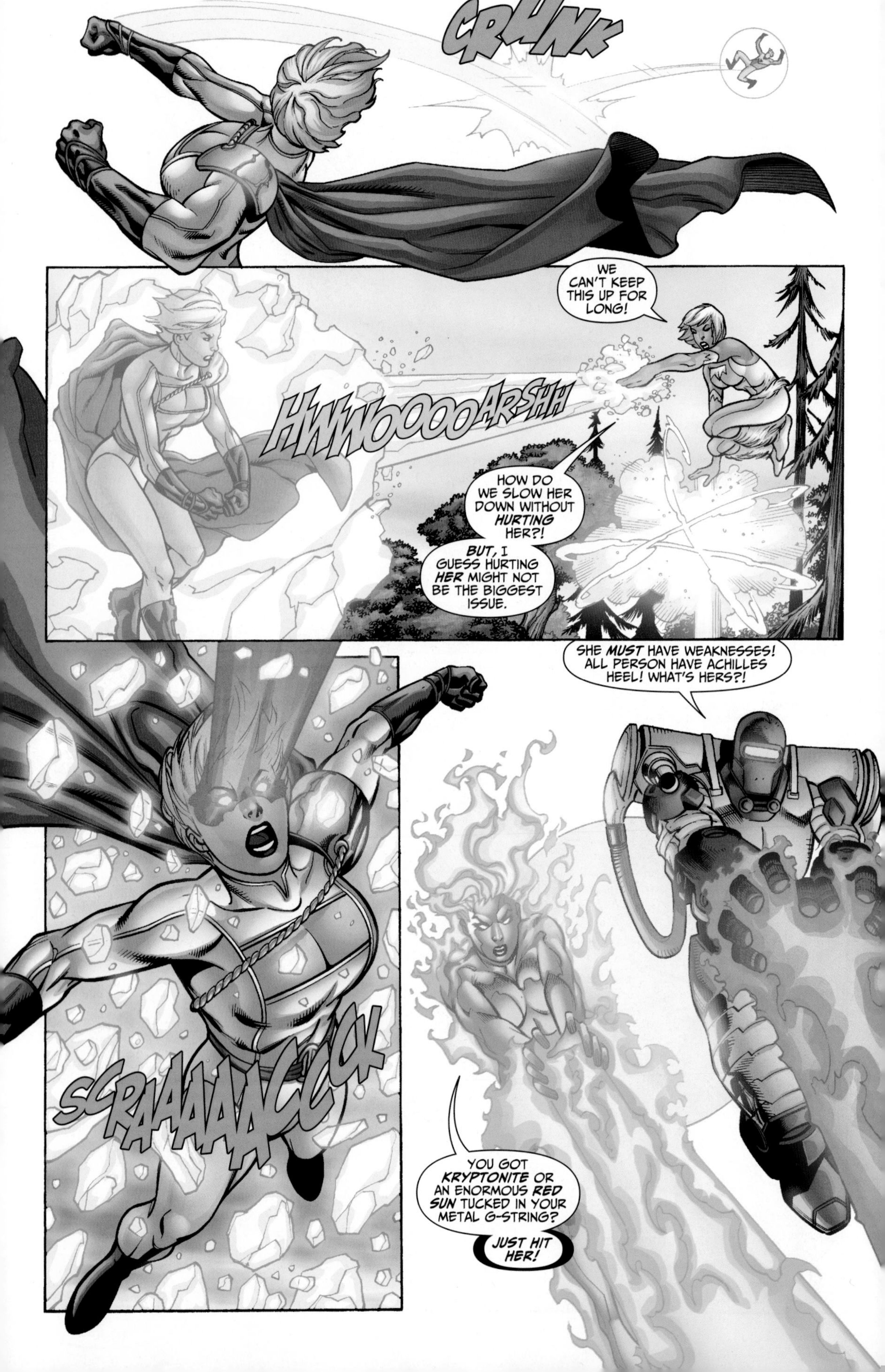
CRUNK
WE CAN'T KEEP THIS UP FOR LONG!
HWWOOOOARSHH
HOW DO WE SLOW HER DOWN WITHOUT *HURTING* HER?!
BUT, I GUESS HURTING *HER* MIGHT NOT BE THE BIGGEST ISSUE.
SHE *MUST* HAVE WEAKNESSES! ALL PERSON HAVE ACHILLES HEEL! WHAT'S HERS?!
SCRAAAAACCCK
YOU GOT *KRYPTONITE* OR AN ENORMOUS *RED SUN* TUCKED IN YOUR METAL G-STRING?
JUST HIT HER!

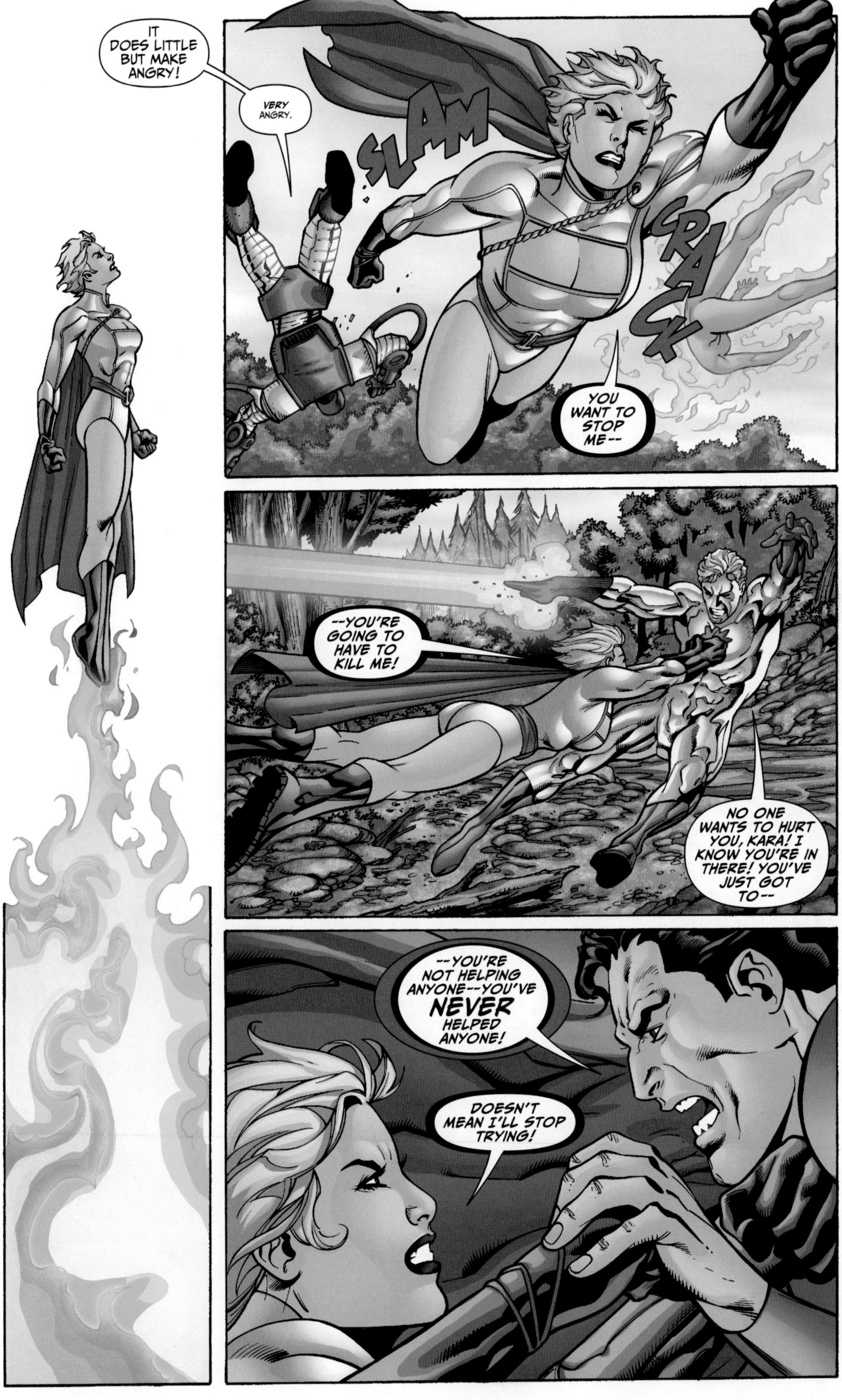
IT DOES LITTLE BUT MAKE ANGRY!
VERY ANGRY.
SLAM
CRACK
YOU WANT TO STOP ME--
--YOU'RE GOING TO HAVE TO KILL ME!
NO ONE WANTS TO HURT YOU, KARA! I KNOW YOU'RE IN THERE! YOU'VE JUST GOT TO--
--YOU'RE NOT HELPING ANYONE--YOU'VE NEVER HELPED ANYONE!
DOESN'T MEAN I'LL STOP TRYING!

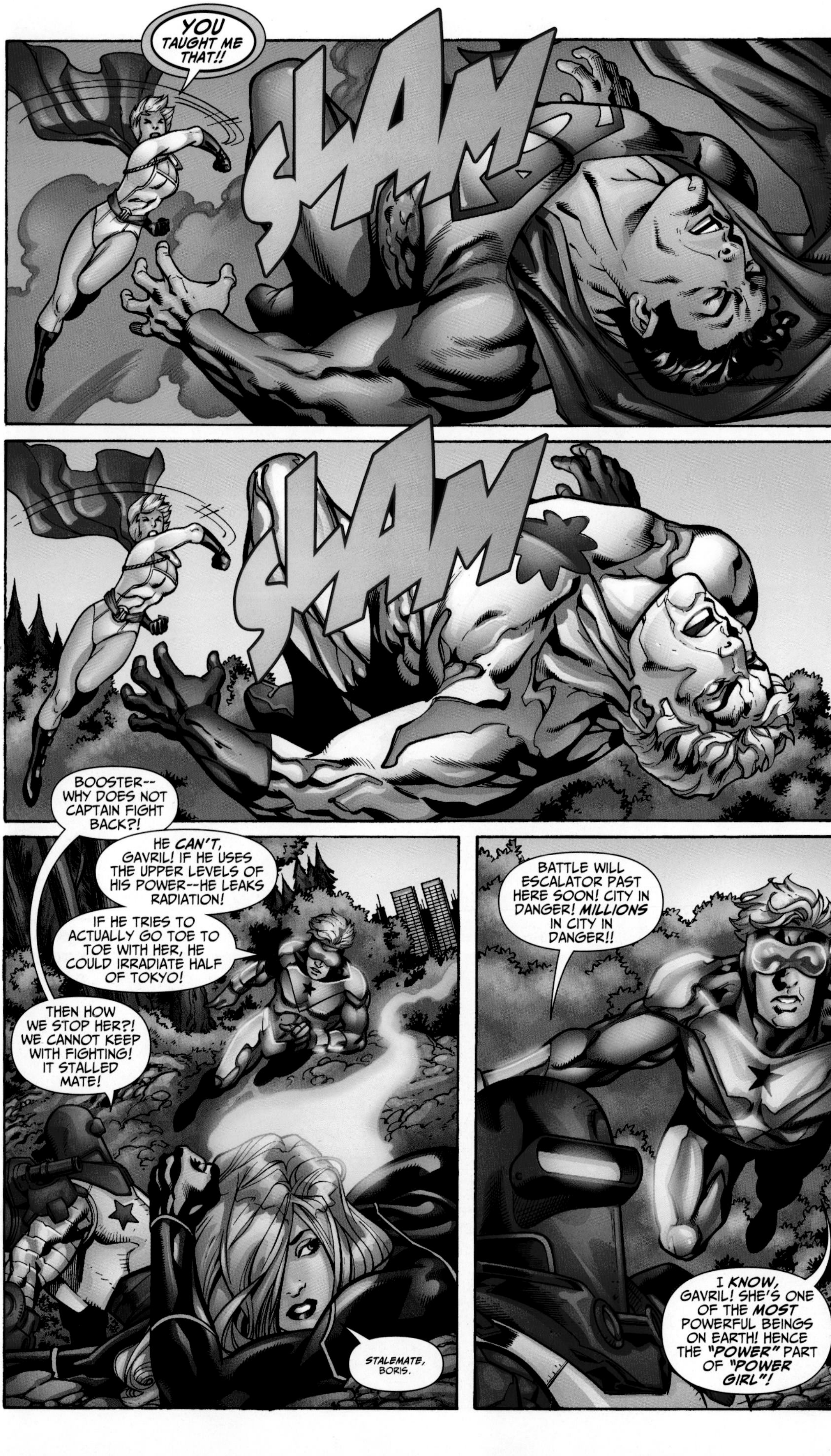
YOU TAUGHT ME THAT!!
SLAM
SLAM
BOOSTER-- WHY DOES NOT CAPTAIN FIGHT BACK?!
HE CAN'T, GAVRIL! IF HE USES THE UPPER LEVELS OF HIS POWER--HE LEAKS RADIATION!
IF HE TRIES TO ACTUALLY GO TOE TO TOE WITH HER, HE COULD IRRADIATE HALF OF TOKYO!
THEN HOW WE STOP HER?! WE CANNOT KEEP WITH FIGHTING! IT STALLED MATE!
STALEMATE, BORIS.
BATTLE WILL ESCALATOR PAST HERE SOON! CITY IN DANGER! MILLIONS IN CITY IN DANGER!!
I KNOW, GAVRIL! SHE'S ONE OF THE MOST POWERFUL BEINGS ON EARTH! HENCE THE "POWER" PART OF "POWER GIRL"!

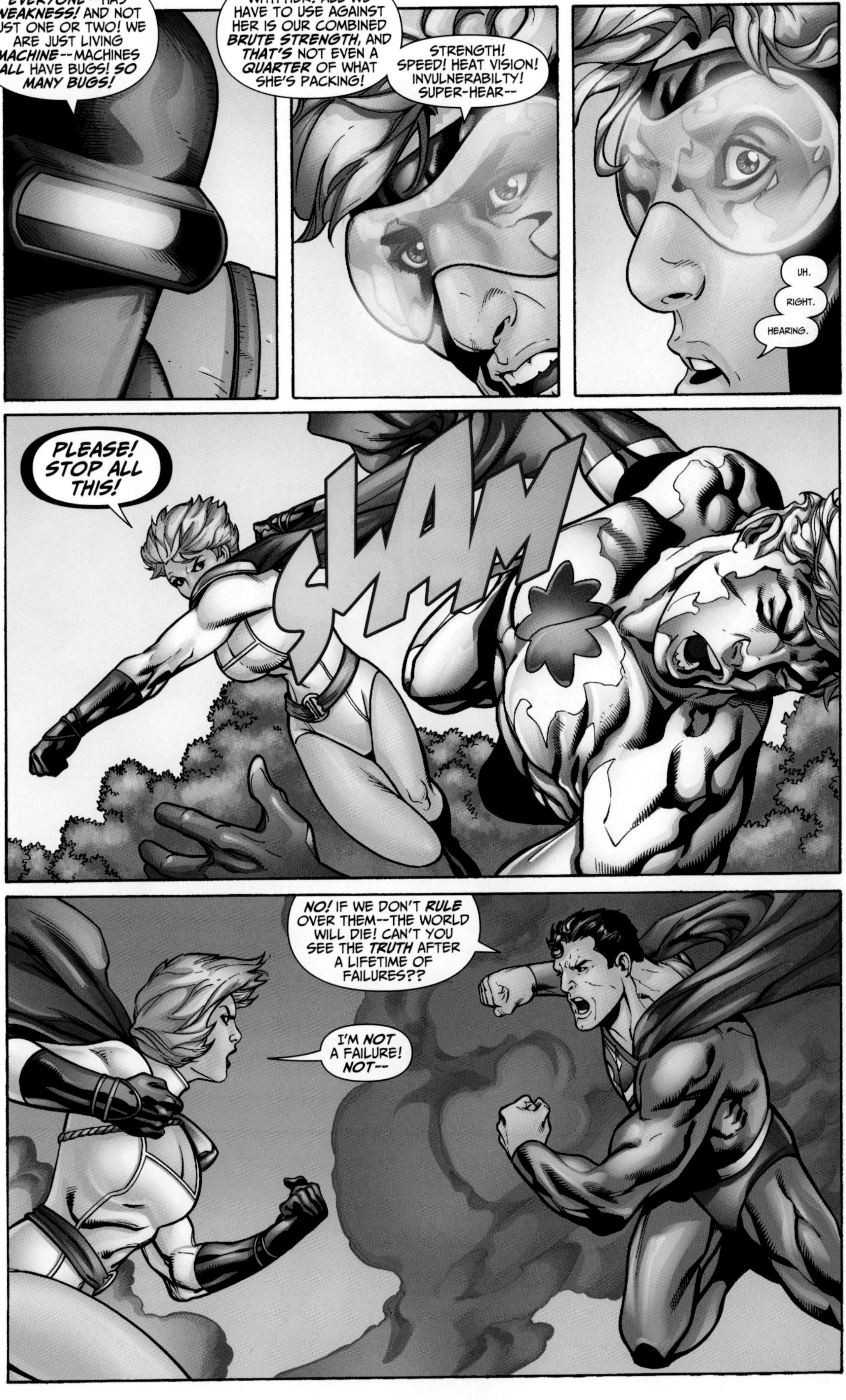
EVERYONE--EVERYONE--HAS WEAKNESS! AND NOT JUST ONE OR TWO! WE ARE JUST LIVING MACHINE--MACHINES ALL HAVE BUGS! SO MANY BUGS!
NOT WITH HER! ALL WE HAVE TO USE AGAINST HER IS OUR COMBINED BRUTE STRENGTH, AND THAT'S NOT EVEN A QUARTER OF WHAT SHE'S PACKING!
STRENGTH! SPEED! HEAT VISION! INVULNERABILTY! SUPER-HEAR--
UH.
RIGHT.
HEARING.
PLEASE! STOP ALL THIS!
SLAM
NO! IF WE DON'T RULE OVER THEM--THE WORLD WILL DIE! CAN'T YOU SEE THE TRUTH AFTER A LIFETIME OF FAILURES??
I'M NOT A FAILURE! NOT--

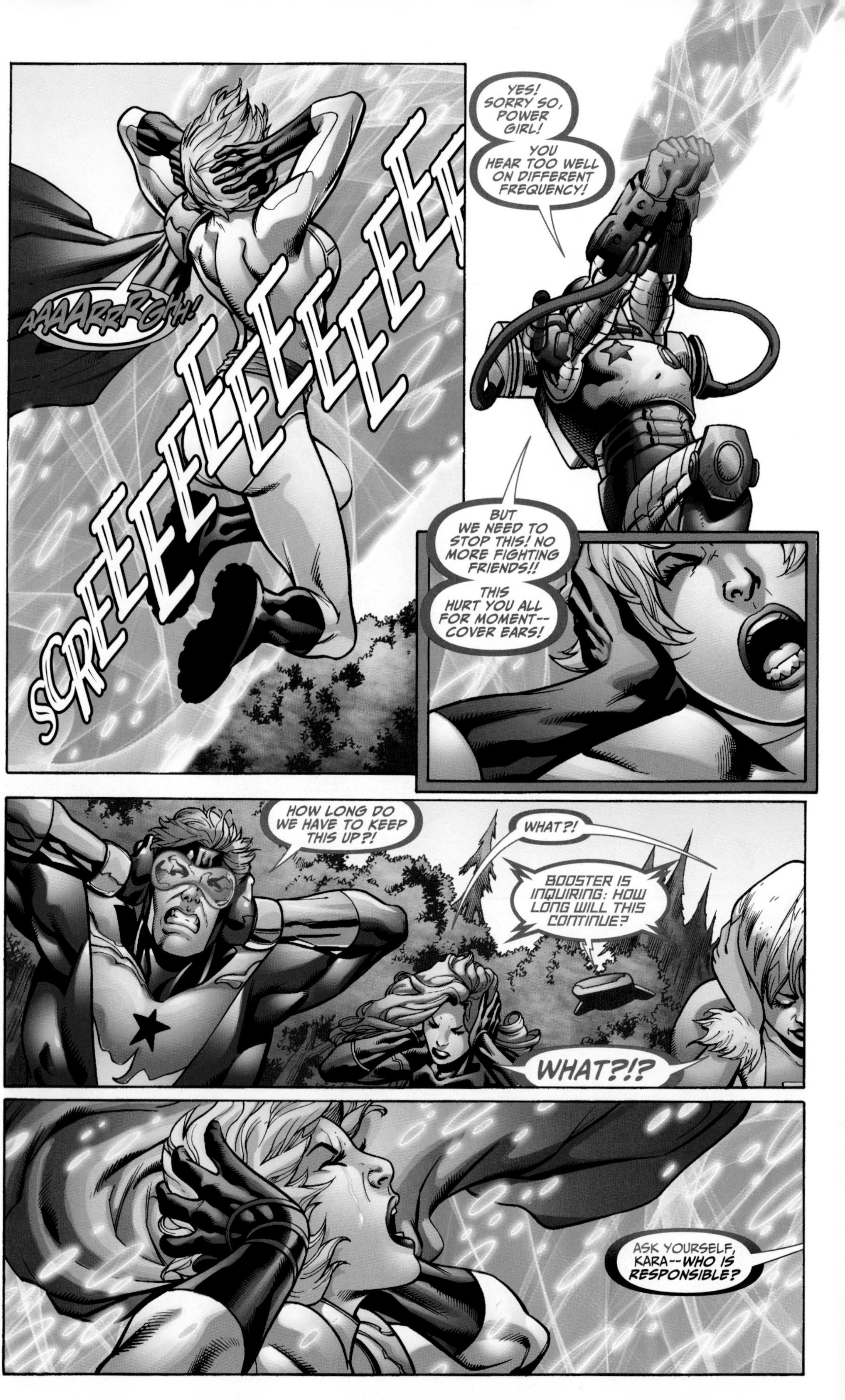
SCREEEEEEEEEEEE
AAAARRRGHH!
YES! SORRY SO, POWER GIRL!
YOU HEAR TOO WELL ON DIFFERENT FREQUENCY!
BUT WE NEED TO STOP THIS! NO MORE FIGHTING FRIENDS!!
THIS HURT YOU ALL FOR MOMENT-- COVER EARS!
HOW LONG DO WE HAVE TO KEEP THIS UP?!
WHAT?!
BOOSTER IS INQUIRING: HOW LONG WILL THIS CONTINUE?
WHAT?!?
ASK YOURSELF, KARA--WHO IS RESPONSIBLE?

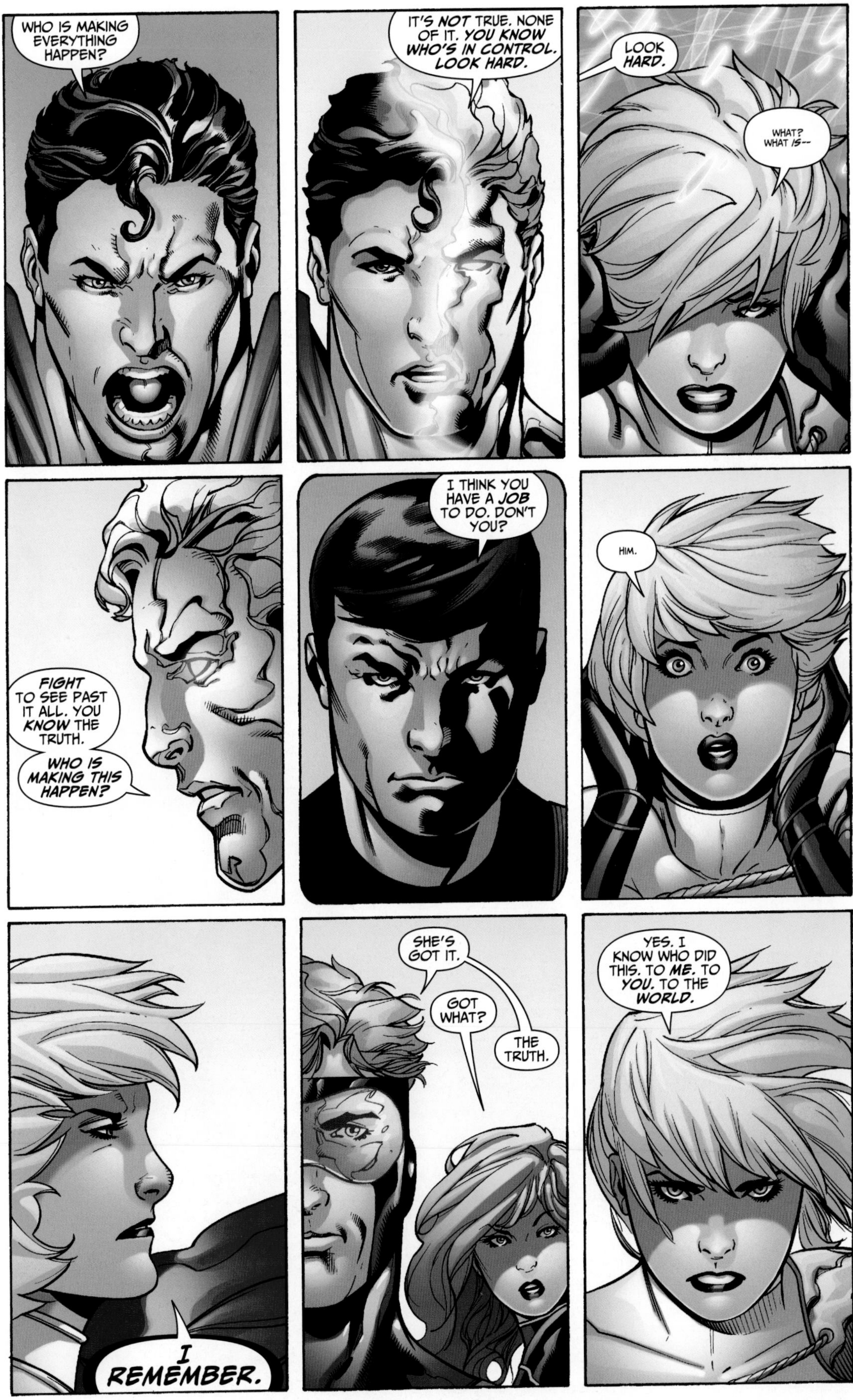
WHO IS MAKING EVERYTHING HAPPEN?
IT'S NOT TRUE. NONE OF IT. YOU KNOW WHO'S IN CONTROL. LOOK HARD.
LOOK HARD.
WHAT? WHAT IS--
FIGHT TO SEE PAST IT ALL. YOU KNOW THE TRUTH.
WHO IS MAKING THIS HAPPEN?
I THINK YOU HAVE A JOB TO DO. DON'T YOU?
HIM.
I REMEMBER.
SHE'S GOT IT.
GOT WHAT?
THE TRUTH.
YES. I KNOW WHO DID THIS. TO ME. TO YOU. TO THE WORLD.

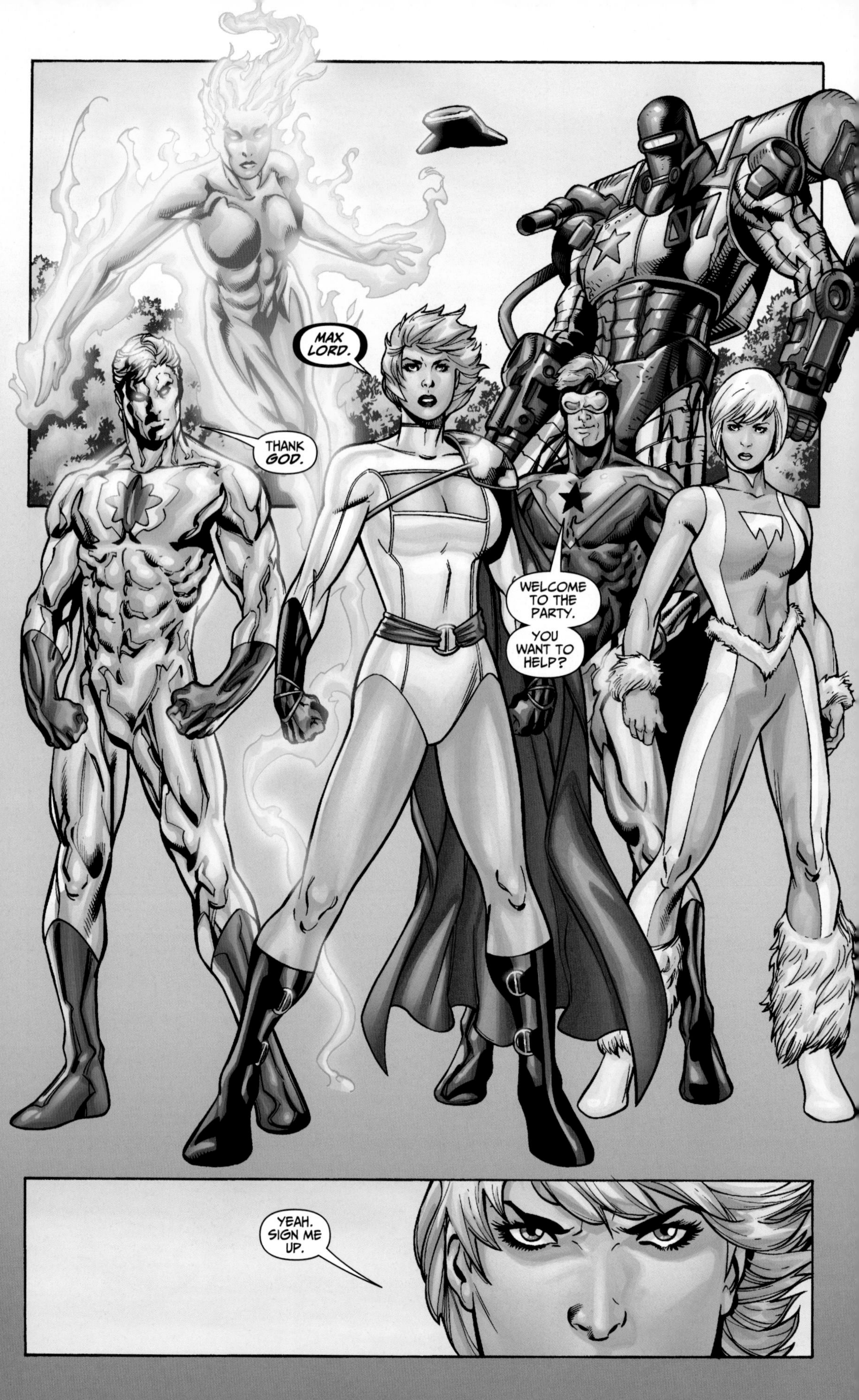

MAX LORD.
THANK GOD.
WELCOME TO THE PARTY.
YOU WANT TO HELP?
YEAH. SIGN ME UP.

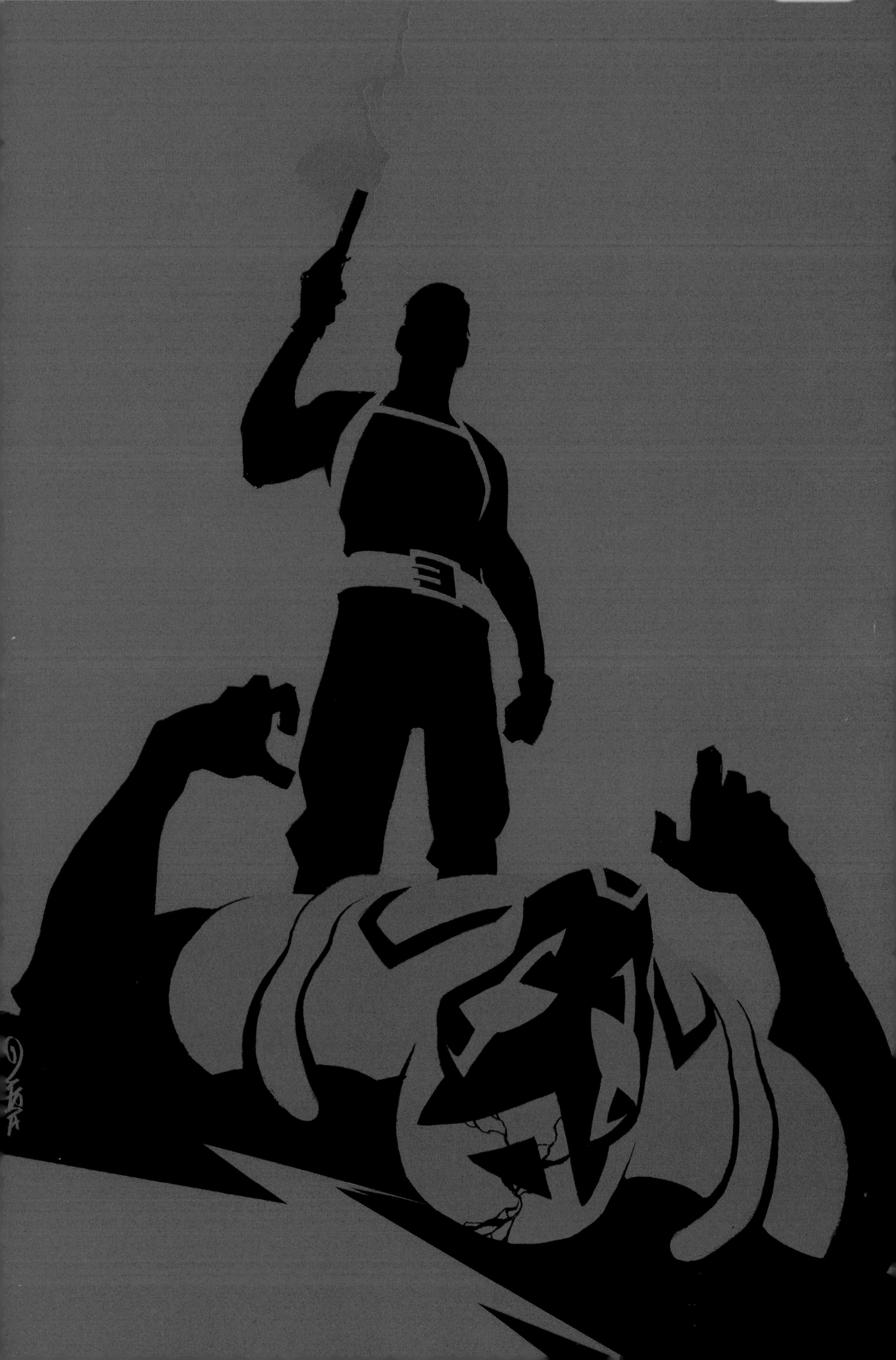

Cover by Dustin Nguyen

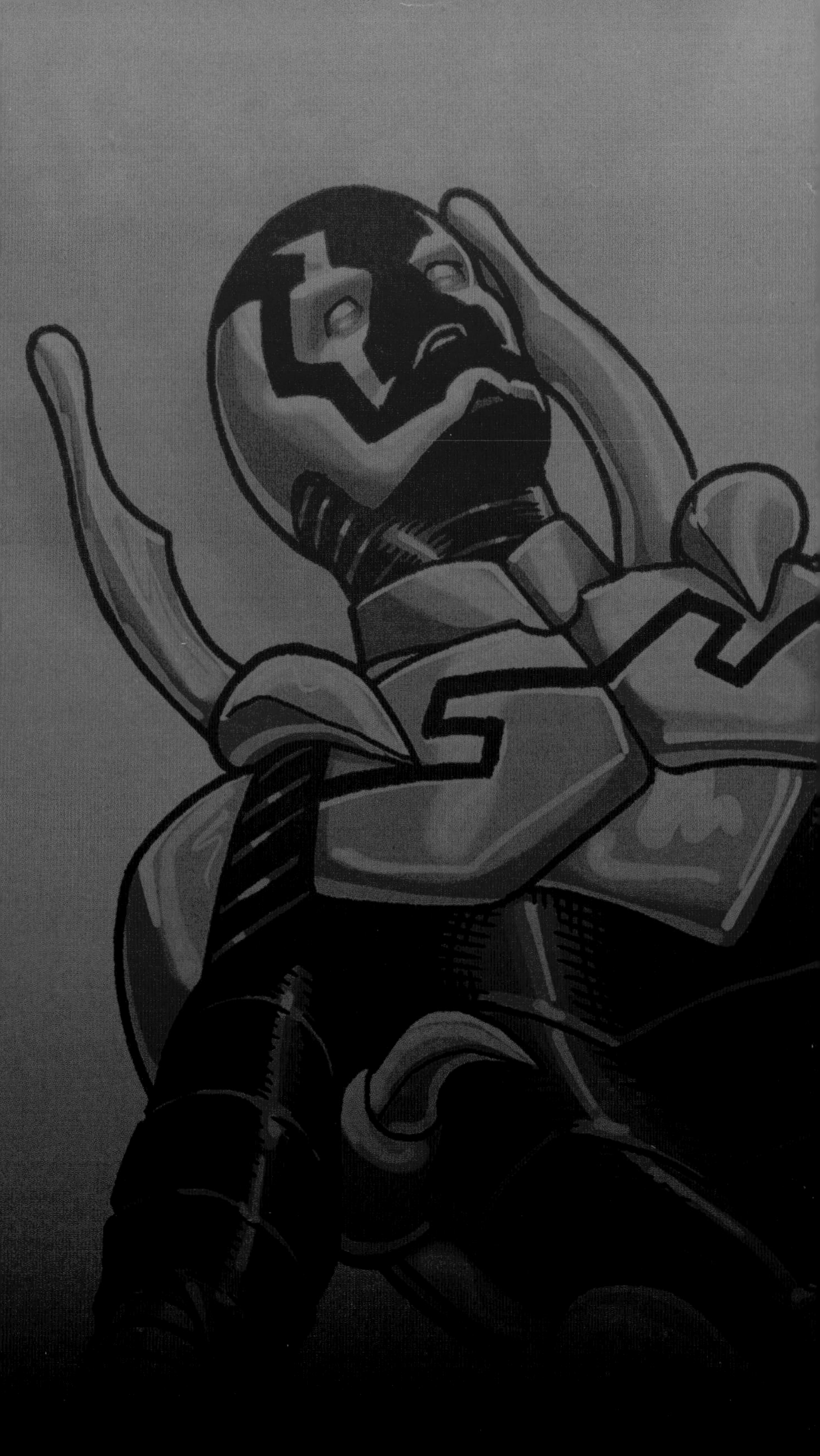

NETEEN:

AND THE LORD TAKETH AWAY

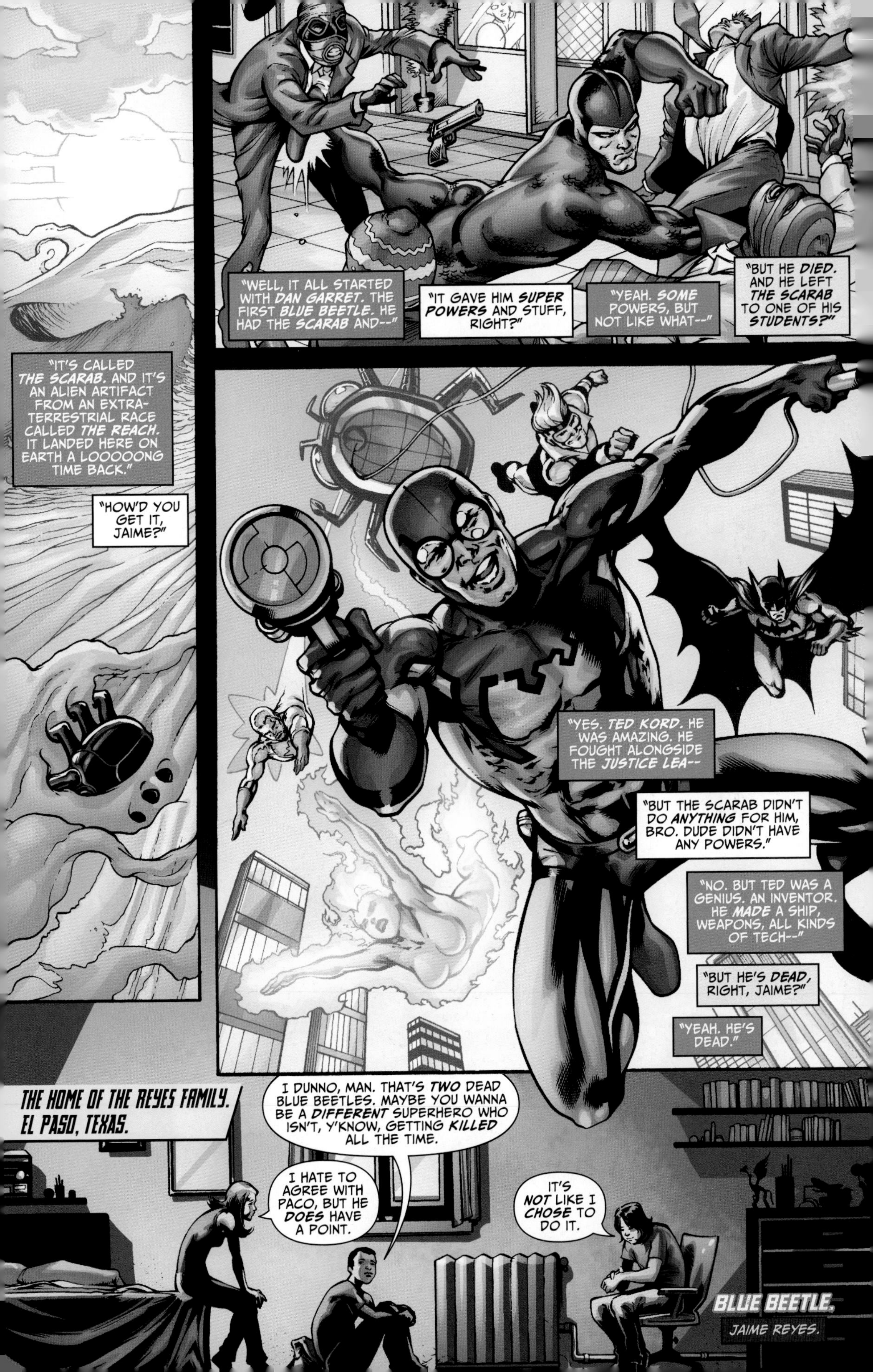
"IT'S CALLED THE SCARAB. AND IT'S AN ALIEN ARTIFACT FROM AN EXTRA-TERRESTRIAL RACE CALLED THE REACH. IT LANDED HERE ON EARTH A LOOOOONG TIME BACK."
"HOW'D YOU GET IT, JAIME?"
"WELL, IT ALL STARTED WITH DAN GARRET. THE FIRST BLUE BEETLE. HE HAD THE SCARAB AND--"
"IT GAVE HIM SUPER POWERS AND STUFF, RIGHT?"
"YEAH. SOME POWERS, BUT NOT LIKE WHAT--"
"BUT HE DIED. AND HE LEFT THE SCARAB TO ONE OF HIS STUDENTS?"
"YES. TED KORD. HE WAS AMAZING. HE FOUGHT ALONGSIDE THE JUSTICE LEA--
"BUT THE SCARAB DIDN'T DO ANYTHING FOR HIM, BRO. DUDE DIDN'T HAVE ANY POWERS."
"NO. BUT TED WAS A GENIUS. AN INVENTOR. HE MADE A SHIP, WEAPONS, ALL KINDS OF TECH--"
"BUT HE'S DEAD, RIGHT, JAIME?"
"YEAH. HE'S DEAD."
THE HOME OF THE REYES FAMILY. EL PASO, TEXAS.
I DUNNO, MAN. THAT'S TWO DEAD BLUE BEETLES. MAYBE YOU WANNA BE A DIFFERENT SUPERHERO WHO ISN'T, Y'KNOW, GETTING KILLED ALL THE TIME.
I HATE TO AGREE WITH PACO, BUT HE DOES HAVE A POINT.
IT'S NOT LIKE I CHOSE TO DO IT.
BLUE BEETLE.
JAIME REYES.

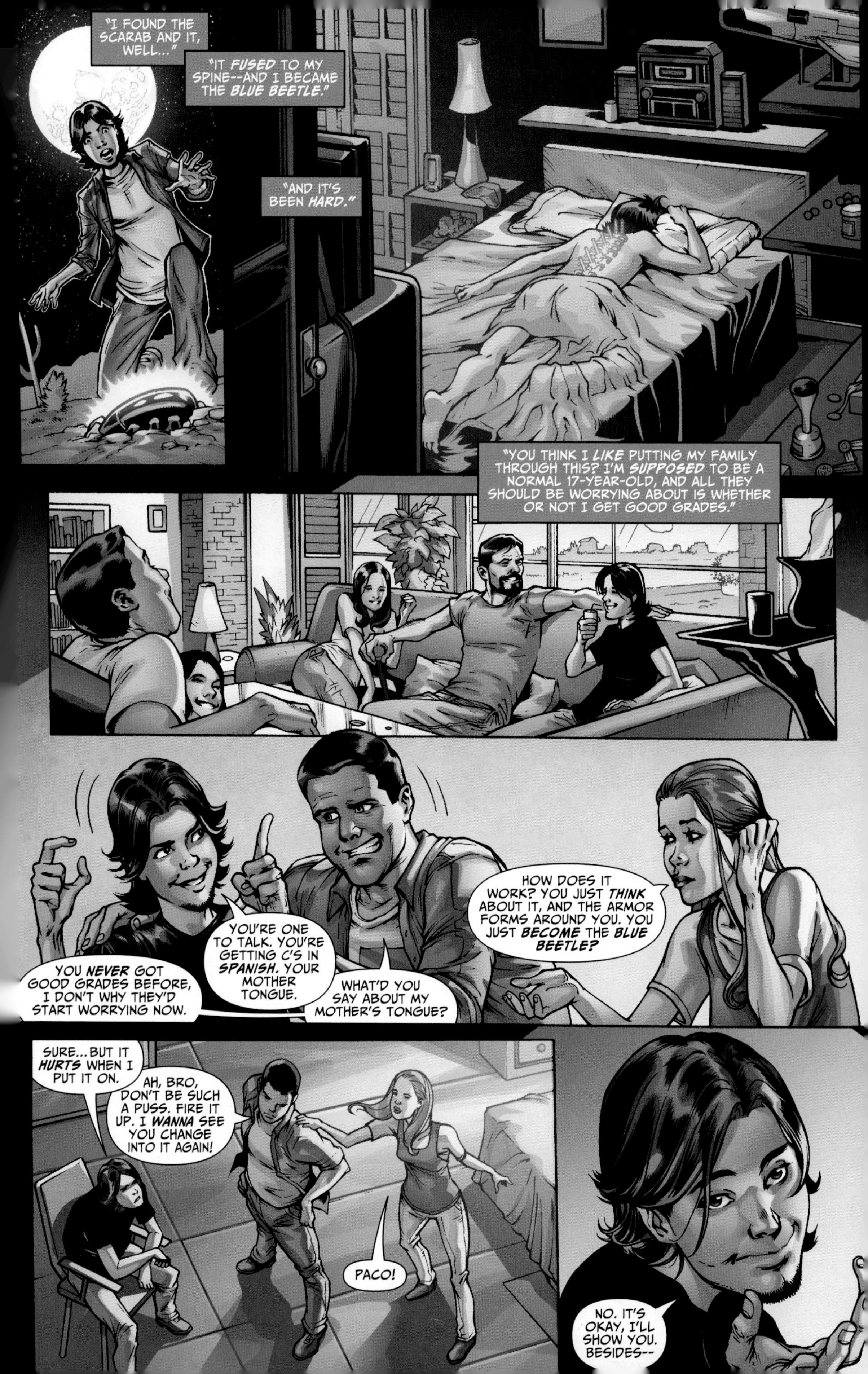
"I FOUND THE SCARAB AND IT, WELL..."
"IT FUSED TO MY SPINE--AND I BECAME THE BLUE BEETLE."
"AND IT'S BEEN HARD."
"YOU THINK I LIKE PUTTING MY FAMILY THROUGH THIS? I'M SUPPOSED TO BE A NORMAL 17-YEAR-OLD, AND ALL THEY SHOULD BE WORRYING ABOUT IS WHETHER OR NOT I GET GOOD GRADES."
YOU NEVER GOT GOOD GRADES BEFORE, I DON'T WHY THEY'D START WORRYING NOW.
YOU'RE ONE TO TALK. YOU'RE GETTING C'S IN SPANISH. YOUR MOTHER TONGUE.
WHAT'D YOU SAY ABOUT MY MOTHER'S TONGUE?
HOW DOES IT WORK? YOU JUST THINK ABOUT IT, AND THE ARMOR FORMS AROUND YOU. YOU JUST BECOME THE BLUE BEETLE?
SURE... BUT IT HURTS WHEN I PUT IT ON.
AH, BRO, DON'T BE SUCH A PUSS. FIRE IT UP. I WANNA SEE YOU CHANGE INTO IT AGAIN!
PACO!
NO. IT'S OKAY, I'LL SHOW YOU. BESIDES--

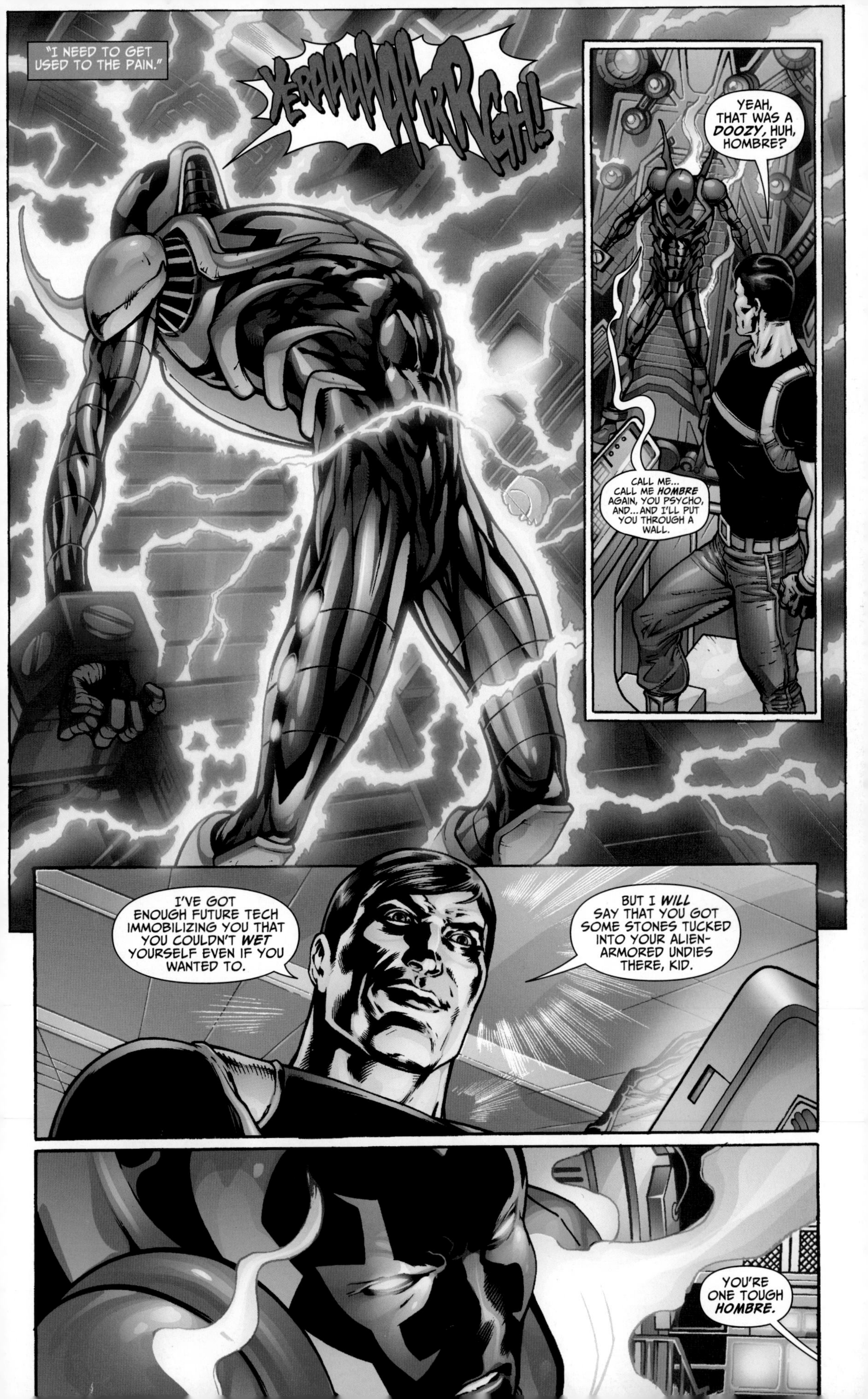
"I NEED TO GET USED TO THE PAIN."
YERAAAAAAAARRRGH!
YEAH, THAT WAS A DOOZY, HUH, HOMBRE?
CALL ME... CALL ME HOMBRE AGAIN, YOU PSYCHO, AND... AND I'LL PUT YOU THROUGH A WALL.
I'VE GOT ENOUGH FUTURE TECH IMMOBILIZING YOU THAT YOU COULDN'T WET YOURSELF EVEN IF YOU WANTED TO.
BUT I WILL SAY THAT YOU GOT SOME STONES TUCKED INTO YOUR ALIEN-ARMORED UNDIES THERE, KID.
YOU'RE ONE TOUGH HOMBRE.

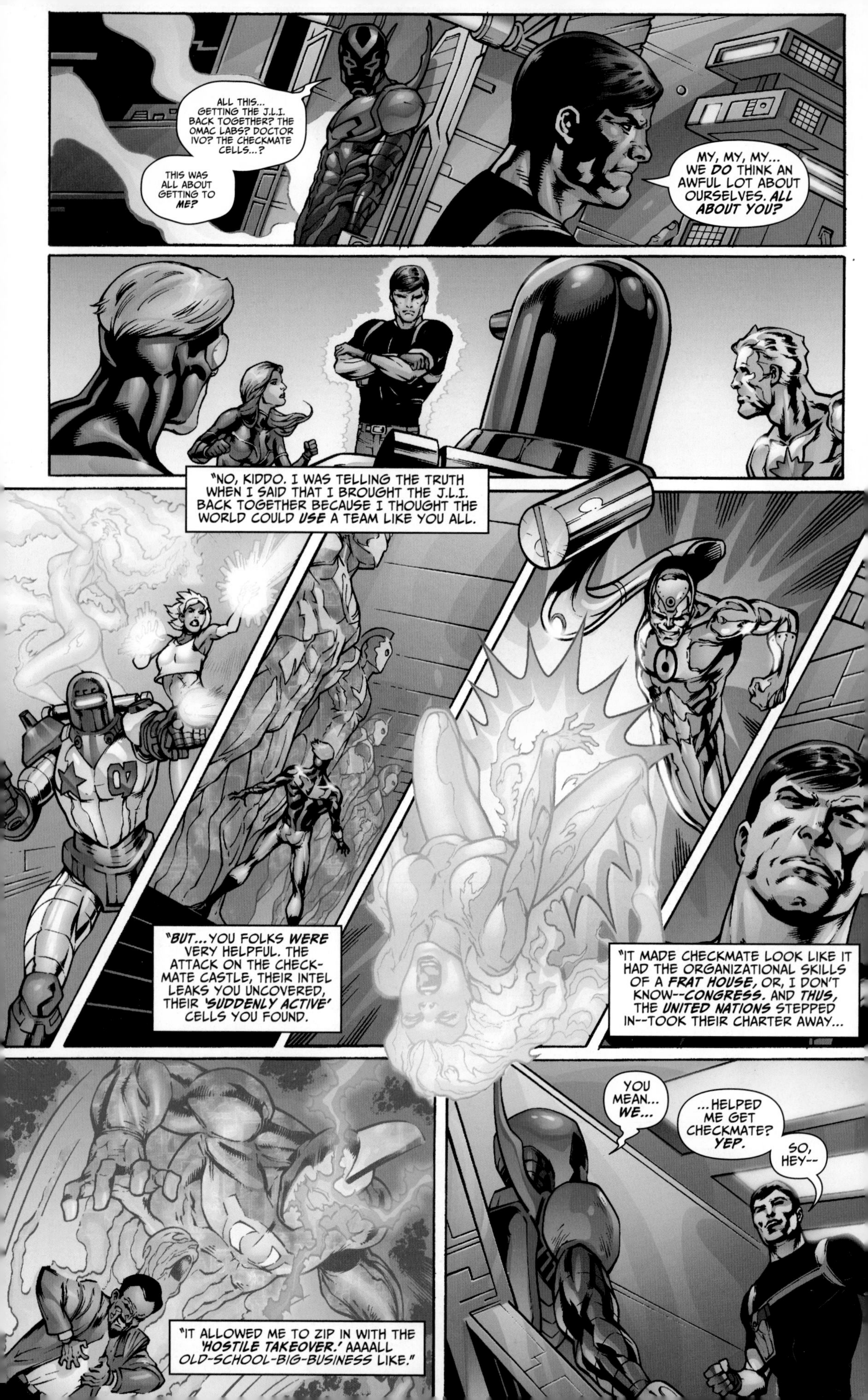
ALL THIS... GETTING THE J.L.I. BACK TOGETHER? THE OMAC LABS? DOCTOR IVO? THE CHECKMATE CELLS...?
THIS WAS ALL ABOUT GETTING TO ME?
MY, MY, MY... WE DO THINK AN AWFUL LOT ABOUT OURSELVES. ALL ABOUT YOU?
"NO, KIDDO. I WAS TELLING THE TRUTH WHEN I SAID THAT I BROUGHT THE J.L.I. BACK TOGETHER BECAUSE I THOUGHT THE WORLD COULD USE A TEAM LIKE YOU ALL.
"BUT...YOU FOLKS WERE VERY HELPFUL. THE ATTACK ON THE CHECK-MATE CASTLE, THEIR INTEL LEAKS YOU UNCOVERED, THEIR 'SUDDENLY ACTIVE' CELLS YOU FOUND.
"IT MADE CHECKMATE LOOK LIKE IT HAD THE ORGANIZATIONAL SKILLS OF A FRAT HOUSE, OR, I DON'T KNOW--CONGRESS. AND THUS, THE UNITED NATIONS STEPPED IN--TOOK THEIR CHARTER AWAY...
"IT ALLOWED ME TO ZIP IN WITH THE 'HOSTILE TAKEOVER.' AAAALL OLD-SCHOOL-BIG-BUSINESS LIKE."
YOU MEAN... WE...
...HELPED ME GET CHECKMATE? YEP.
SO, HEY--

THANK YOU!

KERAAAAHRRGH!

T-ZAAACK

I'VE GOT IT! I THINK I'VE *FINALLY* LOCATED WHAT COULD BE DEFINED AS THE ARMOR'S *NERVOUS* SYSTEM.

HURTS...HURTS SO BAD...NEVER HURT SO MUCH IN MY WHOLE--

!@)--0+-~'!

WHAT? WHAT WAS--

!@#$%&*

HEY, IS THAT YOU? SCARAB, YOU THERE? YOU AWAKE? YOU--

1 POINT 1 POINT 1 POINT 1 POINT--SYSTEM REBOOT ENGAGED--

OH, I NEVER THOUGHT I'D MISS THE CREEPY LIFELESS MONO-TONE OF YOUR VOICE--HEY--

I CAN MOVE...MY FINGER-- OR AT LEAST--GOD, FEELS LIKE A MILLIMETER OF--

DUDE! CAN WE SEND A SIGNAL?

NEGATIVE. REBOOT IN PROCESS.

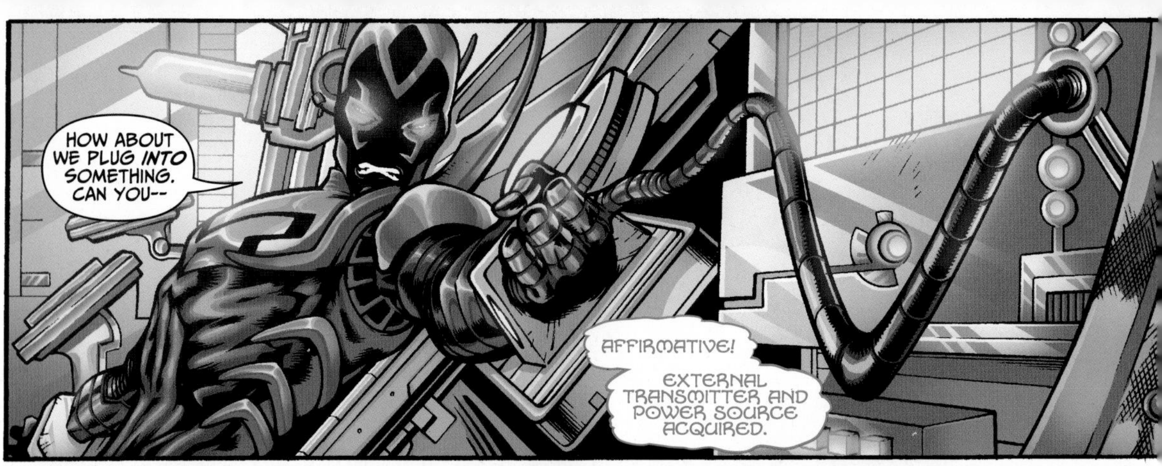
HOW ABOUT WE PLUG *INTO* SOMETHING. CAN YOU--
AFFIRMATIVE!
EXTERNAL TRANSMITTER AND POWER SOURCE ACQUIRED.

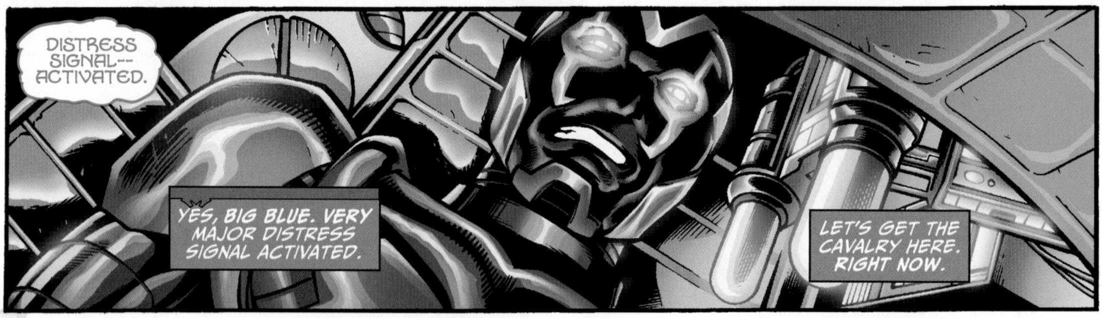
DISTRESS SIGNAL-- ACTIVATED.
YES, BIG BLUE. VERY MAJOR DISTRESS SIGNAL ACTIVATED.
LET'S GET THE CAVALRY HERE. **RIGHT NOW.**

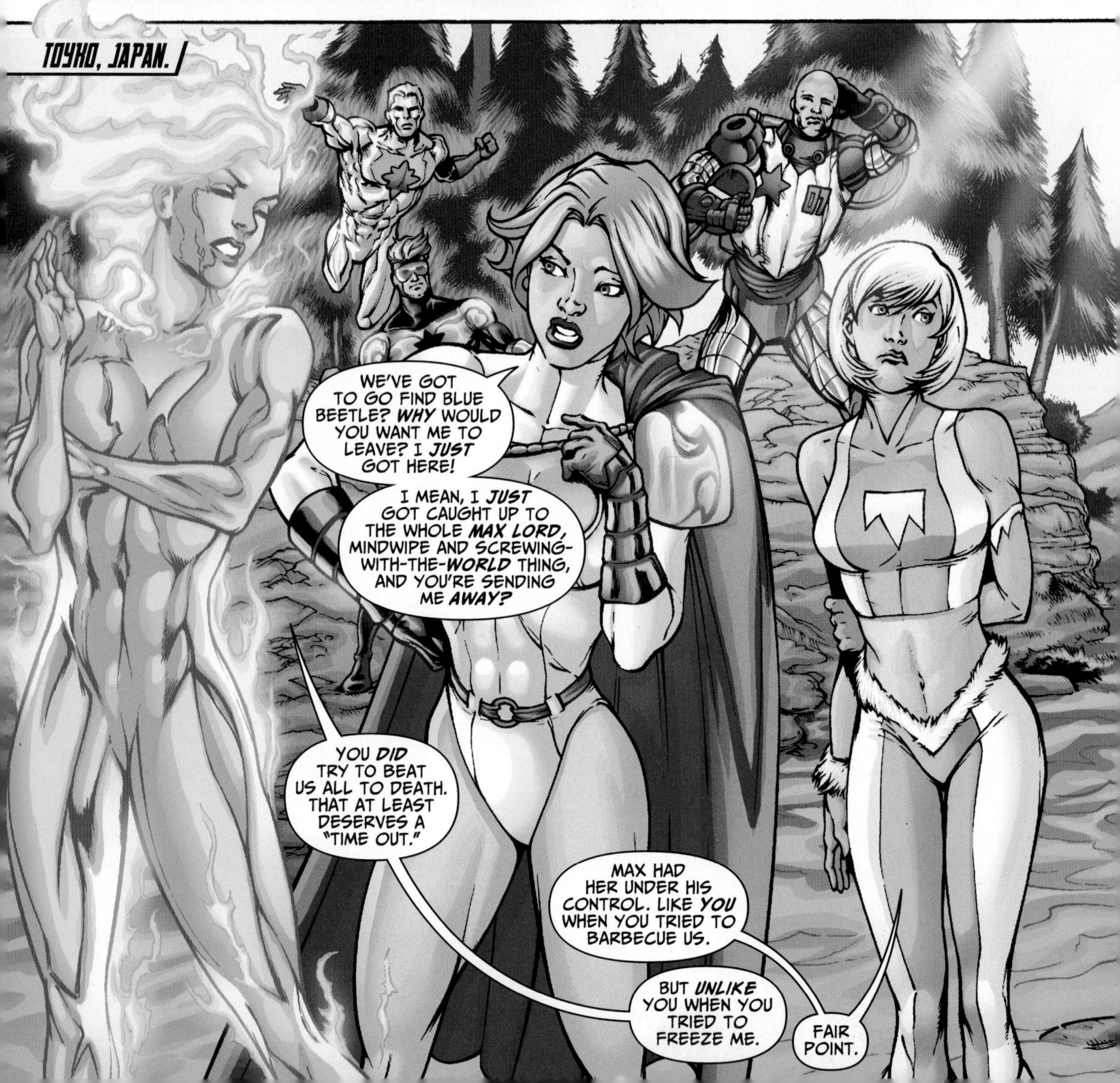
TOYKO, JAPAN.
WE'VE GOT TO GO FIND BLUE BEETLE? *WHY* WOULD YOU WANT ME TO LEAVE? I *JUST* GOT HERE!
I MEAN, I *JUST* GOT CAUGHT UP TO THE WHOLE *MAX LORD*, MINDWIPE AND SCREWING-WITH-THE-*WORLD* THING, AND YOU'RE SENDING ME *AWAY?*
YOU *DID* TRY TO BEAT US ALL TO DEATH. THAT AT LEAST DESERVES A "TIME OUT."
MAX HAD HER UNDER HIS CONTROL. LIKE *YOU* WHEN YOU TRIED TO BARBECUE US.
BUT *UNLIKE* YOU WHEN YOU TRIED TO FREEZE ME.
FAIR POINT.

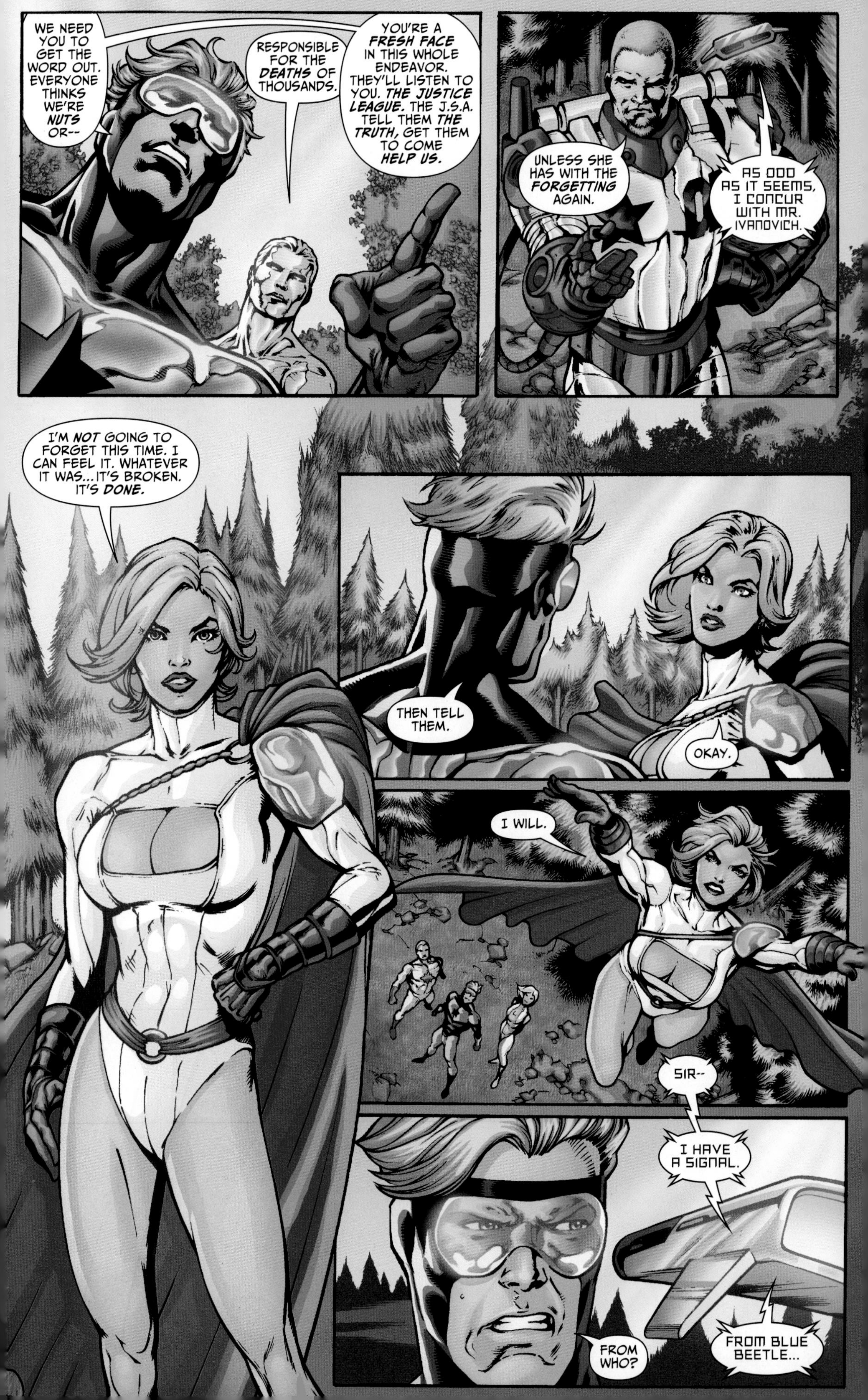
WE NEED YOU TO GET THE WORD OUT. EVERYONE THINKS WE'RE NUTS OR--
RESPONSIBLE FOR THE DEATHS OF THOUSANDS.
YOU'RE A FRESH FACE IN THIS WHOLE ENDEAVOR. THEY'LL LISTEN TO YOU. THE JUSTICE LEAGUE. THE J.S.A. TELL THEM THE TRUTH, GET THEM TO COME HELP US.
UNLESS SHE HAS WITH THE FORGETTING AGAIN.
AS ODD AS IT SEEMS, I CONCUR WITH MR. IVANOVICH.
I'M NOT GOING TO FORGET THIS TIME. I CAN FEEL IT. WHATEVER IT WAS...IT'S BROKEN. IT'S DONE.
THEN TELL THEM.
OKAY.
I WILL.
SIR--
I HAVE A SIGNAL.
FROM WHO?
FROM BLUE BEETLE...

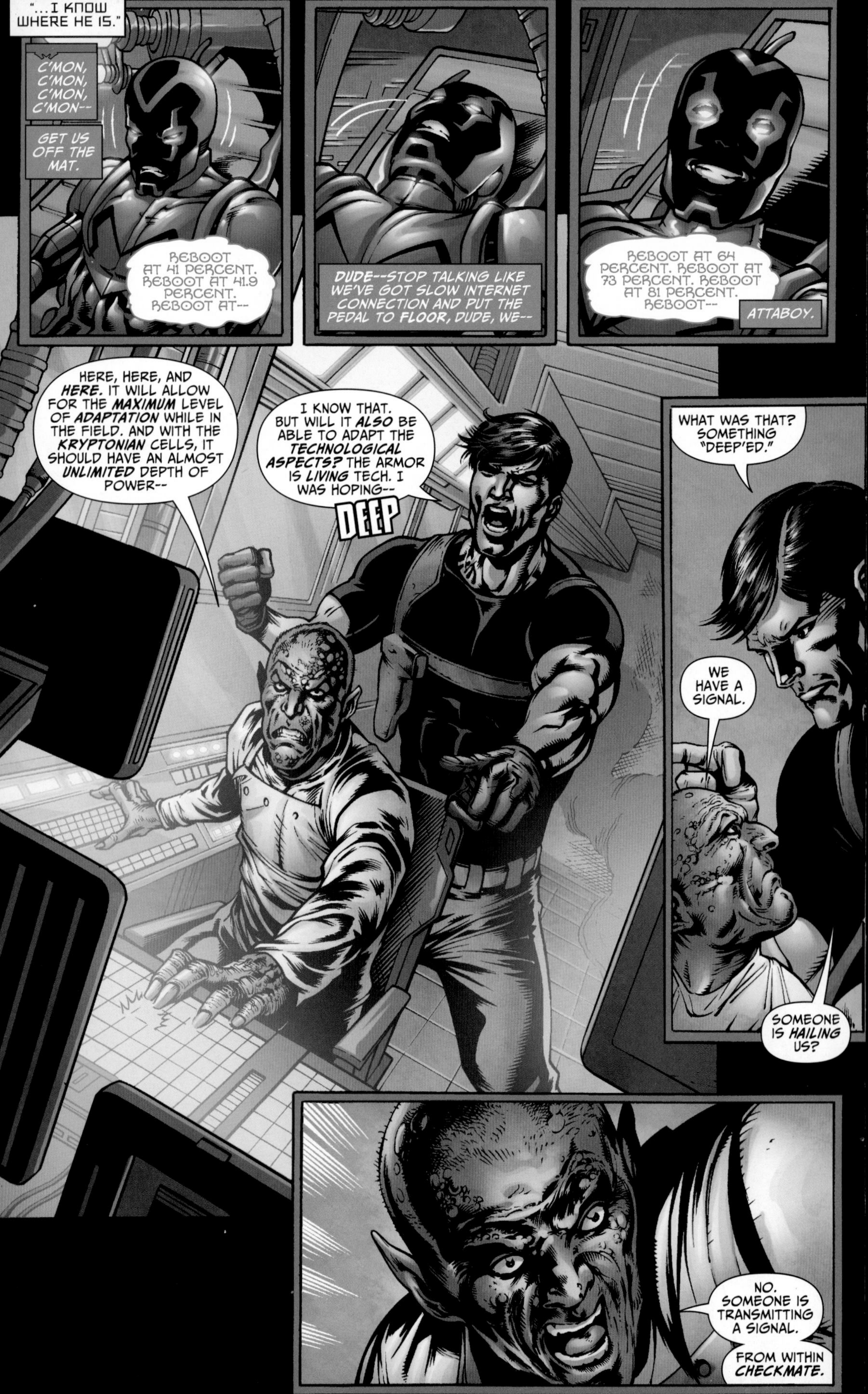
"...I KNOW WHERE HE IS."
C'MON, C'MON, C'MON, C'MON--
GET US OFF THE MAT.
REBOOT AT 41 PERCENT. REBOOT AT 41.9 PERCENT. REBOOT AT--
DUDE--STOP TALKING LIKE WE'VE GOT SLOW INTERNET CONNECTION AND PUT THE PEDAL TO FLOOR, DUDE, WE--
REBOOT AT 64 PERCENT. REBOOT AT 73 PERCENT. REBOOT AT 81 PERCENT. REBOOT--
ATTABOY.
HERE, HERE, AND HERE. IT WILL ALLOW FOR THE MAXIMUM LEVEL OF ADAPTATION WHILE IN THE FIELD. AND WITH THE KRYPTONIAN CELLS, IT SHOULD HAVE AN ALMOST UNLIMITED DEPTH OF POWER--
I KNOW THAT. BUT WILL IT ALSO BE ABLE TO ADAPT THE TECHNOLOGICAL ASPECTS? THE ARMOR IS LIVING TECH. I WAS HOPING--
DEEP
WHAT WAS THAT? SOMETHING "DEEP'ED."
WE HAVE A SIGNAL.
SOMEONE IS HAILING US?
NO. SOMEONE IS TRANSMITTING A SIGNAL.
FROM WITHIN CHECKMATE.

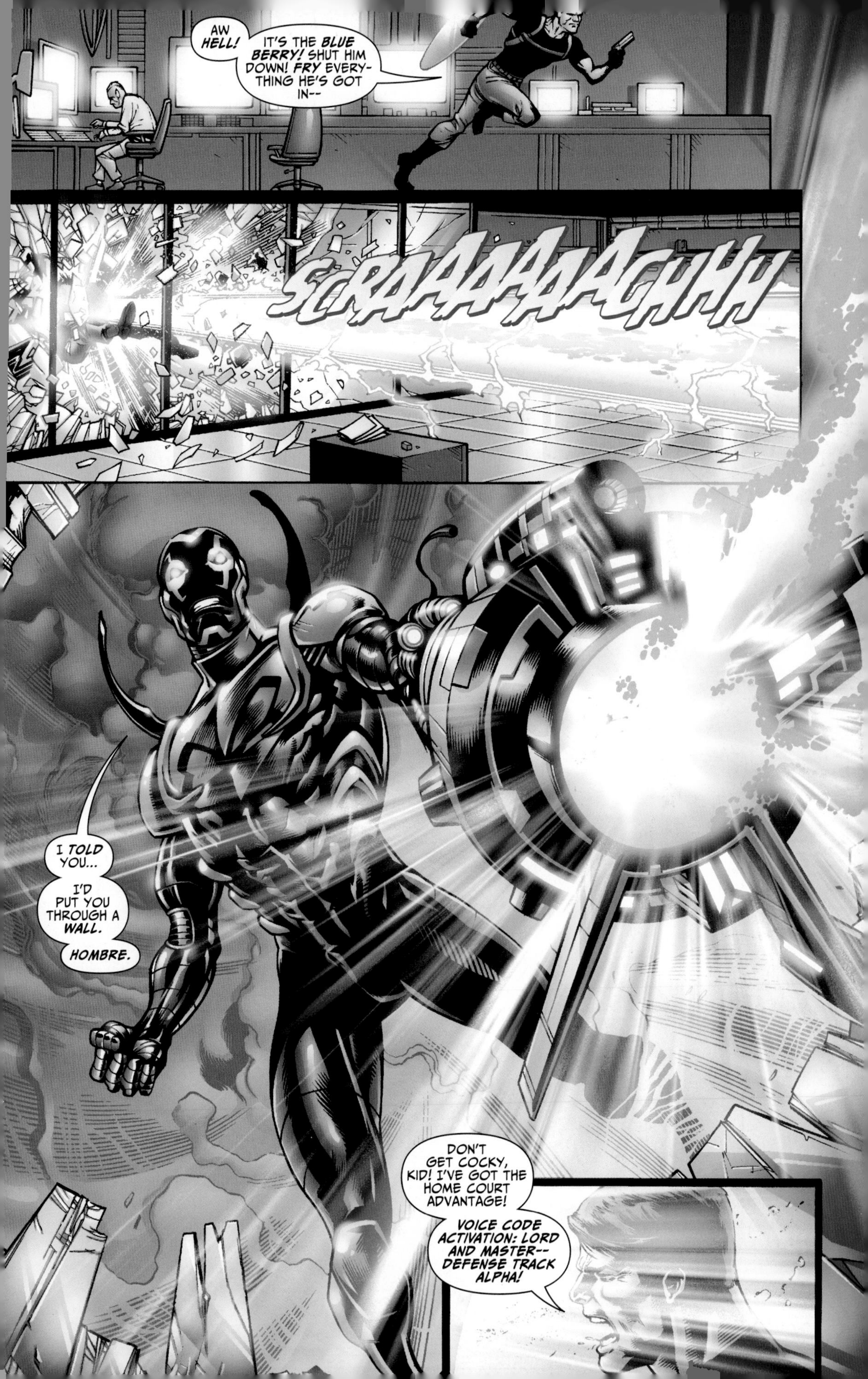
AW HELL!
IT'S THE BLUE BERRY! SHUT HIM DOWN! FRY EVERYTHING HE'S GOT IN--
SCRAAAAAAACHHH
I TOLD YOU...
I'D PUT YOU THROUGH A WALL.
HOMBRE.
DON'T GET COCKY, KID! I'VE GOT THE HOME COURT ADVANTAGE!
VOICE CODE ACTIVATION: LORD AND MASTER-- DEFENSE TRACK ALPHA!

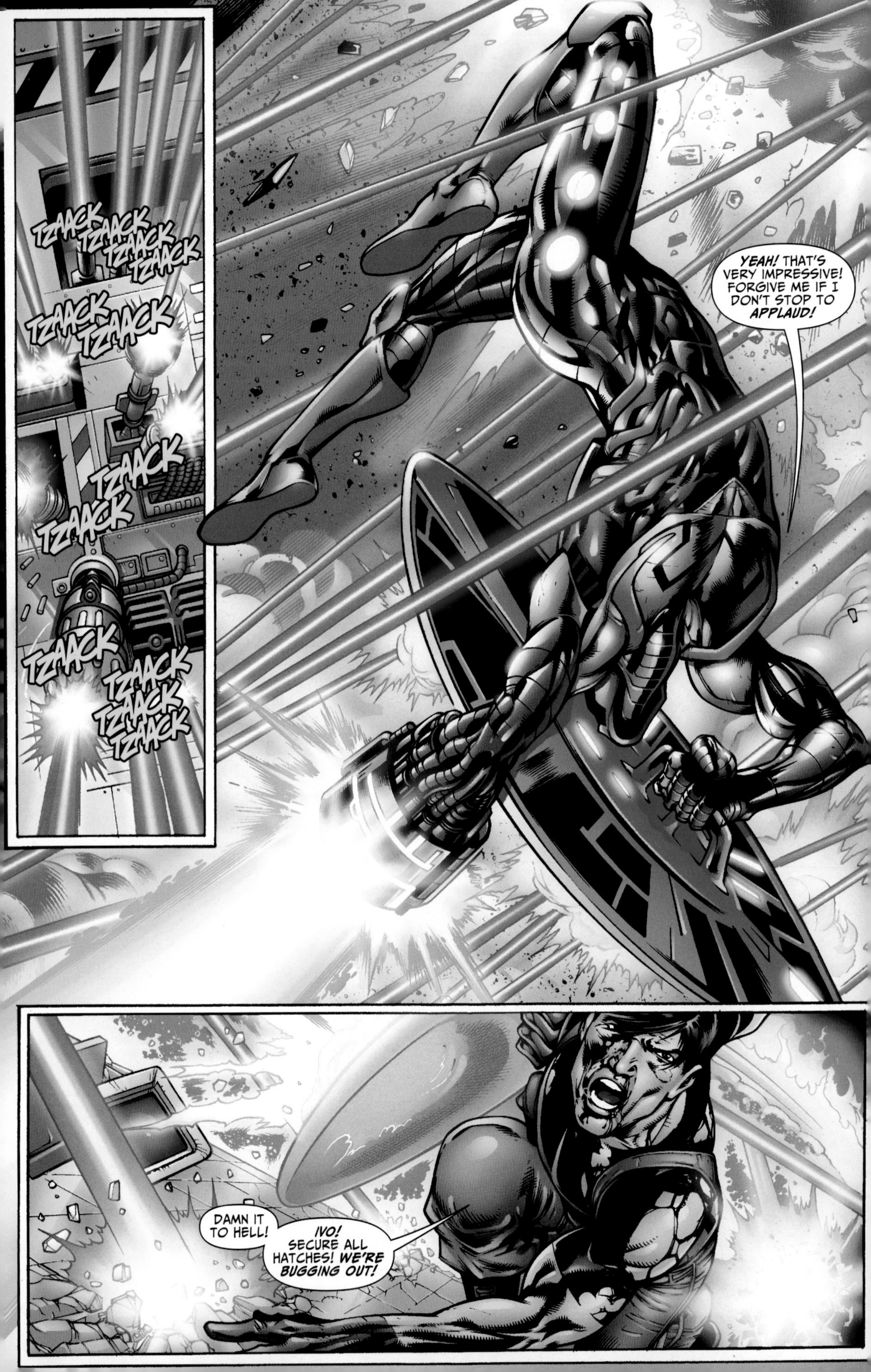
TZAACK TZAACK TZAACK TZAACK
TZAACK TZAACK
TZAACK TZAACK
TZAACK TZAACK TZAACK TZAACK
YEAH! THAT'S VERY IMPRESSIVE! FORGIVE ME IF I DON'T STOP TO APPLAUD!
DAMN IT TO HELL!
IVO! SECURE ALL HATCHES! WE'RE BUGGING OUT!

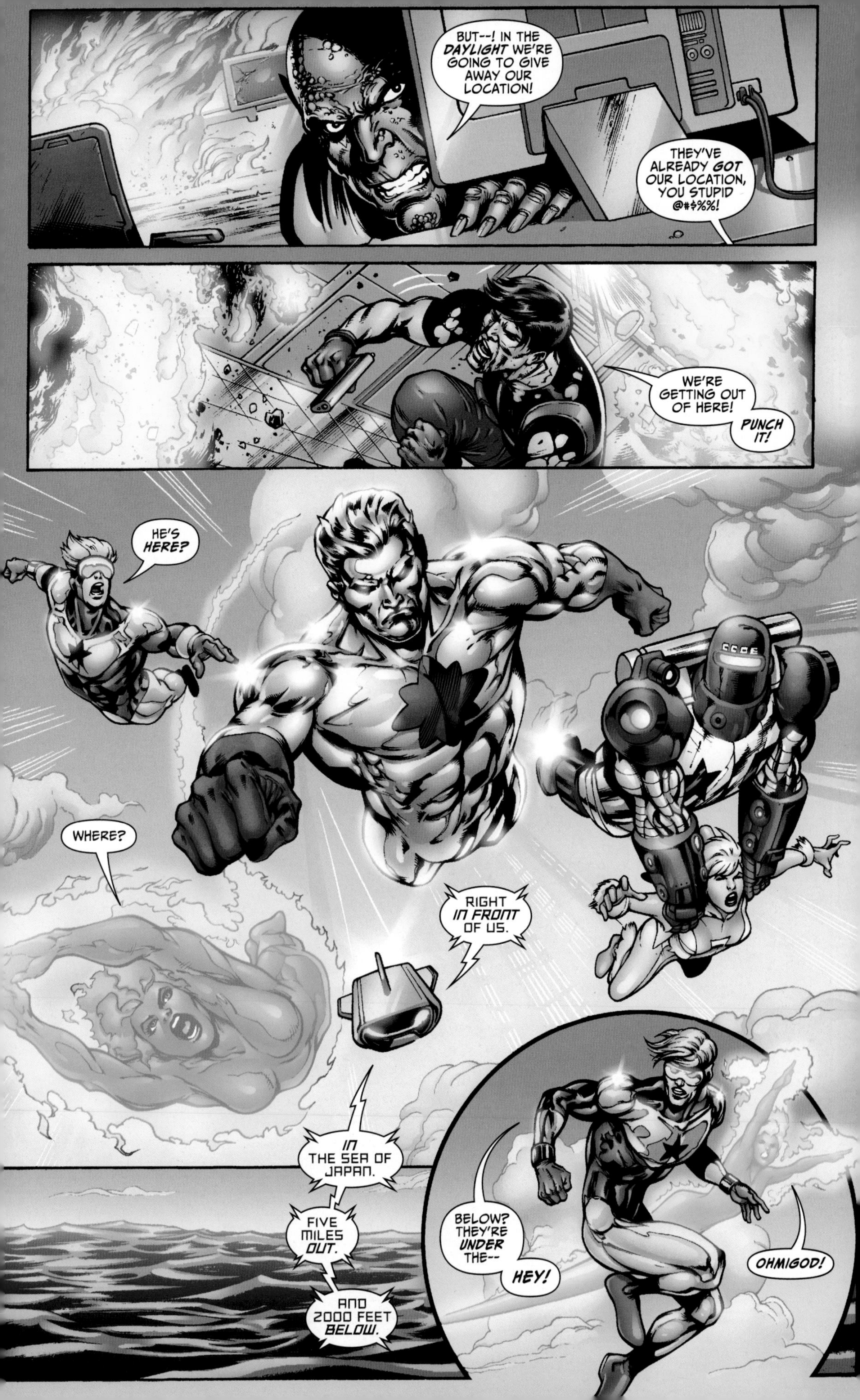
BUT--! IN THE DAYLIGHT WE'RE GOING TO GIVE AWAY OUR LOCATION!
THEY'VE ALREADY GOT OUR LOCATION, YOU STUPID @#$%%!
WE'RE GETTING OUT OF HERE!
PUNCH IT!
HE'S HERE?
WHERE?
RIGHT IN FRONT OF US.
IN THE SEA OF JAPAN.
FIVE MILES OUT.
AND 2000 FEET BELOW.
BELOW? THEY'RE UNDER THE--
HEY!
OHMIGOD!

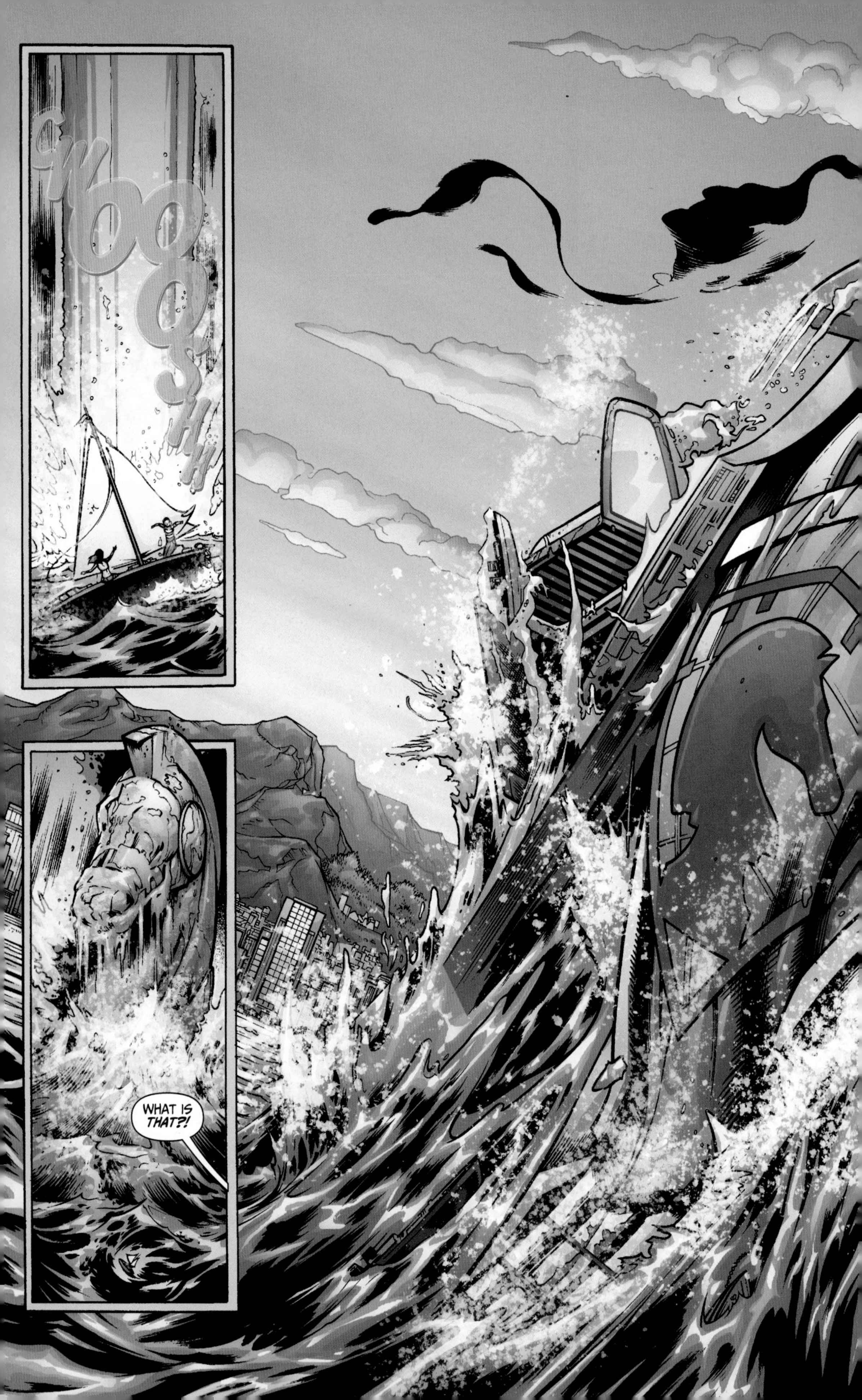
GWOOOSHHH
WHAT IS THAT?!

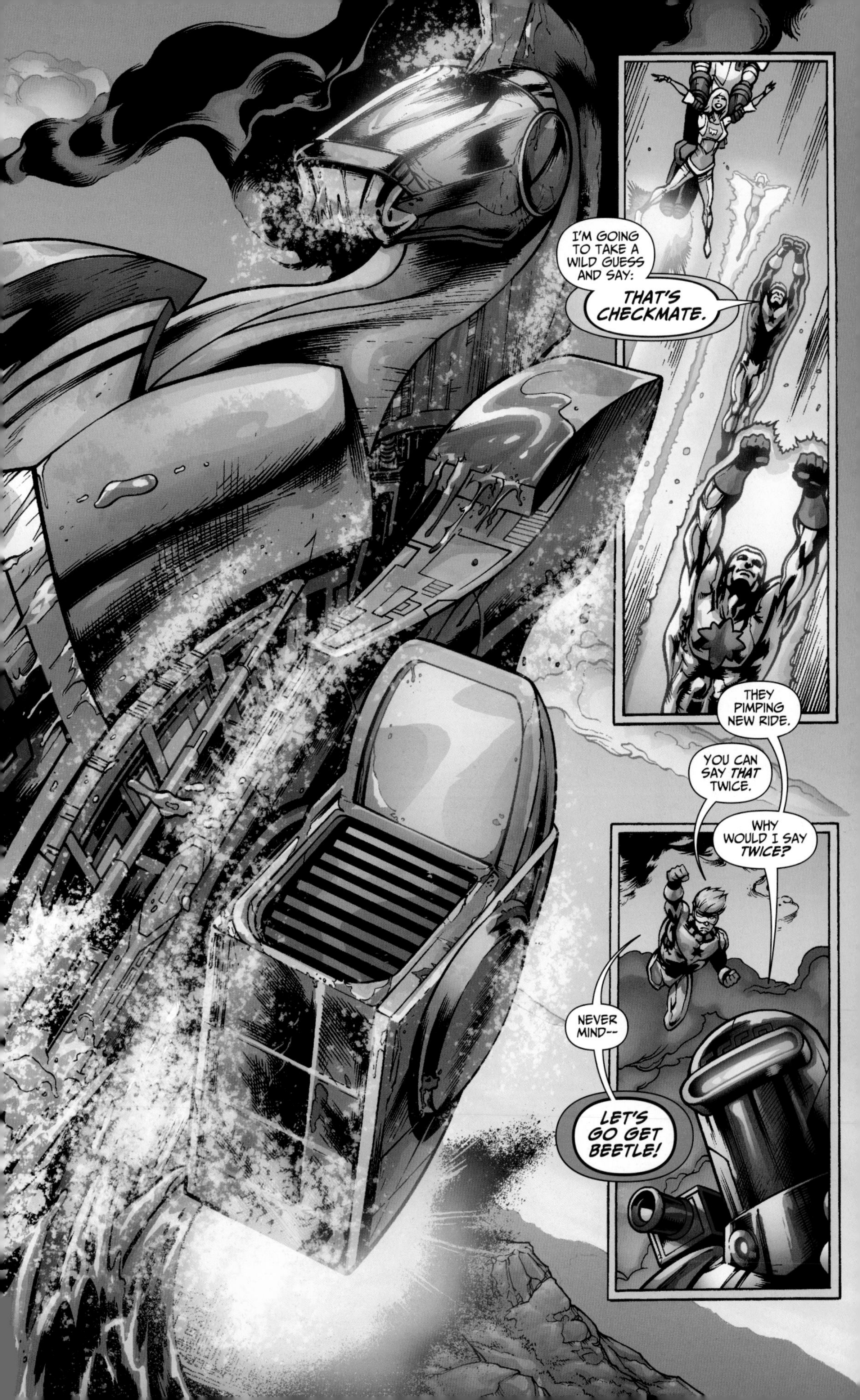

I'M GOING TO TAKE A WILD GUESS AND SAY:
THAT'S CHECKMATE.
THEY PIMPING NEW RIDE.
YOU CAN SAY THAT TWICE.
WHY WOULD I SAY TWICE?
NEVER MIND--
LET'S GO GET BEETLE!

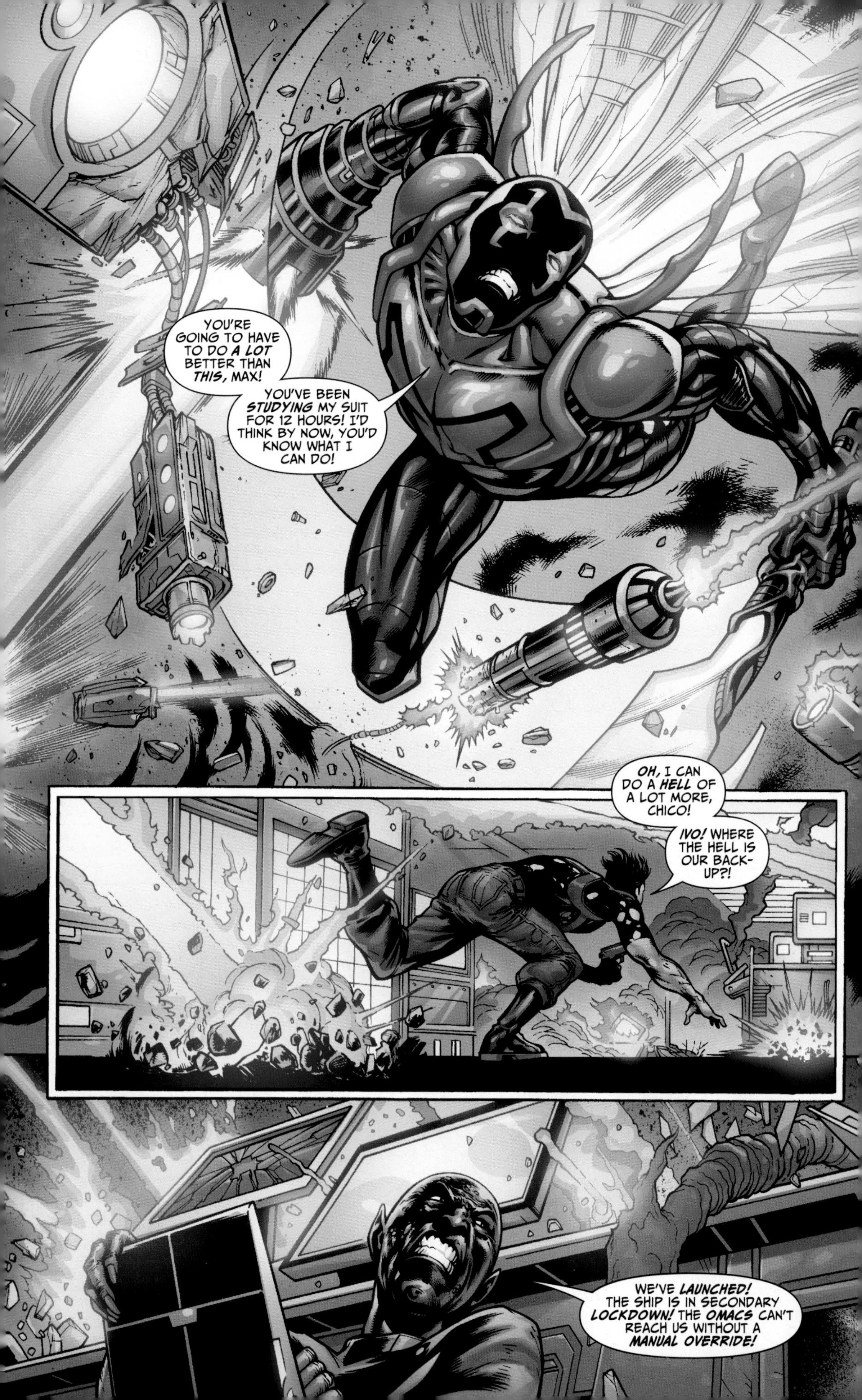
YOU'RE GOING TO HAVE TO DO A LOT BETTER THAN THIS, MAX!
YOU'VE BEEN STUDYING MY SUIT FOR 12 HOURS! I'D THINK BY NOW, YOU'D KNOW WHAT I CAN DO!
OH, I CAN DO A HELL OF A LOT MORE, CHICO!
IVO! WHERE THE HELL IS OUR BACK-UP?!
WE'VE LAUNCHED! THE SHIP IS IN SECONDARY LOCKDOWN! THE OMACS CAN'T REACH US WITHOUT A MANUAL OVERRIDE!

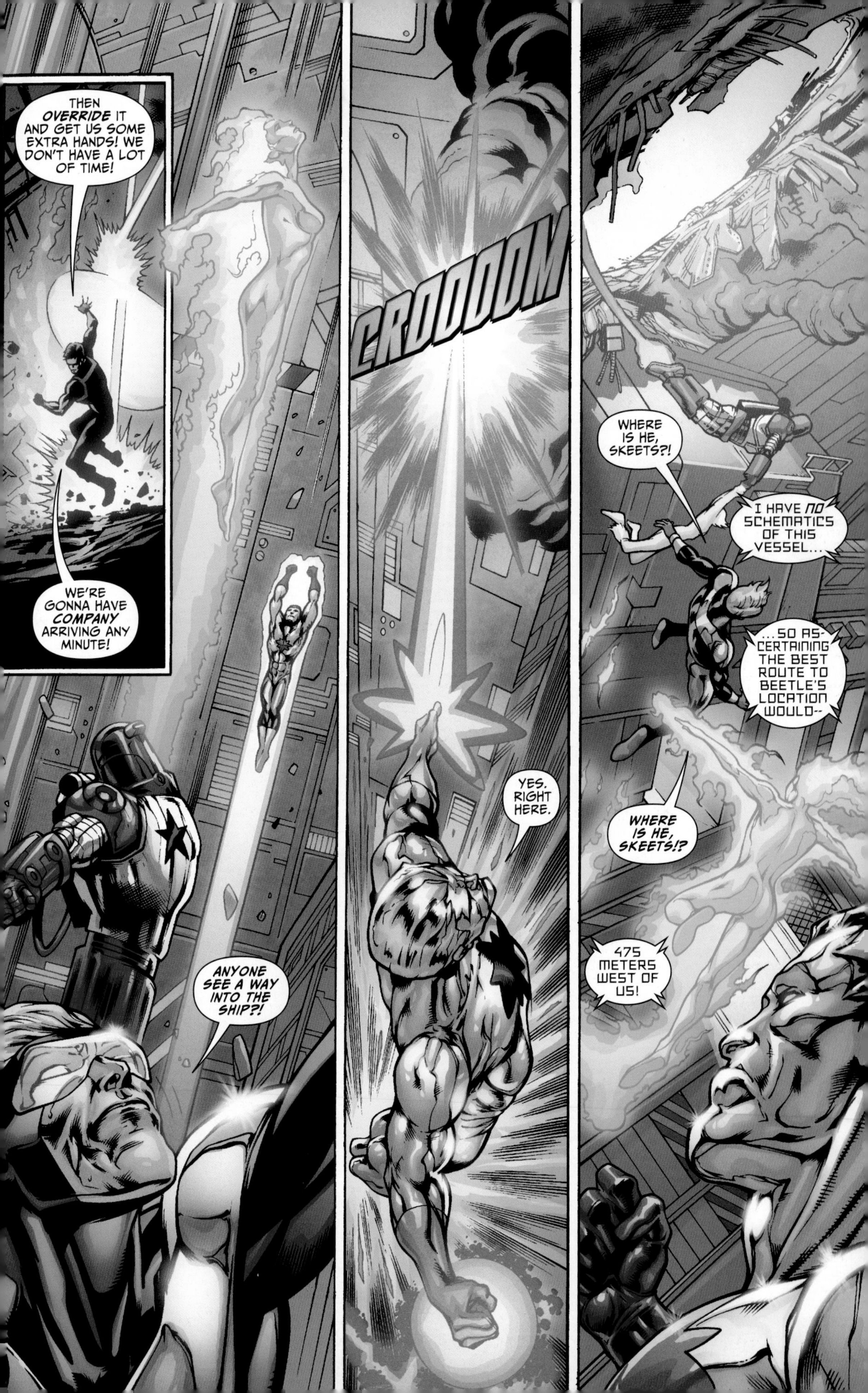
THEN OVERRIDE IT AND GET US SOME EXTRA HANDS! WE DON'T HAVE A LOT OF TIME!
WE'RE GONNA HAVE COMPANY ARRIVING ANY MINUTE!
ANYONE SEE A WAY INTO THE SHIP?!
CROOOOM
YES. RIGHT HERE.
WHERE IS HE, SKEETS?!
I HAVE NO SCHEMATICS OF THIS VESSEL...
...SO ASCERTAINING THE BEST ROUTE TO BEETLE'S LOCATION WOULD--
WHERE IS HE, SKEETS!?
475 METERS WEST OF US!

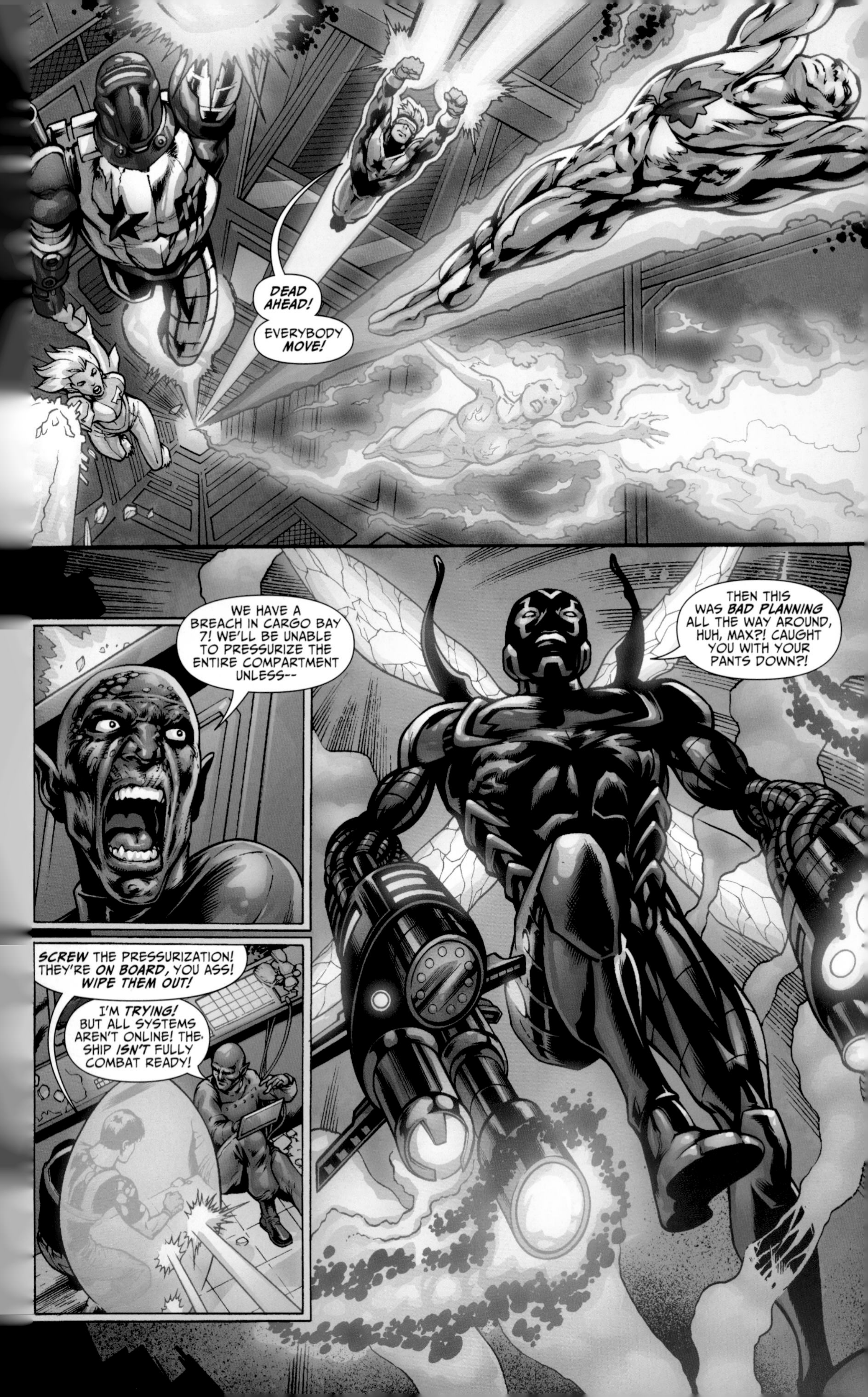
DEAD AHEAD!
EVERYBODY MOVE!
WE HAVE A BREACH IN CARGO BAY 7! WE'LL BE UNABLE TO PRESSURIZE THE ENTIRE COMPARTMENT UNLESS--
SCREW THE PRESSURIZATION! THEY'RE ON BOARD, YOU ASS! WIPE THEM OUT!
I'M TRYING! BUT ALL SYSTEMS AREN'T ONLINE! THE SHIP ISN'T FULLY COMBAT READY!
THEN THIS WAS BAD PLANNING ALL THE WAY AROUND, HUH, MAX?! CAUGHT YOU WITH YOUR PANTS DOWN?!

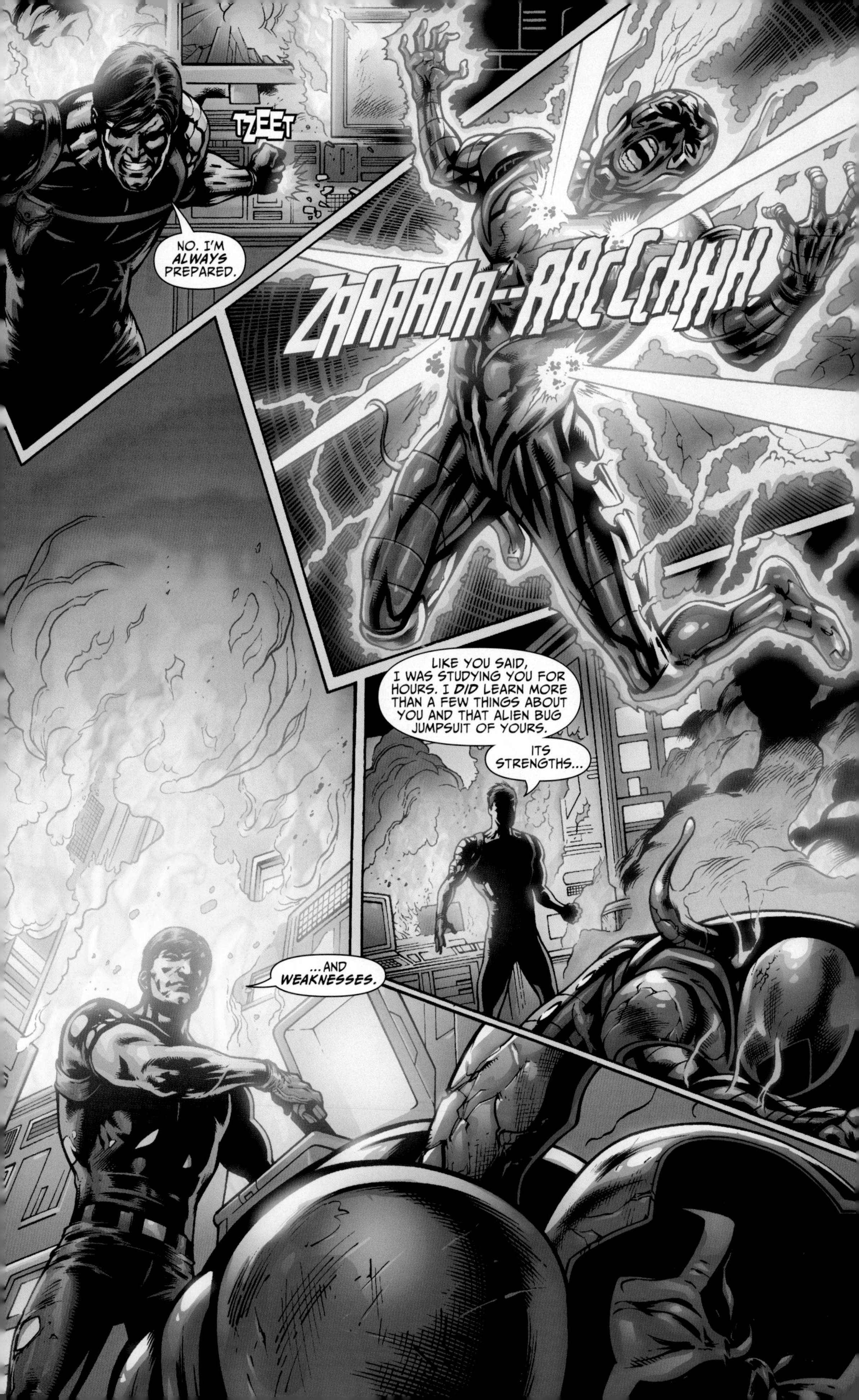
TZEET
NO. I'M ALWAYS PREPARED.
ZAAAAAA-AACCCHHH
LIKE YOU SAID, I WAS STUDYING YOU FOR HOURS. I DID LEARN MORE THAN A FEW THINGS ABOUT YOU AND THAT ALIEN BUG JUMPSUIT OF YOURS.
ITS STRENGTHS...
...AND WEAKNESSES.

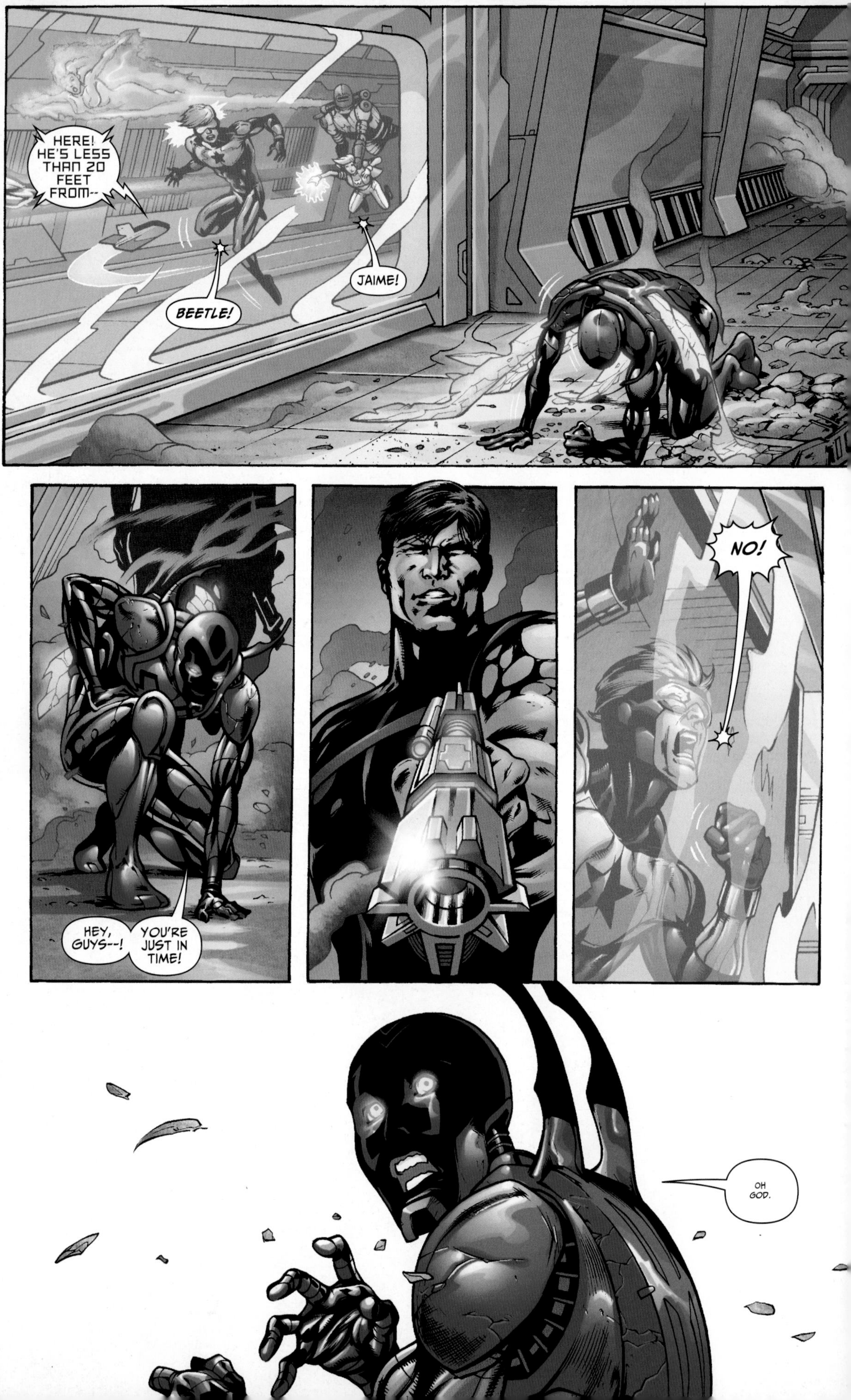

HERE! HE'S LESS THAN 20 FEET FROM--
BEETLE!
JAIME!
HEY, GUYS--!
YOU'RE JUST IN TIME!
NO!
OH GOD.

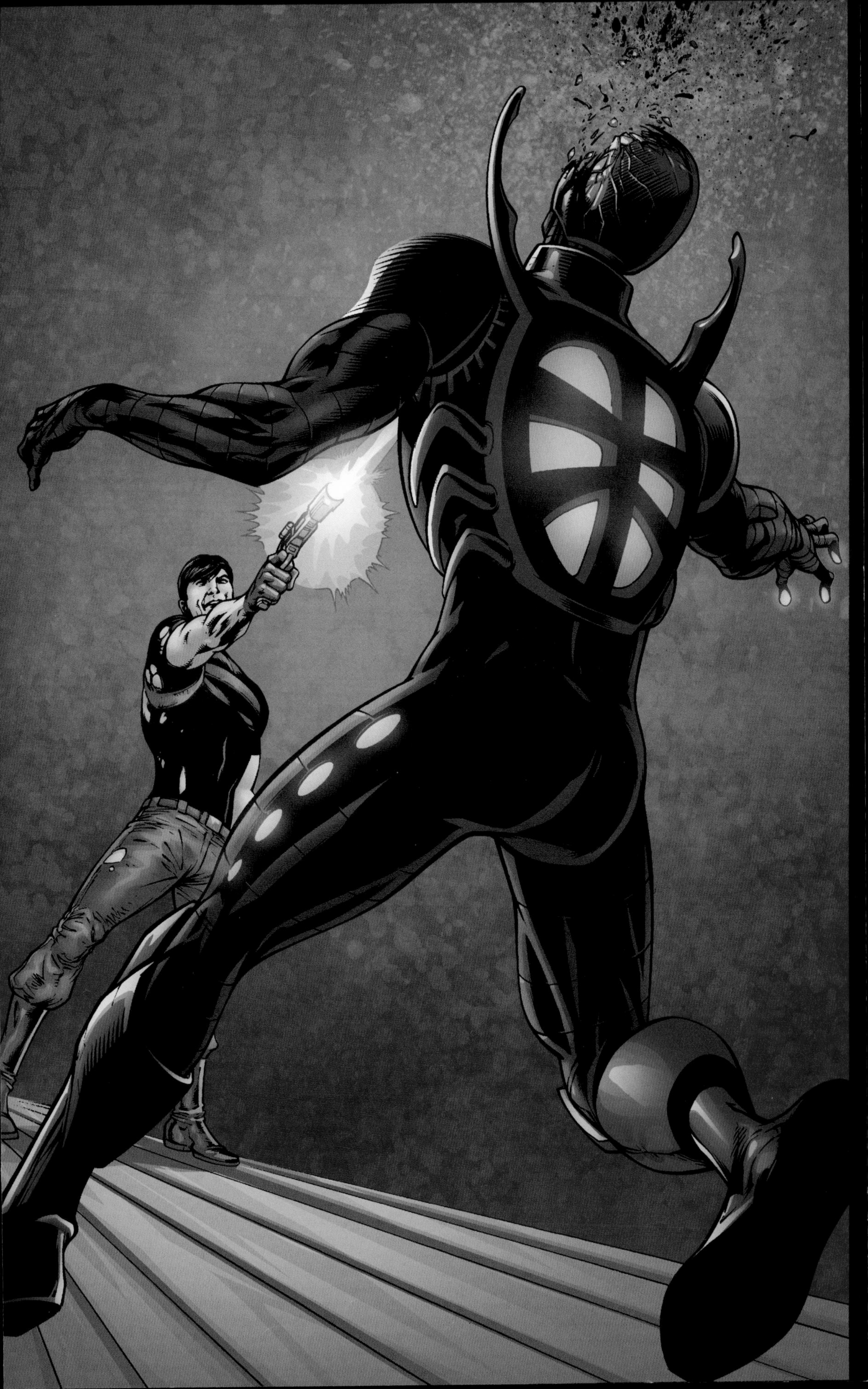

JAIME!

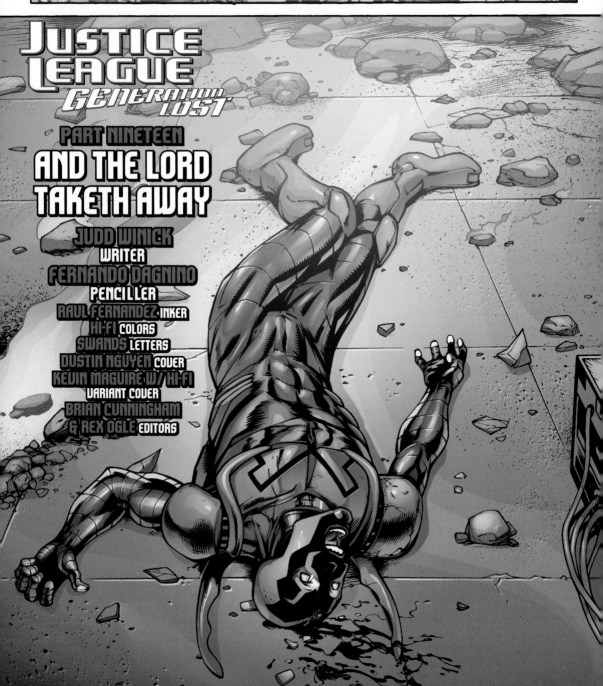

JUSTICE LEAGUE
GENERATION LOST

PART NINETEEN
AND THE LORD TAKETH AWAY

JUDD WINICK
WRITER

FERNANDO DAGNINO
PENCILLER

RAUL FERNANDEZ INKER

HI-FI COLORS

SWANDS LETTERS

DUSTIN NGUYEN COVER

KEVIN MAGUIRE W/ HI-FI
VARIANT COVER

BRIAN CUNNINGHAM
& REX OGLE EDITORS

Cover by Dustin Nguyen

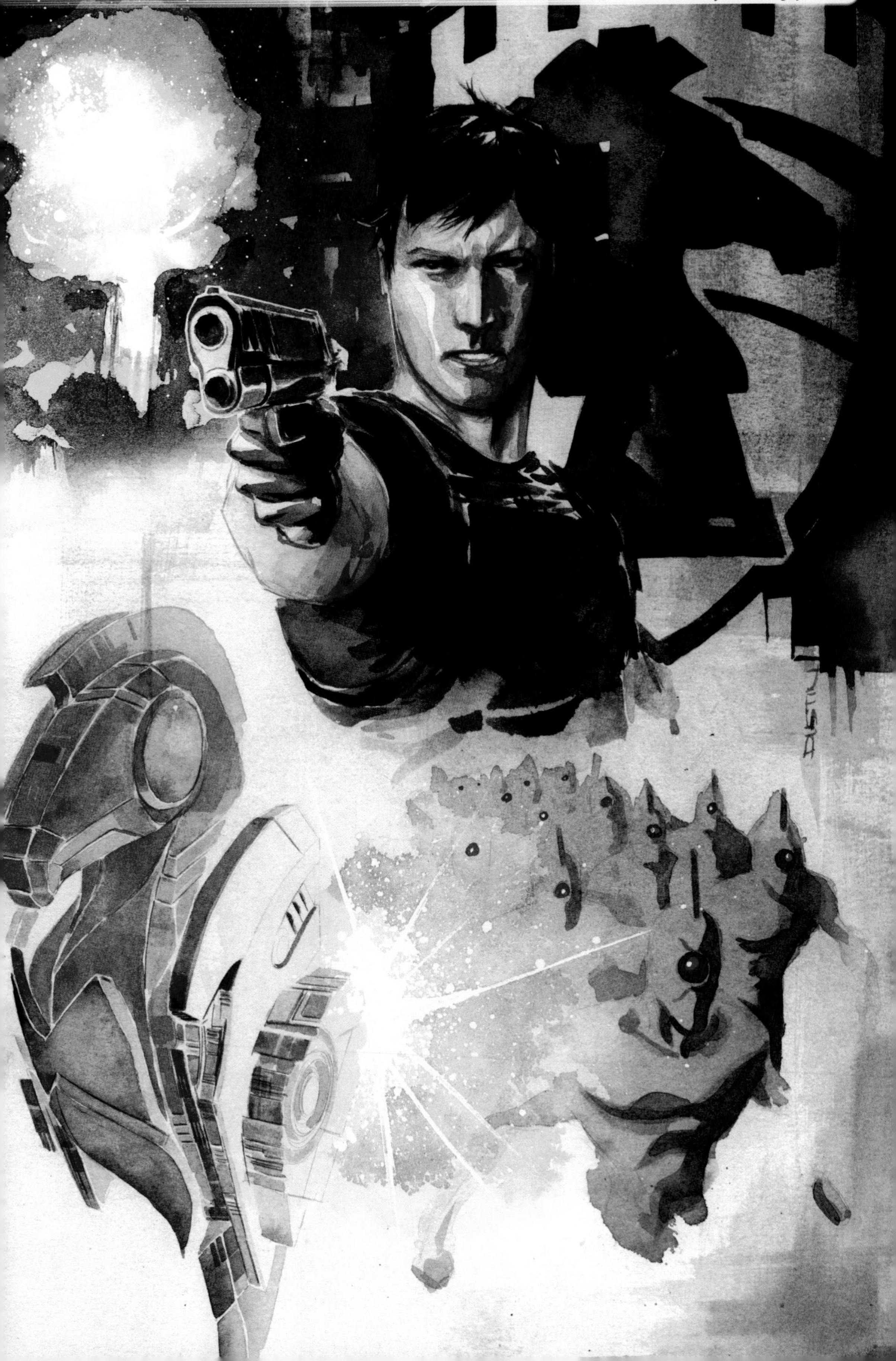

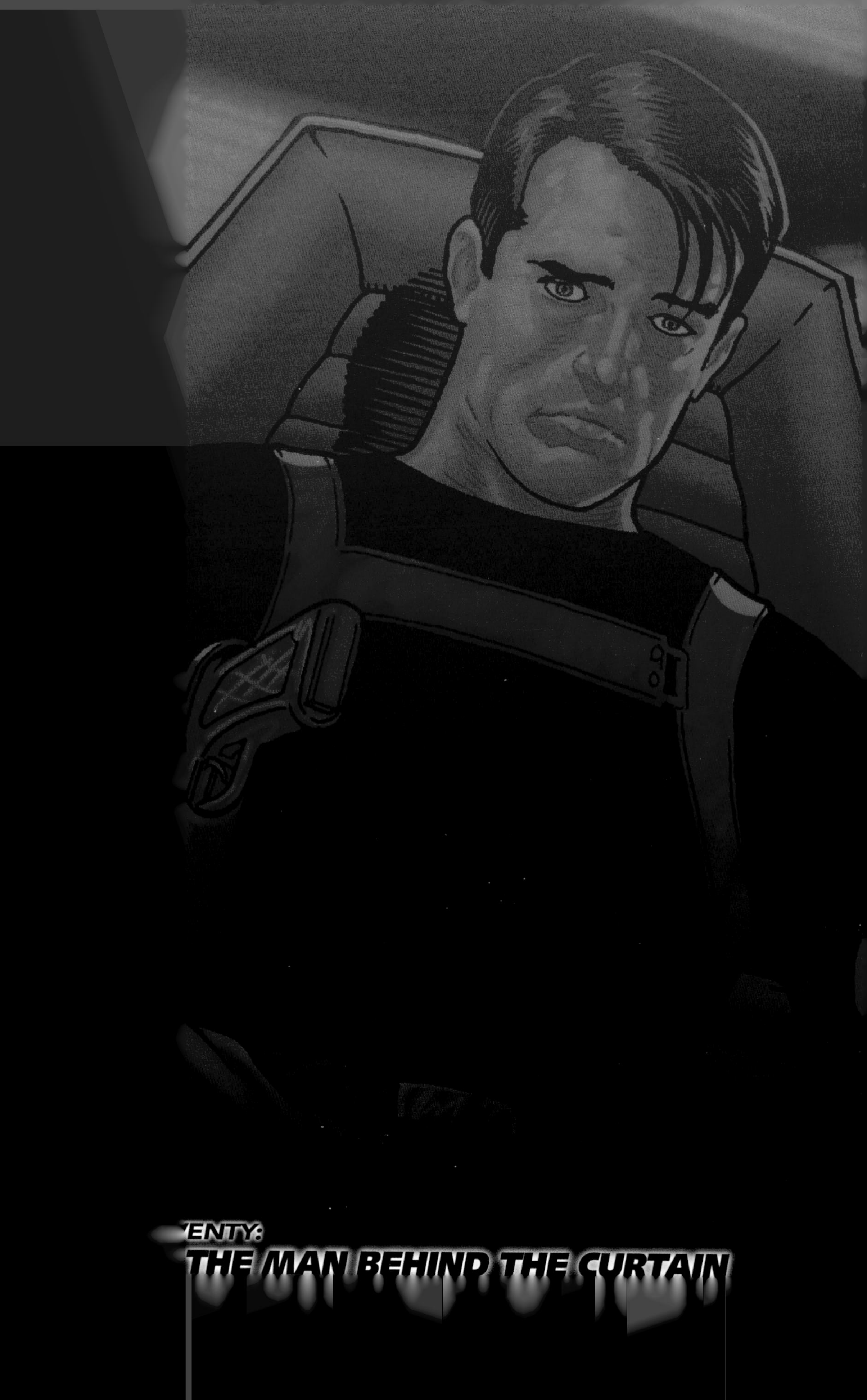

ENTY:
THE MAN BEHIND THE CURTAIN

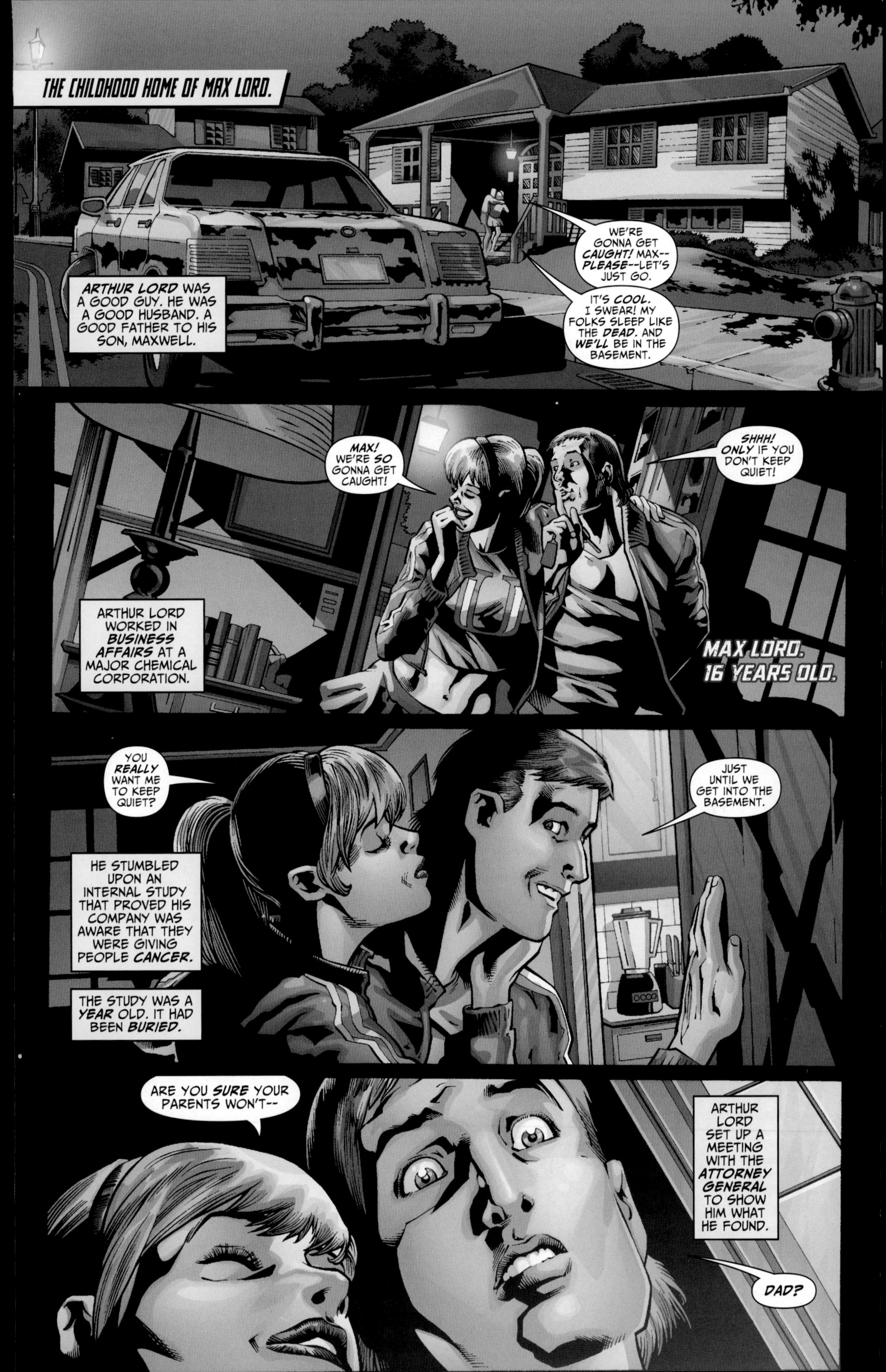
THE CHILDHOOD HOME OF MAX LORD.
WE'RE GONNA GET CAUGHT! MAX-- PLEASE--LET'S JUST GO.
ARTHUR LORD WAS A GOOD GUY. HE WAS A GOOD HUSBAND. A GOOD FATHER TO HIS SON, MAXWELL.
IT'S COOL. I SWEAR! MY FOLKS SLEEP LIKE THE DEAD. AND WE'LL BE IN THE BASEMENT.
MAX! WE'RE SO GONNA GET CAUGHT!
SHHH! ONLY IF YOU DON'T KEEP QUIET!
ARTHUR LORD WORKED IN BUSINESS AFFAIRS AT A MAJOR CHEMICAL CORPORATION.
MAX LORD. 16 YEARS OLD.
YOU REALLY WANT ME TO KEEP QUIET?
JUST UNTIL WE GET INTO THE BASEMENT.
HE STUMBLED UPON AN INTERNAL STUDY THAT PROVED HIS COMPANY WAS AWARE THAT THEY WERE GIVING PEOPLE CANCER.
THE STUDY WAS A YEAR OLD. IT HAD BEEN BURIED.
ARE YOU SURE YOUR PARENTS WON'T--
ARTHUR LORD SET UP A MEETING WITH THE ATTORNEY GENERAL TO SHOW HIM WHAT HE FOUND.
DAD?

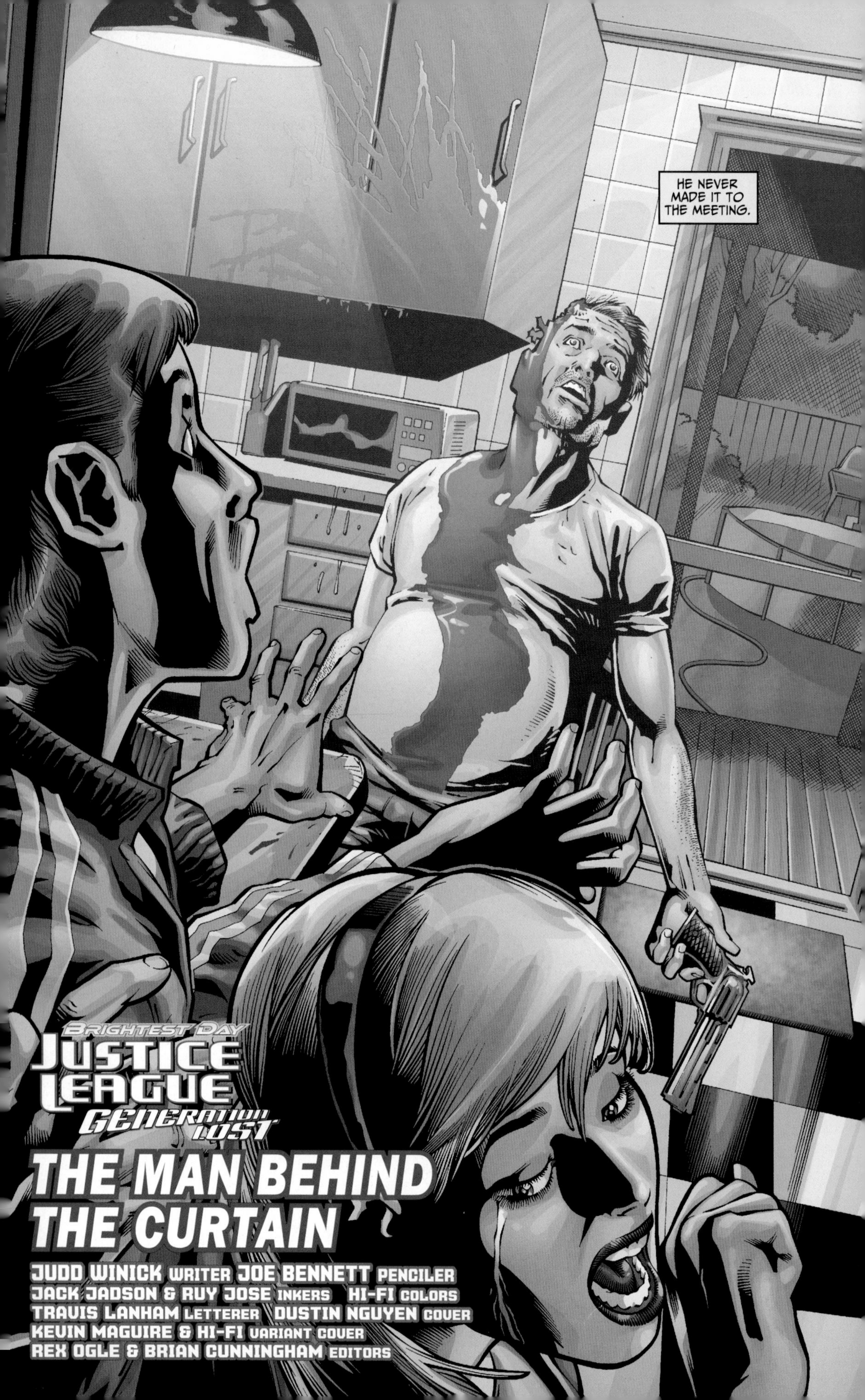
HE NEVER MADE IT TO THE MEETING.
BRIGHTEST DAY
JUSTICE LEAGUE
GENERATION LOST
THE MAN BEHIND THE CURTAIN
JUDD WINICK WRITER JOE BENNETT PENCILER
JACK JADSON & RUY JOSE INKERS HI-FI COLORS
TRAVIS LANHAM LETTERER DUSTIN NGUYEN COVER
KEVIN MAGUIRE & HI-FI VARIANT COVER
REX OGLE & BRIAN CUNNINGHAM EDITORS

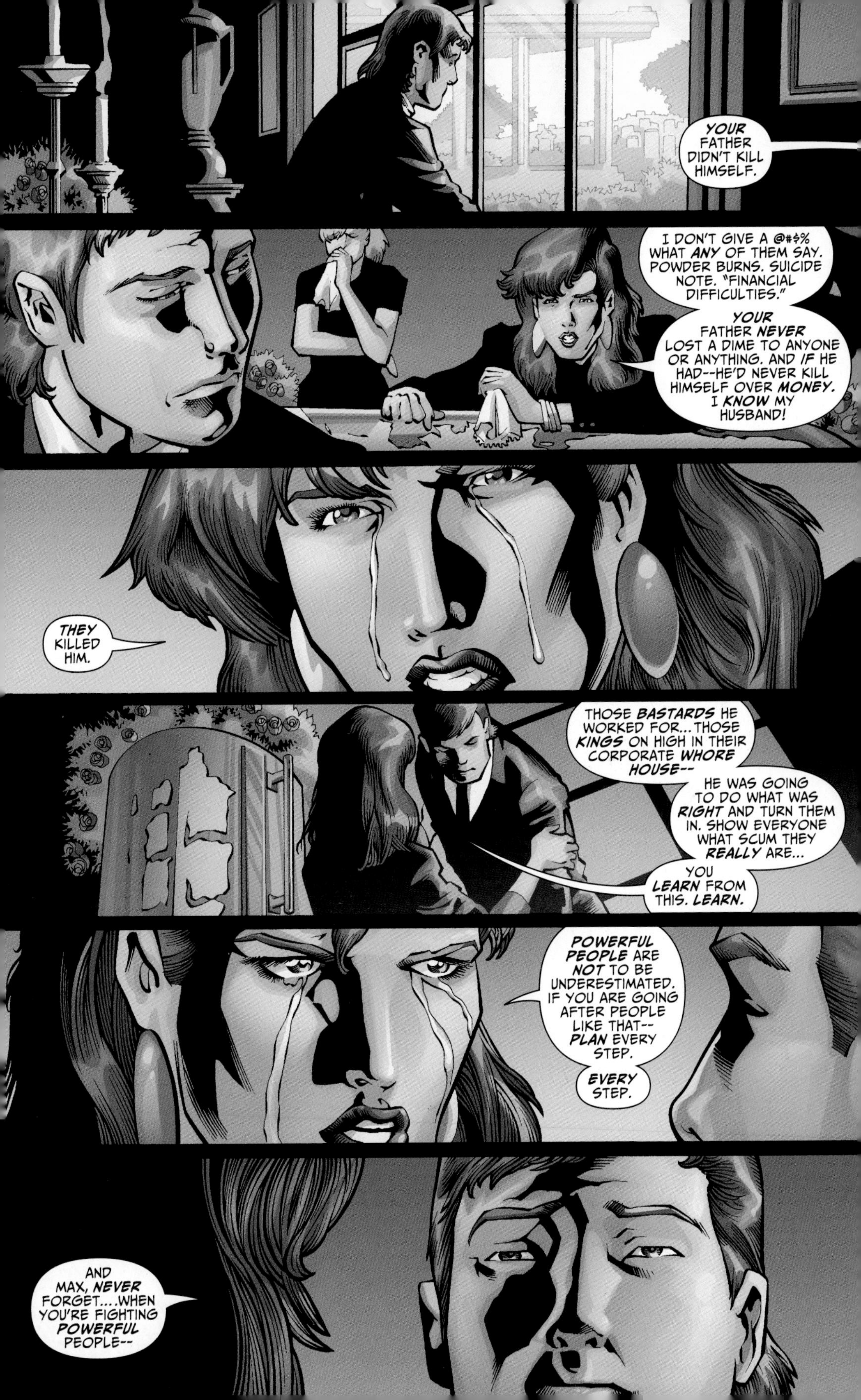
YOUR FATHER DIDN'T KILL HIMSELF.
I DON'T GIVE A @#$% WHAT ANY OF THEM SAY. POWDER BURNS. SUICIDE NOTE. "FINANCIAL DIFFICULTIES."
YOUR FATHER NEVER LOST A DIME TO ANYONE OR ANYTHING. AND IF HE HAD--HE'D NEVER KILL HIMSELF OVER MONEY. I KNOW MY HUSBAND!
THEY KILLED HIM.
THOSE BASTARDS HE WORKED FOR... THOSE KINGS ON HIGH IN THEIR CORPORATE WHORE HOUSE--
HE WAS GOING TO DO WHAT WAS RIGHT AND TURN THEM IN. SHOW EVERYONE WHAT SCUM THEY REALLY ARE...
YOU LEARN FROM THIS. LEARN.
POWERFUL PEOPLE ARE NOT TO BE UNDERESTIMATED. IF YOU ARE GOING AFTER PEOPLE LIKE THAT-- PLAN EVERY STEP.
EVERY STEP.
AND MAX, NEVER FORGET....WHEN YOU'RE FIGHTING POWERFUL PEOPLE--

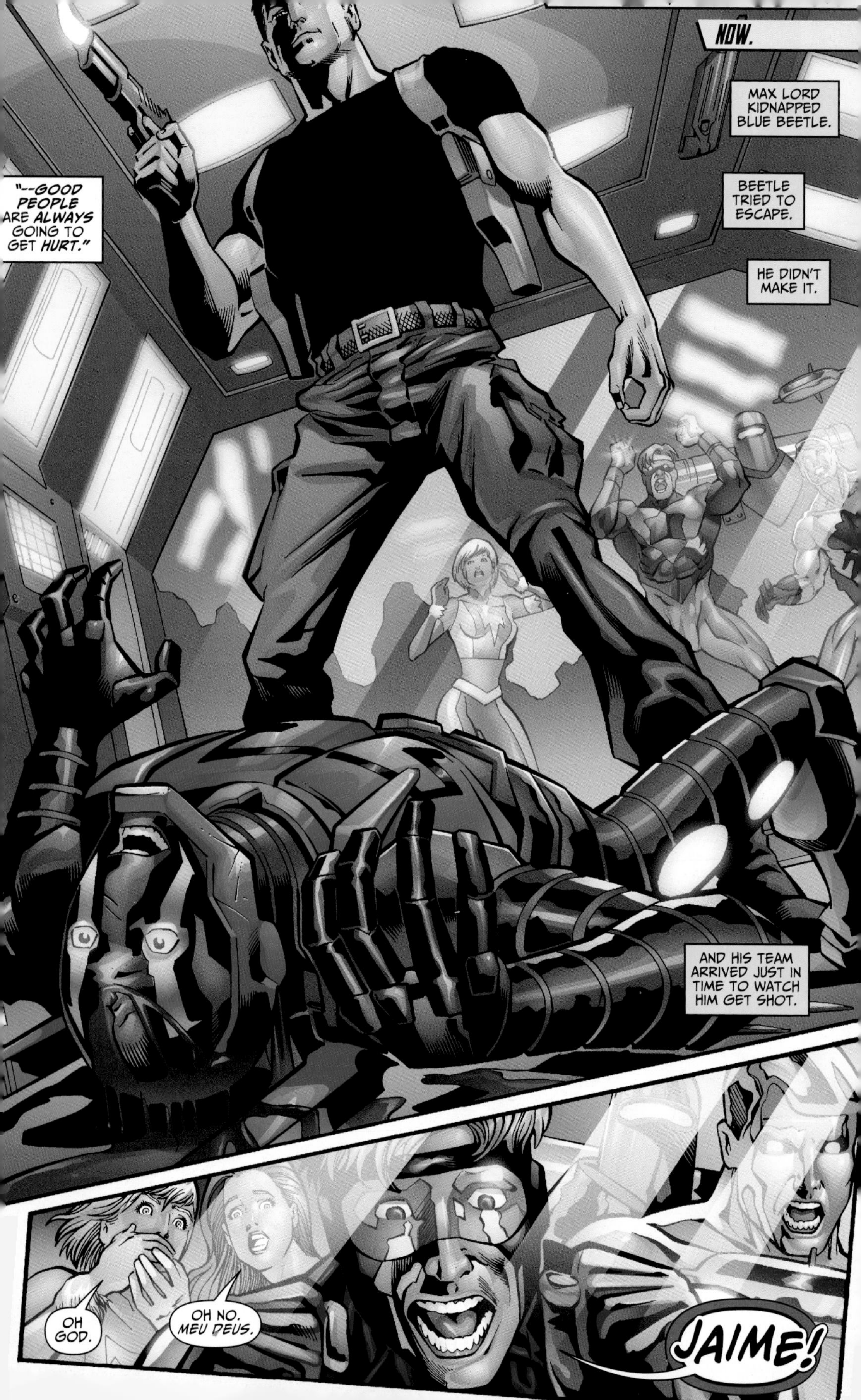
NOW.
"--GOOD PEOPLE ARE ALWAYS GOING TO GET HURT."
MAX LORD KIDNAPPED BLUE BEETLE.
BEETLE TRIED TO ESCAPE.
HE DIDN'T MAKE IT.
AND HIS TEAM ARRIVED JUST IN TIME TO WATCH HIM GET SHOT.
OH GOD.
OH NO. MEU DEUS.
JAIME!

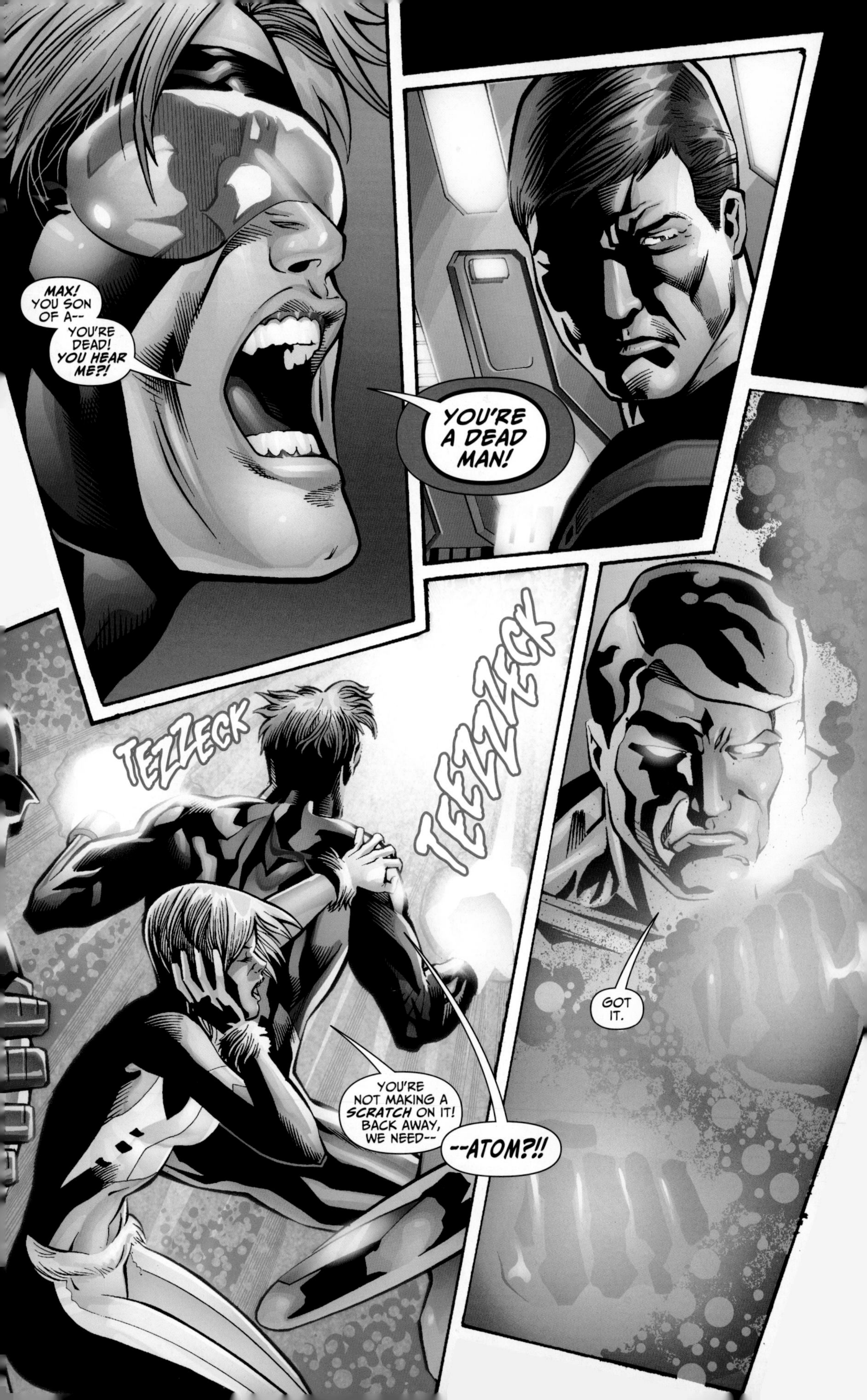
MAX! YOU SON OF A--
YOU'RE DEAD! YOU HEAR ME?!
YOU'RE A DEAD MAN!
TEZZLECK
TEEZZZECK
GOT IT.
YOU'RE NOT MAKING A SCRATCH ON IT! BACK AWAY, WE NEED--
--ATOM?!!

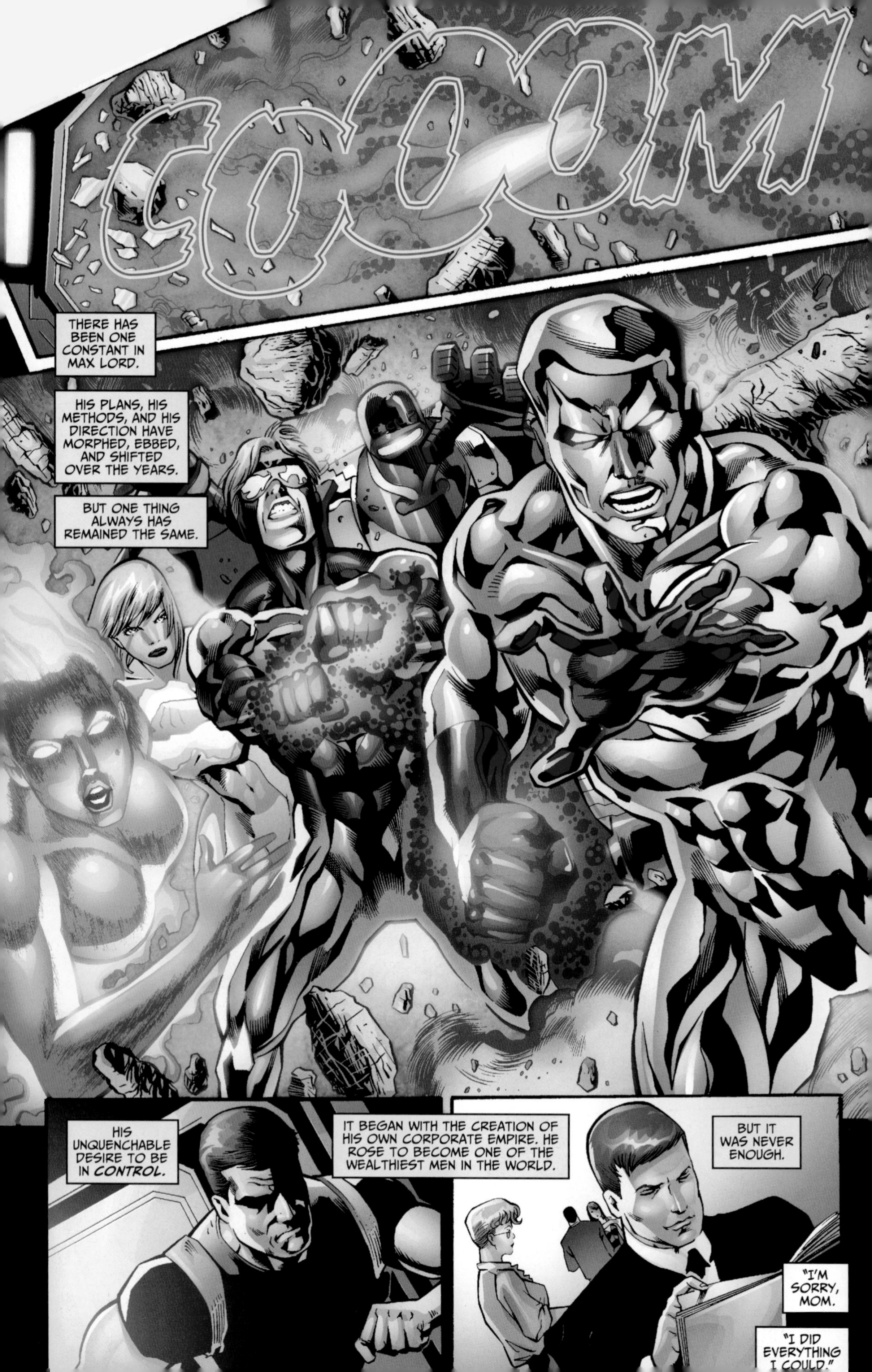

GOOOOM
THERE HAS BEEN ONE CONSTANT IN MAX LORD.
HIS PLANS, HIS METHODS, AND HIS DIRECTION HAVE MORPHED, EBBED, AND SHIFTED OVER THE YEARS.
BUT ONE THING ALWAYS HAS REMAINED THE SAME.
HIS UNQUENCHABLE DESIRE TO BE IN *CONTROL*.
IT BEGAN WITH THE CREATION OF HIS OWN CORPORATE EMPIRE. HE ROSE TO BECOME ONE OF THE WEALTHIEST MEN IN THE WORLD.
BUT IT WAS NEVER ENOUGH.
"I'M SORRY, MOM.
"I DID EVERYTHING I COULD."

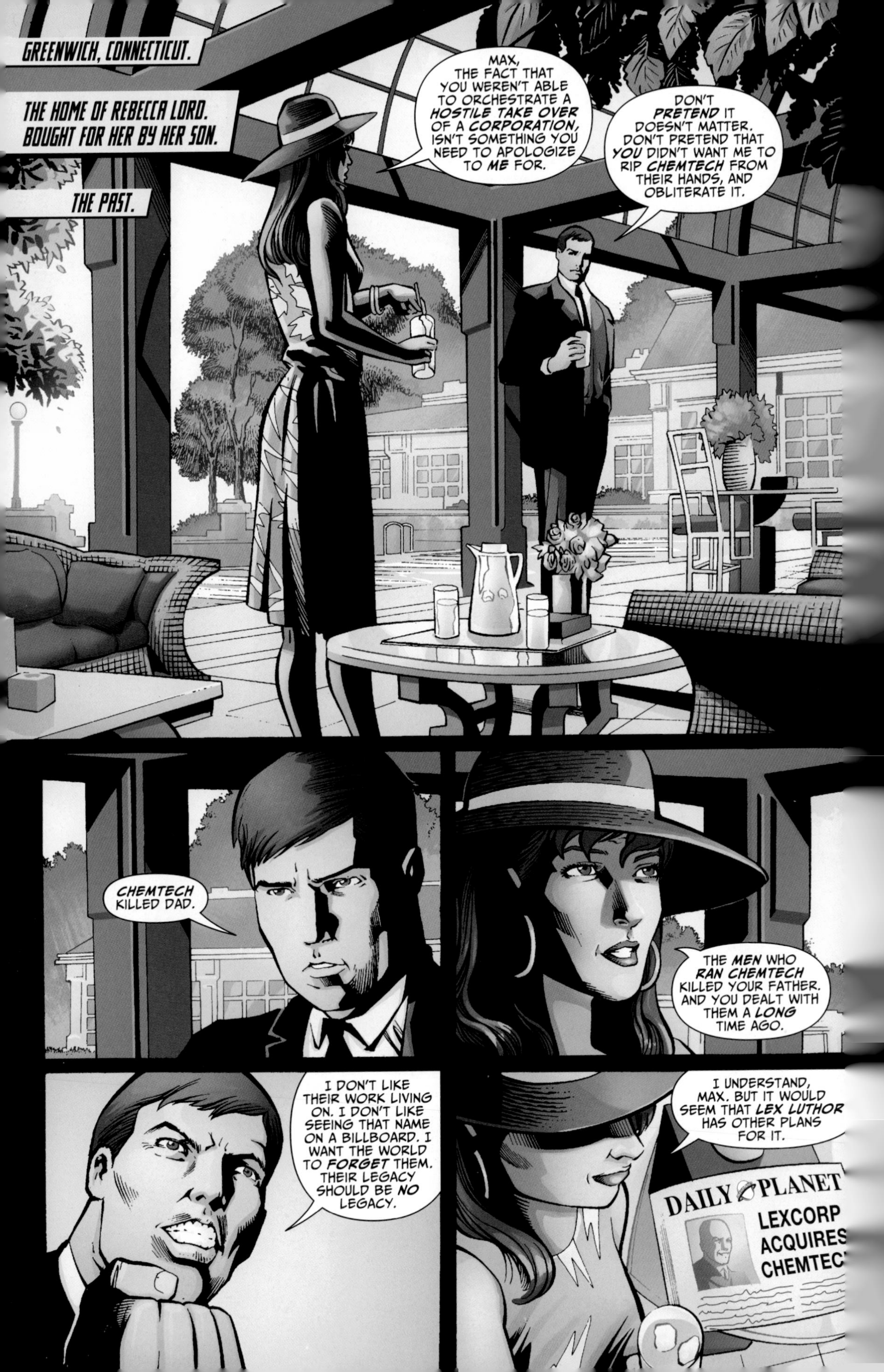
GREENWICH, CONNECTICUT.
THE HOME OF REBECCA LORD. BOUGHT FOR HER BY HER SON.
THE PAST.
MAX, THE FACT THAT YOU WEREN'T ABLE TO ORCHESTRATE A HOSTILE TAKE OVER OF A CORPORATION, ISN'T SOMETHING YOU NEED TO APOLOGIZE TO ME FOR.
DON'T PRETEND IT DOESN'T MATTER. DON'T PRETEND THAT YOU DIDN'T WANT ME TO RIP CHEMTECH FROM THEIR HANDS, AND OBLITERATE IT.
CHEMTECH KILLED DAD.
THE MEN WHO RAN CHEMTECH KILLED YOUR FATHER. AND YOU DEALT WITH THEM A LONG TIME AGO.
I DON'T LIKE THEIR WORK LIVING ON. I DON'T LIKE SEEING THAT NAME ON A BILLBOARD. I WANT THE WORLD TO FORGET THEM. THEIR LEGACY SHOULD BE NO LEGACY.
I UNDERSTAND, MAX. BUT IT WOULD SEEM THAT LEX LUTHOR HAS OTHER PLANS FOR IT.
DAILY PLANET
LEXCORP ACQUIRES

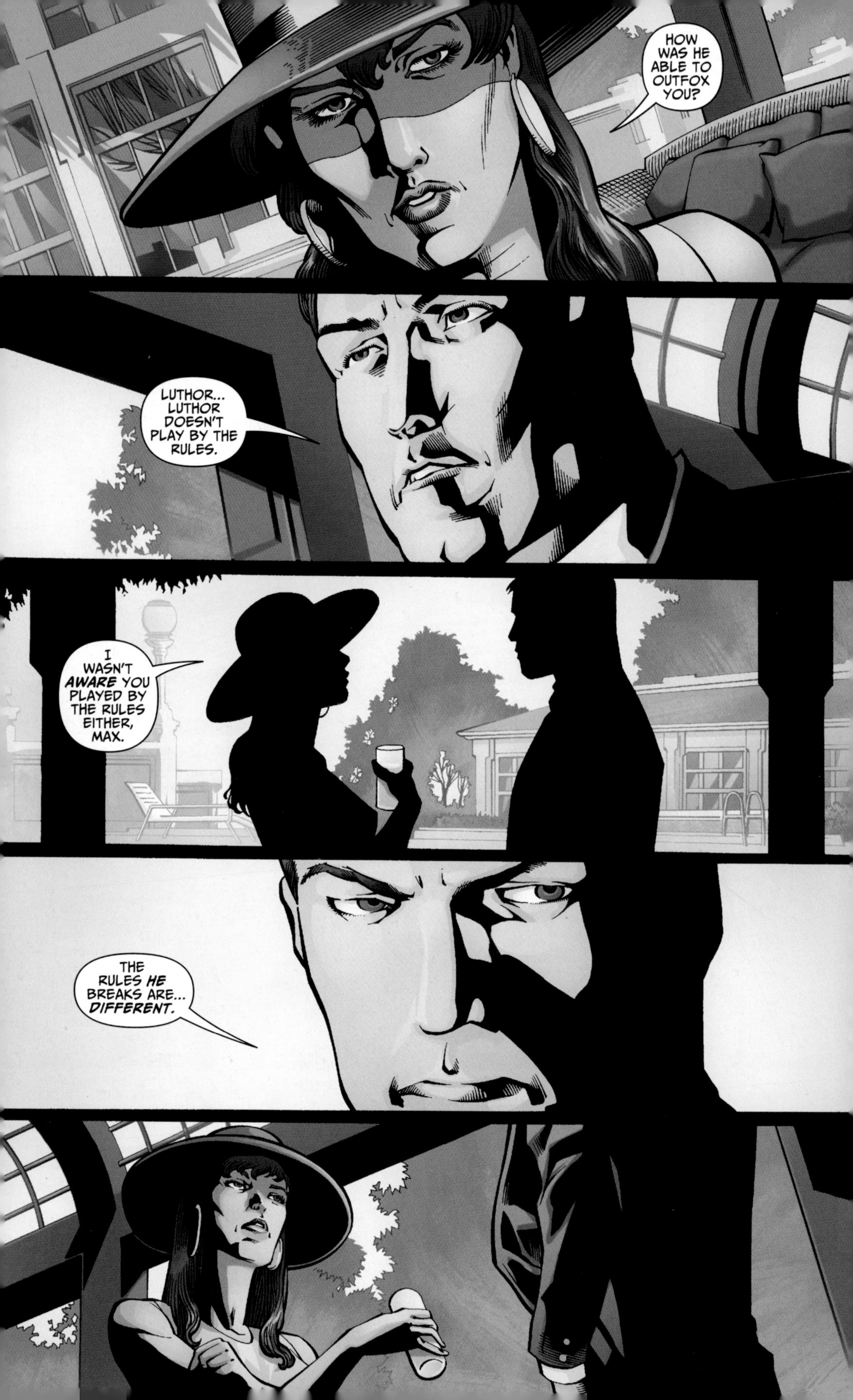
HOW WAS HE ABLE TO OUTFOX YOU?
LUTHOR... LUTHOR DOESN'T PLAY BY THE RULES.
I WASN'T AWARE YOU PLAYED BY THE RULES EITHER, MAX.
THE RULES HE BREAKS ARE... DIFFERENT.

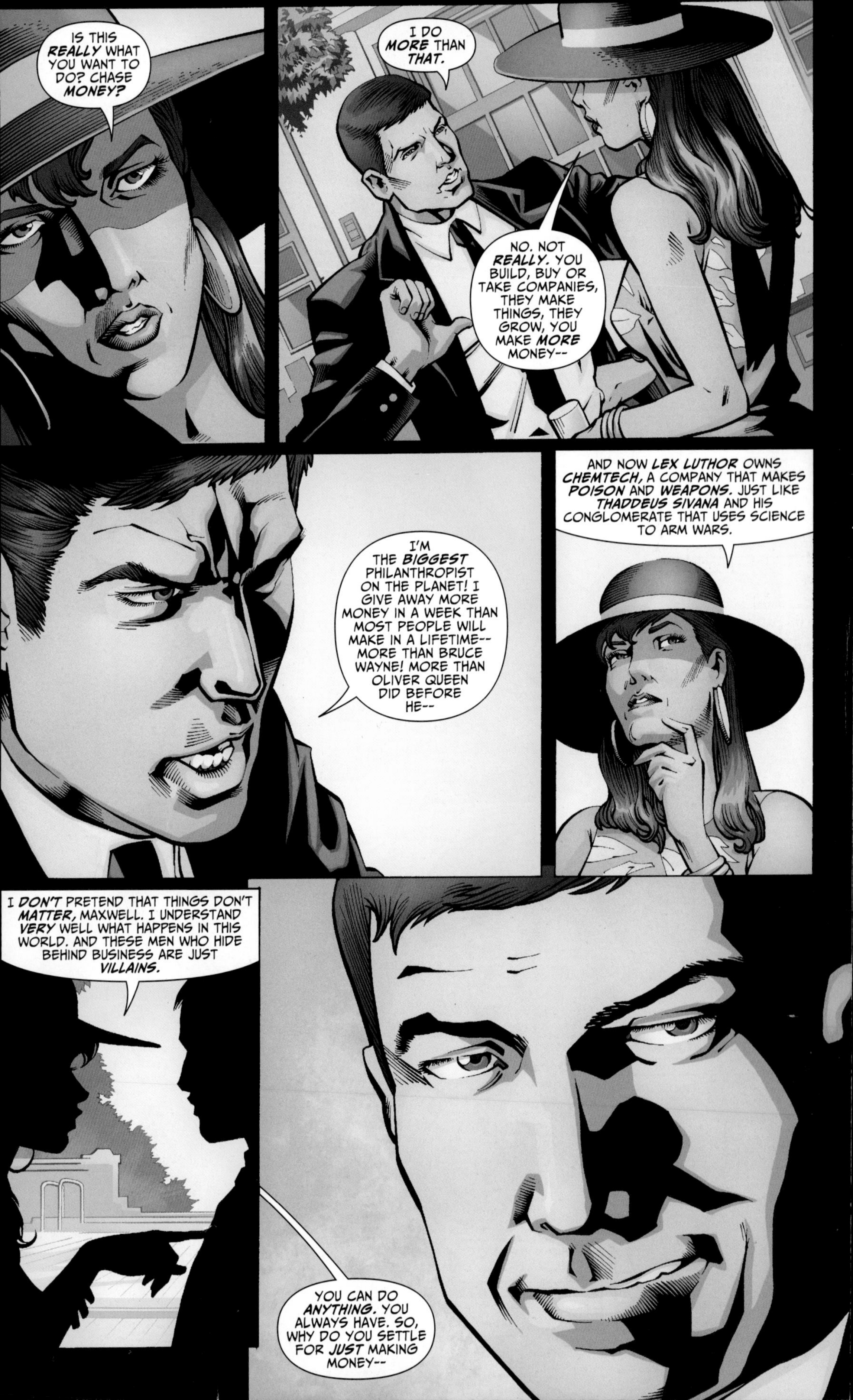
IS THIS REALLY WHAT YOU WANT TO DO? CHASE MONEY?
I DO MORE THAN THAT.
NO. NOT REALLY. YOU BUILD, BUY OR TAKE COMPANIES, THEY MAKE THINGS, THEY GROW, YOU MAKE MORE MONEY--
I'M THE BIGGEST PHILANTHROPIST ON THE PLANET! I GIVE AWAY MORE MONEY IN A WEEK THAN MOST PEOPLE WILL MAKE IN A LIFETIME-- MORE THAN BRUCE WAYNE! MORE THAN OLIVER QUEEN DID BEFORE HE--
AND NOW LEX LUTHOR OWNS CHEMTECH, A COMPANY THAT MAKES POISON AND WEAPONS. JUST LIKE THADDEUS SIVANA AND HIS CONGLOMERATE THAT USES SCIENCE TO ARM WARS.
I DON'T PRETEND THAT THINGS DON'T MATTER, MAXWELL. I UNDERSTAND VERY WELL WHAT HAPPENS IN THIS WORLD. AND THESE MEN WHO HIDE BEHIND BUSINESS ARE JUST VILLAINS.
YOU CAN DO ANYTHING. YOU ALWAYS HAVE. SO, WHY DO YOU SETTLE FOR JUST MAKING MONEY--

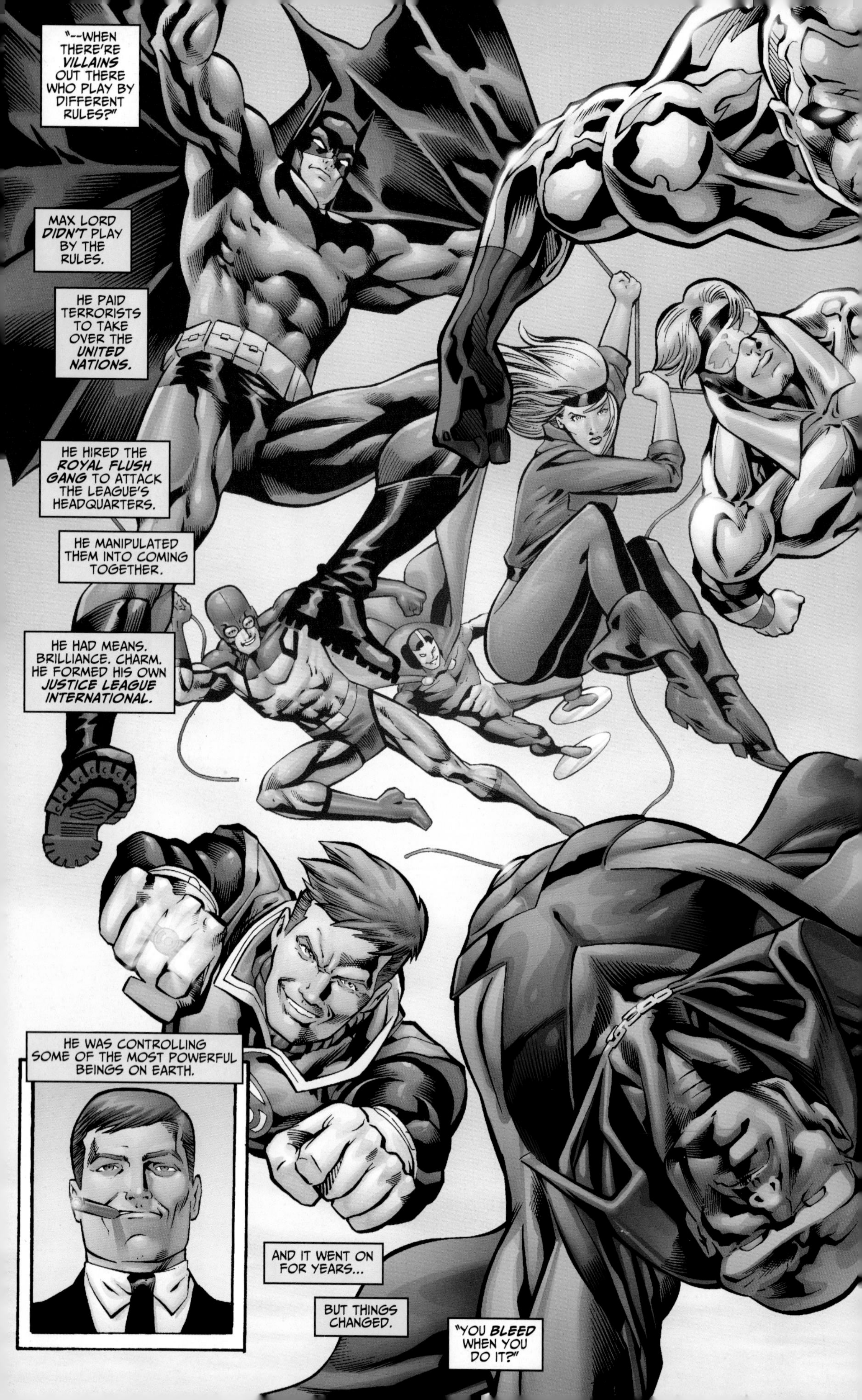
"--WHEN THERE'RE VILLAINS OUT THERE WHO PLAY BY DIFFERENT RULES?"
MAX LORD DIDN'T PLAY BY THE RULES.
HE PAID TERRORISTS TO TAKE OVER THE UNITED NATIONS.
HE HIRED THE ROYAL FLUSH GANG TO ATTACK THE LEAGUE'S HEADQUARTERS.
HE MANIPULATED THEM INTO COMING TOGETHER.
HE HAD MEANS. BRILLIANCE. CHARM. HE FORMED HIS OWN JUSTICE LEAGUE INTERNATIONAL.
HE WAS CONTROLLING SOME OF THE MOST POWERFUL BEINGS ON EARTH.
AND IT WENT ON FOR YEARS...
BUT THINGS CHANGED.
"YOU BLEED WHEN YOU DO IT?"

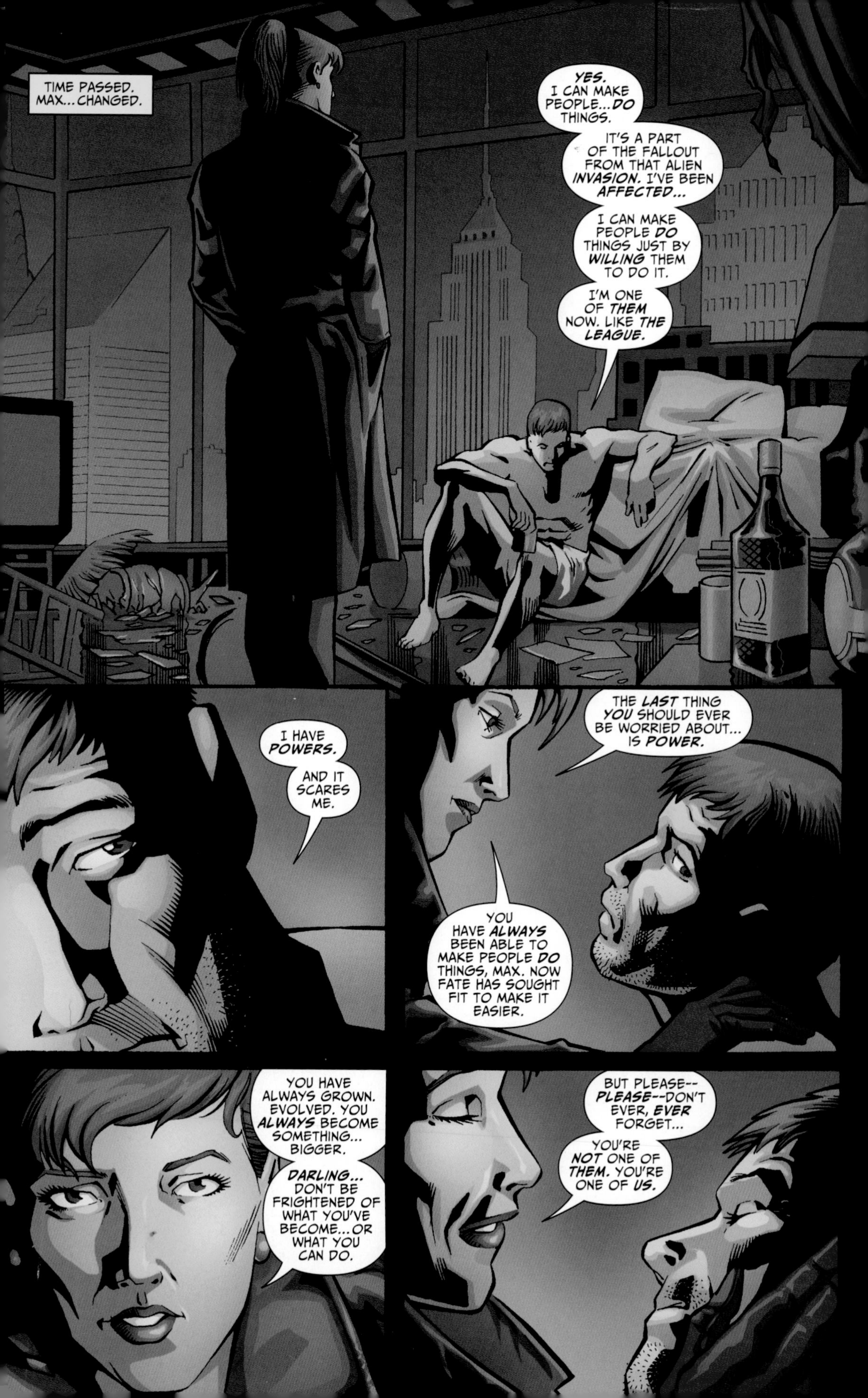
TIME PASSED. MAX...CHANGED.
YES. I CAN MAKE PEOPLE...DO THINGS.
IT'S A PART OF THE FALLOUT FROM THAT ALIEN INVASION. I'VE BEEN AFFECTED...
I CAN MAKE PEOPLE DO THINGS JUST BY WILLING THEM TO DO IT.
I'M ONE OF THEM NOW. LIKE THE LEAGUE.
I HAVE POWERS.
AND IT SCARES ME.
THE LAST THING YOU SHOULD EVER BE WORRIED ABOUT... IS POWER.
YOU HAVE ALWAYS BEEN ABLE TO MAKE PEOPLE DO THINGS, MAX. NOW FATE HAS SOUGHT FIT TO MAKE IT EASIER.
YOU HAVE ALWAYS GROWN. EVOLVED. YOU ALWAYS BECOME SOMETHING... BIGGER.
DARLING... DON'T BE FRIGHTENED OF WHAT YOU'VE BECOME...OR WHAT YOU CAN DO.
BUT PLEASE--PLEASE--DON'T EVER, EVER FORGET...
YOU'RE NOT ONE OF THEM. YOU'RE ONE OF US.

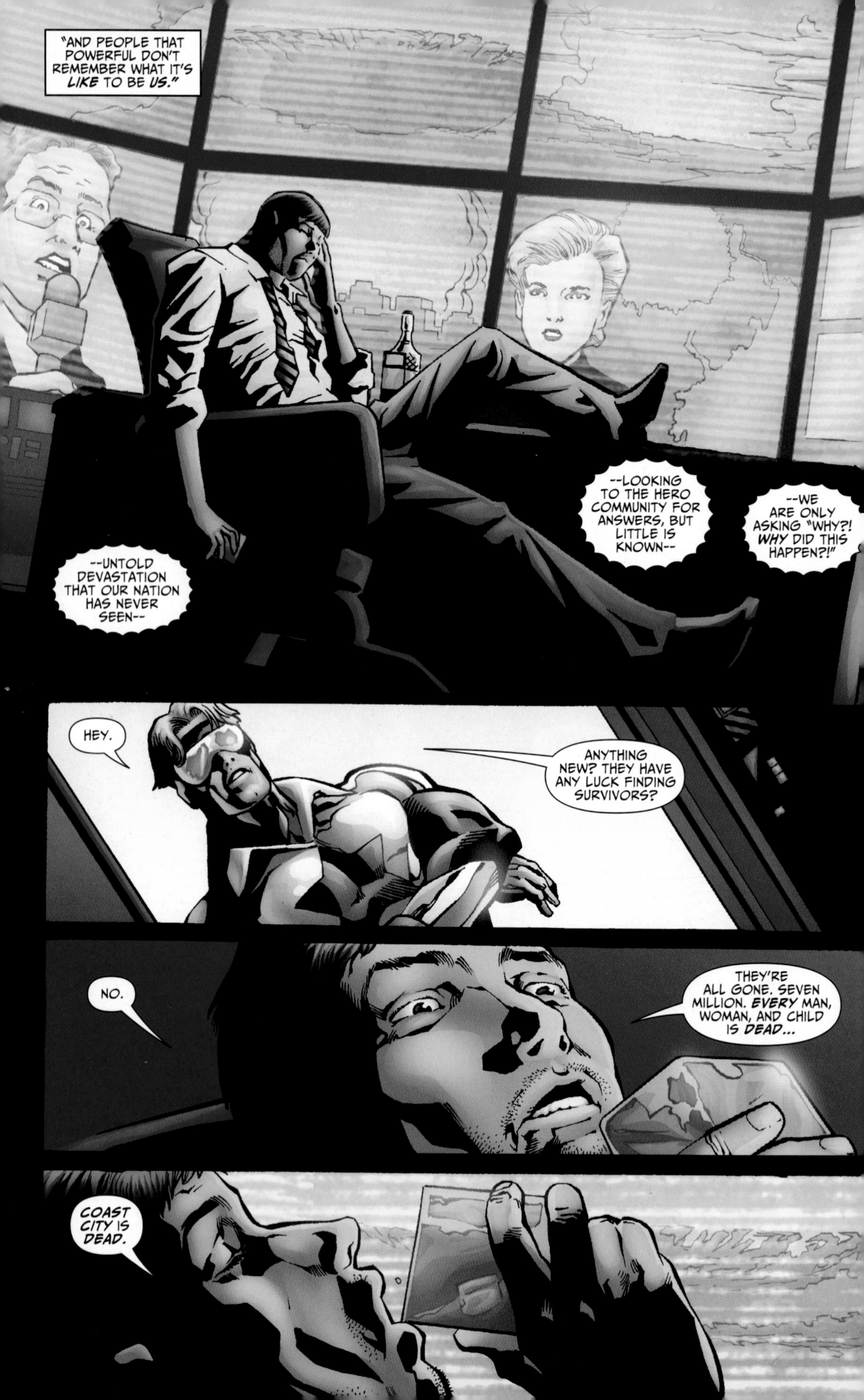
"AND PEOPLE THAT POWERFUL DON'T REMEMBER WHAT IT'S *LIKE* TO BE *US.*"
--UNTOLD DEVASTATION THAT OUR NATION HAS NEVER SEEN--
--LOOKING TO THE HERO COMMUNITY FOR ANSWERS, BUT LITTLE IS KNOWN--
--WE ARE ONLY ASKING "WHY?! *WHY* DID THIS HAPPEN?!"
HEY.
ANYTHING NEW? THEY HAVE ANY LUCK FINDING SURVIVORS?
NO.
THEY'RE ALL GONE. SEVEN MILLION. *EVERY* MAN, WOMAN, AND CHILD IS *DEAD...*
COAST CITY IS *DEAD.*

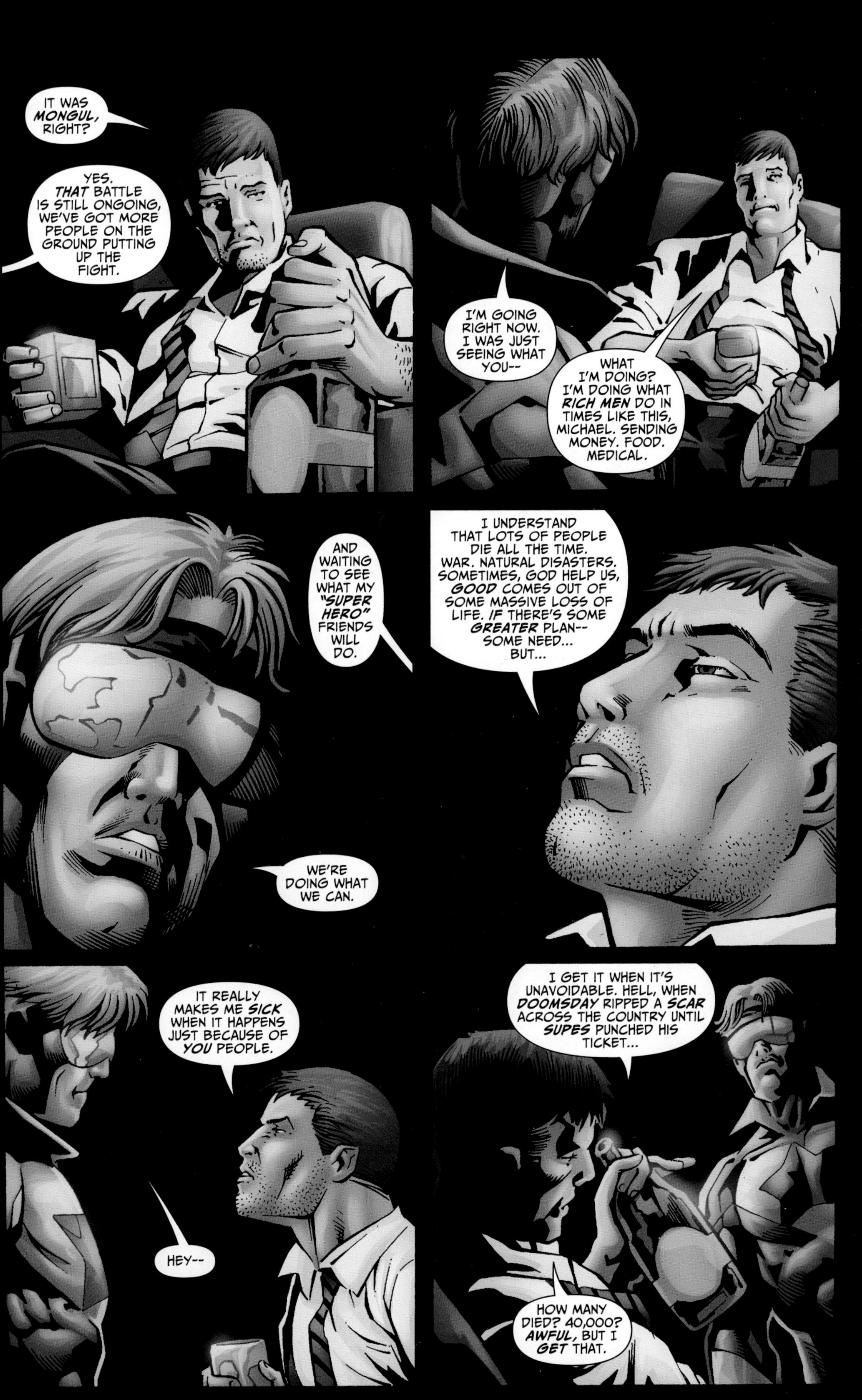
IT WAS MONGUL, RIGHT?
YES. THAT BATTLE IS STILL ONGOING, WE'VE GOT MORE PEOPLE ON THE GROUND PUTTING UP THE FIGHT.
I'M GOING RIGHT NOW. I WAS JUST SEEING WHAT YOU--
WHAT I'M DOING? I'M DOING WHAT RICH MEN DO IN TIMES LIKE THIS, MICHAEL. SENDING MONEY. FOOD. MEDICAL.
AND WAITING TO SEE WHAT MY "SUPER HERO" FRIENDS WILL DO.
WE'RE DOING WHAT WE CAN.
I UNDERSTAND THAT LOTS OF PEOPLE DIE ALL THE TIME. WAR. NATURAL DISASTERS. SOMETIMES, GOD HELP US, GOOD COMES OUT OF SOME MASSIVE LOSS OF LIFE. IF THERE'S SOME GREATER PLAN-- SOME NEED... BUT...
IT REALLY MAKES ME SICK WHEN IT HAPPENS JUST BECAUSE OF YOU PEOPLE.
HEY--
I GET IT WHEN IT'S UNAVOIDABLE. HELL, WHEN DOOMSDAY RIPPED A SCAR ACROSS THE COUNTRY UNTIL SUPES PUNCHED HIS TICKET...
HOW MANY DIED? 40,000? AWFUL, BUT I GET THAT.

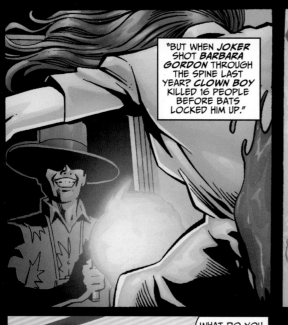

"BUT WHEN *JOKER* SHOT *BARBARA GORDON* THROUGH THE SPINE LAST YEAR? *CLOWN BOY* KILLED 16 PEOPLE BEFORE BATS LOCKED HIM UP."

"OR WHEN JOHN STEWART'S *ARROGANCE* CAUSED BILLIONS TO DIE WHEN *XANSHI* BLEW UP."

WHAT DO YOU THINK *THOSE* GAMES ARE ABOUT?

YOU EVER WONDER IF YOU GUYS-- JUST BY *BEING AROUND*--ARE DOING MORE *HARM* THAN *GOOD?*

MAX, I KNOW YOU'RE UPSET. THIS IS A *NIGHTMARE.* BUT YOU CAN'T GIVE UP HOPE. WE DO WHAT WE CAN. *YOU* DO WHAT YOU CAN AND WE--

MY *MOTHER* LIVED IN *COAST CITY.*

MAX.

OH MY GOD. MAX. I AM SO SORRY.

IS THERE ANYTHING I CAN DO?

YES, MICHAEL. YOU CAN *FORGET* THAT WE EVER HAD THIS CONVERSATION.

YES... FORGET...

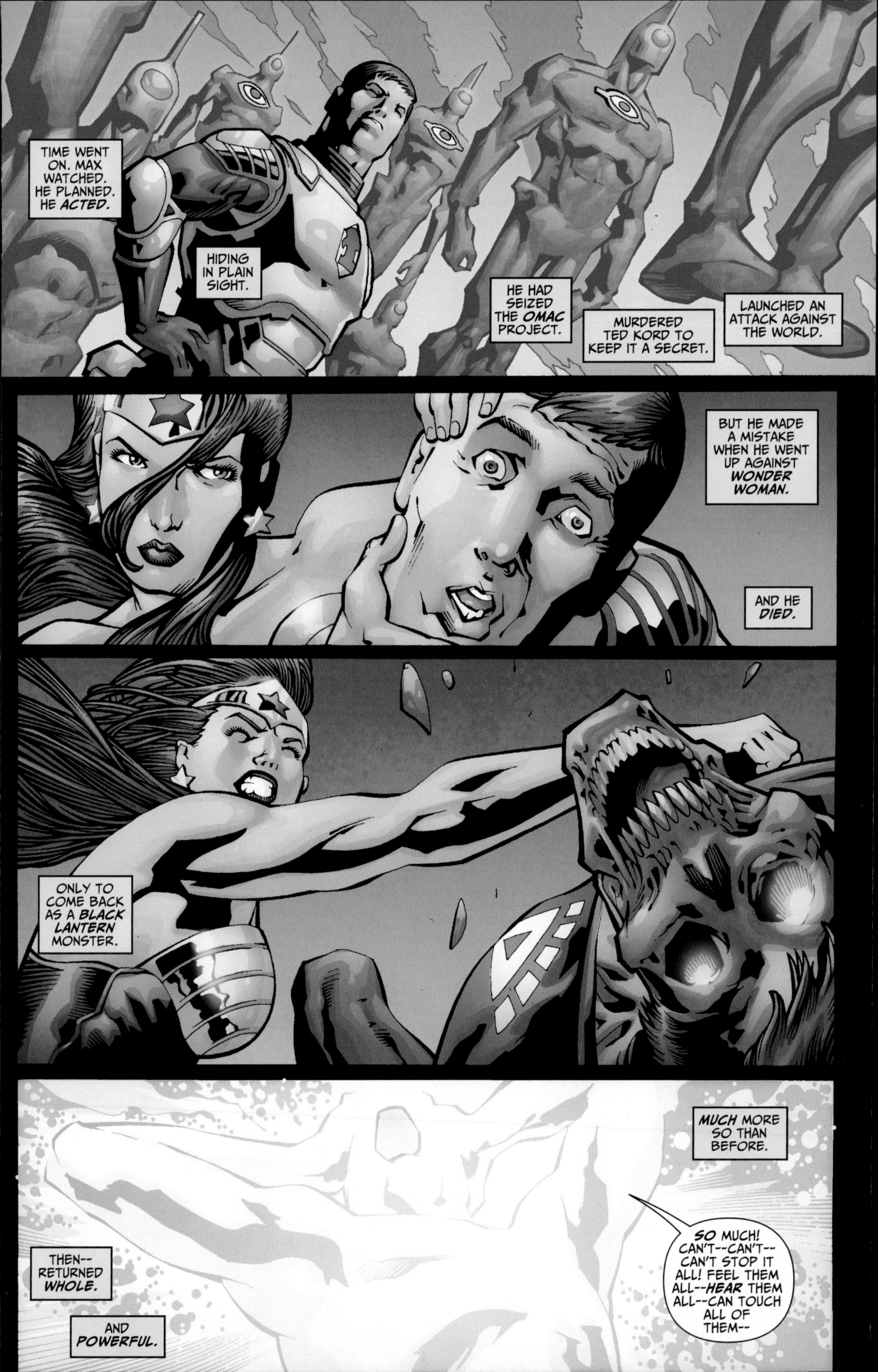

TIME WENT ON. MAX WATCHED. HE PLANNED. HE *ACTED.*
HIDING IN PLAIN SIGHT.
HE HAD SEIZED THE *OMAC* PROJECT.
MURDERED TED KORD TO KEEP IT A SECRET.
LAUNCHED AN ATTACK AGAINST THE WORLD.
BUT HE MADE A MISTAKE WHEN HE WENT UP AGAINST *WONDER WOMAN.*
AND HE *DIED.*
ONLY TO COME BACK AS A *BLACK LANTERN* MONSTER.
MUCH MORE SO THAN BEFORE.
THEN-- RETURNED *WHOLE.*
AND *POWERFUL.*
SO MUCH! CAN'T--CAN'T-- CAN'T STOP IT ALL! FEEL THEM ALL--*HEAR* THEM ALL--CAN TOUCH ALL OF THEM--

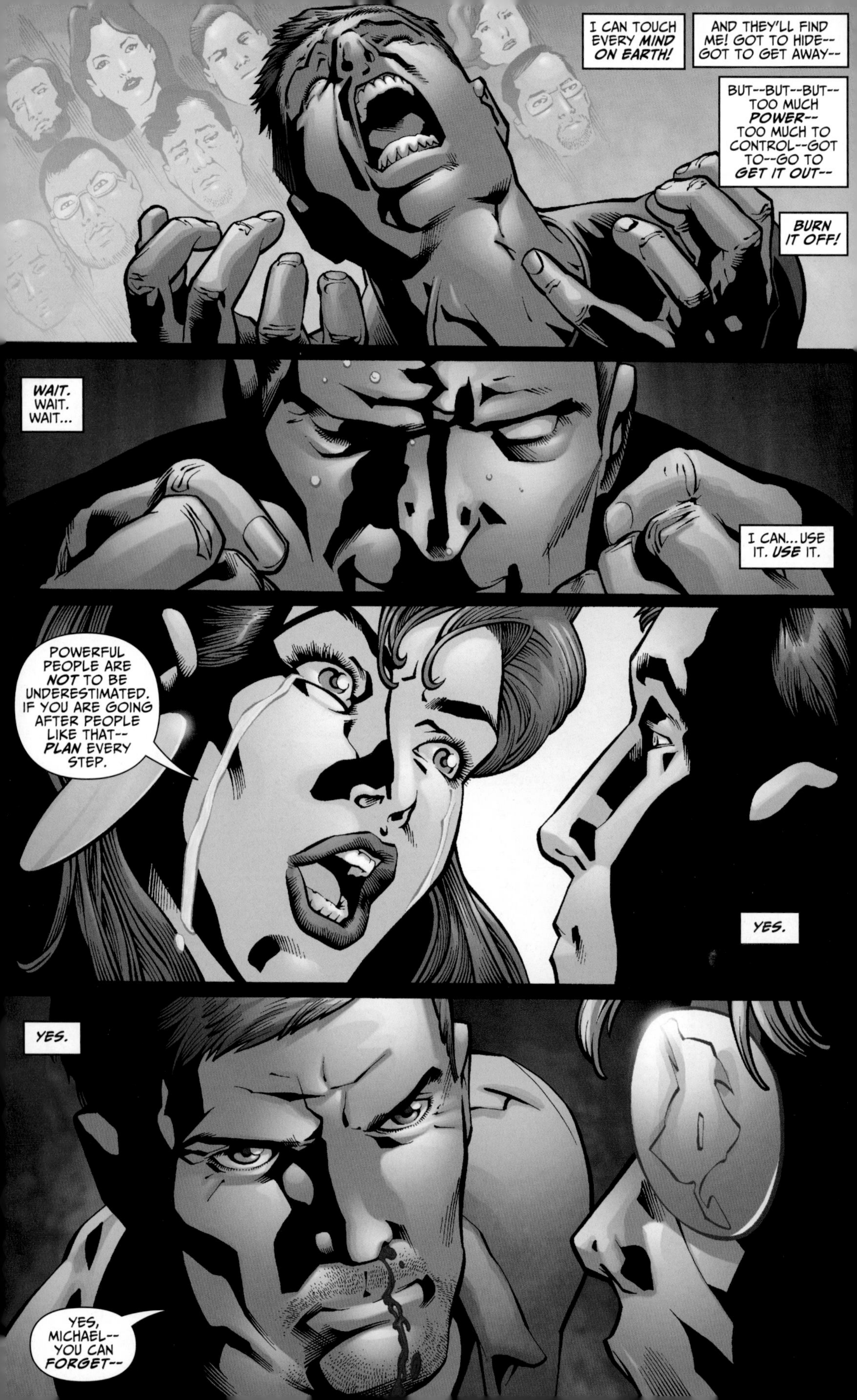

I CAN TOUCH EVERY MIND ON EARTH!
AND THEY'LL FIND ME! GOT TO HIDE--GOT TO GET AWAY--
BUT--BUT--BUT--TOO MUCH POWER--TOO MUCH TO CONTROL--GOT TO--GO TO GET IT OUT--
BURN IT OFF!
WAIT. WAIT. WAIT...
I CAN...USE IT. USE IT.
POWERFUL PEOPLE ARE NOT TO BE UNDERESTIMATED. IF YOU ARE GOING AFTER PEOPLE LIKE THAT--PLAN EVERY STEP.
YES.
YES.
YES, MICHAEL--YOU CAN FORGET--

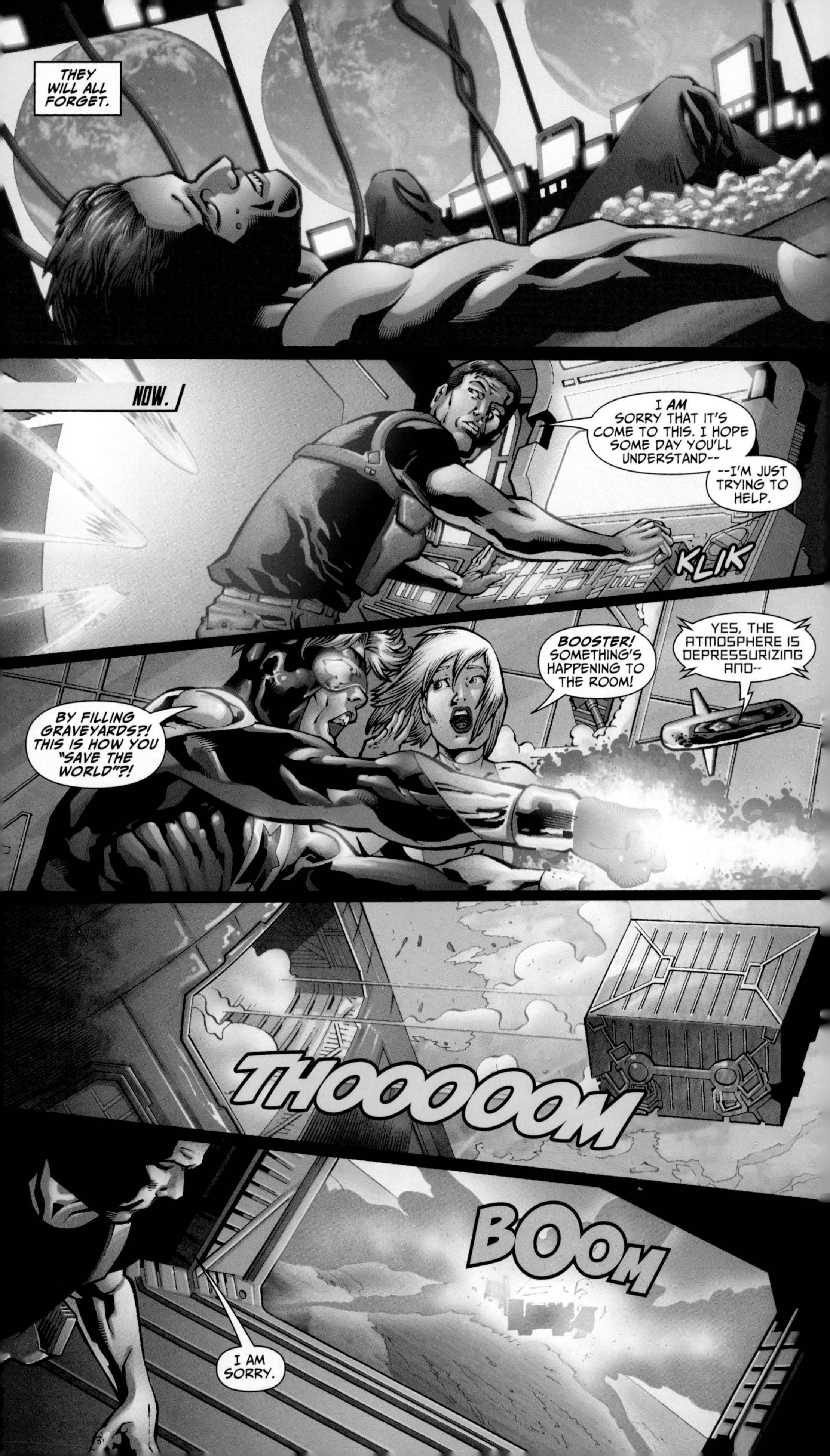
THEY WILL ALL FORGET.
NOW.
I AM SORRY THAT IT'S COME TO THIS. I HOPE SOME DAY YOU'LL UNDERSTAND--
--I'M JUST TRYING TO HELP.
KLIK
BY FILLING GRAVEYARDS?! THIS IS HOW YOU "SAVE THE WORLD"?!
BOOSTER! SOMETHING'S HAPPENING TO THE ROOM!
YES, THE ATMOSPHERE IS DEPRESSURIZING AND--
THOOOOOM
BOOM
I AM SORRY.

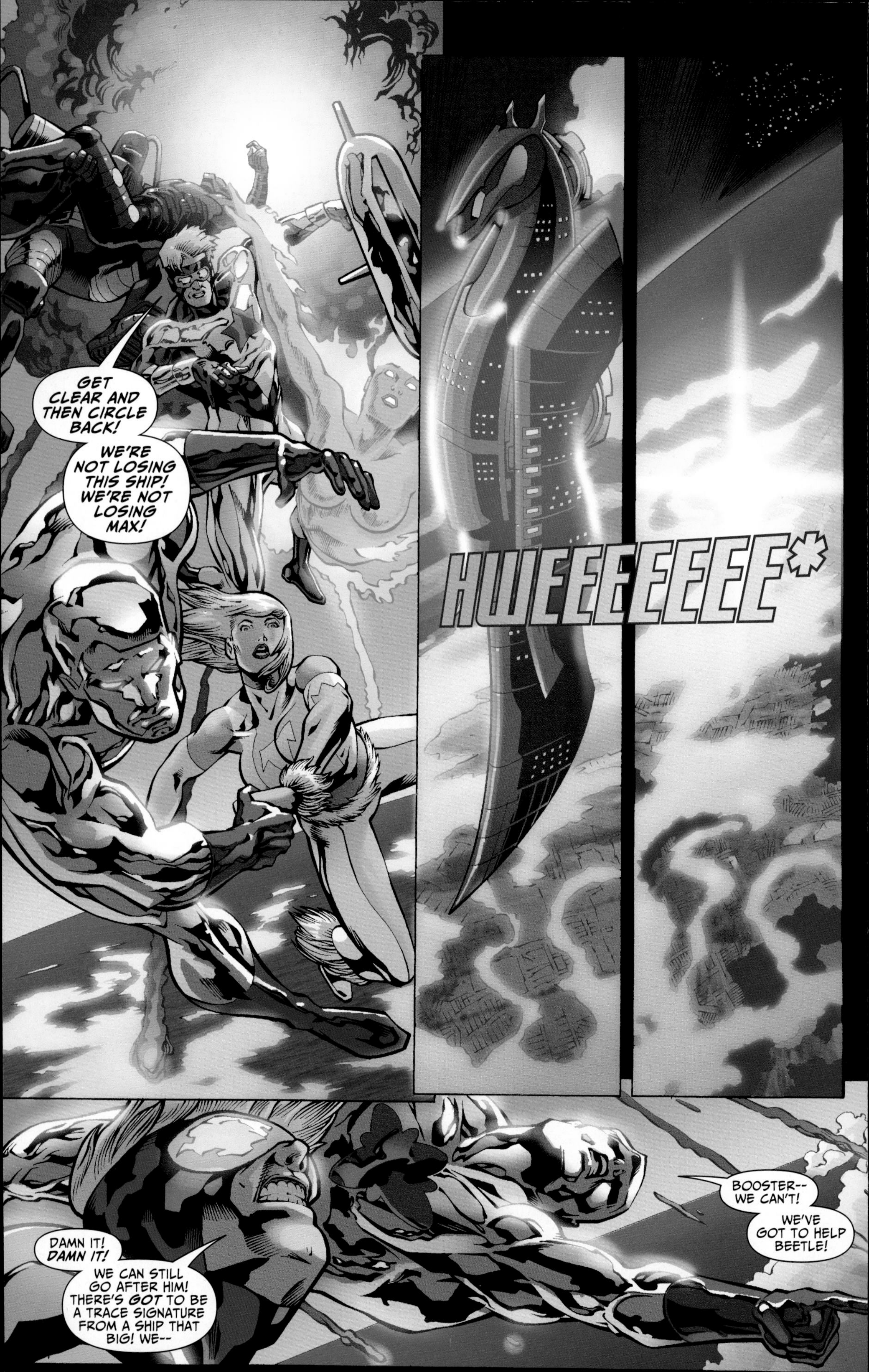
GET CLEAR AND THEN CIRCLE BACK!
WE'RE NOT LOSING THIS SHIP! WE'RE NOT LOSING MAX!
HWEEEEEEE*
BOOSTER-- WE CAN'T!
WE'VE GOT TO HELP BEETLE!
DAMN IT! DAMN IT!
WE CAN STILL GO AFTER HIM! THERE'S GOT TO BE A TRACE SIGNATURE FROM A SHIP THAT BIG! WE--

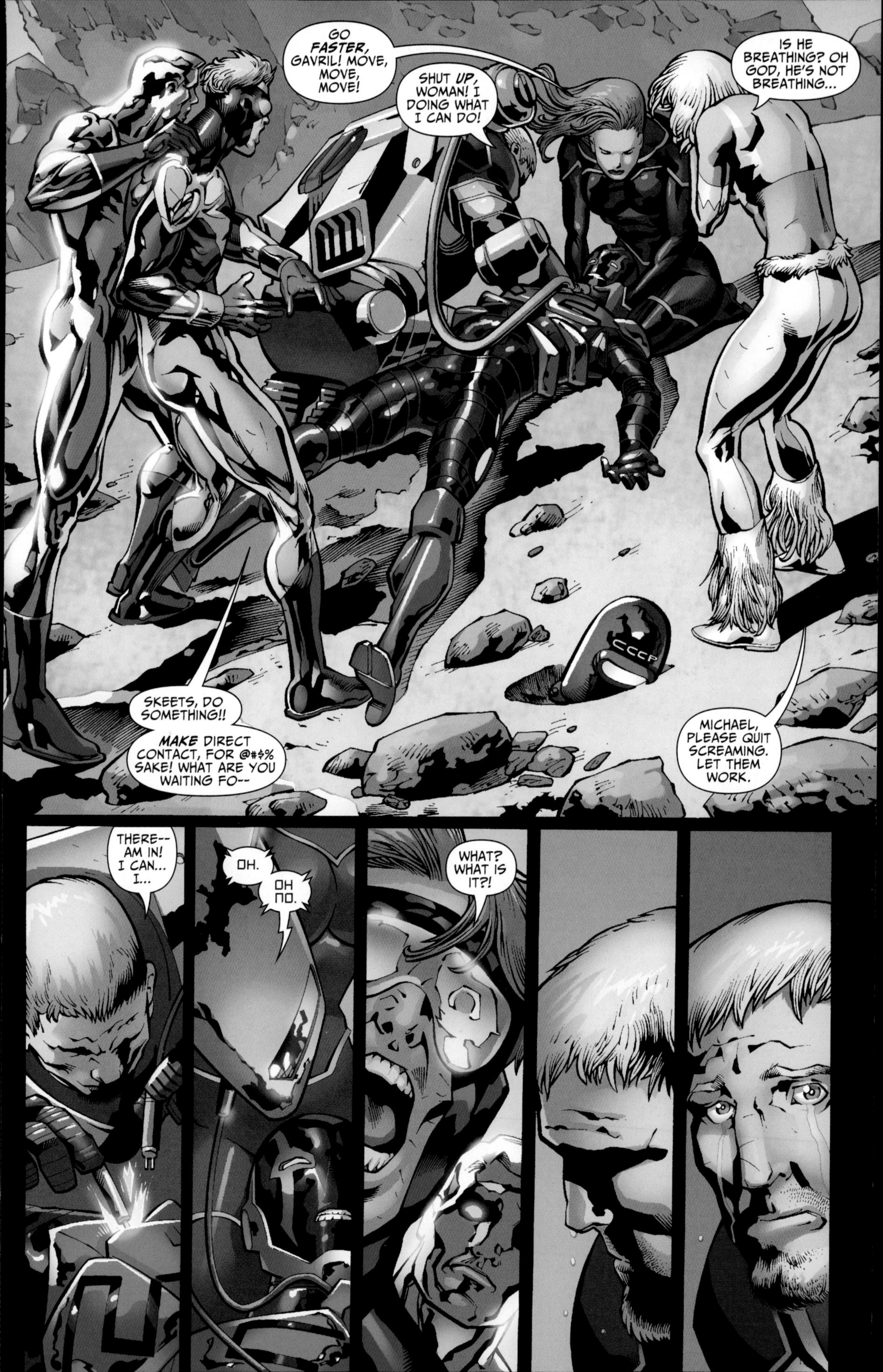
GO **FASTER**, GAVRIL! MOVE, MOVE, MOVE!
SHUT **UP**, WOMAN! I DOING WHAT I CAN DO!
IS HE BREATHING? OH GOD, HE'S NOT BREATHING...
CCCP
SKEETS, DO SOMETHING!!
MAKE DIRECT CONTACT, FOR @#$% SAKE! WHAT ARE YOU WAITING FO--
MICHAEL, PLEASE QUIT SCREAMING. LET THEM WORK.
THERE-- AM IN! I CAN... I...
OH.
OH NO.
WHAT? WHAT IS IT?!

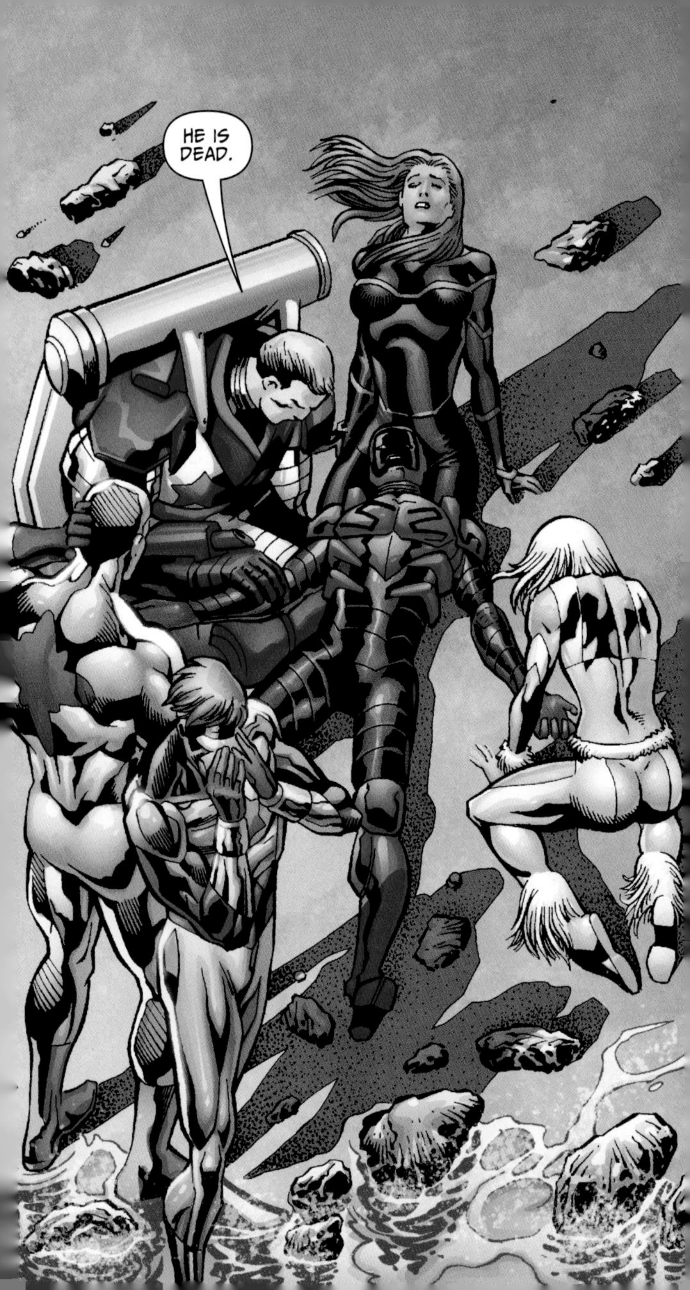
HE IS DEAD.

Cover by Dustin Nguyen

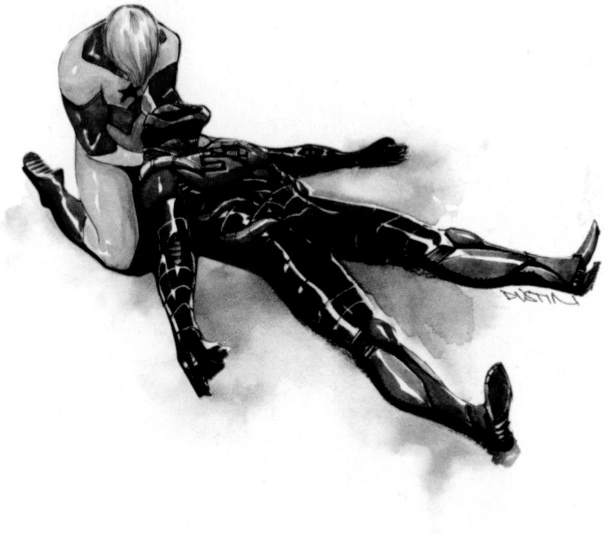

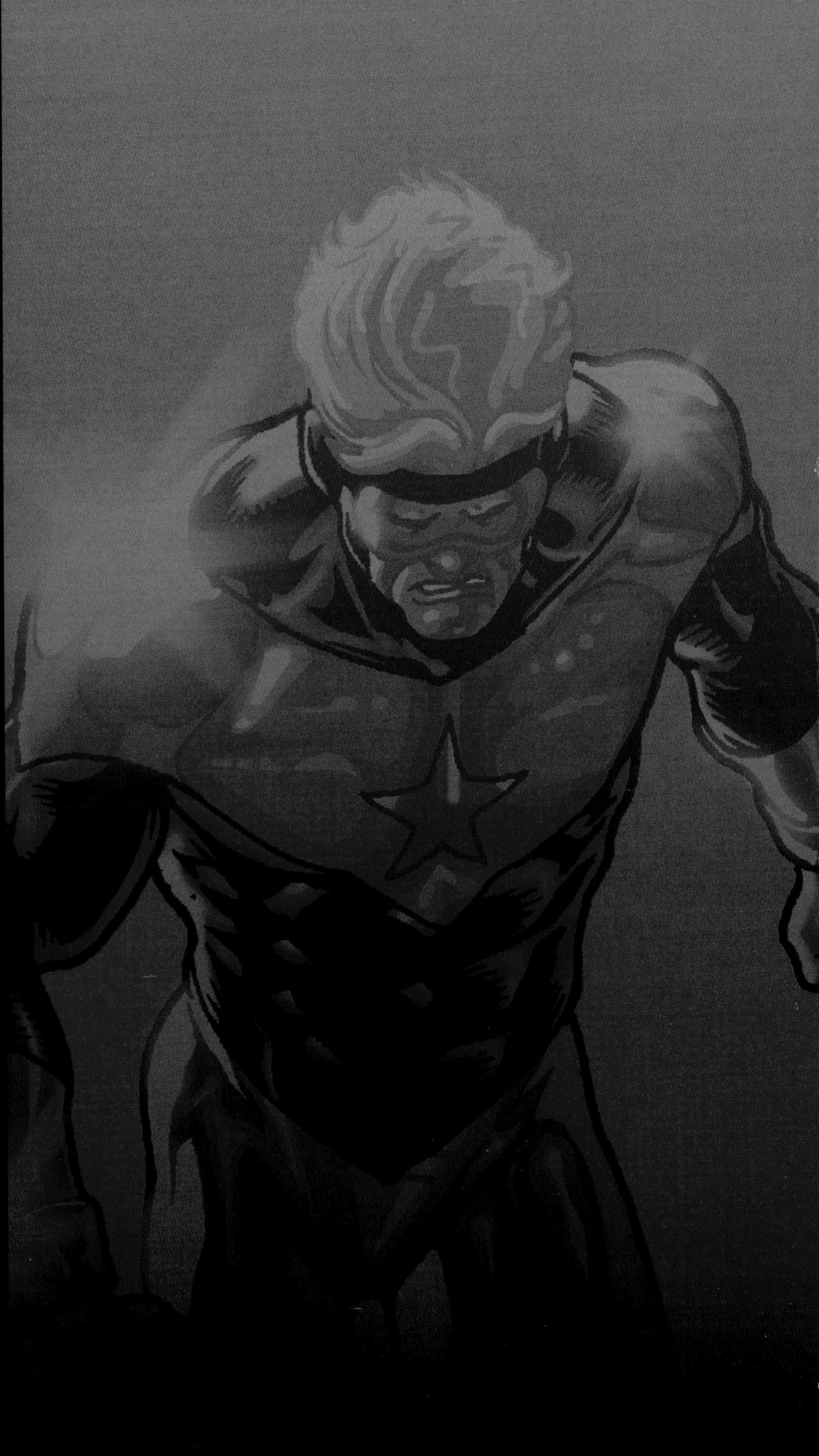

PART TWENTY-ONE:
THE DARK OF MORNING'S LIGHT

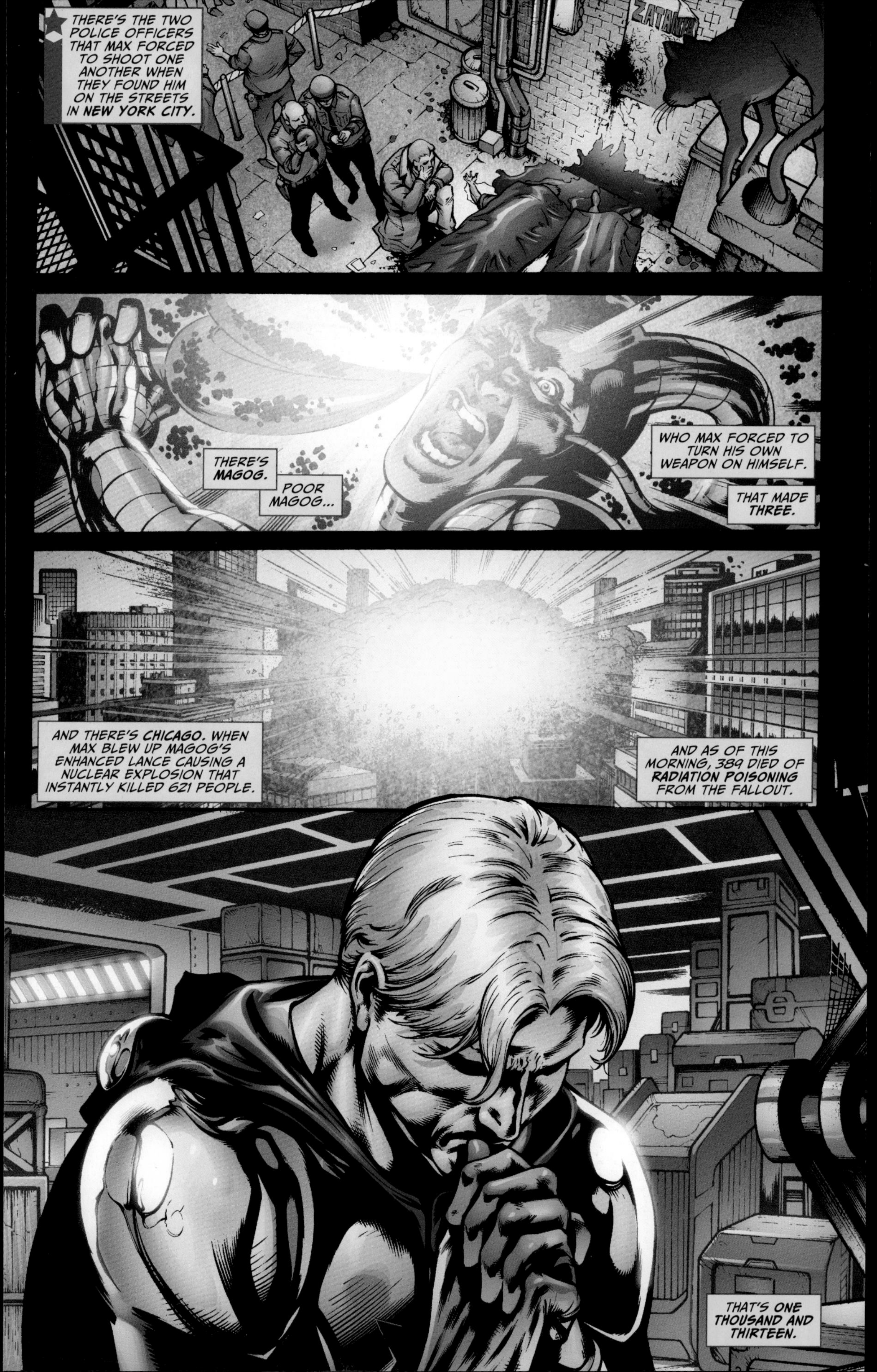
THERE'S THE TWO POLICE OFFICERS THAT MAX FORCED TO SHOOT ONE ANOTHER WHEN THEY FOUND HIM ON THE STREETS IN NEW YORK CITY.
ZATANNA
THERE'S MAGOG.
POOR MAGOG...
WHO MAX FORCED TO TURN HIS OWN WEAPON ON HIMSELF.
THAT MADE THREE.
AND THERE'S CHICAGO. WHEN MAX BLEW UP MAGOG'S ENHANCED LANCE CAUSING A NUCLEAR EXPLOSION THAT INSTANTLY KILLED 621 PEOPLE.
AND AS OF THIS MORNING, 389 DIED OF RADIATION POISONING FROM THE FALLOUT.
THAT'S ONE THOUSAND AND THIRTEEN.

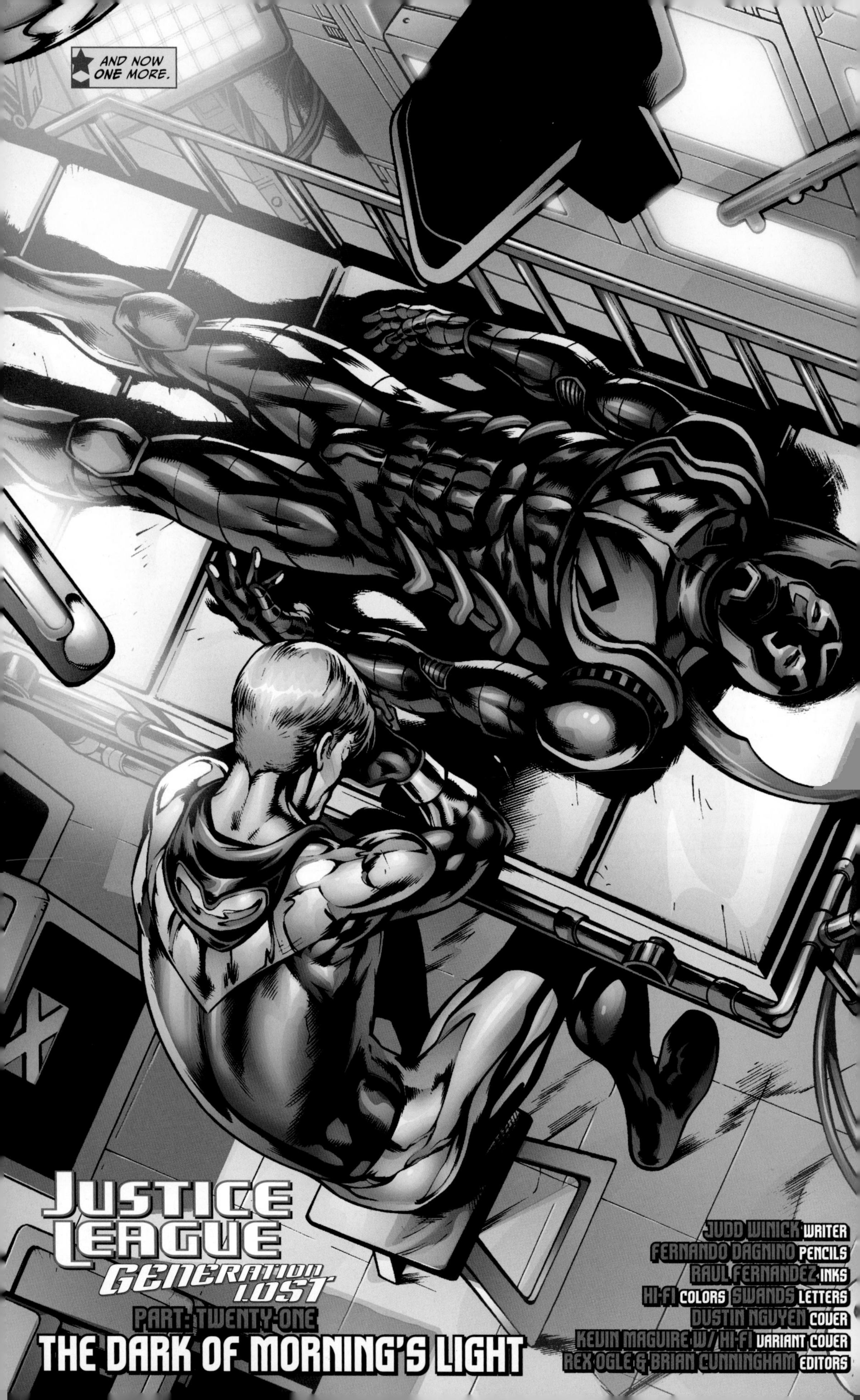
AND NOW ONE MORE.
JUSTICE LEAGUE
GENERATION LOST
PART: TWENTY-ONE
THE DARK OF MORNING'S LIGHT
JUDD WINICK WRITER
FERNANDO DAGNINO PENCILS
RAUL FERNANDEZ INKS
HI-FI COLORS SWANDS LETTERS
DUSTIN NGUYEN COVER
KEVIN MAGUIRE W/ HI-FI VARIANT COVER
REX OGLE & BRIAN CUNNINGHAM EDITORS

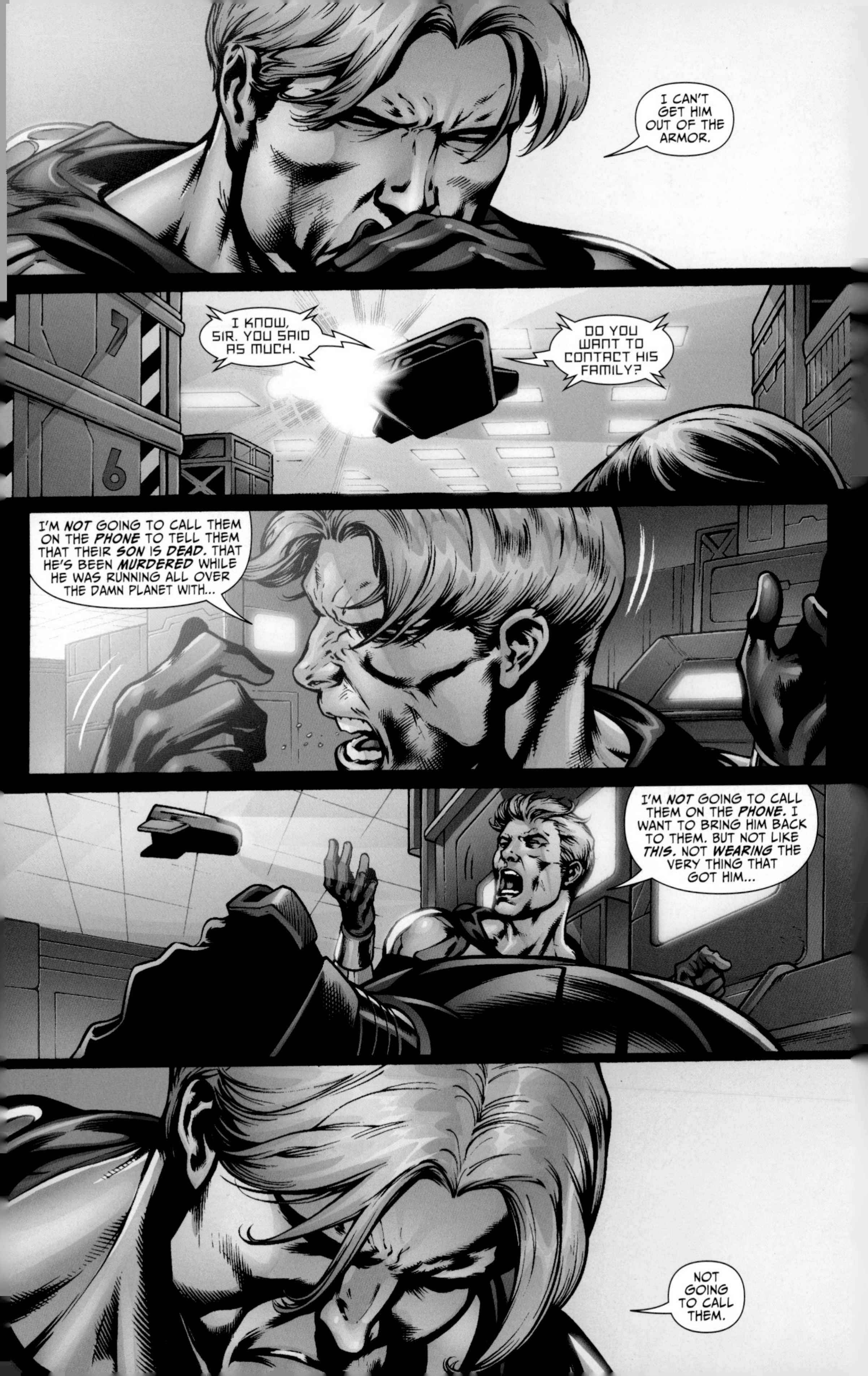
I CAN'T GET HIM OUT OF THE ARMOR.
I KNOW, SIR. YOU SAID AS MUCH.
DO YOU WANT TO CONTACT HIS FAMILY?
I'M *NOT* GOING TO CALL THEM ON THE *PHONE* TO TELL THEM THAT THEIR *SON* IS *DEAD*. THAT HE'S BEEN *MURDERED* WHILE HE WAS RUNNING ALL OVER THE DAMN PLANET WITH...
I'M *NOT* GOING TO CALL THEM ON THE *PHONE*. I WANT TO BRING HIM BACK TO THEM. BUT NOT LIKE *THIS*. NOT *WEARING* THE VERY THING THAT GOT HIM...
NOT GOING TO CALL THEM.

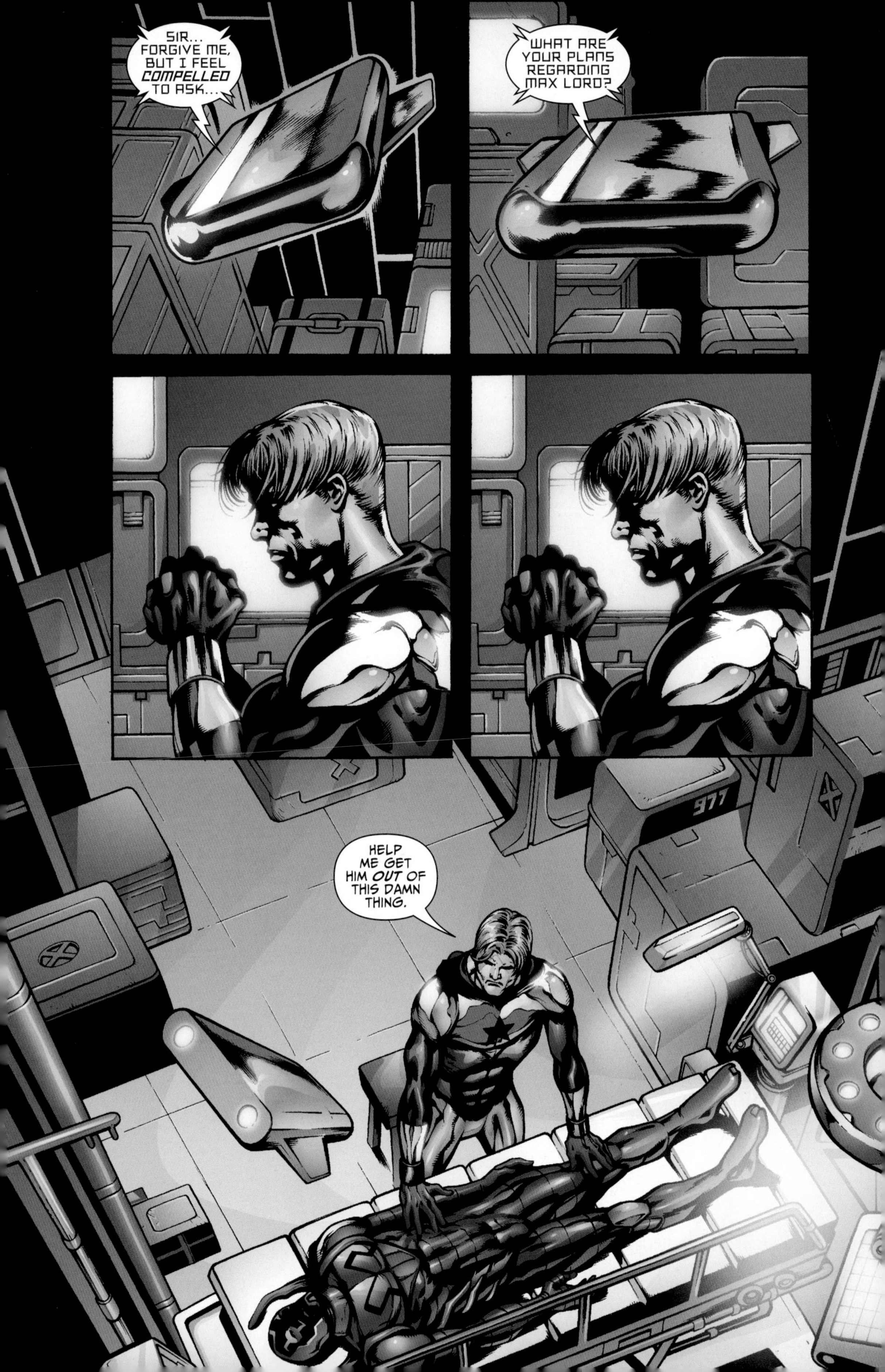
SIR... FORGIVE ME, BUT I FEEL *COMPELLED* TO ASK...
WHAT ARE YOUR PLANS REGARDING MAX LORD?
HELP ME GET HIM *OUT* OF THIS DAMN THING.

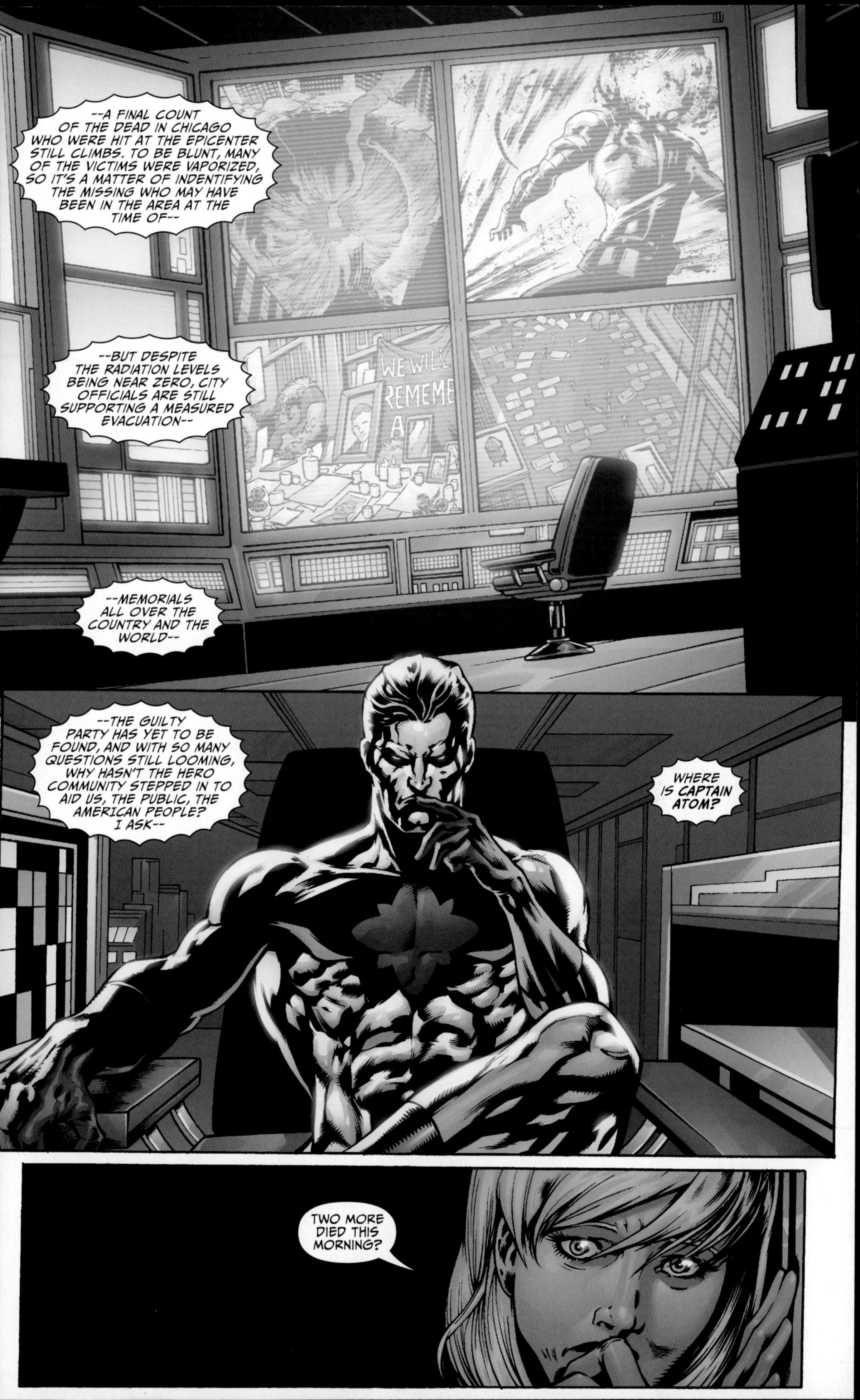
--A FINAL COUNT OF THE DEAD IN CHICAGO WHO WERE HIT AT THE EPICENTER STILL CLIMBS. TO BE BLUNT, MANY OF THE VICTIMS WERE VAPORIZED, SO IT'S A MATTER OF INDENTIFYING THE MISSING WHO MAY HAVE BEEN IN THE AREA AT THE TIME OF--
WE WILL REMEME A
--BUT DESPITE THE RADIATION LEVELS BEING NEAR ZERO, CITY OFFICIALS ARE STILL SUPPORTING A MEASURED EVACUATION--
--MEMORIALS ALL OVER THE COUNTRY AND THE WORLD--
--THE GUILTY PARTY HAS YET TO BE FOUND, AND WITH SO MANY QUESTIONS STILL LOOMING, WHY HASN'T THE HERO COMMUNITY STEPPED IN TO AID US, THE PUBLIC, THE AMERICAN PEOPLE? I ASK--
WHERE IS CAPTAIN ATOM?
TWO MORE DIED THIS MORNING?

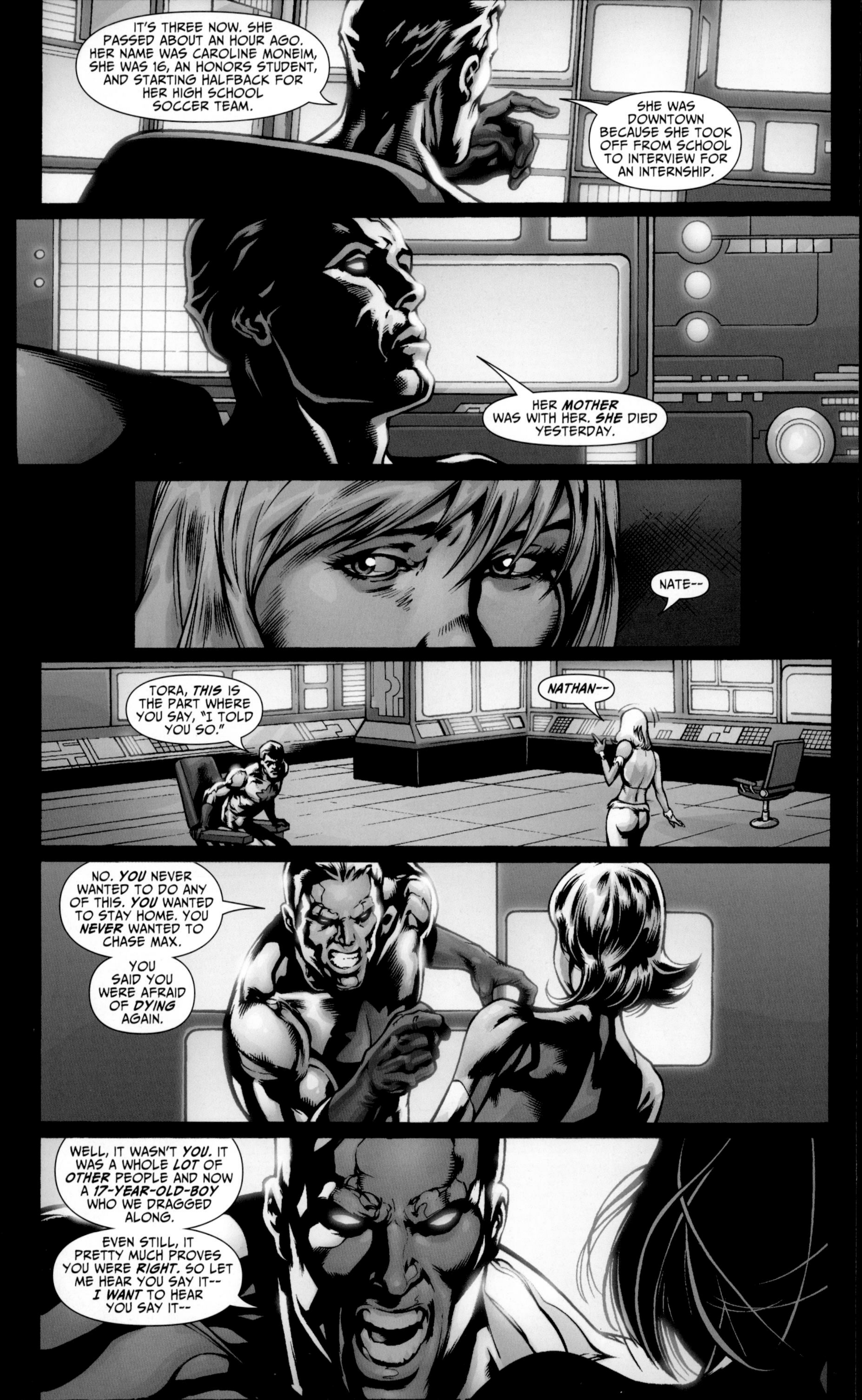
IT'S THREE NOW. SHE PASSED ABOUT AN HOUR AGO. HER NAME WAS CAROLINE MONEIM, SHE WAS 16, AN HONORS STUDENT, AND STARTING HALFBACK FOR HER HIGH SCHOOL SOCCER TEAM.
SHE WAS DOWNTOWN BECAUSE SHE TOOK OFF FROM SCHOOL TO INTERVIEW FOR AN INTERNSHIP.
HER MOTHER WAS WITH HER. SHE DIED YESTERDAY.
NATE--
TORA, THIS IS THE PART WHERE YOU SAY, "I TOLD YOU SO."
NATHAN--
NO. YOU NEVER WANTED TO DO ANY OF THIS. YOU WANTED TO STAY HOME. YOU NEVER WANTED TO CHASE MAX.
YOU SAID YOU WERE AFRAID OF DYING AGAIN.
WELL, IT WASN'T YOU. IT WAS A WHOLE LOT OF OTHER PEOPLE AND NOW A 17-YEAR-OLD-BOY WHO WE DRAGGED ALONG.
EVEN STILL, IT PRETTY MUCH PROVES YOU WERE RIGHT. SO LET ME HEAR YOU SAY IT-- I WANT TO HEAR YOU SAY IT--

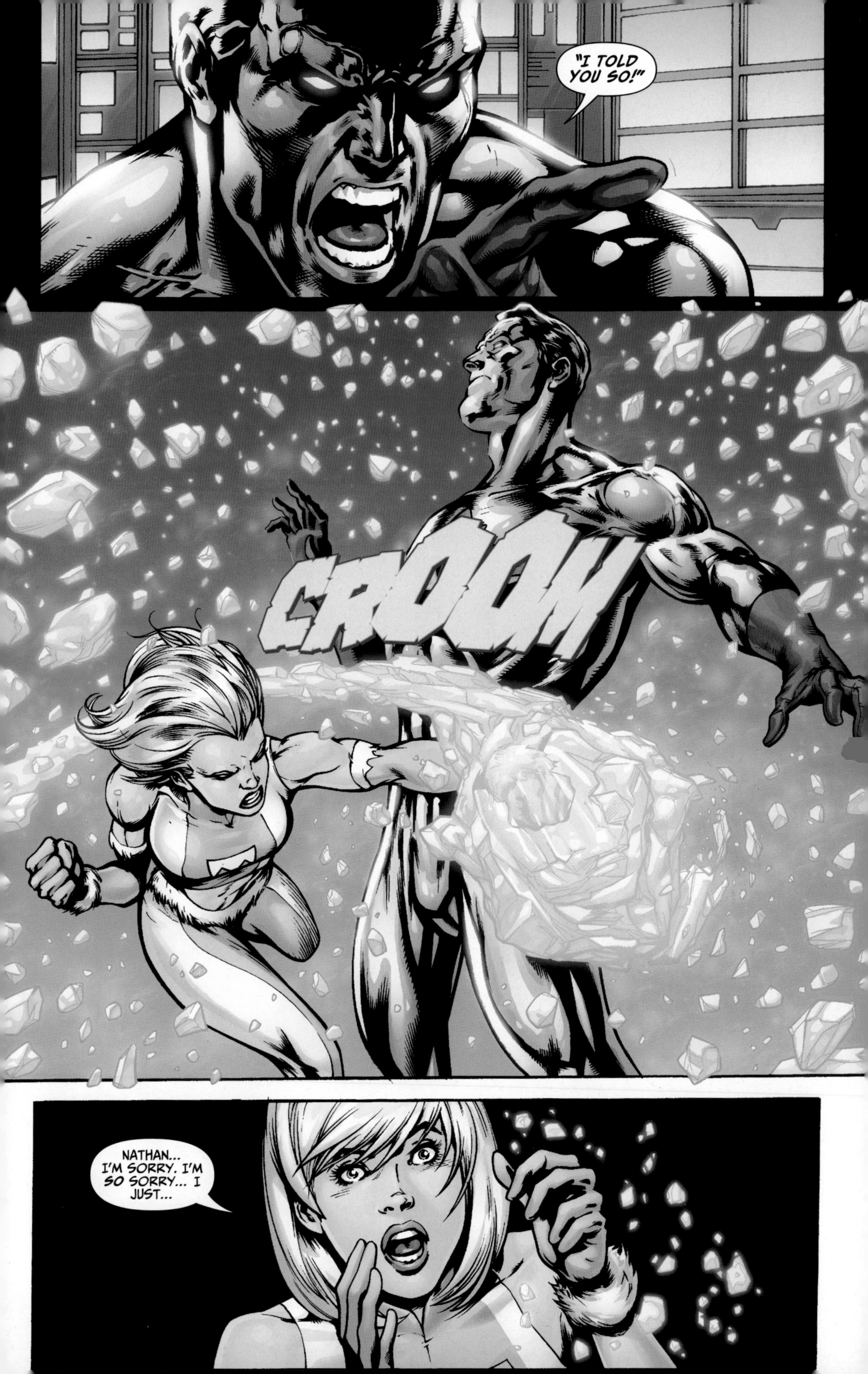
"I TOLD YOU SO!"
CROOM
NATHAN... I'M SORRY. I'M SO SORRY... I JUST...

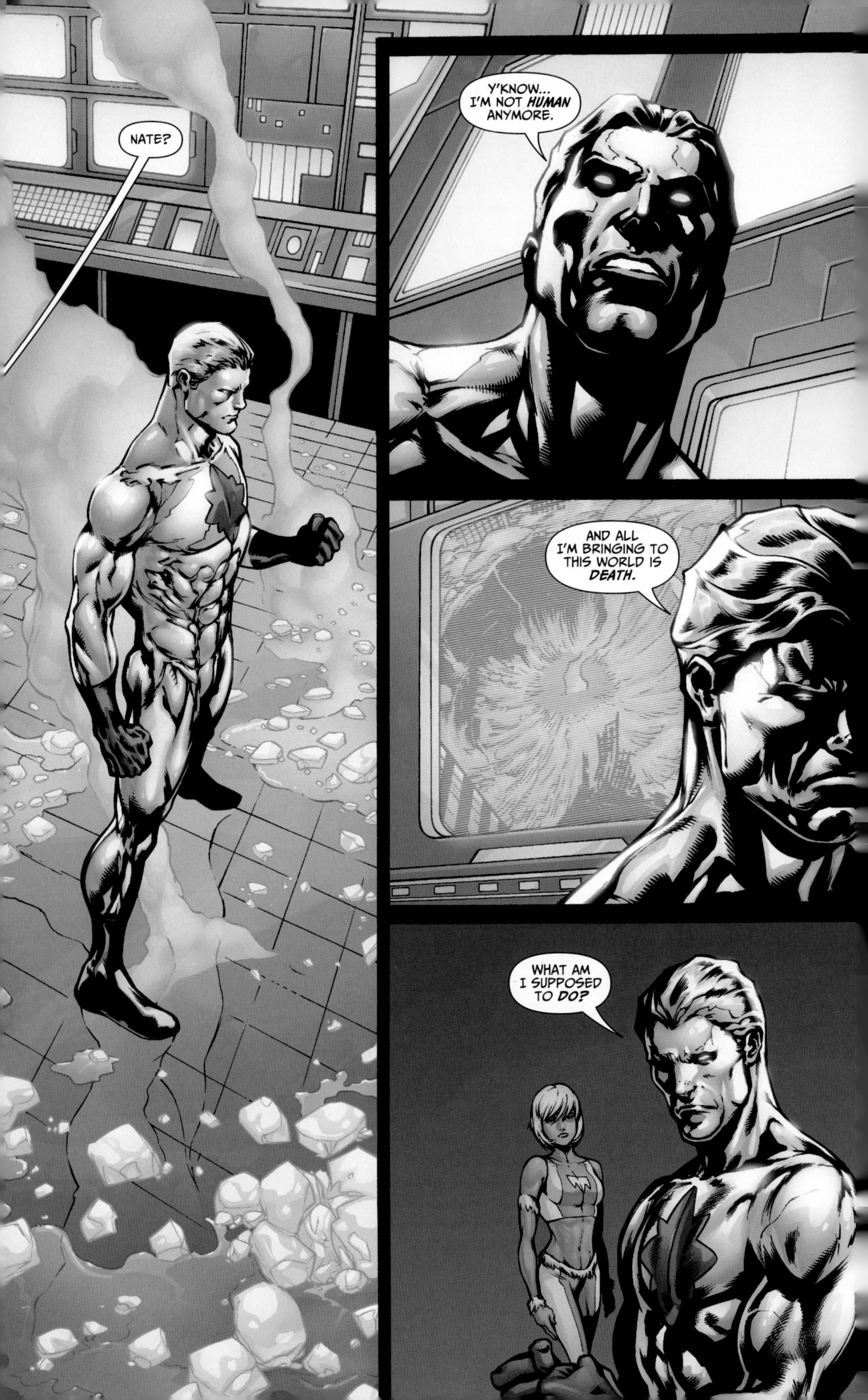
NATE?
Y'KNOW... I'M NOT *HUMAN* ANYMORE.
AND ALL I'M BRINGING TO THIS WORLD IS *DEATH.*
WHAT AM I SUPPOSED TO *DO?*

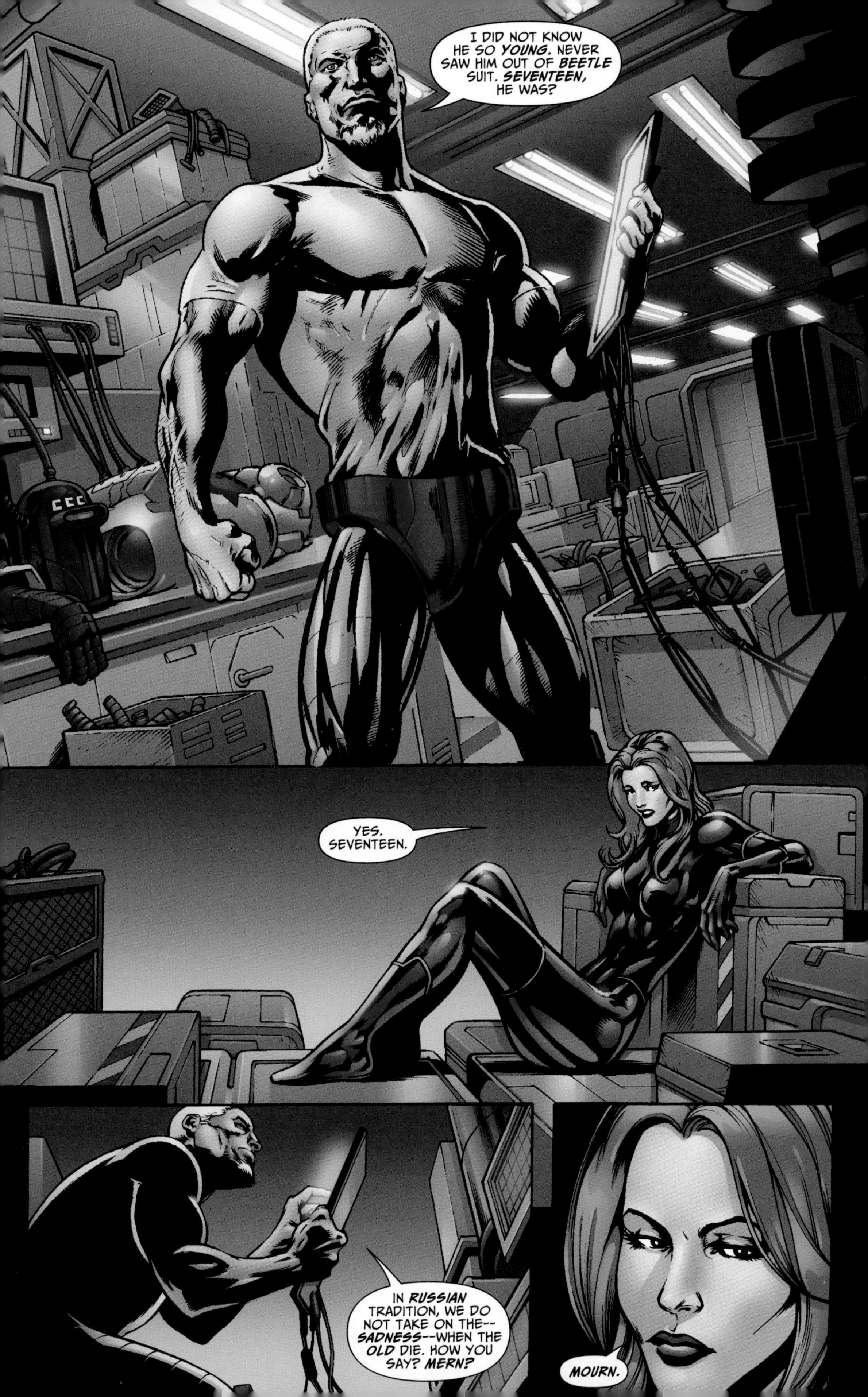
I DID NOT KNOW HE SO *YOUNG*. NEVER SAW HIM OUT OF *BEETLE* SUIT. *SEVENTEEN,* HE WAS?
YES. SEVENTEEN.
IN *RUSSIAN* TRADITION, WE DO NOT TAKE ON THE-- *SADNESS*--WHEN THE *OLD* DIE. HOW YOU SAY? *MERN?*
MOURN.

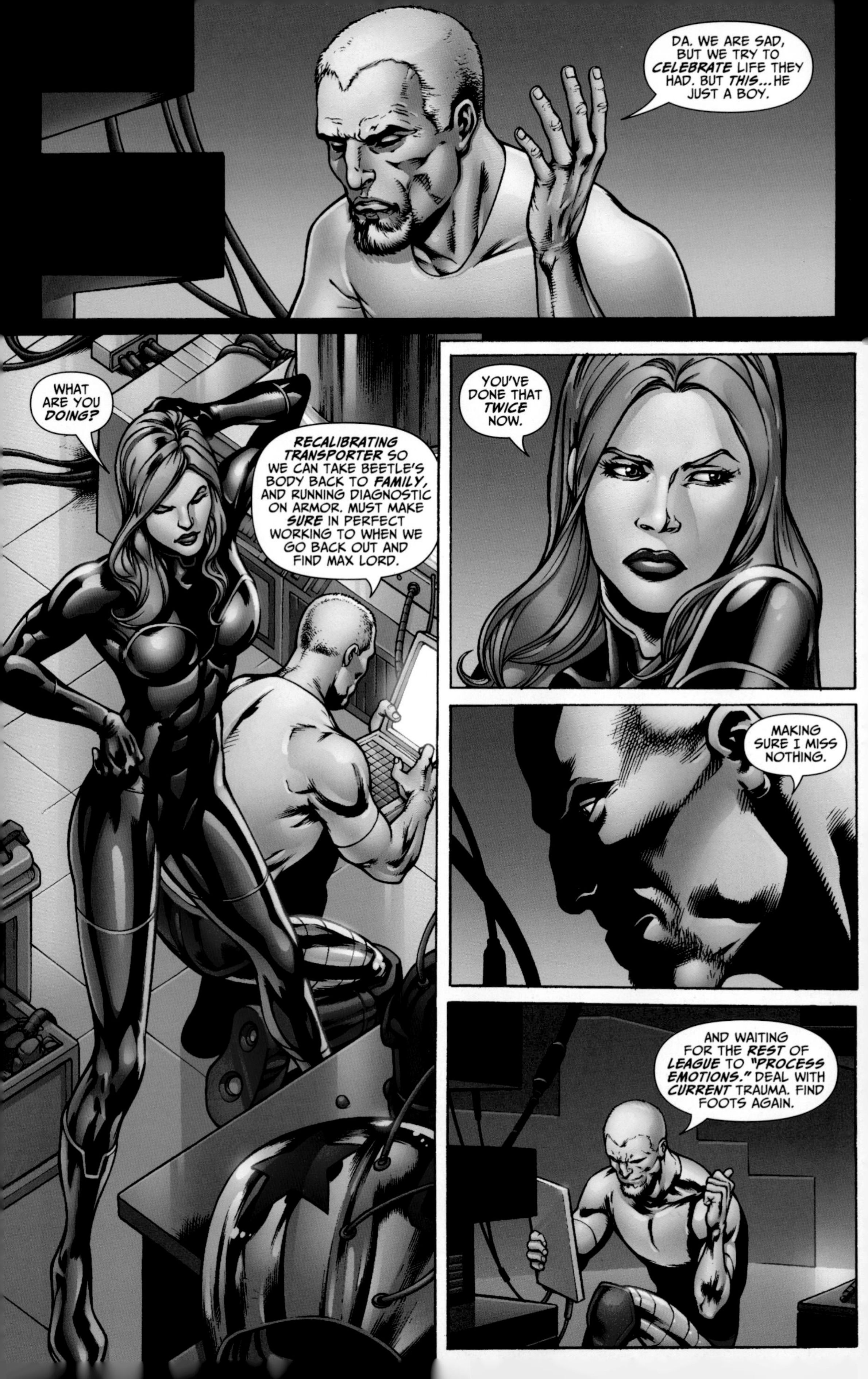
DA. WE ARE SAD, BUT WE TRY TO *CELEBRATE* LIFE THEY HAD. BUT *THIS*... HE JUST A BOY.
WHAT ARE YOU *DOING?*
RECALIBRATING TRANSPORTER SO WE CAN TAKE BEETLE'S BODY BACK TO *FAMILY*, AND RUNNING DIAGNOSTIC ON ARMOR. MUST MAKE *SURE* IN PERFECT WORKING TO WHEN WE GO BACK OUT AND FIND MAX LORD.
YOU'VE DONE THAT *TWICE* NOW.
MAKING SURE I MISS NOTHING.
AND WAITING FOR THE *REST* OF *LEAGUE* TO *"PROCESS EMOTIONS."* DEAL WITH *CURRENT* TRAUMA. FIND FOOTS AGAIN.

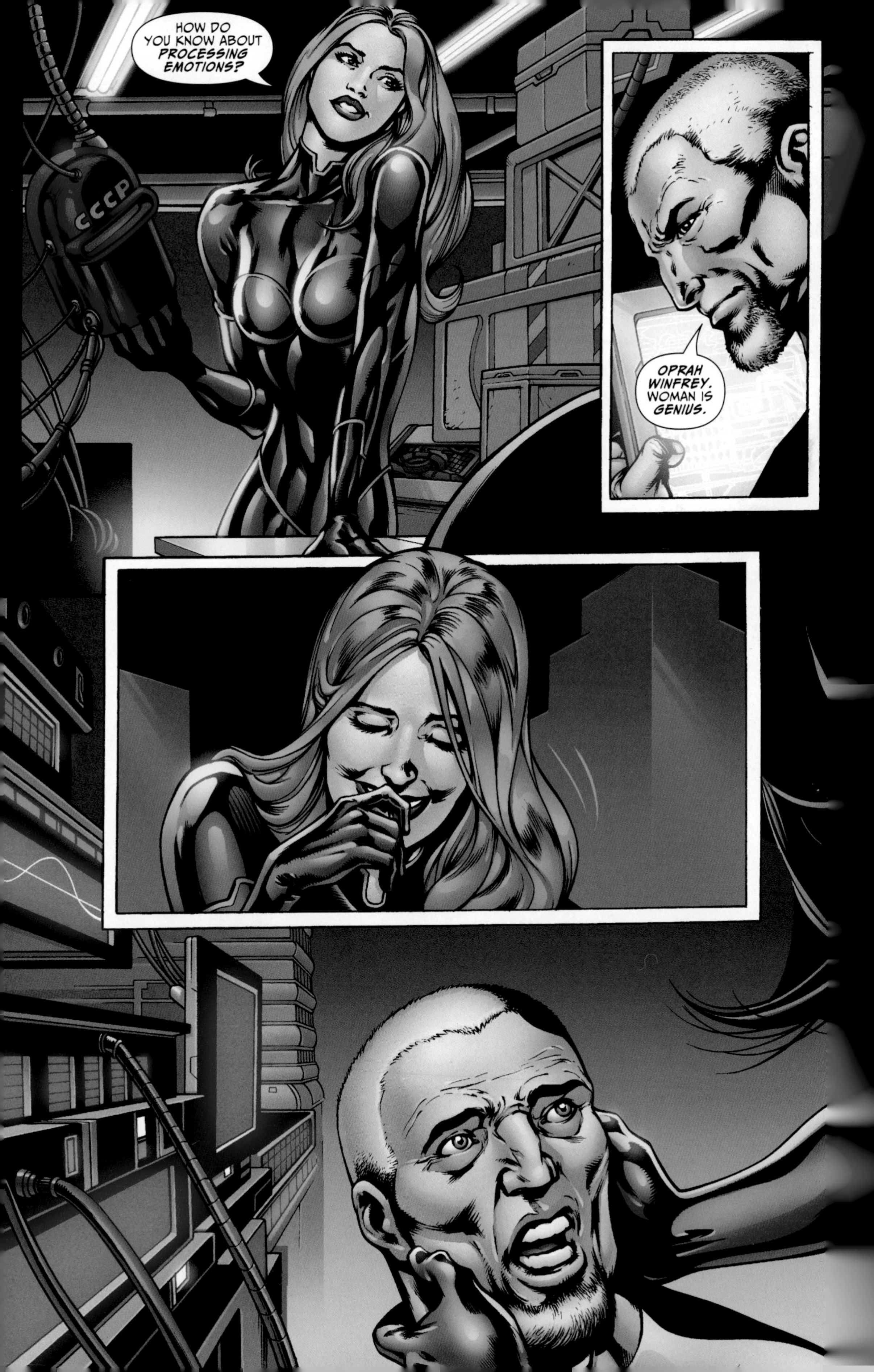
HOW DO YOU KNOW ABOUT PROCESSING EMOTIONS?
OPRAH WINFREY. WOMAN IS GENIUS.
CCCP

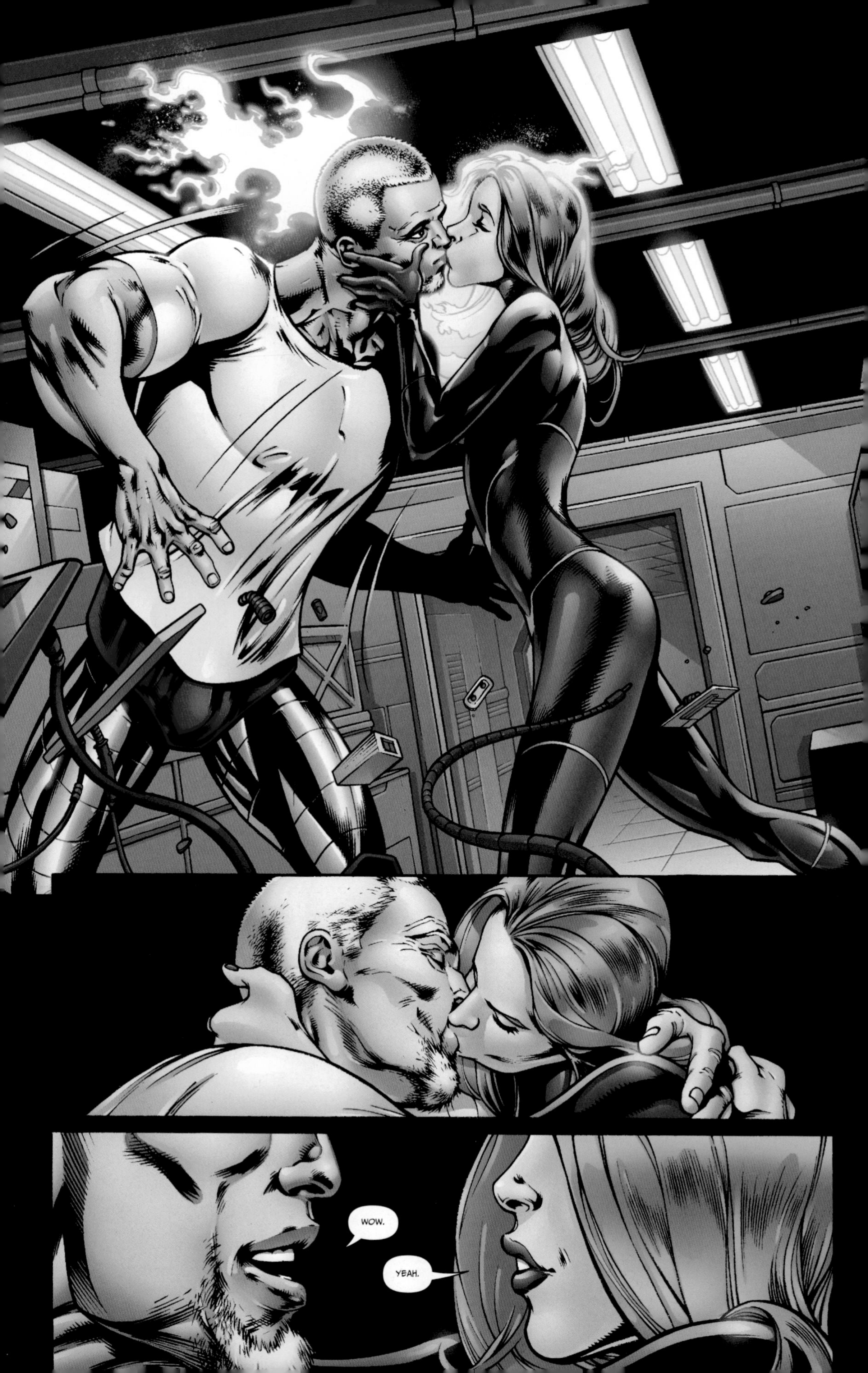
WOW.
YEAH.

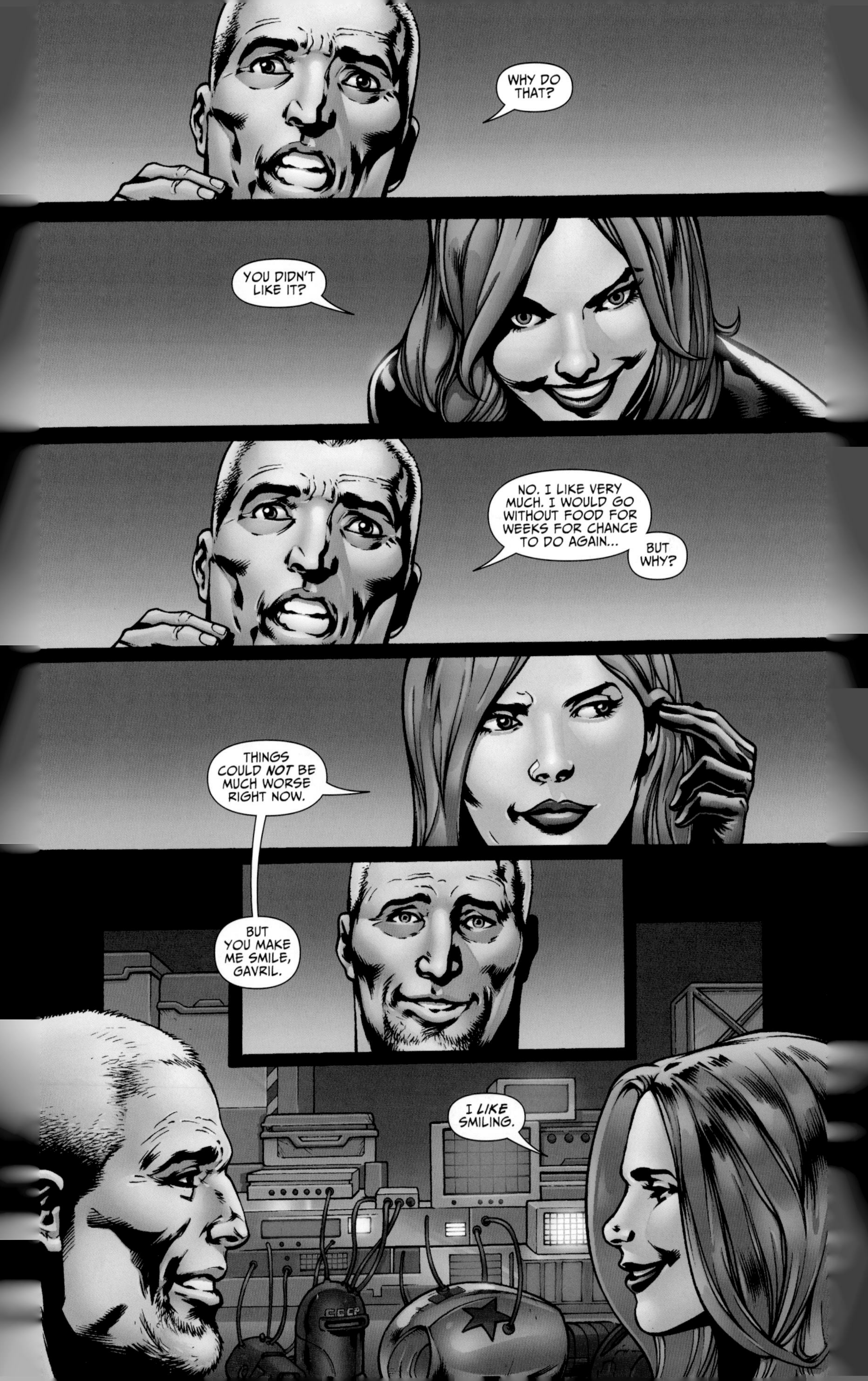
WHY DO THAT?
YOU DIDN'T LIKE IT?
NO. I LIKE VERY MUCH. I WOULD GO WITHOUT FOOD FOR WEEKS FOR CHANCE TO DO AGAIN...
BUT WHY?
THINGS COULD NOT BE MUCH WORSE RIGHT NOW.
BUT YOU MAKE ME SMILE, GAVRIL.
I LIKE SMILING.

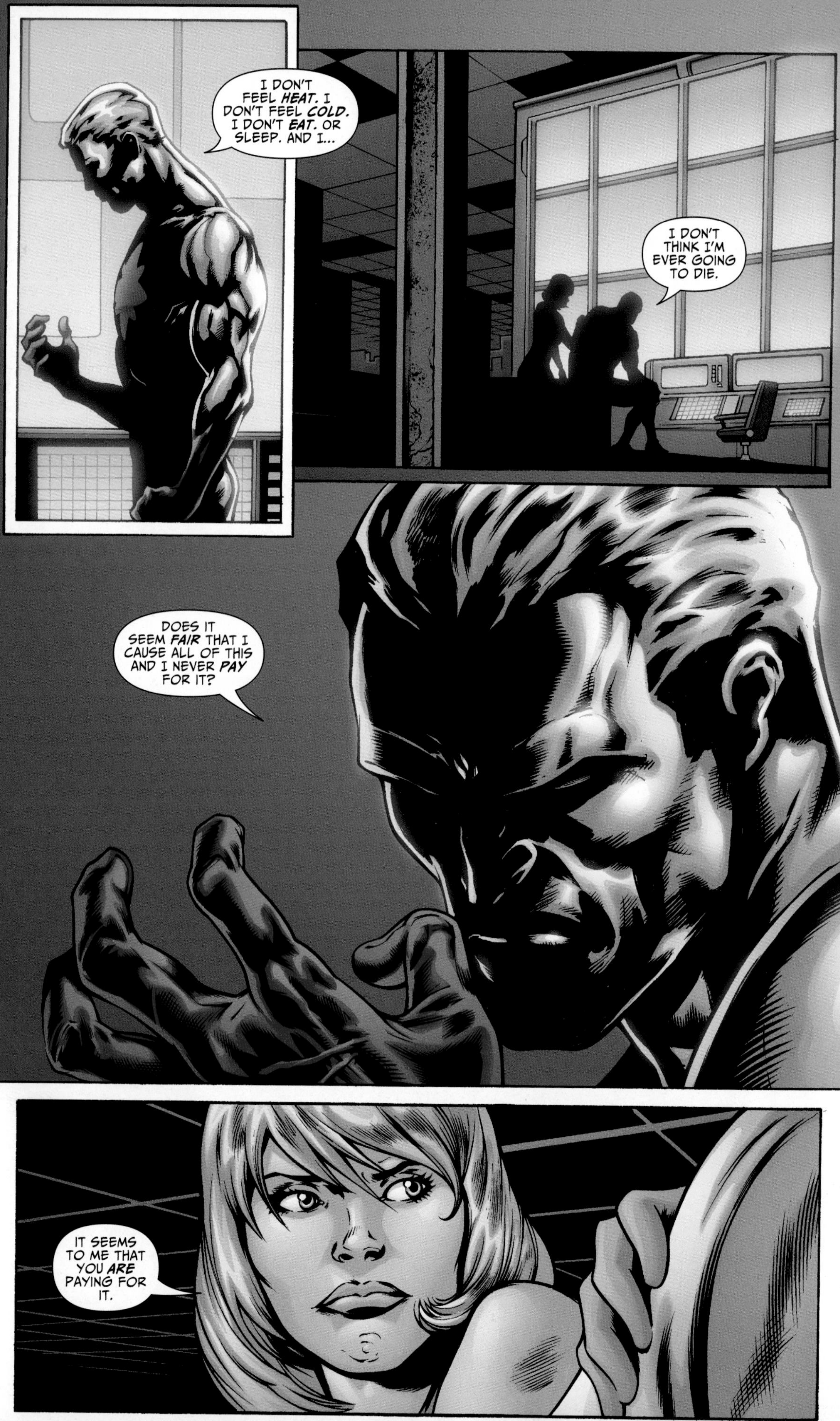
I DON'T FEEL *HEAT*. I DON'T FEEL *COLD*. I DON'T *EAT*. OR SLEEP. AND I...
I DON'T THINK I'M EVER GOING TO DIE.
DOES IT SEEM *FAIR* THAT I CAUSE ALL OF THIS AND I NEVER *PAY* FOR IT?
IT SEEMS TO ME THAT YOU *ARE* PAYING FOR IT.

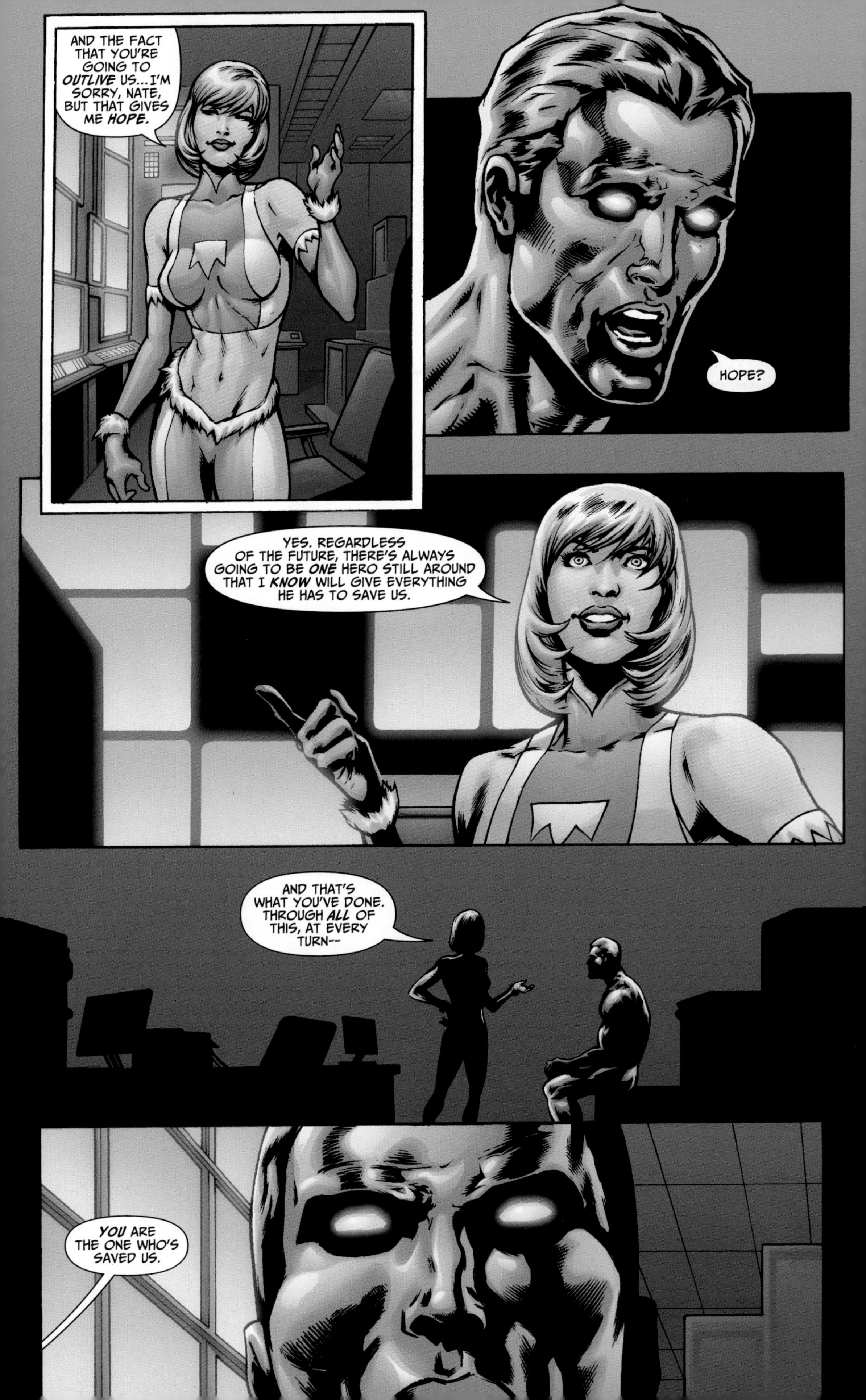
AND THE FACT THAT YOU'RE GOING TO *OUTLIVE* US...I'M SORRY, NATE, BUT THAT GIVES ME *HOPE.*
HOPE?
YES. REGARDLESS OF THE FUTURE, THERE'S ALWAYS GOING TO BE *ONE* HERO STILL AROUND THAT I *KNOW* WILL GIVE EVERYTHING HE HAS TO SAVE US.
AND THAT'S WHAT YOU'VE DONE. THROUGH *ALL* OF THIS, AT EVERY TURN--
YOU ARE THE ONE WHO'S SAVED US.

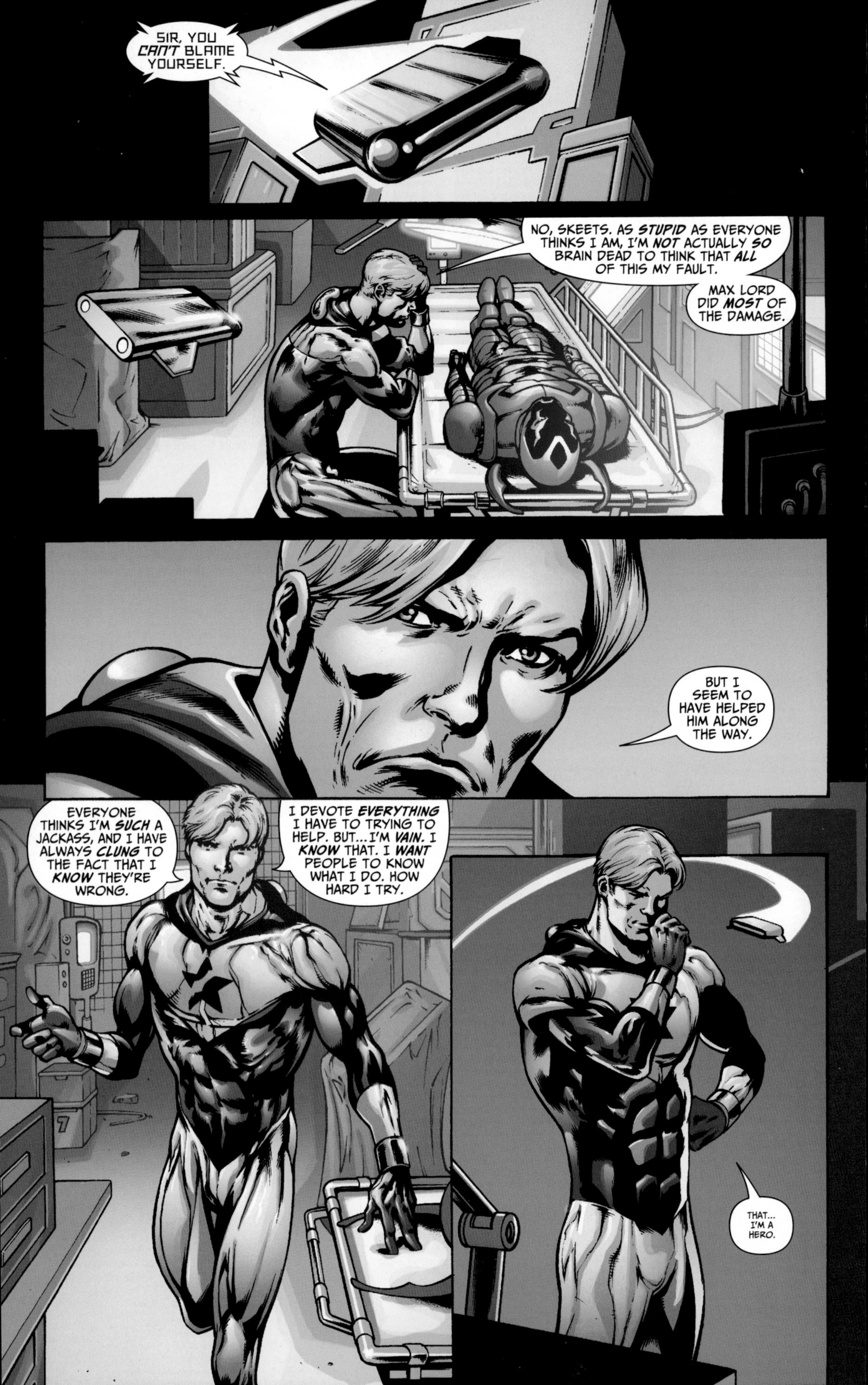
SIR, YOU CAN'T BLAME YOURSELF.
NO, SKEETS. AS STUPID AS EVERYONE THINKS I AM, I'M NOT ACTUALLY SO BRAIN DEAD TO THINK THAT ALL OF THIS MY FAULT.
MAX LORD DID MOST OF THE DAMAGE.
BUT I SEEM TO HAVE HELPED HIM ALONG THE WAY.
EVERYONE THINKS I'M SUCH A JACKASS, AND I HAVE ALWAYS CLUNG TO THE FACT THAT I KNOW THEY'RE WRONG.
I DEVOTE EVERYTHING I HAVE TO TRYING TO HELP. BUT... I'M VAIN. I KNOW THAT. I WANT PEOPLE TO KNOW WHAT I DO. HOW HARD I TRY.
THAT... I'M A HERO.

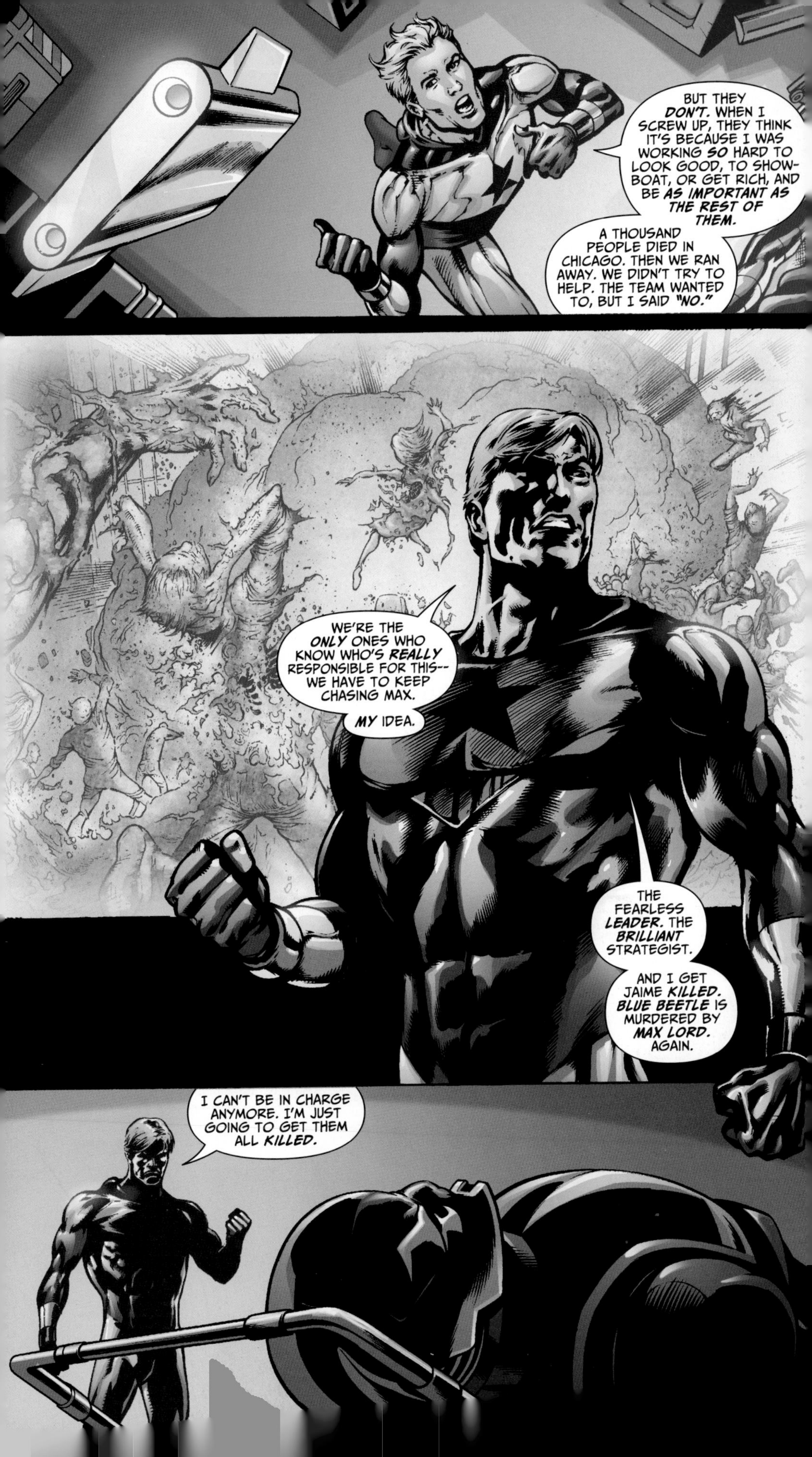

BUT THEY DON'T. WHEN I SCREW UP, THEY THINK IT'S BECAUSE I WAS WORKING SO HARD TO LOOK GOOD, TO SHOW-BOAT, OR GET RICH, AND BE AS IMPORTANT AS THE REST OF THEM.
A THOUSAND PEOPLE DIED IN CHICAGO. THEN WE RAN AWAY. WE DIDN'T TRY TO HELP. THE TEAM WANTED TO, BUT I SAID "NO."
WE'RE THE ONLY ONES WHO KNOW WHO'S REALLY RESPONSIBLE FOR THIS-- WE HAVE TO KEEP CHASING MAX.
MY IDEA.
THE FEARLESS LEADER. THE BRILLIANT STRATEGIST.
AND I GET JAIME KILLED. BLUE BEETLE IS MURDERED BY MAX LORD. AGAIN.
I CAN'T BE IN CHARGE ANYMORE. I'M JUST GOING TO GET THEM ALL KILLED.

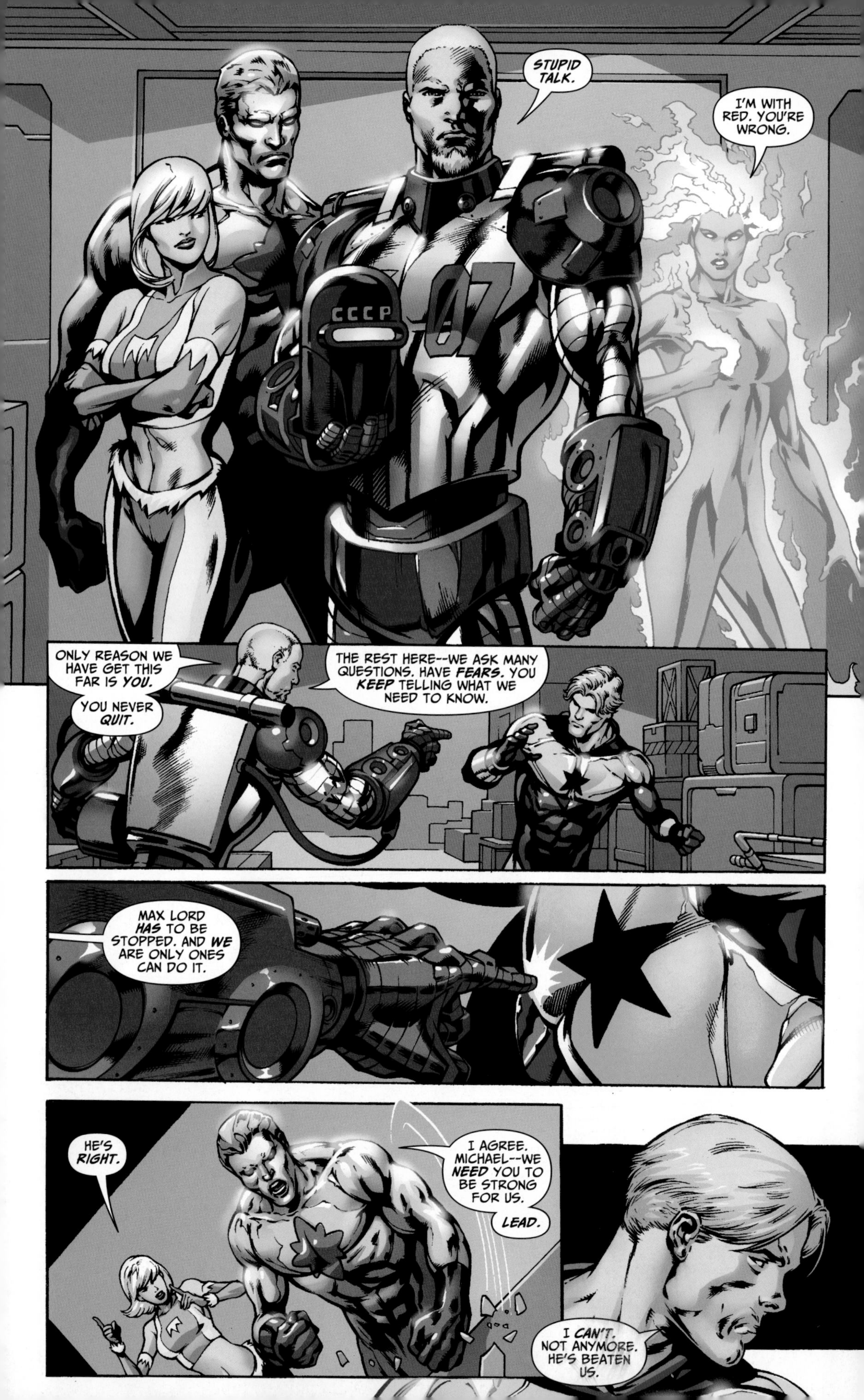
STUPID TALK.
I'M WITH RED. YOU'RE WRONG.
ONLY REASON WE HAVE GET THIS FAR IS YOU.
YOU NEVER QUIT.
THE REST HERE--WE ASK MANY QUESTIONS. HAVE FEARS. YOU KEEP TELLING WHAT WE NEED TO KNOW.
MAX LORD HAS TO BE STOPPED. AND WE ARE ONLY ONES CAN DO IT.
HE'S RIGHT.
I AGREE. MICHAEL--WE NEED YOU TO BE STRONG FOR US.
LEAD.
I CAN'T. NOT ANYMORE. HE'S BEATEN US.

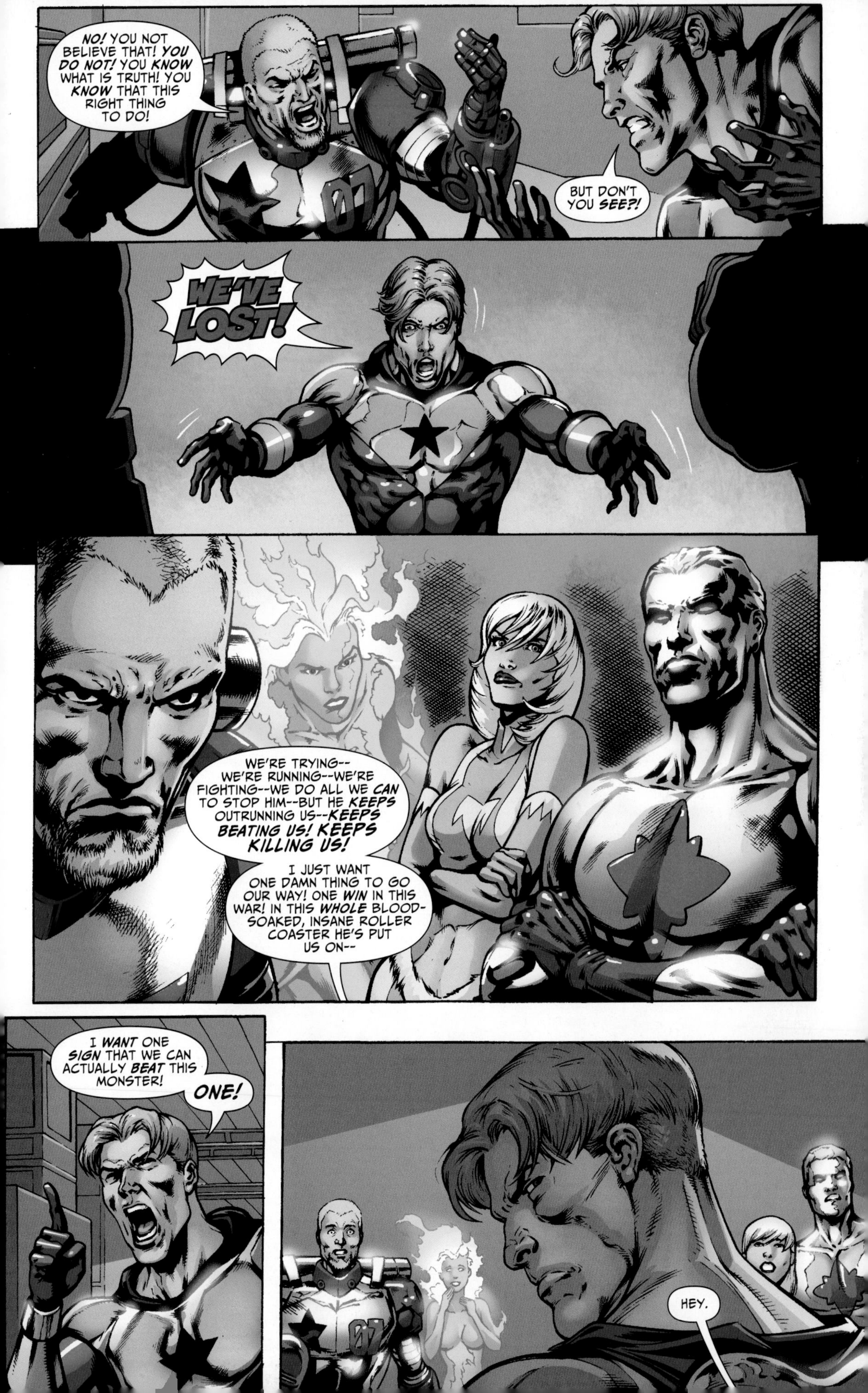
NO! YOU NOT BELIEVE THAT! YOU DO NOT! YOU KNOW WHAT IS TRUTH! YOU KNOW THAT THIS RIGHT THING TO DO!
BUT DON'T YOU SEE?!
WE'VE LOST!
WE'RE TRYING-- WE'RE RUNNING--WE'RE FIGHTING--WE DO ALL WE CAN TO STOP HIM--BUT HE KEEPS OUTRUNNING US--KEEPS BEATING US! KEEPS KILLING US!
I JUST WANT ONE DAMN THING TO GO OUR WAY! ONE WIN IN THIS WAR! IN THIS WHOLE BLOOD-SOAKED, INSANE ROLLER COASTER HE'S PUT US ON--
I WANT ONE SIGN THAT WE CAN ACTUALLY BEAT THIS MONSTER!
ONE!
HEY.

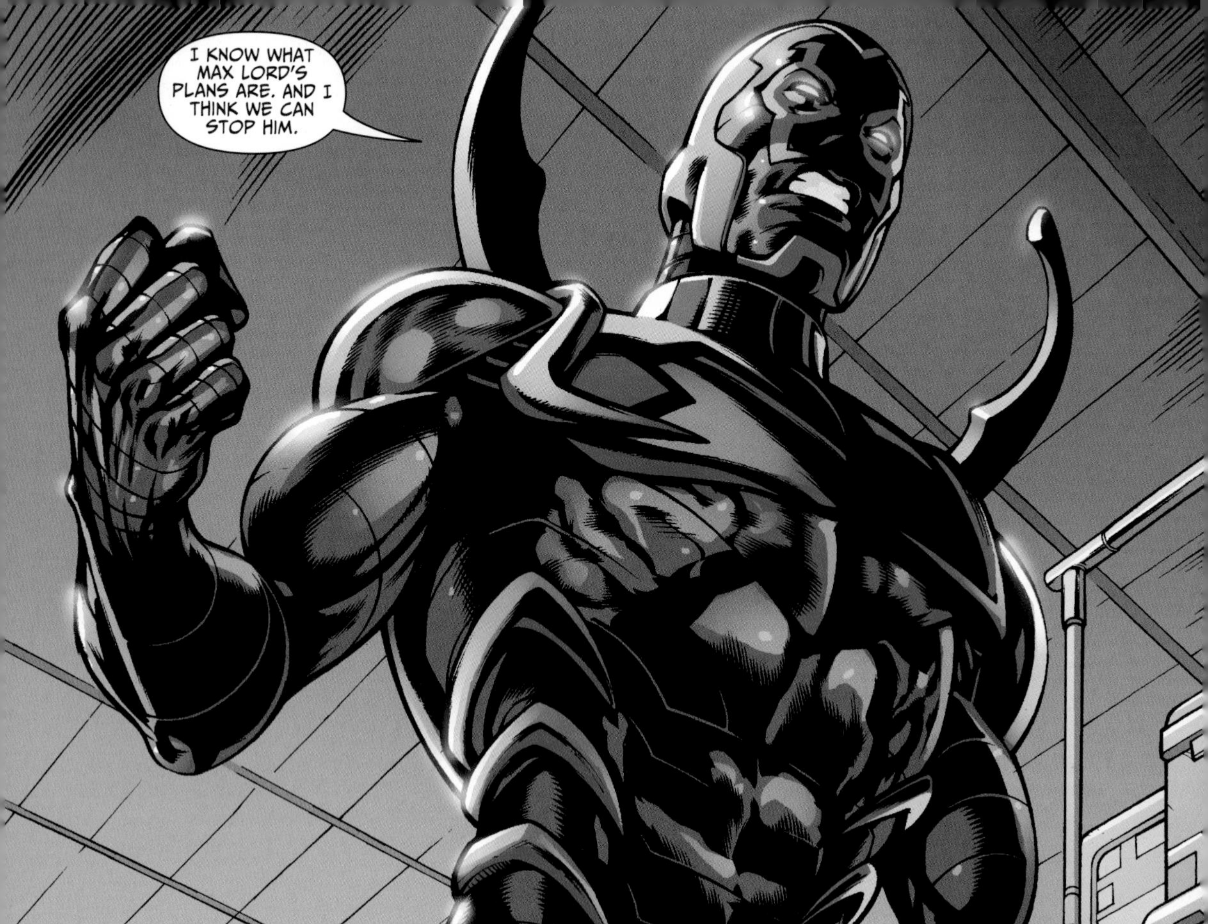
I KNOW WHAT MAX LORD'S PLANS ARE. AND I THINK WE CAN STOP HIM.

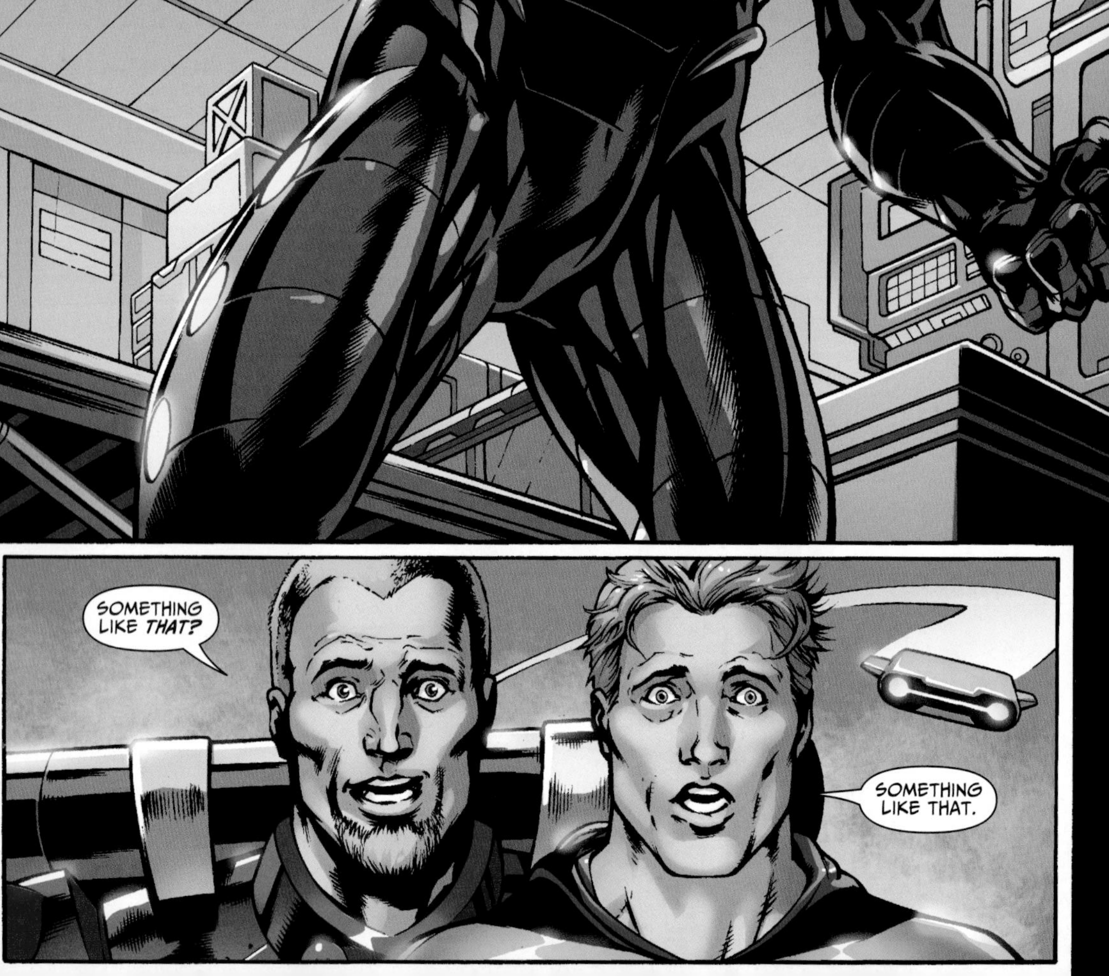
SOMETHING LIKE *THAT?*
SOMETHING LIKE THAT.

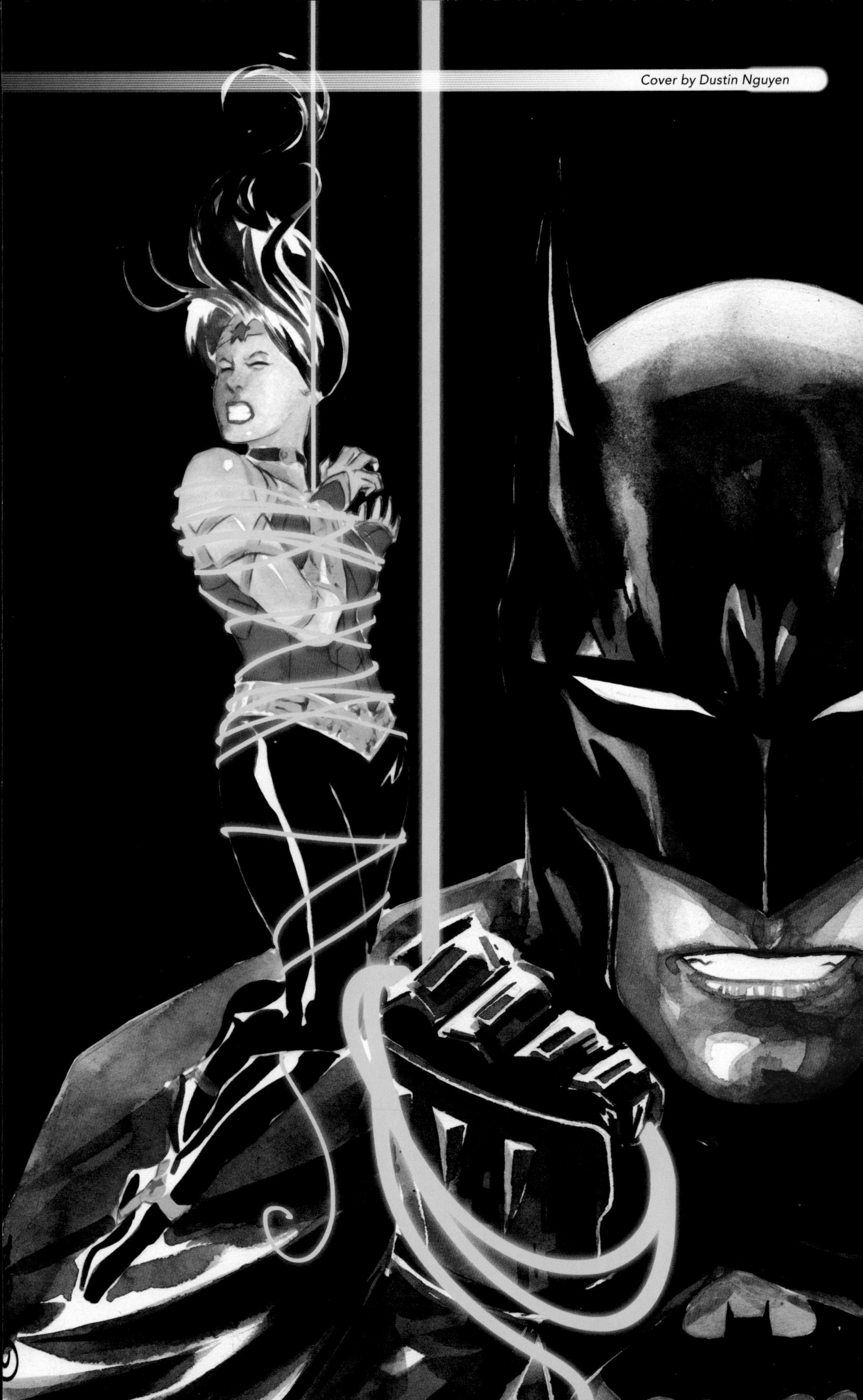

Cover by Dustin Nguyen

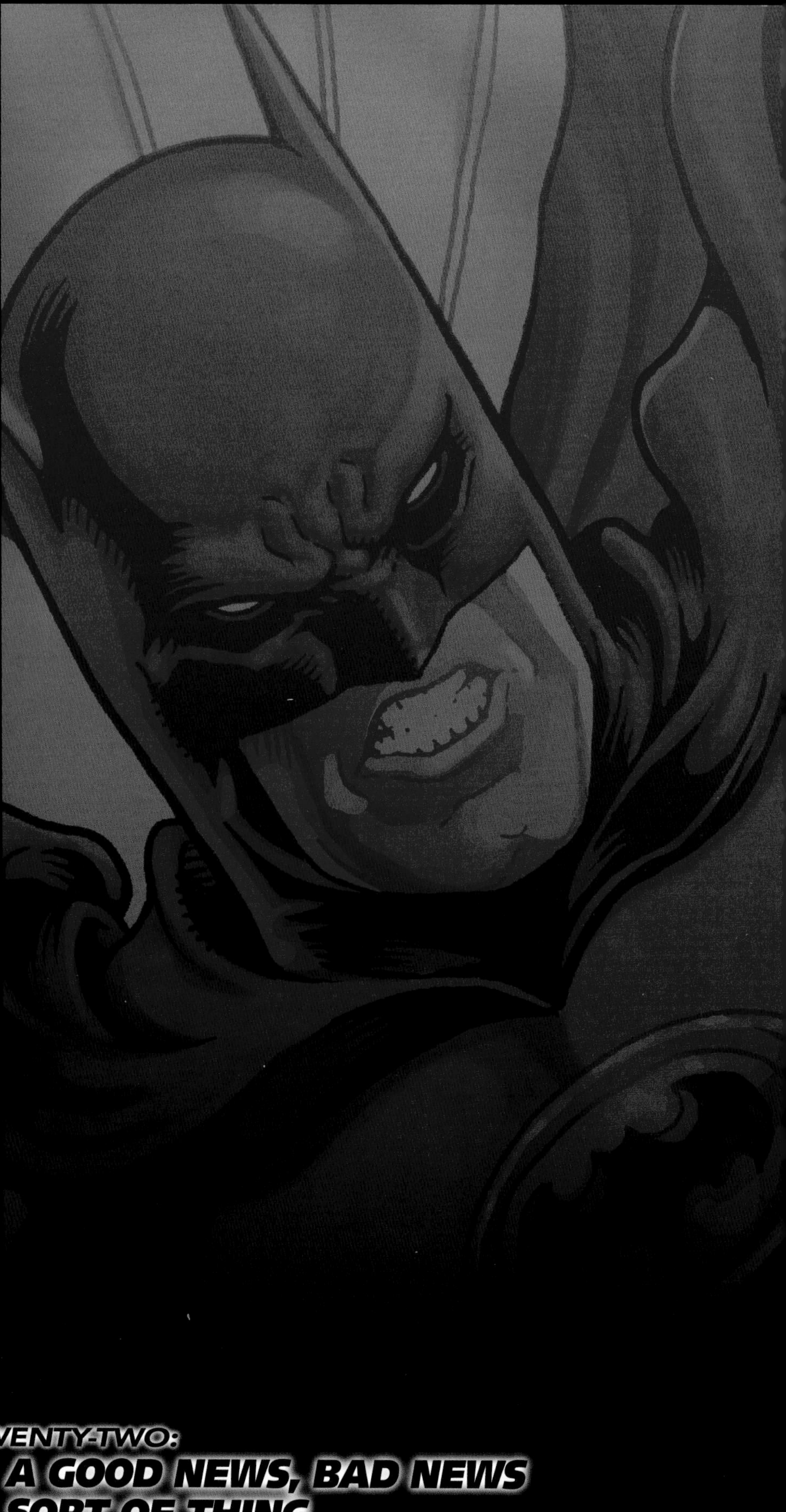

PART TWENTY-TWO:

A GOOD NEWS, BAD NEWS SORT OF THING

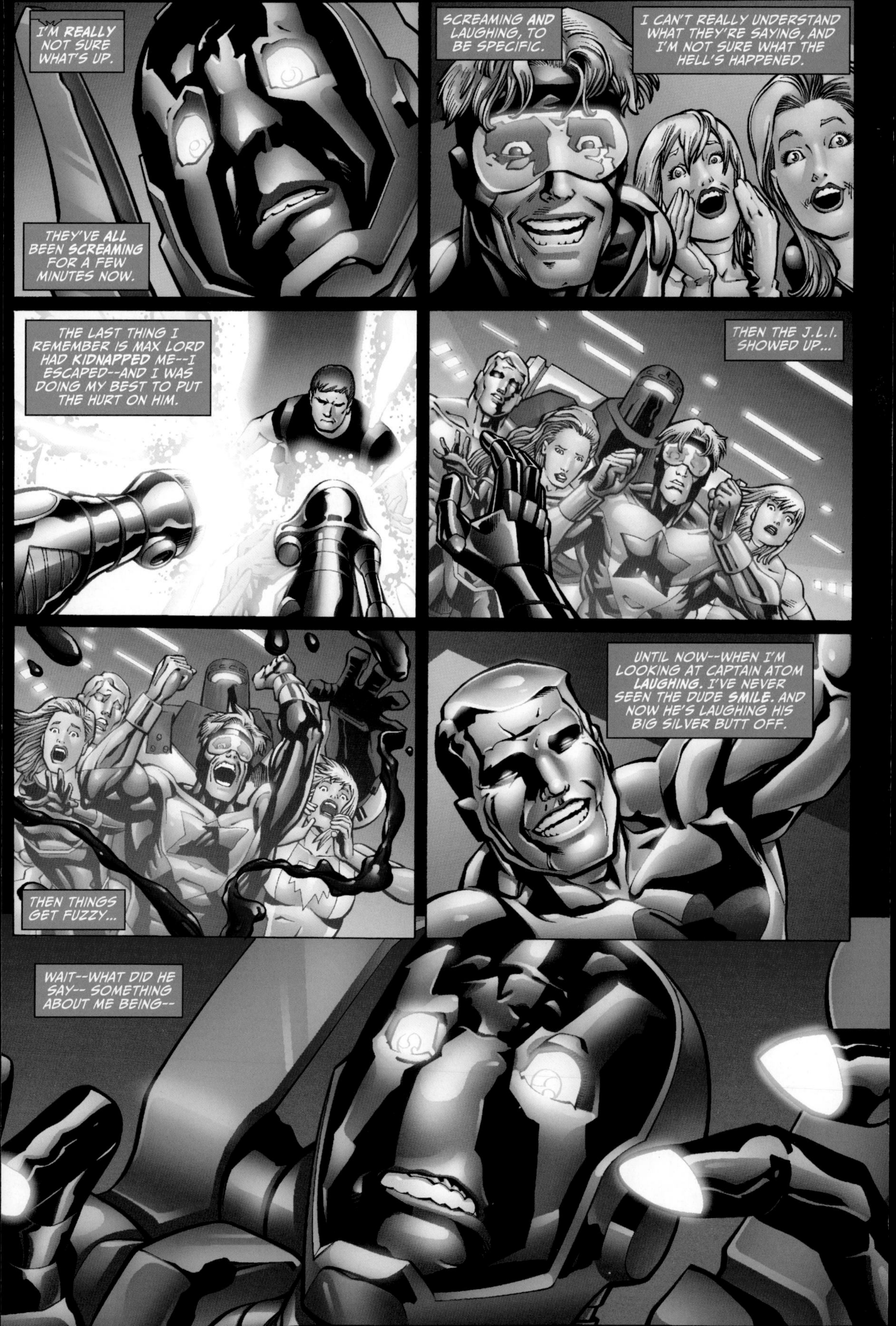
I'M REALLY NOT SURE WHAT'S UP.
THEY'VE ALL BEEN SCREAMING FOR A FEW MINUTES NOW.
SCREAMING AND LAUGHING, TO BE SPECIFIC.
I CAN'T REALLY UNDERSTAND WHAT THEY'RE SAYING, AND I'M NOT SURE WHAT THE HELL'S HAPPENED.
THE LAST THING I REMEMBER IS MAX LORD HAD KIDNAPPED ME--I ESCAPED--AND I WAS DOING MY BEST TO PUT THE HURT ON HIM.
THEN THE J.L.I. SHOWED UP...
THEN THINGS GET FUZZY...
UNTIL NOW--WHEN I'M LOOKING AT CAPTAIN ATOM LAUGHING. I'VE NEVER SEEN THE DUDE SMILE. AND NOW HE'S LAUGHING HIS BIG SILVER BUTT OFF.
WAIT--WHAT DID HE SAY-- SOMETHING ABOUT ME BEING--

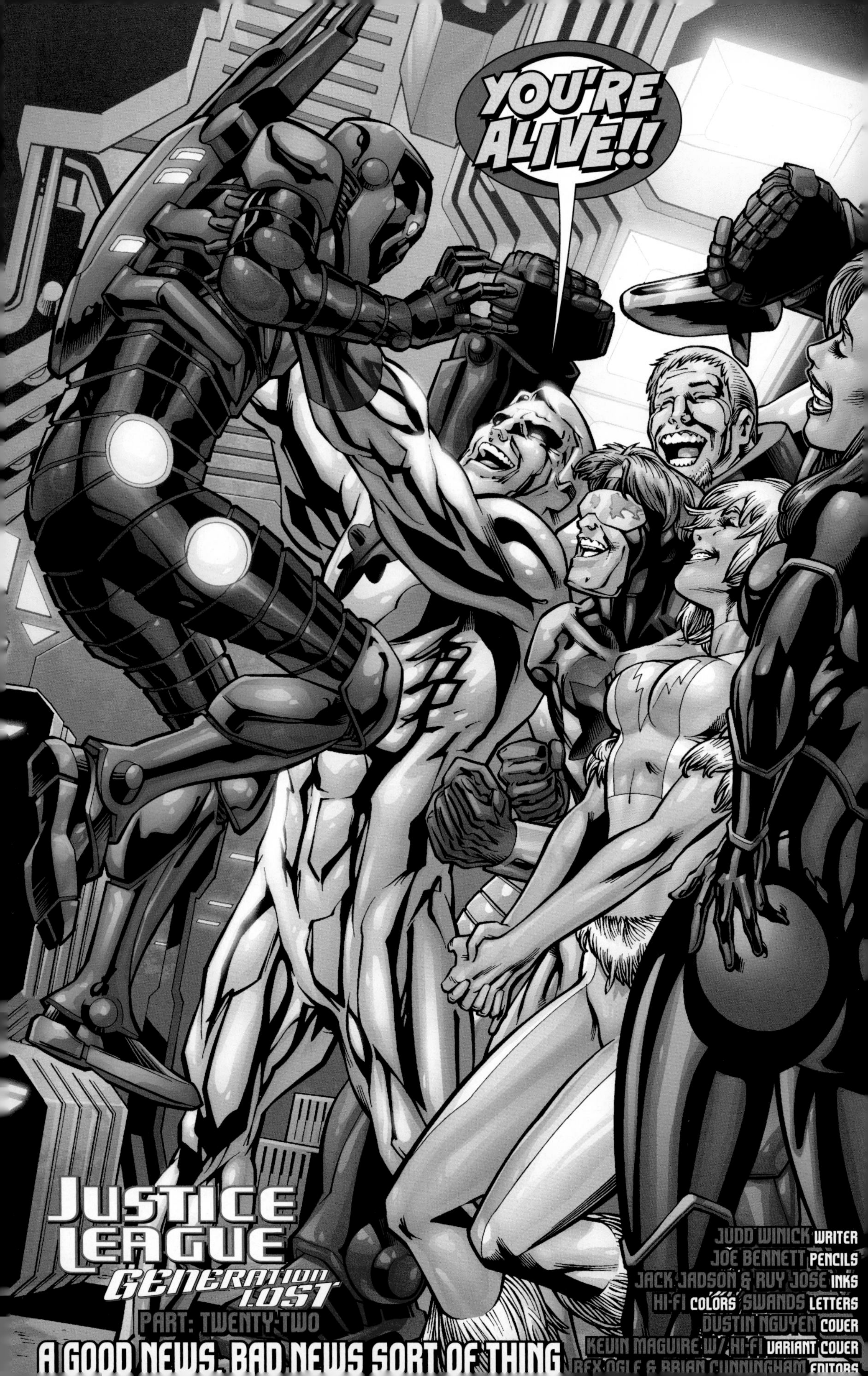
YOU'RE ALIVE!!
JUSTICE LEAGUE
GENERATION LOST
PART: TWENTY-TWO
A GOOD NEWS, BAD NEWS SORT OF THING
JUDD WINICK WRITER
JOE BENNETT PENCILS
JACK JADSON & RUY JOSE INKS
HI-FI COLORS SWANDS LETTERS
DUSTIN NGUYEN COVER
KEVIN MAGUIRE W/ HI-FI VARIANT COVER
REX OGLE & BRIAN CUNNINGHAM EDITORS

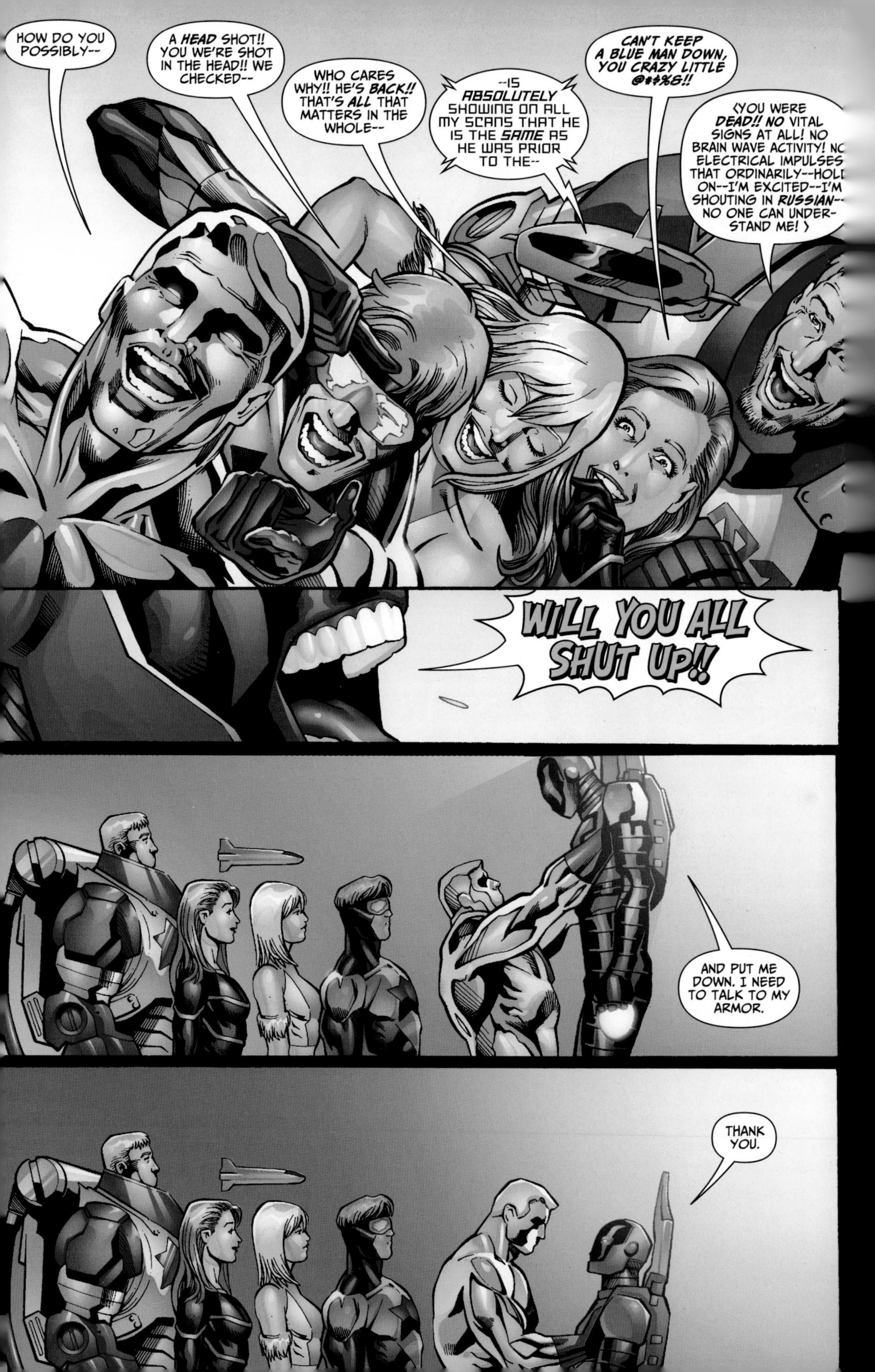
HOW DO YOU POSSIBLY--
A HEAD SHOT!! YOU WE'RE SHOT IN THE HEAD!! WE CHECKED--
WHO CARES WHY!! HE'S BACK!! THAT'S ALL THAT MATTERS IN THE WHOLE--
--IS ABSOLUTELY SHOWING ON ALL MY SCANS THAT HE IS THE SAME AS HE WAS PRIOR TO THE--
CAN'T KEEP A BLUE MAN DOWN, YOU CRAZY LITTLE @#$%&!!
‹YOU WERE DEAD!! NO VITAL SIGNS AT ALL! NO BRAIN WAVE ACTIVITY! NO ELECTRICAL IMPULSES THAT ORDINARILY--HOLD ON--I'M EXCITED--I'M SHOUTING IN RUSSIAN--NO ONE CAN UNDERSTAND ME!›
WILL YOU ALL SHUT UP!!
AND PUT ME DOWN. I NEED TO TALK TO MY ARMOR.
THANK YOU.

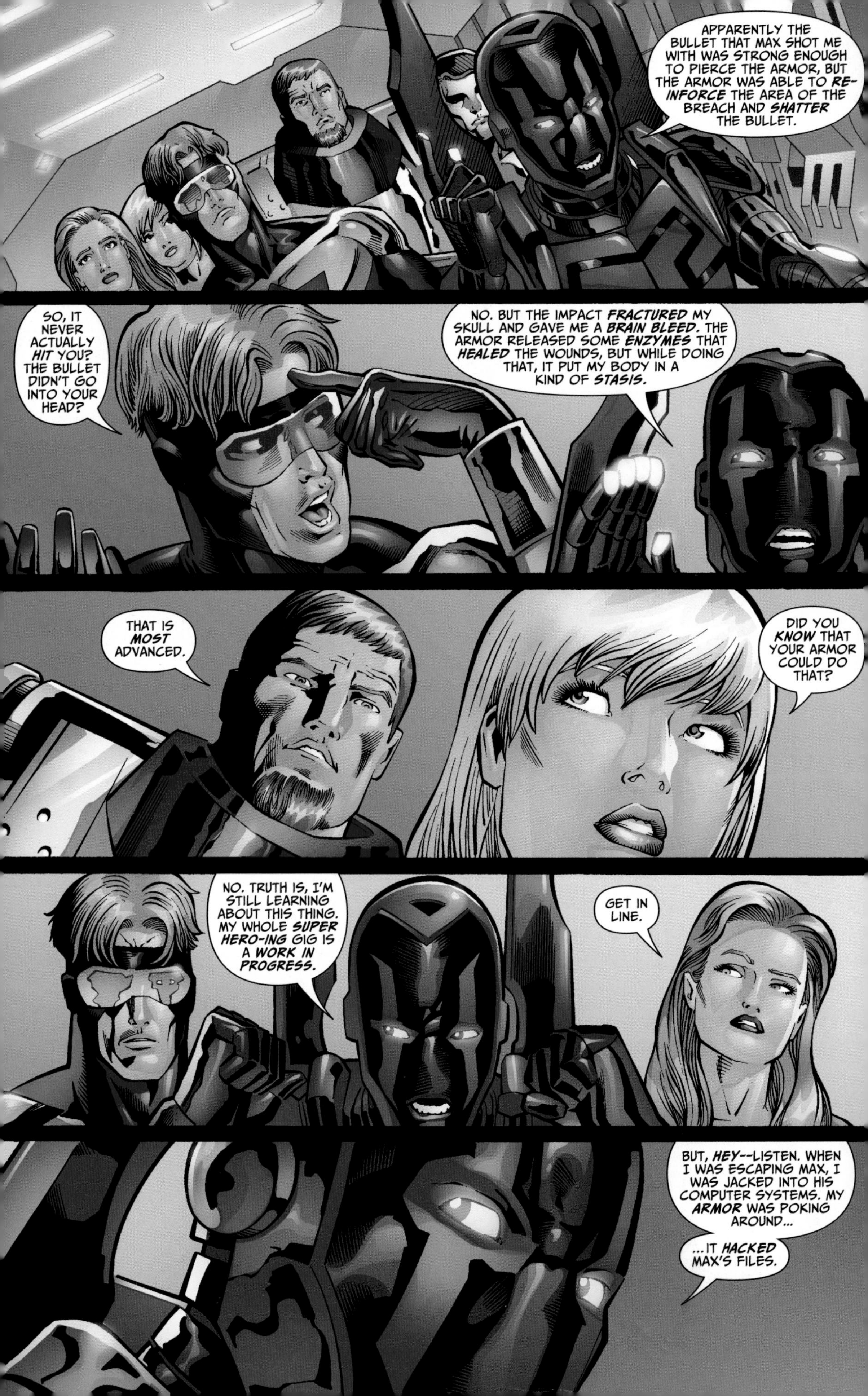
APPARENTLY THE BULLET THAT MAX SHOT ME WITH WAS STRONG ENOUGH TO PIERCE THE ARMOR, BUT THE ARMOR WAS ABLE TO RE-INFORCE THE AREA OF THE BREACH AND SHATTER THE BULLET.
SO, IT NEVER ACTUALLY HIT YOU? THE BULLET DIDN'T GO INTO YOUR HEAD?
NO. BUT THE IMPACT FRACTURED MY SKULL AND GAVE ME A BRAIN BLEED. THE ARMOR RELEASED SOME ENZYMES THAT HEALED THE WOUNDS, BUT WHILE DOING THAT, IT PUT MY BODY IN A KIND OF STASIS.
THAT IS MOST ADVANCED.
DID YOU KNOW THAT YOUR ARMOR COULD DO THAT?
NO. TRUTH IS, I'M STILL LEARNING ABOUT THIS THING. MY WHOLE SUPER HERO-ING GIG IS A WORK IN PROGRESS.
GET IN LINE.
BUT, HEY--LISTEN. WHEN I WAS ESCAPING MAX, I WAS JACKED INTO HIS COMPUTER SYSTEMS. MY ARMOR WAS POKING AROUND...
...IT HACKED MAX'S FILES.

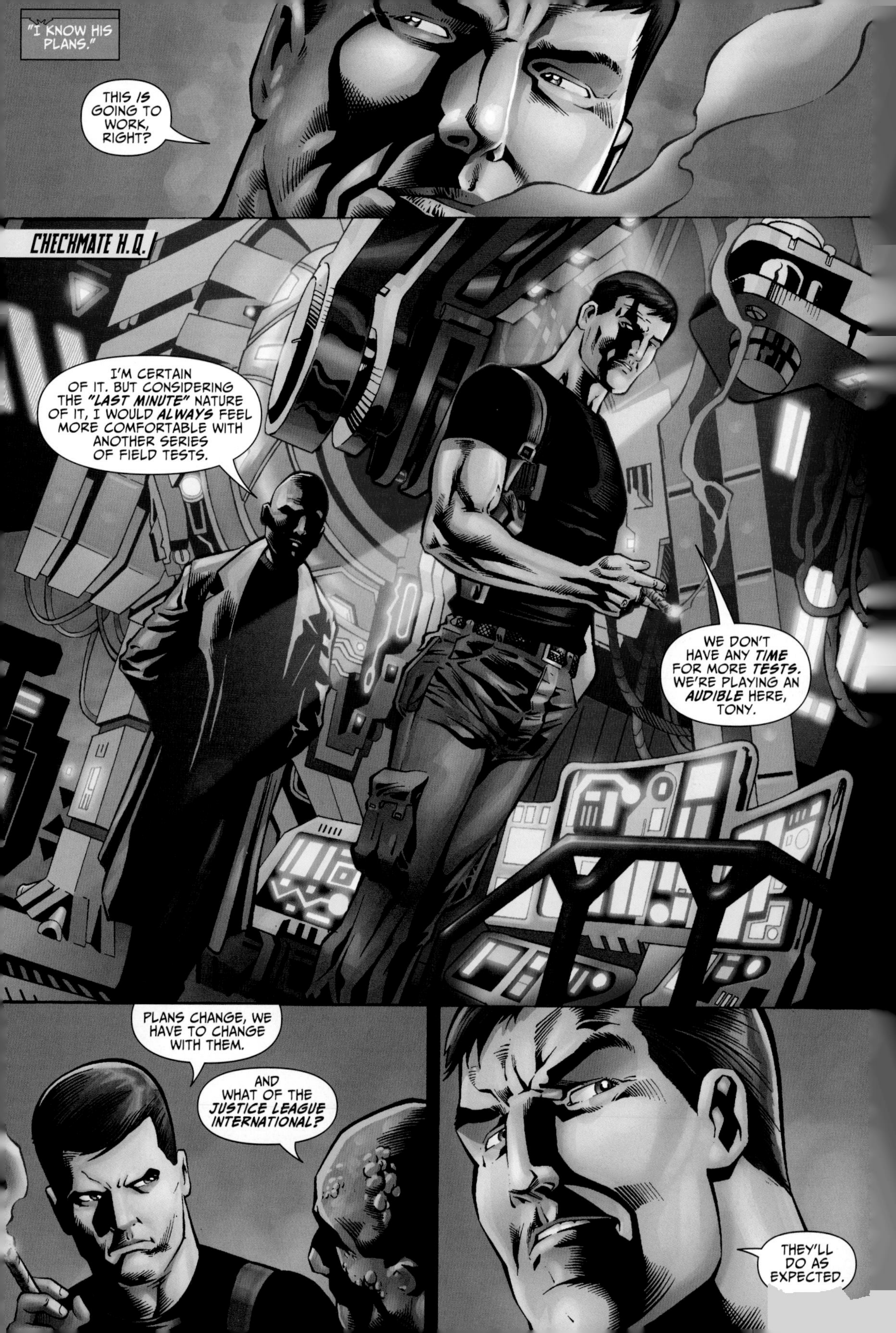
"I KNOW HIS PLANS."
THIS *IS* GOING TO WORK, RIGHT?
CHECKMATE H.Q.
I'M CERTAIN OF IT. BUT CONSIDERING THE *"LAST MINUTE"* NATURE OF IT, I WOULD *ALWAYS* FEEL MORE COMFORTABLE WITH ANOTHER SERIES OF FIELD TESTS.
WE DON'T HAVE ANY *TIME* FOR MORE *TESTS.* WE'RE PLAYING AN *AUDIBLE* HERE, TONY.
PLANS CHANGE, WE HAVE TO CHANGE WITH THEM.
AND WHAT OF THE *JUSTICE LEAGUE INTERNATIONAL?*
THEY'LL DO AS EXPECTED.

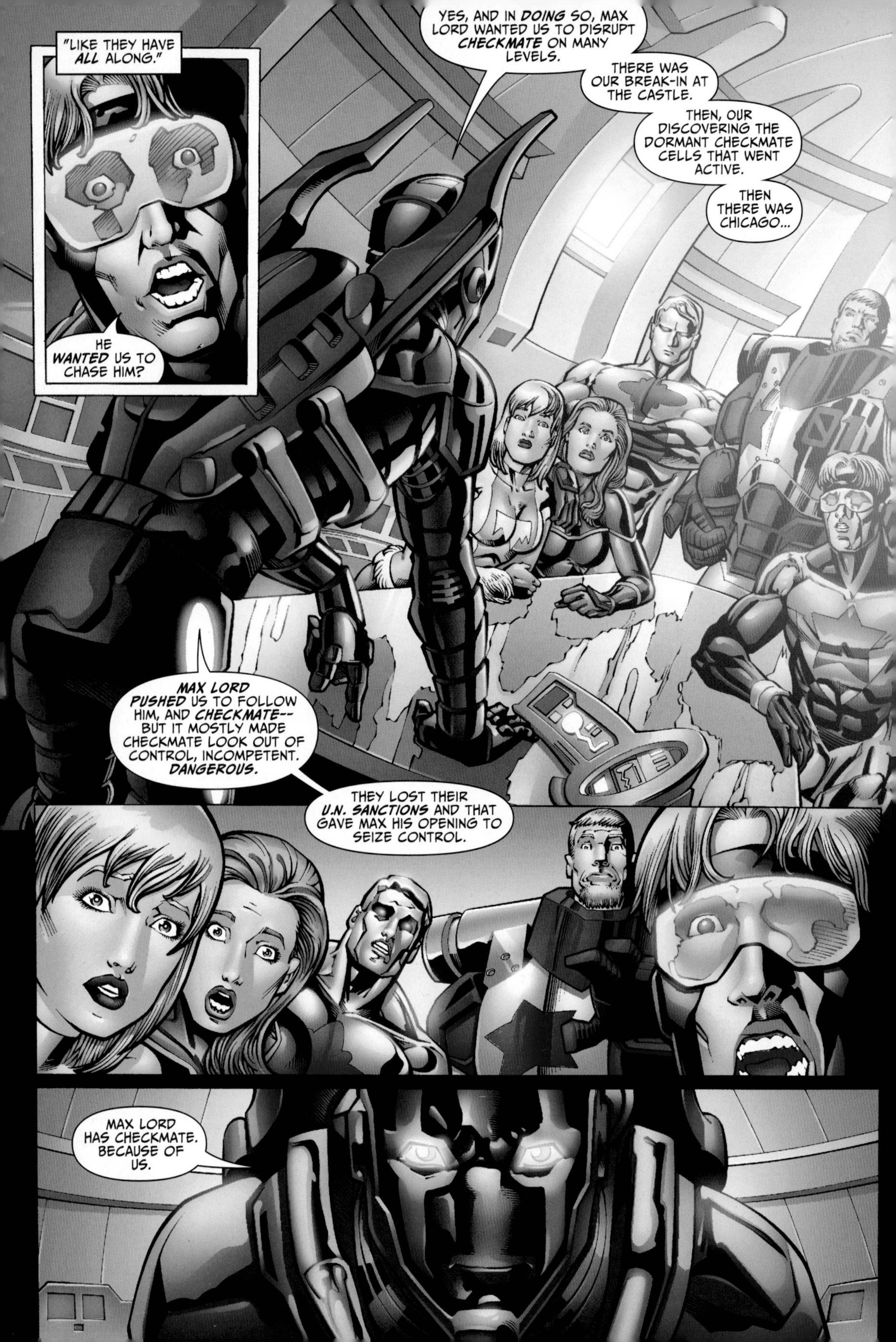
"LIKE THEY HAVE ALL ALONG."
HE WANTED US TO CHASE HIM?
YES, AND IN DOING SO, MAX LORD WANTED US TO DISRUPT CHECKMATE ON MANY LEVELS.
THERE WAS OUR BREAK-IN AT THE CASTLE.
THEN, OUR DISCOVERING THE DORMANT CHECKMATE CELLS THAT WENT ACTIVE.
THEN THERE WAS CHICAGO...
MAX LORD PUSHED US TO FOLLOW HIM, AND CHECKMATE-- BUT IT MOSTLY MADE CHECKMATE LOOK OUT OF CONTROL, INCOMPETENT. DANGEROUS.
THEY LOST THEIR U.N. SANCTIONS AND THAT GAVE MAX HIS OPENING TO SEIZE CONTROL.
MAX LORD HAS CHECKMATE. BECAUSE OF US.

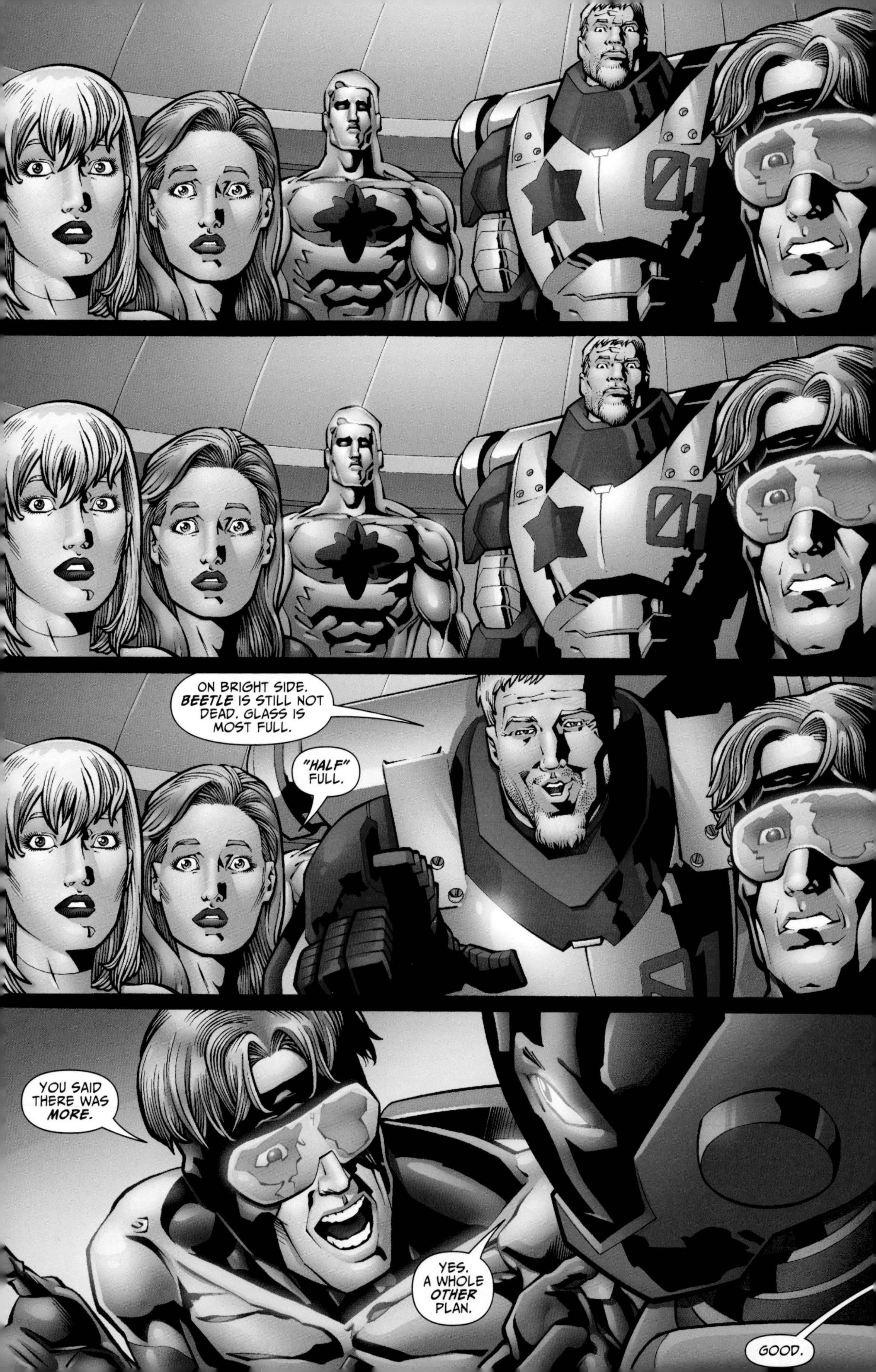
ON BRIGHT SIDE. *BEETLE* IS STILL NOT DEAD. GLASS IS MOST FULL.
"HALF" FULL.
YOU SAID THERE WAS *MORE.*
YES. A WHOLE *OTHER* PLAN.
GOOD.

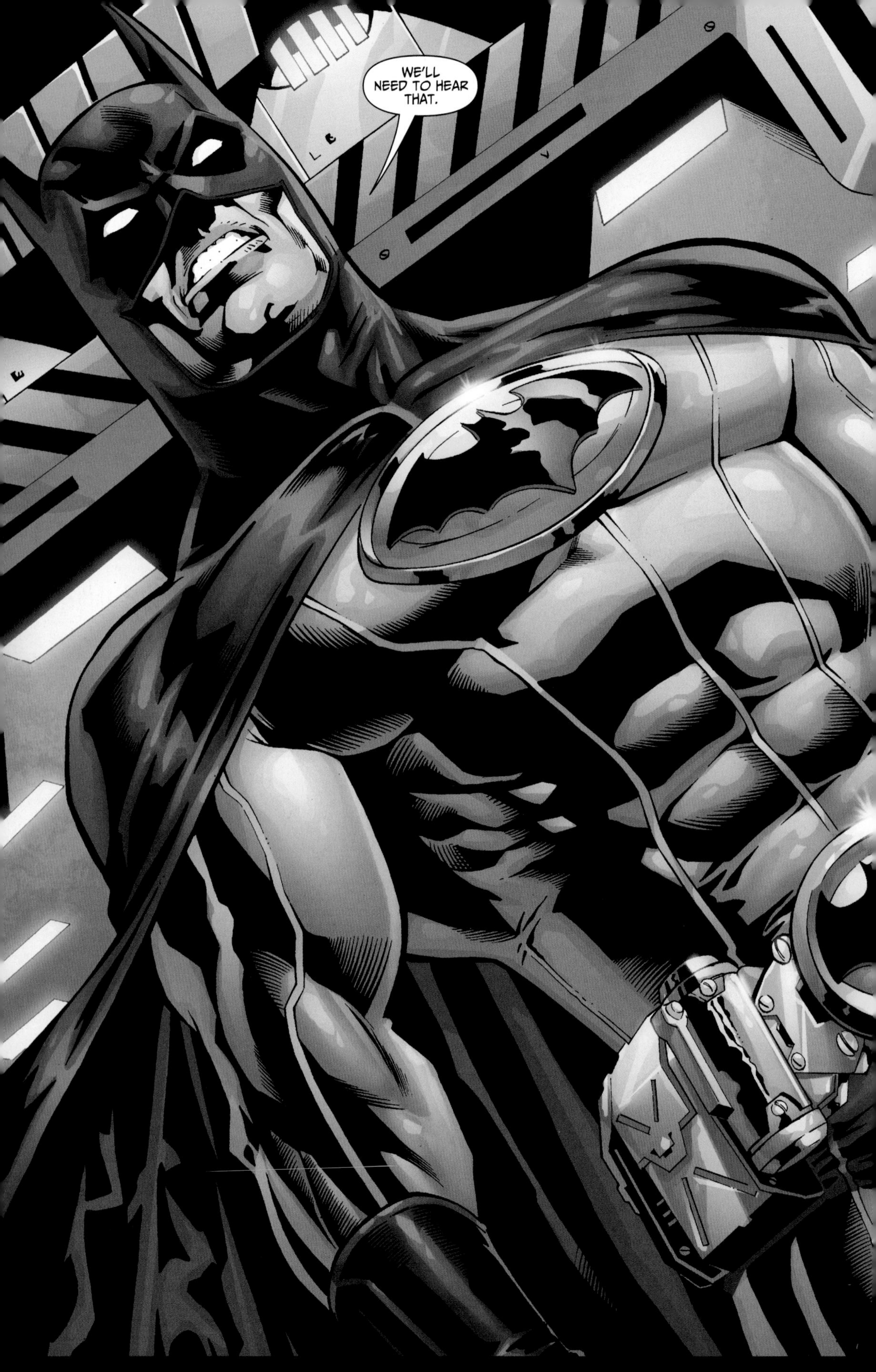
WE'LL NEED TO HEAR THAT.

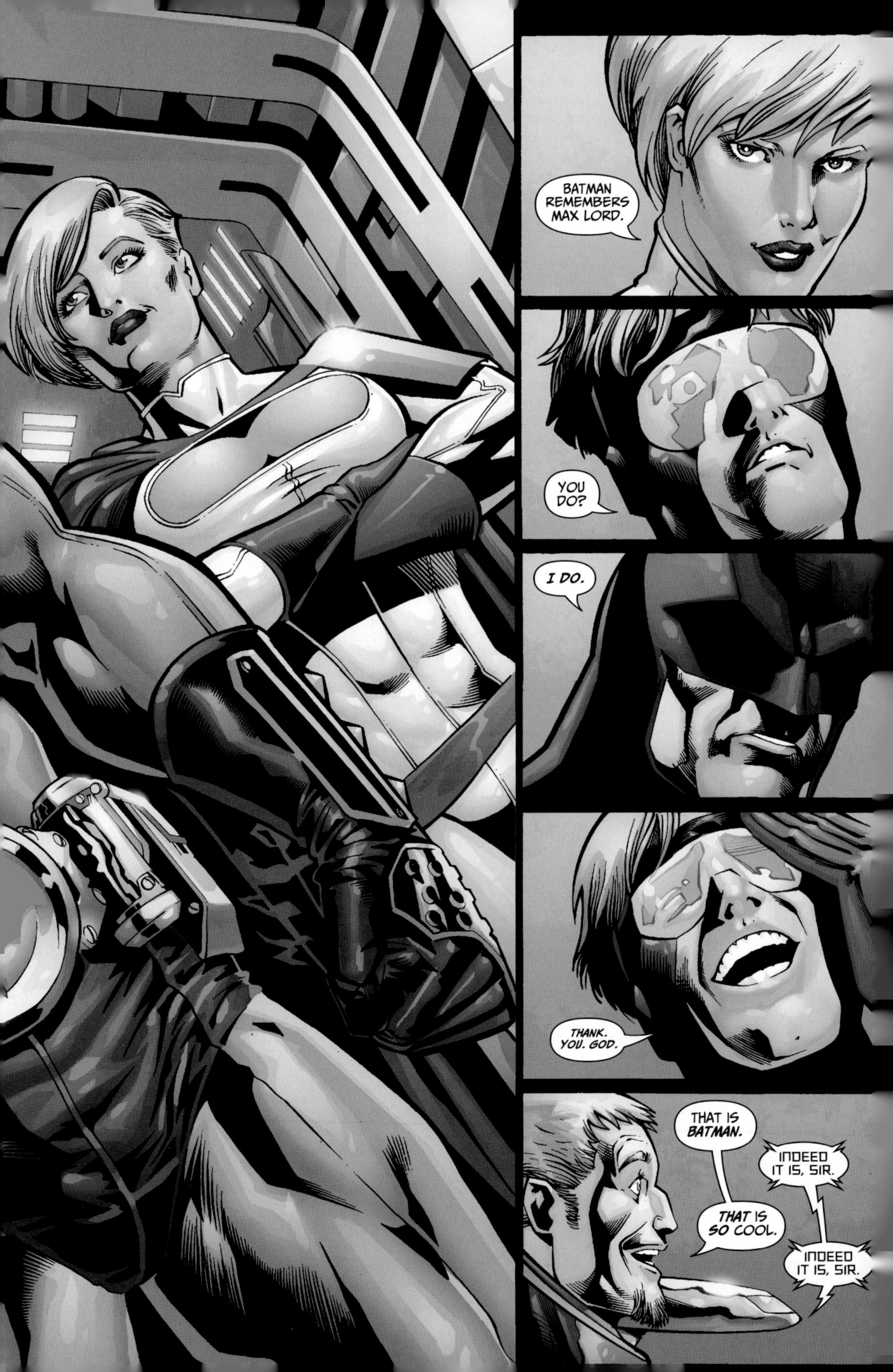

BATMAN REMEMBERS MAX LORD.
YOU DO?
I DO.
THANK. YOU. GOD.
THAT IS BATMAN.
INDEED IT IS, SIR.
THAT IS SO COOL.
INDEED IT IS, SIR.

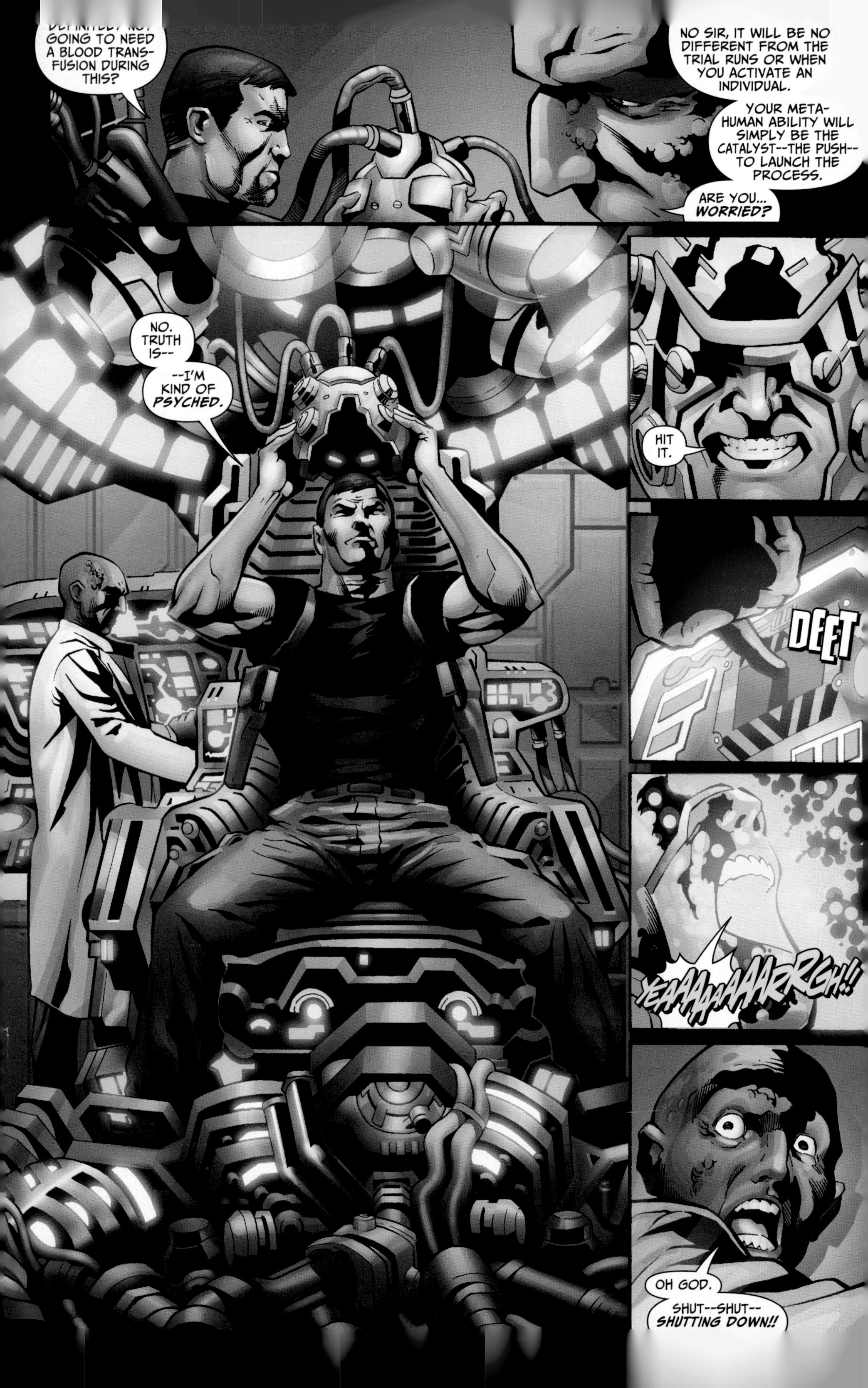
DEFINITELY NOT GOING TO NEED A BLOOD TRANSFUSION DURING THIS?
NO SIR, IT WILL BE NO DIFFERENT FROM THE TRIAL RUNS OR WHEN YOU ACTIVATE AN INDIVIDUAL.
YOUR META-HUMAN ABILITY WILL SIMPLY BE THE CATALYST--THE PUSH--TO LAUNCH THE PROCESS.
ARE YOU... WORRIED?
NO. TRUTH IS--
--I'M KIND OF PSYCHED.
HIT IT.
DEET
YEAAAAAAAARRGH!!
OH GOD.
SHUT--SHUT--SHUTTING DOWN!!

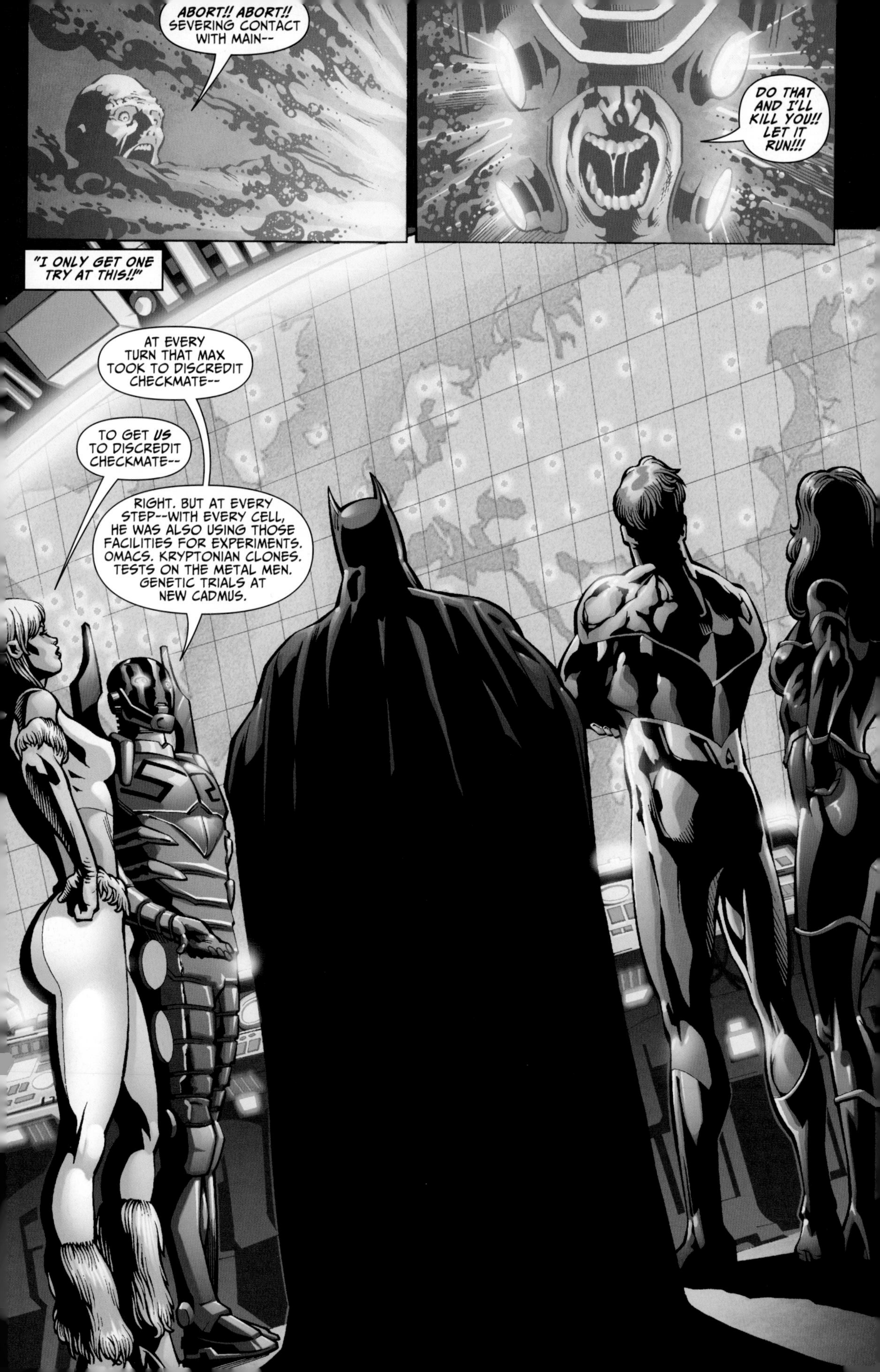
ABORT!! ABORT!! SEVERING CONTACT WITH MAIN--
DO THAT AND I'LL KILL YOU!! LET IT RUN!!!
"I ONLY GET ONE TRY AT THIS!!"
AT EVERY TURN THAT MAX TOOK TO DISCREDIT CHECKMATE--
TO GET US TO DISCREDIT CHECKMATE--
RIGHT. BUT AT EVERY STEP--WITH EVERY CELL, HE WAS ALSO USING THOSE FACILITIES FOR EXPERIMENTS. OMACS. KRYPTONIAN CLONES. TESTS ON THE METAL MEN. GENETIC TRIALS AT NEW CADMUS.

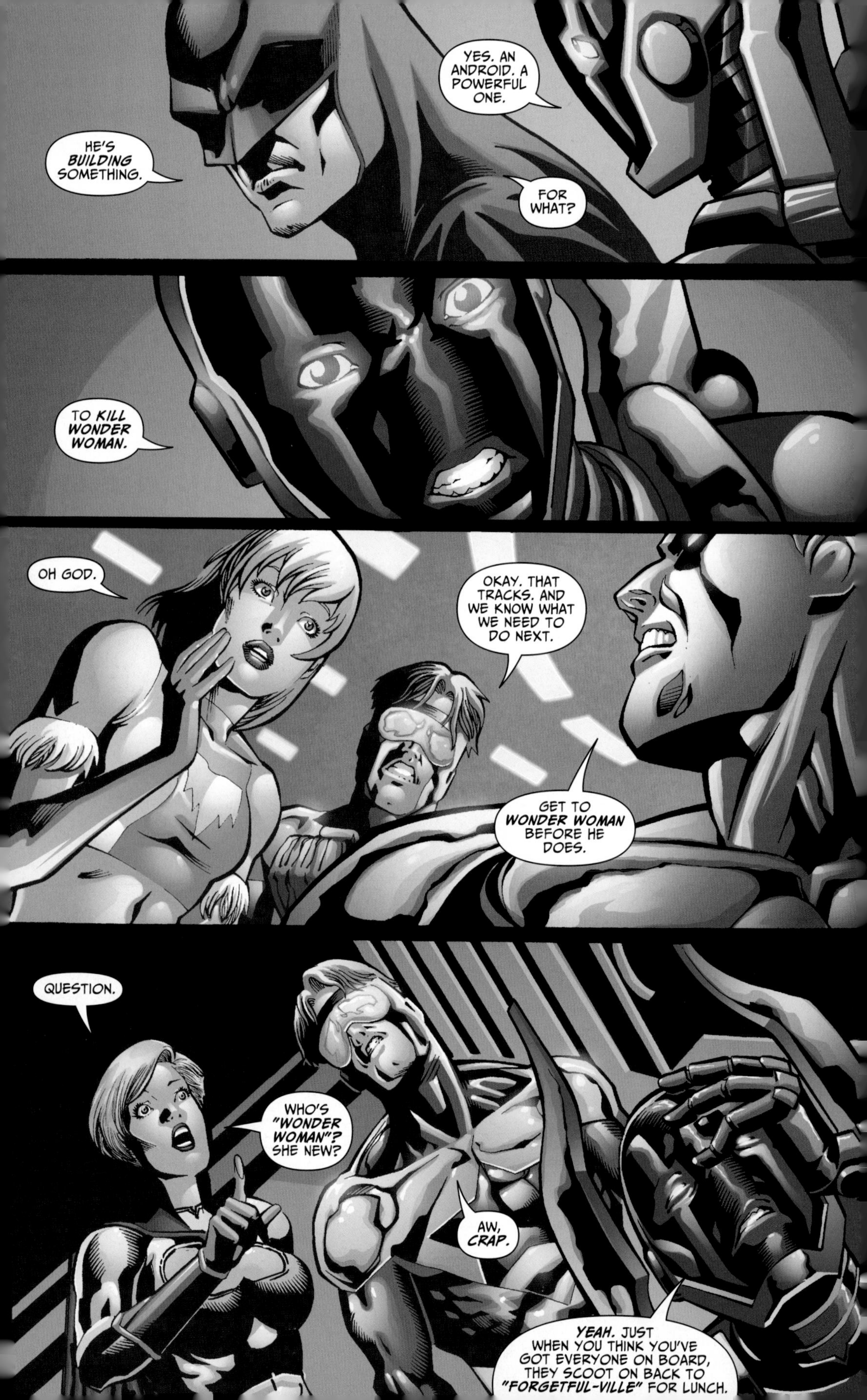
HE'S BUILDING SOMETHING.
YES. AN ANDROID. A POWERFUL ONE.
FOR WHAT?
TO KILL WONDER WOMAN.
OH GOD.
OKAY. THAT TRACKS. AND WE KNOW WHAT WE NEED TO DO NEXT.
GET TO WONDER WOMAN BEFORE HE DOES.
QUESTION.
WHO'S "WONDER WOMAN"? SHE NEW?
AW, CRAP.
YEAH. JUST WHEN YOU THINK YOU'VE GOT EVERYONE ON BOARD, THEY SCOOT ON BACK TO "FORGETFUL-VILLE" FOR LUNCH.

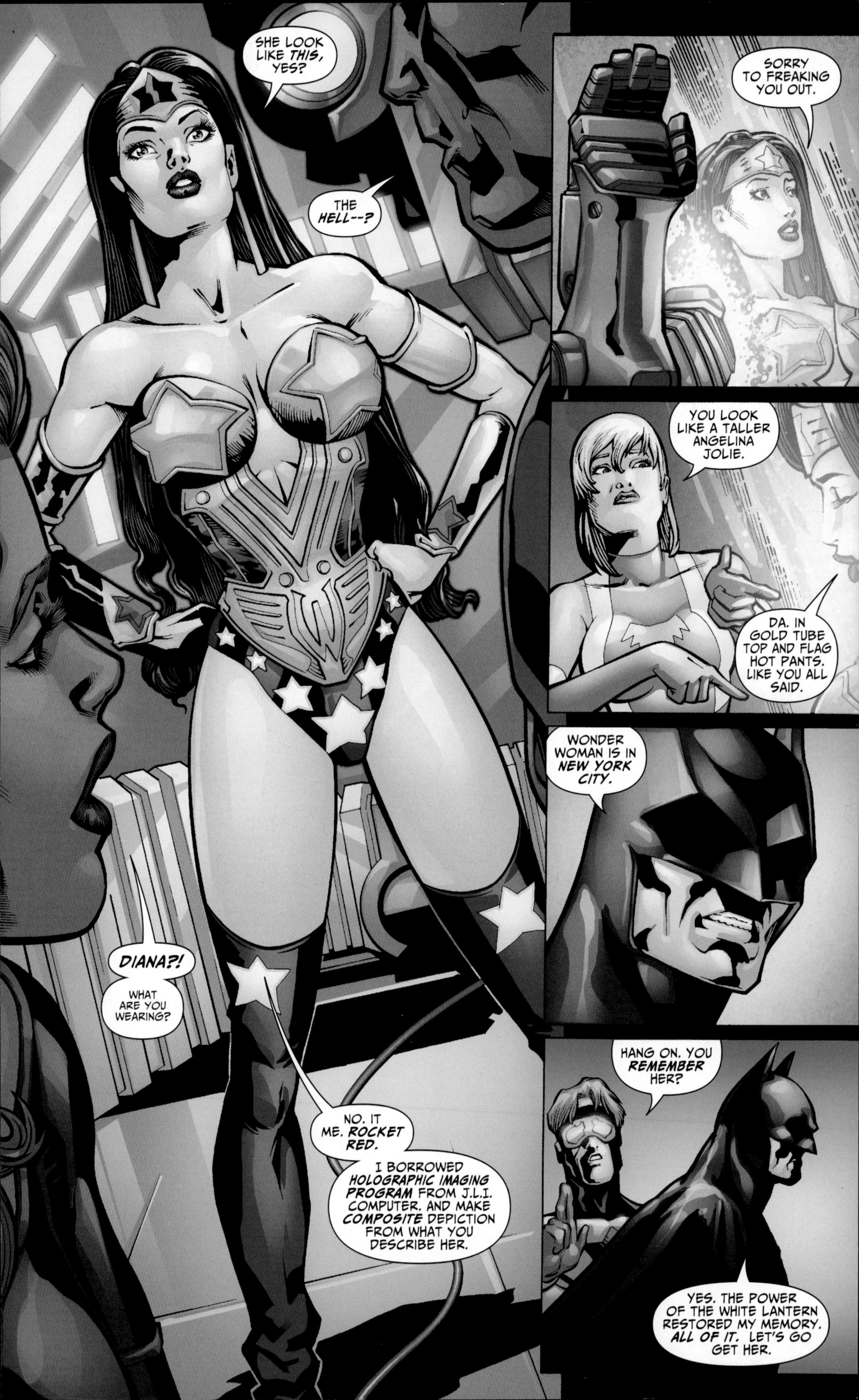
SHE LOOK LIKE THIS, YES?
THE HELL--?
DIANA?!
WHAT ARE YOU WEARING?
NO. IT ME. ROCKET RED.
I BORROWED HOLOGRAPHIC IMAGING PROGRAM FROM J.L.I. COMPUTER. AND MAKE COMPOSITE DEPICTION FROM WHAT YOU DESCRIBE HER.
SORRY TO FREAKING YOU OUT.
YOU LOOK LIKE A TALLER ANGELINA JOLIE.
DA. IN GOLD TUBE TOP AND FLAG HOT PANTS. LIKE YOU ALL SAID.
WONDER WOMAN IS IN NEW YORK CITY.
HANG ON. YOU REMEMBER HER?
YES. THE POWER OF THE WHITE LANTERN RESTORED MY MEMORY. ALL OF IT. LET'S GO GET HER.

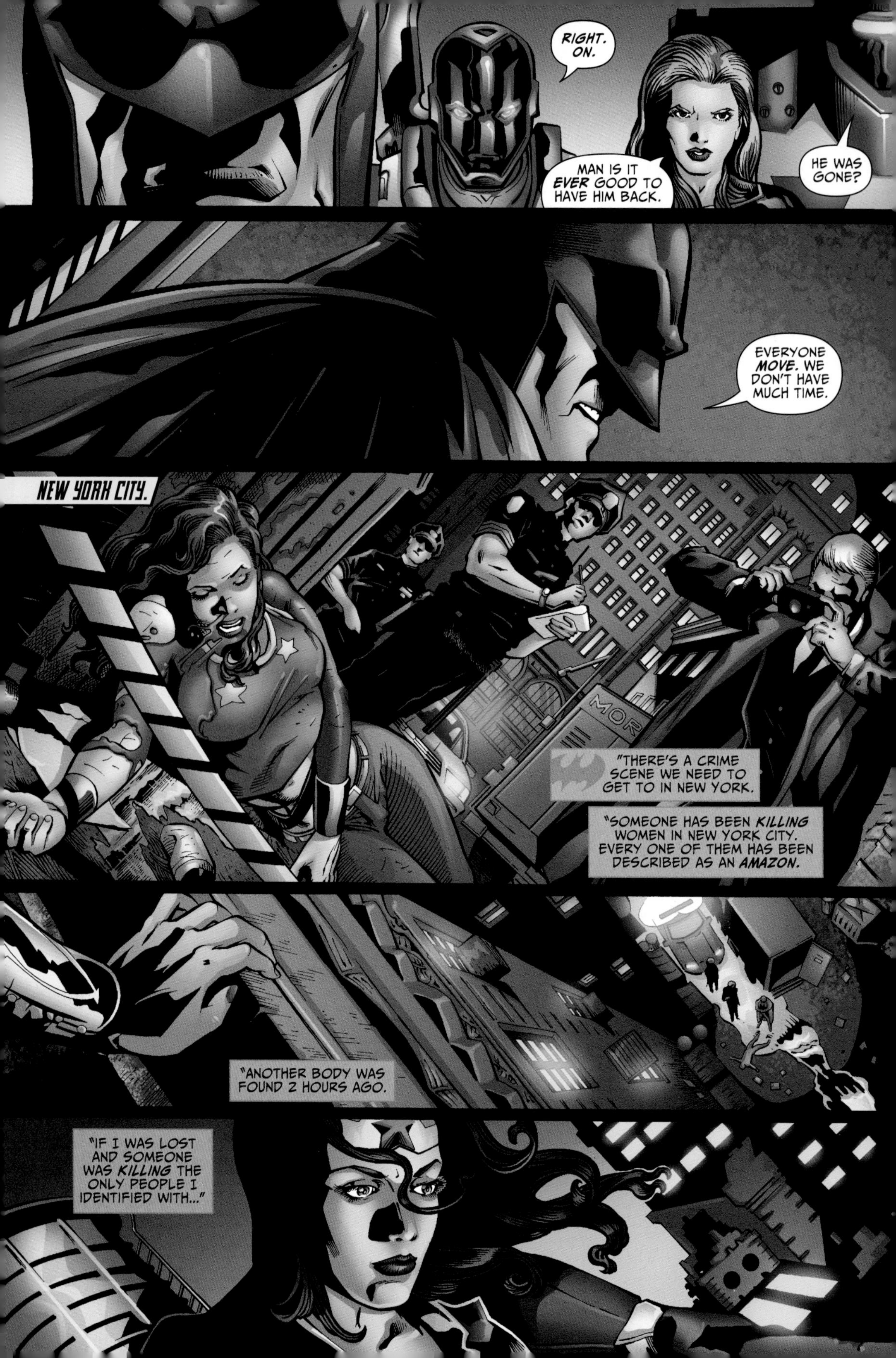
RIGHT. ON.
MAN IS IT EVER GOOD TO HAVE HIM BACK.
HE WAS GONE?
EVERYONE MOVE. WE DON'T HAVE MUCH TIME.
NEW YORK CITY.
MOR
"THERE'S A CRIME SCENE WE NEED TO GET TO IN NEW YORK.
"SOMEONE HAS BEEN KILLING WOMEN IN NEW YORK CITY. EVERY ONE OF THEM HAS BEEN DESCRIBED AS AN AMAZON.
"ANOTHER BODY WAS FOUND 2 HOURS AGO.
"IF I WAS LOST AND SOMEONE WAS KILLING THE ONLY PEOPLE I IDENTIFIED WITH..."

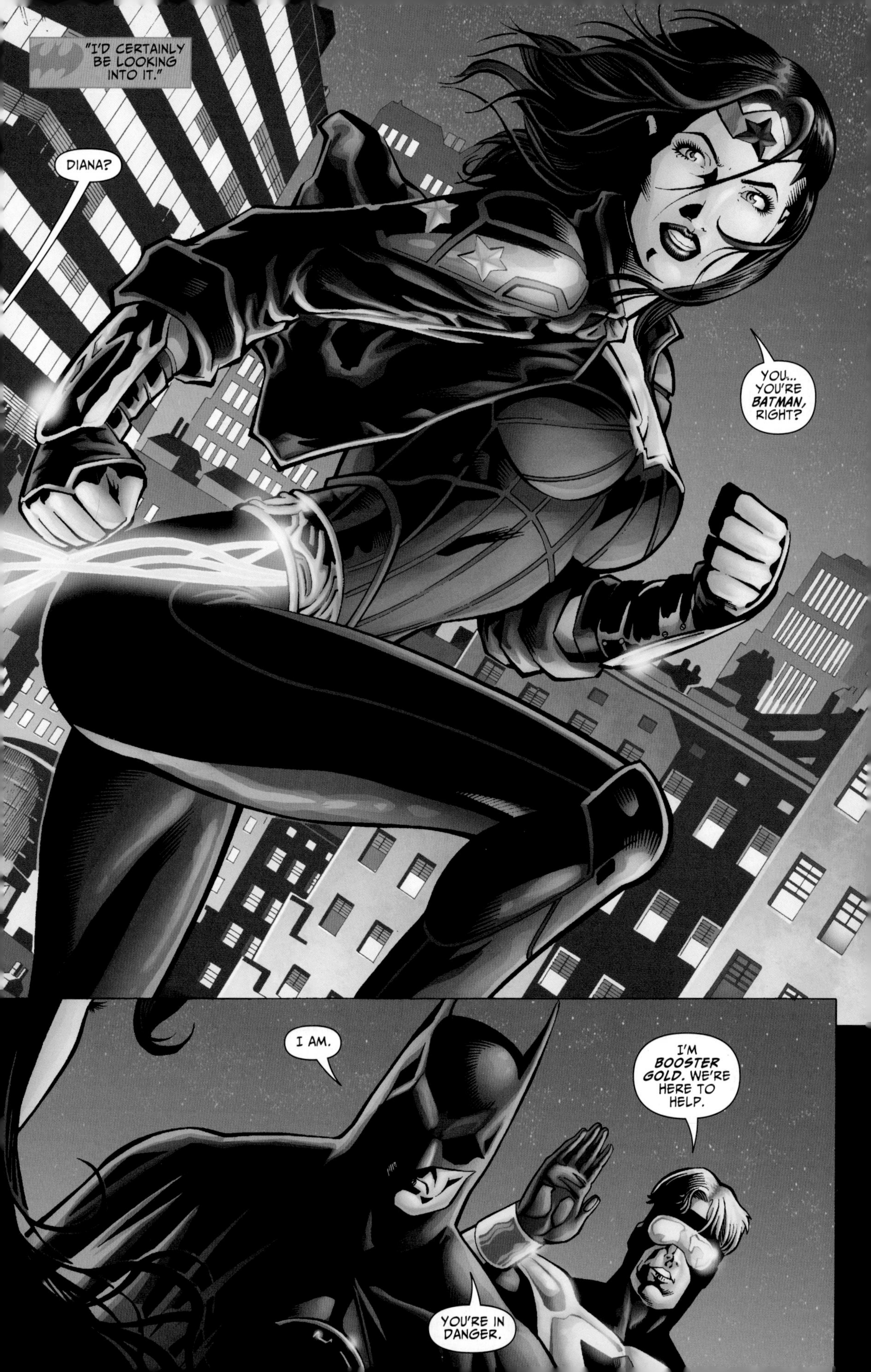
"I'D CERTAINLY BE LOOKING INTO IT."
DIANA?
YOU... YOU'RE BATMAN, RIGHT?
I AM.
I'M BOOSTER GOLD. WE'RE HERE TO HELP.
YOU'RE IN DANGER.

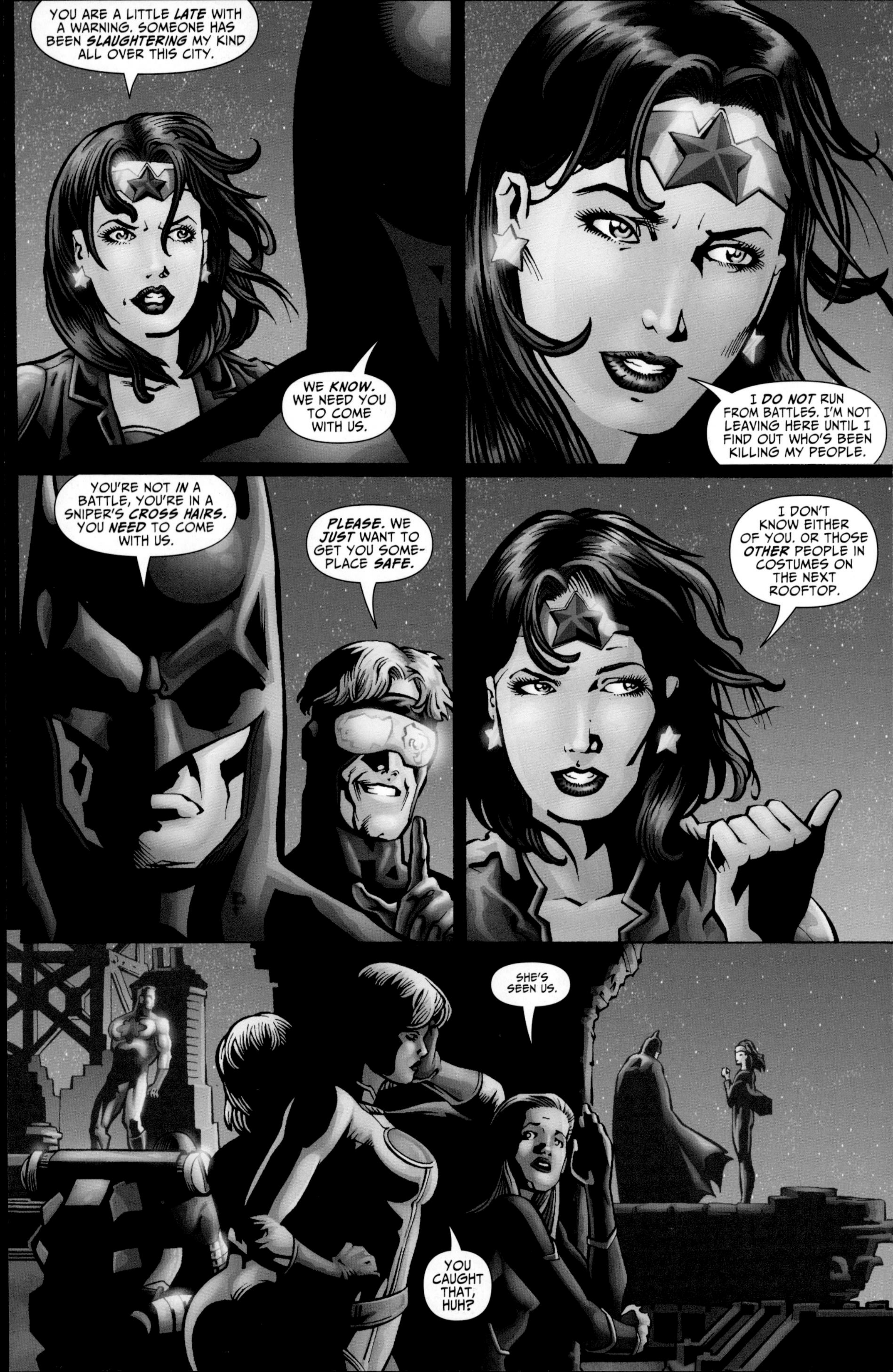
YOU ARE A LITTLE LATE WITH A WARNING. SOMEONE HAS BEEN SLAUGHTERING MY KIND ALL OVER THIS CITY.
WE KNOW. WE NEED YOU TO COME WITH US.
I DO NOT RUN FROM BATTLES. I'M NOT LEAVING HERE UNTIL I FIND OUT WHO'S BEEN KILLING MY PEOPLE.
YOU'RE NOT IN A BATTLE, YOU'RE IN A SNIPER'S CROSS HAIRS. YOU NEED TO COME WITH US.
PLEASE. WE JUST WANT TO GET YOU SOME-PLACE SAFE.
I DON'T KNOW EITHER OF YOU. OR THOSE OTHER PEOPLE IN COSTUMES ON THE NEXT ROOFTOP.
SHE'S SEEN US.
YOU CAUGHT THAT, HUH?

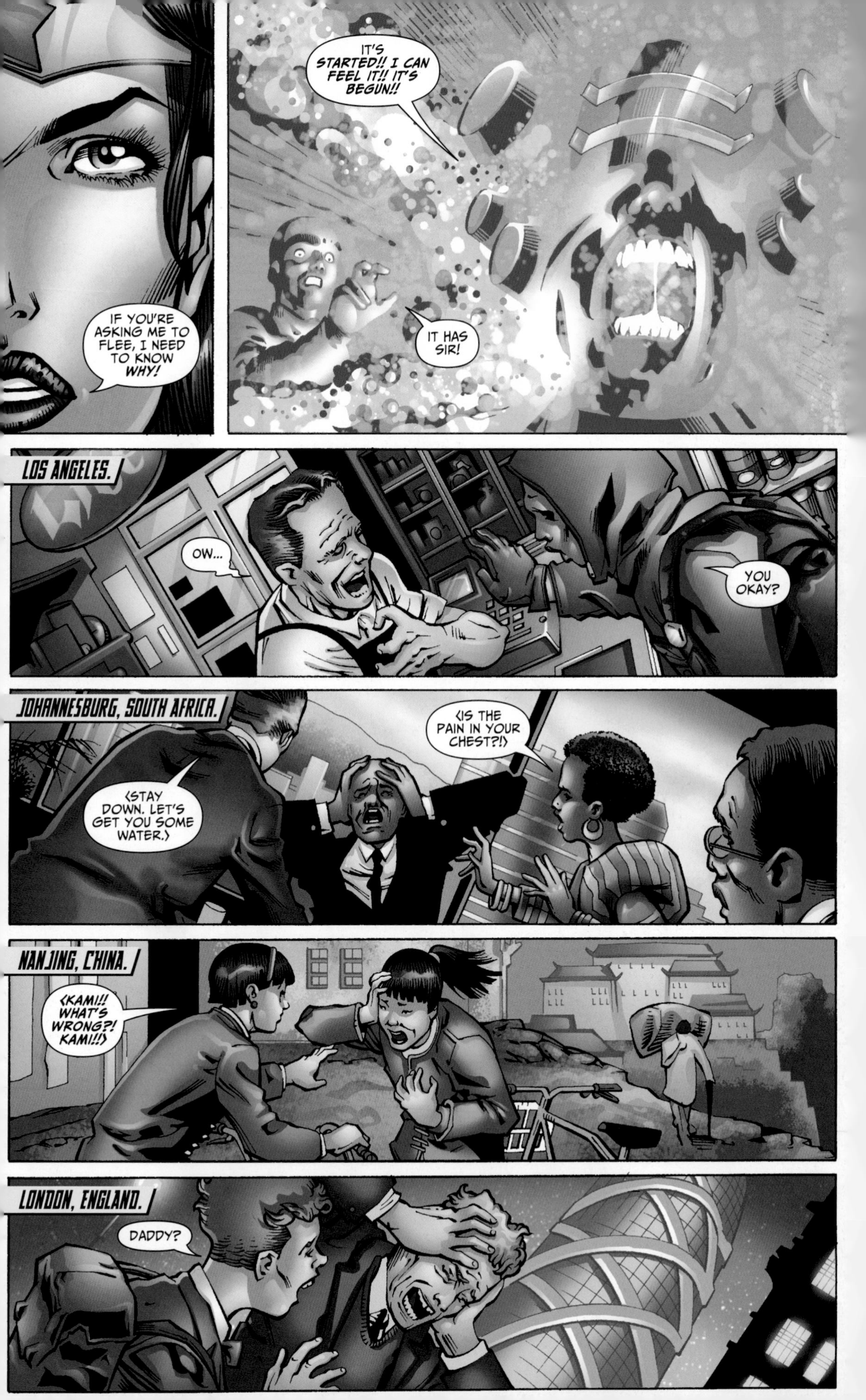
IF YOU'RE ASKING ME TO FLEE, I NEED TO KNOW WHY!
IT'S STARTED!! I CAN FEEL IT!! IT'S BEGUN!!
IT HAS SIR!
LOS ANGELES.
OW...
YOU OKAY?
JOHANNESBURG, SOUTH AFRICA.
‹IS THE PAIN IN YOUR CHEST?!›
‹STAY DOWN. LET'S GET YOU SOME WATER.›
NANJING, CHINA.
‹KAMI!! WHAT'S WRONG?! KAMI!!›
LONDON, ENGLAND.
DADDY?

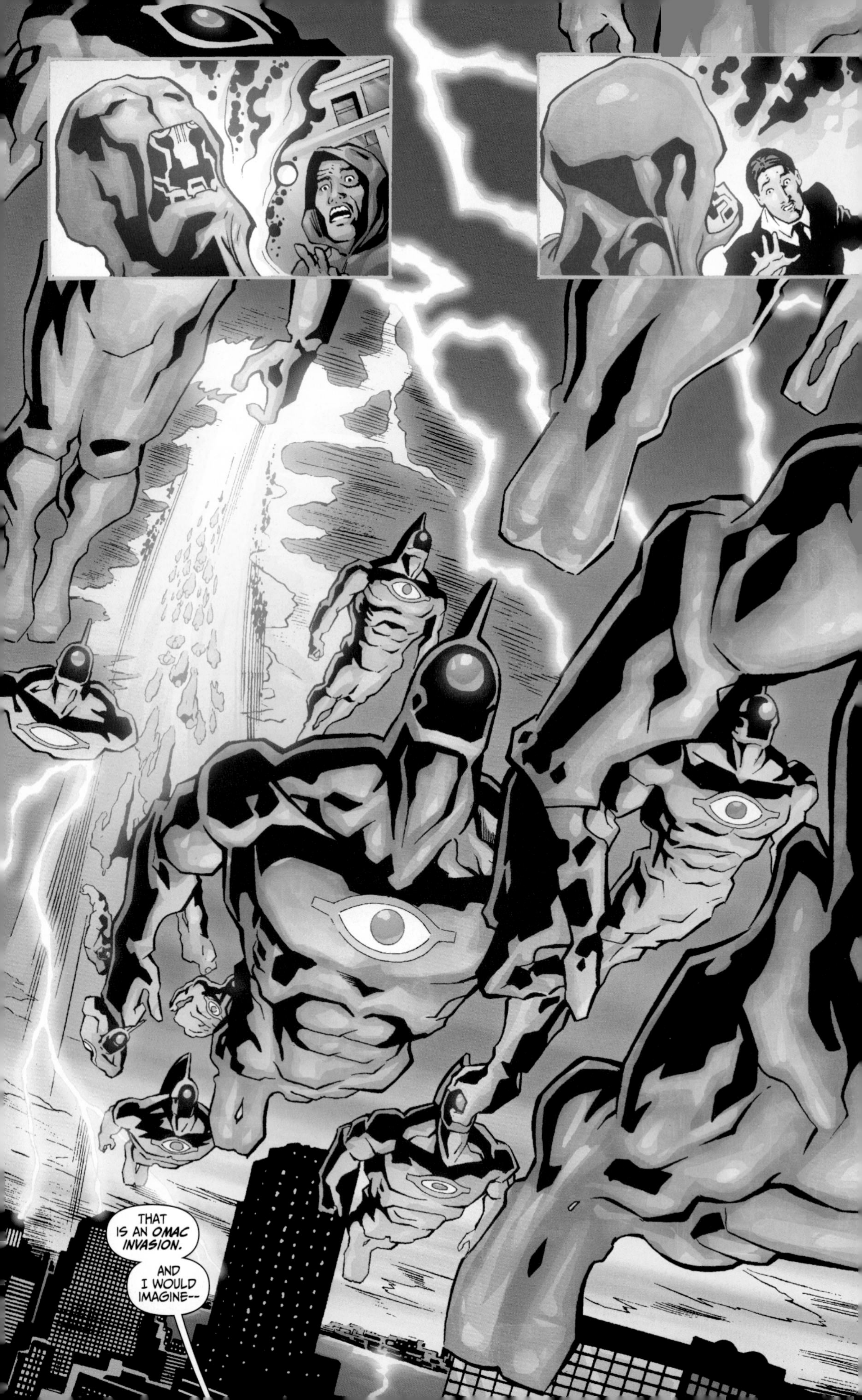
THAT IS AN *OMAC INVASION.*
AND I WOULD IMAGINE--

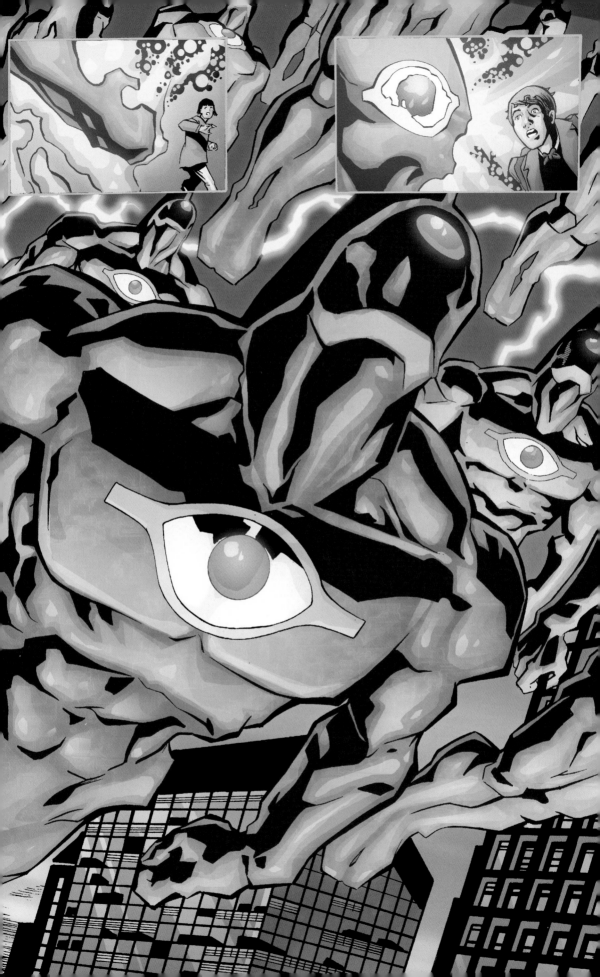

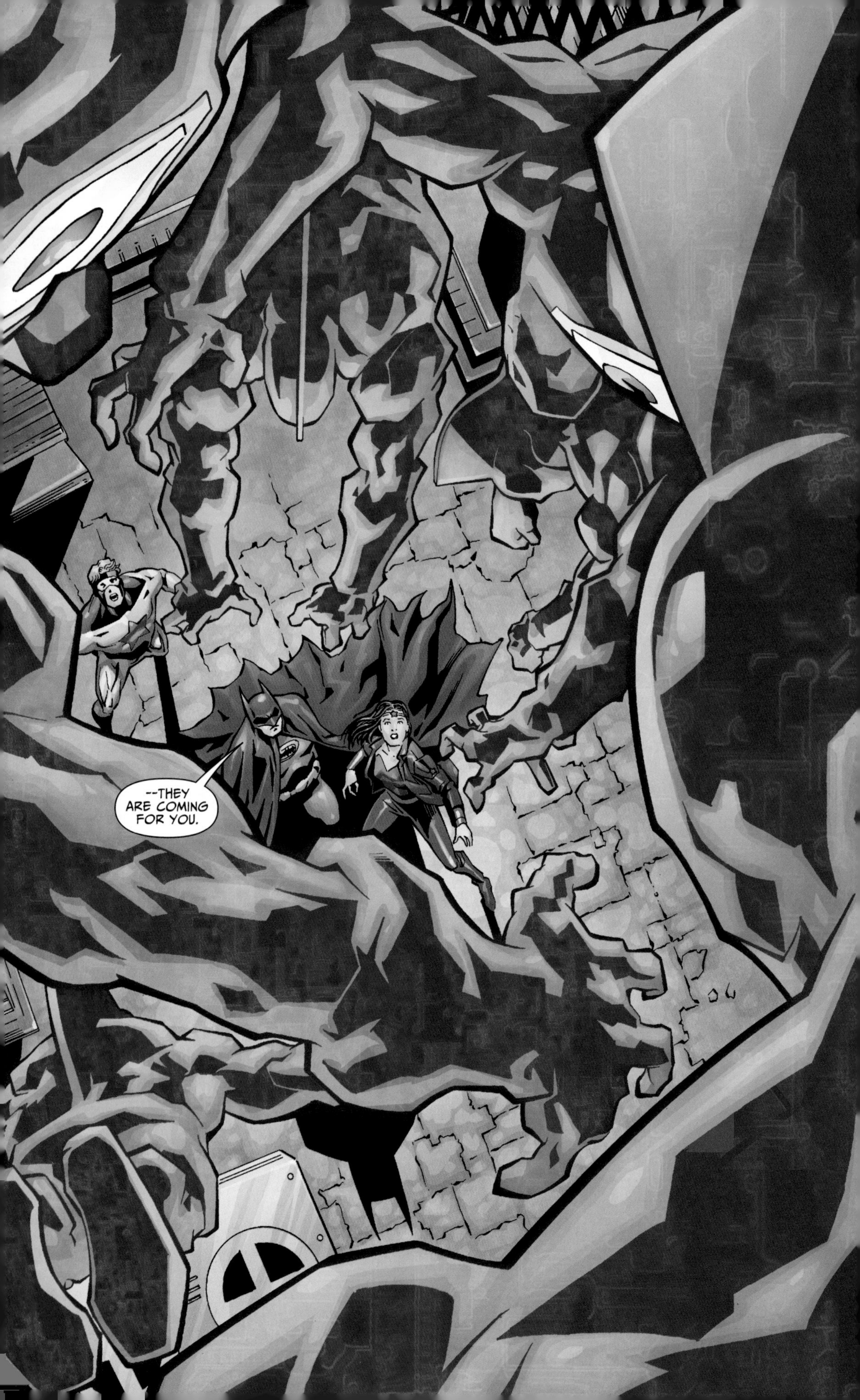
--THEY ARE COMING FOR YOU.

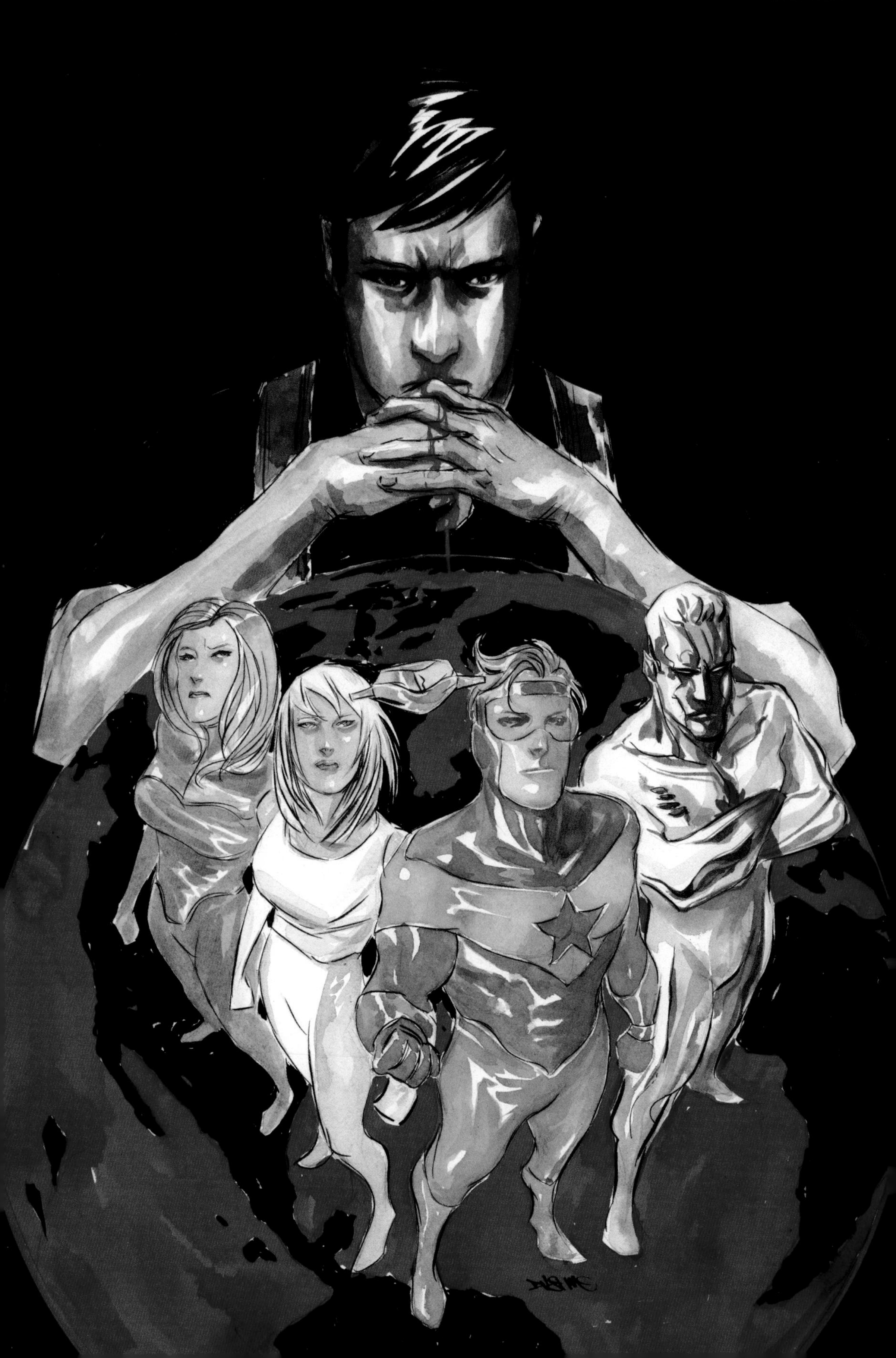

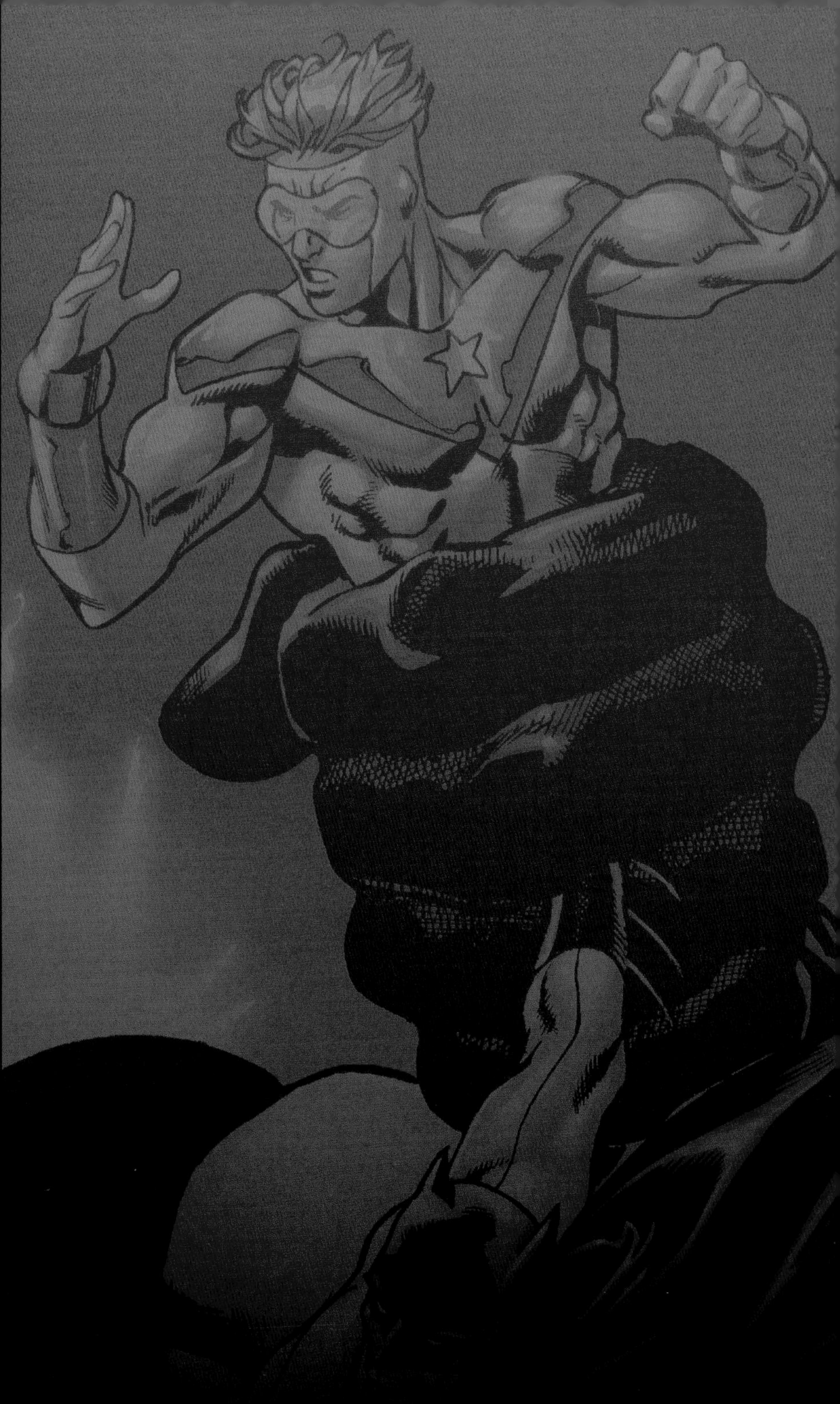

PART TWENTY-THREE:
CAUGHT

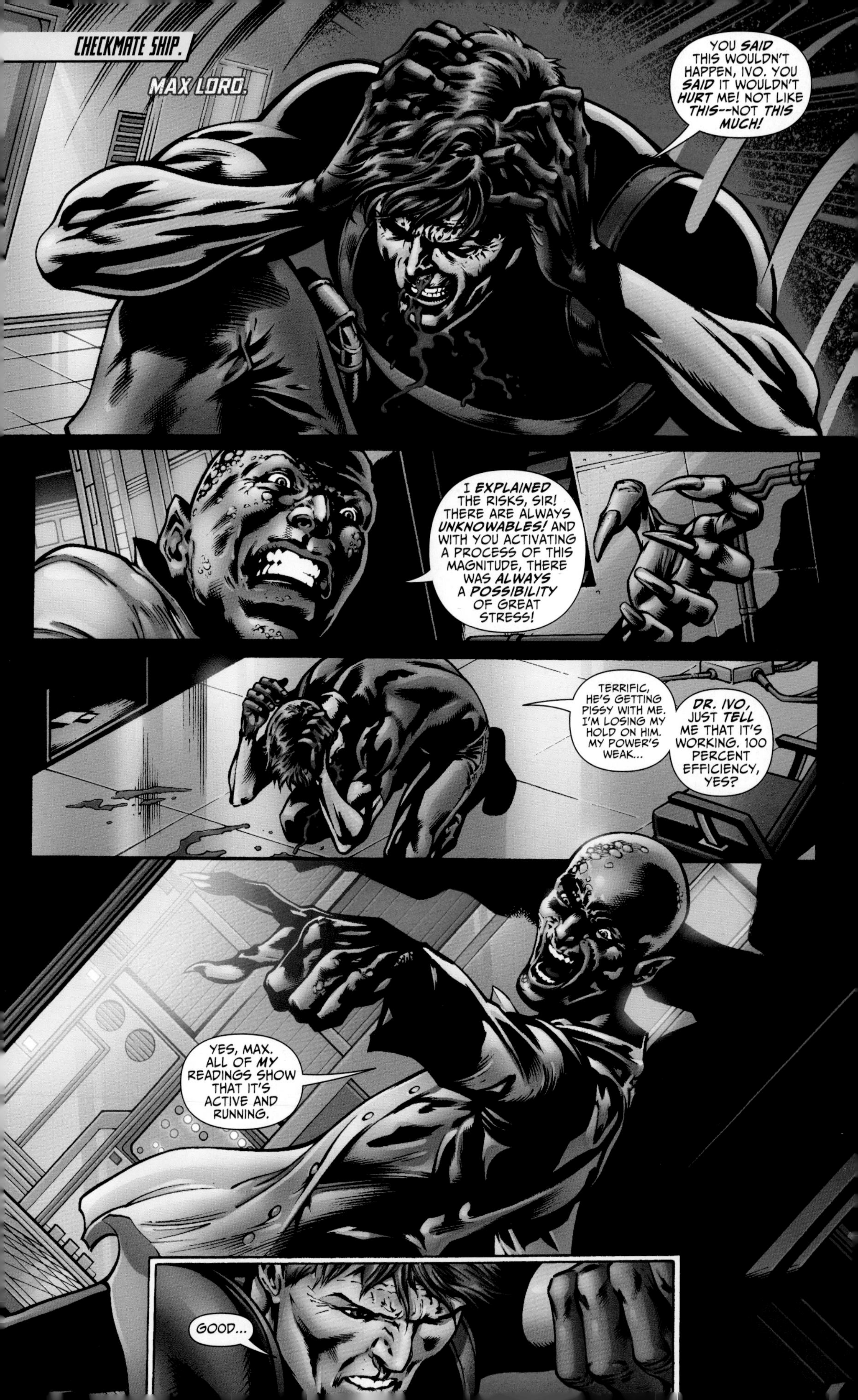
CHECKMATE SHIP.
MAX LORD.
YOU SAID THIS WOULDN'T HAPPEN, IVO. YOU SAID IT WOULDN'T HURT ME! NOT LIKE THIS--NOT THIS MUCH!
I EXPLAINED THE RISKS, SIR! THERE ARE ALWAYS UNKNOWABLES! AND WITH YOU ACTIVATING A PROCESS OF THIS MAGNITUDE, THERE WAS ALWAYS A POSSIBILITY OF GREAT STRESS!
TERRIFIC, HE'S GETTING PISSY WITH ME. I'M LOSING MY HOLD ON HIM. MY POWER'S WEAK...
DR. IVO, JUST TELL ME THAT IT'S WORKING. 100 PERCENT EFFICIENCY, YES?
YES, MAX. ALL OF MY READINGS SHOW THAT IT'S ACTIVE AND RUNNING.
GOOD...

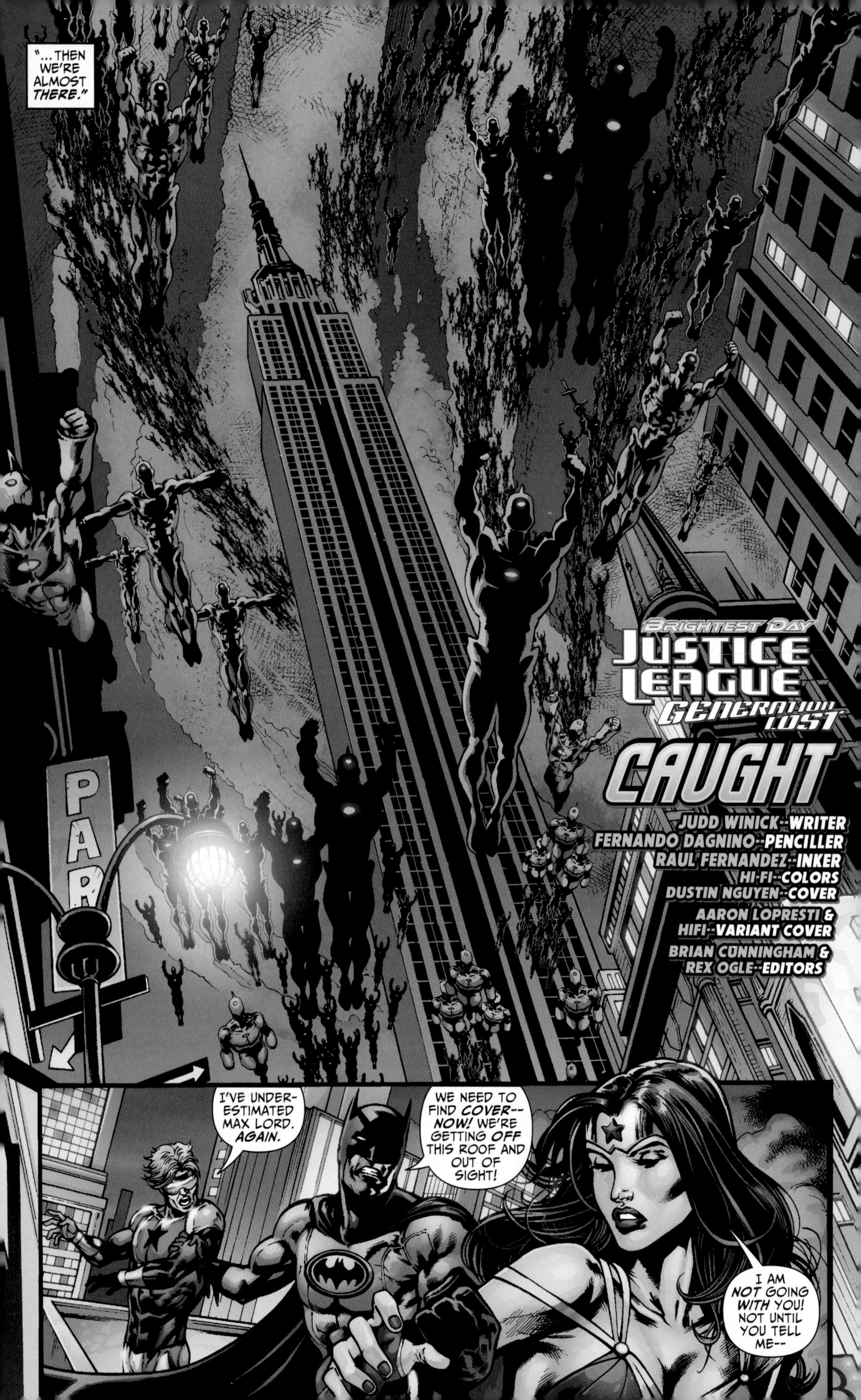
"...THEN WE'RE ALMOST THERE."
BRIGHTEST DAY
JUSTICE LEAGUE
GENERATION LOST
CAUGHT
JUDD WINICK--WRITER
FERNANDO DAGNINO--PENCILLER
RAUL FERNANDEZ--INKER
HI-FI--COLORS
DUSTIN NGUYEN--COVER
AARON LOPRESTI & HIFI--VARIANT COVER
BRIAN CUNNINGHAM & REX OGLE--EDITORS
I'VE UNDER-ESTIMATED MAX LORD. AGAIN.
WE NEED TO FIND COVER-- NOW! WE'RE GETTING OFF THIS ROOF AND OUT OF SIGHT!
I AM NOT GOING WITH YOU! NOT UNTIL YOU TELL ME--

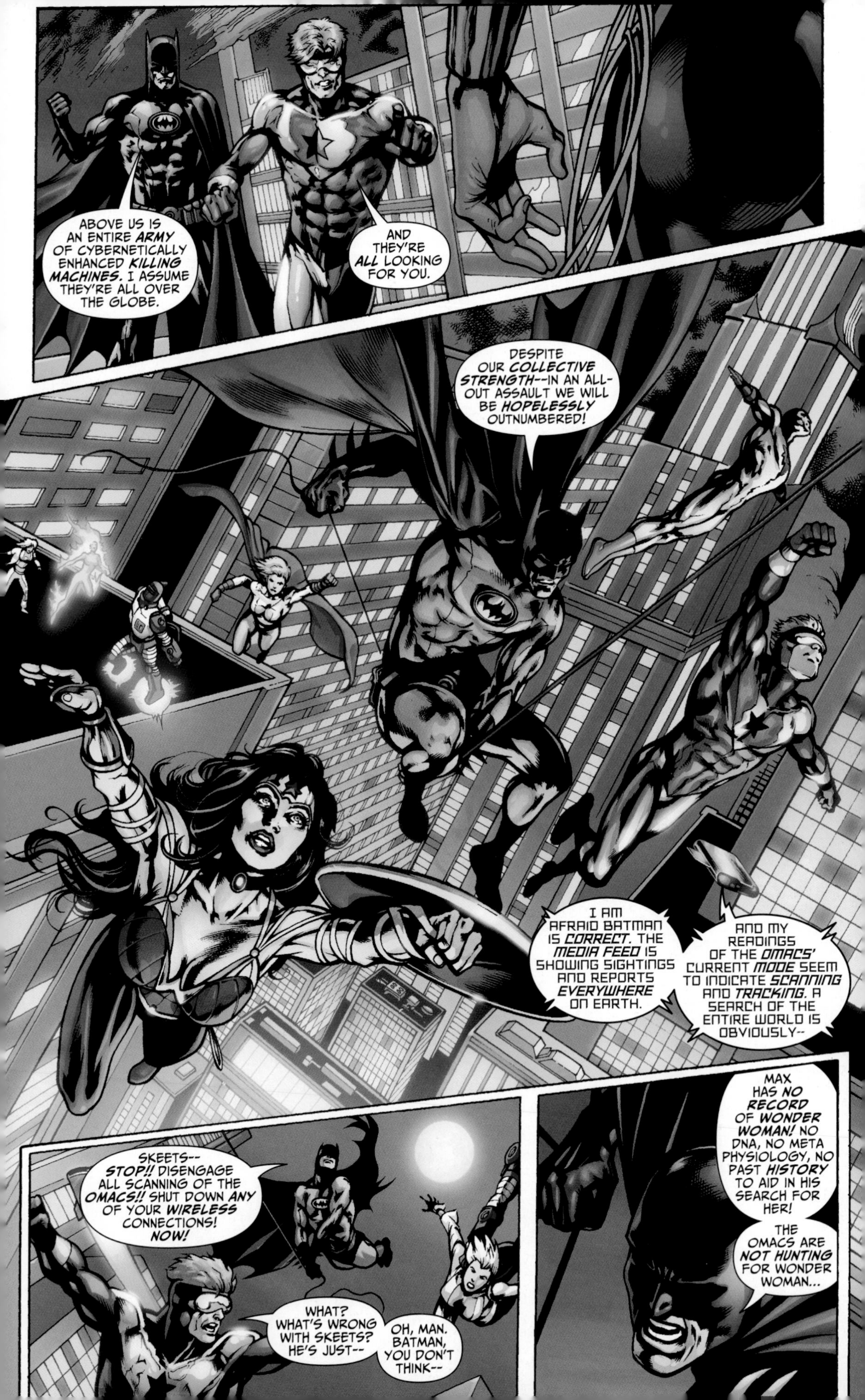

ABOVE US IS AN ENTIRE ARMY OF CYBERNETICALLY ENHANCED KILLING MACHINES. I ASSUME THEY'RE ALL OVER THE GLOBE.
AND THEY'RE ALL LOOKING FOR YOU.
DESPITE OUR COLLECTIVE STRENGTH--IN AN ALL-OUT ASSAULT WE WILL BE HOPELESSLY OUTNUMBERED!
I AM AFRAID BATMAN IS CORRECT. THE MEDIA FEED IS SHOWING SIGHTINGS AND REPORTS EVERYWHERE ON EARTH.
AND MY READINGS OF THE OMACS' CURRENT MODE SEEM TO INDICATE SCANNING AND TRACKING. A SEARCH OF THE ENTIRE WORLD IS OBVIOUSLY--
SKEETS--STOP!! DISENGAGE ALL SCANNING OF THE OMACS!! SHUT DOWN ANY OF YOUR WIRELESS CONNECTIONS! NOW!
WHAT? WHAT'S WRONG WITH SKEETS? HE'S JUST--
OH, MAN. BATMAN, YOU DON'T THINK--
MAX HAS NO RECORD OF WONDER WOMAN! NO DNA, NO META PHYSIOLOGY, NO PAST HISTORY TO AID IN HIS SEARCH FOR HER!
THE OMACS ARE NOT HUNTING FOR WONDER WOMAN...

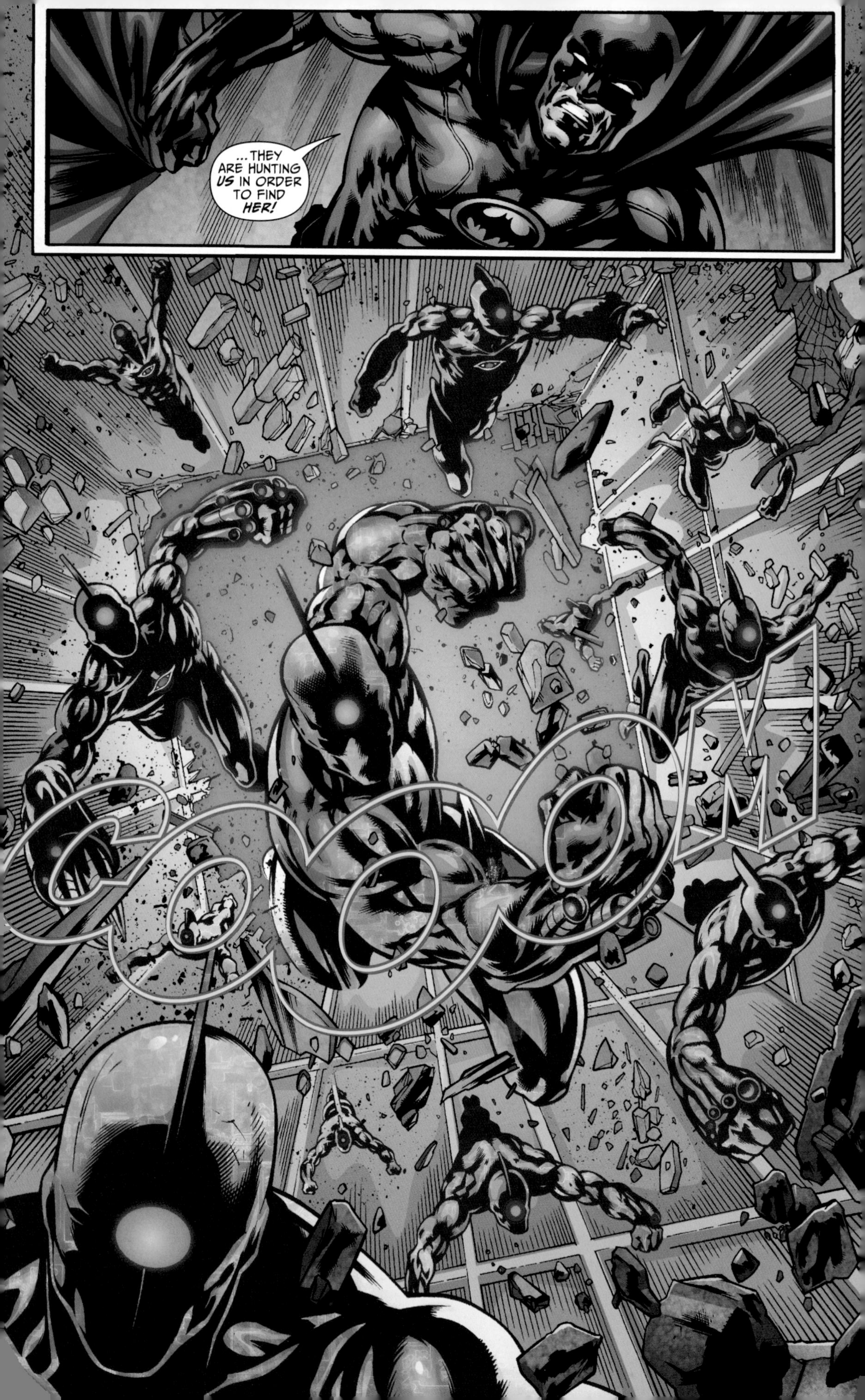
...THEY ARE HUNTING US IN ORDER TO FIND HER!
COOOOM

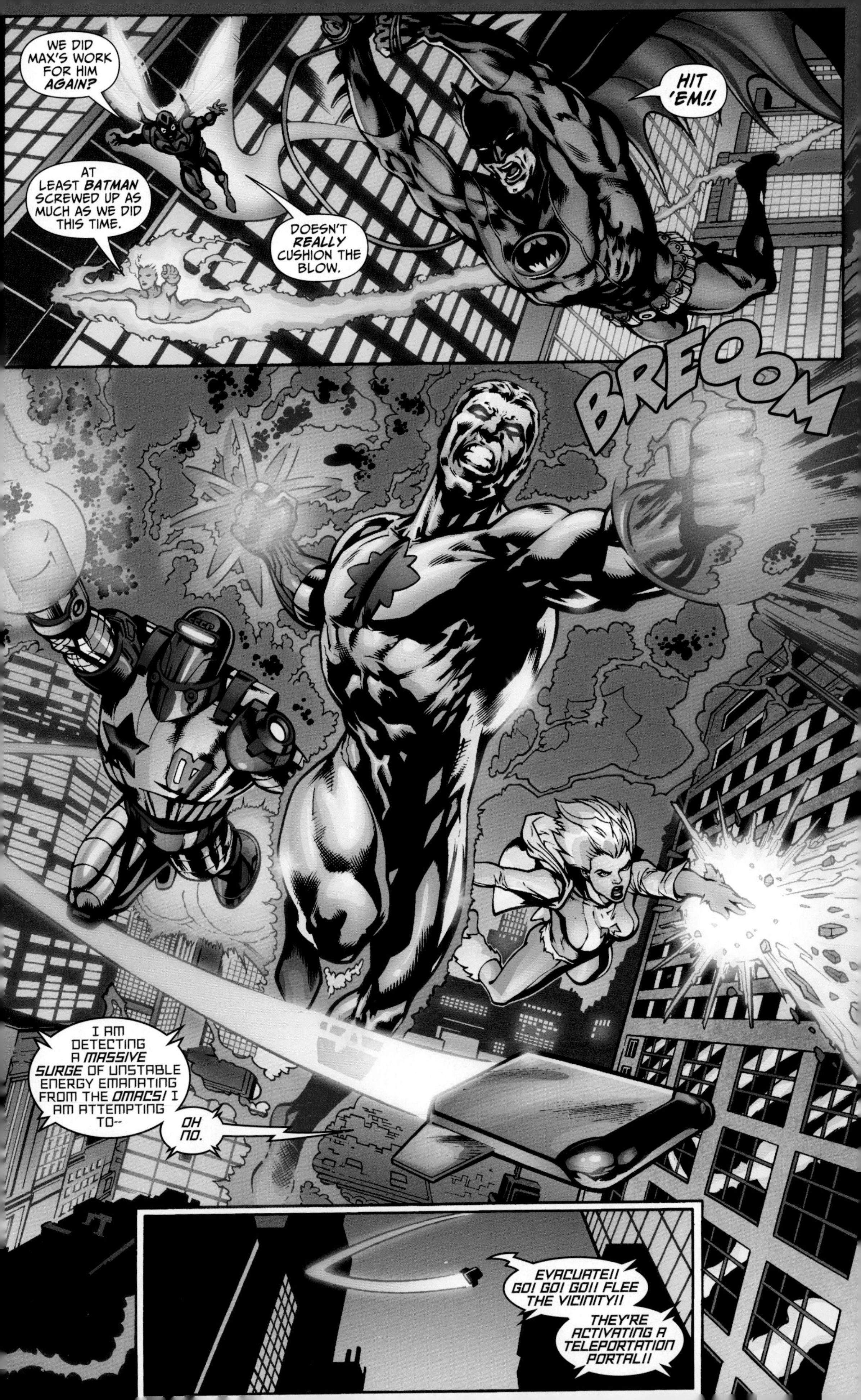
WE DID MAX'S WORK FOR HIM AGAIN?
HIT 'EM!!
AT LEAST BATMAN SCREWED UP AS MUCH AS WE DID THIS TIME.
DOESN'T REALLY CUSHION THE BLOW.
BREOOOM
I AM DETECTING A MASSIVE SURGE OF UNSTABLE ENERGY EMANATING FROM THE OMACS! I AM ATTEMPTING TO--
OH NO.
EVACUATE!! GO! GO! GO!! FLEE THE VICINITY!!
THEY'RE ACTIVATING A TELEPORTATION PORTAL!!

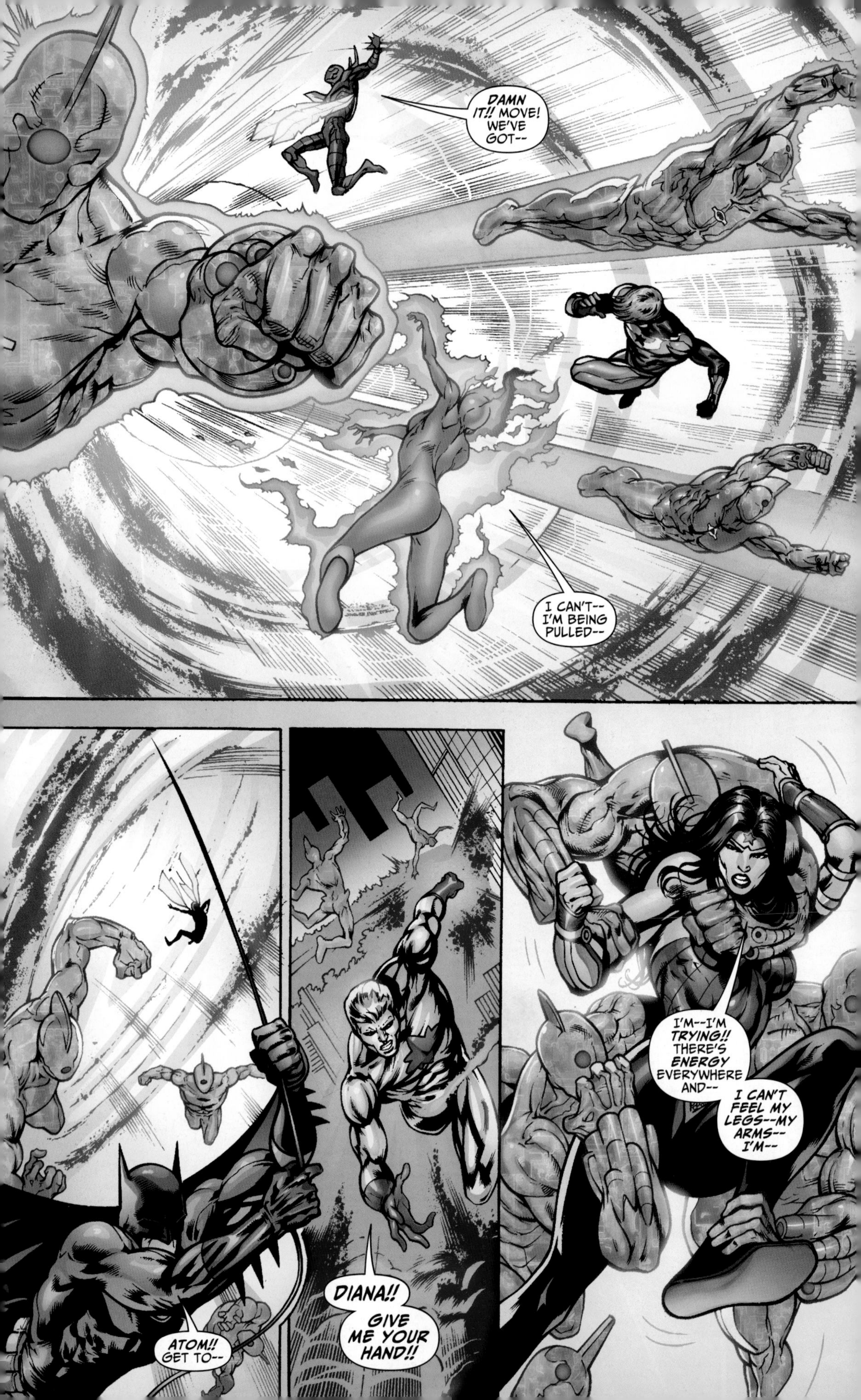
DAMN IT!! MOVE! WE'VE GOT--
I CAN'T-- I'M BEING PULLED--
ATOM!! GET TO--
DIANA!!
GIVE ME YOUR HAND!!
I'M--I'M TRYING!! THERE'S ENERGY EVERYWHERE AND--
I CAN'T FEEL MY LEGS--MY ARMS-- I'M--

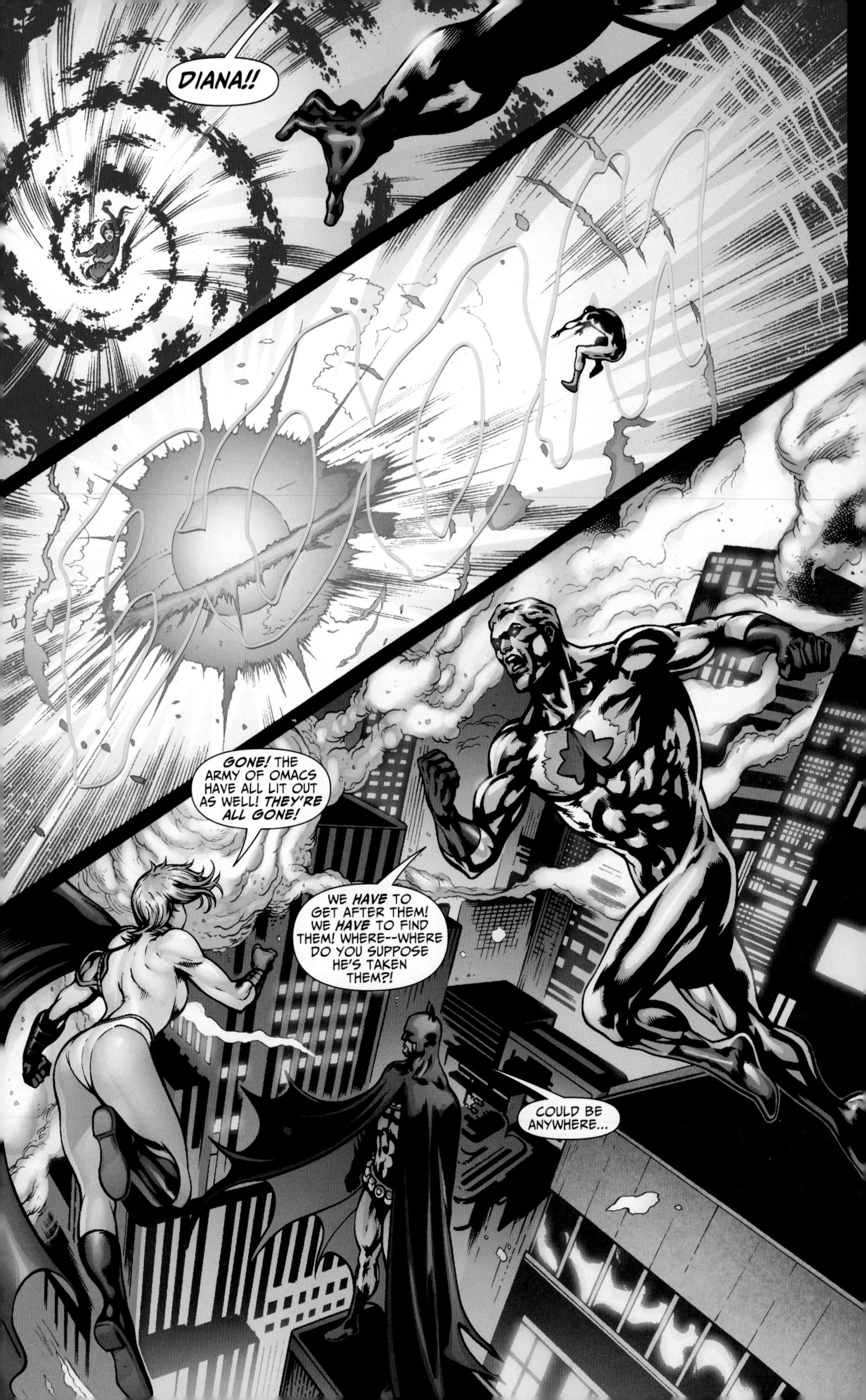
DIANA!!
GONE! THE ARMY OF OMACS HAVE ALL LIT OUT AS WELL! THEY'RE ALL GONE!
WE HAVE TO GET AFTER THEM! WE HAVE TO FIND THEM! WHERE--WHERE DO YOU SUPPOSE HE'S TAKEN THEM?!
COULD BE ANYWHERE...

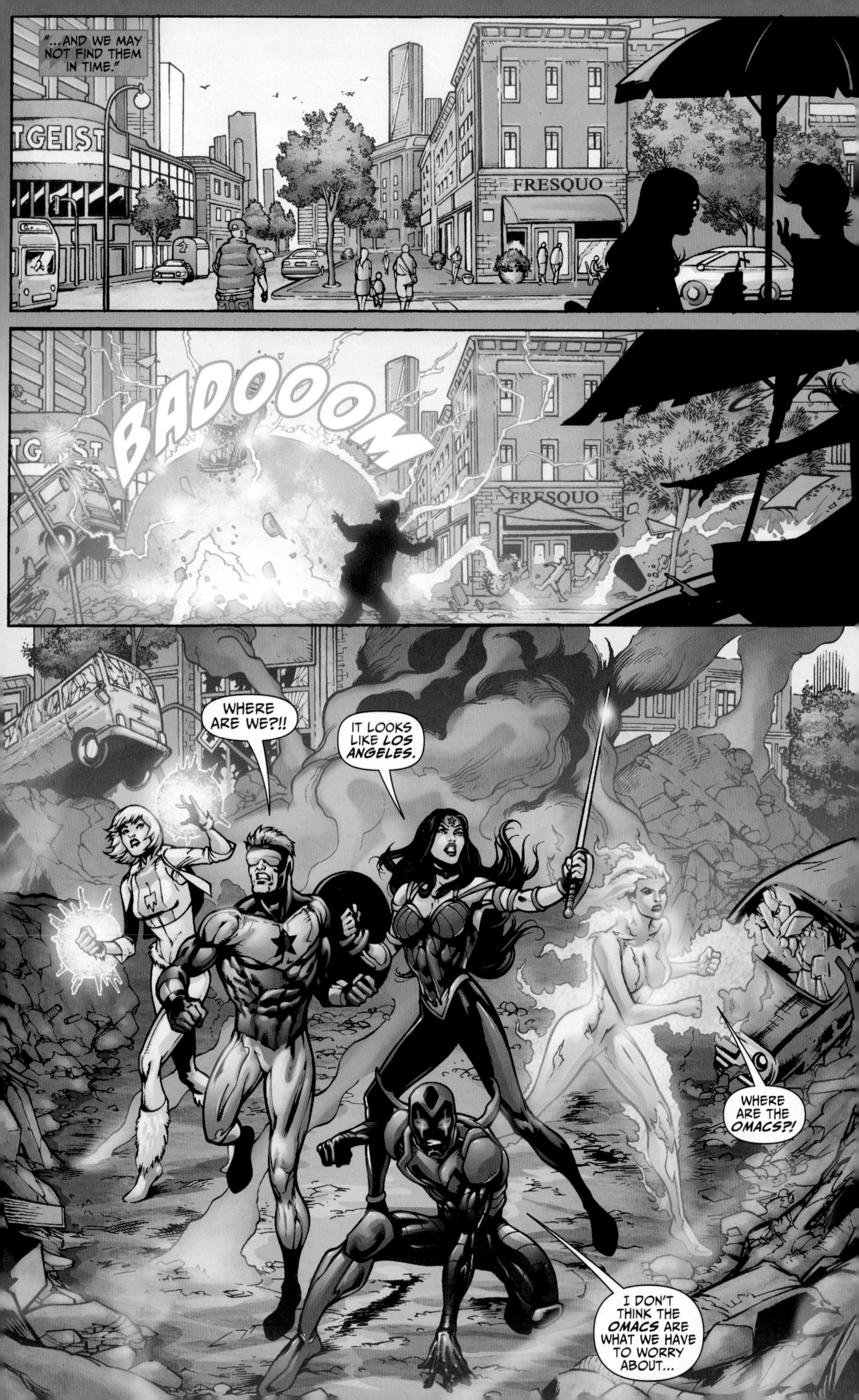
"...AND WE MAY NOT FIND THEM IN TIME."
TGEIST
FRESQUO
BADOOOM
WHERE ARE WE?!!
IT LOOKS LIKE LOS ANGELES.
WHERE ARE THE OMACS?!
I DON'T THINK THE OMACS ARE WHAT WE HAVE TO WORRY ABOUT...

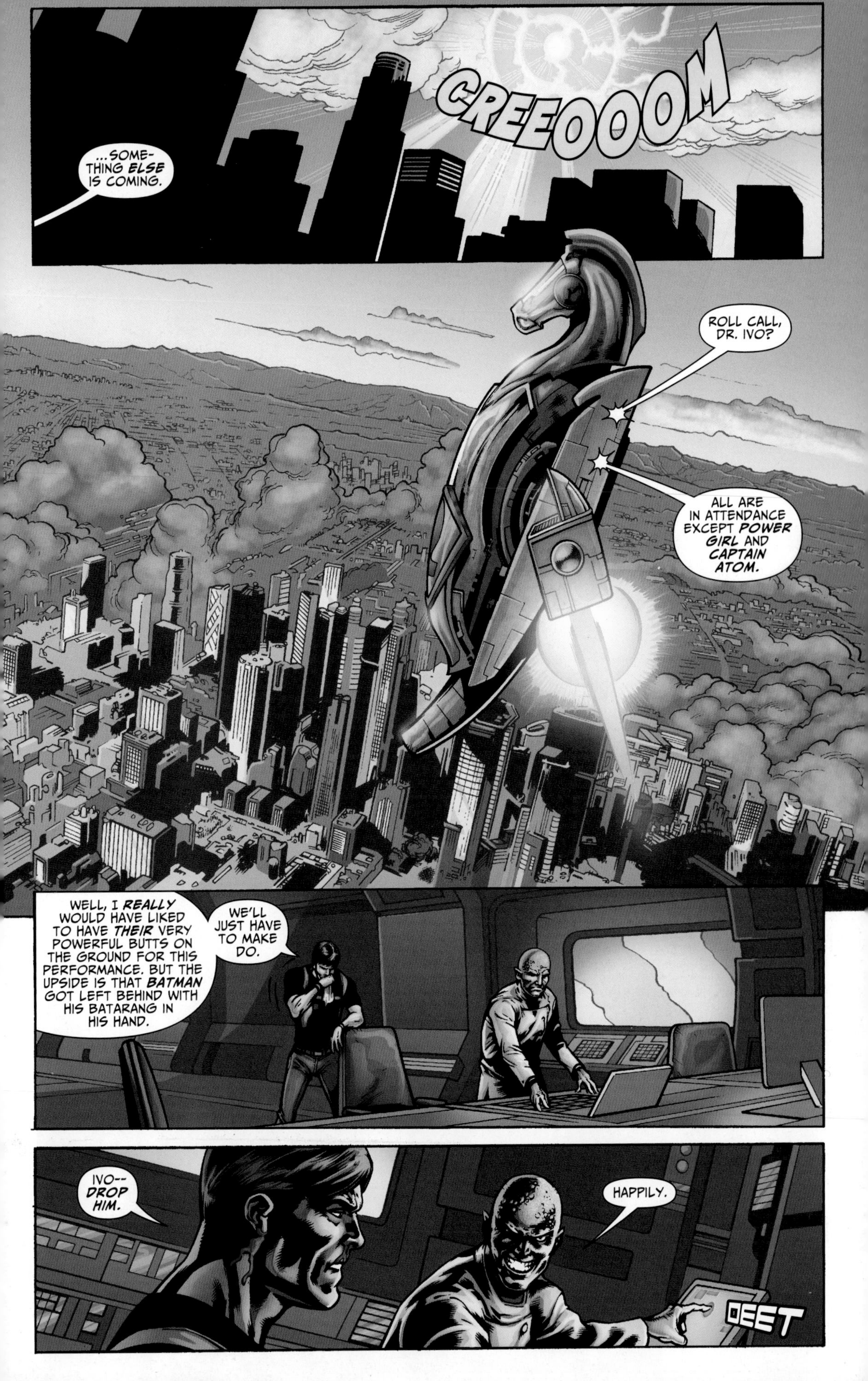
CREEOOOM
...SOMETHING ELSE IS COMING.
ROLL CALL, DR. IVO?
ALL ARE IN ATTENDANCE EXCEPT POWER GIRL AND CAPTAIN ATOM.
WELL, I REALLY WOULD HAVE LIKED TO HAVE THEIR VERY POWERFUL BUTTS ON THE GROUND FOR THIS PERFORMANCE. BUT THE UPSIDE IS THAT BATMAN GOT LEFT BEHIND WITH HIS BATARANG IN HIS HAND.
WE'LL JUST HAVE TO MAKE DO.
IVO-- DROP HIM.
HAPPILY.
BEEP

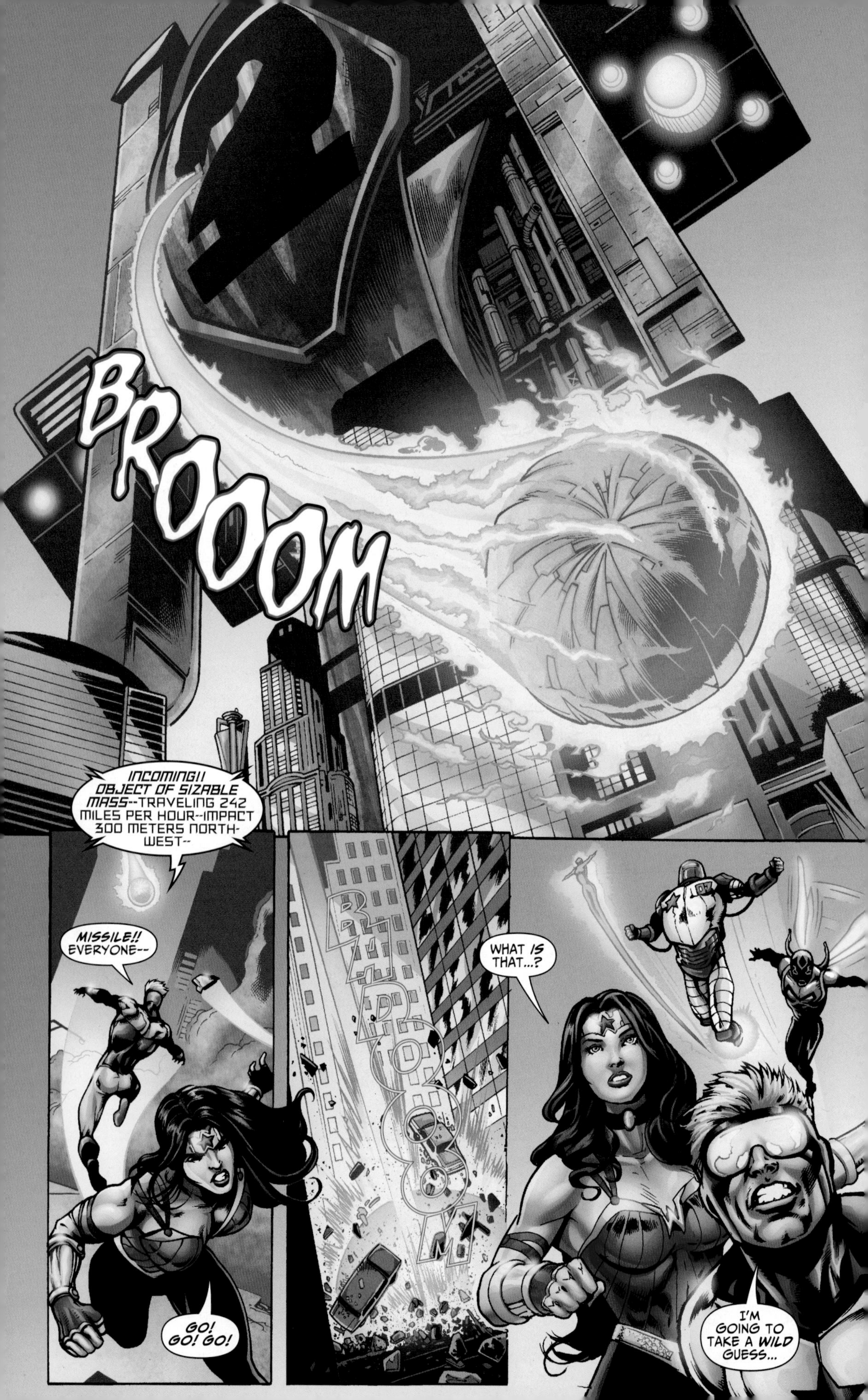
BROOOOM
INCOMING!! OBJECT OF SIZABLE MASS--TRAVELING 242 MILES PER HOUR--IMPACT 300 METERS NORTH-WEST--
MISSILE!! EVERYONE--
GO! GO! GO!
BROOOM
WHAT IS THAT...?
I'M GOING TO TAKE A WILD GUESS...

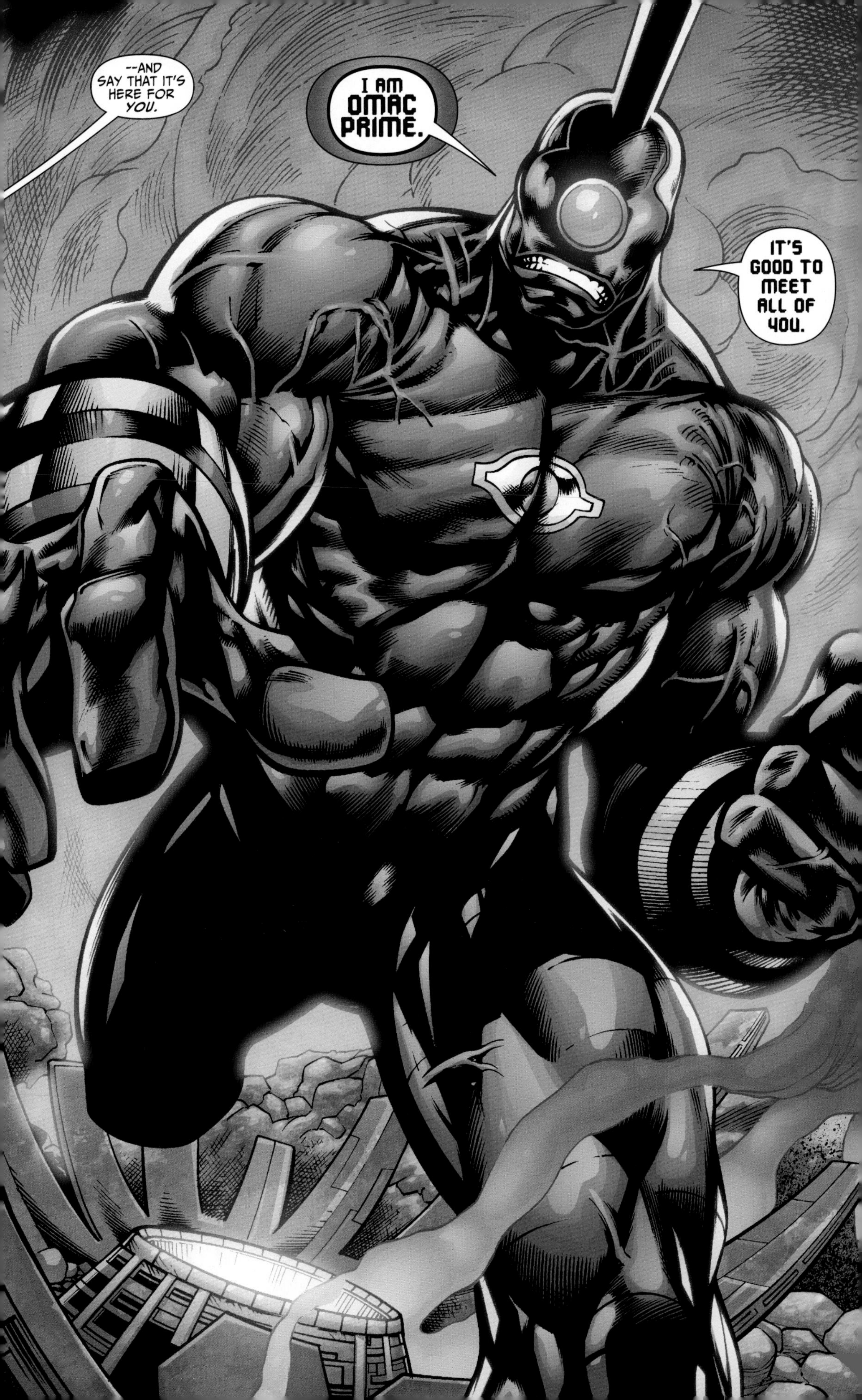
--AND SAY THAT IT'S HERE FOR *YOU.*
I AM OMAC PRIME.
IT'S GOOD TO MEET ALL OF YOU.

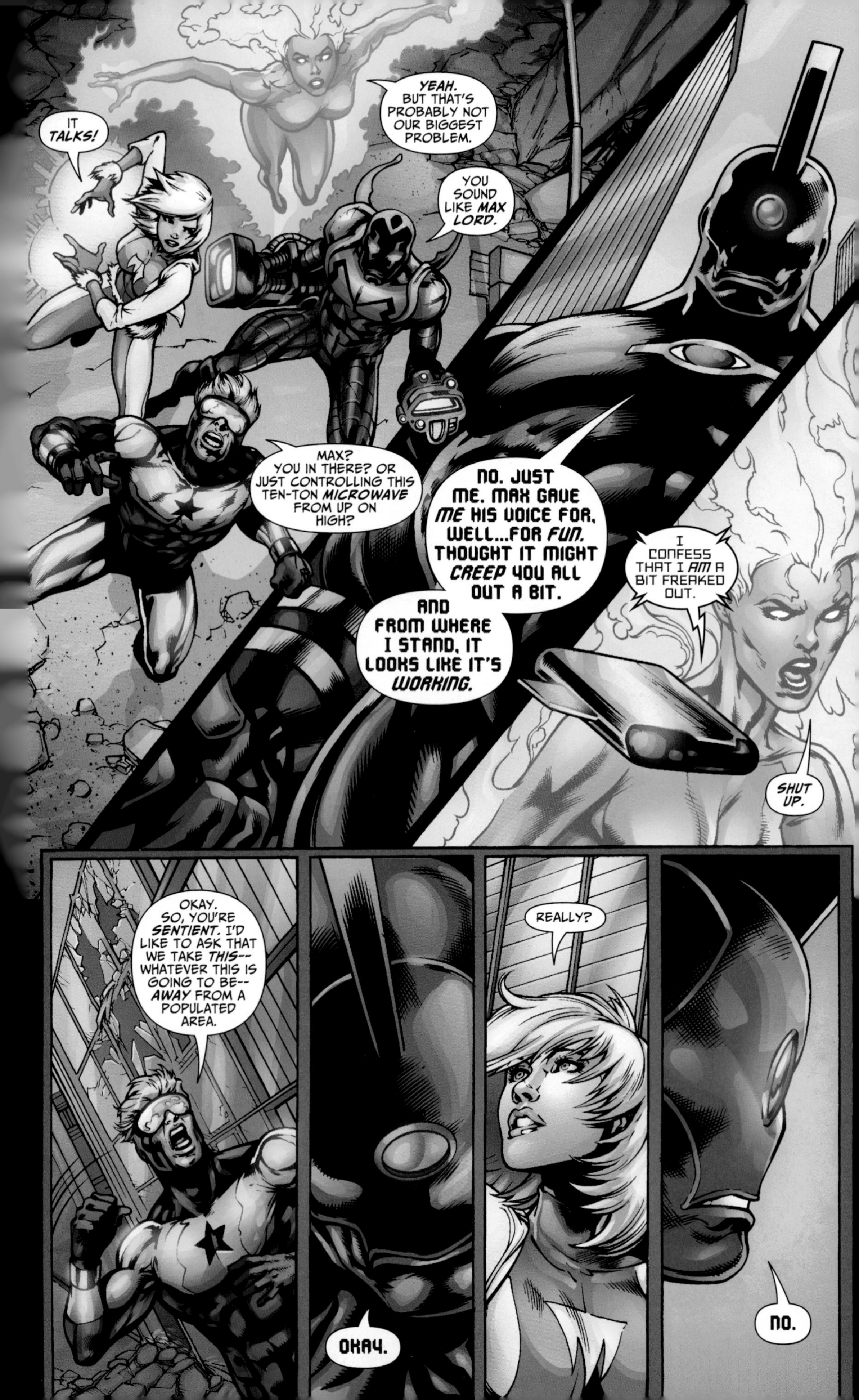
IT TALKS!
YEAH. BUT THAT'S PROBABLY NOT OUR BIGGEST PROBLEM.
YOU SOUND LIKE MAX LORD.
MAX? YOU IN THERE? OR JUST CONTROLLING THIS TEN-TON MICROWAVE FROM UP ON HIGH?
NO. JUST ME. MAX GAVE ME HIS VOICE FOR, WELL...FOR FUN. THOUGHT IT MIGHT CREEP YOU ALL OUT A BIT.
AND FROM WHERE I STAND, IT LOOKS LIKE IT'S WORKING.
I CONFESS THAT I AM A BIT FREAKED OUT.
SHUT UP.
OKAY. SO, YOU'RE SENTIENT. I'D LIKE TO ASK THAT WE TAKE THIS-- WHATEVER THIS IS GOING TO BE-- AWAY FROM A POPULATED AREA.
OKAY.
REALLY?
NO.

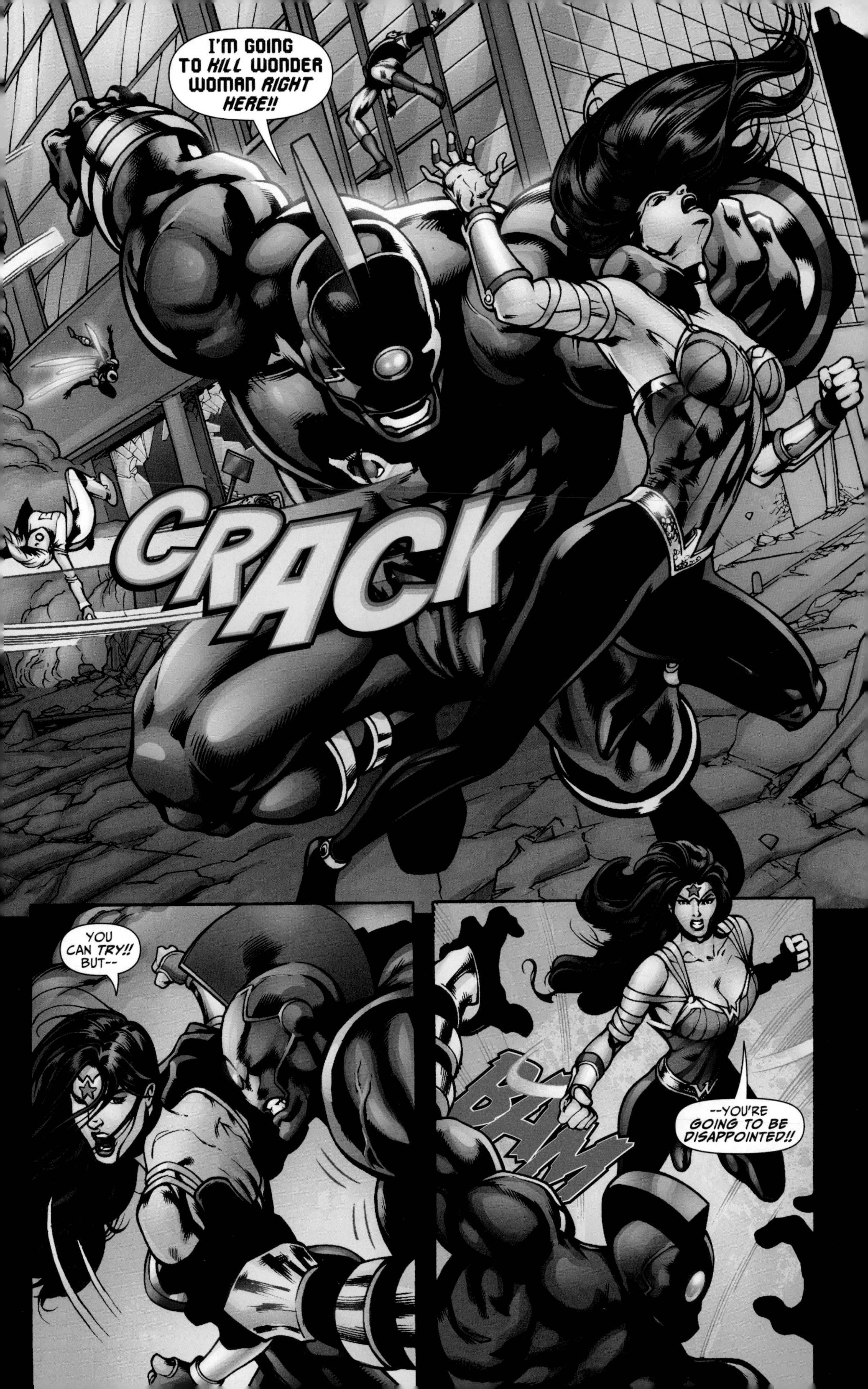
I'M GOING TO KILL WONDER WOMAN RIGHT HERE!!
CRACK
YOU CAN TRY!! BUT--
BAM
--YOU'RE GOING TO BE DISAPPOINTED!!

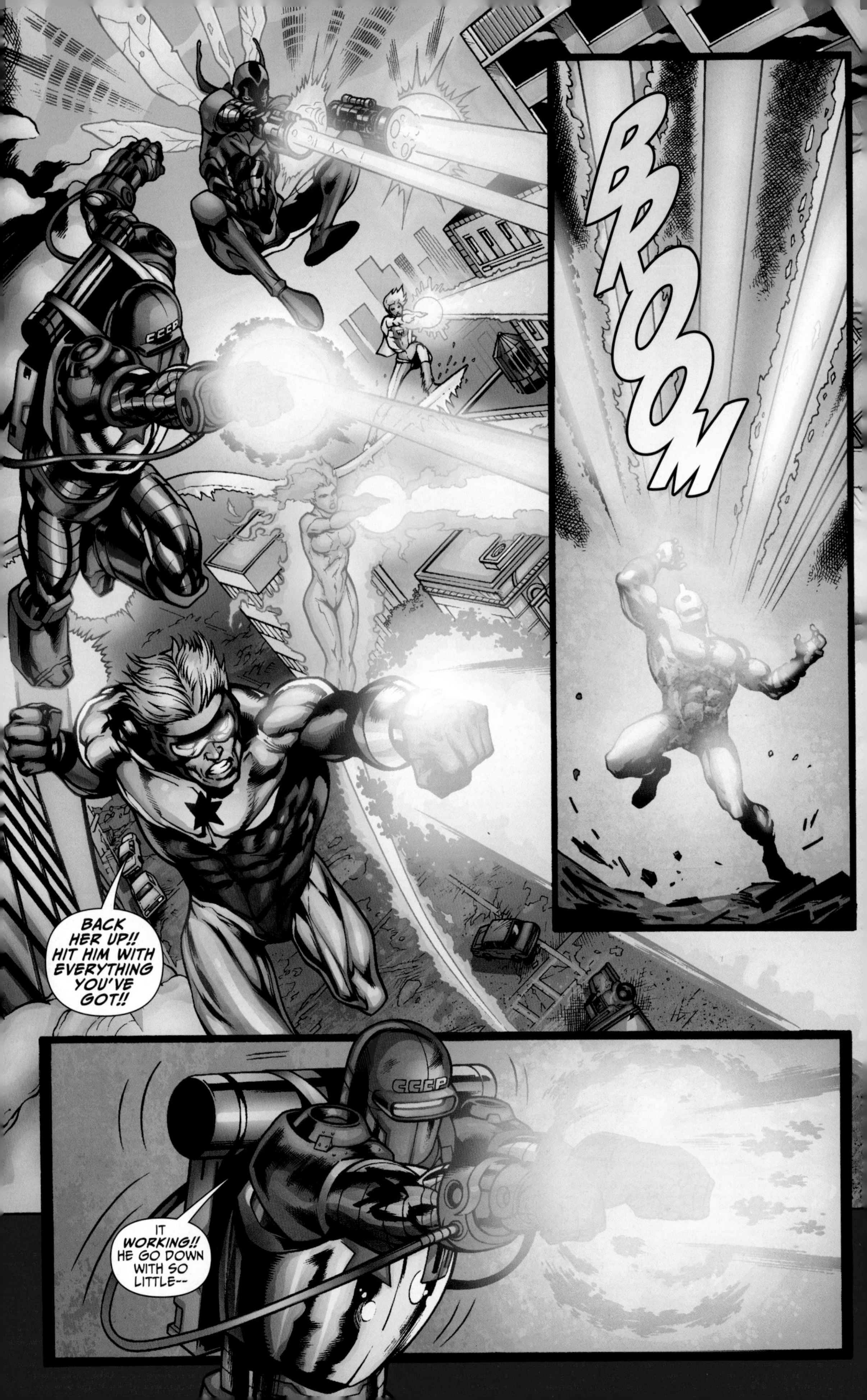
BROOOM
BACK HER UP!! HIT HIM WITH EVERYTHING YOU'VE GOT!!
IT WORKING!! HE GO DOWN WITH SO LITTLE--

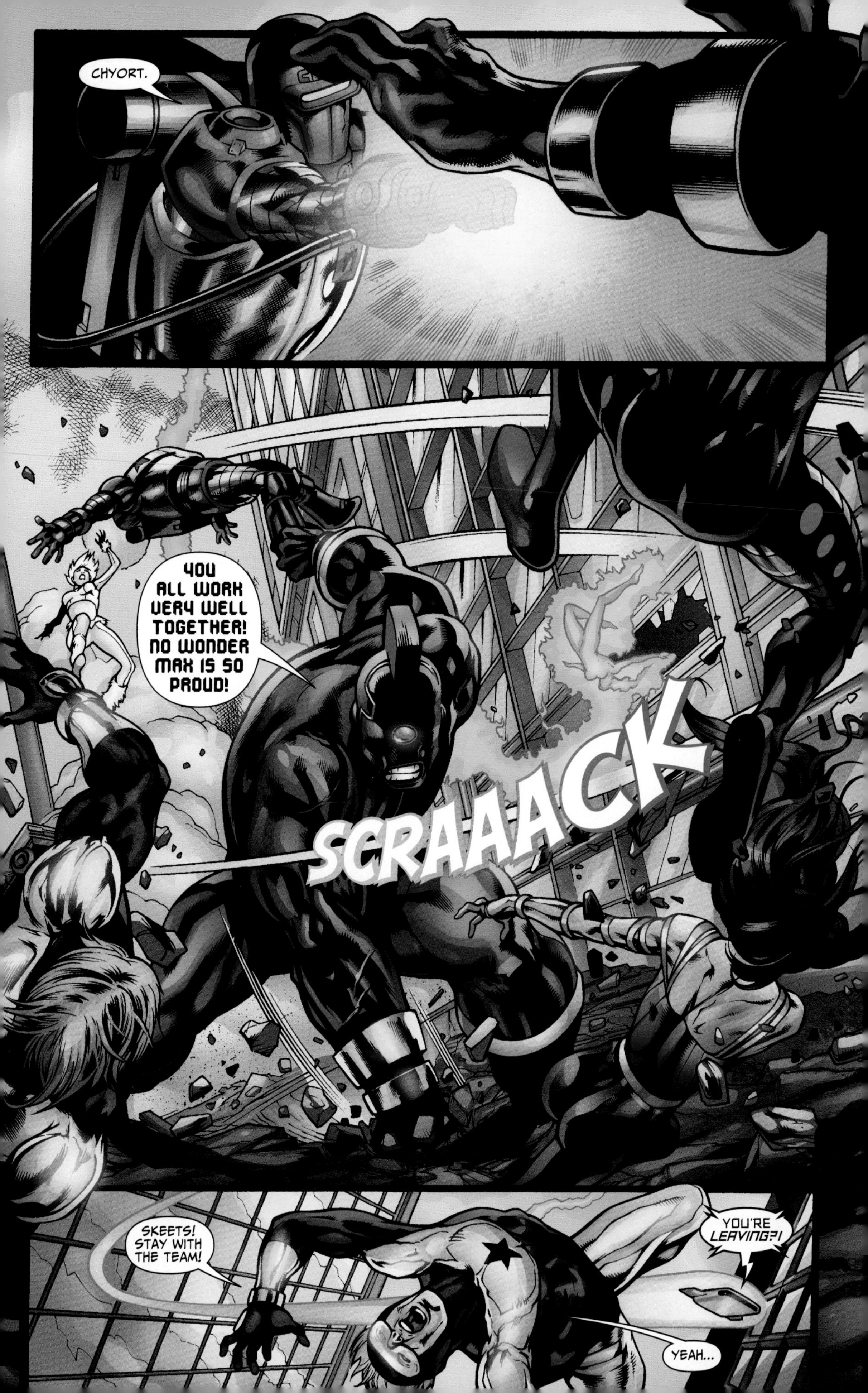
CHYORT.
YOU ALL WORK VERY WELL TOGETHER! NO WONDER MAX IS SO PROUD!
SCRAAACK
SKEETS! STAY WITH THE TEAM!
YOU'RE LEAVING?!
YEAH...

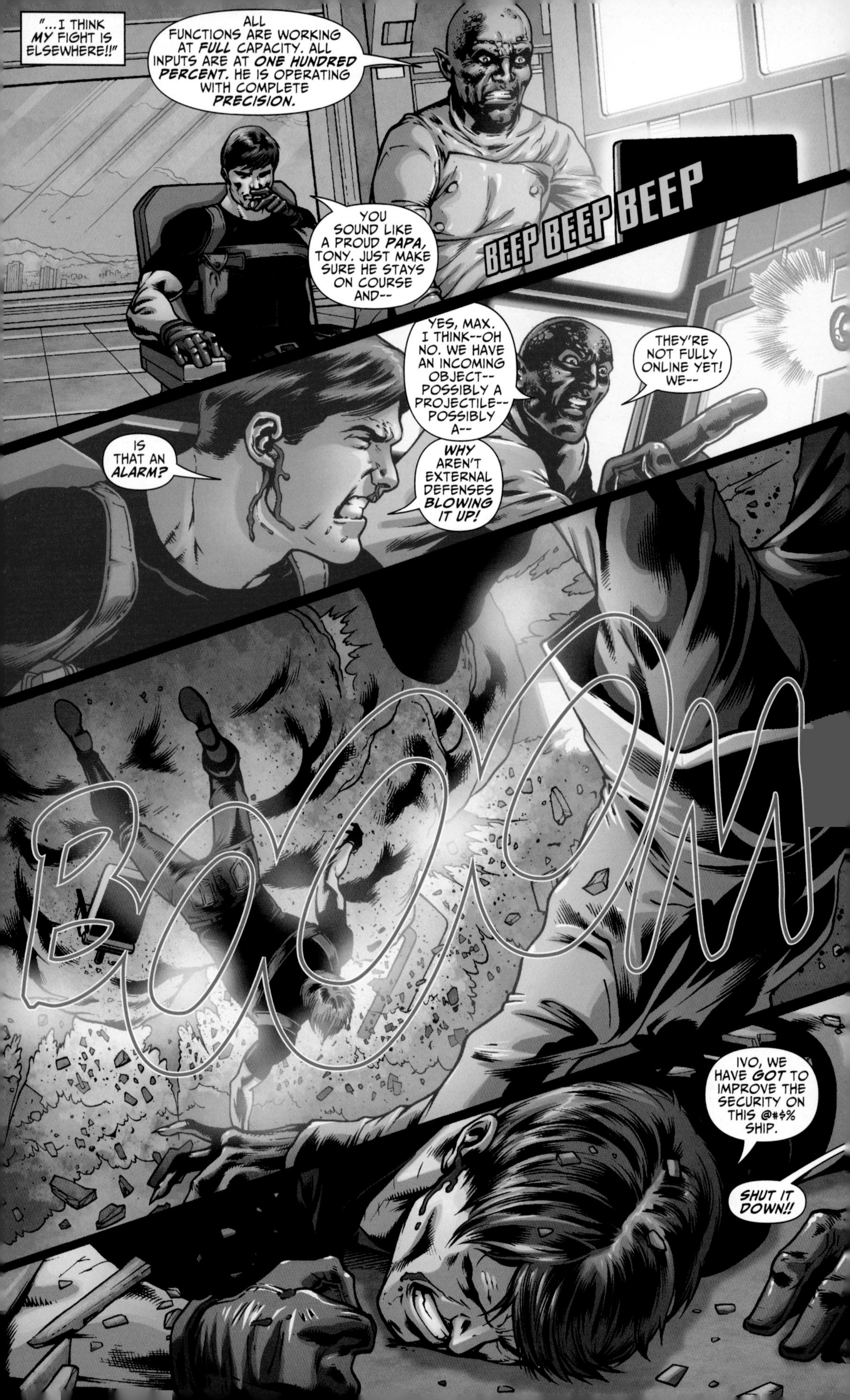
"...I THINK MY FIGHT IS ELSEWHERE!!"
ALL FUNCTIONS ARE WORKING AT FULL CAPACITY. ALL INPUTS ARE AT ONE HUNDRED PERCENT. HE IS OPERATING WITH COMPLETE PRECISION.
YOU SOUND LIKE A PROUD PAPA, TONY. JUST MAKE SURE HE STAYS ON COURSE AND--
BEEP BEEP BEEP
YES, MAX. I THINK--OH NO. WE HAVE AN INCOMING OBJECT--POSSIBLY A PROJECTILE--POSSIBLY A--
THEY'RE NOT FULLY ONLINE YET! WE--
IS THAT AN ALARM?
WHY AREN'T EXTERNAL DEFENSES BLOWING IT UP!
BOOOM
IVO, WE HAVE GOT TO IMPROVE THE SECURITY ON THIS @#$% SHIP.
SHUT IT DOWN!!

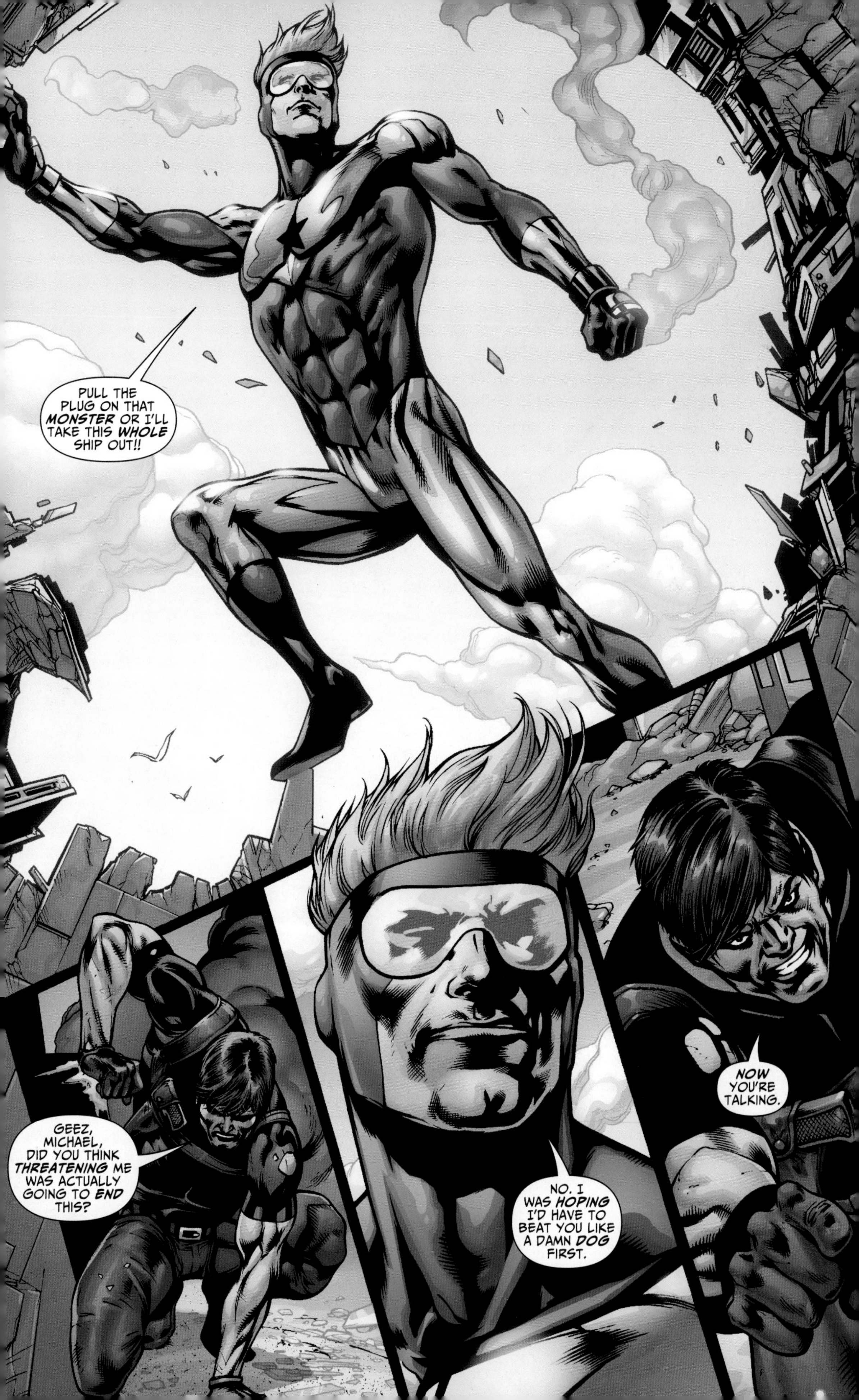
PULL THE PLUG ON THAT MONSTER OR I'LL TAKE THIS WHOLE SHIP OUT!!
GEEZ, MICHAEL, DID YOU THINK THREATENING ME WAS ACTUALLY GOING TO END THIS?
NO. I WAS HOPING I'D HAVE TO BEAT YOU LIKE A DAMN DOG FIRST.
NOW YOU'RE TALKING.

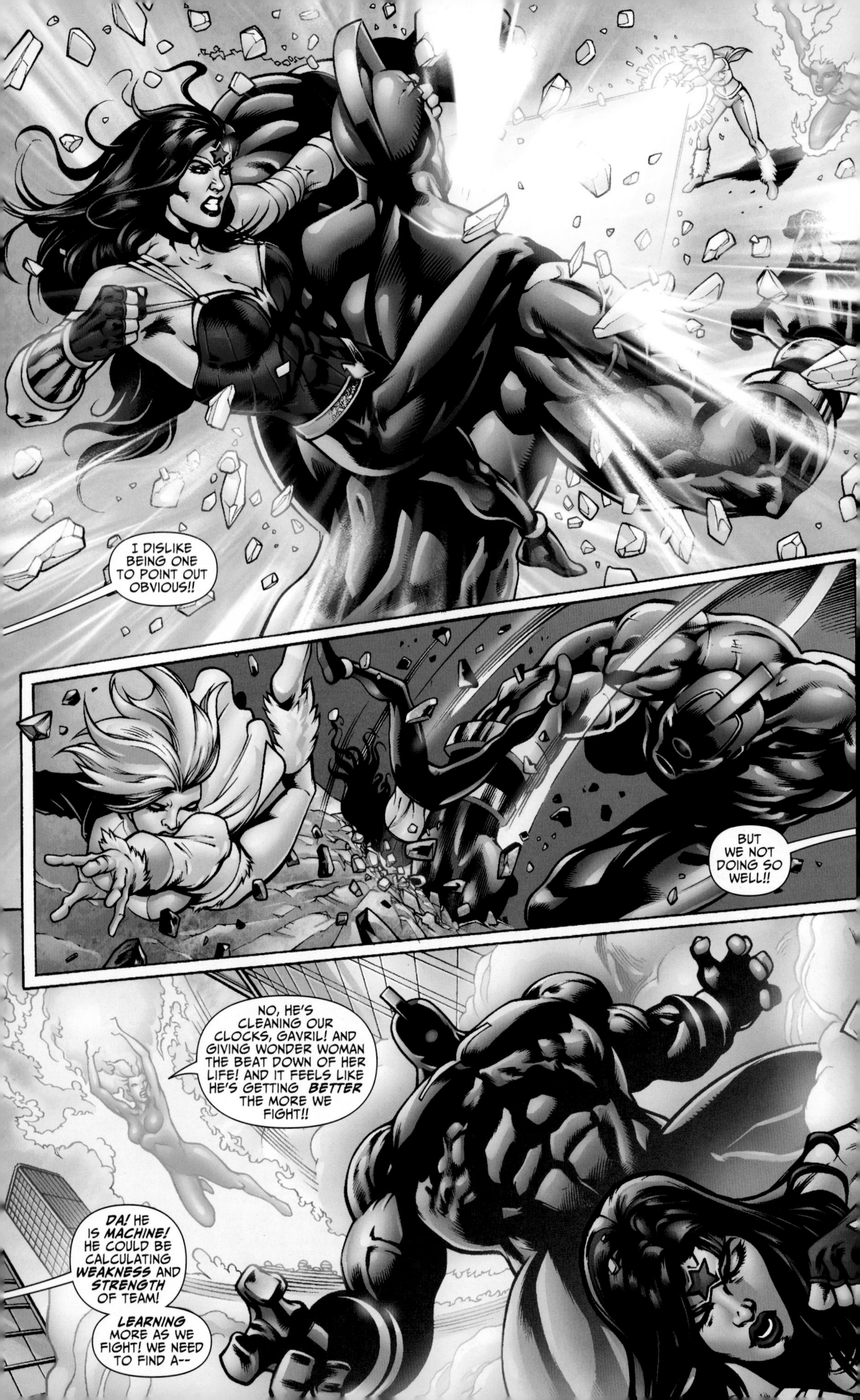
I DISLIKE BEING ONE TO POINT OUT OBVIOUS!!
BUT WE NOT DOING SO WELL!!
NO, HE'S CLEANING OUR CLOCKS, GAVRIL! AND GIVING WONDER WOMAN THE BEAT DOWN OF HER LIFE! AND IT FEELS LIKE HE'S GETTING BETTER THE MORE WE FIGHT!!
DA! HE IS MACHINE! HE COULD BE CALCULATING WEAKNESS AND STRENGTH OF TEAM!
LEARNING MORE AS WE FIGHT! WE NEED TO FIND A--

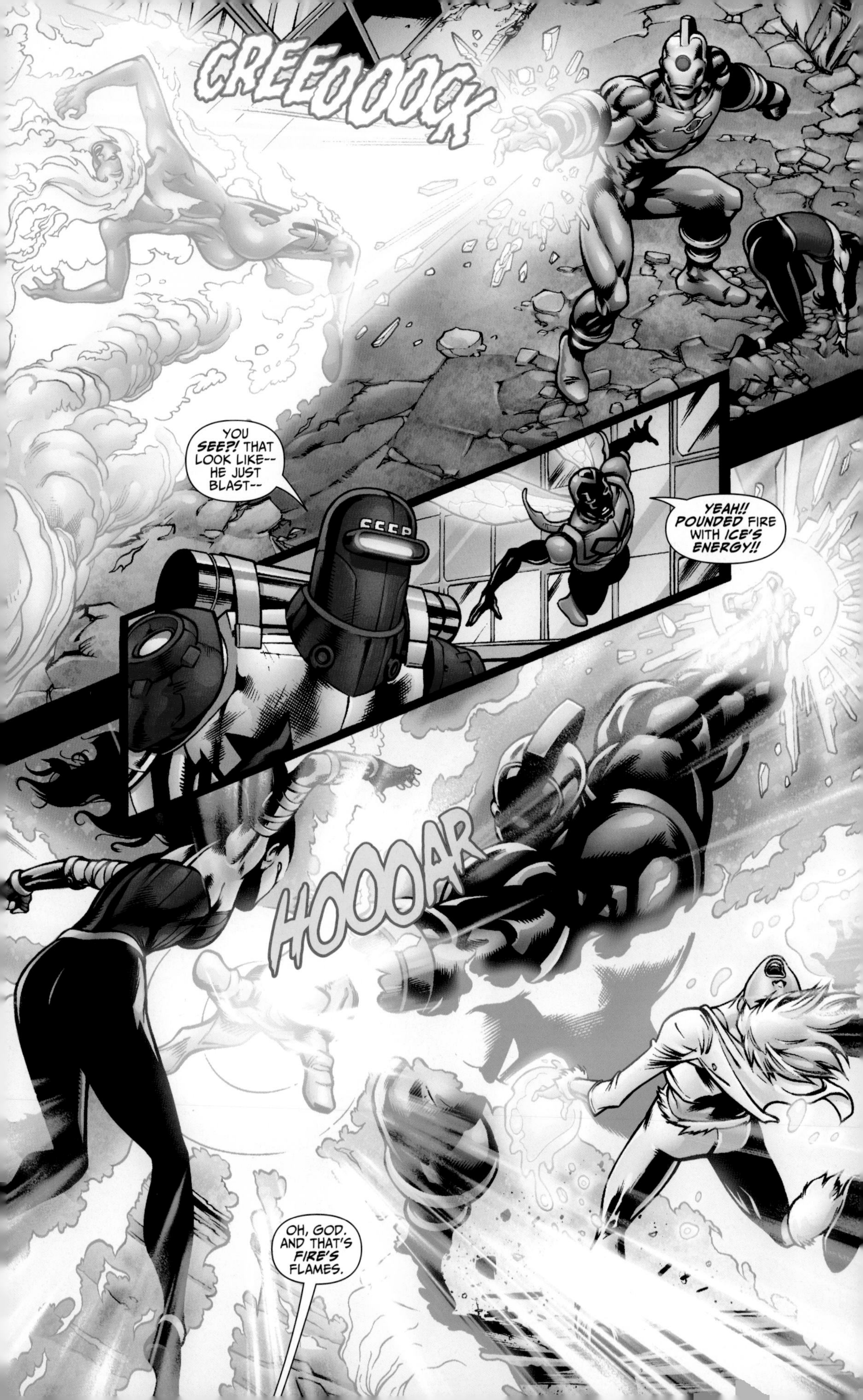
CREEOOOCK
YOU SEE?! THAT LOOK LIKE-- HE JUST BLAST--
YEAH!! POUNDED FIRE WITH ICE'S ENERGY!!
HOOOAR
OH, GOD. AND THAT'S FIRE'S FLAMES.

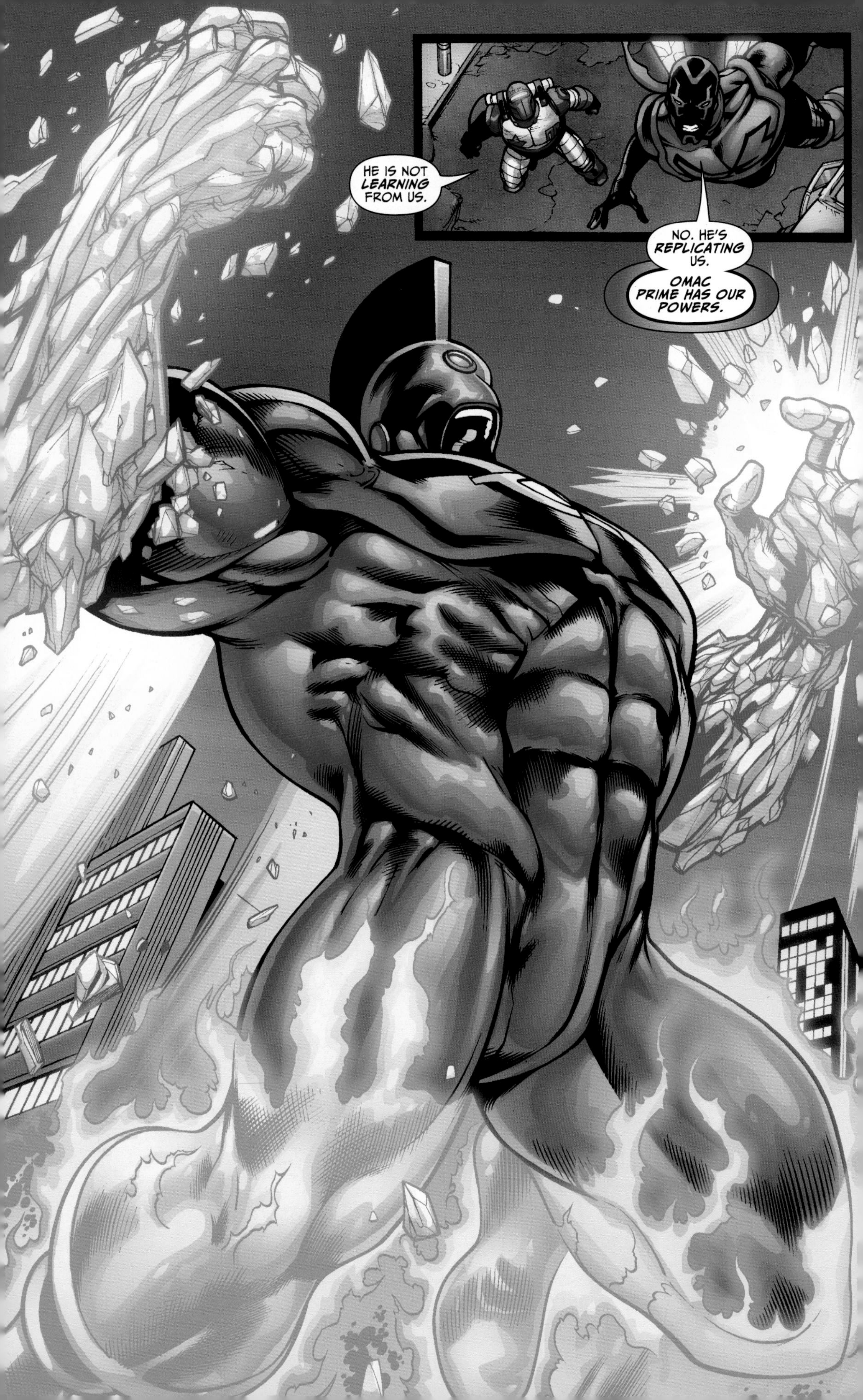
HE IS NOT LEARNING FROM US.
NO. HE'S REPLICATING US.
OMAC PRIME HAS OUR POWERS.

Cover by Dustin Nguyen

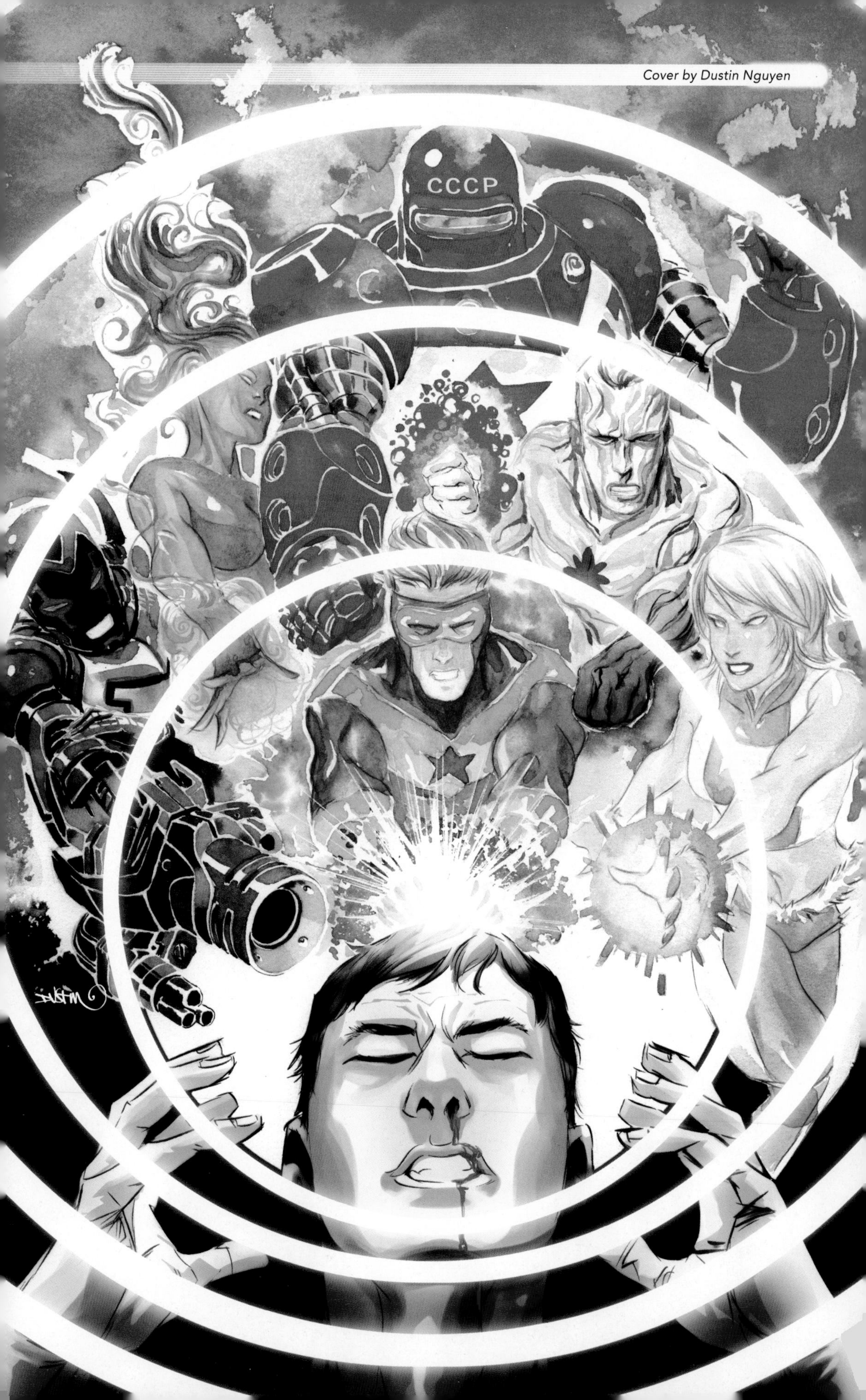
CCCP
DUSTIN

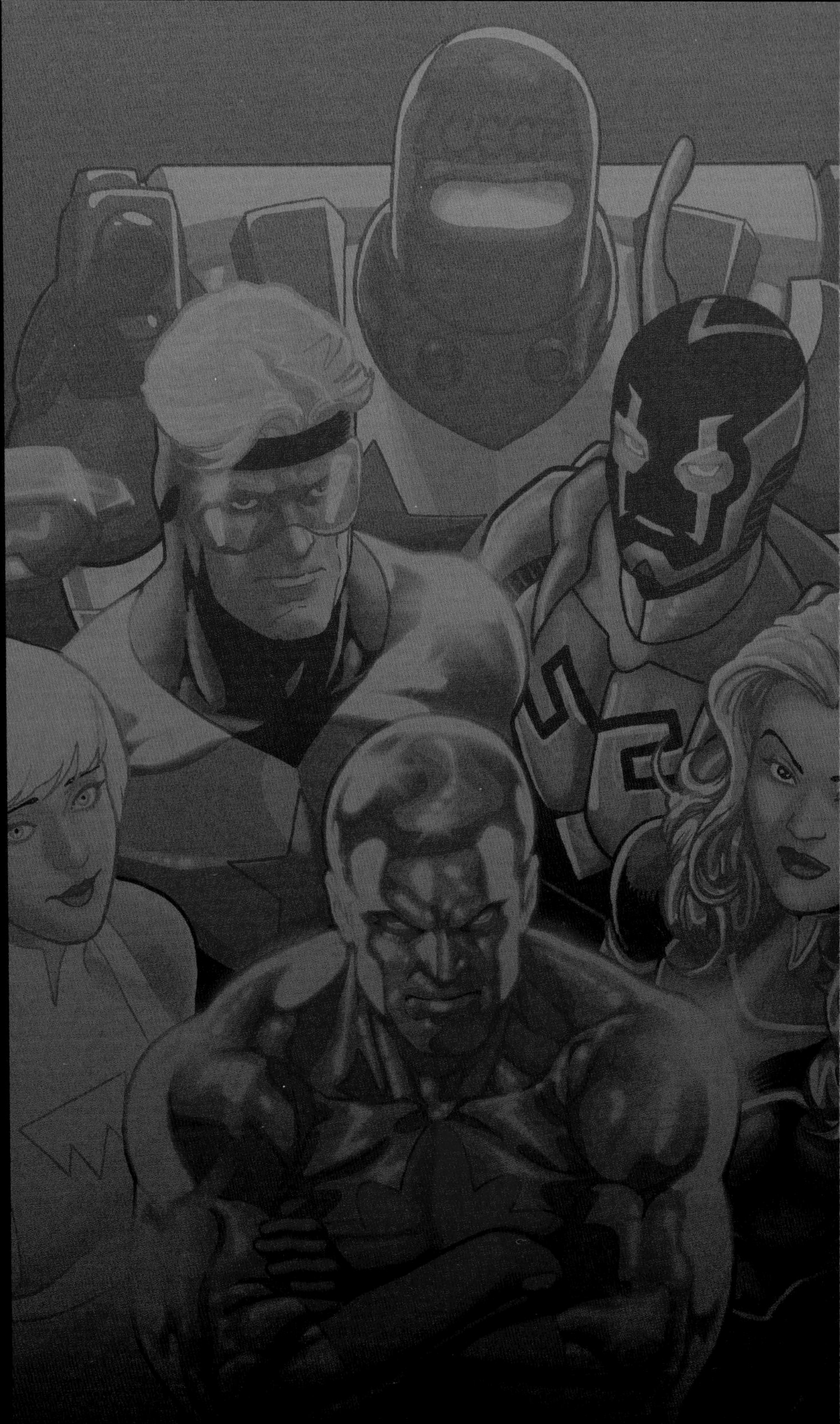

PART TWENTY-FOUR:

IT ALL COMES DOWN TO THIS!

HE WANTED SOMETHING THAT COULD KILL *WONDER WOMAN*. HE WAS WARY OF *FORCING* SOMEONE TO DO IT BY CONTROLLING THEIR MINDS. LAST TIME THAT ACTUALLY GOT HIM *KILLED*.

SO HE DECIDED TO *BUILD* SOMETHING.

HE MADE CAREFUL STUDY OF HIS *OMACS*...

...AND OF *THE METAL MEN* AND THE SPONTANEITY OF THEIR *NEUROLOGICAL* PROCESS.

HE ADAPTED THE GENETIC BUILDING BLOCKS OF *PROJECT CADMUS* AND THE *CREATURE COMMANDOS*...

...AS WELL AS *BLUE BEETLE'S* ALIEN ARMOR AND ITS SHAPESHIFTING ABILITIES.

AND THEN THERE WAS SCIENTIST *DR. ANTHONY IVO*. LONG AGO HE INVENTED *AMAZO*, THE ANDROID THAT COULD MIMIC THE ABILITIES OF METAHUMANS.

AND WITH ALL THAT...*MAX LORD* HAD HIS CREATION--

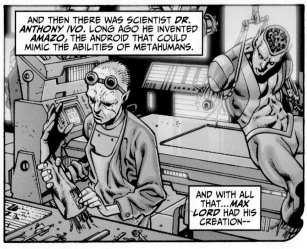

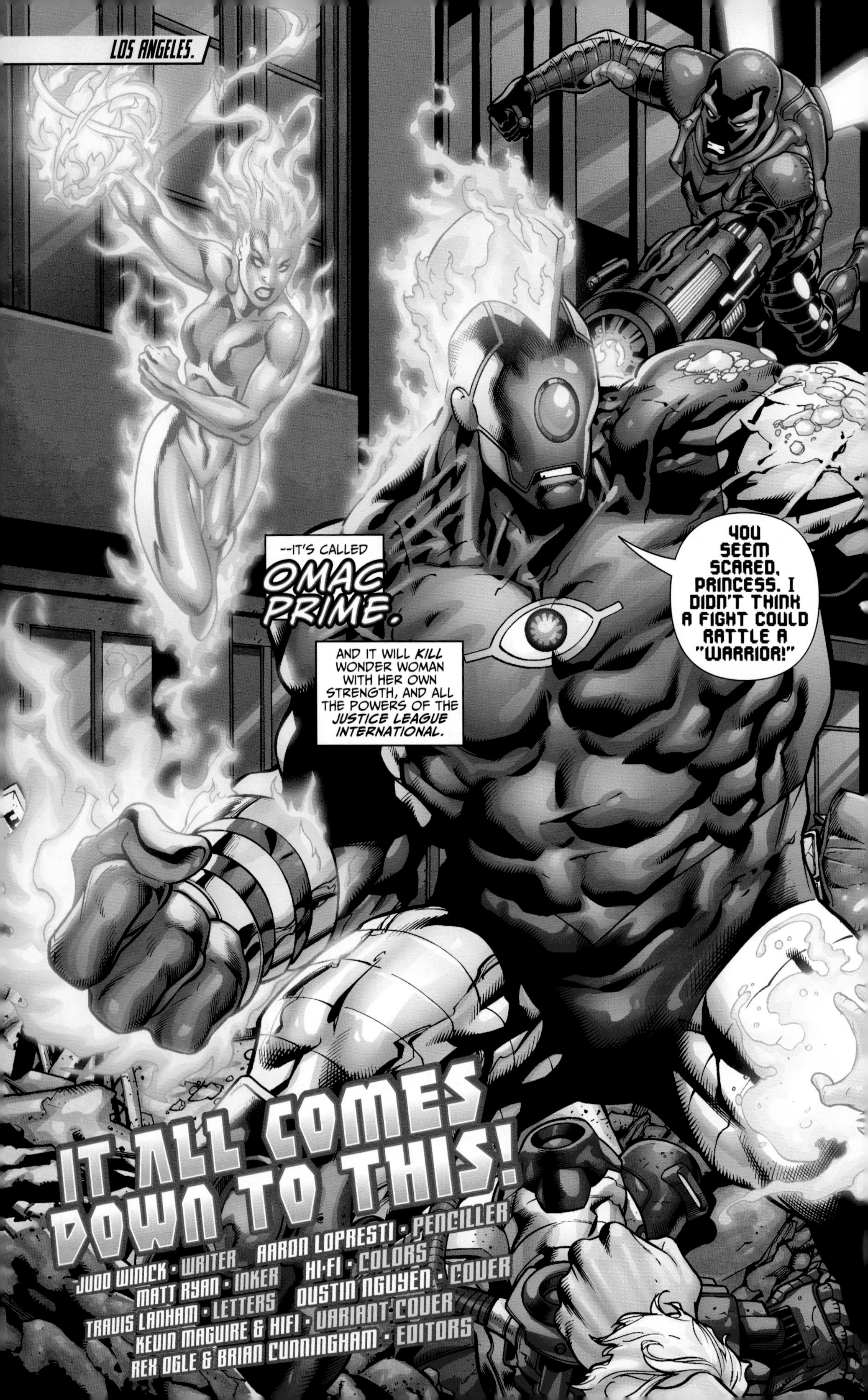

LOS ANGELES.
--IT'S CALLED OMAC PRIME.
AND IT WILL KILL WONDER WOMAN WITH HER OWN STRENGTH, AND ALL THE POWERS OF THE JUSTICE LEAGUE INTERNATIONAL.
YOU SEEM SCARED, PRINCESS. I DIDN'T THINK A FIGHT COULD RATTLE A "WARRIOR!"
IT ALL COMES DOWN TO THIS!
JUDD WINICK · WRITER AARON LOPRESTI · PENCILLER
MATT RYAN · INKER HI-FI · COLORS
TRAVIS LANHAM · LETTERS DUSTIN NGUYEN · COVER
KEVIN MAGUIRE & HIFI · VARIANT COVER
REX OGLE & BRIAN CUNNINGHAM · EDITORS

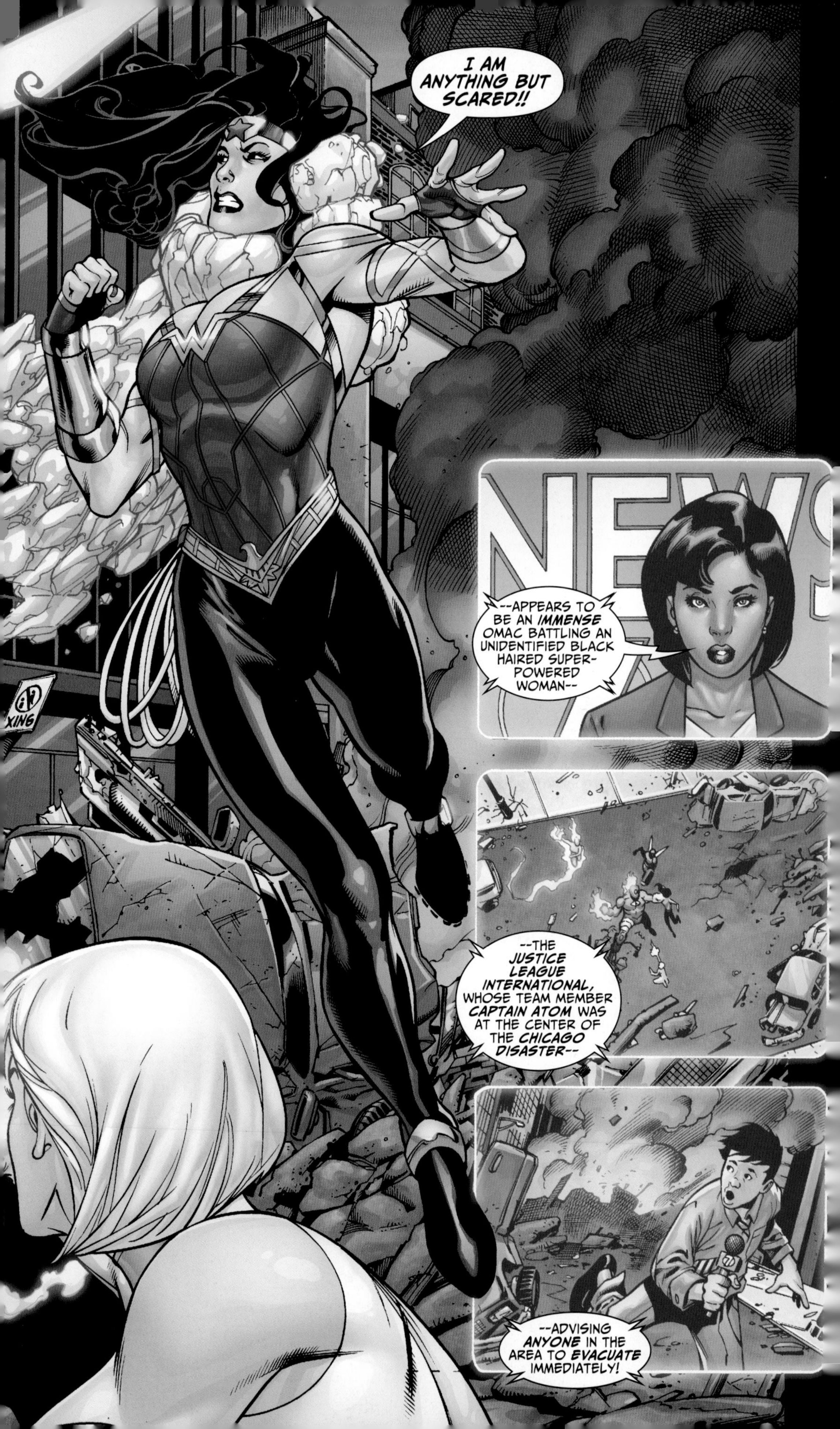
I AM ANYTHING BUT SCARED!!
XING
NEWS
--APPEARS TO BE AN IMMENSE OMAC BATTLING AN UNIDENTIFIED BLACK HAIRED SUPER-POWERED WOMAN--
--THE JUSTICE LEAGUE INTERNATIONAL, WHOSE TEAM MEMBER CAPTAIN ATOM WAS AT THE CENTER OF THE CHICAGO DISASTER--
--ADVISING ANYONE IN THE AREA TO EVACUATE IMMEDIATELY!

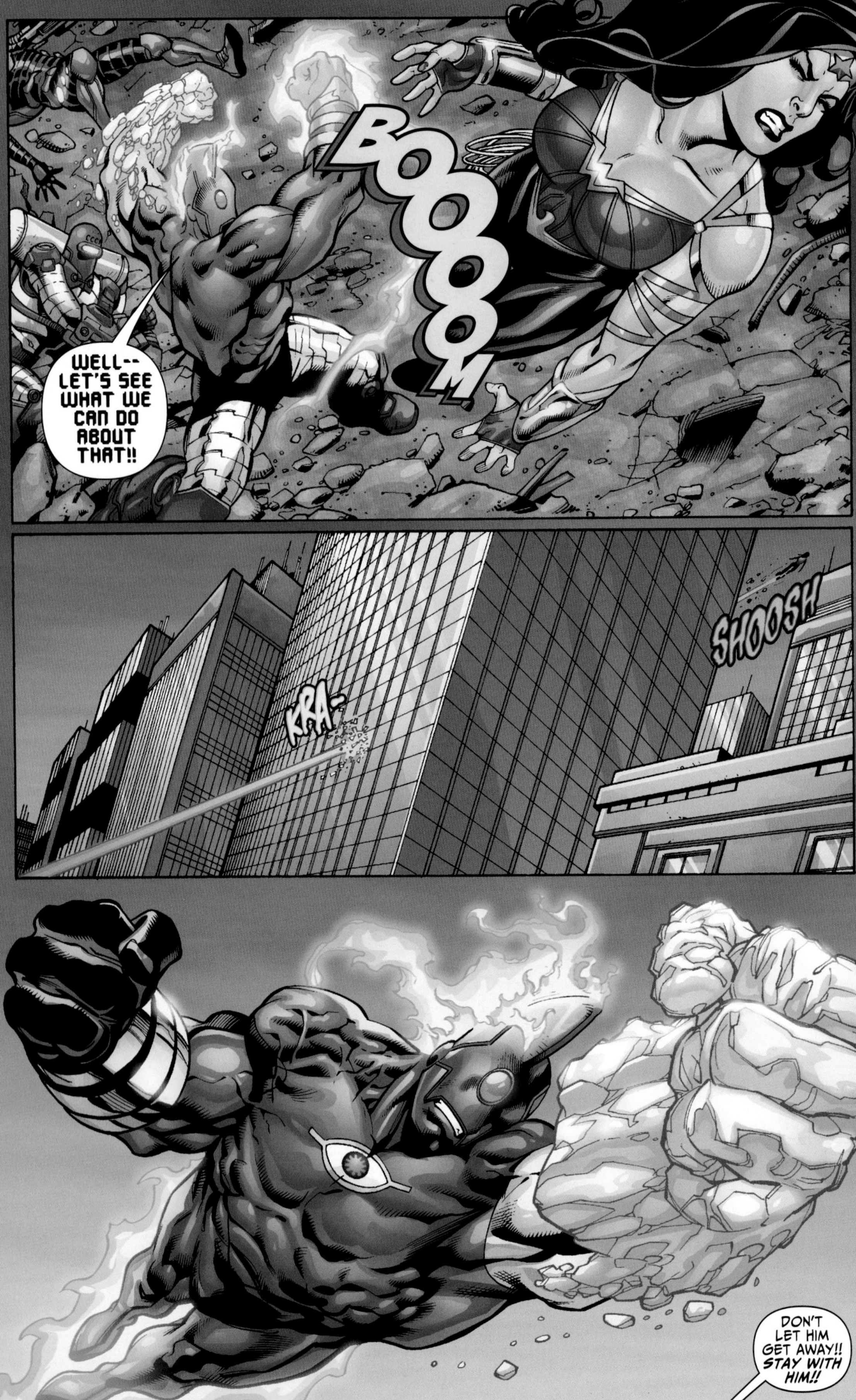
BOOOOOM
WELL-- LET'S SEE WHAT WE CAN DO ABOUT THAT!!
KRA-
SHOOSH
DON'T LET HIM GET AWAY!! STAY WITH HIM!!

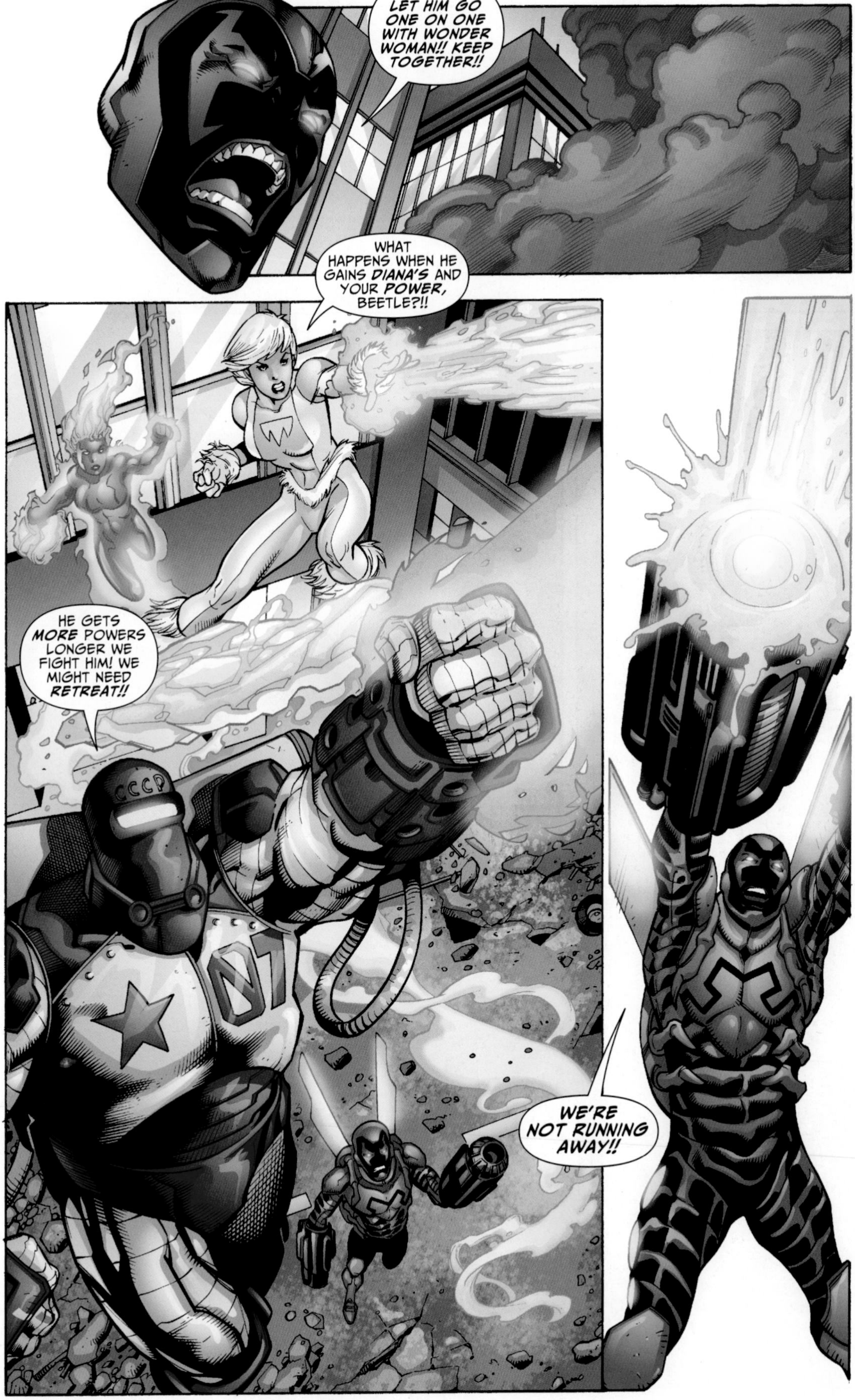
DON'T LET HIM GO ONE ON ONE WITH WONDER WOMAN!! KEEP TOGETHER!!
WHAT HAPPENS WHEN HE GAINS DIANA'S AND YOUR POWER, BEETLE?!!
HE GETS MORE POWERS LONGER WE FIGHT HIM! WE MIGHT NEED RETREAT!!
WE'RE NOT RUNNING AWAY!!
CCCP
07

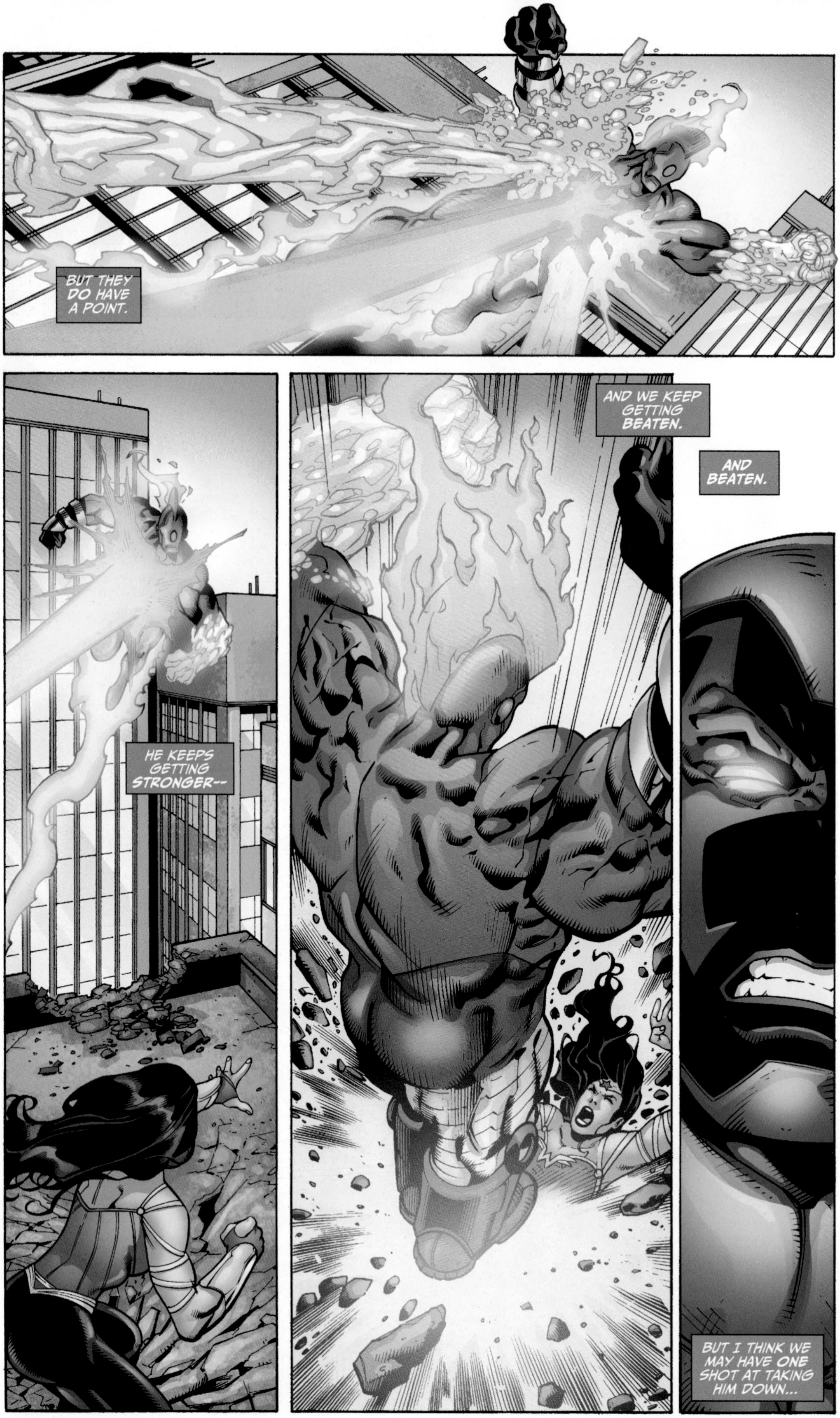
BUT THEY DO HAVE A POINT.
HE KEEPS GETTING STRONGER--
AND WE KEEP GETTING BEATEN.
AND BEATEN.
BUT I THINK WE MAY HAVE ONE SHOT AT TAKING HIM DOWN...

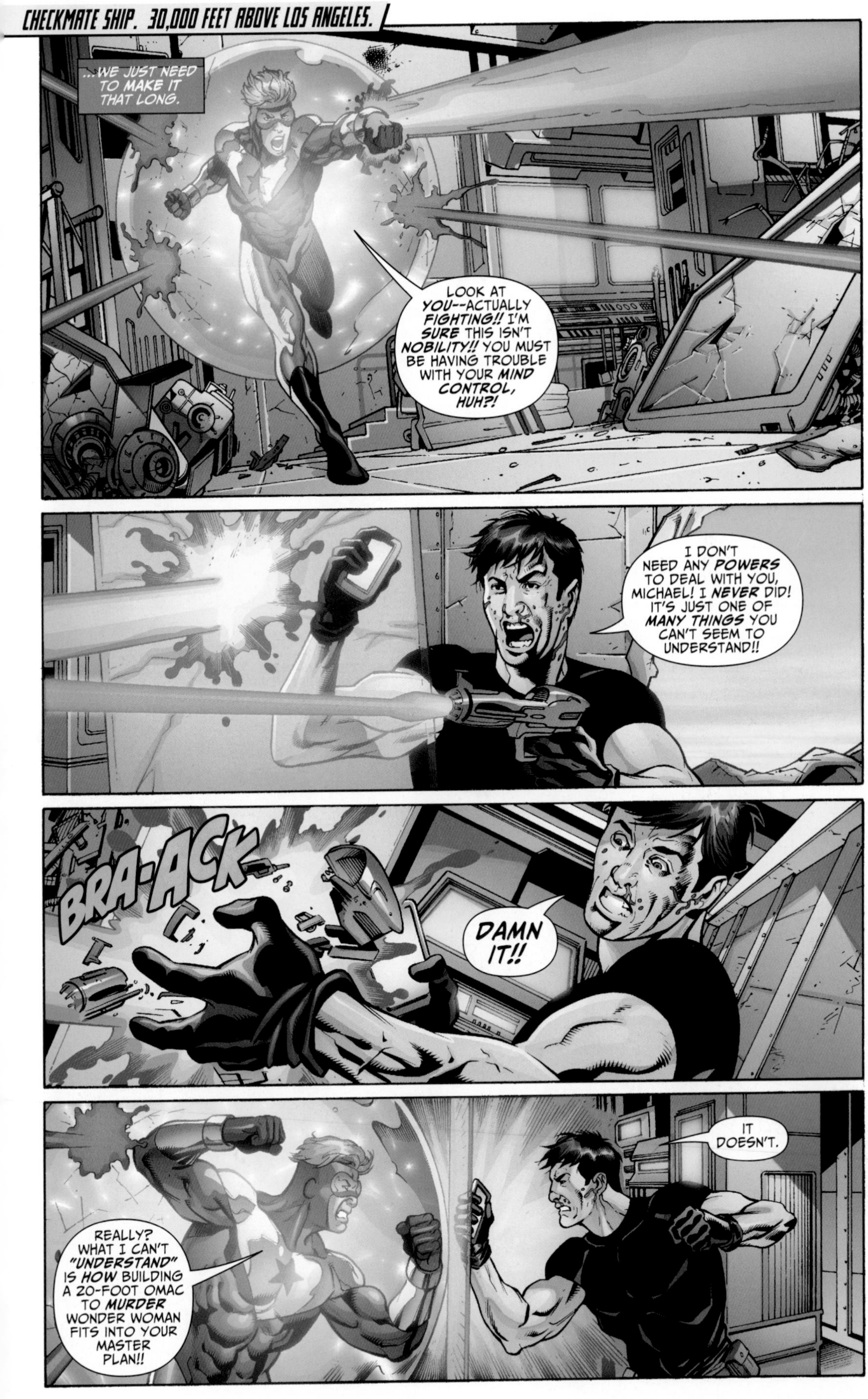
CHECKMATE SHIP. 30,000 FEET ABOVE LOS ANGELES.
...WE JUST NEED TO MAKE IT THAT LONG.
LOOK AT YOU--ACTUALLY FIGHTING!! I'M SURE THIS ISN'T NOBILITY!! YOU MUST BE HAVING TROUBLE WITH YOUR MIND CONTROL, HUH?!
I DON'T NEED ANY POWERS TO DEAL WITH YOU, MICHAEL! I NEVER DID! IT'S JUST ONE OF MANY THINGS YOU CAN'T SEEM TO UNDERSTAND!!
BRA-ACK
DAMN IT!!
REALLY? WHAT I CAN'T "UNDERSTAND" IS HOW BUILDING A 20-FOOT OMAC TO MURDER WONDER WOMAN FITS INTO YOUR MASTER PLAN!!
IT DOESN'T.

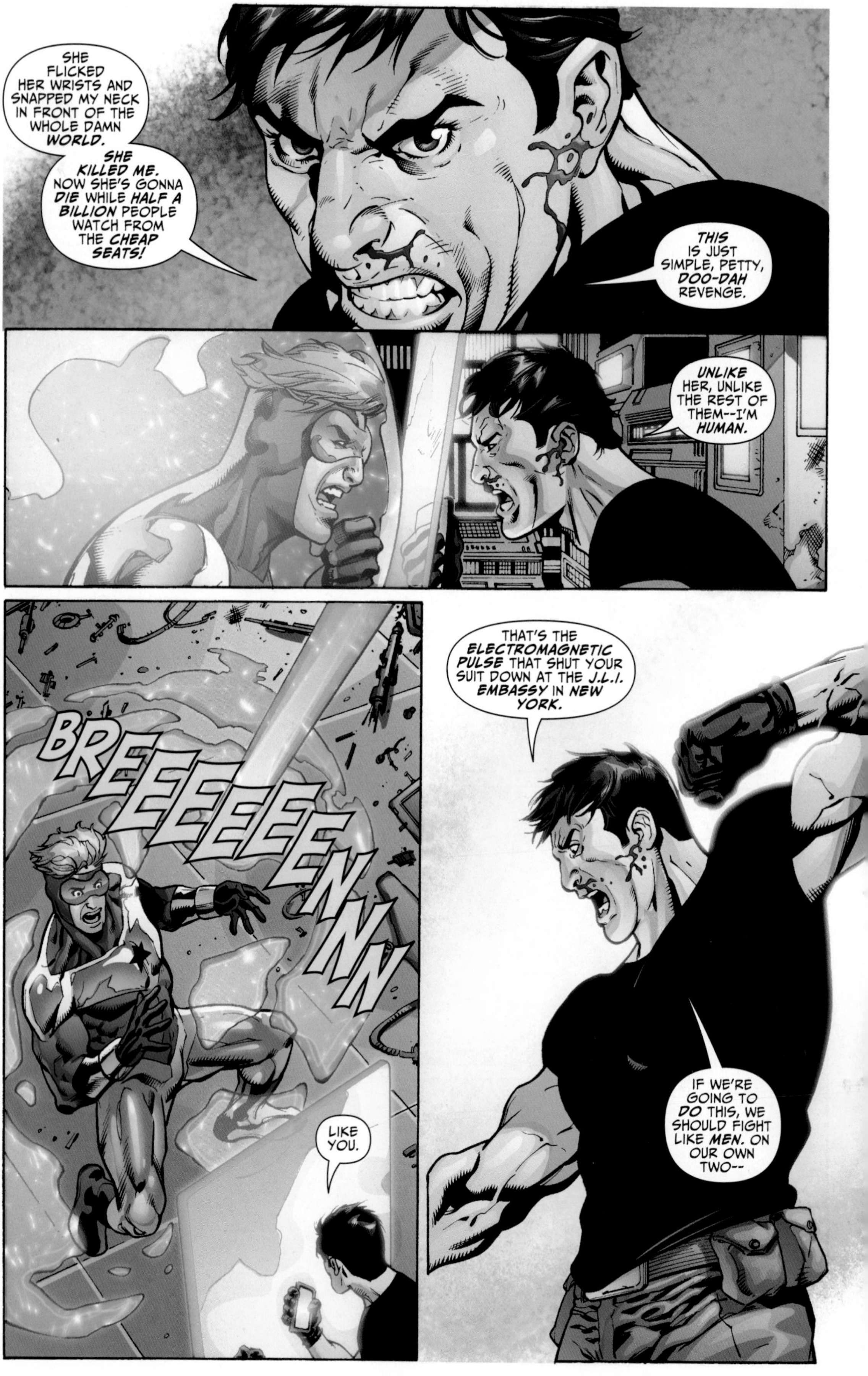
SHE FLICKED HER WRISTS AND SNAPPED MY NECK IN FRONT OF THE WHOLE DAMN WORLD.
SHE KILLED ME. NOW SHE'S GONNA DIE WHILE HALF A BILLION PEOPLE WATCH FROM THE CHEAP SEATS!
THIS IS JUST SIMPLE, PETTY, DOO-DAH REVENGE.
UNLIKE HER, UNLIKE THE REST OF THEM--I'M HUMAN.
BREEEEEEENNN
LIKE YOU.
THAT'S THE ELECTROMAGNETIC PULSE THAT SHUT YOUR SUIT DOWN AT THE J.L.I. EMBASSY IN NEW YORK.
IF WE'RE GOING TO DO THIS, WE SHOULD FIGHT LIKE MEN. ON OUR OWN TWO--

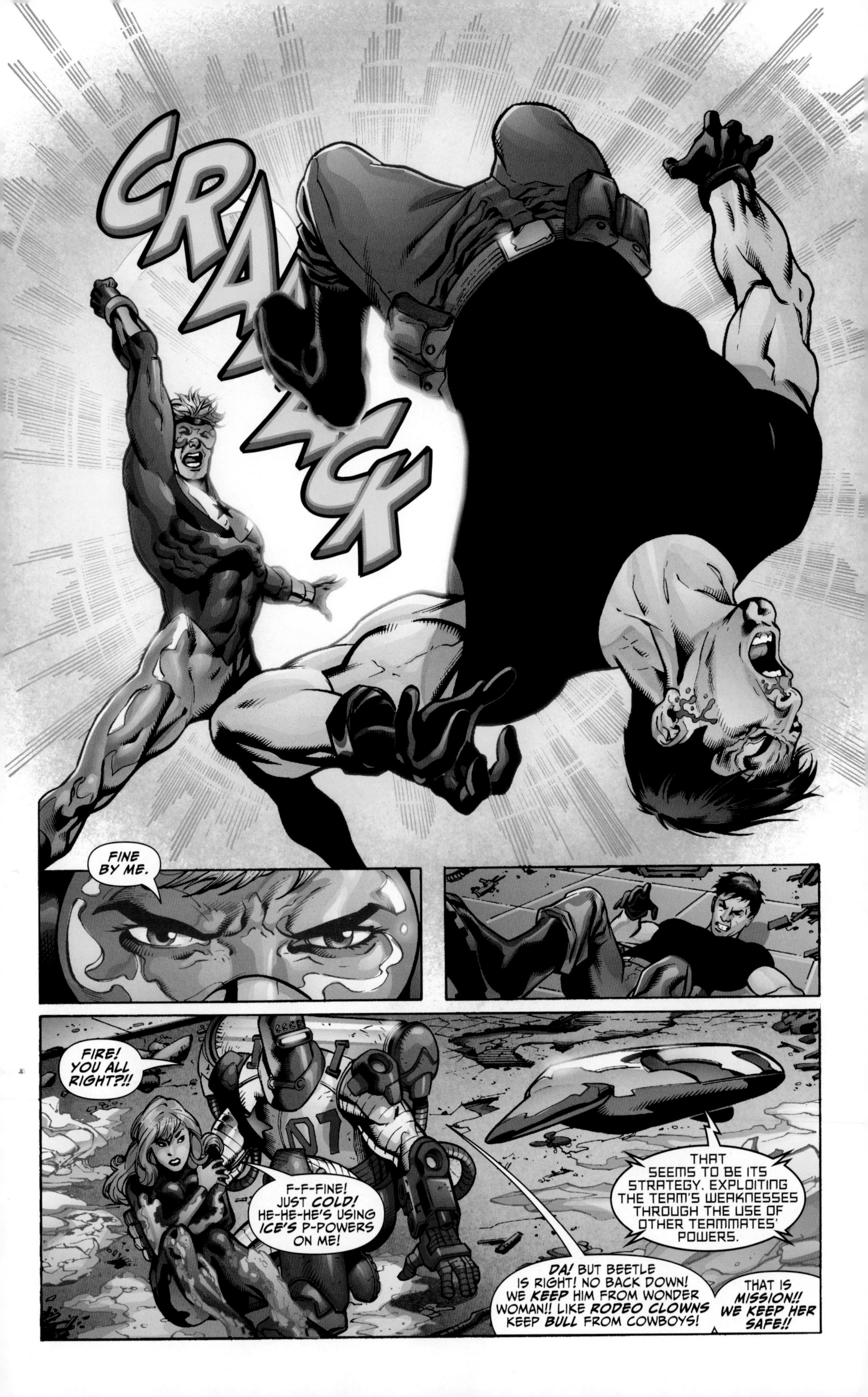

CRAAACK
FINE BY ME.
FIRE! YOU ALL RIGHT?!!
F-F-FINE! JUST COLD! HE-HE-HE'S USING ICE'S P-POWERS ON ME!
THAT SEEMS TO BE ITS STRATEGY. EXPLOITING THE TEAM'S WEAKNESSES THROUGH THE USE OF OTHER TEAMMATES' POWERS.
DA! BUT BEETLE IS RIGHT! NO BACK DOWN! WE KEEP HIM FROM WONDER WOMAN!! LIKE RODEO CLOWNS KEEP BULL FROM COWBOYS!
THAT IS MISSION!! WE KEEP HER SAFE!!

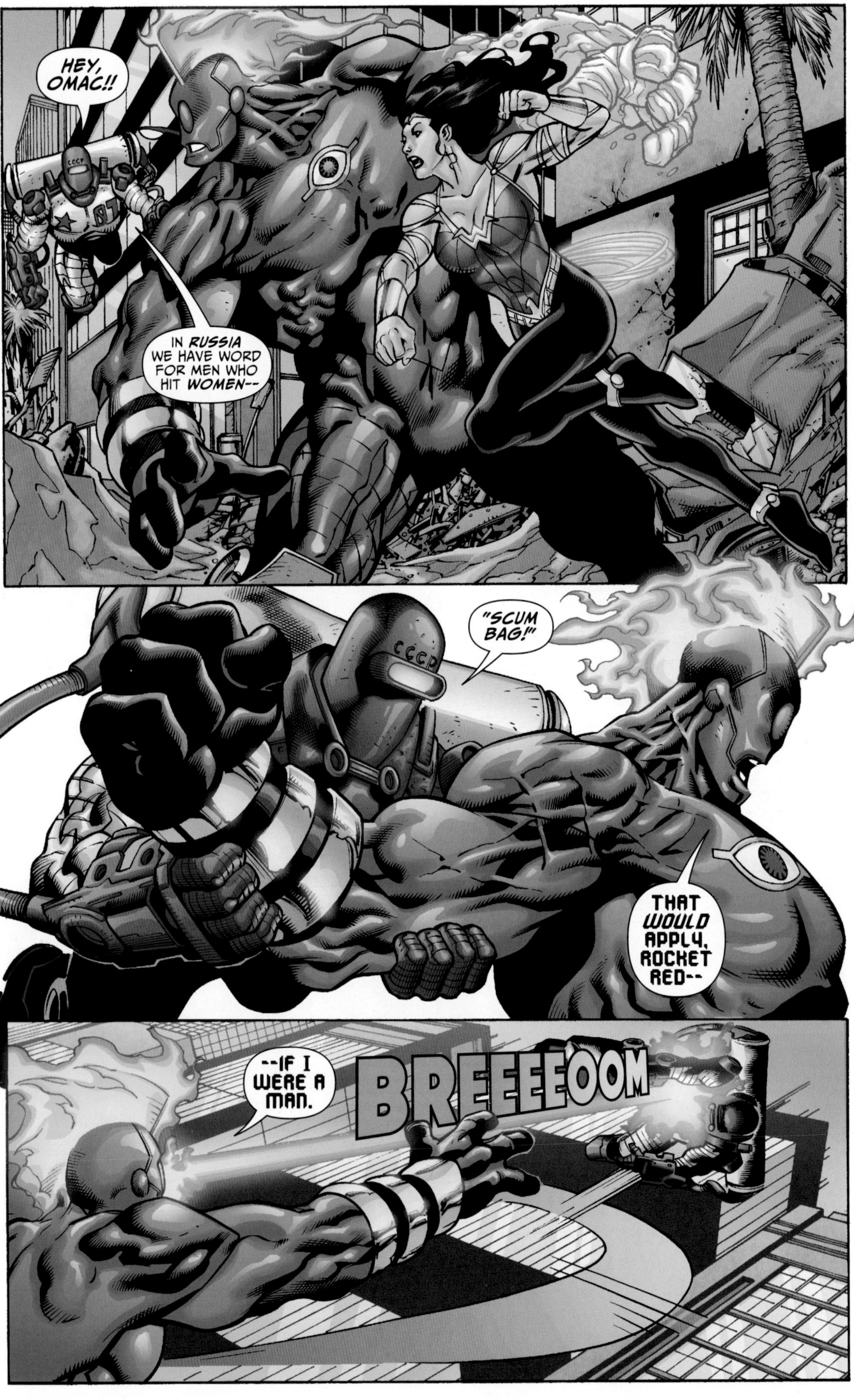
HEY, OMAC!!
IN RUSSIA WE HAVE WORD FOR MEN WHO HIT WOMEN--
"SCUM BAG!"
THAT WOULD APPLY, ROCKET RED--
--IF I WERE A MAN.
BREEEEOOM

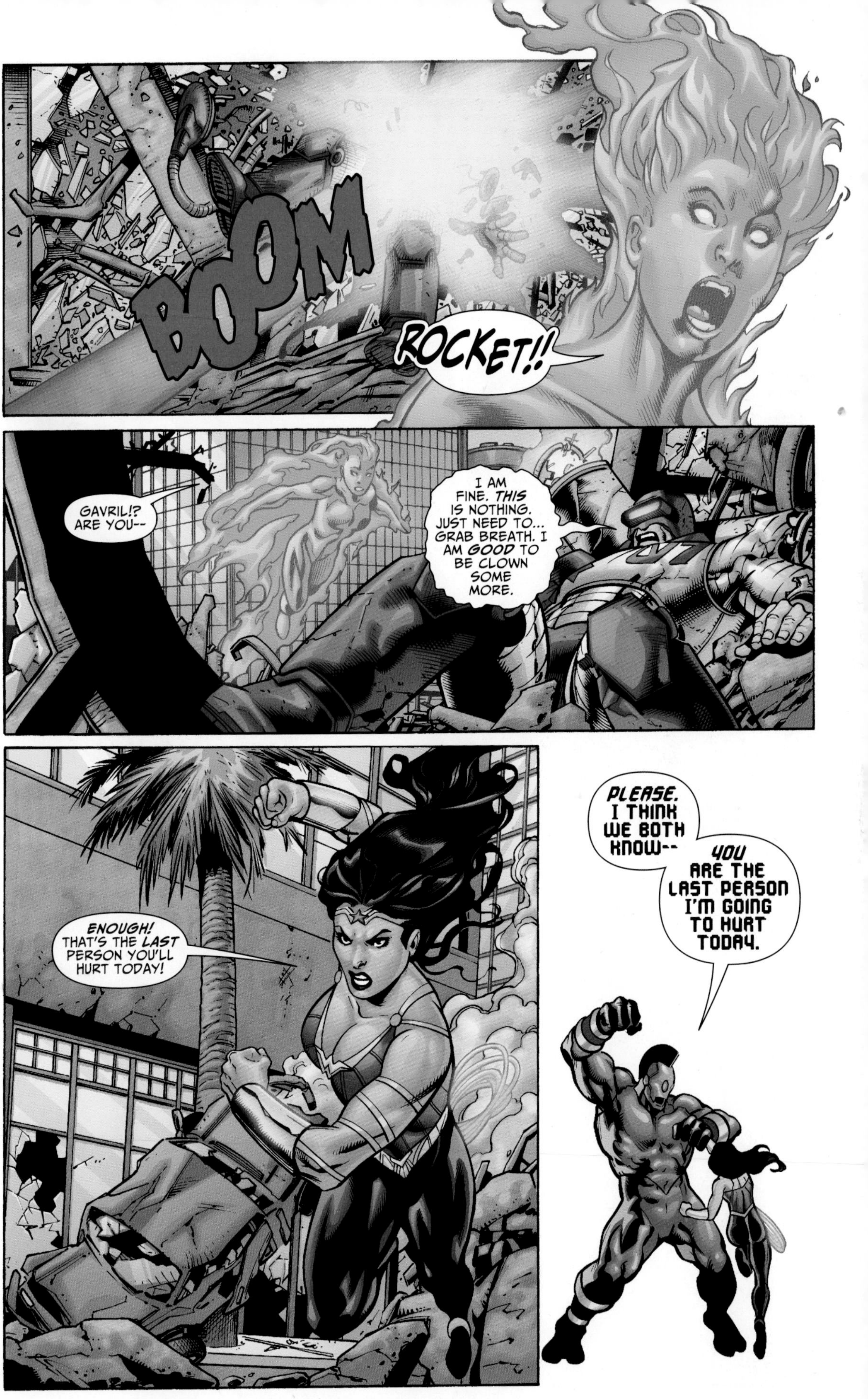
BOOM
ROCKET!!
GAVRIL!? ARE YOU--
I AM FINE. THIS IS NOTHING. JUST NEED TO... GRAB BREATH. I AM GOOD TO BE CLOWN SOME MORE.
ENOUGH! THAT'S THE LAST PERSON YOU'LL HURT TODAY!
PLEASE. I THINK WE BOTH KNOW--
YOU ARE THE LAST PERSON I'M GOING TO HURT TODAY.

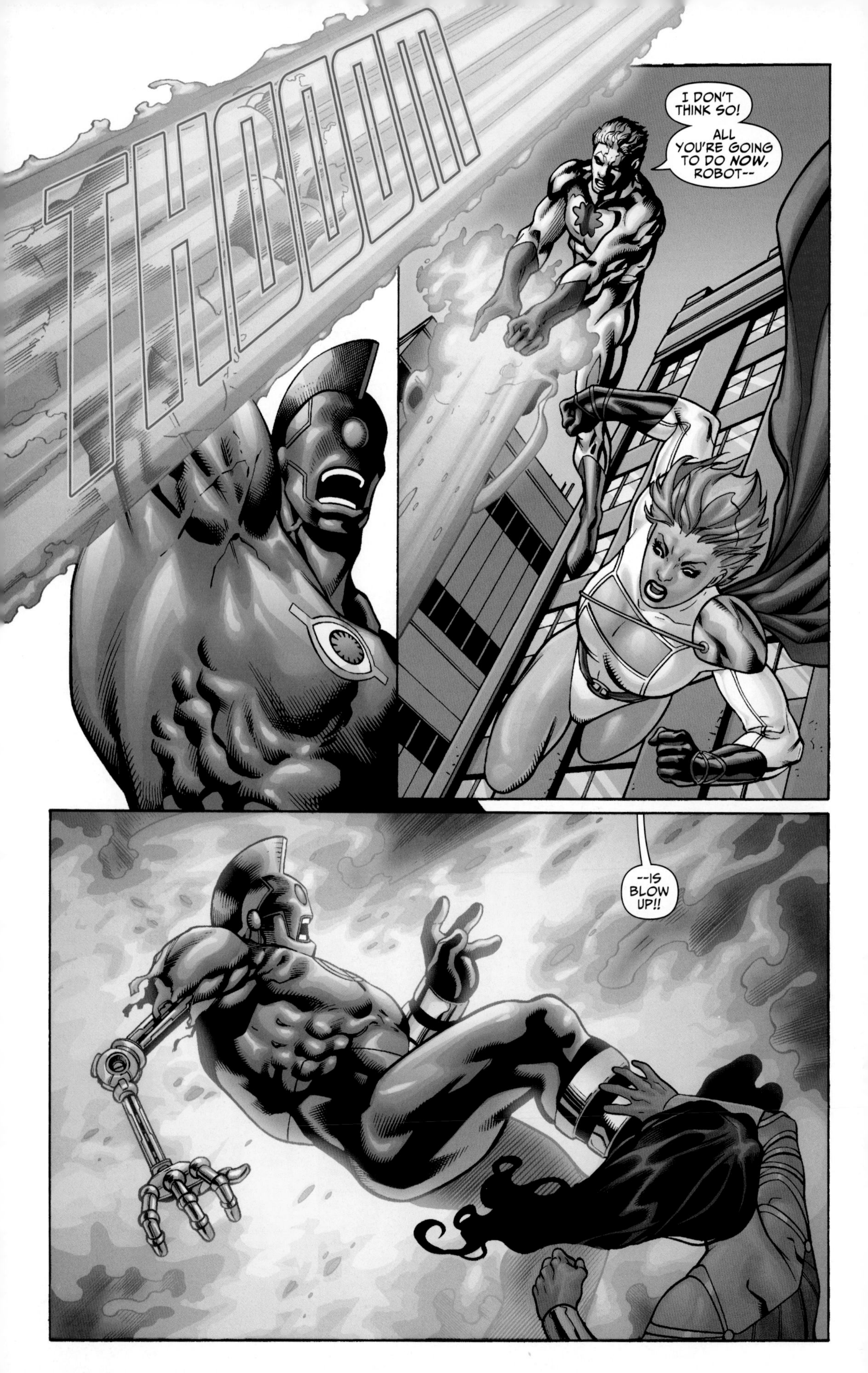
THOOOM
I DON'T THINK SO!
ALL YOU'RE GOING TO DO NOW, ROBOT--
--IS BLOW UP!!

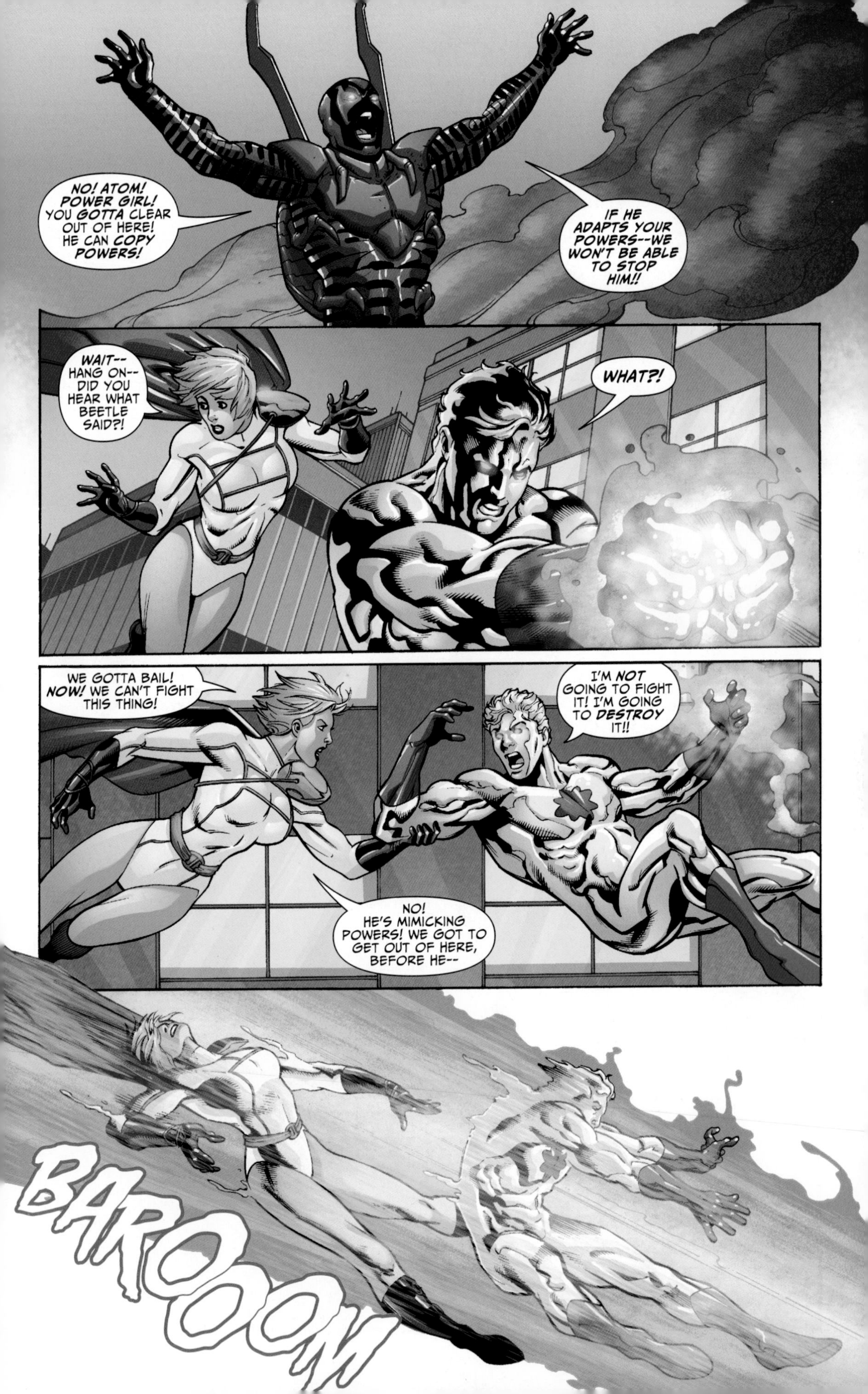
NO! ATOM! POWER GIRL! YOU GOTTA CLEAR OUT OF HERE! HE CAN COPY POWERS!
IF HE ADAPTS YOUR POWERS--WE WON'T BE ABLE TO STOP HIM!!
WAIT-- HANG ON-- DID YOU HEAR WHAT BEETLE SAID?!
WHAT?!
WE GOTTA BAIL! NOW! WE CAN'T FIGHT THIS THING!
I'M NOT GOING TO FIGHT IT! I'M GOING TO DESTROY IT!!
NO! HE'S MIMICKING POWERS! WE GOT TO GET OUT OF HERE, BEFORE HE--
BAROOOM

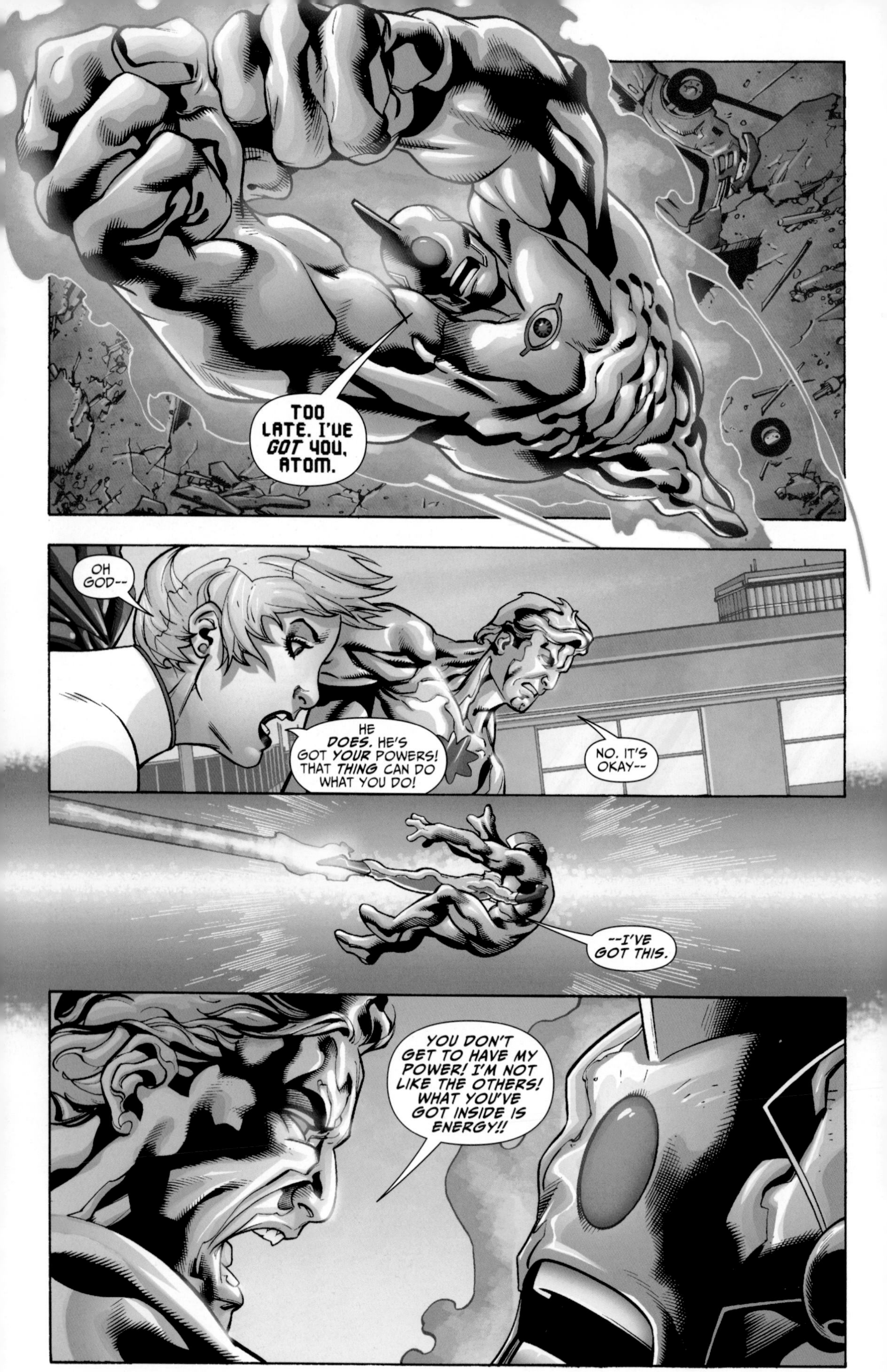
TOO LATE. I'VE GOT YOU, ATOM.
OH GOD--
HE DOES. HE'S GOT YOUR POWERS! THAT THING CAN DO WHAT YOU DO!
NO. IT'S OKAY--
--I'VE GOT THIS.
YOU DON'T GET TO HAVE MY POWER! I'M NOT LIKE THE OTHERS! WHAT YOU'VE GOT INSIDE IS ENERGY!!

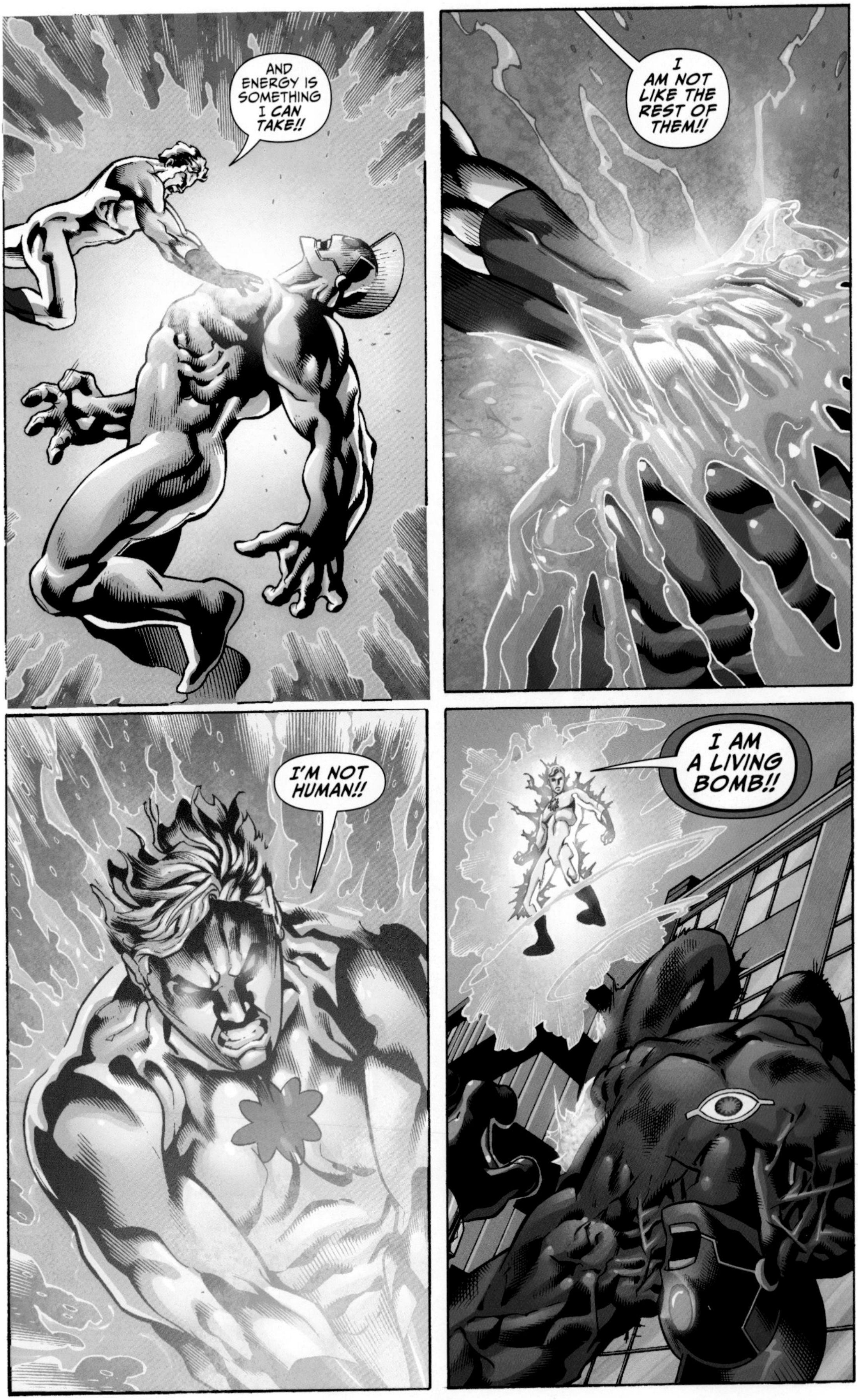
AND ENERGY IS SOMETHING I CAN TAKE!!
I AM NOT LIKE THE REST OF THEM!!
I'M NOT HUMAN!!
I AM A LIVING BOMB!!

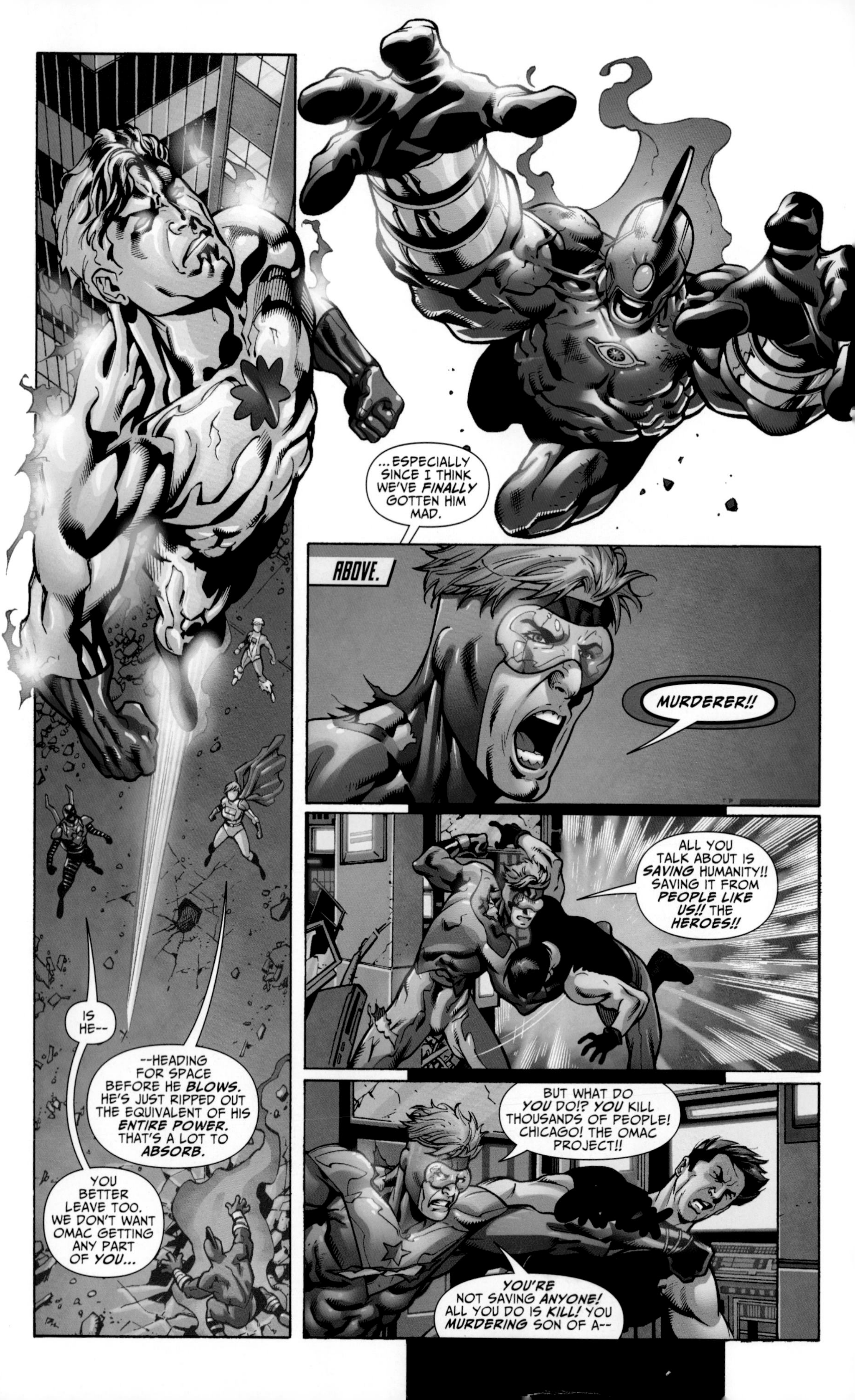
...ESPECIALLY SINCE I THINK WE'VE FINALLY GOTTEN HIM MAD.
ABOVE.
MURDERER!!
ALL YOU TALK ABOUT IS SAVING HUMANITY!! SAVING IT FROM PEOPLE LIKE US!! THE HEROES!!
BUT WHAT DO YOU DO!? YOU KILL THOUSANDS OF PEOPLE! CHICAGO! THE OMAC PROJECT!!
YOU'RE NOT SAVING ANYONE! ALL YOU DO IS KILL! YOU MURDERING SON OF A--
IS HE--
--HEADING FOR SPACE BEFORE HE BLOWS. HE'S JUST RIPPED OUT THE EQUIVALENT OF HIS ENTIRE POWER. THAT'S A LOT TO ABSORB.
YOU BETTER LEAVE TOO. WE DON'T WANT OMAC GETTING ANY PART OF YOU...

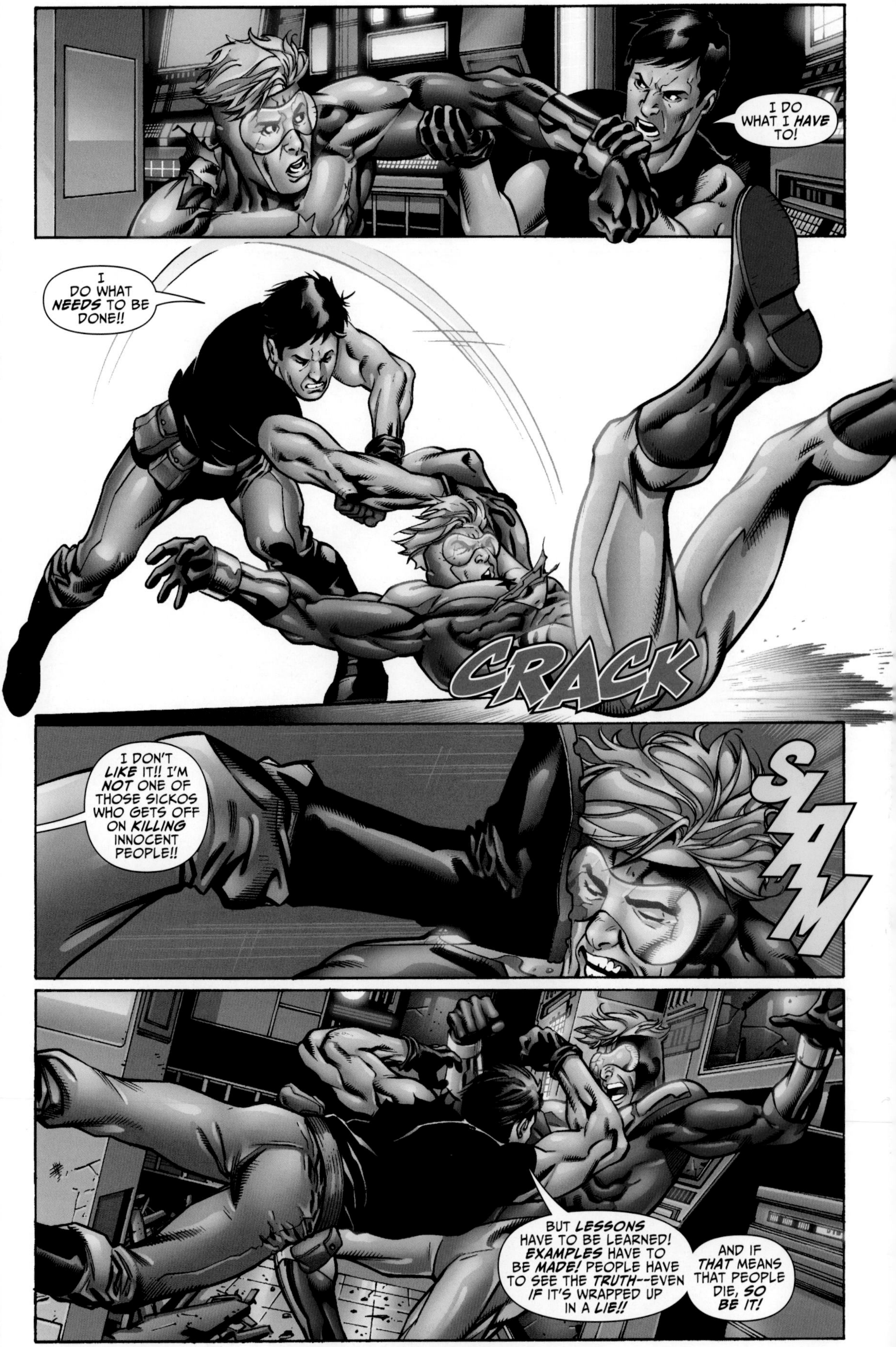
I DO WHAT I HAVE TO!
I DO WHAT NEEDS TO BE DONE!!
CRACK
I DON'T LIKE IT!! I'M NOT ONE OF THOSE SICKOS WHO GETS OFF ON KILLING INNOCENT PEOPLE!!
SLAM
BUT LESSONS HAVE TO BE LEARNED! EXAMPLES HAVE TO BE MADE! PEOPLE HAVE TO SEE THE TRUTH--EVEN IF IT'S WRAPPED UP IN A LIE!!
AND IF THAT MEANS THAT PEOPLE DIE, SO BE IT!

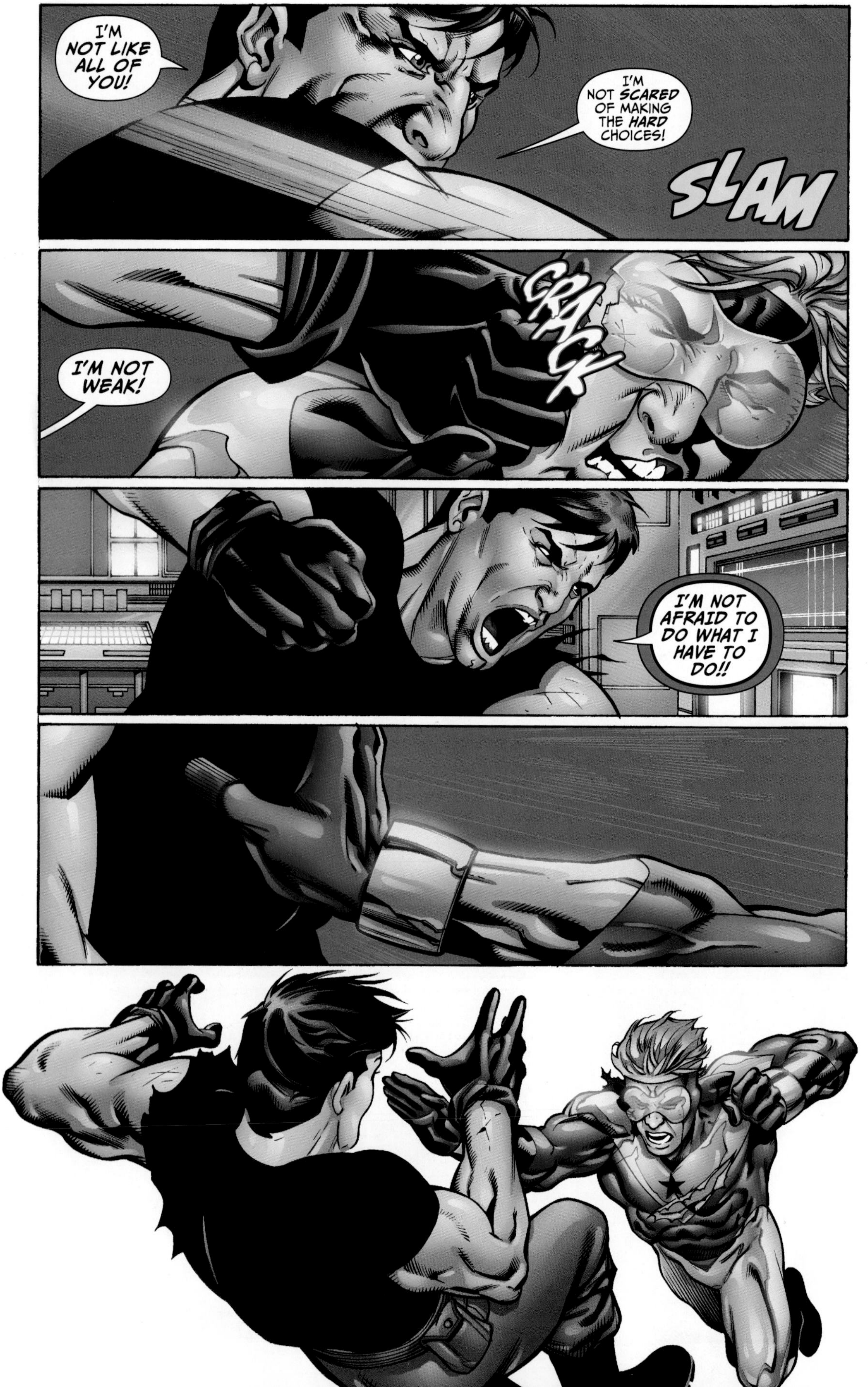
I'M NOT LIKE ALL OF YOU!
I'M NOT SCARED OF MAKING THE HARD CHOICES!
SLAM
CRACK
I'M NOT WEAK!
I'M NOT AFRAID TO DO WHAT I HAVE TO DO!!

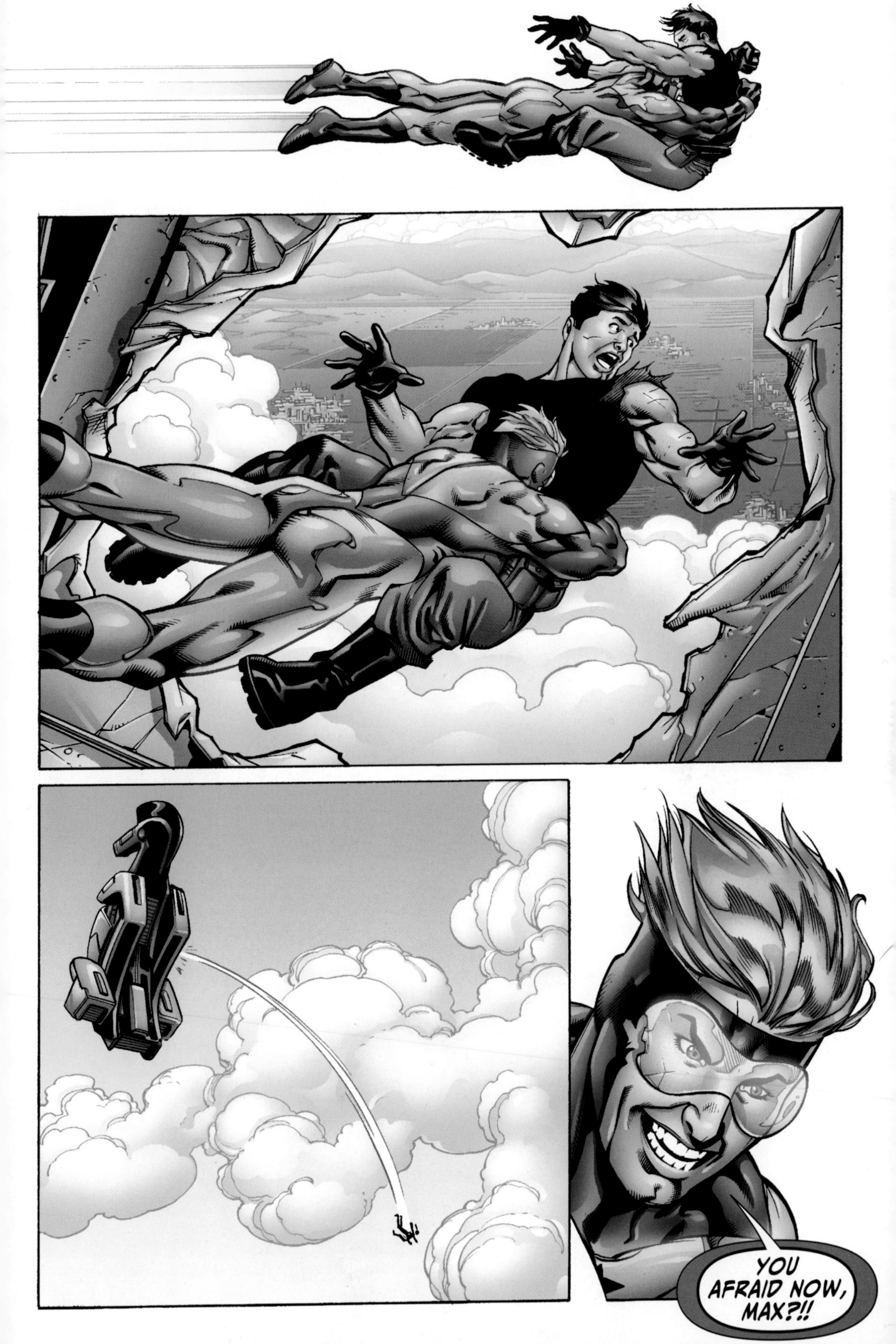
YOU AFRAID NOW, MAX?!!

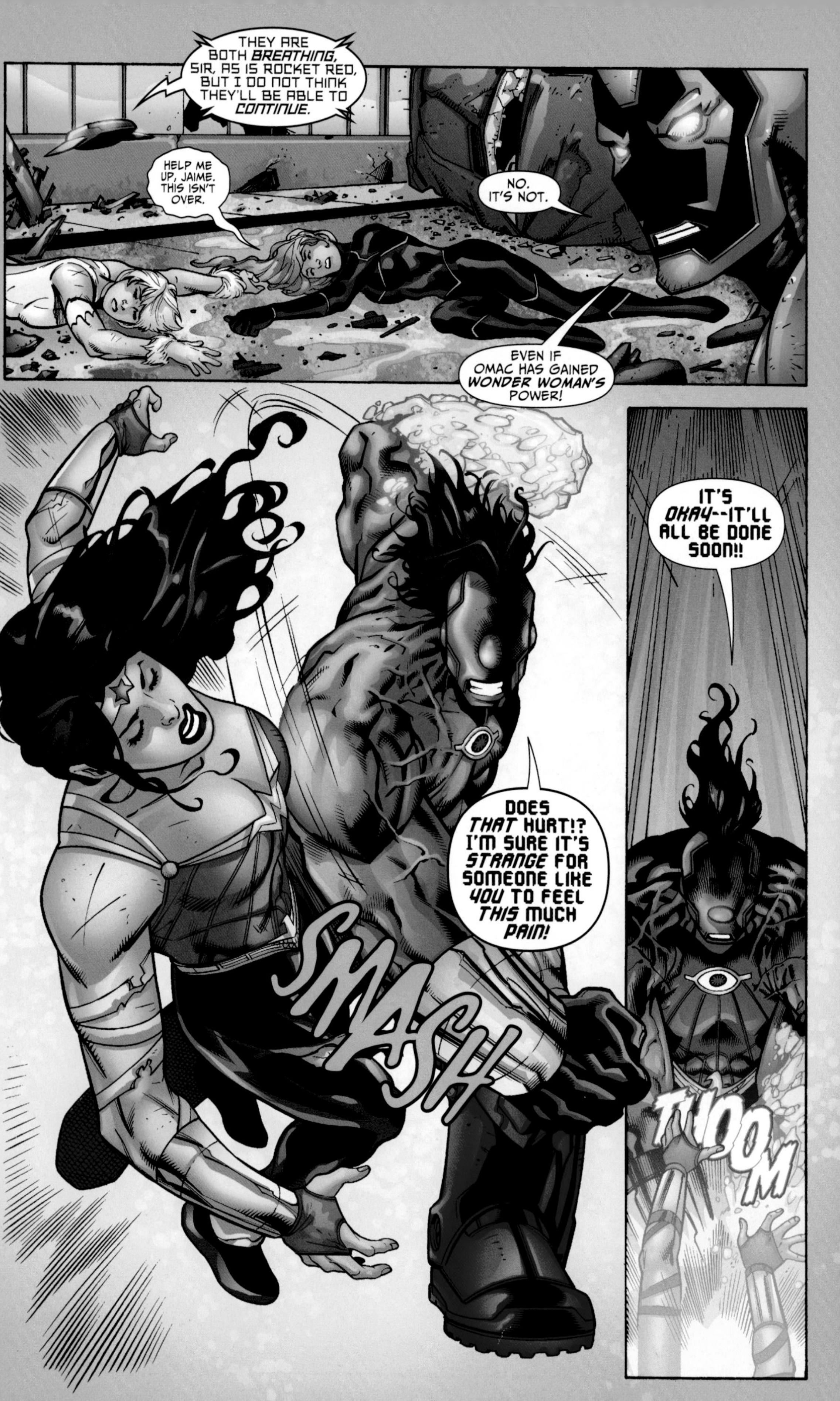
THEY ARE BOTH BREATHING, SIR, AS IS ROCKET RED, BUT I DO NOT THINK THEY'LL BE ABLE TO CONTINUE.
HELP ME UP, JAIME. THIS ISN'T OVER.
NO. IT'S NOT.
EVEN IF OMAC HAS GAINED WONDER WOMAN'S POWER!
DOES THAT HURT!? I'M SURE IT'S STRANGE FOR SOMEONE LIKE YOU TO FEEL THIS MUCH PAIN!
SMASH
IT'S OKAY--IT'LL ALL BE DONE SOON!!
THOOM

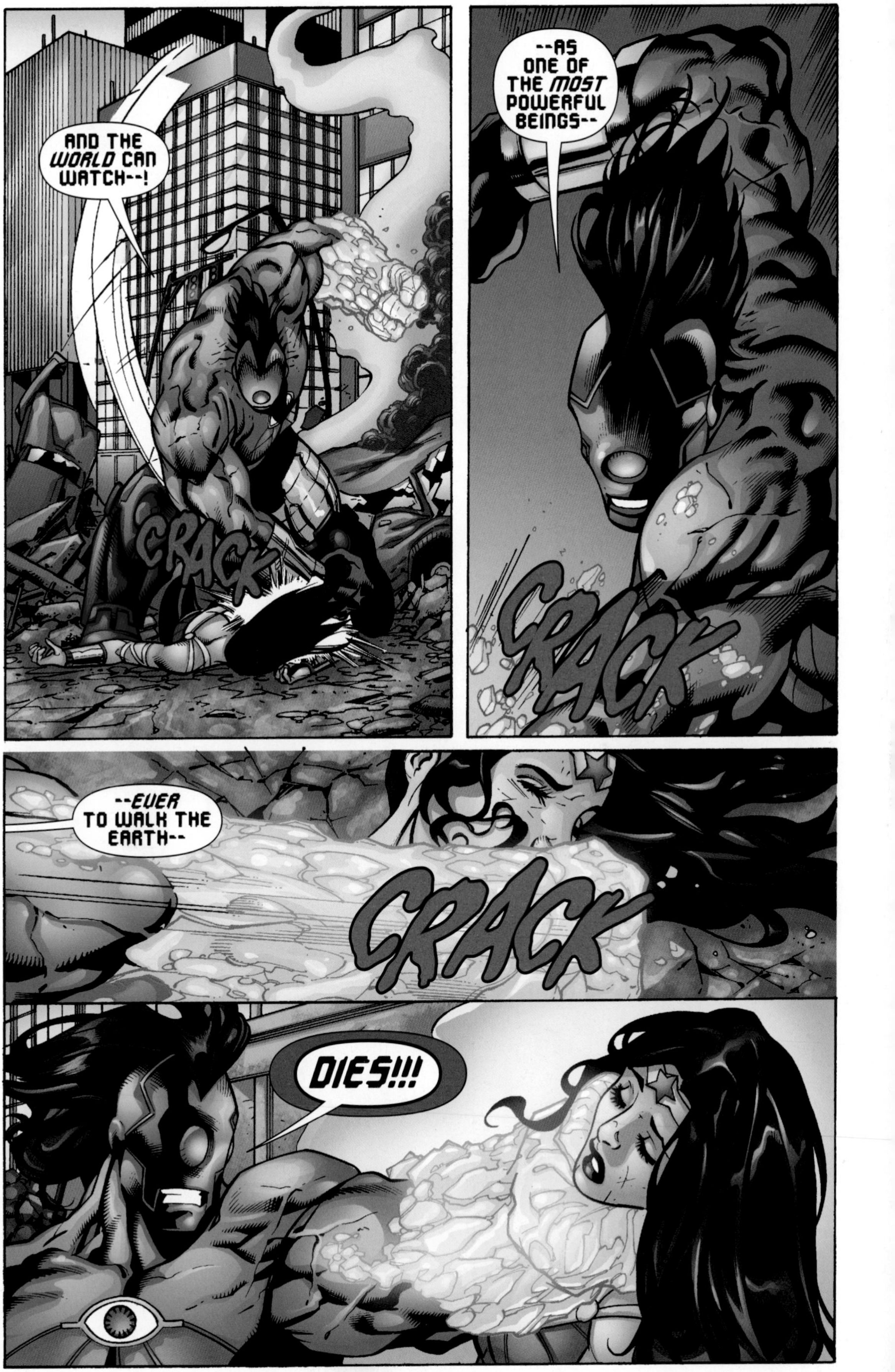
AND THE WORLD CAN WATCH--!
CRACK
--AS ONE OF THE MOST POWERFUL BEINGS--
CRACK
--EVER TO WALK THE EARTH--
CRACK
DIES!!!

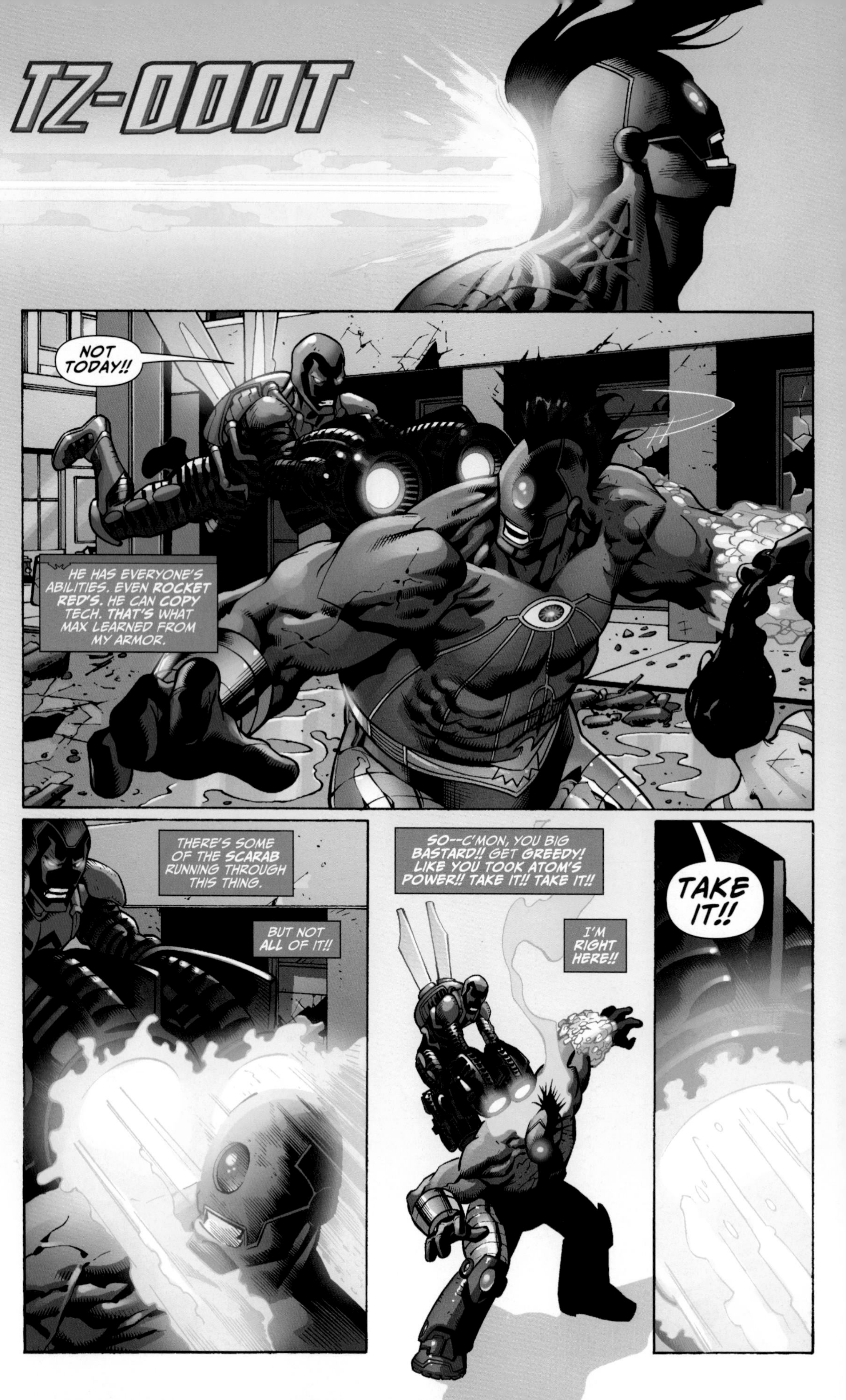
TZ-DOOT
NOT TODAY!!
HE HAS EVERYONE'S ABILITIES. EVEN ROCKET RED'S. HE CAN COPY TECH. THAT'S WHAT MAX LEARNED FROM MY ARMOR.
THERE'S SOME OF THE SCARAB RUNNING THROUGH THIS THING.
BUT NOT ALL OF IT!!
SO--C'MON, YOU BIG BASTARD!! GET GREEDY! LIKE YOU TOOK ATOM'S POWER!! TAKE IT!! TAKE IT!!
I'M RIGHT HERE!!
TAKE IT!!

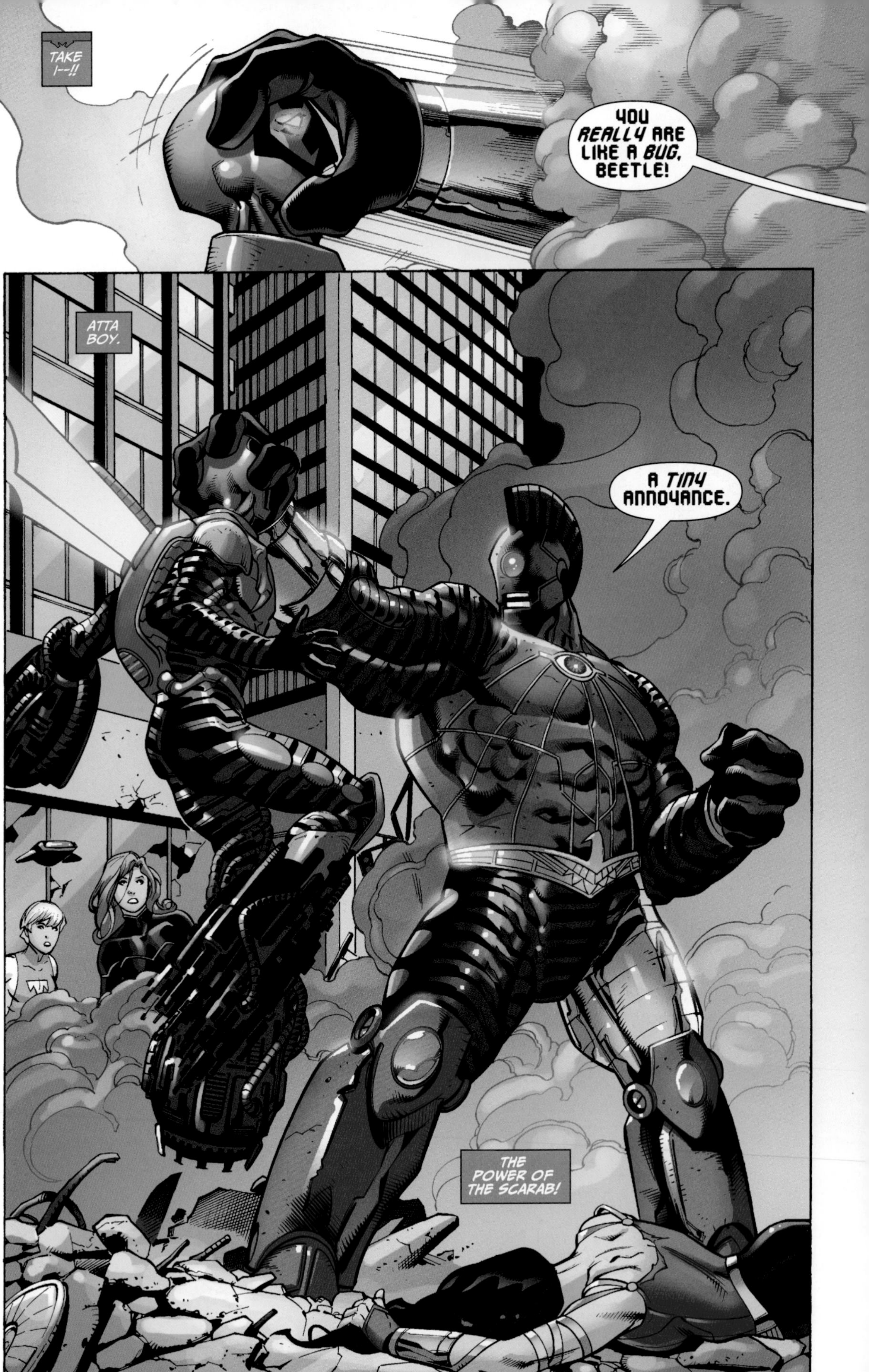
TAKE I--!!
YOU REALLY ARE LIKE A BUG, BEETLE!
ATTA BOY.
A TINY ANNOYANCE.
THE POWER OF THE SCARAB!

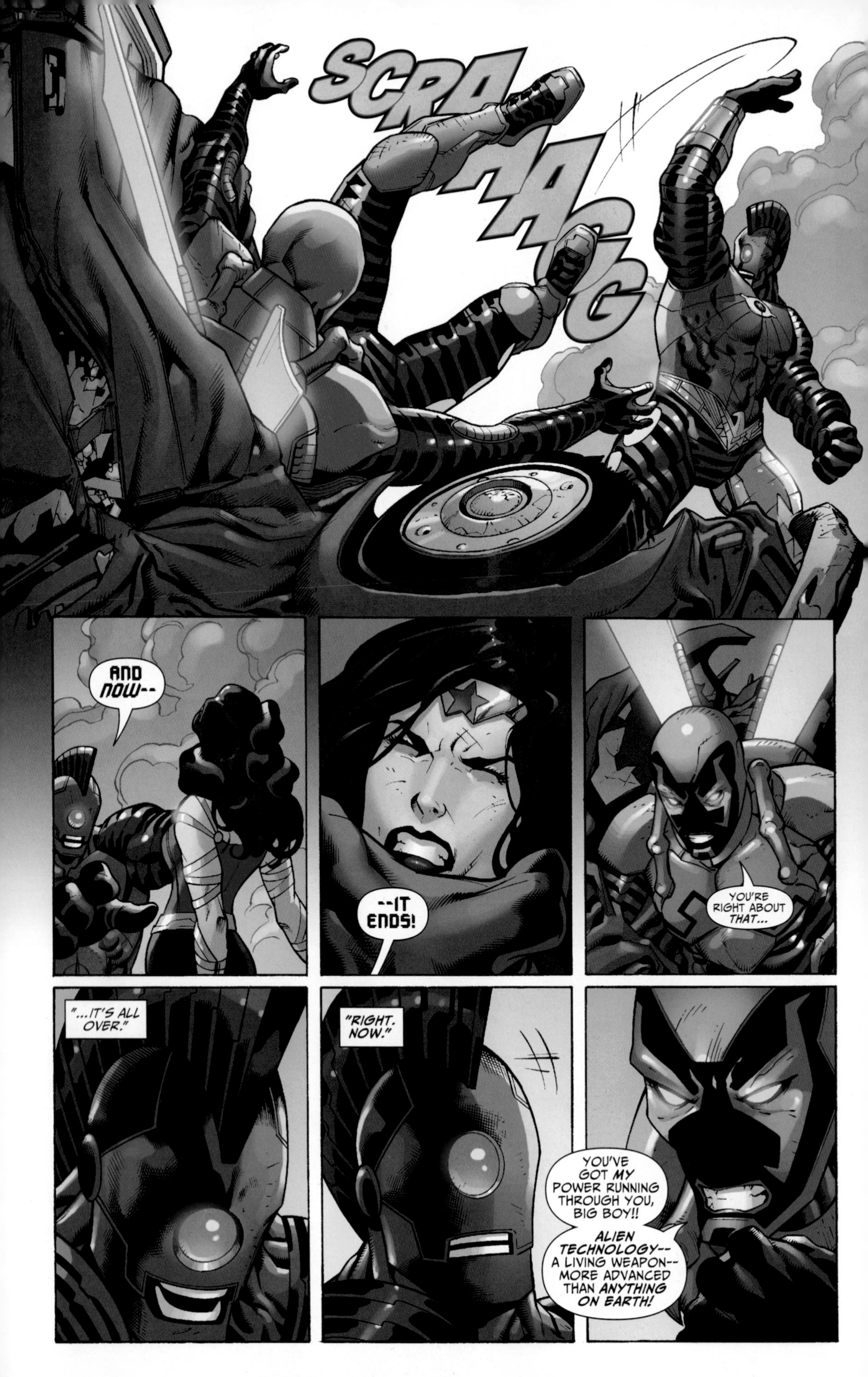
SCRA
AAG
AND NOW--
--IT ENDS!
YOU'RE RIGHT ABOUT THAT...
"...IT'S ALL OVER."
"RIGHT. NOW."
YOU'VE GOT MY POWER RUNNING THROUGH YOU, BIG BOY!!
ALIEN TECHNOLOGY-- A LIVING WEAPON-- MORE ADVANCED THAN ANYTHING ON EARTH!

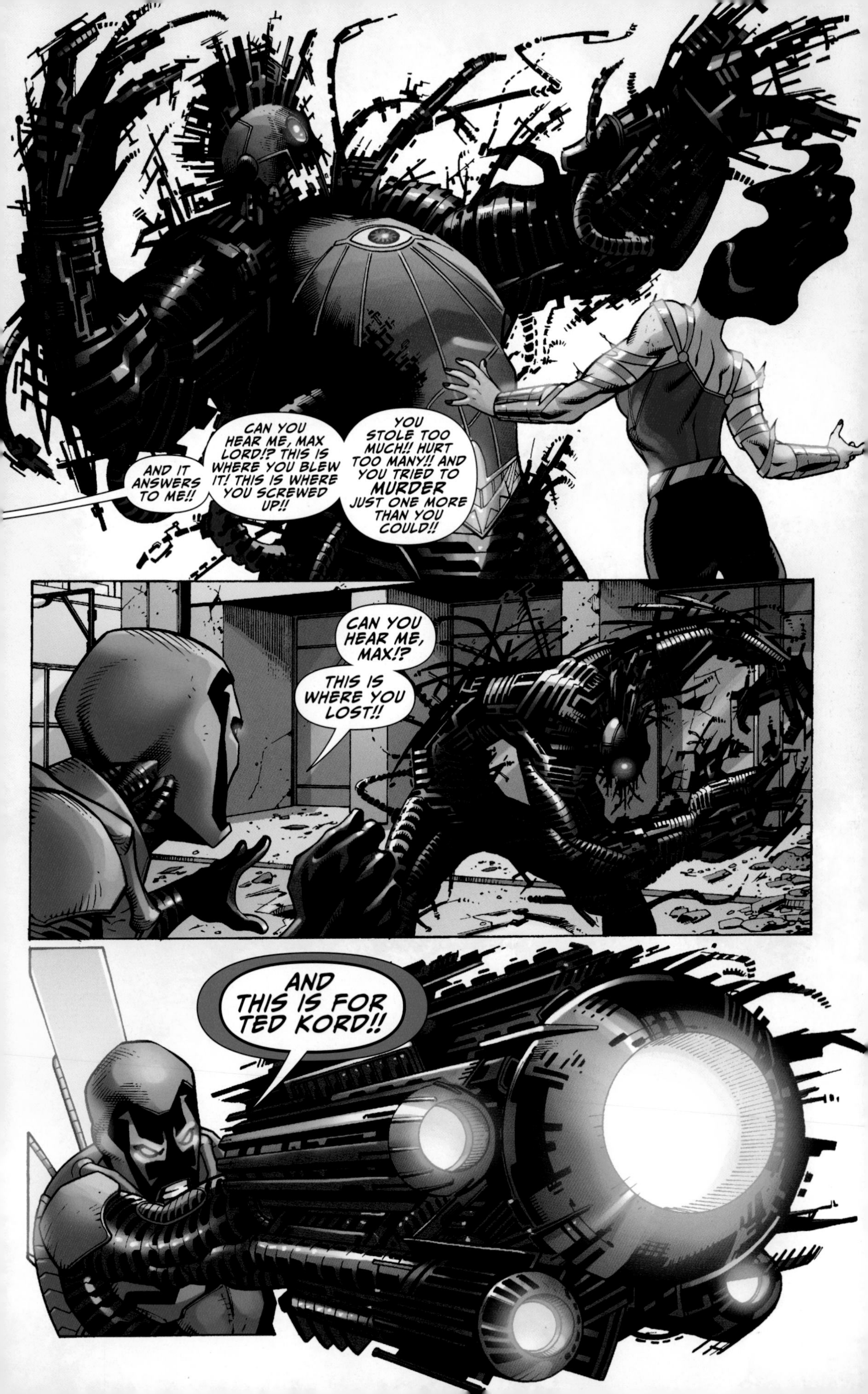
AND IT ANSWERS TO ME!!
CAN YOU HEAR ME, MAX LORD!? THIS IS WHERE YOU BLEW IT! THIS IS WHERE YOU SCREWED UP!!
YOU STOLE TOO MUCH!! HURT TOO MANY!! AND YOU TRIED TO MURDER JUST ONE MORE THAN YOU COULD!!
CAN YOU HEAR ME, MAX!?
THIS IS WHERE YOU LOST!!
AND THIS IS FOR TED KORD!!

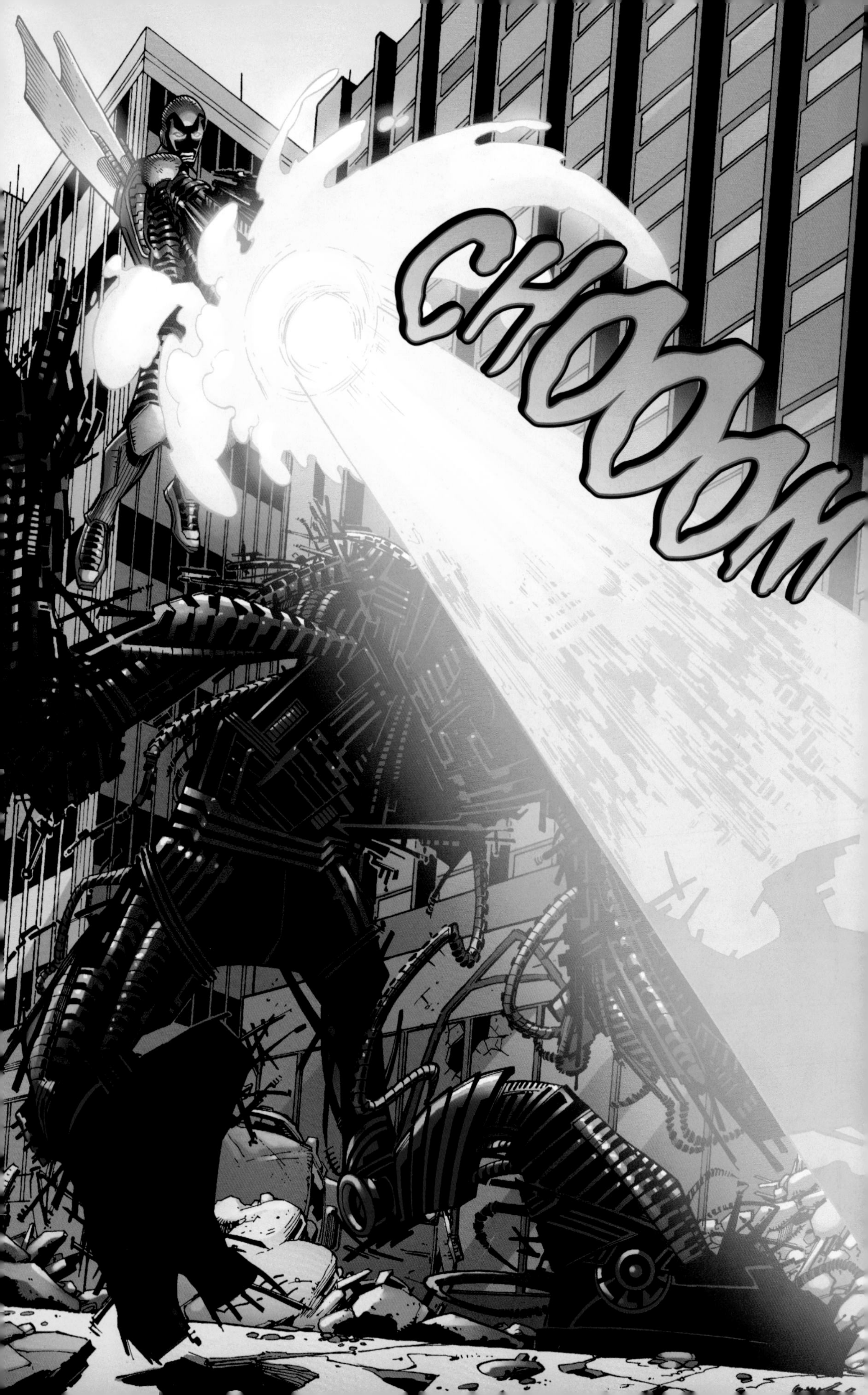
CHOOOM

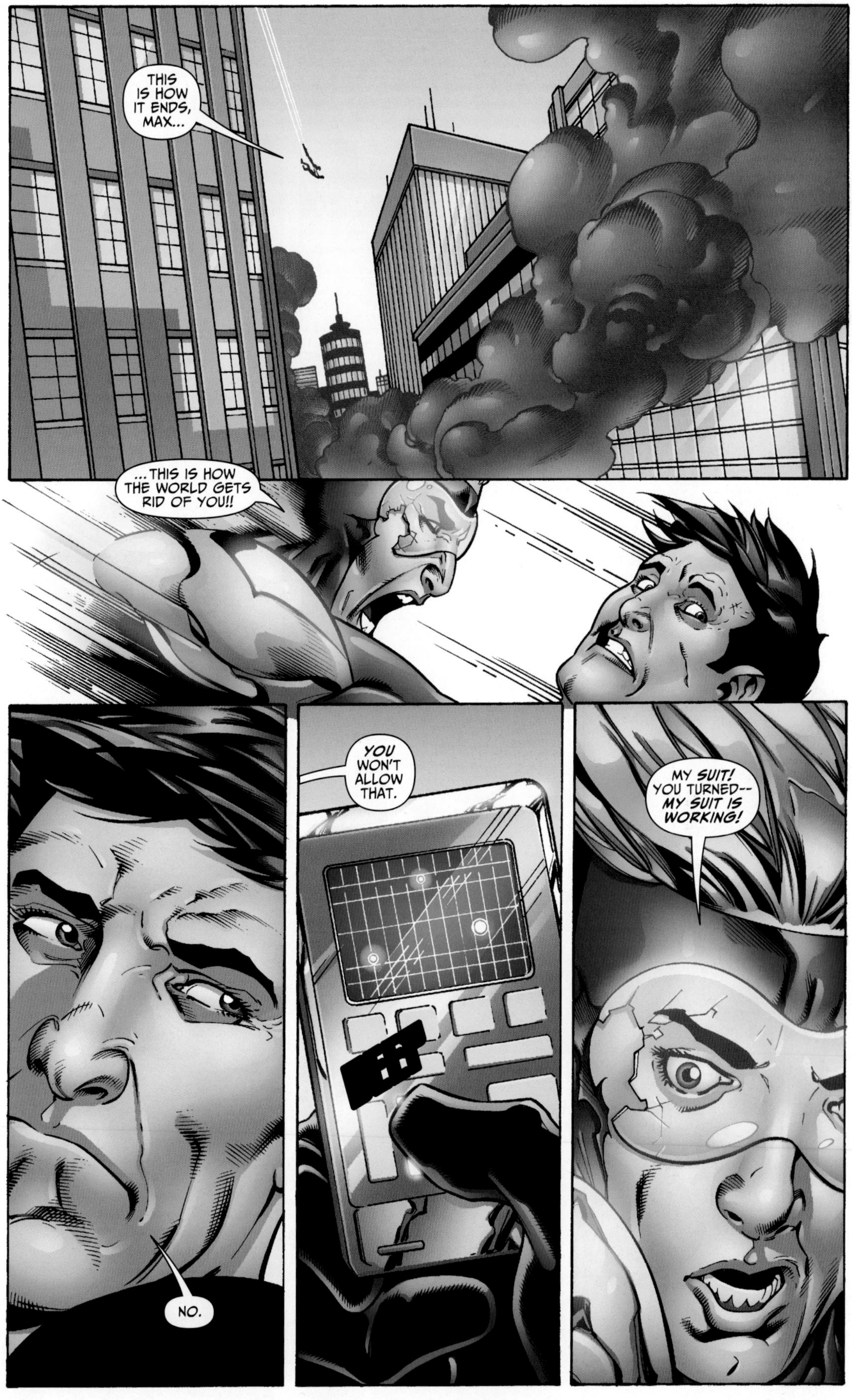
THIS IS HOW IT ENDS, MAX...
...THIS IS HOW THE WORLD GETS RID OF YOU!!
NO.
YOU WON'T ALLOW THAT.
MY SUIT! YOU TURNED-- MY SUIT IS WORKING!

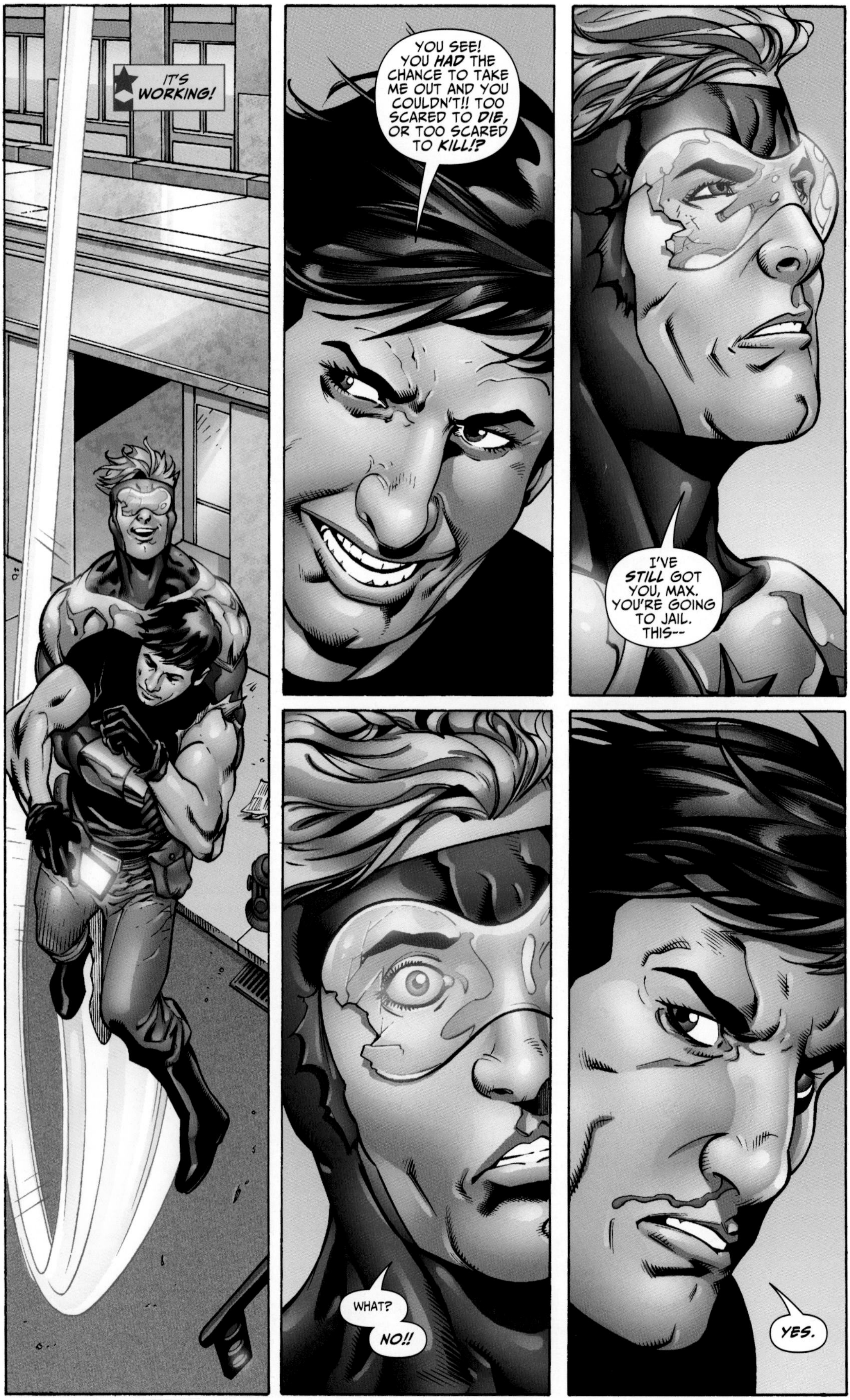
IT'S WORKING!
YOU SEE! YOU HAD THE CHANCE TO TAKE ME OUT AND YOU COULDN'T!! TOO SCARED TO DIE, OR TOO SCARED TO KILL!?
I'VE STILL GOT YOU, MAX. YOU'RE GOING TO JAIL. THIS--
WHAT?
NO!!
YES.

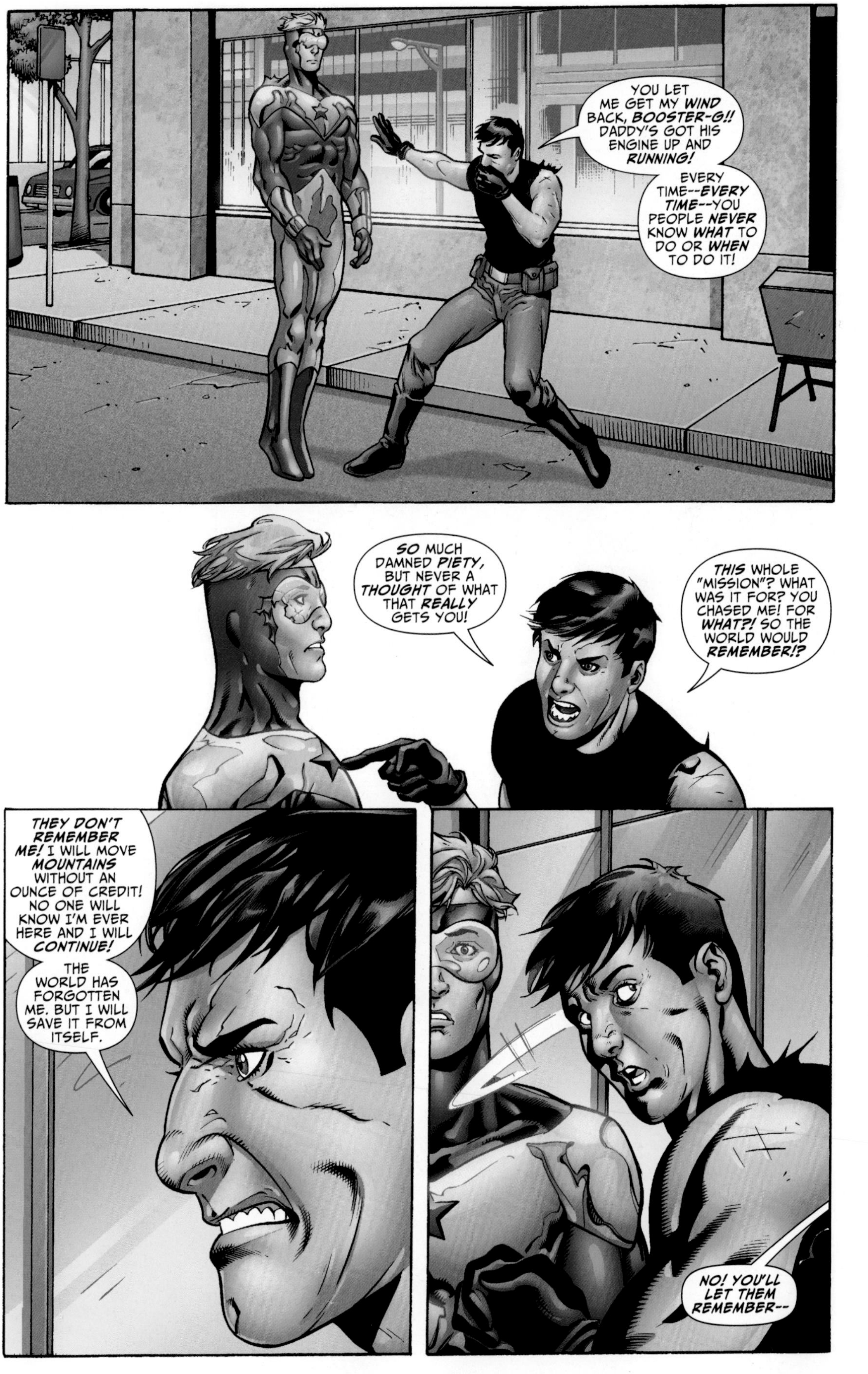
YOU LET ME GET MY WIND BACK, BOOSTER-G!! DADDY'S GOT HIS ENGINE UP AND RUNNING!
EVERY TIME--EVERY TIME--YOU PEOPLE NEVER KNOW WHAT TO DO OR WHEN TO DO IT!
SO MUCH DAMNED PIETY, BUT NEVER A THOUGHT OF WHAT THAT REALLY GETS YOU!
THIS WHOLE "MISSION"? WHAT WAS IT FOR? YOU CHASED ME! FOR WHAT?! SO THE WORLD WOULD REMEMBER!?
THEY DON'T REMEMBER ME! I WILL MOVE MOUNTAINS WITHOUT AN OUNCE OF CREDIT! NO ONE WILL KNOW I'M EVER HERE AND I WILL CONTINUE!
THE WORLD HAS FORGOTTEN ME. BUT I WILL SAVE IT FROM ITSELF.
NO! YOU'LL LET THEM REMEMBER--

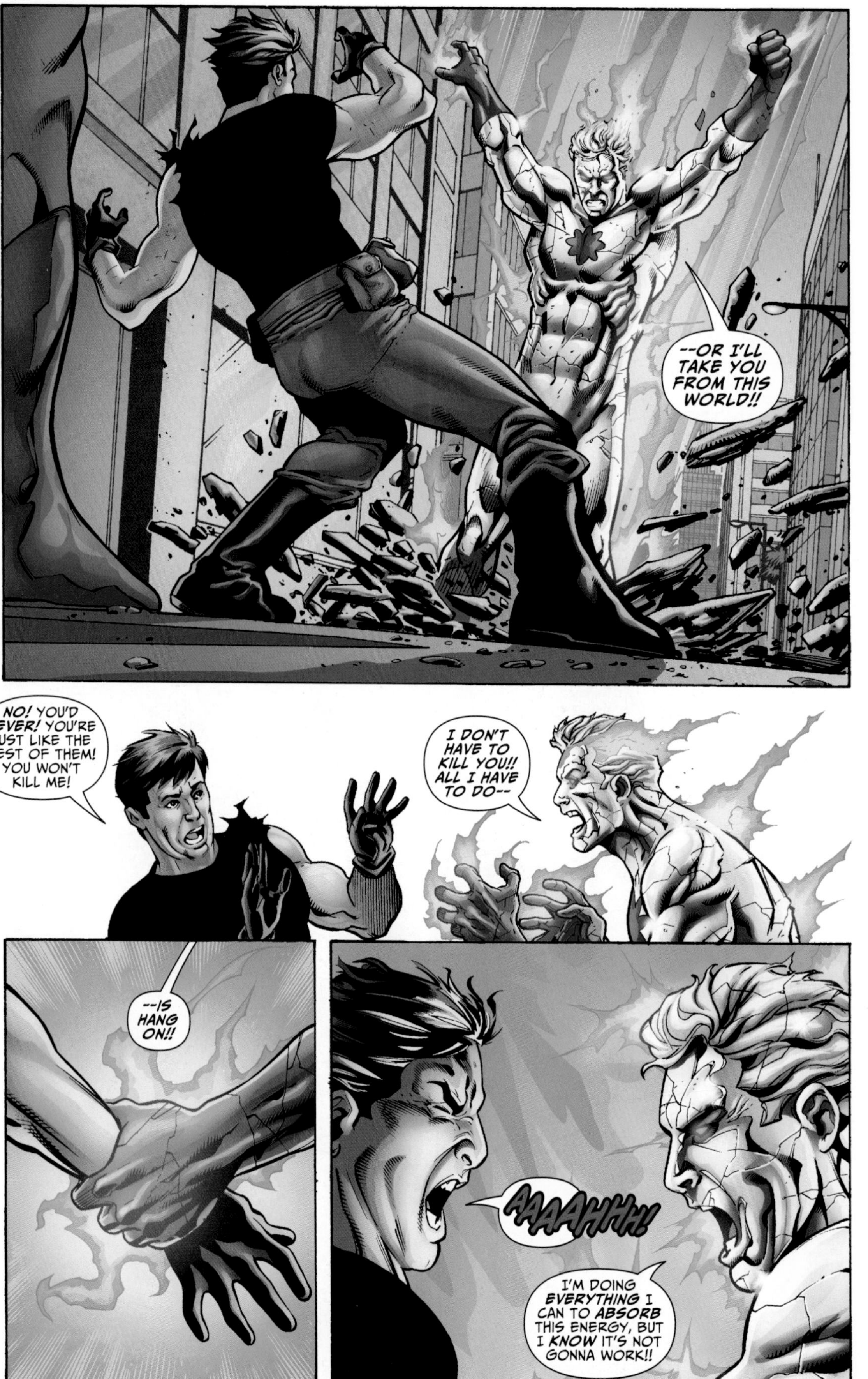
--OR I'LL TAKE YOU FROM THIS WORLD!!
NO! YOU'D NEVER! YOU'RE JUST LIKE THE REST OF THEM! YOU WON'T KILL ME!
I DON'T HAVE TO KILL YOU!! ALL I HAVE TO DO--
--IS HANG ON!!
AAAAHHH!
I'M DOING EVERYTHING I CAN TO ABSORB THIS ENERGY, BUT I KNOW IT'S NOT GONNA WORK!!

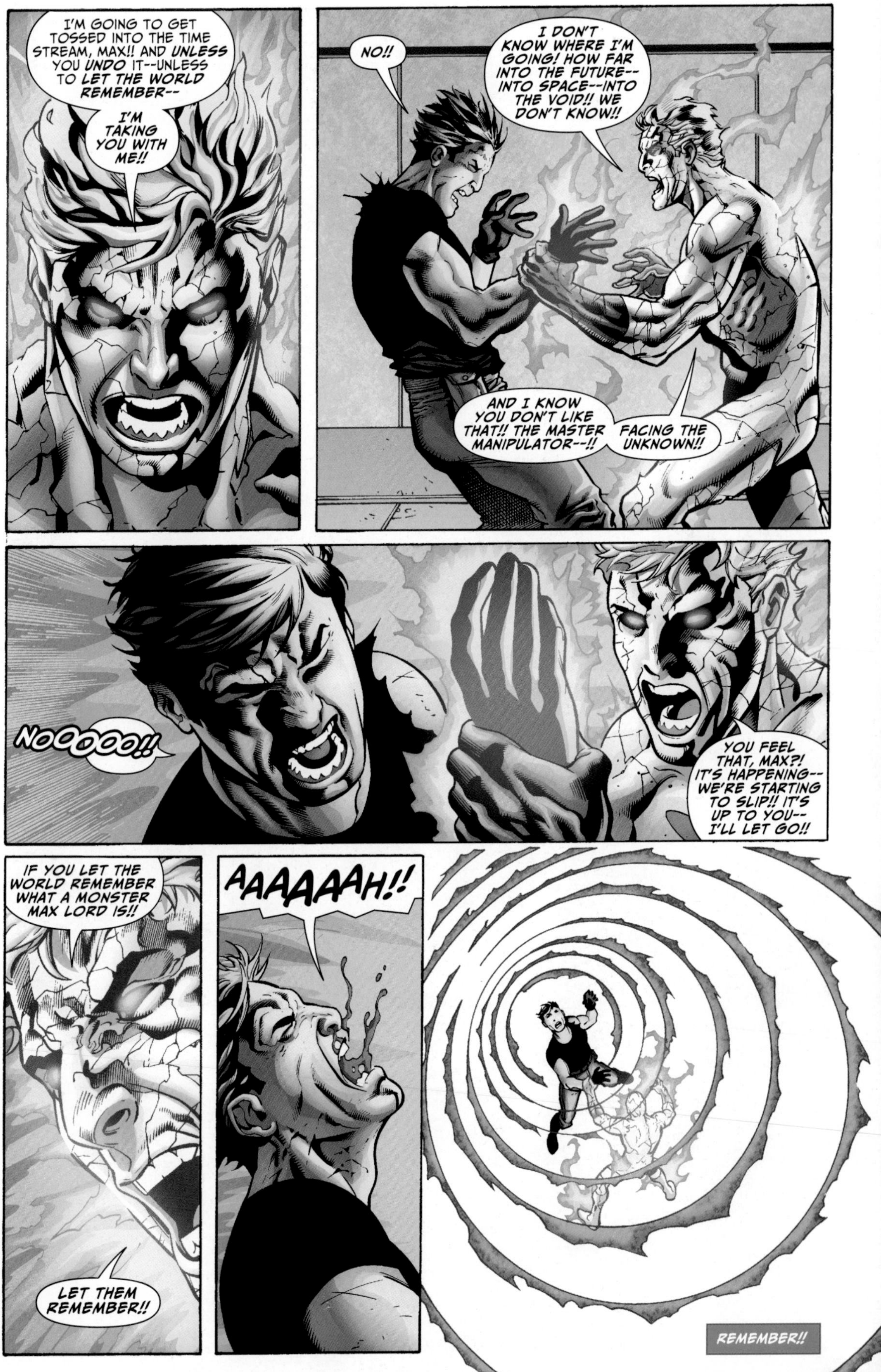
I'M GOING TO GET TOSSED INTO THE TIME STREAM, MAX!! AND UNLESS YOU UNDO IT--UNLESS TO LET THE WORLD REMEMBER--
I'M TAKING YOU WITH ME!!
NO!!
I DON'T KNOW WHERE I'M GOING! HOW FAR INTO THE FUTURE--INTO SPACE--INTO THE VOID!! WE DON'T KNOW!!
AND I KNOW YOU DON'T LIKE THAT!! THE MASTER MANIPULATOR--!!
FACING THE UNKNOWN!!
NOOOOO!!
YOU FEEL THAT, MAX?! IT'S HAPPENING--WE'RE STARTING TO SLIP!! IT'S UP TO YOU--I'LL LET GO!!
IF YOU LET THE WORLD REMEMBER WHAT A MONSTER MAX LORD IS!!
LET THEM REMEMBER!!
AAAAAAH!!
REMEMBER!!

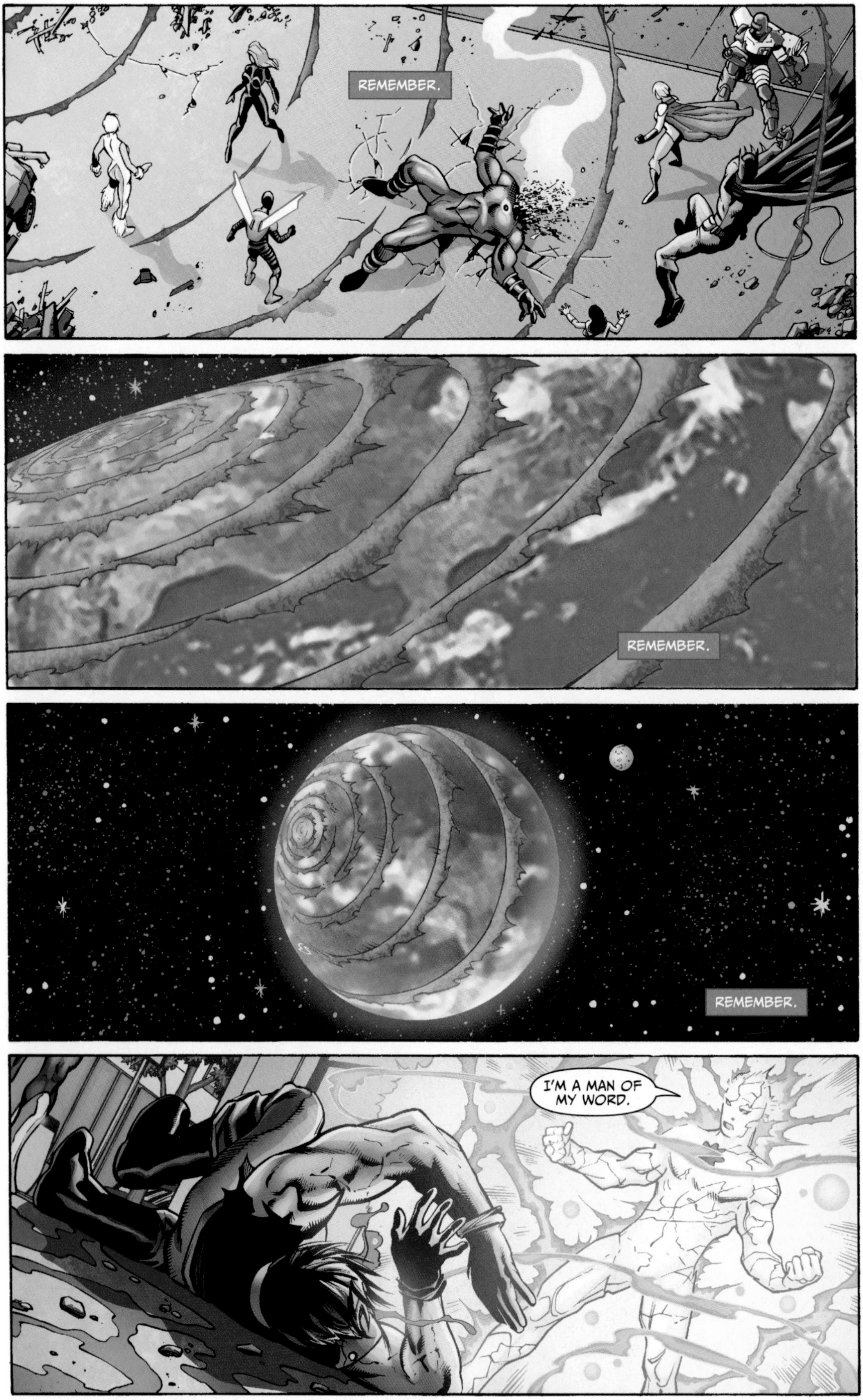
REMEMBER.
REMEMBER.
REMEMBER.
I'M A MAN OF MY WORD.

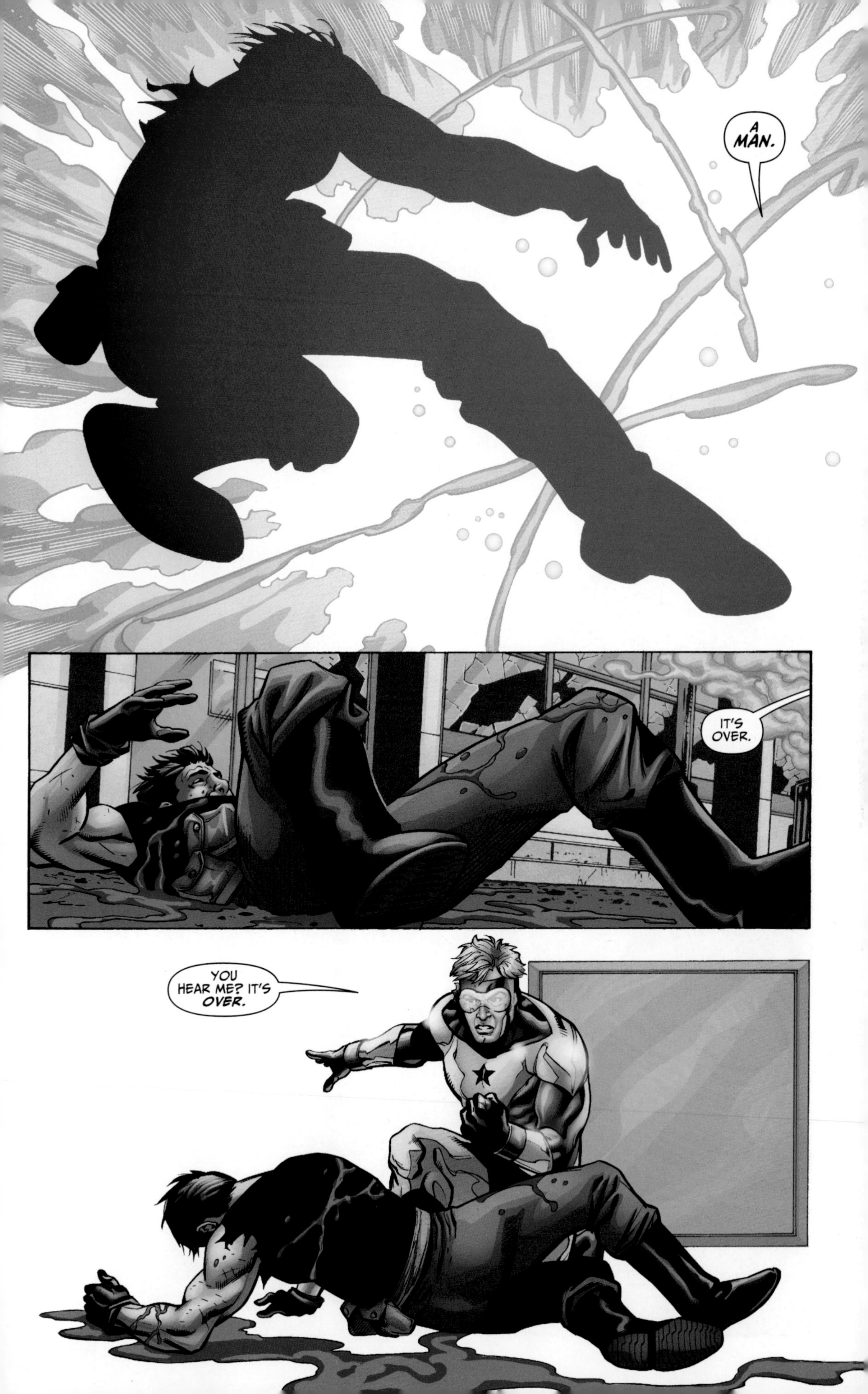
A MAN.
IT'S OVER.
YOU HEAR ME? IT'S OVER.

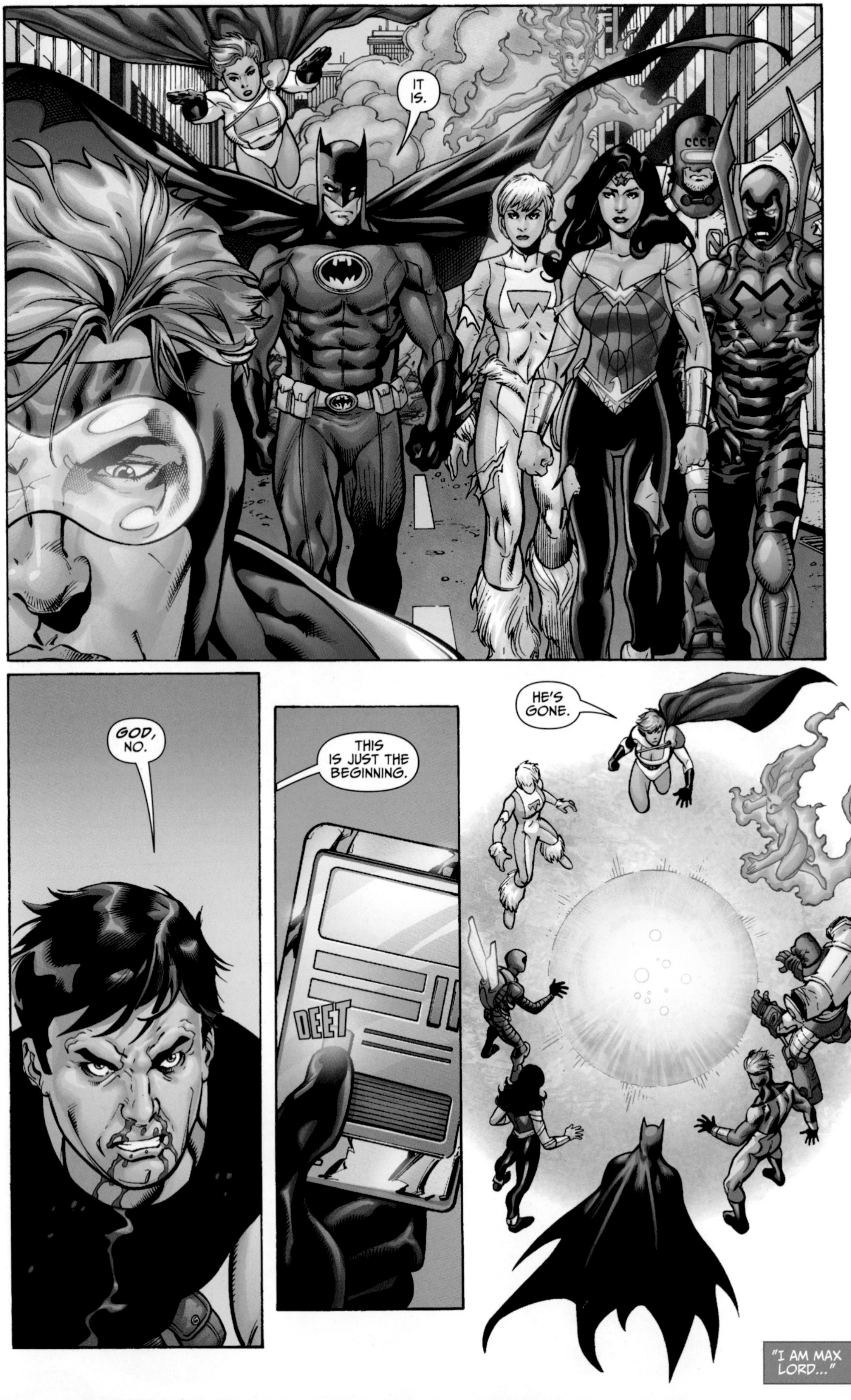
IT IS.
GOD, NO.
THIS IS JUST THE BEGINNING.
DEET
HE'S GONE.
"I AM MAX LORD..."

...MUCH HAS BEEN SAID ABOUT ME OF LATE, AND VERY LITTLE OF IT IS *TRUE*.

YOU'VE HEARD THAT I AM A *CRIMINAL MASTERMIND*. THAT I AM A *MURDERER*. THAT I'VE RETURNED FROM THE *DEAD*.

LET ME TELL ALL OF YOU--I AM A *CITIZEN*. I HAVE *NEVER* TAKEN A LIFE, AND I'M JUST A *REGULAR GUY*. *SUPERMAN* MIGHT BE ABLE TO COME BACK FROM THE GRAVE, BUT I'M *NOT* SUPERMAN.

THESE *FALSEHOODS* HAVE BEEN SPREAD BY THOSE WHO I DISAGREE WITH. THE COMMUNITY OF *SUPER HEROES*. WHY? I CAN ONLY GUESS BECAUSE I TAKE ISSUE WITH WHAT THEY DO.

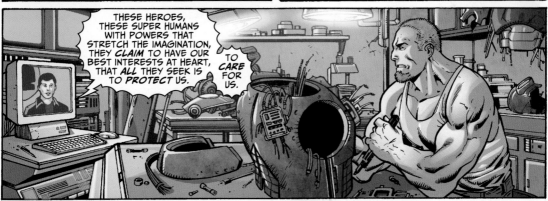

THESE HEROES, THESE SUPER HUMANS WITH POWERS THAT STRETCH THE IMAGINATION, THEY *CLAIM* TO HAVE OUR BEST INTERESTS AT HEART, THAT *ALL* THEY SEEK IS TO *PROTECT* US.

TO *CARE* FOR US.

AND MANY DO. LIKE THE *JUSTICE LEAGUE INTERNATIONAL*. THESE ARE PROTECTORS WE CAN *TRUST*.

THEY HAVE BEEN LINKED TO THE RECENT CATASTROPHE IN *CHICAGO*.

BUT THE TRUTH IS A SO-CALLED HERO, *MAGOG*, WHO WASN'T A *MADMAN* OR BENT ON REVENGE... HE WAS SIMPLY A MAN WITH *GREAT* POWER WHO PICKED THE EQUIVALENT OF A *BAR FIGHT* WITH CAPTAIN ATOM... AND *KILLED* A THOUSAND PEOPLE!

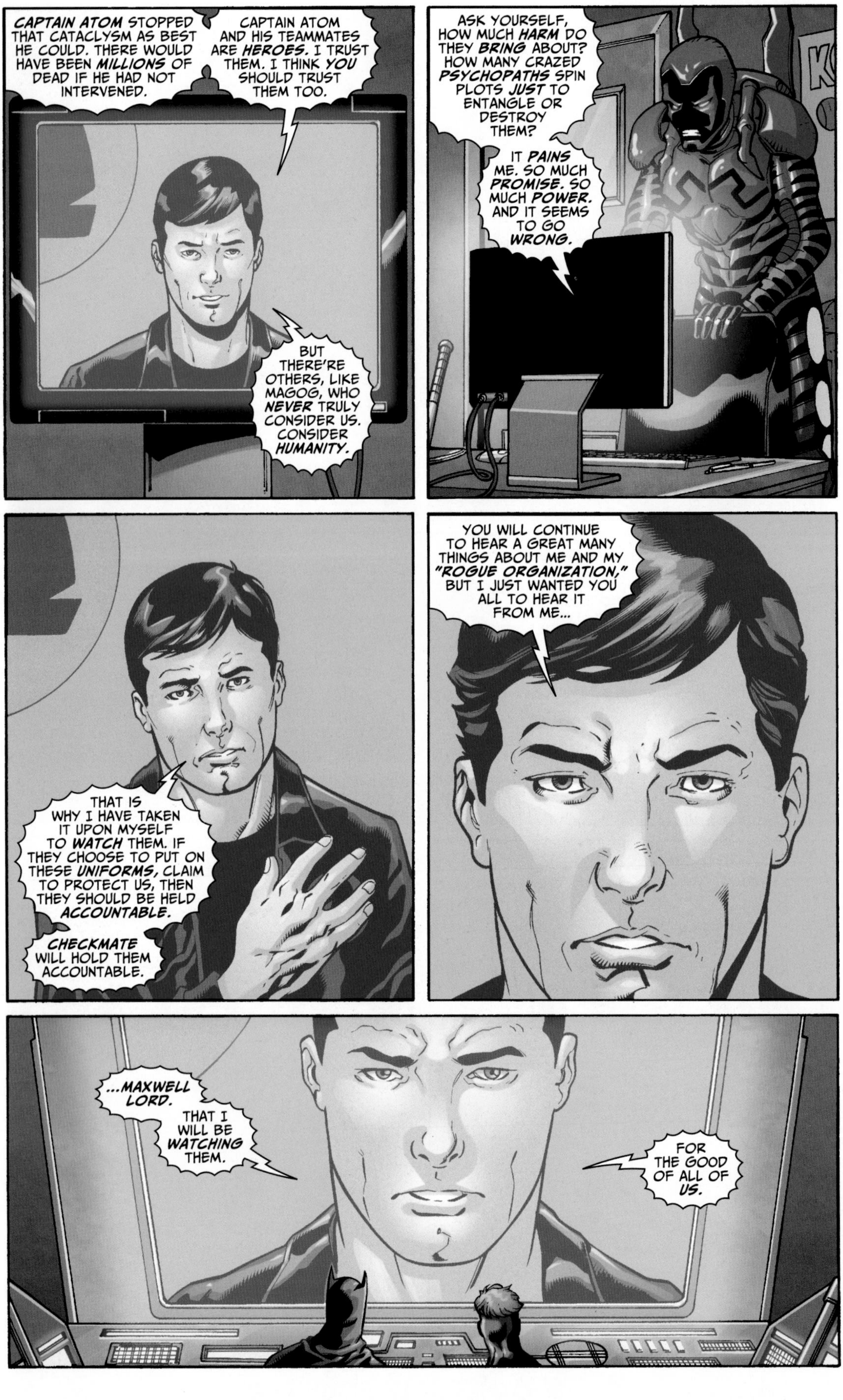
CAPTAIN ATOM STOPPED THAT CATACLYSM AS BEST HE COULD. THERE WOULD HAVE BEEN MILLIONS OF DEAD IF HE HAD NOT INTERVENED.
CAPTAIN ATOM AND HIS TEAMMATES ARE HEROES. I TRUST THEM. I THINK YOU SHOULD TRUST THEM TOO.
BUT THERE'RE OTHERS, LIKE MAGOG, WHO NEVER TRULY CONSIDER US. CONSIDER HUMANITY.
ASK YOURSELF, HOW MUCH HARM DO THEY BRING ABOUT? HOW MANY CRAZED PSYCHOPATHS SPIN PLOTS JUST TO ENTANGLE OR DESTROY THEM?
IT PAINS ME. SO MUCH PROMISE. SO MUCH POWER. AND IT SEEMS TO GO WRONG.
THAT IS WHY I HAVE TAKEN IT UPON MYSELF TO WATCH THEM. IF THEY CHOOSE TO PUT ON THESE UNIFORMS, CLAIM TO PROTECT US, THEN THEY SHOULD BE HELD ACCOUNTABLE.
CHECKMATE WILL HOLD THEM ACCOUNTABLE.
YOU WILL CONTINUE TO HEAR A GREAT MANY THINGS ABOUT ME AND MY "ROGUE ORGANIZATION," BUT I JUST WANTED YOU ALL TO HEAR IT FROM ME...
...MAXWELL LORD.
THAT I WILL BE WATCHING THEM.
FOR THE GOOD OF ALL OF US.

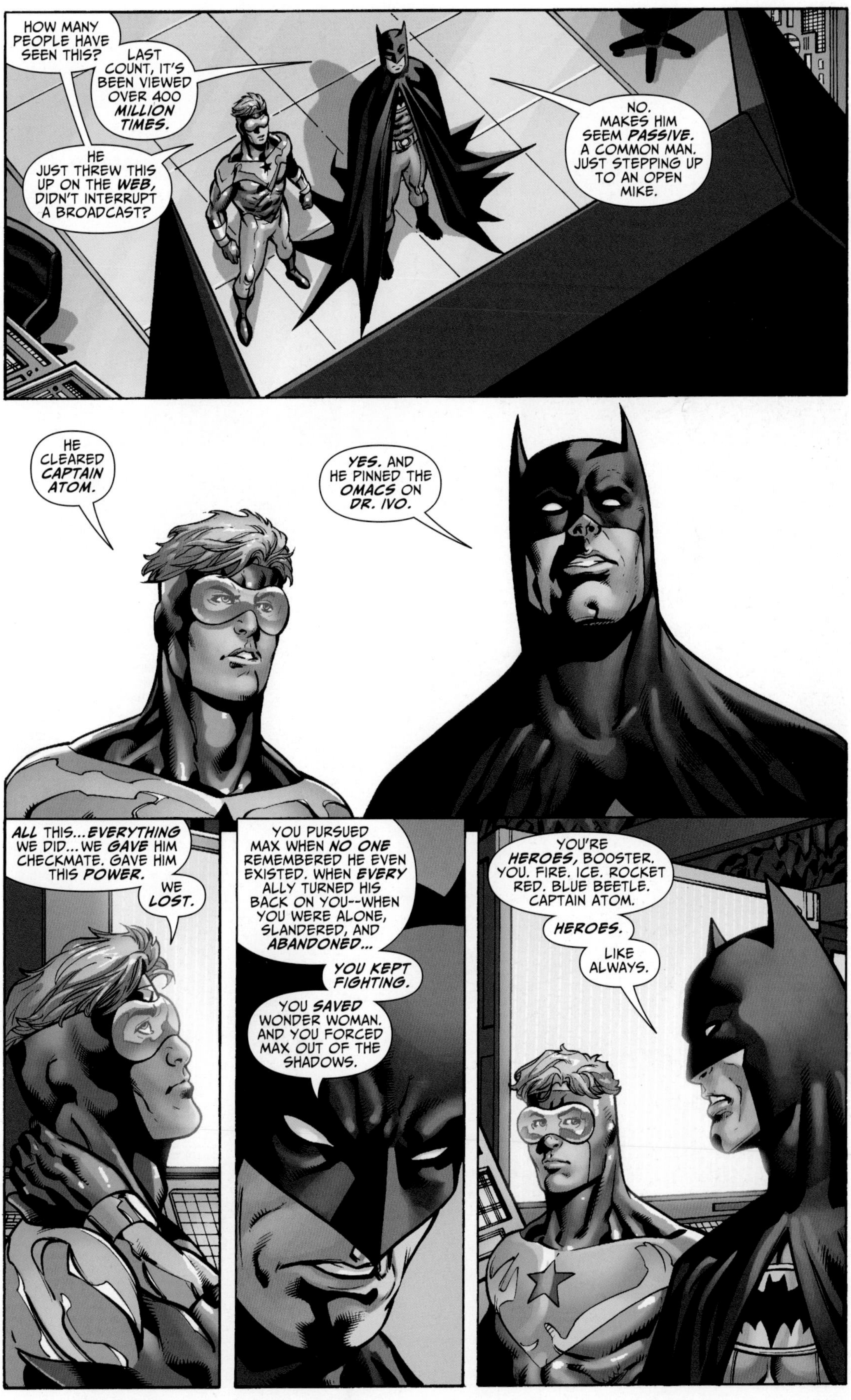
HOW MANY PEOPLE HAVE SEEN THIS?
LAST COUNT, IT'S BEEN VIEWED OVER 400 MILLION TIMES.
HE JUST THREW THIS UP ON THE WEB, DIDN'T INTERRUPT A BROADCAST?
NO. MAKES HIM SEEM PASSIVE. A COMMON MAN. JUST STEPPING UP TO AN OPEN MIKE.
HE CLEARED CAPTAIN ATOM.
YES. AND HE PINNED THE OMACS ON DR. IVO.
ALL THIS...EVERYTHING WE DID...WE GAVE HIM CHECKMATE. GAVE HIM THIS POWER.
WE LOST.
YOU PURSUED MAX WHEN NO ONE REMEMBERED HE EVEN EXISTED. WHEN EVERY ALLY TURNED HIS BACK ON YOU--WHEN YOU WERE ALONE, SLANDERED, AND ABANDONED...
YOU KEPT FIGHTING.
YOU SAVED WONDER WOMAN. AND YOU FORCED MAX OUT OF THE SHADOWS.
YOU'RE HEROES, BOOSTER. YOU. FIRE. ICE. ROCKET RED. BLUE BEETLE. CAPTAIN ATOM.
HEROES.
LIKE ALWAYS.

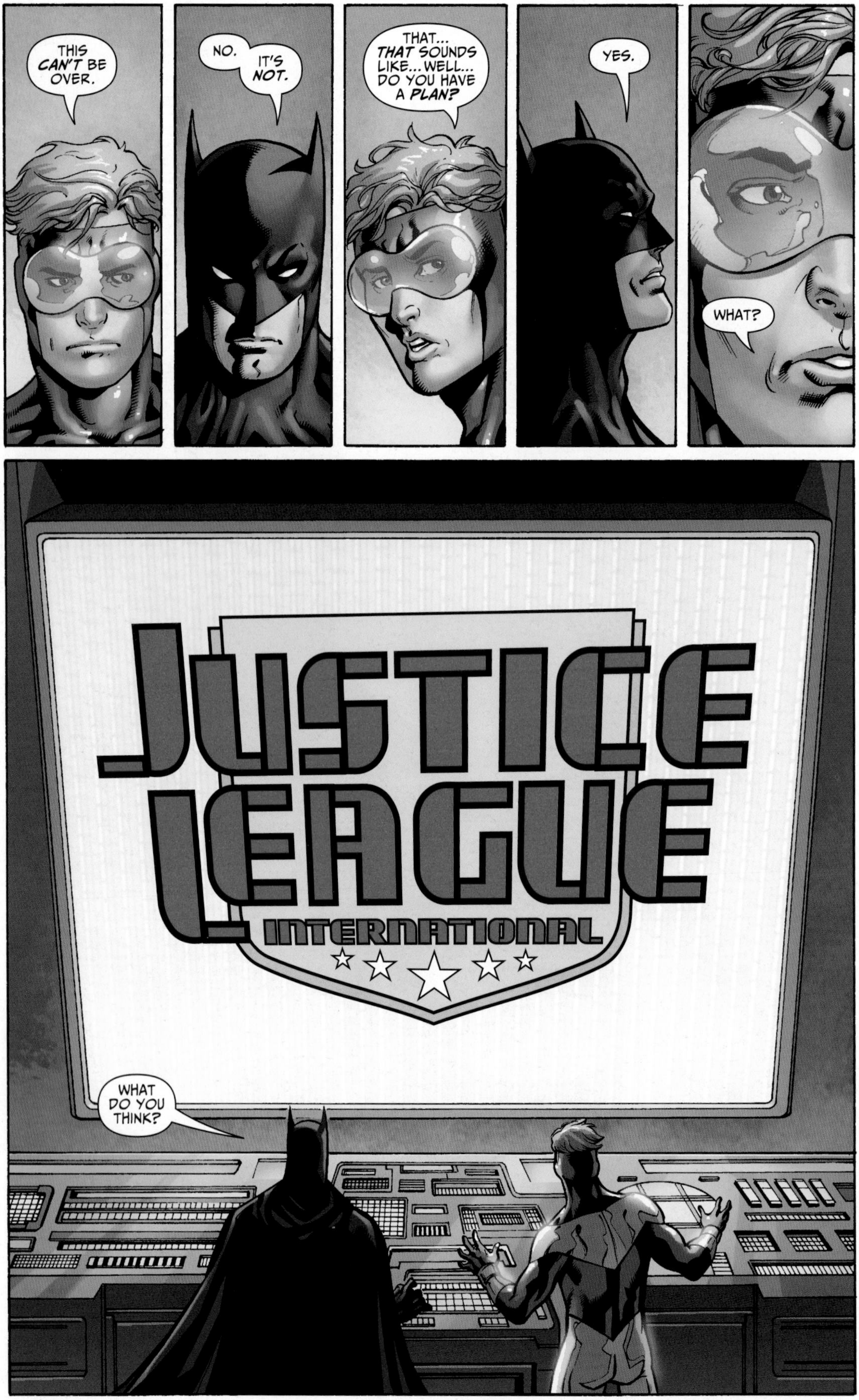
THIS CAN'T BE OVER.
NO.
IT'S NOT.
THAT... THAT SOUNDS LIKE...WELL... DO YOU HAVE A PLAN?
YES.
WHAT?
JUSTICE LEAGUE
INTERNATIONAL
WHAT DO YOU THINK?

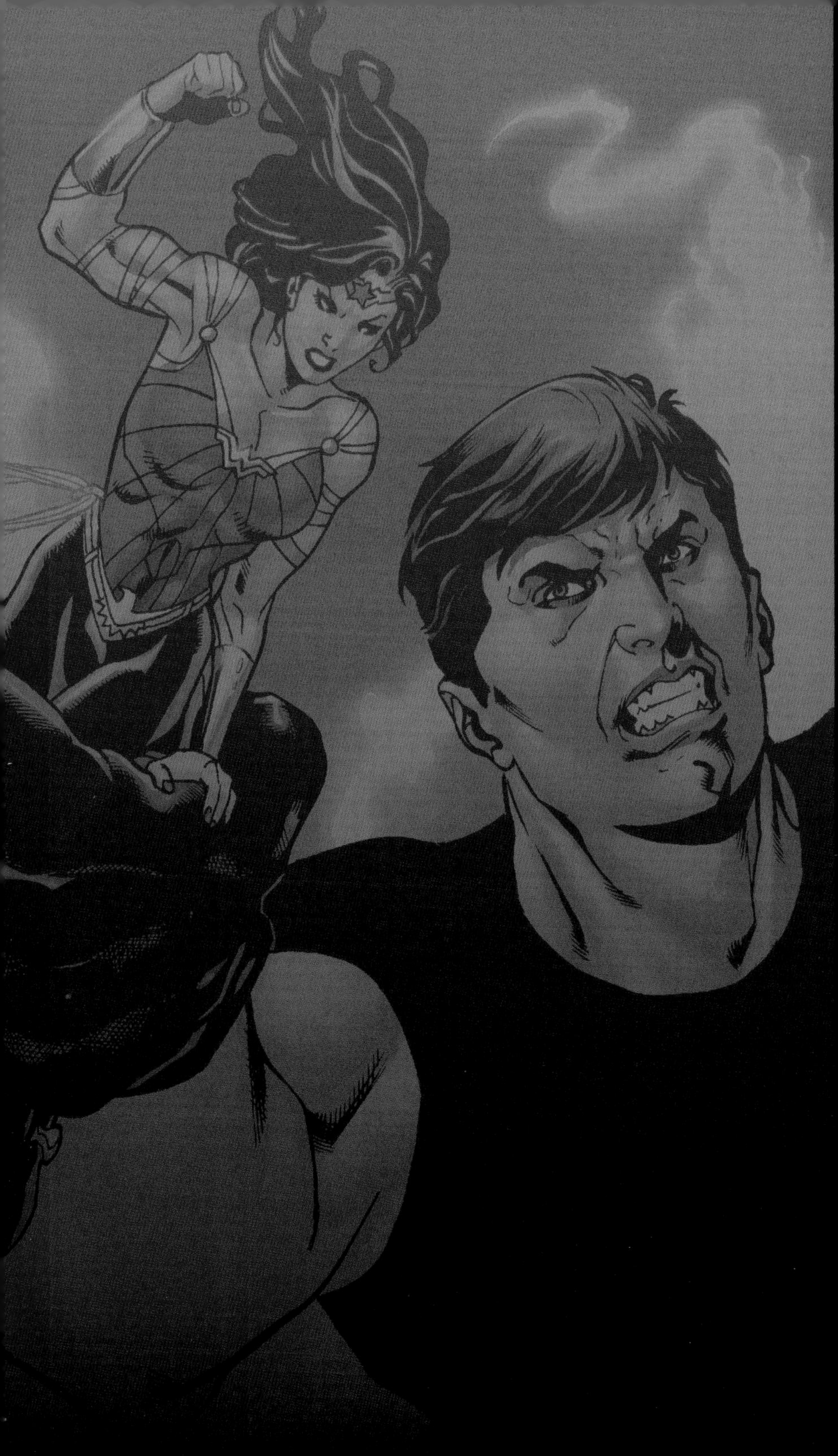

VARIANT COVER GALLERY

JUSTICE LEAGUE: GENERATION LOST 13 by Kevin Maguire & Hi-Fi

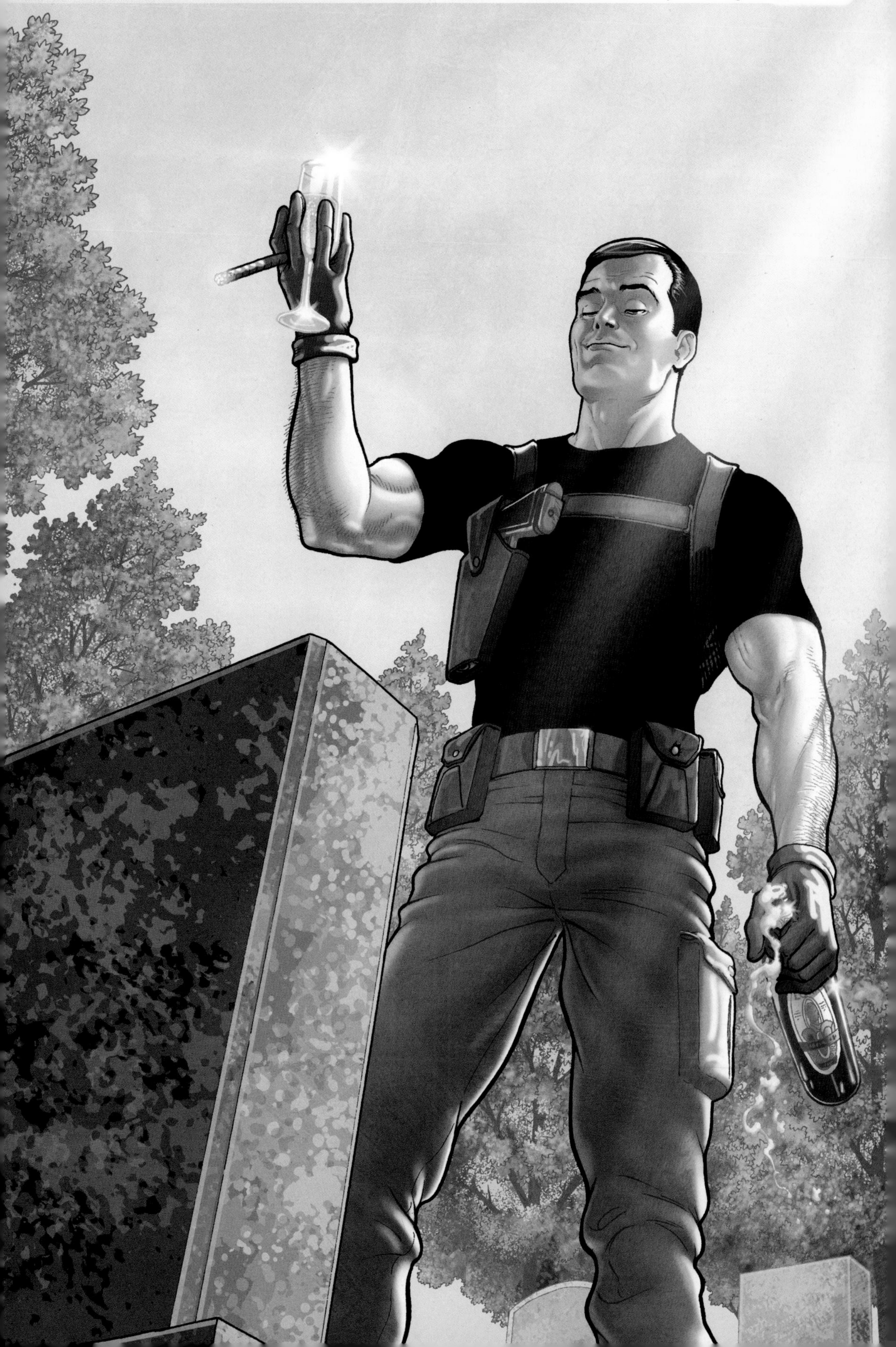

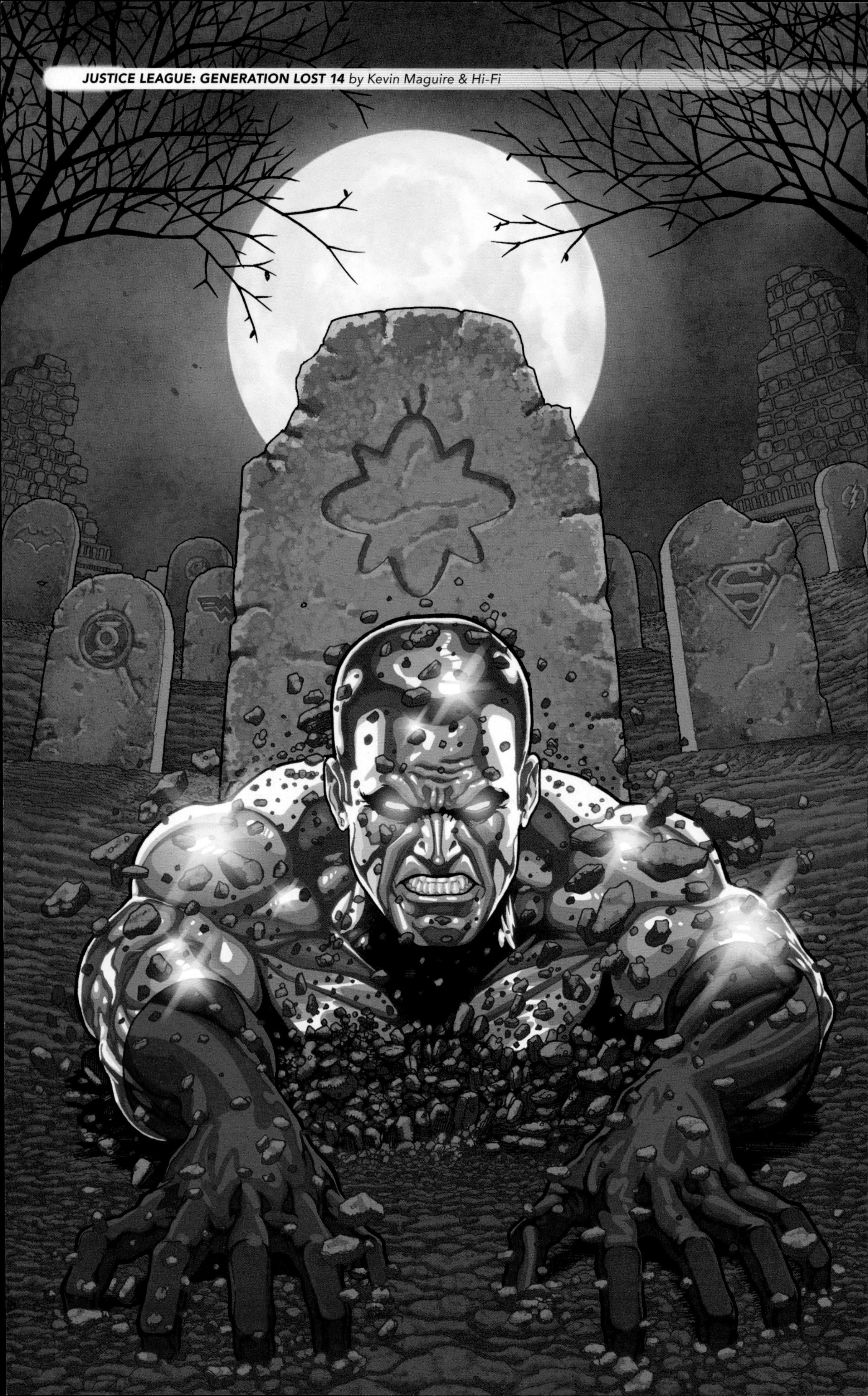

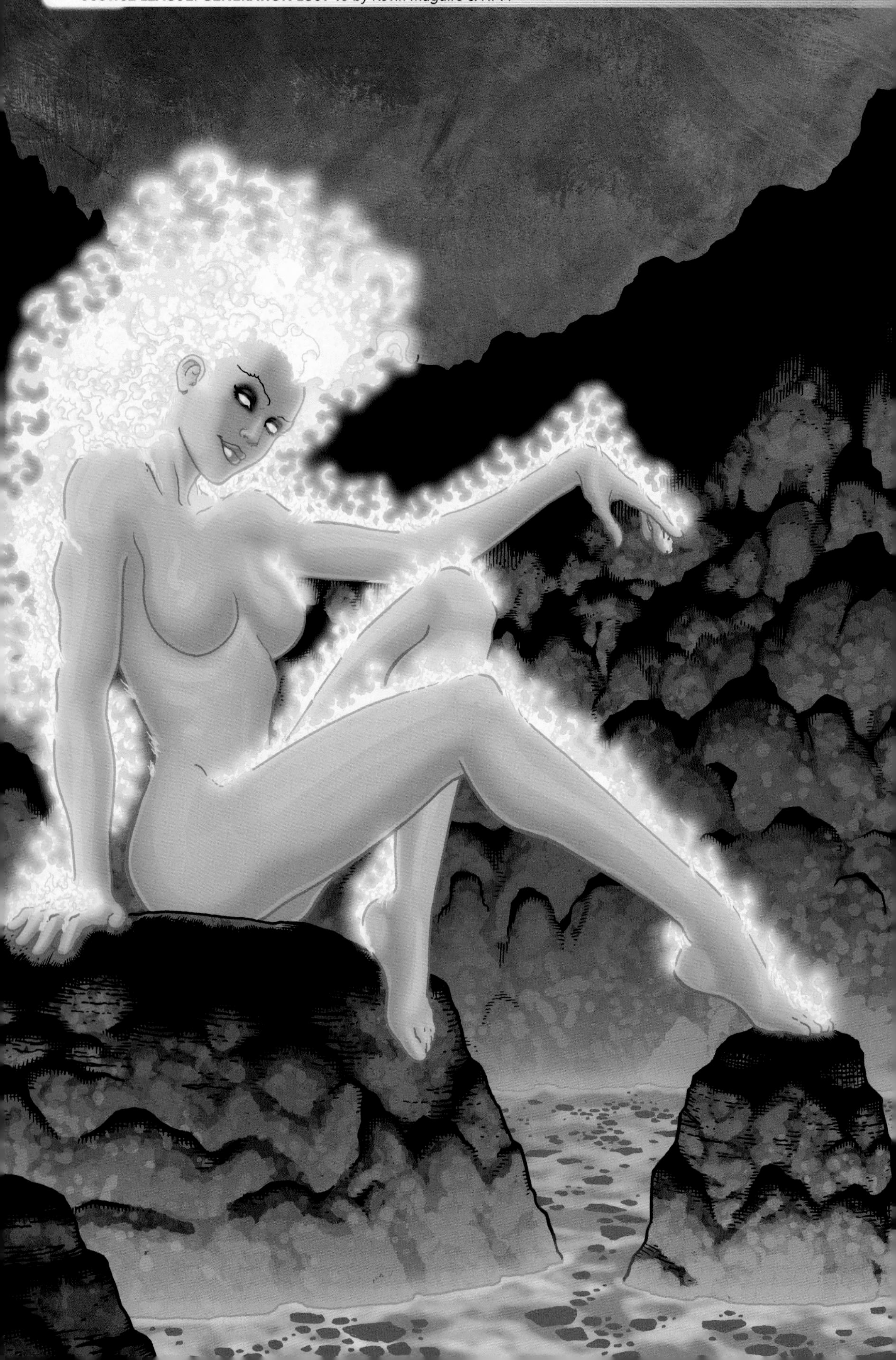

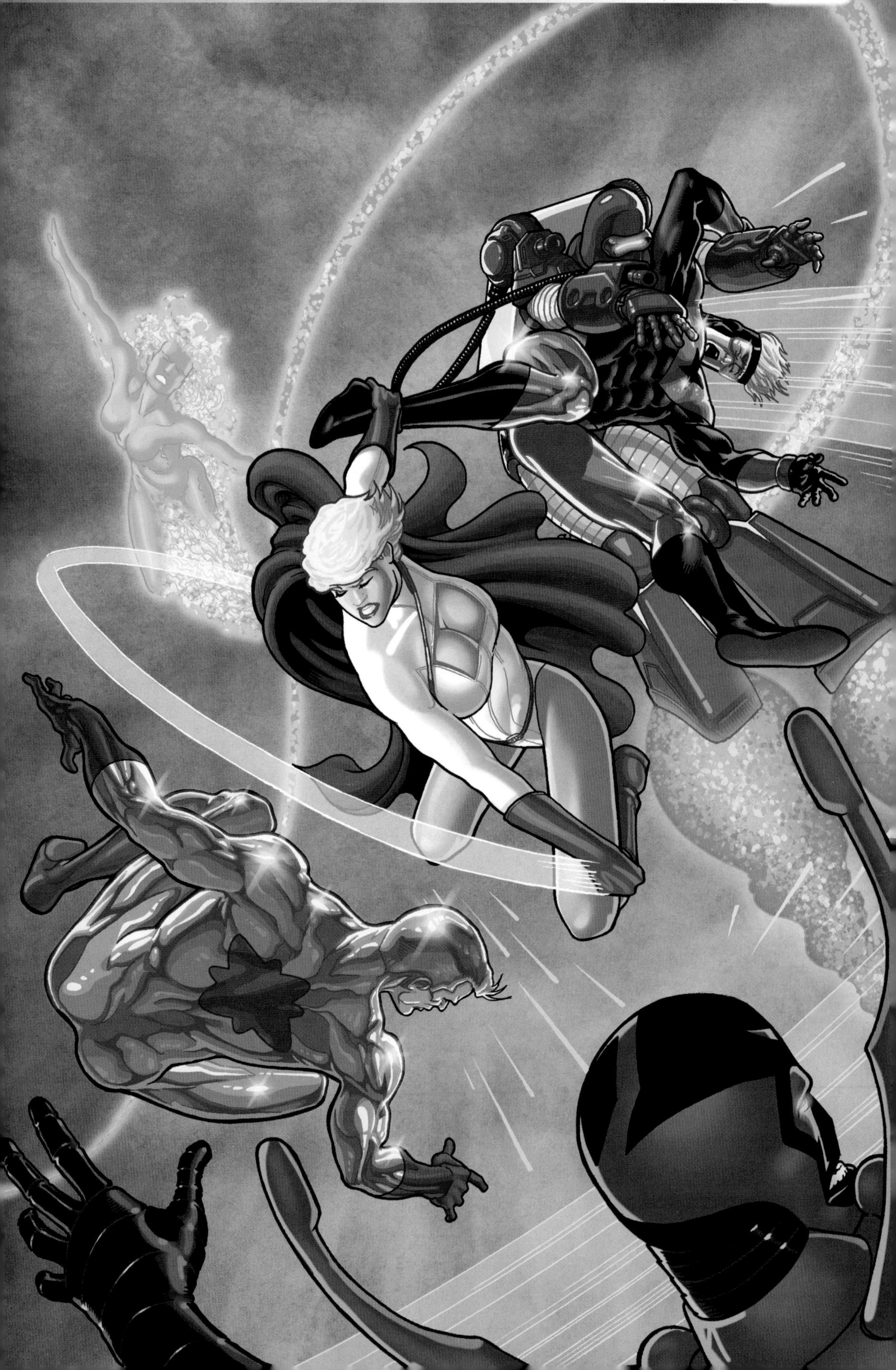

JUSTICE LEAGUE: GENERATION LOST 18 by Kevin Maguire & Hi-Fi

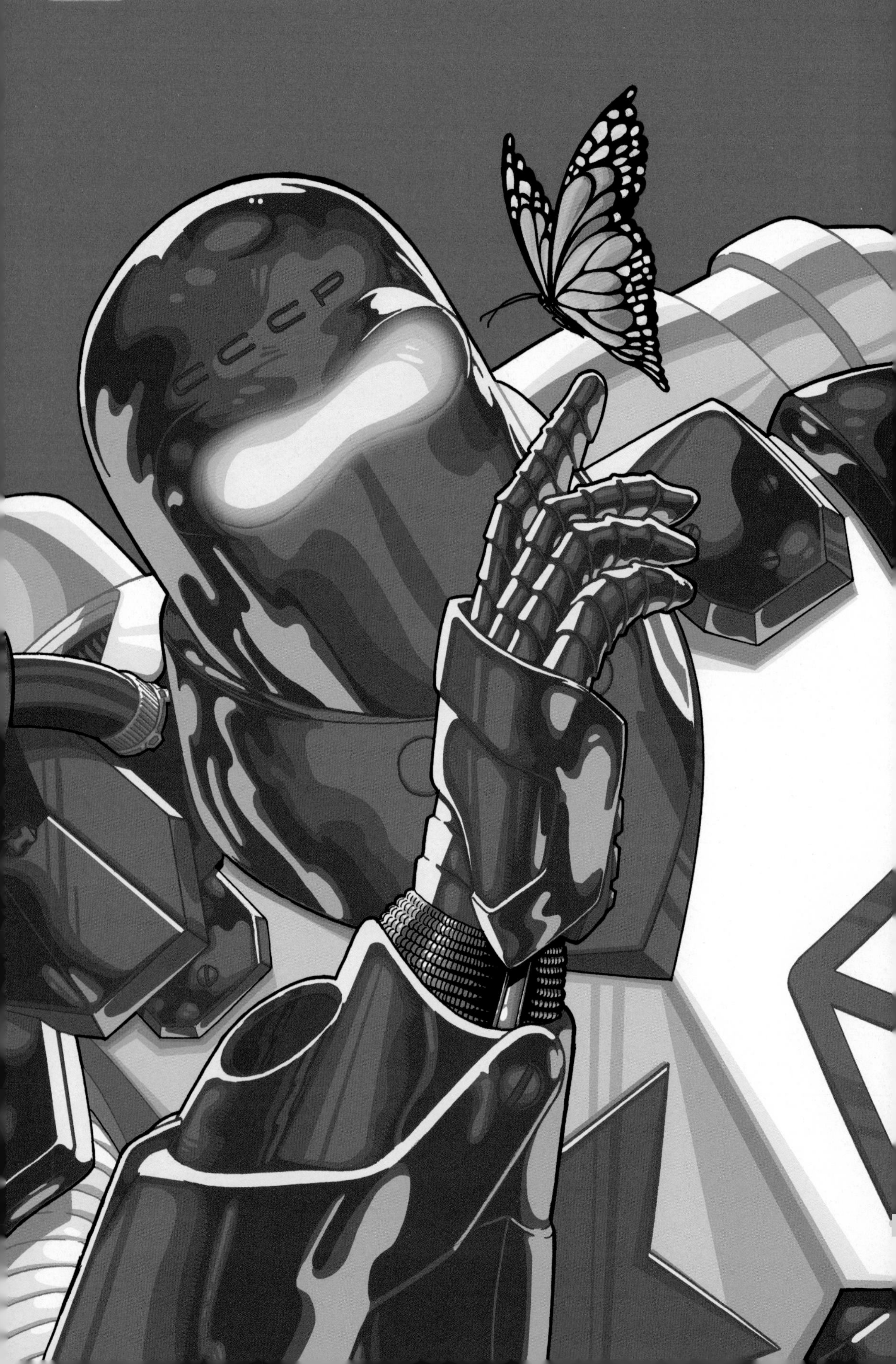

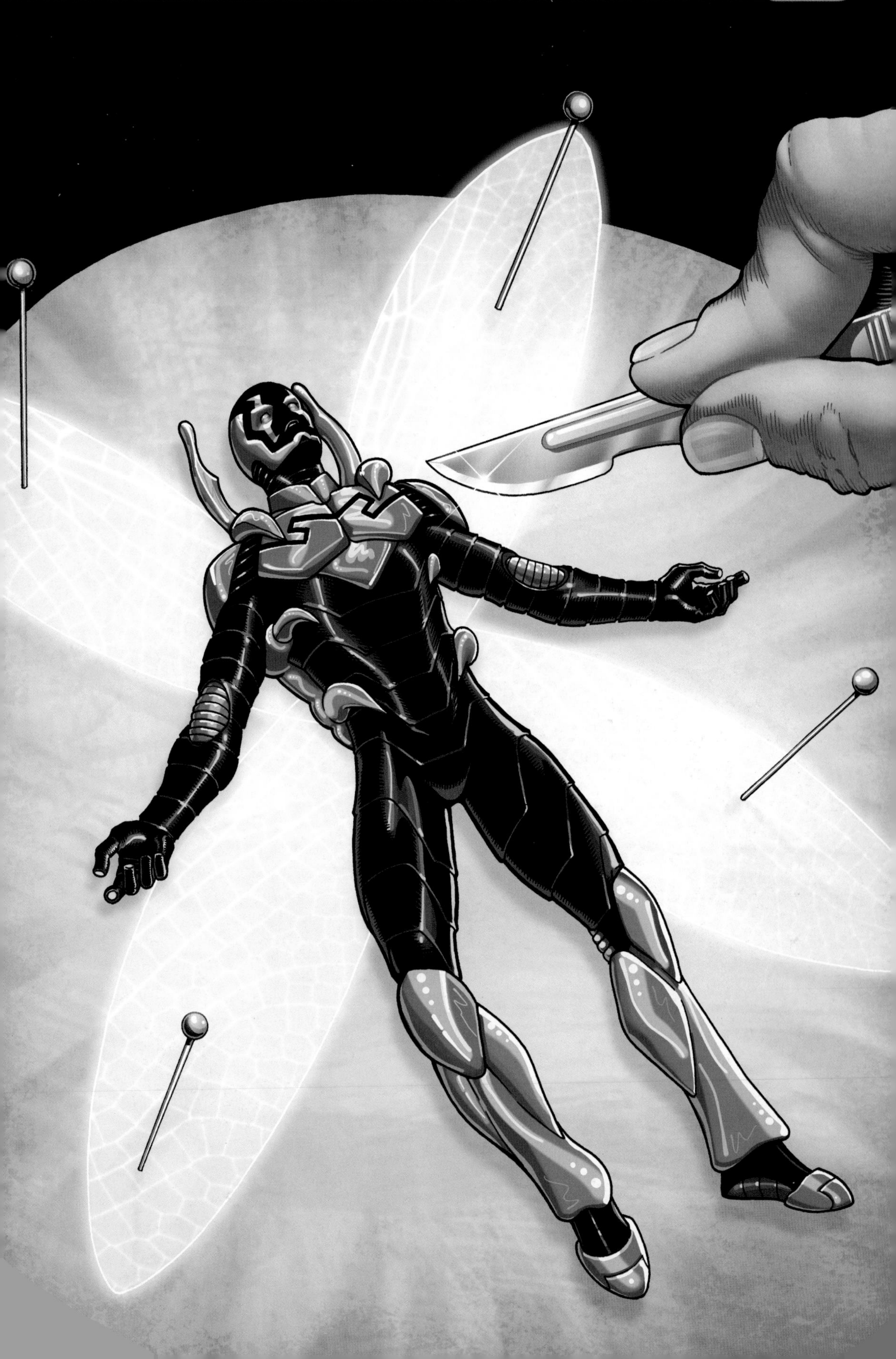

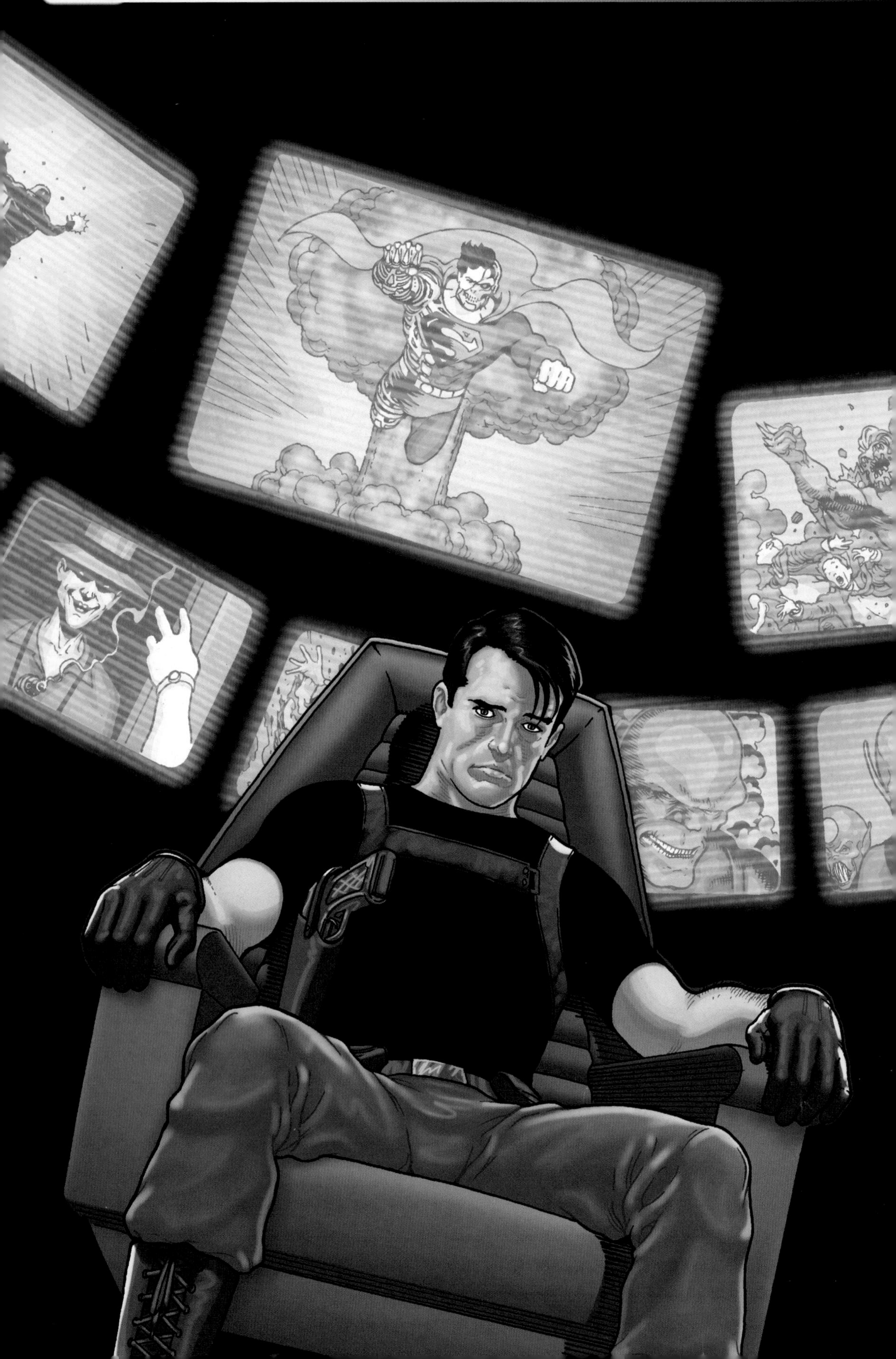

JUDD WINICK
WRITER

**JOE BENNETT
FERNANDO DAGNINO
AARON LOPRESTI**
PENCILLERS

**JACK JADSON & RUY JOSÉ
RAUL FERNANDEZ
MATT RYAN**
INKERS

HI-FI
COLORIST

**SAL CIPRIANO
SWANDS
TRAVIS LANHAM
JOHN J. HILL**
LETTERERS

AARON LOPRESTI with **HI-FI**
COLLECTION COVER

LEAGUE

ON LOST

VOLUME
TWO

Rex Ogle Brian Cunningham *Editors – Original series*
Ian Sattler *Director Editorial, Special Projects and Archival Editions*
Robbin Brosterman *Design Director-Books* | **Curtis King Jr.** *Publication Design*

Eddie Berganza *Executive Editor* | **Bob Harras** *VP – Editor in Chief*

Diane Nelson *President* | **Dan DiDio** and **Jim Lee** *Co-Publishers*
Geoff Johns *Chief Creative Officer* | **John Rood** *Executive VP – Sales, Marketing and Business Development*
Amy Genkins *Senior VP – Business and Legal Affairs* | **Nairi Gardiner** *Senior VP – Finance*
Jeff Boison *VP – Publishing Operations* | **Mark Chiarello** *VP – Art Direction and Design*
John Cunningham *VP – Marketing* | **Terri Cunningham** *VP – Talent Relations and Services*
Alison Gill *Senior VP – Manufacturing and Operations* | **David Hyde** *VP – Publicity*
Hank Kanalz *Senior VP – Digital* | **Jay Kogan** *VP – Business and Legal Affairs, Publishing*
Jack Mahan *VP – Business Affairs, Talent* | **Nick Napolitano** *VP – Manufacturing Administration*
Sue Pohja *VP – Book Sales* | **Courtney Simmons** *Senior VP – Publicity* | **Bob Wayne** *VP – Sales*

JUSTICE LEAGUE: GENERATION LOST Volume Two

DC COMICS 1700 Broadway, New York, NY 10019
A Warner Bros. Entertainment Company

Printed by RR Donnelley, Salem, VA, USA.
9/9/11. First printing.

HC ISBN: 978-1-4012-3283-2
SC ISBN: 978-1-4012-3458-4

SUSTAINABLE
FORESTRY
INITIATIVE

Certified Chain of Custody
Promoting Sustainable
Forest Management

Fiber used in this product line meets the
sourcing requirements of the SFI program.

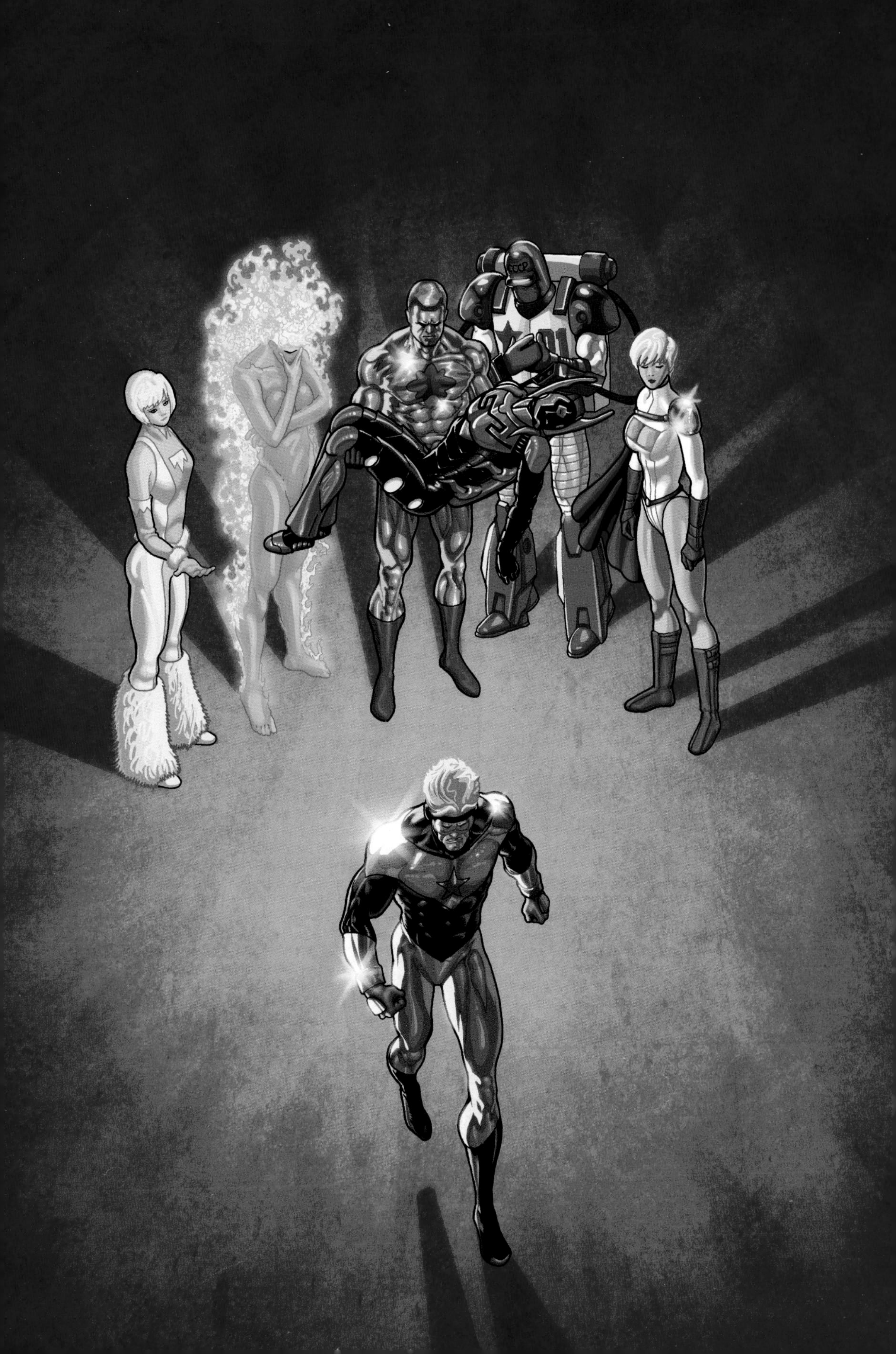

JUSTICE LEAGUE: GENERATION LOST 22 by Kevin Maguire & Hi-Fi

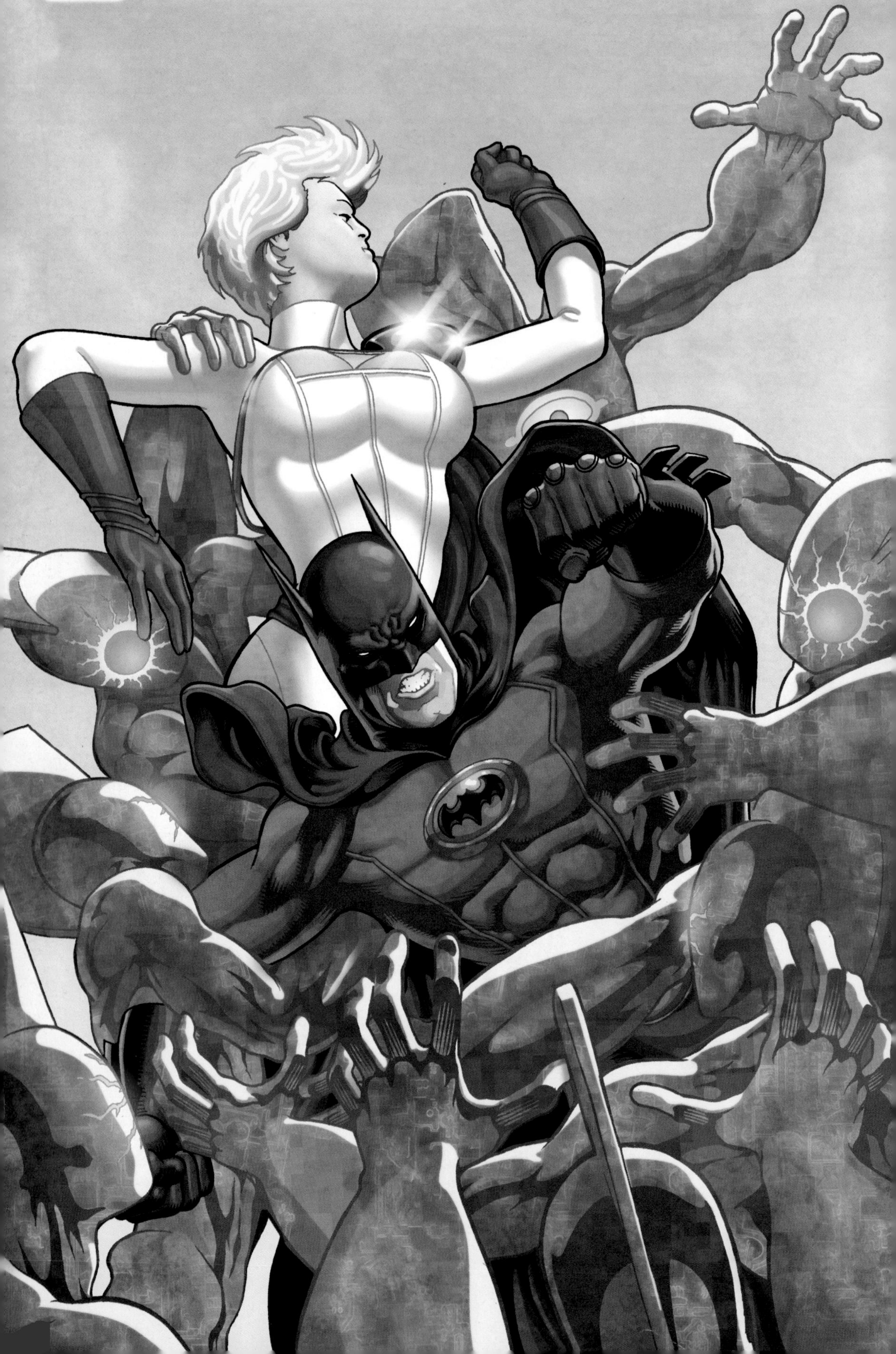

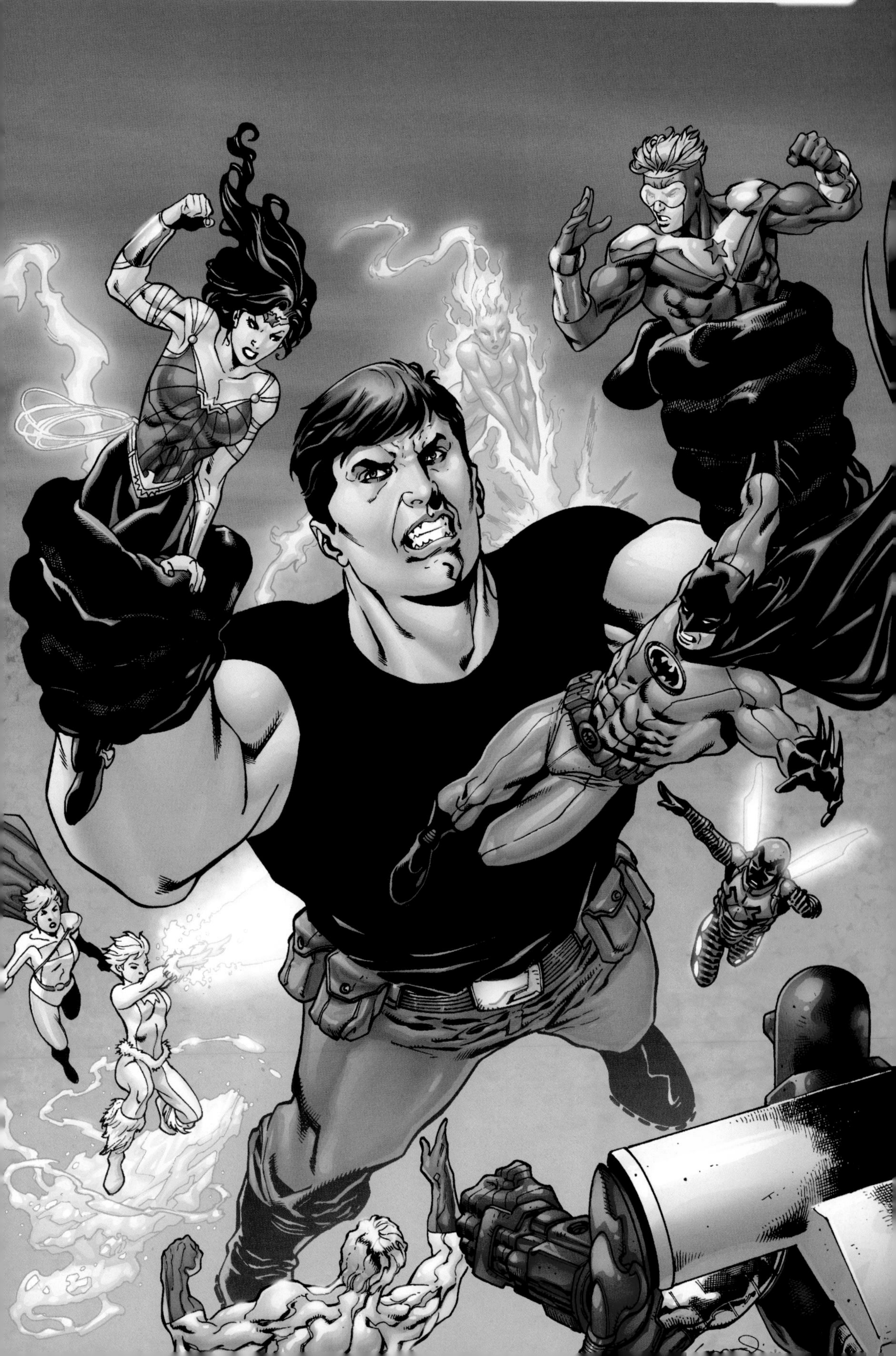

***JUSTICE LEAGUE: GENERATION LOST* 24** by Kevin Maguire & Hi-Fi

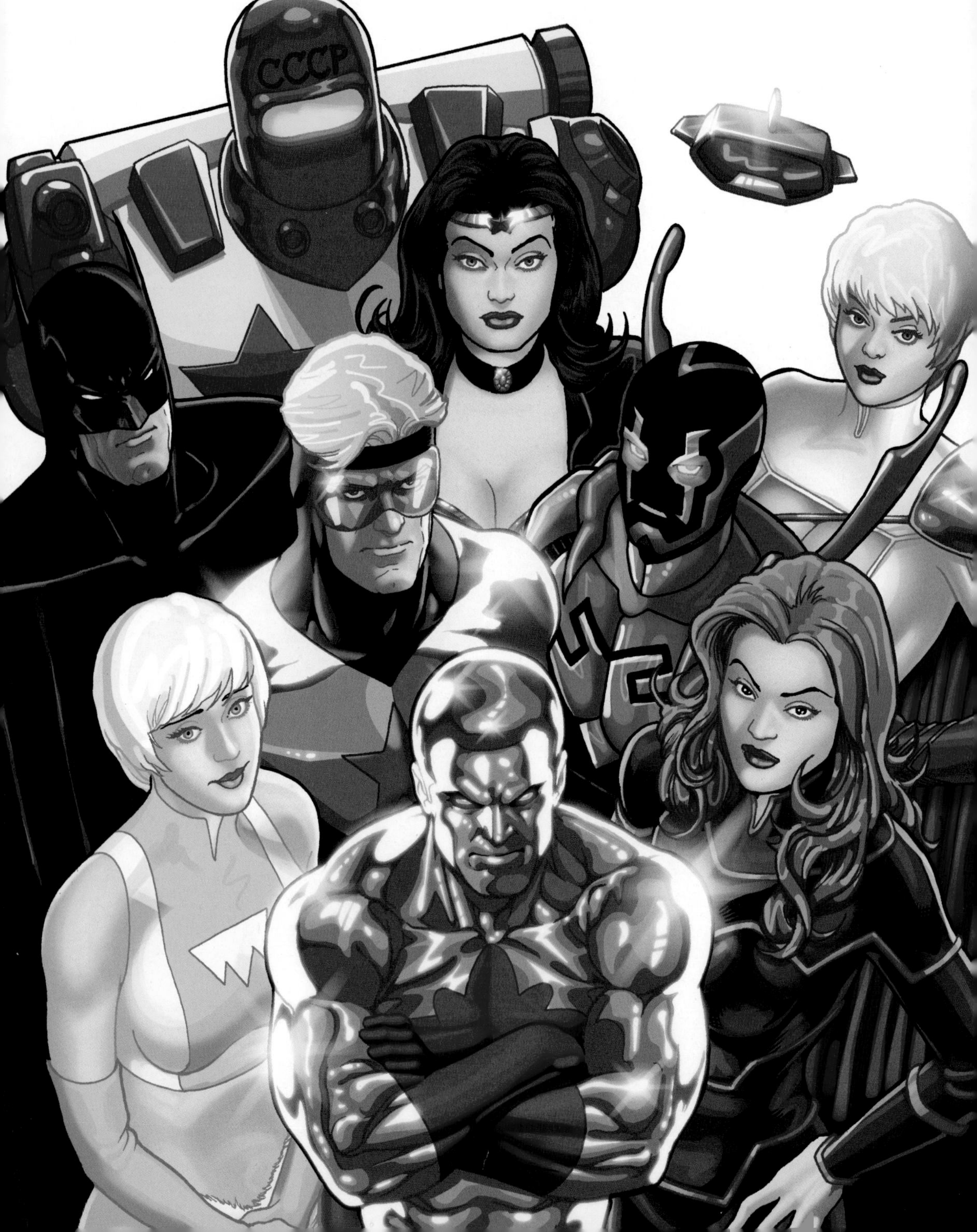
CCCP

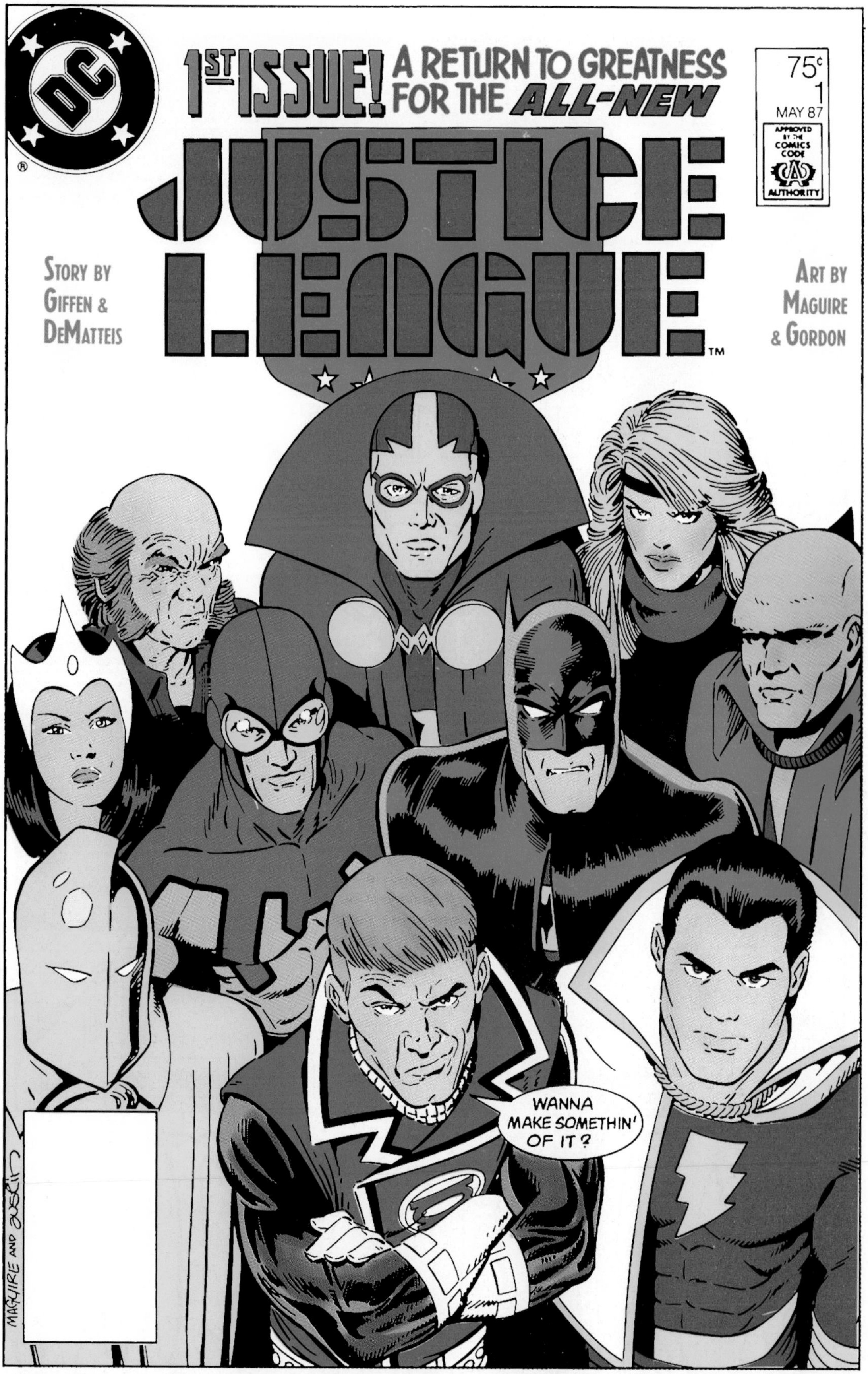
DC
1ST ISSUE! A RETURN TO GREATNESS FOR THE ALL-NEW
JUSTICE LEAGUE™
75¢
1
MAY 87
APPROVED BY THE COMICS CODE AUTHORITY
STORY BY GIFFEN & DEMATTEIS
ART BY MAGUIRE & GORDON
WANNA MAKE SOMETHIN' OF IT?

See how the original Justice League International first began in this classic excerpt from Justice League #1!

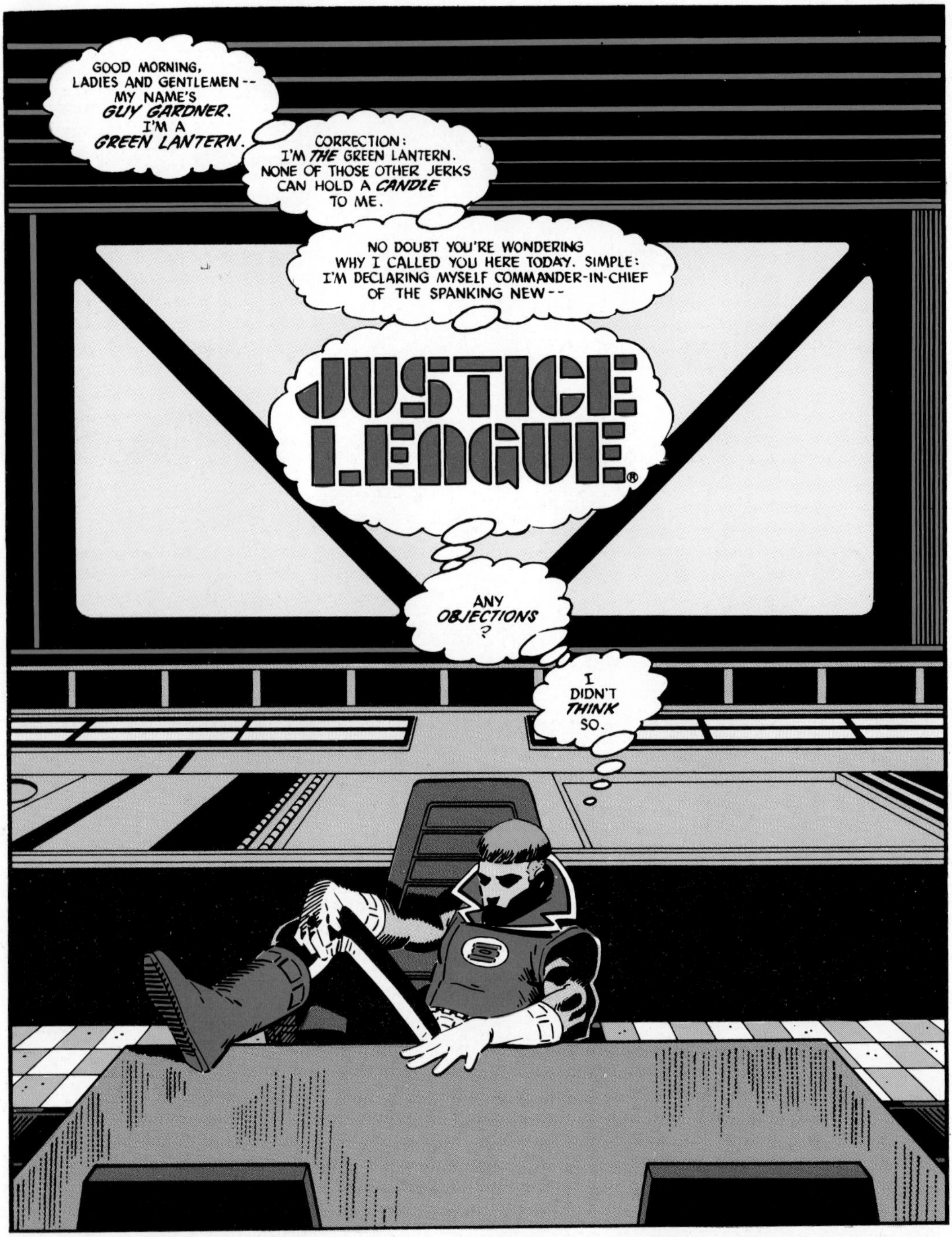
GOOD MORNING, LADIES AND GENTLEMEN-- MY NAME'S GUY GARDNER. I'M A GREEN LANTERN.
CORRECTION: I'M THE GREEN LANTERN. NONE OF THOSE OTHER JERKS CAN HOLD A CANDLE TO ME.
NO DOUBT YOU'RE WONDERING WHY I CALLED YOU HERE TODAY. SIMPLE: I'M DECLARING MYSELF COMMANDER-IN-CHIEF OF THE SPANKING NEW--
JUSTICE LEAGUE®
ANY OBJECTIONS?
I DIDN'T THINK SO.

BORN AGAIN

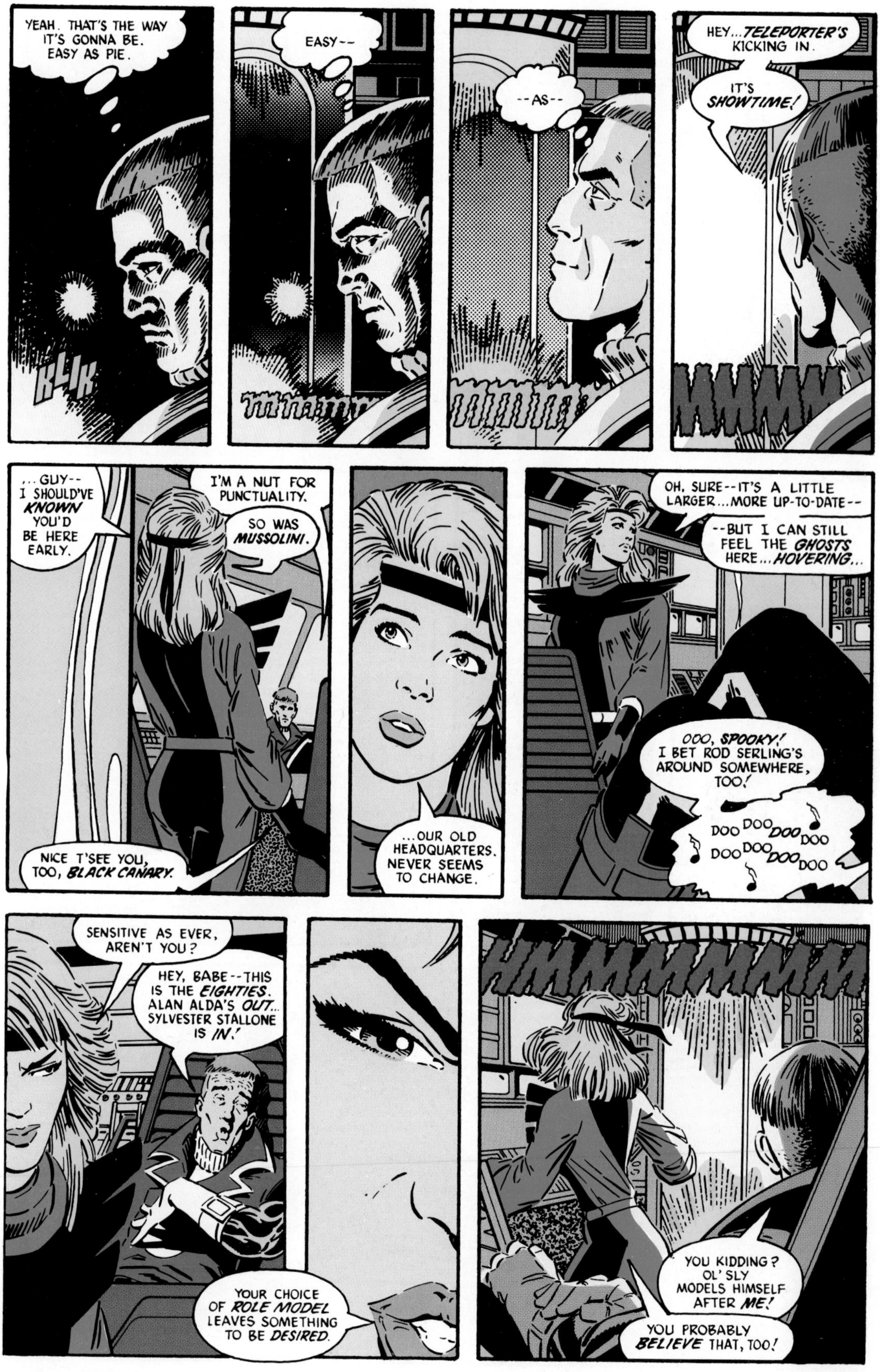

YEAH. THAT'S THE WAY IT'S GONNA BE. EASY AS PIE.
KLIK
EASY--
--AS--
HEY...TELEPORTER'S KICKING IN.
IT'S SHOWTIME!
MMMM
...GUY--
I SHOULD'VE KNOWN YOU'D BE HERE EARLY.
I'M A NUT FOR PUNCTUALITY.
SO WAS MUSSOLINI.
NICE T'SEE YOU, TOO, BLACK CANARY.
...OUR OLD HEADQUARTERS. NEVER SEEMS TO CHANGE.
OH, SURE--IT'S A LITTLE LARGER...MORE UP-TO-DATE--
--BUT I CAN STILL FEEL THE GHOSTS HERE...HOVERING...
OOO, SPOOKY! I BET ROD SERLING'S AROUND SOMEWHERE, TOO!
DOO DOO DOO DOO
DOO DOO DOO DOO
SENSITIVE AS EVER, AREN'T YOU?
HEY, BABE--THIS IS THE EIGHTIES. ALAN ALDA'S OUT... SYLVESTER STALLONE IS IN!
YOUR CHOICE OF ROLE MODEL LEAVES SOMETHING TO BE DESIRED.
HMMMMMMM
YOU KIDDING? OL' SLY MODELS HIMSELF AFTER ME!
YOU PROBABLY BELIEVE THAT, TOO!

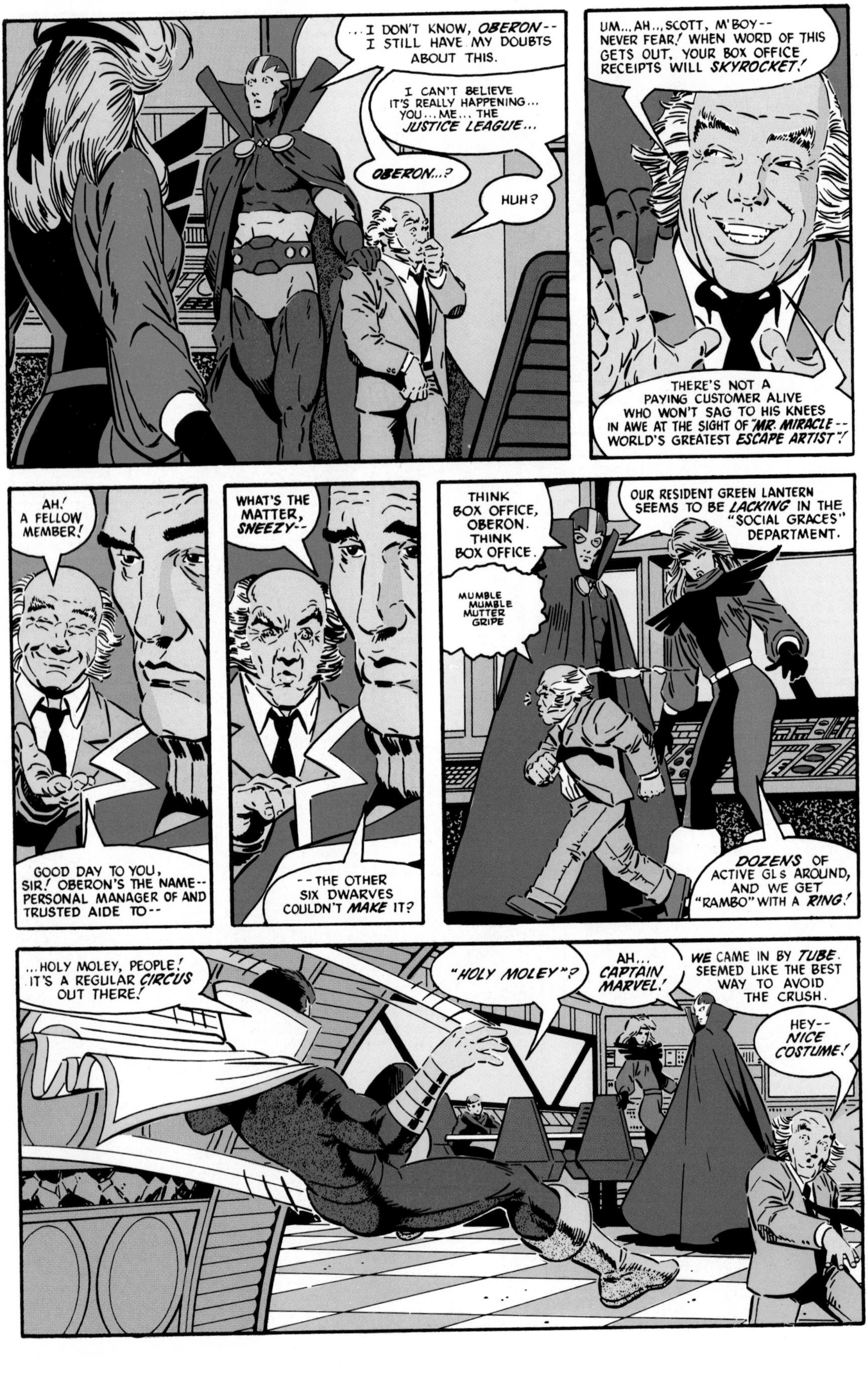
...I DON'T KNOW, OBERON--
I STILL HAVE MY DOUBTS ABOUT THIS.
I CAN'T BELIEVE IT'S REALLY HAPPENING... YOU...ME... THE JUSTICE LEAGUE...
OBERON...?
HUH?
UM...AH...SCOTT, M'BOY--NEVER FEAR! WHEN WORD OF THIS GETS OUT, YOUR BOX OFFICE RECEIPTS WILL SKYROCKET!
THERE'S NOT A PAYING CUSTOMER ALIVE WHO WON'T SAG TO HIS KNEES IN AWE AT THE SIGHT OF "MR. MIRACLE"--WORLD'S GREATEST ESCAPE ARTIST"!
AH! A FELLOW MEMBER!
GOOD DAY TO YOU, SIR! OBERON'S THE NAME--PERSONAL MANAGER OF AND TRUSTED AIDE TO--
WHAT'S THE MATTER, SNEEZY--
--THE OTHER SIX DWARVES COULDN'T MAKE IT?
THINK BOX OFFICE, OBERON. THINK BOX OFFICE.
MUMBLE MUMBLE MUTTER GRIPE
OUR RESIDENT GREEN LANTERN SEEMS TO BE LACKING IN THE "SOCIAL GRACES" DEPARTMENT.
DOZENS OF ACTIVE GLs AROUND, AND WE GET "RAMBO" WITH A RING!
...HOLY MOLEY, PEOPLE! IT'S A REGULAR CIRCUS OUT THERE!
"HOLY MOLEY"?
AH... CAPTAIN MARVEL!
WE CAME IN BY TUBE. SEEMED LIKE THE BEST WAY TO AVOID THE CRUSH.
HEY--NICE COSTUME!

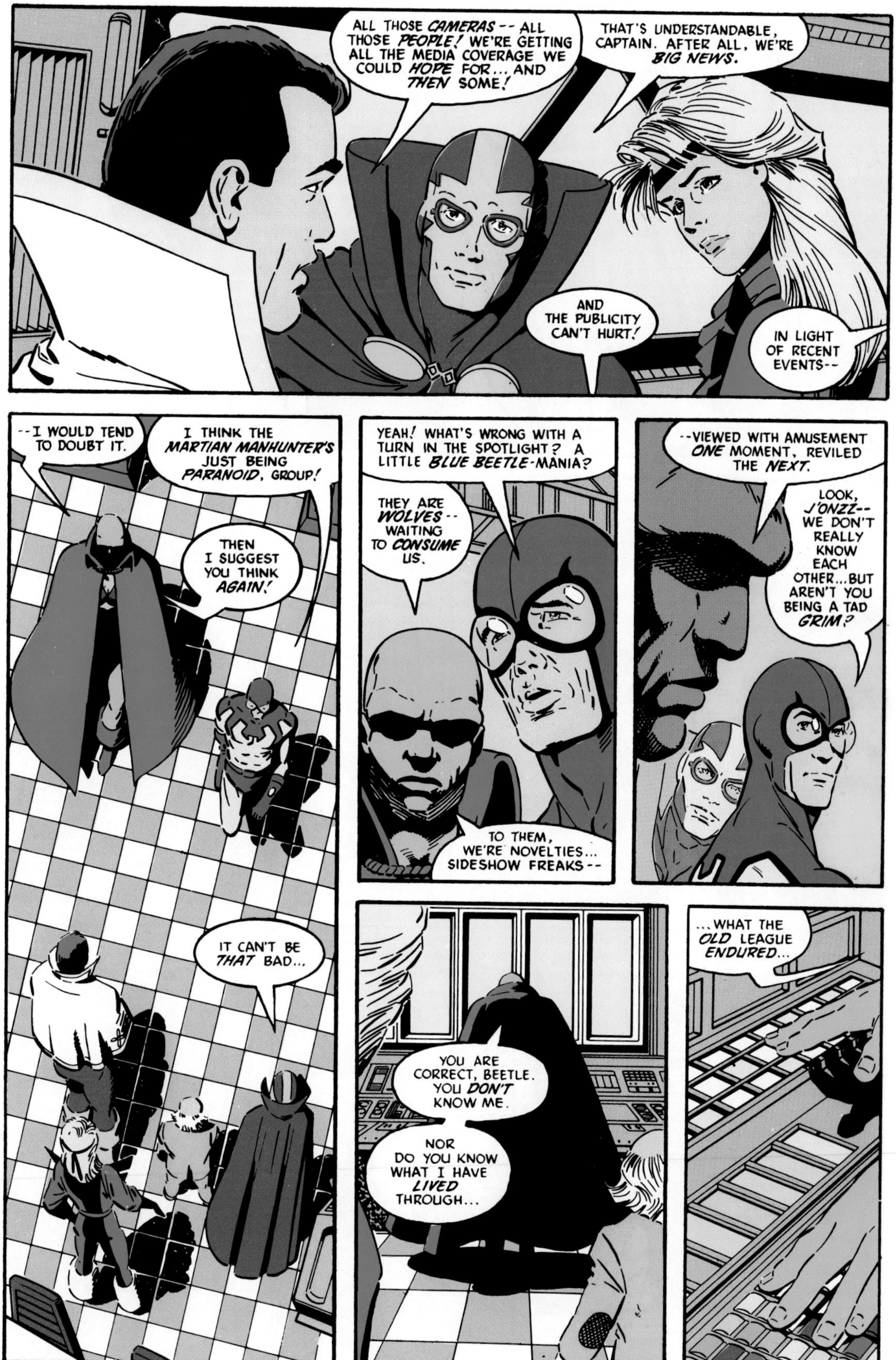
ALL THOSE CAMERAS -- ALL THOSE PEOPLE! WE'RE GETTING ALL THE MEDIA COVERAGE WE COULD HOPE FOR... AND THEN SOME!
THAT'S UNDERSTANDABLE, CAPTAIN. AFTER ALL, WE'RE BIG NEWS.
AND THE PUBLICITY CAN'T HURT!
IN LIGHT OF RECENT EVENTS--
--I WOULD TEND TO DOUBT IT.
I THINK THE MARTIAN MANHUNTER'S JUST BEING PARANOID, GROUP!
THEN I SUGGEST YOU THINK AGAIN!
IT CAN'T BE THAT BAD...
YEAH! WHAT'S WRONG WITH A TURN IN THE SPOTLIGHT? A LITTLE BLUE BEETLE-MANIA?
THEY ARE WOLVES -- WAITING TO CONSUME US.
TO THEM, WE'RE NOVELTIES... SIDESHOW FREAKS--
--VIEWED WITH AMUSEMENT ONE MOMENT, REVILED THE NEXT.
LOOK, J'ONZZ-- WE DON'T REALLY KNOW EACH OTHER...BUT AREN'T YOU BEING A TAD GRIM?
YOU ARE CORRECT, BEETLE. YOU DON'T KNOW ME.
NOR DO YOU KNOW WHAT I HAVE LIVED THROUGH...
...WHAT THE OLD LEAGUE ENDURED...

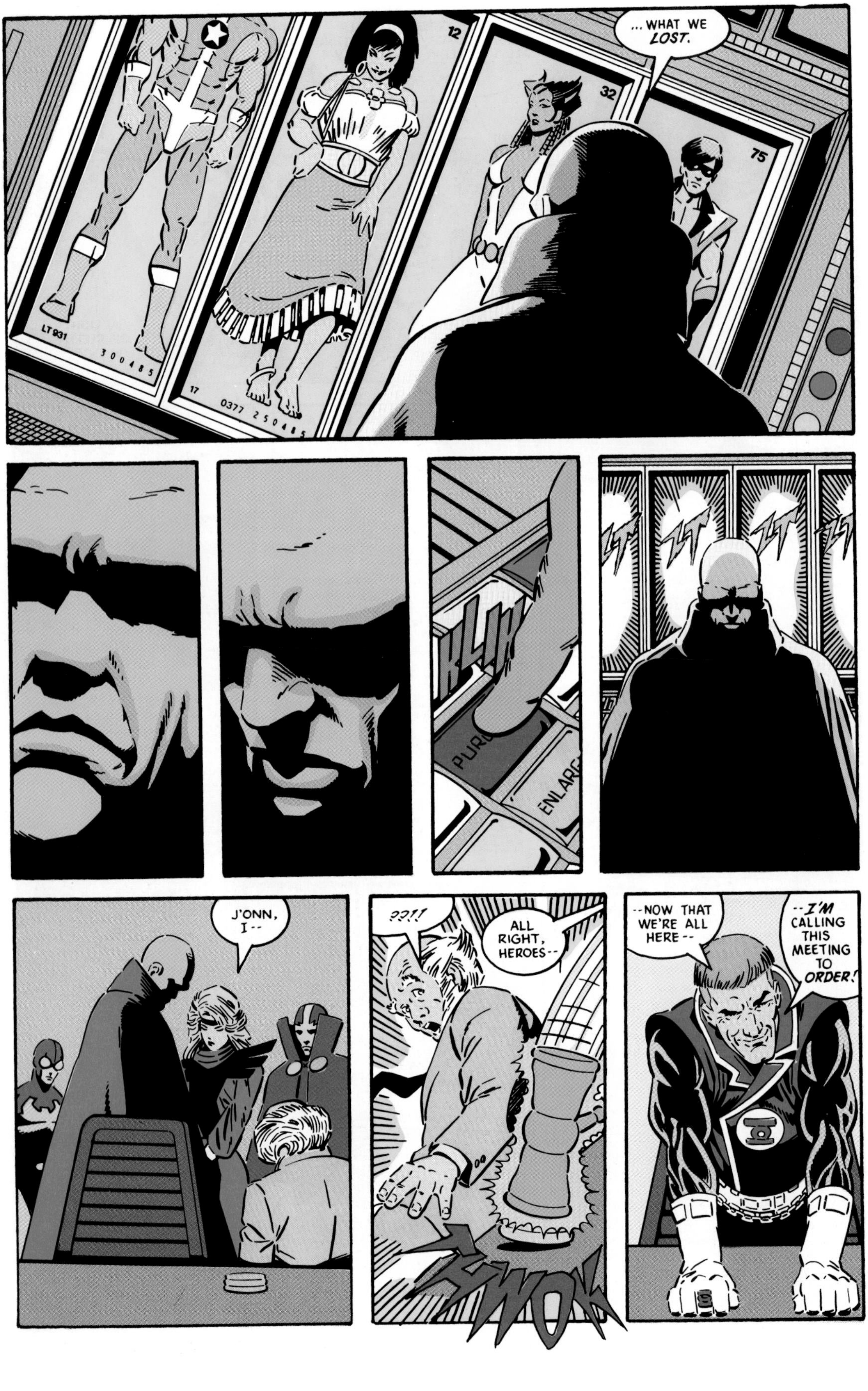
...WHAT WE LOST.
LT 931
300485
17
0377 250485
12
32
75
KLIK
PURG
ENLARG
J'ONN, I--
??!!
ALL RIGHT, HEROES--
WHOK
--NOW THAT WE'RE ALL HERE--
--I'M CALLING THIS MEETING TO ORDER!

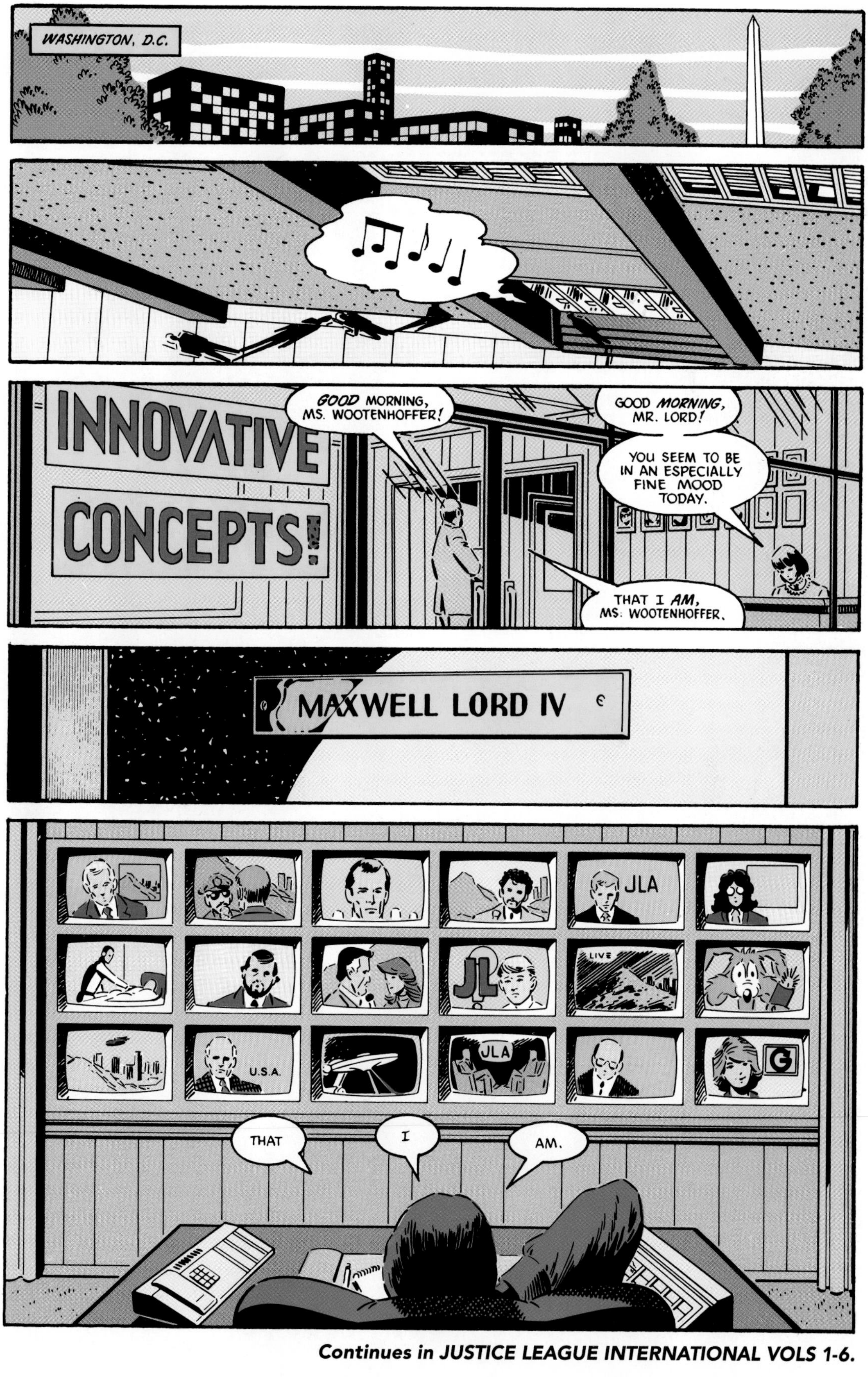
WASHINGTON, D.C.
INNOVATIVE CONCEPTS!
GOOD MORNING, MS. WOOTENHOFFER!
GOOD MORNING, MR. LORD!
YOU SEEM TO BE IN AN ESPECIALLY FINE MOOD TODAY.
THAT I AM, MS. WOOTENHOFFER.
MAXWELL LORD IV
JLA
LIVE
JL
U.S.A.
JLA
G
THAT
I
AM.

Continues in JUSTICE LEAGUE INTERNATIONAL VOLS 1-6.

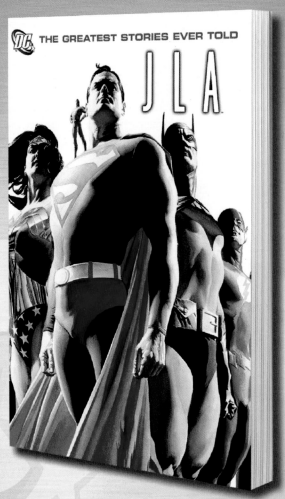

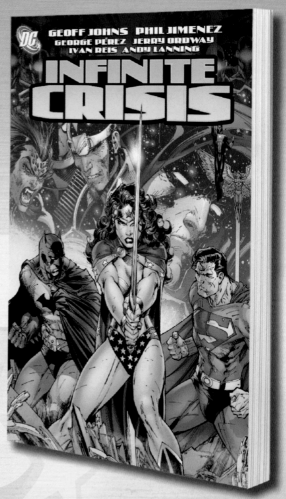